Fodor's

ISRAEL

8th Edition

Fodor's Travel Publications New York, Toronto, London, Sydney, Auckland

www.fodors.com

هال
Cardamom

Eugene Fodor: The Spy Who Loved Travel

As Fodor's celebrates our 75th anniversary, we are honoring the colorful and adventurous life of Eugene Fodor, who revolutionized guidebook publishing in 1936 with his first book, *On the Continent, The Entertaining Travel Annual.*

Eugene Fodor's life seemed to leap off the pages of a great spy novel. Born in Hungary, he spoke six languages and graduated from the Sorbonne and the London School of Economics. During World War II he joined the Office of Strategic Services, the budding spy agency for the United States. He commanded the team that went behind enemy lines to liberate Prague, and recommended to Generals Eisenhower, Bradley, and Patton that Allied troops move to the capital city. After the war, Fodor worked as a spy in Austria, posing as a U.S. diplomat.

In 1949 Eugene Fodor—with the help of the CIA—established Fodor's Modern Guides. He was passionate about travel and wanted to bring his insider's knowledge of Europe to a new generation of sophisticated Americans who wanted to explore and seek out experiences beyond their borders. Among his innovations were annual updates, consulting local experts, and including cultural and historical perspectives and an emphasis on people—not just sites. As Fodor described it, "The main interest and enjoyment of foreign travel lies not only in 'the sites,' . . . but in contact with people whose customs, habits, and general outlook are different from your own."

Eugene Fodor died in 1991, but his legacy, Fodor's Travel, continues. It is now one of the world's largest and most trusted brands in travel information, covering more than 600 destinations worldwide in guidebooks, on Fodors.com, and in ebooks and iPhone apps. Technology and the accessibility of travel may be changing, but Eugene Fodor's unique storytelling skills and reporting style are behind every word of today's Fodor's guides.

Our editors and writers continue to embrace Eugene Fodor's vision of building personal relationships through travel. We invite you to join the Fodor's community at fodors.com/community and share your experiences with like-minded travelers. Tell us when we're right. Tell us when we're wrong. And share fantastic travel secrets that aren't yet in Fodor's. Together, we will continue to deepen our understanding of our world.

Happy 75th Anniversary, Fodor's! Here's to many more.

Tim Jarrell, Publisher

FODOR'S ISRAEL

Editors: Linda Cabasin, Caroline Trefler

Editorial contributor: Mark Sullivan
Writers: Benjamin Balint, Judy Balint, Sarah Bronson, Judy Stacey Goldman, Dina Kraft, Mike Rogoff, Jessica Steinberg, Adeena Sussman

Production Editor: Evangelos Vasilakis
Maps & Illustrations: Henry Colomb and Mark Stroud, Moon Street Photography; David Lindroth, *cartographers;* Bob Blake, Rebecca Baer, *map editors;* William Wu, *information graphics*
Design: Fabrizio La Rocca, *creative director*; Guido Caroti, Siobhan O'Hare, *art directors*; Tina Malaney, Nora Rosansky, Chie Ushio, *designers*; Melanie Marin, *senior picture editor*
Cover Photo: (Jewish Quarter, Old City, Jerusalem): Index Stock Imagery RF/ photolibrary.com
Production Manager: Angela L. McLean

COPYRIGHT

8th Edition

ISBN 978-0-307-48059-0

ISSN 0071-6588

SPECIAL SALES

This book is available at special discounts for bulk purchases for sales promotions or premiums. Special editions, including personalized covers, excerpts of existing books, and corporate imprints, can be created in large quantities for special needs. For more information, write to Special Markets/Premium Sales, 1745 Broadway, MD 6-2, New York, NY 10019, or e-mail specialmarkets@randomhouse.com.

AN IMPORTANT TIP & AN INVITATION

Although all prices, opening times, and other details in this book are based on information supplied to us at press time, changes occur all the time in the travel world, and Fodor's cannot accept responsibility for facts that become outdated or for inadvertent errors or omissions. So **always confirm information when it matters,** especially if you're making a detour to visit a specific place. Your experiences—positive and negative—matter to us. If we have missed or misstated something, **please write to us.** Share your opinion instantly through our online feedback center at fodors.com/contact-us.

PRINTED IN COLOMBIA

10 9 8 7 6 5 4 3 2 1

CONTENTS

Fodor's Features

MAPS

ABOUT THIS BOOK

Our Ratings

At Fodor's, we spend considerable time choosing the best places in a destination so you don't have to. By default, anything we recommend in this book is worth visiting. But some sights, properties, and experiences are so great that we've recognized them with additional accolades. Orange Fodor's Choice stars indicate our top recommendations; black stars highlight places we deem Highly Recommended; and Best Bets call attention to top properties in various categories. Disagree with any of our choices? Care to nominate a new place? Visit our feedback center at www.fodors.com/feedback.

Hotels

Hotels have private bath, phone, and TV; and we specify when they offer meal plans. BP is a full breakfast; CP is a Continental breakfast; and MAP is a breakfast and dinner. We always list facilities but not whether you'll be charged an extra fee to use them.

Restaurants

Unless we state otherwise, restaurants are open for lunch and dinner daily. We mention dress only when there's a specific requirement and reservations only when they're essential or not accepted—it's always best to book ahead.

Credit Cards

We assume that restaurants and hotels accept credit cards. If not, we'll note it in the review.

Budget Well

Hotel and restaurant price categories from ¢ to $$$$ are defined in the opening pages of the respective chapters. For attractions, we always give standard adult admission fees; reductions are usually available for children, students, and senior citizens.

Listings

- ★ Fodor's Choice
- ★ Highly recommended
- ✉ Physical address
- ✣ Directions or Map coordinates
- 📫 Mailing address
- ☎ Telephone
- 📠 Fax
- 🌐 On the Web
- ✎ E-mail
- 🎟 Admission fee
- ⏲ Open/closed times
- Ⓜ Metro stations
- ▭ No credit cards

Hotels & Restaurants

- 🏨 Hotel
- 🛏 Number of rooms
- 👍 Facilities
- 🍽 Meal plans
- ✕ Restaurant
- ✍ Reservations
- 👔 Dress code
- 🚬 Smoking

Outdoors

- ⛳ Golf
- ⛺ Camping

Other

- ☺ Family-friendly
- ⇨ See also
- ✉ Branch address
- ☞ Take note

Experience Israel

1

ISRAEL TODAY

Israel and the Palestinians Reopen Talks

Almost two decades of sporadic dialog between Israel and the Palestinians, often interrupted by violence, have not brought peace much closer. Agreement remains elusive on the core issues of security, defined borders, sharing Jerusalem, Palestinian refugees, Jewish settlements in the West Bank, and water sources.

The resumption of direct peace talks between Israel and the Palestinians in September 2010 was met by some apathy, cynicism and even hostility in both communities. The Israeli government determined to continue construction in Jewish West Bank settlements; the Palestinians retorted that they would abandon the talks; U.S. envoy George Mitchell, a key negotiator in Northern Ireland, cheerfully shared (at this writing) that there was more progress behind the scenes than appeared. Peace remains a challenge.

A Vibrant Economy

Israel's founding fathers were socialists, with deep roots in its early agrarian economy. But poor in natural resources—though natural gas has recently been discovered offshore—Israel always relied on the human factor. Diamond-cutting was an early initiative of Jewish refugees from pre-war and Nazi-occupied Holland and Belgium, and Israel produces 40% of the world's cut and polished stones. The real story, however, is high-tech.Israel is third on the list of NASDAQ-listed companies, after the United States and Canada. Israeli high-tech companies with attractive expertise are constantly being snapped up by big foreign corporations.

Sophisticated, technology-based agriculture has also done very well, but its share of the country's exports has dropped from 60% in the 1950s to under 2% today as the economy has burgeoned and reinvented itself. Israel is now defining itself as a source for clean technology, with companies engaged in solar power, wastewater, electric car, fuel cell, and fuel consumption technologies.

The country's financial environment, including vigilant bank regulation, helped it weather the recent global crisis better than most. The Israel shekel remained remarkably strong, and relations with the European Union were upgraded. At the same time, one out of every five Israeli families lives below the poverty line. The gap between the haves and have-nots is high, and real wealth and influence are concentrated in the hands of the very few. There is public awareness of the problem, yet in a Gallup World Poll, conducted in 155 countries between 2005 and 2009 to find the world's happiest societies, Israel tied for eighth place with Canada, Australia and Switzerland.

Greening Israel

From its earliest years of statehood, Israel had to consider its lack of natural water resources and find ways to compensate, from using drip irrigation for crops and gardens to utilizing rooftop solar panels for heating water. As clean technology, environmental products, and green concepts have become popular, Israel has kept apace, with water treatment technologies that are used locally and exported, as well as solar energy installations in the Negev Desert.

Green housing is also taking root, from private initiatives using natural materials such as mud bricks to government green building standards requiring the use of recycled materials, solar electricity panels, and energy-efficient insulation. Cities

are widening their recycling programs, encouraging bikers, and improving public transportation. Municipalities are also making room for community gardens while banning watering private lawns. Organic farms have become a trend, providing seasonal produce.

A New Immigrant Issue

Modern Israel was born in 1948 as a Jewish nation-state. The country's Jewish population tripled in the first decade of independence, absorbing refugees from postwar Europe and a hostile Middle East. Beginning in 1989, three-quarters of a million people immigrated from the former Soviet Union under the "homecoming" clauses of the Law of Return. Tens of thousands of Jews from remote Ethiopia were woven into Israel's colorful social fabric in the same period.

More recently, African refugees and illegals, and Asians with expired work visas, have presented Israeli authorities with new challenges. In the absence of clear legal guidelines, the resident permit policy has been inconsistent, and the deportation process of illegals problematic. What has moved many Israelis are the hundreds of children of foreign workers who were born in Israel, speak fluent Hebrew, and know no other home. It's the complex problem of illegal immigrants versus the tradition of harboring the homeless—a poignant issue for Jewish Israelis.

The Gaza Conundrum

The Palestinians have been divided. The secular Fatah faction, the nominal leadership, is dominant in the West Bank. Hamas, an extreme Islamicist group that rejects any accommodation with Israel, took control of the Gaza Strip in 2007. Rocket attacks from Gaza against civilian targets in Israel became more frequent. The Israeli military retaliation in late 2008 continues to reverberate in diplomatic circles. Rocket attacks were drastically reduced, but fresh supplies of ground-to-air and anti-tank missiles are coming into the Gaza Strip from Egyptian Sinai through smugglers' tunnels. In 2011, Fatah and Hamas signed a peace agreement, creating uncertainty for Israel and hope for their own.

Israel's Other Neighbors

The start of 2011 brought surprising changes to the Middle East, with protests known as the Arab Spring that have at this writing overthrown the heads of state in Tunisia and Egypt. Those uprisings have had little effect on Israel, which continues to feel relieved that ultra-hostile, almost-nuclear Iran doesn't live next door, but its surrogates do. Hezbollah, a militant Lebanese Shi'ite organization, has been harassing Israel since the early 1980s, even after Israel's full withdrawal from Lebanese territory in 2000. A massive confrontation between the two in 2006 bled both sides, but brought some quiet to Israel's northern front. Hezbollah (at this writing) is a partner in Lebanon's ruling coalition, giving that government—in Israel's view—shared responsibility for attacks against Israel.

While neighboring Syria has kept its border with Israel quiet since the mid-1970s, it is a conduit for resupplying the Hezbollah with long-range missiles, compliments of Iran. The recent uprisings in Syria could hinder that relative quiet, but it's too soon to tell. Meanwhile, Israel continues to signal Syria that it is interested in defusing tensions. An eventual peace agreement with Syria would entail Israel returning the Golan Heights, captured in 1967.

WHAT'S WHERE

Tel Aviv

The following numbers refer to chapters.

2 Jerusalem. The walls of the Old City embrace sites sacred to Judaism, Christianity, and Islam, but Israel's capital is more than its ancient places. Rub shoulders in the vibrant markets, sip coffee in a stone courtyard, and poke around modern museums and malls of a city suspended between East and West, past and present.

3 Around Jerusalem and the Dead Sea. Treat yourself to three different desert experiences: exploring King Herod's mountaintop palace-citadel of Masada, floating in the Dead Sea, and frolicking under waterfalls in the Ein Gedi canyon. Day trips to Bethlehem and to wineries west of Jerusalem are other memorable options.

4 Tel Aviv. The beautiful beaches and seaside promenade, alive with cafés and good times, hug the Mediterranean. The "city that never sleeps" is Israel's cultural and entertainment center. Don't miss its Bauhaus architecture, charming old neighborhoods, and first-class restaurants and nightlife.

5 Haifa and the Northern Coast. Although you're never far from a Mediterranean beach, take time to see the sights in Haifa, like the Baha'i Shrine and Gardens, and in Akko's medieval Old City. South of Haifa are Roman Caesarea and the Mt. Carmel wine country.

6 Lower Galilee. Verdant valleys, rolling hills, and the freshwater Sea of Galilee are counterpoints to the historical riches in this northern part of Israel. Hike the Arbel cliffs, explore archaeology at Beit She'an and Zippori, and visit Nazareth and the famed sites of Jesus' ministry. At night, enjoy dinner by the lake.

Capernaum

7 Upper Galilee and the Golan. Historical treasures, quaint bed-and-breakfasts, and the great outdoors are some of the best reasons for visiting Israel's northeast corner. The mountaintop city of Tzfat (Safed), cradle of Jewish mysticism, and Rosh Pina, a delightful restored village, are two primary sites.

8 Eilat and the Negev. Visiting the Negev is about experiencing the desert's stunning geological treasures, and enjoying Eilat's gorgeous beaches and Red Sea coral reefs. Take a side trip to ancient Petra, in nearby Jordan, to see its temples and tombs carved out of red sandstone cliffs.

Negev desert

LEBANON
SYRIA
JORDAN
EGYPT
GAZA
WEST BANK
GOLAN HEIGHTS
UNDOF Zone (U.N. Disengagement Observer Force)
Mediterranean Sea
Sea of Galilee
Dead Sea
Jordan River
Yarmuk River
Dan
Kiryat Shmona
Rosh Hanikra
Nahariya
Meron
Ma'alot
Tzfat
Akko
Gamla
Haifa
Tiberias
Ein Hod
Nazareth
Afula
Umm el Fahm
Bet She'an
Jenin
Netanya
Tulkarm
Qalqilya
Herzliya Pituach
Nablus/ Shechem
Ramat Gan
Petah Tikva
Tel Aviv
Amman
Lod
Rishon Lezion
Ramallah
Jericho
Ashdod
JERUSALEM
Ashkelon
Bethlehem
Kiryat Gat
Hebron
Gaza
Ein Gedi
Masada
Beersheva
Ein Bokek
Mashabei Sadeh
Dimona
Nizzana
Sde Boker
Hatzeva
Ein Yahav
Mitzpe Ramon
Petra
Lotan
Eilat
Aqaba
0
30 miles
30 km

ISRAEL PLANNER

Getting Here

International flights land at Ben Gurion International Airport, about 10 mi from Tel Aviv and about 27 mi from Jerusalem.

Security checks on airlines flying to Israel are stringent. Be prepared for what might sound like personal questions about your itinerary, packing habits, and desire to travel to Israel. Remember that the staff is concerned with protecting you, and be patient.

A taxi is the quickest and most convenient way to get to and from the airport. Fares to Jerusalem are NIS 280 ($70) for the 45-minute trip and approximately NIS 185 ($50) to Tel Aviv. Another option is the 10-passenger Nesher that shuttles between Jerusalem and Ben Gurion and costs NIS 50 ($12).

If you depart for the airport from central Tel Aviv by car or taxi at rush hour (7–9 am, 5–7 pm), note that the roads can get clogged. Allow 45 minutes for a trip that would otherwise take only about 20 minutes.

The train is a money saver if you're heading for Tel Aviv. A one-way ticket is NIS 14 ($3.50) and takes about 25 minutes.

Getting Around

You can get almost anywhere in Israel by bus, and the Central Bus Station is a fixture in most towns: ask for the *tahana merkazit*. Egged handles all of the country's bus routes; in Tel Aviv there's also Dan. Both intercity and urban buses run from 5:30 am to 12:30 am Sunday to Thursday.

Note: Public transportation is suspended during the Jewish Sabbath (Shabbat), from about two hours before sundown Friday to sundown Saturday, although some lines run minibuses in Tel Aviv. Haifa, with a large Arab population, also has some Shabbat service.

Taxis can be a good option on Shabbat—they're plentiful, relatively inexpensive, and can be hailed on the street. Drivers must use the meter according to law. *Sheruts* are shared taxis or minivans that run fixed routes at a set rate; some can be booked in advance.

The train from Tel Aviv to Jerusalem is a scenic, 1-hour-and-45-minute trip—not the quickest way to travel between the two cities. Commuter trains run efficiently between other cities; the majority of service runs along the coast, from Nahariya south and then inland to Beersheva. Signs at train stations are posted in English. Reservations are not accepted.

For more information on getting here and around, turn to Travel Smart Israel.

DRIVING DISTANCES/TIMES IN ISRAEL		
Eilat to Tel Aviv	220 mi (354 km)	5.5 hrs
Tel Aviv to Jerusalem	36 mi (58 km)	50 mins
Jerusalem to Ben Gurion Airport	27 mi (43 km)	45 mins
Ben Gurion Airport to Tel Aviv	10 mi (16 km)	25 mins
Tel Aviv to Haifa	52 mi (84 km)	1.25 hrs
Haifa to Tiberias	35 mi (56 km)	50 mins
Tiberias to Jerusalem	109 mi (175 km)	2 hrs
Jerusalem to Eilat	190 mi (306 km)	4.5 hrs
Jerusalem to Masada	30 mi (48 km)	1 hr
Haifa to Nazareth	23 mi (37 km)	55 mins

Dining

Unless otherwise noted, the restaurants listed in this guide are open daily for lunch (*arukhat tzohorayim*) and dinner (*arukhat erev*), and prices are in Israeli shekels (NIS). In Israel, many restaurants are *kosher* and will display a dated kosher certificate. These restaurants serve dishes that include either dairy products or meat—but neither is ever served together. Fish can be served with either dairy products or meat, except shellfish, which is a nonkosher food and is not served in kosher restaurants. In the cities, cafés are generally open Sunday to Thursday 8 am to midnight. Kosher cafés close two hours before the Sabbath; nonkosher places keep regular hours. Restaurants serving lunch and dinner usually open at noon and close around midnight or 1 am. Israelis eat dinner fairly late, and it's not uncommon to wait for a table at 10 pm.

Lodging

Nearly all hotel rooms in Israel have private bathrooms with a combined shower and tub. The best hotels have a swimming pool, a health club, and tennis courts; and with rare exceptions in major cities, most hotels have parking facilities. Almost all the large Israeli hotels are certified kosher, and most include a traditional Israeli breakfast. The lodgings we list are the cream of the crop in each price category. We always list the facilities that are available—but we don't specify whether they cost extra: when pricing accommodations, always ask what's included and what costs extra. *Price-category information is given in each chapter.* Prices are in dollars, as paying bills at hotels in foreign currency eliminates the Value-Added Tax (VAT). Unless otherwise noted, all lodgings have a private bathroom, a room phone, and a television.

WHAT IT COSTS

	¢	$	$$	$$$	$$$$
Restaurants	under NIS 32	NIS 32–NIS 49	NIS 50–NIS 75	NIS 76–NIS 100	over NIS 100
Hotels	under $120	$120–$200	$201–$300	$301–$400	over $400

Restaurant prices are per person for a main course at dinner in NIS (Israeli shekels). Hotel prices are in U.S. dollars, for two people in a standard double room in high season. Non-Israeli citizens paying in foreign currency are exempt from the 16% VAT tax on hotel rooms.

When to Go

Israel has several high seasons, but each attracts different types of visitors. The Jewish New Year (Rosh Hashanah) and Sukkot usually fall in September or October, bringing Jewish travelers wanting to celebrate in the Holy Land. Christmas and New Year is a favorite time for Christian pilgrims. In April or March, when Passover and Easter generally coincide, Christian and Jewish tourists crowd religious sites in Jerusalem and the Galilee. July and August are the hottest months, and Israel becomes swamped with beachgoers. The weather is perfect in late September and October, and from April to mid-June, when days are warm enough without being too hot, and nights are comfortable. May and June are in between high seasons and prices are more affordable. The weather is still splendid, and historical sites and other attractions are yet to be filled with tourists.

Renting a Car

Renting a car is a good idea only if you plan to thoroughly explore the country but not within big cities. At the time of this writing, gas costs NIS 6.50 per liter. (Self-service is always cheaper). Most important, double check if coverage applies if you plan to drive in the West Bank. *For more information, turn to Travel Smart.*

ISRAEL MADE EASY

Customs of the Country

Western-style social graces are not the strong suit of the average Israeli. But, despite the country's legendary informality, the traditions and customs of its many ethnic and religious communities form an entire corpus of social norms. Sensitivity to those norms can open doors; ignoring them may cause offense. The best example is the modest dress code required (especially for women) in conservative religious environments—Muslim holy places, some churches and monasteries, and (strictest of all) ultra-Orthodox Jewish shrines and neighborhoods. Covered shoulders, modest necklines, and either full-length pants or (safest) skirts below the knees are de rigueur.

Eating Out

Restaurants that abide by kosher dietary regulations, to satisfy a particular clientele, close for Friday dinner and Saturday lunch (Sabbath ends at dark). Kosher hotel eateries remain open, but will not offer menu items that require cooking on the spot. "Kosher" has nothing to do with particular cuisines but with certain restrictions (no pork or shellfish, no dairy and meat products on the same menu, and more). Kosher restaurants today not only have to compete with nonkosher rivals but also must satisfy an increasingly demanding kosher clientele, so the variety of kosher food is growing. Tipping is 12% minimum. Mostly, this is expected in cash, but adding it to the bill is becoming more common, especially in Tel Aviv. There is great coffee all over Israel. Latte is called "hafuch"; and if you want black coffee, ask for "filter" coffee or Americano. Tap water is safe throughout Israel.

Greetings

Israelis do not stand on ceremony, and greet each other warmly with either a slap on the back (for men) or an air kiss on both cheeks (for women). Tourists are usually greeted with a handshake. Ultra-Orthodox Jewish men won't acknowledge women, and very religious Jews of either gender do not shake hands or mingle socially with members of the opposite sex.

Israelis are known for their bluntness. That openness extends to discussions on religion and politics, too, so don't be afraid to speak your mind (but expect candor in return).

The Jewish Sabbath

The Sabbath extends from sundown Friday until dark on Saturday. Most shops and restaurants in Jewish neighborhoods close, but Arab areas in Jerusalem's Old City, and towns like Nazareth and Akko, will be bustling. While Jerusalem quiets down by Friday afternoon, Tel Aviv remains lively, although bus services are suspended in both cities. Sunday is the first day of the regular work- and school week.

Language

Hebrew is the national language of Israel, but travelers can get by with English. Virtually every hotel has English-speaking staff, as do most restaurants and many shops in the major cities. In smaller towns and rural areas it might be more challenging. A few words of Hebrew, such as *toda* (thank you), *bevakasha* (please), and *shalom* (hello or goodbye) will be warmly appreciated.

Arabic is Israel's other official language, spoken by Arabs, Druze, and a dwindling number of Jews with family roots in Arab lands. Because Israel is a nation of

immigrants, mistakes and various accents are tolerated cheerfully.

Israelis use a lot of hand gestures when they talk. A common gesture is to turn the palm upwards and press the thumb and three fingers together to mean "wait a minute"; this has no negative connotations. Just as harmless is the Israeli who says "I don't believe you" to express that something is unbelievably wonderful.

Money and Shopping

The Israeli shekel (designated NIS) is the currency, but the U.S. dollar is accepted in places accustomed to dealing with tourists. At press time, $1 is equal to NIS 3.45. Rates for hotels, guiding services, and car rentals are always quoted and paid for in foreign currency, thus avoiding the 16% local VAT. Many better stores offer a government VAT refund on purchases above US$100, claimable at the airport duty-free or at the Jordanian border. Licensed exchange booths on busy streets or in shopping malls are convenient places to change money; banks offer lines, unhelpful hours and unattractive rates. Although ATM transaction fees may be higher abroad than at home, ATM rates are excellent because they're based on wholesale rates offered only by major banks. Avoid buying gold, silver, gemstones, and antiquities in bazaars (like Jerusalem's Old City souk), where things aren't always what they seem and prices fluctuate wildly.

Safety

Israel is news, it seems—for better or for worse. To be sure, there have been several major security situations over the last decade or so, but intense media coverage has sometimes exaggerated the scope and significance of this or that localized incident. Much of the populace seems unmoved, however. At this writing, the country has enjoyed a considerable period of calm. In Jerusalem, the Old City can be thronged during the day and virtually empty at night. Spend your evenings elsewhere. The Arab neighborhoods of East Jerusalem are perhaps not as welcoming as they were once, but unless there is some general security issue at the time, the daytime wanderer should not encounter anything more serious than pickpockets.

At the time of this writing, Israeli authorities were barring their citizens from visiting Palestinian autonomous areas such as Bethlehem and Jericho, but tourists can take an Arab cab and this guidebook. Your concierge or Israeli tour guide may be able to set up a Palestinian guide on the other side. There are standard security checks along the roads to the West Bank, and car rental companies generally do not allow their vehicles to cross into those areas.

Expect to have your handbags searched as a matter of course when you enter bus and train terminals, department stores, places of entertainment, museums, and public buildings. These checks are generally quick and courteous.

Visiting Sacred Sites

Muslim sites are generally closed for tourists on Friday, the Muslim holy day. Avoid the Muslim Quarter of Jerusalem's Old City between noon and 2 pm on Fridays, when the flow of worshippers in the streets can be uncomfortable or even rowdy. Some Christian sites close on Sunday; others open after morning worship. Many Jewish religious sites, museums, and historical sites close early on Friday: some remain closed through Saturday (the Jewish Sabbath).

ISRAEL TOP ATTRACTIONS

A

B

C

D

E

Old City, Jerusalem

(A) The golden stones are saturated with Jerusalem's millennia of history. Explore the Church of the Holy Sepulcher, mingle with Jewish worshippers at the Western Wall, and stroll the Temple Mount to admire its Muslim shrines. Time spent exploring the winding alleyways, bustling markets, and storied buildings of the Old City is both a fascinating history primer and a lesson in the challenges of coexistence.

Masada and the Dead Sea

(B) The view and the ancient remains of King Herod's mountaintop palace-fortress are reason enough to climb Masada, as a predawn hike or by swift cable car, but the echoes of the Jewish rebellion against Rome make Masada what it is. Float in the hyperbrine of the nearby Dead Sea, and then frolic in Ein Gedi's fresh waterfalls. It all makes for a memorable day of contrasts and superlatives.

Makhtesh Ramon

(C) In the heart of the Negev desert, the Ramon Crater—formed when an ancient ocean above it migrated northward—includes multicolored rock formations, breathtaking hills and valleys, wadis (mostly dry river beds), fossil formations, and many flora and fauna unique to the region. It's great for a guided hike, a Jeep tour, or some camel riding.

The Sea of Galilee

(D) This shimmering freshwater lake, known in Hebrew as the *Kinneret*, is linked to many events in the life of Jesus. Pilgrims flock to its shores, sail its waters, and gather for baptism at the River Jordan where it leaves the lake.

Baha'i Shrine and Gardens

(E) Adherents of the Baha'i faith, which believes in the unity of humankind, built this showpiece in Haifa, combining a show-stopping acre of manicured grounds

F

G

J

H

I

with an ornate, gold-domed shrine sure to impress visitors and true believers alike.

Caesarea

(F) King Herod built the great port city over 2,000 years ago, naming it for Caesar Augustus. The renovated Roman theater is back in business; scuba enthusiasts can see elements of the Herodian port; and an ancient aqueduct slices across a pretty beach. Crusader fortifications mix with latter-day restaurants and galleries to create a serene, picturesque getaway.

Western Wall

(G) Jews the world over flock to the only remaining relic of the complex that housed the ancient Holy Temple in Jerusalem. Every day, hundreds of handwritten paper notes covered with personal prayers are stuffed into the wall's cracks.

Church of the Holy Sepulcher

(H) Five of the fourteen Stations of the Cross—including the site of Jesus' crucifixion and burial—are found within this Crusader-era church in Jerusalem's Old City. Six denominations of Christianity are represented here, each with distinct chapels and religious rites.

Old City, Akko

(I) The picturesque port city has seen it all: Canaanites and Greeks, Crusaders and Napoleon, Turks and Brits. Visit the excellently preserved medieval quarters; browse the copperware shops; eat hummus and seafood; explore the small port, the Turkish bathhouse, and the British prison from which Jewish resistance fighters broke out in the 1940s.

Dome of the Rock

(J) In Jerusalem an enormous plaza, on the site of the Temple Mount, holds the al-Aqsa Mosque, the third-holiest site in Islam and an active house of worship, and the gold-topped Dome of the Rock. Exploring the plaza is well worthwhile, although the shrines are currently closed to non-Muslims.

QUINTESSENTIAL ISRAEL

Falafel

Falafel sandwiches are a fast-food staple in Israel, and stands are found from the busy streets of downtown Tel Aviv to the ultra-Orthodox areas of Jerusalem and the Eilat beach promenade.

It starts with a scoop of seasoned chickpeas mashed into small spheres that are quickly fried in oil then thrust—six or so—into a pita. Patrons give a nod or a "no thanks" to some hummus or *harif* (hot sauce), and to each of the colorful accompaniments: finely chopped cucumbers and tomatoes, shredded cabbage (white or red), parsley, pickles, and even french fries stuffed on top. Some establishments give you little bowls to fill with extra side dishes. Many customers drizzle their creation with self-serve sauces: *amba* (spicy pickled mango) and tahini. Be sure to have a few extra napkins ready, and assume the falafel position before taking your first bite: leaning forward well away from clothing and shoes.

The Sabra Personality

Israelis are reputed to have prickly personalities. Although you will hear the word *savlanut* (patience) bandied about, natives don't seem to be blessed with an overabundance of that quality.

An old saying tries to explain the character of Israelis, masters of the short retort, by comparing it to the prickly pear, a cactus known as the *sabra*, which is thorny on the outside but sweet on the inside. By extension, native-born Israelis are known as sabras. Fortunately, this national tendency toward abruptness is tempered with a generous dose of Mediterranean warmth. But there's a trick to dealing with the perceived cold shoulder: persevere. A welcome thaw is likely to be close at hand.

Israel is more than holy sites and turbulent politics; to get a sense of the country, familiarize yourself with some of the features in daily life.

Markets and Bargaining

Israel's open-air markets are just the place to soak up local culture while shopping for snacks to stock your hotel room. Many produce markets also have stalls selling cheap clothing and other textiles. Machaneh Yehuda in Jerusalem and Tel Aviv's Carmel Market are famous. For markets that sell decorative brass, ceramic and glass items, beads, embroidered dresses, and jackets or secondhand funky clothes, head to Jerusalem's Old City or the Jaffa Flea Market.

Bargaining can be fun—but there are some useful pointers. Never answer the question "how much do you want to pay?" When the seller names a price, come back with about half. If the seller balks, be prepared to walk out; if you're called back, they want to make a sale. If you're in a hurry, vendors will know it and won't drop the price. Not every vendor will be in the mood for the bargaining game: Don't begin the process unless your intentions are serious.

Café Culture

Café sitting is an integral part of Israeli life, especially in the cities where it seems as if there's one on every corner. The locals love their *café hafuch* (latte: literally, "upside-down coffee"). In many cafés a request for cappuccino gets you the same beverage, perhaps with more froth and a shake of cinnamon. Rival Israeli coffee chains have multiplied like crazy across the country since the late '90s. The coffee, invariably made in Italian machines, is usually excellent. Unlike European cafés where the waiters get antsy if you stay too long, in Israel you can sit unhassled. Most cafés offer reasonably priced full breakfasts, sandwiches, main-dish salads, quiche, pizza, and soup. There are also upscale bistro-cafés, great for everything from a glass of wine to a heartier meal.

IF YOU LIKE

Archaeology

For earlier Israeli generations, archaeology was something of a national sport. It's still riveting to walk where the ancients did—and often you can read about the very site in the Bible.

Old Testament stuff doesn't get better than **Megiddo,** with its 25 strata of history. Get a free brochure with your ticket, and take a few minutes in the tiny museum. Explore Second Temple period remains at **Masada** (again, take the brochure—and find 30 minutes for the wonderful museum), near the Dead Sea, and monumental masonry and audiovisuals at the **Jerusalem Archaeological Park** (Davidson Center). On the Mediterranean, **Caesarea,** with its Roman theater, hippodrome, sunken harbor, mosaics and Crusader ruins, is a must-see for many. **Capernaum,** by the Sea of Galilee, was a Jewish town with New Testament echoes: minimal explanations, but an ancient synagogue and church remains evoke the story.

If a hands-on excavation, dirt and all, appeals to the Indiana Jones within you, Archaeological Seminars has a year-round Dig for a Day program—actually three hours of fun—in the caves of **Beit Guvrin–Maresha National Park.** More heavy-duty digs require a one-week minimum commitment from its volunteers; some insist on a month. Most are scheduled for the spring or summer. For a list of expeditions looking for pay-your-own-way labor, browse the Internet and follow the links; they change from year to year.

In Jerusalem, reinforce your newfound archaeological expertise with a visit (best with a docent) to the **Israel Museum**'s excellent Archaeological Wing, or the neighboring **Bible Lands Museum.**

The Great Outdoors

Think green. After a tour of the cities and sites, visit one or more of Israel's tranquil nature reserves to mellow out and commune with the flora and fauna. It's also a great way to experience the diversity of the countryside.

The Hula Valley, in the Upper Galilee, is the best-watered part of the country. **Tel Dan Nature Reserve** is a fairyland of brooks and streams. It also has impressive biblical ramparts and a high place as an added bonus.

The **Banias** (officially the Hermon Stream Nature Reserve) seeps out softly beneath Mt. Hermon, right at a shrine to Pan, and then churns its way south. An easy trail offers great views of waterfalls and cataracts.

Israel is a major bird migration route from northeastern Europe to Africa in the autumn, and back again in the spring. Many of the estimated 500 million frequent flyers rest awhile in the wetlands **Hula Nature Reserve** (where you sometimes get tantalizing views of water buffalo, wolves and water creatures) and nearby Agmon Ha-Hula, popular with pelicans and noisy cranes.

On the Golan Heights, eagles and griffon vultures nest in the craggy **Gamla Nature Reserve.** View a fine waterfall, and visit remains of one of the oldest synagogues ever found.

Do you like caves? The small but exquisite **Soreq Cave** (Avshalom Reserve), not far from Jerusalem, boasts almost every type of stalactite formation known.

Desert Adventures

The desert has its own subtle beauty. No wonder that contemplative religions were born there, or that hermits sought solitude on its hillsides. Your excursion can be as short as a few hours or as long as a day, or several days. Tours can be booked through travel agents or through your hotel, but some tours don't operate in the hot summers. On all hikes, make sure you wear a hat and good walking shoes, and drink plenty of water.

The booming silence of **Makhtesh Ramon,** the wild canyons behind **Eilat,** and the enormous ravines of the Judean Desert attract serious hikers, but should not be done alone. Consider an organized hike with (for example) the **Society for the Protection of Nature in Israel.**

Running water in the desert is pure magic. The photo-op canyon of **Ein Avdat,** near Sde Boker, south of Beersheba, is easily accessible. The **Ein Gedi** oasis, near the Dead Sea, offers a twofer: the shorter but often crowded Nahal David, and the much longer, more primeval Nahal Arugot trail. Both have natural freshwater pools and waterfalls, and are home to ibex (wild goats) and hyrax (small furry creatures).

Hai Bar, a nature reserve 30 minutes north of Eilat, breeds biblical animals that are now endangered species. The horned addax and oryx, and the ostrich and the Somali wild ass may be released into the wild once numbers justify it. Predators—animals, birds and reptiles—are kept in a zoolike environment. Tour alone or (better) with a local guide.

If you prefer to travel by other means than by foot, you can sign up to see the desert by Jeep. Another option is a camel trip into the Negev northwest of Eilat.

Sacred Spaces

Sanctity comes in different forms in the Holy Land, and its sights, sounds, smells and textures make for a multisensory experience as well. Some pilgrims find the hubbub at many sites disconcerting, but keep in mind that most places were not pristine and ethereal in their day either.

For Christians of every denomination, Israel offers a unique opportunity to follow in the footsteps of Jesus. From the **Sea of Galilee** to the Jordan River and **Nazareth,** scripture comes alive. Ride a boat, explore ancient **Capernaum,** and contemplate the landscape where Jesus preached. In Jerusalem, the **Garden of Gethsemane,** the **Via Dolorosa,** and the **Church of the Holy Sepulcher** evoke the scenes of Jesus' final days. The **Garden Tomb** is a mandatory stop for many Protestants.

For the Jewish faith, the holiest place in the world is the **Western Wall,** a remnant of Jerusalem's ancient Temple Mount. Graves traditionally identified with biblical figures, Talmudic sages, and medieval rabbis dot the Galilee. The tombs of King David in Jerusalem and Rabbi Shimon Bar Yochai on **Mt. Meron** in Upper Galilee are famous. But for many Jews, the entire land, rather than individual sites, is biblical and blessed.

The black-domed **al-Aqsa Mosque,** in Jerusalem's Haram esh-Sharif (or Temple Mount), is the third-holiest place in Islam. The golden **Dome of the Rock** nearby is built on the spot where the Prophet Muhammad is believed to have ascended to the heavens to receive the teachings of Islam.

The landmark gold-domed **Baha'i Shrine** on the slopes of Mt. Carmel, in Haifa, covers the tomb of the Bab, the forerunner of the Baha'i faith. Its gardens provide a serene environment for this gentle faith.

ISRAEL: PEOPLE, RELIGION, AND STATE

"I could not conceive of a small country having so large a history," wrote Mark Twain after his visit to the Holy Land in 1867. The rich history certainly fascinates, as does the complex political situation despite, or because of, its constant sense of urgency. But beyond that are the people, a varied population of 7.7 million, representing a startlingly wide array of ethnicities, nationalities, religious beliefs, and lifestyles. The diversity of Israel's population is one of the country's greatest strengths—and one of its essential challenges. It may explain, for example, why defining a national identity is still a work in progress, even after more than sixty years.

Creating a Nation

Israel's founding generation saw the country as a modern reincarnation of the ancient Jewish nation-state. Israel was the "Promised Land" of Abraham and Moses, the Israelite kingdom of David and Solomon, and the home of Jesus of Nazareth and the Jewish Talmudic sages. Although the Jewish presence in the country has been unbroken for more than 3,000 years, several massive exiles—first by the Babylonians in 586 BC and then by the Romans in AD 70—created a Diaspora, a dispersion of the Jewish people throughout the world. The sense of historical roots still resonates for many, probably most, Jewish Israelis; and bringing their brethren home has been a national priority from the beginning.

The attachment to the ancient homeland, and a yearning for the restoration of "Zion and Jerusalem," weaves through the entire fabric of Jewish history and religious tradition. Over the centuries, many Jews trickled back to Eretz Yisrael (the Land of Israel), while others looked forward to fulfilling their dream of return in some future—many felt imminent—messianic age. Not all were prepared to wait for divine intervention, however, and in the late 19th century, a variety of Jewish nationalist organizations emerged, bent on creating a home for their people in Israel (then the district of Palestine in the vast Ottoman Empire). Zionism was created as a political movement to give structure and impetus to that idea.

Some early Zionist leaders, like founding father Theodor Herzl, believed that the urgent priority was simply a Jewish haven safe from persecution, wherever that haven might be. Argentina was suggested, and Great Britain offered Uganda. In light of Jewish historical and emotional links to the land of Israel, most Zionists rejected these "territorialist" proposals.

The establishment of the State of Israel did not, of course, meet with universal rejoicing. To the Arab world, it was anathema, an alien implant in a Muslim Middle East. Palestinian Arabs today mark Israel's independence as the *Nakba*, the Catastrophe, a moment in time when their own national aspirations were thwarted. For many ultra-Orthodox Jews, the founding of Israel was an arrogant preempting of God's divine plan; and to make matters worse, the new state was blatantly secular, despite its concessions to religious interests. This internal battle over the character of the Jewish state, and the implacable hostility of Israel's neighbors—which has resulted in more than six decades of unremitting conflict—have been the two main issues engaging the country since its birth.

The Israeli People

Roughly 5.8 million of Israel's citizens—a little more than 75%—are Jewish. Some trace their family roots back many

generations on local soil; others are first- to fourth-generation *olim* (immigrants) from dozens of different countries. The first modern pioneers arrived from Russia in 1882, purchased land, and set about developing it with romantic zeal. A decade or two later, inspired by the socialist ideas then current in Eastern Europe, a much larger wave founded the first *kibbutzim*—collective villages or communes. In time, these fiercely idealistic farmers became something of a moral elite, having little financial power but providing a greatly disproportionate percentage of the country's political leadership, military officer cadre, and intelligentsia.

The kibbutz ideology has pretty much run out of steam. A more personally ambitious younger generation has increasingly eschewed the communal lifestyle in favor of the lures of the big city. In the vast majority of the 270 or so kibbutzim across the country, modern economic realities have undermined the old socialist structure, and a high degree of privatization is the order of the day.

The State of Israel was founded in 1948, just three years after the end of World War II and the Holocaust, in which the Nazis annihilated fully two-thirds of European Jewry. In light of the urgency of providing a haven for remnants of those shattered communities, the Law of Return was passed in 1950 granting any Jew automatic right to Israeli citizenship.

Most of the immigrants before Israel's independence in 1948 were Ashkenazi Jews (of Central or Eastern European descent), but the biggest wave in the first decade of statehood came from the Arab lands of North Africa and the Middle East. Israel's Jewish population—600,000 at the time of independence—doubled within 3½ years and tripled within ten.

In the late 1980s and early '90s, a wave of about three-quarters of a million Jews moved to Israel from the former Soviet Union. The Russian influence is felt everywhere in Israel today, not least in the fields of technology and classical music. In the early 1980s, a smaller group of Jews from the long-isolated Ethiopian community trekked across Sudan, on their odyssey to the dreamed-of "Jerusalem." Many perished en route. Another 14,500 were airlifted into Israel over one weekend in 1991. Their challenge—and that of Israeli society—has been their integration into a modern technological society.

The vast majority of Israel's 1.5 million Arabic-speaking citizens are Muslims (among them about 120,000 Bedouin), followed by 120,000 Druze (a separate religious group), and about 100,000 Christian Arabs. Most Israeli Arabs live in the mixed Jewish-Arab towns of Jaffa, Ramla, Lod, Haifa, and Akko; a number of good-sized towns and villages on the eastern edge of the coastal plain; in Nazareth and throughout the Lower Galilee; and, in the case of the Bedouin, in the Negev Desert. The extent to which they are integrated with Israeli Jews often depends on location. In Haifa, for example, there is little tension between the two ethnic groups. On the other hand, Jerusalem's quarter-million Arab residents are Palestinian not Israeli, and the situation is more fraught. All Israeli Arabs are equal under the law, and vote for and serve in the *Knesset*, the Israeli parliament.

However, social and economic gaps between the Arab and Jewish sectors do exist, and Arab complaints of government neglect and unequal allocation of

ISRAEL: PEOPLE, RELIGION, AND STATE

resources have sometimes spilled into angry street demonstrations and other antiestablishment activity. The Muslims in Israel are mainstream Sunnis and regarded as both politically and religiously moderate by the standards of the region. Nevertheless, in recent years there has been some radicalization of the community's youth, who identify politically with the Palestinian liberation movement and/or religiously with the Islamic revival that has swept the Middle East.

Of the Christian Arabs, most belong to the Greek Catholic, Greek Orthodox, or Roman Catholic churches; a handful of Eastern denominations and a few small Protestant groups account for the rest. The Western Christian community is minuscule, consisting mainly of clergy, and temporary sojourners such as diplomats.

Israel's Druze, though Arabic-speaking, follow a separate and secret religion that broke from Islam about 1,000 years ago. Larger kindred communities exist in long-hostile Syria and Lebanon, but Israeli Druze have solidly identified with Israel, and the community's young men are routinely drafted into the Israeli army.

The Arab community itself is not liable for military service, partly in order to avoid the risk of battlefield confrontations with kinsmen from neighboring countries; between the lines, however, lies the fear that Israeli Arabs in uniform may experience a sense of dual loyalty.

Judaism in Israel

There is no firm separation of religion and state in Israel. Matters of personal status—marriage, divorce, adoption, and conversion—are the preserve of the religious authorities of the community concerned. For this reason there is no civil marriage; if one partner does not convert to the faith of the other, the couple must marry abroad. Within the Jewish community, such functions fall under the supervision of the Orthodox chief rabbinate, much to the dismay of members of the tiny but growing Conservative and Reform movements, and of the large number of nonobservant Jews.

Almost half of all Israeli Jews call themselves secular. The religiously observant—strict adherence to Sabbath laws and dietary laws, regular attendance at worship services, and so on—account for about 20 percent. At least another one-third of the Jewish population identify themselves as "traditional," meaning they observe some Jewish customs to some extent, often as a nod to Jewish heritage or out of a sense of family duty. Ultra-Orthodox (*haredi* in Hebrew) is the smaller of the two mainstreams that make up the Orthodox Jewish community. The men are easily recognized by their black hats and garb. Their parallel universe embraces religion as a 24/7 lifestyle. Their independent school system, 80% government-funded, teaches only religious subjects. While some haredi men do go out to work, many have committed themselves to full-time study.

The confrontation between secular Israelis and the ultra-Orthodox has escalated over the years, as the religious community tries to impose its vision of how a Jewish state should behave. One volatile issue is the Orthodox contention that only someone who meets the Orthodox definition of a Jew (either born of a Jewish mother or converted by strict Orthodox procedures) should be eligible for Israeli citizenship under the Law of Return. The real resentment, however, is reserved for the political

clout and budgets that the haredim have gained as the price of coalition politics, and their almost total refusal to serve in the military on the grounds of continuing religious studies. By contrast, the modern Orthodox—in Israel they prefer to be known as "religious Zionists"—tend to be gung-ho Israeli patriots, serve in the military, and are strongly identified with the hard-line settler movement in the West Bank and elsewhere. Unlike the haredim, modern Orthodox men and women are fully immersed in Israeli society. Modern Orthodox men dress in "regular" clothes, but typically wear *kippot* or skullcaps on their heads. Women in both religious communities dress very modestly.

Israeli Government

Israel prides itself on being the only true democracy in the Middle East, but it sometimes seems bent on tearing itself apart politically in the democratic process. This is how the system works (or doesn't): once every four years, prior to national elections, every contesting party publishes a list of its candidates for the 120-member Knesset, in a hierarchy determined by the party's own convention. There are no constituencies or voting districts; each party that breaks the minimum threshold of 2% of the national vote gets in, winning the same percentage of Knesset seats as its proportion of nationwide votes (hence the description of the system as "proportional representation").

The good news is that the system is intensely democratic. A relatively small grouping of like-minded voters countrywide can elect an MK (Member of the Knesset) to represent its views. The largest party able to gain a parliamentary majority through a coalition with other parties forms the government, and its leader becomes the prime minister.

The bad news is that the system spawns a plethora of small parties, whose collective support the government needs in order to rule. Since no party has ever won enough seats to rule alone, Israeli governments have always been based on compromise, with small parties exerting a degree of political influence often quite out of proportion to their actual size. Attempts to change the system have been doomed, because the small parties, which stand to lose if the system is changed, are precisely those on whose support the current government depends.

The religious divide in the Jewish community carries over into the Knesset, where religion is a central plank in the platform of several parties. The other and arguably more active ideological "fault line" divides Israeli society into a dovish liberal left (currently much weakened), a hard-line right wing of ultranationalists, and a fluctuating political center that sometimes knows what it is not, but not too often what it is. Where you stand on the left-right spectrum reflects your views on the Israel-Palestinian issue: dovish or hawkish, yea or nay to a Palestinian state, dismantle West Bank settlements or keep building them, divide Jerusalem or keep it all. In a country where security, the Jewishness of Israel, and its democratic character have always been the main issues, these ideological-political distinctions have critical ramifications. Of late, even essential characteristics of a democratic society—the independence of the judiciary, for example—have come under attack from ultraconservatives. Liberals are concerned.

ISRAEL'S TOP EXPERIENCES

Rooftopping in Jerusalem

Historical Jerusalem is about shrines and antiquities, but some 35,000 people live within the Old City walls. From the Ramparts Walk, you can get a look into the courtyards and gardens that lie behind the bolted iron doors you pass on the street. The towers and domes of the city's main faith communities pierce sweeping panoramas.

Shopping in the Market

A walk through a produce market may sometimes feel like a contact sport, but this is hands-down the best way to experience real commerce that combines Middle Eastern–style salesmanship with top-quality products. Spices, dried fruits, nuts, produce, cheeses, and meats are sold from stalls crowded one up against the other. Best are Jerusalem's Machaneh Yehuda and Tel Aviv's Carmel Market.

Floating in the Dead Sea

The Dead Sea is so called for the fact that no living thing can survive in its briney brew. The lake has become a mecca for those who believe in its curative properties; but even if you don't suffer from skin or muscular ailments, bobbing like a cork in the supersaturated water is an utterly relaxing (if slightly bizarre) experience. Reading a newspaper while doing it makes a great photograph as well.

Eating Israeli Breakfast

Israelis don't eat this sumptuously at home, but the "Israeli breakfast" served at most hotels has grown out of local healthy habits of yogurts, fruit, cheeses, eggs, and salads (yes, for breakfast). The often-elaborate hotel buffets began adding baked goods, smoked fish, eggs made to order, a variety of breads and juices, and (Western influence!) cereal and pancakes or waffles. It's a superb way to start your day.

Exploring Tel Aviv's Old Neighborhoods

Tel Aviv's old neighborhoods—situated largely in the south—tell the tale of the development of a modern city that celebrated its 100th anniversary in 2009. Now gentrifying after years of neglect, areas such as Neveh Tzedek fuse architectural preservation and modern progress. There's also plenty of good dining and shopping.

Hiking the Desert

Deserts offer deep silence, minimalist landscapes, sparse vegetation, and rare animal life. Therein lies their magic: the Great Escape. There's a lot of desert in little Israel. Nature reserves like Ein Gedi's two canyons (near the Dead Sea) and Ein Avdat (in the Negev) add the miracle of running water to the enormous crags.

Touring a Winery

Israeli grape growing and wine production can be traced to biblical times. There's no better way to sample the country's vintages than to tour its wineries, from large operations with dozens of varieties to boutique, limited-production establishments. Reservations need to be made for tours and tastings at all but the largest wineries.

Checking out the Beach Scene in Eilat

The bikinis, the Speedos, the sarongs, the sunglasses—it's the Riviera with local flair. Eilat is a respite for on-the-go Israelis who love nothing more than to spend a few days eating chips (french fries), and dipping into the Red Sea—all set to the *plonk-plonk* soundtrack of *matkot,* the Israeli paddleball game that may as well be a national sport.

ISRAEL LODGING PRIMER

Israel has plenty of hotels belonging to major international hotel chains and smaller national networks, as well as independently run lodgings. Some are utilitarian, but some recent trends are a rise in distinctive boutique hotels and in luxury properties. In contrast, options such as kibbutz hotels and bed-and-breakfasts (known as *zimmers* in Israel) offer a glimpse into local life and a more leisurely experience. *For specific contacts, see Accommodations in Travel Smart Israel.*

Israel's Ministry of Tourism has begun to institute a system that should be in place by the end of 2012. The government has already started to rate the country's 9,000 B&Bs, starting with those in the Galilee. They are ranked A, B, or C, based on size and the facilities offered.

Apartment and House Rentals

Short-term rentals are popular, especially in Jerusalem and Tel Aviv and particularly for families who would otherwise be taking two or three hotel rooms. Options range from basic studios to mansions, and most are privately owned. Agents give you the biggest selection, but it's also possible to find accommodations through listing services.

Bed-and-Breakfasts

Over the past decade, thousands of zimmers have sprung up, especially in the Galilee and the Golan. These are intimate cabins, usually featuring one or two bedrooms, a kitchenette, a hot tub, and an outdoor lounging area. Prices are not necessarily lower than hotels, but if it's peace and quiet you're after, these may be just the thing.

Many of Israel's *kibbutzim* (communal settlements) have opened B&Bs. Private-home owners are also increasingly opening their doors to guests.

Christian Hospices

Lodgings called Christian hospices (meaning hostelries, not facilities for the ill) provide accommodations and sometimes meals; these are mainly in Jerusalem and the Galilee. Some hospices are real bargains, while others are merely reasonable; facilities range from spare to luxurious. They give preference to pilgrimage groups, but most will accept secular travelers when space is available.

Home Exchanges and Vacation Rentals

With a direct home exchange you stay in someone else's home while they stay in yours. More common in Israel is the vacation rental. You're not actually staying in someone's full-time residence, just their weekend place or an investment rental.

Hostels

Youth hostels in Israel compete with hotels and guesthouses. Many hostels provide family rooms with private baths. All are air-conditioned; some have communal cooking facilities; and all provide meals. It's worth coming equipped with a valid Hostelling International membership card—otherwise, the attractive, modern hostels charge guesthouse prices. Even without a card, however, hostels are a good deal.

Kibbutz Hotels

Around the country, kibbutz hotels offer budget-level accommodations in peaceful, sometimes lovely settings. Most have large lawns, swimming pools, and athletic facilities. Some offer lectures about the history of kibbutzim and tours of the settlements and the surrounding areas.

FLAVORS OF ISRAEL

Most Israelis divide the day into at least six excuses to eat. There's breakfast, a 10 am snack, a quick lunch, a 5 pm coffee break (around the time that the Western world is calling for a cocktail), a full dinner, and a snack before bed, just for good measure. Satisfying this appetite is made easier by the great grab-and-go food with soul, including crispy falafel, sold on Israel's streets and in small food joints.

A good number of Israel's restaurants are kosher, and conform to Jewish dietary laws. Essentially, kosher restaurants do not serve food that mixes milk and meat. Fish and eggs can be served with either, although note that some fish (skate, for example) and all shellfish are not kosher. Most restaurants that identify themselves as strictly kosher may not be open on the Jewish Sabbath. The majority of hotels countrywide serve kosher food. Bon appétit, or, as they say here, *betayavon!*

Israeli Breakfast

The classic "Israeli breakfast" is legendary, but fewer busy Israelis have time to make it at home these days. You will mostly find it at hotels, B&Bs, and cafés. Hotel buffets will include bowls of brightly colored "Israeli" salads, platters of cheeses, piles of fresh fruit, granola, hot and cold cereals, baskets of various breads and baked goods ranging from cinnamon or chocolate twists to quiche, smoked fish, fresh fruit juices, made-to-order eggs (*betza ayin*, or "egg like an eye," means a fried egg, *chavitah* is omelet, and *mekushkash* is scrambled), and pancakes (locals pour on chocolate sauce). Country lodgings such as B&Bs offer homemade versions, and city coffeehouses specialize in the Israeli breakfast, accompanied by croissants and cappuccino, often served until 1 pm—and sometimes all day.

The Essential Cup of Coffee

Gone are the days when the only coffee available was a tiny cup of *botz*, or mud. You can have that, too (ask for café Turki), but Israel has a coffee culture on a par with Europe's. Most places use Italian machines; the past decade has seen the advent of Western-style coffeeshop chains, the biggest being Aroma, Café Hillel, and Café Joe. You can have a robust and flavorful cappuccino (known as *hafuch*, or upside-down); an Americano should you be homesick; espresso; and in the summer, iced coffee known as *barad*, a slushy chilled confection made with crushed ice. Soy milk is often available, as is decaf (*natoul* in Hebrew). In the Old City of Jerusalem and Arab establishments, espresso is made with the addition of a pinch of cardamom, or *hel*.

Israeli Salad

There are several different kinds of chopped salads in Israel, but there's one classic, and there's no question that this is a trademark dish. Its origins probably lie with Arab cuisine; basically it's a combination of fresh cucumbers, tomatoes, and onion, but the secret's in the chopping—each ingredient must be chopped small and evenly. Cooks who fly in the face of tradition might add chopped parsley and mint, and bits of chopped lemon. Then the salad is dashed with quality olive oil and fresh lemon juice and a sprinkle of salt and pepper or *za'atar*, a Middle Eastern spice blend made with dried hyssop, oregano and sesame seeds. It can be eaten on its own with white cheese and bread before work, spooned into a pita with falafel and hummus at any time of day, and with the main dish at most every meal.

Grilled Meats and Steaks

Virtually every town has at least one Middle Eastern grill restaurant, where you can find kebab, skewered grilled chicken (dark meat baby chicken, or *pargit,* is a favorite), lamb, beef, mixed grill or spit-grilled shawarma, generally prepared with turkey seasoned with lamb fat, cumin, coriander, and other spices.

If you want a good steak, don't worry: order entrecôte and see for yourself. You can even get a good hamburger these days. In Jerusalem, around the open fruit and vegetable market, are grilled-meat eateries famous for their chicken and beef on skewers, called *shipudim*, and their *meu'rav Yerushalmi* (Jerusalem mixed grill), a mélange of chicken hearts, livers, and spleen.

Seafood

There are fish restaurants all over the country, but locals say the best ones are in cities and towns that border the Mediterranean (like Tel Aviv, Jaffa, Ashdod, Haifa, and Akko), around the Kinneret (Sea of Galilee), and in Eilat. In nonkosher restaurants the chance of finding shrimp, squid and other nonkosher fish on the menu have increased substantially.

Salatim

The world *salat* in Hebrew means salad. But many small dishes, served cold, as an appetizer, are called *salatim*. It's basically a mezze. In less fancy restaurants, and often in fish and grilled-meat places, these are slung onto the table along with a basket of pita before you've even managed to get comfortable. They're usually free, but ask. Dig into selections such as two or three types of eggplant, hot Turkish condiments in red or green, cumin-flecked carrot salad, tahini-enriched hummus, fried cauliflower, pickled vegetables, and cracked-wheat salad (tabbouleh), but leave room for the main course, too.

Cheeses

Holy Land cows are hard at work providing milk for cheeses, and these top the list, followed by goat and sheep milk cheese and, last but not least, the healthy buffalo cheese—mostly mozzarella. Soft white cheeses reign supreme. An Israeli favorite is *gvina levana*, a spreadable white cheese available in a variety of fat percentages. A few famous cheeses are Bulgarit (goat), on the salty side; Brinza (half goat, half sheep); Tzfatit, originally made in the northern city of Tzfat, not too salty; the ubiquitous goat cheese, feta; and Tom (goat), a zingy white cheese.

Wines

There's a surfeit of choice when it comes to excellent wine in Israel, made from all the major international grape varieties in five main wine regions from north to south. *For more information, see the Wines of Israel feature in Chapter 5.*

World Cuisine

The last decade or so has brought fusion cuisines to Israel—a superb blend of local flavors and ingredients with French-Italian-Asian or Californian influences—designed by young Israeli chefs, many of whom have studied abroad.

Although gourmet restaurants dot the Galilee, Golan, Jerusalem, and other parts of the country, it's definitely worth saving up to eat at one of Tel Aviv's top establishments. These restaurants are most often pricey, and though dressing up is never necessary, feel free. The locals also adore sushi, and Japanese restaurants and fast-food sushi joints abound. If you like to poke around, try some home-cooked ethnic foods—like Moroccan, Persian, Bucharian, or Tripolitan (Libyan) fare.

ISRAEL WITH KIDS

Fortunately it's easy to keep the kids busy in Israel. Let them expend energy exploring Crusader castles or caves in nature reserves. For fun on the water, try rafting on the Jordan River—and there are the beaches, of course. Check the Friday papers' entertainment guides (they have a children's section) for up-to-date information.

Eating Out

Restaurants are often happy to accommodate those seeking super-simple fare, like pasta, or chicken schnitzel and fries. Fast food is easily accessible and doesn't have to be junk. Falafel or shawarma, kebabs, and cheese or potato-filled pastries called *bourekas* are very common, and pizza parlors abound.

Nature (and Old Stuff)

Israel's nature reserves and national parks (🌐 *www.parks.org.il*) have plenty for the whole family to do. In the north, you can cycle around a part of the restored Hula Lake (at the site called Agmon Ha'Hula); laugh and learn at the fun 3-D movie about bird migrations at the **Hula Nature Reserve;** kayak or raft the placid waters of the **Jordan River;** and bounce around some awesome landscapes in a Jeep or a 4x4 dune buggy. (The Negev Desert and Eilat Mountains offer comparable off-road experiences.) Explore the medieval **Nimrod's Castle** on the slopes of Mt. Hermon, or **Belvoir** overlooking the Upper Jordan Valley.

Standouts in the south are the oases and walking trails of **Ein Gedi** (with a bonus of bathing under fresh waterfalls) and Ein Avdat. The wondrous **Masada,** Herod's mountaintop palace-fortress, is a real treat and can be reached by foot along the steep Snake Path (recommended for older kids), but there is always the cable car.

Walking is a lively and easy activity to do anywhere. Top in Jerusalem is the Old Testament-period **City of David,** south of the Old City. It's a maze of rock-hewn corridors, ending with a 30-minute wade in the spring water of Hezekiah's Tunnel. (There is a dry exit, too.) The **Ramparts Walk** offers views of the Old City's residential quarters as well as of new Jerusalem outside the walls. Smaller kids can do part of it (with strict adult supervision). In Tel Aviv, the **Tel Aviv Port** is great for coffee and a stroll—and even little kids can run around (with a bit of adult attention) while you enjoy iced drinks and the balmy weather.

Museums

A dirty word among kids? Maybe so, but the following museums might change some minds.

JERUSALEM

In West Jerusalem, the **Israel Museum's Youth Wing** has outdoor play areas as well as exhibitions, often interactive, and a "recycling room" where children can use their creative energy freely. Great rainy-day options include the Bloomfield Science Museum in Givat Ram.

TEL AVIV

The **Eretz Israel Museum** has a series of pavilions on its campus, each with a different theme: pottery, coins, glass, folklore, anthropology, and more. It also has a planetarium—complete with moon rocks.

The **Observatory on the 49th floor of the Azrieli Towers** isn't really a museum, but it offers a cute animated 3-D fantasy movie about Tel Aviv, and a stunning view of the entire metropolis.

HAIFA

The **National Museum of Science and Technology (Technoda)**, the **Railway Museum**, and the **National Maritime Museum** are all geared to young and curious minds—of any age!

THE NEGEV

The **Israel Air Force Museum**, at the Hatzerim Air Force base (west of Beersheva), houses a huge collection of IAF airplanes and helicopters—from World War II Spitfires and Mustangs to contemporary F-16s and Cobras. Each exhibit has a story to tell. There is no English Web site, but guided tours in English can be arranged (☎ *08/990–6888* ✉ *info@iaf-museum.org.il*). This could be a stop on the way to or from Eilat, or a doable day trip from Jerusalem or Tel Aviv.

At One with the Animals

In addition to the wonderful **Tisch Family Zoological Gardens** in Jerusalem, with its emphasis on fauna that feature in the Bible or that are native to Israel, the **Ramat Gan Safari** (🌐 *www.safari.co.il*), near Tel Aviv, and the small but delightful **Haifa Educational Zoo**, there are numerous other options for time out with animals.

The **Jerusalem Bird Observatory** (🌐 *www.jbo.org.il*), perched above the Knesset, offers "close encounters" with ringed birds, bird-watching tours, and other tidbits about bird life; night safaris are recommended.

On the grounds of Kibbutz Nir David, at the foot of Mt. Gilboa, is **Gan Garoo Park**, which specializes in native Australian wildlife—kangaroos and wallabies, cockatoos, and more.

In the high Negev desert, near Mitzpe Ramon, and as far as you can get from their native Andes mountains, gentle alpacas wait for you to hand-feed them. At the **Alpaca Farm** you can learn as well about the whole process of raising them and spinning their marvelously soft wool.

Horseback riding is an option pretty much throughout the country. In the Galilee, end a trail—of a few hours or a couple of days—with hot apple pie at **Vered Hagalil** or with a chunky steak at **Bat Yaar**, in the Biriya Forest near Tzfat (Safed). There are numerous outfits that do camel-hump trails in the Negev (near Beersheva and Arad) and down near **Eilat**.

Beaches

You're never too far from a beach in Israel—but check for a lifeguard. This is a given at city beaches, but not at those off the beaten track. Considering it's such a tiny country, the range of different beach experiences is amazing, from the Mediterranean to the Red Sea, to the Sea of Galilee and even the supersalty Dead Sea, where you can float but not swim.

And More . . .

The whole family will enjoy getting their hands dirty at the three-hour **Dig for a Day** (🌐 *www.archesem.com*)—a chance to dig, sift, and examine artifacts.

Off the Tel Aviv–Jerusalem highway at Latrun is **Mini Israel**—hundreds of exact replica models of the main sites around the country, historical, archaeological, and modern. It's great for an all-of-Israel orientation.

In Eilat, venture out to the biblical theme park, **Kings City**, which comes replete with Pharaohs' palaces and temples, Solomon's mines, mazes, and optical illusions.

ISRAEL'S MARKETS

Israel's main markets are found in Jerusalem and Tel Aviv. As for bargaining (not done at produce stalls)—sure, give it a go, but these days it's a hard drive, so decide if you want to have fun playing the game, or not. The difference in price is likely to be less than you think.

Jerusalem

The **Machaneh Yehuda Market** offers produce that is as flavorful as it is colorful. Recent additions to this collection of alleys running off the main market street include a sprinkling of boutique cafés and unusual restaurants, and stalls selling clothes from India. The market, quite a bit cheaper than the supermarket, is a great place to grab some goodies while on the go or for the hotel room later. Think globally: start the fun with an Indian *lassi* (yogurt drink); and try the French cheeses and hearty whole-grain bread. Then you must—but must—end such a meal with a chunk of sweet sesame halvah.

Weaving through the **Old City market** (the *souk*) will cast you even further back in time. Lavish rugs and fabrics, oriental ceramics, blown-glass items, not-so-antique antiques, beads, embroidered kaftans, and leather thongs line the stone alleyways. Be cautious about buying items with an intrinsic value: gold, silver, precious stones, and antiquities may not be as advertised. Almost all the salespeople here speak English, but a polite quip or two thrown at them in Arabic—check the nuances first!—may bring a wonderful smile, and perhaps a little discount. There's hummus and pickles, Arabic coffee and honey-dripping pastries to buy. Go to the Austrian Hospice (actually a guesthouse) at Station III on the Via Dolorosa for real Wiener schnitzel and apple strudel (but don't let them rubberize them in a microwave). Some well-established stores can handle shipping of items. And beware of pickpockets (your passport is best left in the hotel safe).

Tel Aviv

The **Carmel Market,** or Shuk Hacarmel, begins at its top end (Allenby Road), with stalls of clothes and housewares, and then becomes the city's primary produce market, extending almost down to the sea. The scents are sensational—fresh greens (mint, parsley, basil), lemons and other citrus fruit, salty herring, and more. It can get packed—hold onto your belongings, though pickpocketing is not usually the problem here. The shuk borders the Yemenite Quarter, with a host of small eateries offering Yemenite cooking.

You'll find some true artisans at the **Nahalat Binyamin Pedestrian Mall,** primarily a crafts market, along with the unsung peddlers of imported goods. It's a great place to pick up original and reasonably priced gifts. The pedestrian street converges with the Carmel Market at its Allenby Street end. It's lively, with street performers sharing space with shoppers and strollers. Because it is only open on Tuesdays and Fridays, it gets pretty crowded—especially on Fridays and as holidays approach—though the vibe is always cheery.

The **Jaffa Flea Market** in Jaffa is another such shopping option. In the warren of small streets you can shop for—or just take in the view of—rugs, Mideast *finjan* coffee sets (with the tiny cups for that strong, strong coffee), clothes from India, jewelry, retro lamps, and other junk-mixed-with-bargains. Along with stores and stalls are many small workshops—tinsmiths and carpenters, for example.

ISRAEL'S BEST BEACHES

Whether you'd like to take a dip, jog along the boardwalk at dawn or sunset, have a glass of wine or beer at a beach-front café, or just commune with nature, this little country's beaches have something to offer at the Mediterranean and the Red Sea, and inland at the Dead Sea and on the shores of the Sea of Galilee.

The Med: City Beaches

All the major cities along the coastline like Nahariya, Haifa, Netanya, Herzliya, and Tel Aviv have their own licensed beaches with lifeguards, and varying amenities like showers, changing rooms, beachside cafés, restaurants, and sometimes even a boardwalk.

Tel Aviv's beaches are particularly colorful, with a popular boardwalk for children of all ages, and a diverse local and international crowd of singles and families. Along the way you'll find Chinky Beach (with a retro-hippie crowd), a gay beach (to the right of the Tel Aviv Hilton), and slightly farther north, a segregated beach for those of the religious persuasion with separate days for men and women. In summer, there are free movies, concerts, and meditation and yoga classes right on the beach.

The Red and the Dead

There are beaches and water sports galore in the Red Sea, which laps at the southernmost city of Eilat. The North Beach, near the promenade and the major hotels, is delightfully sandy, and a great place to swim or sunbathe, but don't miss Coral Beach Reserve, with a reef so close that in a minute you can snorkel among the great variety of stony coral and subtropical fish. The Dead Sea—actually a hypersalty lake—draws people from all over the world to luxuriate in its waters, hot springs, and black medicinal mud. The southern shores—the lowest point on the surface of the planet—are filled with hotels that offer spas and beach access. To the north, there are several laid-back beaches—Kalya, Neve Midbar, and Mineral—where you can float.

The Sea of Galilee

Placid and shimmering in the sunlight, the Sea of Galilee, or *Kinneret* in Hebrew, is Israel's only natural freshwater lake, and the backdrop for some of the most important sites in the New Testament. Scenery includes the Galilee's lovely mountains and the cliffs of the Golan Heights. Beaches range from rough sand to rocky, many are camper-friendly, and there are large waterparks at Gai Beach and Luna Gal.

Beach Basics

- Sun in this region is stronger than in Europe and most of North America. Don't overdo exposure.
- Don't leave valuables unattended on blankets, in lockers, or in your car.
- Observe the flags at the lifeguard stations: white means bathing is safe, red means swim with caution, and black means bathing forbidden. Take them seriously.
- Don't swim at beaches without lifeguards. In the Mediterranean there are seasons with dangerous undertows, and at times during July and August there is a short jellyfish invasion. Stay out of the water at those times.
- The Israeli national beach game is called *matkot,* which uses wood paddles and a small rubber ball. Fervent players often usurp prime territory just at the shoreline and are oblivious to passersby, so duck to avoid getting hit with the ball!

ISRAEL AND THE PERFORMING ARTS

For such a small country, Israel has a wealth of cultural activity that reflects both the extraordinary diversity of its population and the fact that the state is just over 60 years old. Innovation and experimentation meld with traditional art forms, creating an exciting Israeli art scene in which classical Western meets the new Middle East.

Apart from the top venues in Tel Aviv, Jerusalem, and Haifa, many towns in Israel have a performing arts center where you can catch flagship performers as well as up-and-coming local talent.

Dance

The main venue for Israeli dance of all kinds is the beautiful **Suzanne Dellal Centre for Dance and Theater** (🌐 *www.suzannedellal.org.il*), in Tel Aviv's historic Neveh Tzedek neighborhood.

All the other companies perform at Israel's large concert halls—check the calendar section of the *Jerusalem Post* or *Haaretz* newspapers for schedules.

For classical ballet, look for performances of Israel's veteran classical ballet company, the **Israel Ballet Company** (☎ *03/604–6610*). The **Panov Ballet Theater Company** (☎ *08/854–5180*), founded in 1998, features a repertoire of both classical and contemporary dance under the direction of former Kirov ballet star and company founder, Valery Panov.

If it's strictly modern dance you're looking for, try to catch the **Batsheva Dance Company** in Tel Aviv (☎ *03/510–4037*)—one of Israel's most respected modern dance companies, founded by Martha Graham and Baroness Batsheva De Rothschild—or the **Kibbutz Contemporary Dance Company** (☎ *09/954–0403*).

In Jerusalem, the **Vertigo Dance Company** (☎ *02/624–4176*), based at the Gerard Behar Center, takes the audience into new and unexpected territory through their modern dance interpretations.

The most comprehensive dance event in Israel is the annual **Summer Dance Festival** at the Suzanne Dellal Centre in Tel Aviv, which features more than 80 events in July and August. In the fall, the center hosts **TelAviv Dance**, a three-week showcase of the world's best companies.

Music

Classical and Opera Israel's classical orchestras are world-renowned and often host the best soloists and conductors from around the world. See if you can catch the **Israel Philharmonic Orchestra** (🌐 *www.ipo.co.il*), directed by Zubin Mehta, during one of its many performances in Tel Aviv, Haifa, or Jerusalem.

The **Jerusalem Symphony** (🌐 *www.jso.co.il*) under the direction of Leon Botstein appears regularly all over the country.

In Haifa it's the **Haifa Symphony Orchestra** (🌐 *www.haifasymphony.co.il*) that brings classical music to the north. Music lovers in the center of the country can enjoy the **Israel Symphony Orchestra of Rishon Lezion** (🌐 *www.isorchestra.co.il*), which also serves as the resident orchestra of the Israeli Opera.

The **Tel Aviv Performing Arts Center** is the place to enjoy the Israel Opera (🌐 *www.israel-opera.co.il*), which stages several series of classical operas and operettas throughout the season (November to July).

Popular Music Israeli popular music ranges from rock groups with an international following such as Hadag Hanachash to singers of modern Israeli ballads like

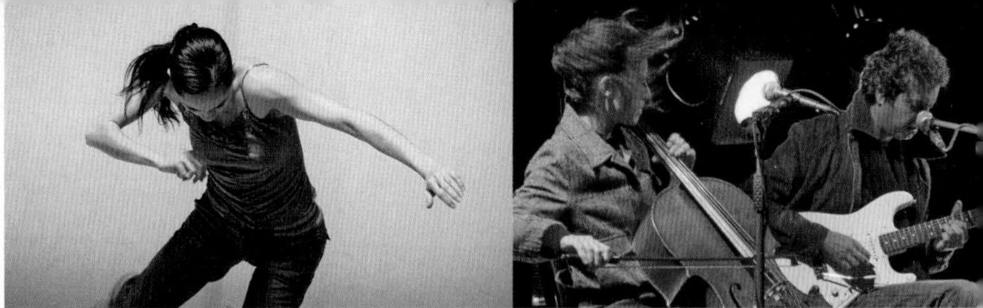

Eviatar Banai, who are well known to locals only. Both will appear at places such as **The Lab** (*Hama'abada*) (☎ *02/629–2001*) in Jerusalem, or the **Goldstar Zappa Club** (☎ *03/649–9550*) in Tel Aviv.

The best popular music festival of the year is the **Ein Gev Festival** in April on the shores of the Sea of Galilee (🌐 *www.eingev.com*).

Israel's best-known pop stars appear every night at the annual **International Arts and Crafts Fair.** The 10-day extravaganza is Jerusalem's main summer festival and takes place just outside the walls of the Old City in mid-August.

Jazz, Ethnic, and World Music There are Israelis with origins in almost every country in the world, and ethnic music is an extremely important part of Israel's musical culture.

Jazz has grown in popularity over the past decade with an influx of accomplished immigrant musicians from Russia and America. Stars like the Idan Raichel Project with his Ethiopian-influenced sound and the Yemenite-flavored Zafa have put Israel on the world music map. Performances are at a variety of venues including **Jerusalem's Confederation House** (☎ *02/642–5206*).

Every November Jerusalem hosts the **International Oud Festival** (🌐 *www.confederationhouse.org*) that highlights ensembles featuring music of the Middle Eastern lute.

For aficionados of vocal music, the village of Abu Ghosh just west of Jerusalem is the place to be in October and May when the beautiful local churches provide the best acoustics for the **Abu Ghosh Music Festival** (🌐 *www.agfestival.co.il*).

The mountaintop town of Tzfat is the setting for the annual **Klezmer Festival** (🌐 *www.*safed.co.il) that takes place mid-August and brings the world's best Jewish musicians together for three days of traditional Jewish music.

Theater

Theater in Israel is almost exclusively staged in Hebrew, with the exception of the **Cameri Theatre of Tel Aviv** (🌐 *www.cameri.co.il*), which presents its most popular productions three times a week with screened simultaneous English translation.

The **Israel Festival** (🌐 *www.israel-festival.org.il*) in Jerusalem is the place to take in an array of the best of the performing arts over two weeks in May. Both Israeli artists and performers from all over the world converge on the capital to showcase the best in music, dance, and theater.

Language won't be a barrier at Jerusalem's annual **International Festival of Puppet Theater** (🌐 *www.traintheater.co.il*) in early August. It showcases the world's best puppet artists.

Film

Israel has a sophisticated and thriving film industry with Israeli movies consistently being nominated for prestigious awards worldwide.

The best places to see the most interesting Israeli films are the **Cinematheques** in Tel Aviv, Haifa, Jerusalem, and Sderot (🌐 *www.jer-cin.org.il*). Most Israeli films have English subtitles.

For real film buffs, plan your visit to Israel to coincide with the prestigious two-week-long **Jerusalem International Film Festival** that takes place in mid-July every year at the Cinematheque or the Jewish Film Festival at the same venue in December.

ISRAEL'S MAJOR HOLIDAYS

Time is figured in different ways in Israel. The Western Gregorian calendar—the solar year from January to December—is the basis of day-to-day life and commerce, but the school year, for example, which runs from September through June, follows the Hebrew lunar calendar. Jewish religious festivals are observed as national public holidays, when businesses and some museums are closed (on Yom Kippur, the Day of Atonement, *all* sites are closed).

The Muslim calendar is also lunar, but without the compensatory leap-year mechanism of its Hebrew counterpart. Muslim holidays thus drift through the seasons and can fall at any time of the year.

Even the Christian calendar is not uniform: Christmas is celebrated on different days by the Roman Catholic (Latin) community, the Greek Orthodox Church, and the Armenian Orthodox Church.

Major Jewish Holidays

The phrase "Not religious" in the text indicates that the holiday might be part of the religious tradition, but few or no public restrictions apply. On holy days, when the text indicates "Religious," most of the Sabbath restrictions apply.

Shabbat (Sabbath) The Day of Rest in Israel is Saturday, the Jewish Sabbath, which begins at sundown Friday and ends at nightfall Saturday. Torah-observant Jews do not cook, travel, answer the telephone, or use money or writing materials during the Shabbat, hence the Sabbath ban on photography at Jewish holy sites like the Western Wall. In Jerusalem, where religious influence is strong, the Downtown area clears out on Friday afternoon, and some religious neighborhoods are even closed to traffic. Kosher restaurants close on the Sabbath, except for the main hotel restaurants, where some menu restrictions apply. In the holy city itself, your dining choices are considerably reduced, but there are more nonkosher eateries open than there used to be. Outside Jerusalem, however, you'll scarcely be affected; in fact, many restaurants do their best business of the week on the Sabbath because nonreligious Israelis take to the roads.

In Arab areas, such as East Jerusalem and Nazareth, Muslims take time off for the week's most important devotions at midday Friday, but the traveler will notice this much less than on Sunday, when most Christian shopkeepers in those towns close their doors. Saturday is market day, and these towns buzz with activity.

There is no public intercity transportation on the Sabbath, although the private *sherut* taxis drive between the main cities. Urban buses operate only in Nazareth and, on a reduced schedule, in Haifa. Shabbat is also the busiest day for nature reserves and national parks—indeed, anywhere the city folk can get away for a day. Keep this in mind if you fancy a long drive; the highways toward the main cities can be choked with returning weekend traffic on Saturday afternoon.

Rosh Hashanah (Jewish New Year) September 29–30, 2011; September 17–18, 2012. This two-day holiday and Yom Kippur are collectively known as the High Holy Days. Rosh Hashanah traditionally begins a 10-day period of introspection and repentance. Observant Jews attend relatively long synagogue services and eat festive meals, including apples and honey to symbolize the hoped-for sweetness of the new year. Nonobservant Jews often use this holiday to picnic and go to the beach.

Yom Kippur (Day of Atonement) October 8, 2011; September 26, 2012. Yom Kippur is the most solemn day of the Jewish year. Observant Jews fast, wear white clothing, avoid leather footwear, and abstain from pleasures of the flesh. Israeli radio and television stations shut down. All sites, entertainment venues, and most restaurants are closed by law. Much of the country comes to a halt, and in Jerusalem and other cities the roads are almost completely empty, aside from emergency vehicles. It is considered a privilege to be invited to someone's house to "break the fast" as the holiday ends, at nightfall.

Sukkoth (Feast of Tabernacles) October 13, 2011; October 1, 2012. Religious. Jews build open-roof huts or shelters called *sukkot* (singular *sukkah*) on porches and in backyards to remember the makeshift lodgings of the biblical Israelites as they wandered in the desert. The more observant will eat as many of their meals as possible in their sukkah; some even sleep there for the duration of the holiday.

Simhat Torah October 20, 2011; October 8, 2012. Religious. The last day of the Sukkoth festival season, this holiday marks the end—and the immediate recommencement—of the annual cycle of the reading of the Torah, the Five Books of Moses. Joyful singing and dancing (often in the street) as people carry the Torah scrolls characterize the evening and morning synagogue services.

Hanukkah December 21–28, 2011; December 9–16, 2012. Not religious. A Jewish rebellion in the 2nd century BC renewed Jewish control of Jerusalem. In the recleansed and rededicated Temple, the tradition tells, a vessel was found with enough oil to burn for a day. It miraculously burned for eight days, hence the eight-day holiday marked by the lighting of an increasing number of candles (on a candelabrum called a *hanukkiah*) from night to night. Schools take a winter break. Shops, businesses, and services all remain open.

Purim March 8, 2012 (celebrated one day later in Jerusalem). Not religious. Children dress up in costumes on the days leading up to Purim. In synagogues and on public television, devout Jews read the Scroll of Esther, the story of the valiant Jewish queen who prevented the massacre of her people in ancient Persia. On Purim day, it's customary to exchange gifts of prepared foods with neighbors and friends. Many towns hold street festivals.

Pesach (Passover) April 7–13, 2012. First and last days religious; dietary restrictions in force throughout. Passover is preceded by vigorous spring-cleaning to remove all traces of leavened bread and related products from the household. During the seven-day holiday itself, no bread is sold in Jewish stores, and the crackerlike matzoh replaces bread in most hotels and restaurants. On the first evening of the holiday, Jewish families gather to retell the ancient story of their people's exodus from Egyptian bondage, and to eat a festive and highly symbolic meal called the seder (Hebrew for order). Hotels have communal seders, and the Ministry of Tourism can sometimes arrange for tourists to join Israeli families for Passover in their homes.

Yom Ha'atzma'ut (Independence Day) April 26, 2012. Not religious. Israel declared independence on May 14, 1948, but the exact date of Yom Ha'atzma'ut every year follows the Hebrew calendar. Although there are gala events, fireworks displays, and military parades all over the country,

ISRAEL'S MAJOR HOLIDAYS

most Israelis go picnicking or swimming. Stores are closed, but public transportation runs and most tourist sites are open.

Shavuot (Feast of Weeks) May 27, 2012. Religious. This holiday, seven weeks after Passover, marks the harvest of the first fruits and, according to tradition, the day on which Moses received the Torah ("the Law") on Mt. Sinai. Many observant Jews stay up all night studying the Torah. It is customary to eat meatless meals with an emphasis on dairy products.

Christian Holidays

Easter April 8, 2012. This major festival celebrates the resurrection of Jesus. The nature and timing of its ceremonies and services are colorfully different in each Christian tradition represented in the Holy Land—Roman Catholic (Latin), Protestant, Greek Orthodox, Armenian Orthodox, Ethiopian, and so on. The date above is observed by the Western churches—Roman Catholic and Protestant. Check the dates for different groups such as the Armenian Orthodox, Greek Orthodox, and Russian Orthodox churches, who base their holidays on the older Julian calendar.

Christmas Except in towns with a large indigenous Christian population, such as Nazareth and Bethlehem, Christmas is not a high-visibility holiday in Israel. The Christmas of the Catholic and Protestant traditions is, of course, celebrated on December 25, but the Greek Orthodox calendar observes it on January 7, and the Armenian Orthodox wait until January 19. Christmas Eve (December 24) is the time for the international choir assembly in Bethlehem's Manger Square, followed by the Roman Catholic midnight mass in the adjacent church. Take a cab to the border crossing (don't forget your passport), and pick up a shared cab to Manger Square on the Palestinian side. Check first with the Israeli Ministry of Tourism information office that the choral event is on schedule.

Muslim Holidays

Muslims observe Friday as their holy day, but it's accompanied by none of the restrictions and far less of the solemnity than those of the Jewish Shabbat and the Christian Sabbath (in their strictest forms). The noontime prayer on Friday is the most important of the week and is typically preceded by a sermon, often broadcast from the loudspeakers of the mosques.

The dates of Muslim holidays shift each year because of the lunar calendar.

Ramadan August 1–30, 2011; July 20–August 18, 2012. This monthlong fast commemorates the month in which the Qur'an was first revealed to Muhammad. Devout Muslims must abstain from food, drink, tobacco, and sex during daylight hours; the three-day festival of Id el-Fitr then marks the conclusion of the period. The dates are affected by the sighting of the new moon and can change slightly at the very last moment. The Muslim holy sites on Jerusalem's Haram esh-Sharif (the Temple Mount) offer only short morning visiting hours during this time and are closed to tourists during Id el-Fitr.

Eid al-Adha November 6, 2011; October 26, 2012. This festival commemorating Abraham's willingness to sacrifice his son marks the end of the annual Haj, or pilgrimage to Mecca. Muslim families throughout Israel celebrate Eid al-Adha by slaughtering a sheep or goat.

GREAT ITINERARIES

BEST OF ISRAEL, WITH THE NEGEV AND EILAT, 11 TO 19 DAYS

Israel is a small but varied country. This itinerary lets you see the high points of Jerusalem and the northern half of the country; you can add the desert if you have the time and inclination.

Jerusalem, 3 to 4 days

You could spend a lifetime in Jerusalem, but three days is probably a good minimum to get a feel for the city and environs. First, spend a day getting an overview of the holy sites of Judaism, Christianity, and Islam. Start with the Western Wall, then go up to the Temple Mount (morning hours) to view the Muslim shrines. Follow the Via Dolorosa to the Church of the Holy Sepulcher. Stop for a Middle Eastern–style lunch in the Christian Quarter before walking down into the Jewish Quarter. (Note: The Temple Mount is closed Friday and Saturday, and some Jewish Quarter sites close early Friday and only reopen Sunday.) Explore the remarkable underworld of biblical (Old Testament) Jerusalem, or if you have a car, pick up one or two of the panoramic views.

On your second day, you can venture farther afield: many consider the Israel Museum and Yad Vashem, including the Holocaust History Museum, essential if you're visiting Jerusalem. Mt. Herzl National Memorial Park is also a meaningful excursion. A good plan is to avoid burnout by doing one of the big museums on Day 2, the other on Day 3. (Note: Yad Vashem and Mt. Herzl are closed Saturday.) Add the Machaneh Yehuda produce market (closed Saturday) and the Knesset menorah.

Your third day can be devoted to the second of the above museums, and sites within an hour of Jerusalem: perhaps a wine tour in the Judean Hills. Or join a dig at Bet Guvrin–Maresha National Park with Archaeological Seminars—and on your way back, visit Mini-Israel, with its hundreds of models of Israeli sites.

The three days suggested for Jerusalem are the bare minimum; a fourth day gives you time to relax and absorb the city—and shop.

The Dead Sea region, 2 days

After getting an early start in your rental car, head east through the stark Judean Desert to Qumran, where the Dead Sea Scrolls were discovered. You can spend an hour (max) touring the ruins and seeing the audiovisual presentation. About 45 minutes south of Qumran along the Dead Sea shore is Ein Gedi, where a leisurely hike to the waterfall and back should take about 1.5 hours, including a dip in a freshwater pool. End the day with a float in the Dead Sea, and spend the night at the Kibbutz Ein Gedi Guest House or one of the fine hotels at Ein Bokek, at the southern end of the lake. A highlight for many are the spa treatments featuring the famously curative Dead Sea mud.

In the morning, hike the Snake Path—or take the cable car—up Masada. The gate to the trail opens before dawn, so you can catch the sunrise at the top if you're limber enough at that hour. Later, head back to Jerusalem to spend the night.

Note: If you don't have a car, one-day bus tours from Jerusalem let you see Masada and the Dead Sea.

The Galilee, 3 days

From Jerusalem, where you've spent the night, make an early start to allow time for all the sites on today's schedule. Retrace your steps down Route 1 East, stopping just north of the Dead Sea–Jerusalem highway at the oasis town of Jericho, the world's oldest city. It's almost worth a trip through this lush town—with its date palms, orange groves, banana plantations, bougainvillea, and papaya trees—just to be able to say "I was there," but Tel Jericho is also a significant archaeological site. Sample the baklava and orange juice. Jericho is in the Palestinian Authority, so check ahead of time for any entry restrictions. (Some car rental agencies do not allow their cars into Palestinian areas.)

Take the Jordan Valley route (Route 90) to the Galilee, stopping en route for a swim at the springs of Gan Hashelosha; then visit the extensive Roman-Byzantine ruins at Beit She'an, where you can have lunch in town or take a sandwich to the site. The Crusader castle of Belvoir will round out the day, and then you can enjoy a lakeside fish dinner in Tiberias, where you'll spend the night.

The next day, spend an hour or two in the far north at the Tel Dan Nature Reserve, with its rushing water and biblical archaeology. Spend the afternoon hiking, or horseback riding at Bat Ya'ar (call ahead to reserve if you want to go trail riding), or kayaking at Hagoshrim or Kfar Blum (seasonal, but no need to reserve). Overnight in Tiberias again, or better yet, farther north in a Hula Valley B&B.

On your third day, you can explore the treasures of Tzfat, with its beautiful vistas, old synagogues, and art and Judaica galleries. Depending on how you spend your day, you can also visit the Golan Heights Winery or do some hiking or bird-watching at Gamla. Overnight in Tiberias or at your Hula Valley B&B.

The Mediterranean Coast and Tel Aviv, 3 days

From Tiberias or your Hula Valley B&B, head west to the coast. Your first stop can be the cable-car ride to the white sea grottoes of Rosh Hanikra. Then travel to Akko, with its Crusader halls and picturesque harbor. Akko is also an excellent place for a fish lunch. Then drive to Haifa for a view from the Dan Panorama hotel at the top of Mt. Carmel. Spend the night in Haifa.

The next day, visit Haifa's Baha'i Shrine and its magnificent gardens, then continue down the coast to visit the village of Zichron Ya'akov, home to the Carmel Wine Cellars and the Bet Aaronsohn Museum. Have lunch and then head to Tel Aviv, stopping at the Roman ruins of Caesarea on the way. In Tel Aviv, you can enjoy a night on the town, perhaps in Neveh Tzedek or Jaffa.

On your third day, take in Tel Aviv's museums, shop, and enjoy a dip in the Mediterranean. From here you can head to the airport if it's time to go home. If you're proceeding on to the desert, spend another night in Tel Aviv and get an early start in the morning.

Add on: The Negev, 2 days

From Tel Aviv, head south toward Beersheva and Route 40. If you're doing this on a Thursday, leave early enough to get to the Beersheva Bedouin market, which is most colorful in the morning. (Beersheva is under two hours' drive from Tel Aviv.) Driving south, stop at Sde Boker, where you can have lunch and see David Ben-Gurion's house and gravesite overlooking the biblical Wilderness of Zin. Near Sde Boker is Ein Avdat, a wilderness oasis that has a trail with stone steps and ladders leading up the magnificent white chalk

canyon. Drive on to Mitzpe Ramon, on the edge of the immense Makhtesh Ramon (Crater). Spend the night here, then enjoy the natural wonders of the Ramon Crater the next day. Spend a second night here as well.

Eilat and environs, 2 to 5 days

Eilat is under three-hour's drive from Mitzpe Ramon. Drive south on Route 40 to where it joins Route 90 and continue south on the Arava Road, which runs along the border with Jordan. Stop at Hai Bar Nature Reserve, and then at Timna Park for a short hike and a view of Solomon's Pillars, arriving in Eilat in the late afternoon. A minimum of two days here allows you to see all the highlights; in three to five days you can have some serious beach or diving time, and take a side trip to Petra, in Jordan. You'll probably want to pick one hotel in Eilat as a base.

TIPS

In the summer, plan to do most of your walking and hiking by midday to avoid the heat.

Make sure to take lots of water, and a hat, when hiking or walking.

Consider flying back to Tel Aviv from Eilat—or fly round-trip to Eilat if you don't have the time or inclination to drive.

Make your hotel/B&B reservations ahead of time, especially in summer and on weekends year-round, when hotels and B&Bs are crowded with vacationing Israelis.

Most hotels in the Dead Sea area and Eilat have spas with a host of treatments; call ahead or book one when you arrive.

You won't need a rental car in the Old City of Jerusalem; navigating and parking can be a challenge, so save the rental car for trips out of town.

The lunarlike red-rock canyons in the hills behind Eilat are great for hiking (but not alone), and there are also plenty of water-sports options: you can snorkel, parasail, or arrange a boat trip to prime dive spots. Day trips to Petra are available through your hotel concierge. Some like more time to explore that extraordinary site, but since you cannot take your rental car across into Jordan, a two-day trip (overnight in Petra) is only doable if you budget for your own guide and car on that side. The return drive from Eilat to Jerusalem via the Arava takes less than five hours, including rest stops.

GREAT ITINERARIES

IN THE FOOTSTEPS OF JESUS, 6 DAYS

Visit the Holy Land, they say, and you'll never read the Bible the same way again; the landscapes and shrines that you'll see, and your encounters with local members of Christian communities at the landmarks of Jesus' life, will have a profound and lasting impact.

Jerusalem and Bethlehem, 2 days

Spend your first day retracing the climax of the story of Jesus in Jerusalem, starting at the Mt. of Olives. This is where Jesus taught, and wept over the city (Luke 19:41), and the tear-shaped Dominus Flevit church commemorates it. The walk down the Mt. of Olives road, also known as the Palm Sunday road, leads to the ancient olive trees in the Garden of Gethsemane, where you can contemplate Jesus' "passion" and arrest.

Follow the Via Dolorosa, stopping at each Station of the Cross, to the Church of the Holy Sepulcher, where most Christians believe Jesus was crucified, buried, and resurrected. The Garden Tomb—the site of Calvary for many Protestants—offers an island of tranquillity. Take your time contemplating the sites; this will not be a rushed day.

The next day, you can explore the Southern Wall excavations at the Jerusalem Archaeological Park, adjacent to the Old City's Dung Gate. Scholars believe Jesus could have walked the stones of the ancient street here, and climbed the Southern Steps to the Temple. Down the hill is the City of David, the Old Testament heart of Jerusalem, including the excavated Area G and Warren's Shaft, and King Hezekiah's water tunnel. The steps of the pool of Siloam, where a blind man had his sight restored (John 9:7–11), were discovered only a few years ago. Add a visit to the Room of the Last Supper on Mt. Zion, up the hill from the Dung Gate, and then have lunch.

In the afternoon, you can visit Bethlehem, the birthplace of Jesus, to see the Church of the Nativity, one of the oldest churches in the world. Bethlehem is in the Palestinian Authority, so bring your passport. Most car rental agencies do not allow their cars into Palestinian areas. It's best to take a taxi to the border crossing east of Jerusalem's Gilo neighborhood. The crossing for tourists is usually uncomplicated, and there are Palestinian taxis waiting on the other side to take you to the church. Or you can opt to spend the afternoon in Jerusalem.

On the way to the Galilee, 1 day

Making an early start, head east through the barren Judean Desert to Qumran, where the Dead Sea Scrolls were found. Some scholars believe John the Baptist may have passed through here, and a visit to the site—you can spend an hour here—is an opportunity to learn about the desert in which Jesus sought solitude, purity, and inspiration.

Then head up the Jordan Valley (Route 90), passing through or near Jericho (depending on political conditions). Jesus also healed a blind man here (Mark 10:46), and had a meal with the tax collector Zacchaeus (Luke 19:1–5). If the security situation isn't favorable, the Israeli soldiers at the checkpoint at Jericho won't allow you in (again, read the newspaper and use common sense). If you skip Jericho, Route 90 swings past it to the east. In Jericho, though, a visit to Tel Jericho, the first conquest of the Israelites in the Holy Land (Joshua 6), is a must.

You can have lunch at the restaurant next to the tell, or at a truck stop on the way north from Jericho.

Then it's on to the ruins at Beit She'an, including the ancient main street, a bathhouse, and mosaics. Not only is this an important Old Testament site, it was also the capital of the Decapolis, a league of 10 Roman cities, among which Jesus taught and healed (Mark 7:31).

Farther north, pilgrims go to Yardenit to be baptized in the Jordan River and remember the baptism of Jesus in these waters. Spend the night in Tiberias.

Sea of Galilee, 1 day

Start the day heading north to the ancient wooden boat at Ginosar, which evokes Gospel descriptions of life on the lake—see, for example, Matthew 9:1. Then, after meditating on Jesus' famous sermon (Matthew 5) in the gardens of the Mount of Beatitudes and its chapel (off Route 90 north of the Sea of Galilee), descend to Tabgha to see the mosaics of the Church of the Multiplication of Loaves and Fishes. From a lakeshore perch at the nearby Church of the Primacy of St. Peter, where Jesus appeared to the disciples after the resurrection (John 21), you can marvel at how Scripture and landscape blend before your eyes.

TIPS

First, and foremost, bring along your Bible; it will get a lot of use.

You won't need a car in Jerusalem, but you will need one for the rest of this itinerary. Your best bet is to pick up a car on the afternoon of the day before you head out of Jerusalem, so that you can make an early start the next day (remember that rental agencies are normally not open on Saturday). The agency will provide you with a basic road map and advice.

Gas stations are numerous, many with convenience stores to stock up on snacks.

GREAT ITINERARIES

Farther east, the ruins of ancient Capernaum—the center of Jesus' local ministry—include a magnificent pillared synagogue (partially restored), and Peter's house.

An archaeological mound across the Jordan River, north of the Sea of Galilee, is ancient Bethsaida, where the Gospels say Jesus healed and taught (Luke 9:10, 10:13). To get there, continue east of Capernaum, cross the Jordan River north of the Sea of Galilee, turn left onto Route 888, and a short distance thereafter turn left to Bethsaida in the Jordan River Park. From there, head back down to the lake and continue around its eastern shore to Kursi National Park and the ruins of a Byzantine church where, it is said, Jesus cast out demons into a herd of swine that stampeded into the water (Matthew 8:28–30).

A good idea for lunch is the fish restaurant at Kibbutz Ein Gev. Ask about a cruise on the lake after lunch (the kibbutz also has a boat company). Spend the night in Tiberias, or at one of the kibbutz guesthouses or B&Bs in the Hula Valley.

The Hula Valley and Banias (Caesarea Philippi), 1 day

The next day, drive through the Hula Valley; it's especially remarkable in the spring when the flowers bloom and bring alive Jesus' famous teaching from the Sermon on the Mount: "Consider the lilies of the field, how they grow" (Matthew 6:28). At the base of Mt. Hermon (which some scholars see as an alternative candidate for the site of the Transfiguration, as described in Mark 9:2–8), northeast of the Hula Valley, is Banias (Caesarea Philippi), where Jesus asked the disciples, "Who do people say I am?" (Matthew 16:13–20). The remains of a pagan Roman shrine are a powerful backdrop for contemplation of that message. Tel Dan, an important city in the biblical Kingdom of Israel, has a beautiful nature reserve. Stay overnight at your B&B or kibbutz hotel in the Hula Valley.

The Galilee Hills and the Coast, 1 day

Head for the hills, connecting to Route 77 and turning south onto Route 754 to Cana to see the church that commemorates Jesus' first miracle: changing water into wine (John 2:1–11). Continue to Nazareth, Jesus' childhood town. The massive modern Church of the Annunciation is built over a rock dwelling where (Catholics believe) the angel Gabriel appeared to Mary (Luke 1:26–38). The Greek Orthodox tradition is that the event took place at the village well, and their church is built over that site, some distance away. Nazareth's restaurants make good lunch stops.

A drive through the lush Jezreel Valley, via Route 60 and then north on Route 65 (the New Testament Valley of Armageddon), brings you to Mt. Tabor, long identified as the Mount of Transfiguration. The valley is named Armageddon (Revelation 16:16), after the archaeological site of Megiddo, now a national park south of Afula on Route 65. The drive back to Jerusalem from Megiddo takes 1.5 hours, using the Route 6 toll road, or you can spend the night in Haifa and return to Jerusalem the next day.

ISRAEL THROUGH THE AGES

Where else in the world can you find the living history of three major religions that have been intertwined for more than 1,000 years? Israel is the crossroads for Christianity, Islam, and Judaism, and many of the remarkable sites here help to tell this country's unique story. One of the best examples can be found in Jerusalem's Old City, where you can visit the Church of the Holy Sepulcher, the Dome of the Rock, and the Western Wall all within a short walk of each other.

1800 BC	1500 BC	1200 BC	900 BC
1800 BC Beginning of Patriarchal Age	13th Century BC Israelite exodus from Egypt	1000 BC David conquers Jerusalem. 950 BC Solomon builds the First Temple	

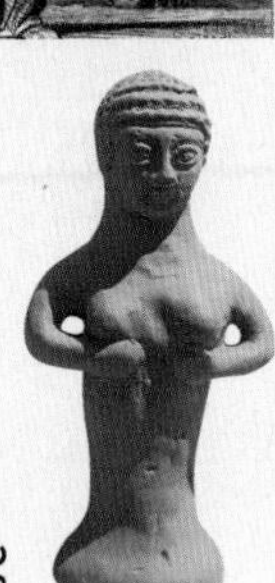

(top left) The Bible—David playing the harp while bringing the Ark of the Covenant from Kirjath-Jearim with other musicians. (bottom) The goddess Asherah was worshipped by some in ancient Israel as the consort of El and in Judah as the consort of Yahweh (some Hebrews baked small cakes for her festival). (right) Artist's depiction of Solomon's court (Ingobertus, c. 880).

1.2 million BC

Prehistory

The land that Israel now occupies served as a land bridge for Homo Erectus on his epic journey out of Africa. The oldest human remains found outside that continent, 1.4 million years old, were unearthed at Ubediya near Lake Kinneret (Sea of Galilee). It was in the Carmel Caves in northern Israel that the only indication of direct contact between Neanderthal Man and Homo Sapiens, 40,000 years ago, has been found, lending credence to the theory that they lived contemporaneously.

■ Visit: Museum at Degania Alef (⇨ Ch.6), Carmel Caves (⇨ Ch.5)

2000–1000 BC

Early Biblical Period

The arrival of Abraham, Isaac, and Jacob marked the beginning of the Patriarchal Age, dated to around 1800 BC. The Israelite exodus from Egypt took place in the 13th century BC. It was at this time that Israel was divided into Canaanite city-kingdoms. As the Israelites established themselves in the hill country, the Philistines, originating in the Aegean, were landing on the coastal plain. Around 1150, the Philistines invaded. A place name deriving from their presence endures to this day—Palestine.

■ Visit: Valley of Ellah (⇨ Ch.3)

1000–928 BC

United Monarchy

David conquered Jerusalem in 1000 BC, united the Israelite tribes into one kingdom, and established his capital here. David's son, Solomon, became king in 968 BC. In 950 BC, Solomon built the First Temple in Jerusalem, the religious center. Shortly after Solomon's death in 928 BC, the kingdom split in two—the northern tribes, which seceded and formed the Kingdom of Israel, and the southern tribes, now known as the Kingdom of Judah.

■ Visit: City of David (⇨ Ch.2), Temple Mount (⇨ Ch.2)

721 BC Assyrians conquer Israel	586 BC Babylonian rule	538 BC Cyrus the Great of Persia conquers Babylonia. Second Temple rebuilt	AD 26 Jesus' Galilean ministry takes place	AD 70 Romans destroy Second Temple. Masada falls in AD 73.
	600 BC	300 BC	0	AD 300

(top left) Hexagonal cylinder of King Sennacherib of Assyria inscribed with an account of his invasion of Palestine and the siege of Jerusalem in the reign of Hezekiah, King of Judah, dated 686 BC. (top center) 1860 engraving of the Western Wall. (top right) Masada. (bottom left) Mosaic in the Church of the Holy Sepulcher, Jerusalem.

928–587 BC

For 200 years, the Kingdom of Israel and the Kingdom of Judah co-existed, though relations were sometimes hostile. But in 721 BC, the Assyrian army, which dominated the region, conquered Israel and took its residents eastward into captivity. The fate of these "ten lost tribes" would be a subject of speculation by scholars thereafter. In 586 BC, the Assyrians were defeated by a new power, the Babylonians. Their king, Nebuchadnezzar, conquered Judah and destroyed Jerusalem and the temple. Those who survived were exiled to the "rivers of Babylon."

538 BC–AD 73

Second Temple Period

This exile ended after only 50 years when Cyrus the Great of Persia conquered Babylonia and permitted the exiles to return to Judah. Jerusalem was rebuilt and a new temple erected. The vast Persian Empire was defeated by Alexander the Great in 333 BC. Judah the Maccabee claimed victory over Hellenistic armies in 165 BC and rededicated the then-desecrated temple. Judean independence brought the Hasmonean dynasty in 142 BC, which the Romans ended when they annexed the country in 63 BC.

Jesus was born in Bethlehem, and 26 years later began his ministry, teaching mostly around the Sea of Galilee. In AD 29, Jesus and his disciples celebrated Passover in Jerusalem; he was arrested, put on trial, and crucified by the Romans soon after.

In AD 66, the Jews rose up against Roman rule. Their fierce revolt failed and Jerusalem and the temple were destroyed in the process, in AD 70. A vestige of the temple compound, the Western Wall, is venerated by Jews to this day. The last Jewish stronghold, Masada, fell three years later.

■ Visit: Sea of Galilee (⇨ Ch.6), Via Dolorosa (⇨ Ch.2), Masada (⇨ Ch.3)

325 Constantine makes Christianity the imperial religion	622 Muhammad's *hejira* and the beginning of Islam		1099 Crusaders conquer Jerusalem
500	700	900	1100

(immediate left) Bar Kochba's coin: top, the Jewish Temple facade with the rising star; reverse: A lulav, the text that reads: "to the freedom of Jerusalem." (top left) Saladin, commander of Muslim forces, battles Christians in the 3rd Crusade. (top right) Richard the Lionheart In battle during the Crusades.

Late Roman & Byzantine Period

AD 73–640

In 132, the Roman emperor Hadrian threatened to rebuild Jerusalem as a pagan city and another Jewish revolt broke out, led by Bar-Kochba. In retribution, Hadrian leveled Jerusalem in 135 and changed the name of the country to Syria Palestina. Many of the remaining Jews were killed, enslaved, or exiled.

It wasn't until the 4th century AD that the Roman emperor Constantine made Christianity the imperial religion. This revived life in the Holy Land, making it a focus of pilgrimage and church construction that included the Church of the Nativity in Bethlehem. In spite of persecution, a vibrant Jewish community still existed.

Muhammad's *hejira* (flight) from Mecca to Medina in Arabia took place in 622, marking the beginning of Islam. This became Year One on the Muslim calendar. When Muhammad died in 632, his followers burst out of Arabia and created a Muslim empire that within a century would extend from India to Spain.

■ Visit: Jerusalem's Cardo (⇨ Ch.2); Caesarea (⇨ Ch.5)

Medieval Period

640–1516

The Dome of the Rock was constructed in Jerusalem in 691 by Caliph Abd al-Malik. In 1099, the Crusaders conquered the city and massacred Jews and Muslims living there. Akko (also called Acre) and Belvoir, in the Lower Galilee, were developed around 1100. Muslim reconquest of the land under the Mamluks began in 1265. In 1291 Akko fell, marking the end of the Crusades. An outstanding period of architecture followed, especially in Jerusalem's Temple Mount (Haram esh-Sharif) and in the Muslim Quarter.

■ Visit: Dome of the Rock (⇨ Ch.2); Al-Aqsa Mosque (⇨ Ch.2); Akko (Ch. 5)

1265 Muslim reconquest begins	Akko falls in 1291, marking the end of the Crusader kingdom	1516 Mamluks defeated in Syria by the Ottoman Turks	1897 First World Zionist Conference

1300 | 1500 | 1700 | 1900

THE PALESTINE POST

STATE OF ISRAEL IS BORN

Most Crowded Hours in Palestine's History

JEWS TAKE OVER SECURITY ZONES

Egyptian Air Force Spitfires Bomb Tel Aviv; One Shot Down

U.S. RECOGNIZES JEWISH STATE

Proclamation by Head Of Government

Special Assembly

2 Columns Cross | Etzion Settlers

(top left) Jewish settlers known as Biluim, in Palestine, 1880s. The 38th Zionist congress, 1933. (bottom left) *Palestine Post* headline announcing declaration of independence in 1948.

1516–1917 Modern Period

In 1516, the Mamluks were defeated in Syria by the Ottoman Turks. Egyptian nationalists took control of Israel in 1832, but were expelled in 1840 with help from European nations. The country's population shifted in the 19th century, when the steamship made access easy.

The first World Zionist Conference, organized by Theodor Herzl, took place in 1897, fueling the idea of a Jewish homeland. In 1909, Tel Aviv was founded, and Degania, the first kibbutz, was established on the southern shore of the Sea of Galilee.

■ Visit: Akko (⇨ Ch.5); Walls of Jerusalem (⇨ Ch.2)

1917–1948 Creation of a Jewish State

The conquest of Palestine by the British in the First World War ushered in many critical changes. In 1917, the British government expressed support in the Balfour Declaration for creation of a Jewish homeland. Arab nationalism began to rise around 1920 in the post-Ottoman Middle East after Ottoman Turkey, which sided with Germany during the first World War, abandoned Palestine. This marked the point at which tension between Jews and Arabs began to increase, peaking in the massacre of Jews in 1920, 1929, and again in 1936. Various Jewish militias formed to counter the violence.

The British "White Paper" of 1938 restricted Jewish immigration and land purchase in Palestine. Tensions with Britain, and clashes between Arabs and Jews, peaked after World War II. The U.N. Partition Plan of 1947 envisioned two states in Palestine, one Jewish and one Arab. With the end of the British mandate in May 1948, David Ben-Gurion, the Palestinian Jewish leader who would later become Israel's first prime minister, declared Israel a Jewish state. Immediately thereafter, Israel survived invasions by the armies of seven Arab countries.

■ Visit: Tel Hai (⇨ Ch.7), Independence Hall, Tel Aviv (⇨ Ch.4), Jordan Valley Kibbutzim (⇨ Ch.5), Ben-Gurion's Desert Home (Ch. 8)

1948 Creation of a Jewish State. David Ben-Gurion elected Israel's first prime minister | 1967 Six-Day War | 1973 Yom Kippur War | 1987 *Intifada* begins | 1994 Oslo Accord | 2000 2nd *Intifada* | 2006 Hamas wins Palestinian election

1930 | 1960 | 1990 | 2020

(left) David Ben-Gurion in 1918. (top right) Knesset, Israeli parliament, Jerusalem. (bottom right) Israeli flag.

1948–1998

The First 50 Years

Fighting ended January, 1949, and a U.N.-supervised cease-fire agreement was signed. Transjordan annexed the West Bank and East Jerusalem; Egypt annexed the Gaza Strip. Palestinian Arabs who fled or were expelled settled in neighboring countries; those who stayed became Israeli citizens. The first elections to the Knesset took place, and David Ben-Gurion was elected prime minister. In 1950, the Knesset enacted the Law of Return, giving any Jew the right to Israeli citizenship.

Around 1964, the Palestine Liberation Organization (PLO) was founded, which sought an independent state for Palestinians and refused to recognize Israel as a state. In 1967, the Six-Day War broke out; Israel occupied territory including the Golan Heights. Egypt and Syria attacked Israel on Yom Kippur in 1973. The Lebanon War in 1982 met with unprecedented Israeli opposition. In 1987, the *intifada* (uprising) brought sustained Palestinian Arab unrest. The Oslo Accords, signed in 1994, involved mutual recognition of Israel and the PLO, as well as Palestinian autonomy in the Gaza Strip and parts of the West Bank.

1998–Present

Israel Today

After Ehud Barak was elected prime minister in 1999, Israel withdrew from Lebanon. The second *intifada* began in 2000 and subsided in 2005, costing more than 3,000 Israeli and Palestinian lives. Current concern is the rise of Hamas, which unexpectedly celebrated a landslide victory in Palestinian elections in January, 2006. Shortly thereafter, the kidnapping of two Israeli soldiers by Hezbollah sparked a 34-day war. Hezbollah's increasing power and peace with Lebanon remain difficult issues for Israel. Despite all this, Israel continues to enjoy a strong economy and healthy tourism.

2

Jerusalem

WORD OF MOUTH

"My family was visiting Israel with a group of other families, and as our tour guide was explaining the amazing history of the church, this little boy separated himself and silently went and lit a candle, symbolizing a prayer, all by himself."

—photo by nicole_pappas, Fodors.com member

WELCOME TO JERUSALEM

TOP REASONS TO GO

★ **The Old City:** For an astonishing montage of religions and cultures, the heart of Jerusalem—with the Holy Sepulcher, Arab bazaar, and Western Wall—has few equals anywhere in the world.

★ **Mt. of Olives:** This classic panorama puts the entire Old City, with the golden Dome of the Rock, squarely within your lens. The view is best with the morning sun behind you.

★ **Machaneh Yehuda:** You can munch a falafel as you watch shoppers swirl and eddy through West Jerusalem's outstanding produce market.

★ **Israel Museum:** The museum, fresh from an enormous renewal, is a winner, with its Dead Sea Scrolls, outdoor model, and a stunning collection of fine art, archaeology, and Judaica.

★ **City of David:** Here you can plunge underground to explore Jerusalem's most ancient remains, and wade the 2,700-year-old water tunnel that once saved the besieged city.

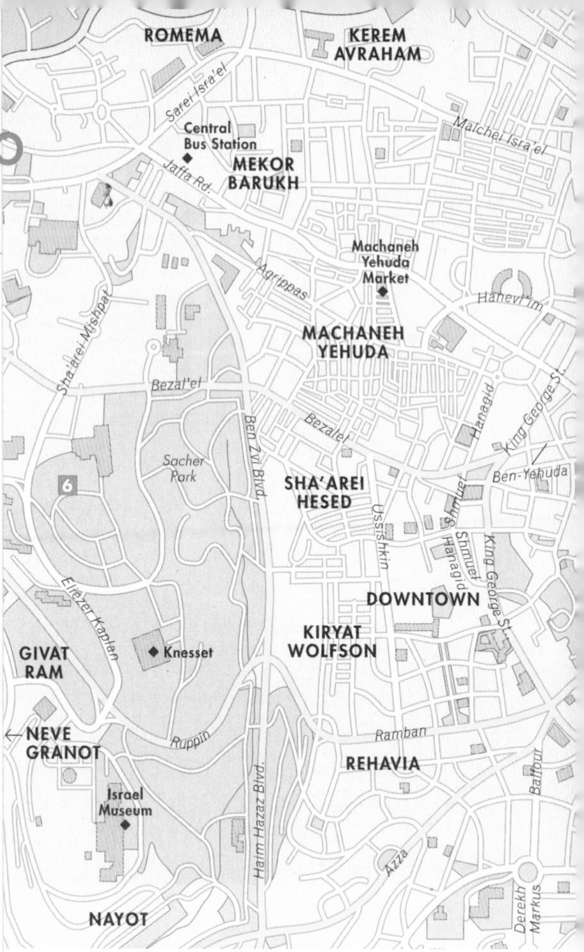

1 Old City classic sights. The walled Old City, with its narrow streets, is what Jerusalem is all about. It is a labyrinth of memories, a bewitching flicker show of colors and cultures, best epitomized by the souk, or bazaar. But it is also the Holy Sepulcher, the Western Wall, and the Dome of the Rock, redolent with religion and seething with history.

2 Jewish Quarter. Excavations in the 1970s unearthed a handful of interesting ancient sites (notably the Herodian Quarter), now integrated into this reconstructed neighborhood in the Old City. Good stores and lots of eateries complete the picture.

3 Tower of David and Mt Zion. Stretching south from Jaffa Gate, this area is a potpourri of interesting minor sights. The Tower of David Museum is the most notable.

4 City of David. At the very core of ancient Jerusalem, outside the Old City walls, this

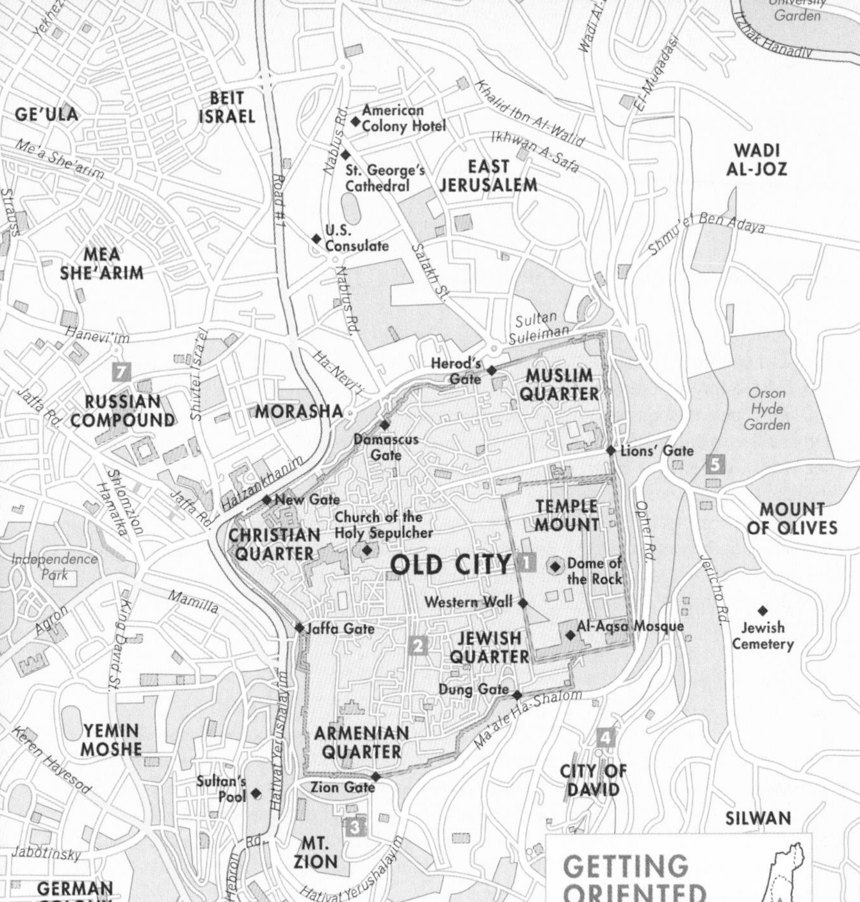

largely underground archaeological adventure would be a banner-headline site anywhere else; in Jerusalem, however, the famous shrines unjustly overshadow it.

5 Mt. of Olives and East Jerusalem. Most visitors, particularly Christians, will identify with two or three particular sites—Gethsemane and the Garden Tomb are the obvious ones. Pick your way down the Mt. of Olives. Rockefeller Museum is a gem.

6 West Jerusalem. Within this extensive side of Jerusalem are several great but unrelated sights, some a few miles apart. Savor the extraordinary Israel Museum and Yad Vashem.

7 Center City. West Jerusalem's Downtown areas have more subtle attractions than the city's postcard snapshots. Check out the Yemin Moshe and Nahalat Shiva neighborhoods, Ben-Yehuda Street, and the Machaneh Yehuda market.

GETTING ORIENTED

Hilly Jerusalem has two centers of gravity—the Old City, on the east side; and the modern Downtown triangle of King George, Ben-Yehuda, and Jaffa streets on the west. Jerusalem is Israel's capital and home to its national institutions, most in Jewish West Jerusalem. East Jerusalem, including the Old City, is largely (but not entirely) Arab. Coexistence is sometimes fragile, and the two communities tend to keep to themselves.

JERUSALEM PLANNER

When to Go

Jerusalem, like Israel in general, is a year-round destination, but the very best months are late March through April, and October through November, when prices are lower and the weather is good, even warm. Winter is colder than in Tel Aviv, but sunny days often follow gloomy ones. Jerusalem gets its own back in the hot, rainless summer months; the inland capital is dry and cools off toward evening. Avoid the main Jewish holidays, when hotels charge peak prices and many tourist attractions change schedules.

Visitor Information

The Tourist Information Office is open Sunday to Thursday 8 to 5, Friday 9 to 1. The Christian Information Centre is open weekdays 8:30 to 5:30, Saturday 8:30 to 12:30.

Contacts **Christian Information Centre** (✉ *Jaffa Gate, Jaffa Gate* ☎ *02/627–2692* 🌐 *http://198.62.75.1/www1/ofm/cic/CICmainin.htm*). **Tourist Information Office** (✉ *Jaffa Gate, Jaffa Gate* ☎ *02/627–1422* 🌐 *http://tour.jerusalem.muni.il*).

Getting Here

See Getting Here and Around in Travel Smart Israel for information about air travel to Israel. Taking the bus from Ben Gurion Airport to Jerusalem is cheap but slow. Board the Egged shuttle (line 5, fare NIS 5.30) for a 10-minute ride to the Ben Gurion Airport El Al Junction, and wait for the Egged bus (line 947, fare NIS 23). It runs to Jerusalem's Central Bus Station. As an easier but often tediously long alternative, 10-seat *sherut* taxis (limo-vans) depart from Ben Gurion Airport when they fill up, and drop passengers at any Jerusalem address for NIS 50. By car, Route 1 is the chief route to Jerusalem from both the west and the east.

Getting Around

Bus Travel: Egged operates the extensive bus service within Jerusalem. The fare is NIS 6.20; you do not need exact change. A cab is more time-effective, and for a group often more cost-effective as well. Egged operates Route 99, a two-hour circle tour of Jerusalem for visitors with 24 stops. The route begins at the Central Bus Station; cost is NIS 60 for one full trip.

Bus Contacts **Egged** (🌐 *www.egged.co.il/eng*).

Car Travel: Walking and taking cabs or a guide-driven tourist limo-van are often more time-effective than a car.

Light Rail Travel: At the time of this writing, Jerusalem's much-delayed light rail system (www.citypass.co.il) was slated to begin operating in 2011. The Red Line, the first to open, will begin at Mt. Scopus and run along Jaffa Street to the main bus station. It will then head southwest on its way to Mt. Herzl and Hadassah Hospital.

Taxi Travel: Taxis can be flagged on the street, ordered by phone, or picked up at a taxi stand or at major hotels. The law requires taxi drivers to use their meters.

Train Travel: Train service between Jerusalem and the coast takes about an hour and 20 minutes—good at rush hour, but 50 minutes slower than the bus at other times. The fare to or from Tel Aviv is NIS 39 round-trip.

For more information, see Travel Smart Israel. For tours, see the box on Sightseeing Tours in Exploring Jerusalem.

Dining

While the range of Jerusalem eateries will never rival that of cosmopolitan Tel Aviv, you can eat very well in the holy city. Middle Eastern food (sometimes mistranslated as "Oriental") is a strong suit. Modern Israeli fare draws on the plethora of fresh produce and the local emphasis on seasonal fruits and vegetables. Proportionately, there are far more kosher establishments than in Tel Aviv, but fear not: the food can be just as varied and delicious, and the dietary restrictions often hardly noticeable.

Lodging

Accommodations range from cheap and simple to high-end deluxe in a variety of settings, from the city center to the almost-rural periphery. Where possible, avoid Jewish holidays—especially the one-week holidays of Passover (March–April) and Sukkot/Tabernacles (September–October), when hotels are full and prices peak.

WHAT IT COSTS

	¢	$	$$	$$$	$$$$
Restaurants	under NIS 32	NIS 32–NIS 49	NIS 50–NIS 75	NIS 76–NIS 100	over NIS 100
Hotels	under $120	$120–$200	$201–$300	$301–$400	over $400

Restaurant prices are per person for a main course at dinner in NIS (Israeli shekels). Hotel prices are in U.S. dollars, for two people in a standard double room in high season. Non-Israeli citizens paying in foreign currency are exempt from the 16% VAT tax on hotel rooms.

Travel Precautions

Individual violence is rare and tourists are not specific targets. Nevertheless, avoid Muslim Quarter backstreets, and be cautious walking the Old City at night (when almost everything is closed anyway). The important weekly Muslim prayers around midday Friday sometimes get passionate if there is a hot Palestinian-Israeli issue in the news. Emotions can spill into the streets of the Muslim Quarter as the crowds leave the al-Aqsa Mosque.

As in any major tourist destination, pickpockets can be a problem: keep purses closed and close to you, and wallets in less accessible pockets. Don't leave valuables in parked cars, and use hotel safes. *For health information, see Travel Smart Israel.*

Planning Your Time

Israel itineraries tend to favor Jerusalem. The Old City alone offers an absorbing two days. Beyond its religious shrines are ancient sites, panoramic walks, and museums. Allow time for poking around the Arab market and the stores of the Jewish Quarter. The immediate environs—the City of David, Mt. of Olives, Mt. Zion, and a few sites north of the Old City walls—can add a day or more. West Jerusalem's spread-out museums, institutions, and attractions take time. Add leisure time and shopping, and you're quickly up to a five- to six-day stay. Jerusalem is also a convenient base for day trips to Masada and the Dead Sea, and even Tel Aviv.

A few tips for maximizing your time: Make a list of must-see sights. Pay attention to opening times and geography, to minimize backtracking. Mix experiences each day, to avoid overdosing on museums, shrines, or archaeology. Above all, take time to let your senses absorb the city. Take time to walk around and sip a coffee at a sidewalk café. Jerusalem is as much about atmosphere as it is a checklist of world-class sights.

By Mike Rogoff
Updated by Jessica Steinberg

Jerusalem is a city suspended between heaven and earth, east and west, past and present—parallel universes of flowing caftans and trendy coffee shops. For some people, Jerusalem is a condition, like being in love; for others, it is a state of mind, a constant tension between rival flags and faiths, or members of the same faith. You may feel moved, energized, or swept into the maelstrom of contemporary issues—but the city will not leave you unaffected.

The word *unique* is easy to throw around, but Jerusalem has a real claim on it. The 5,000-year-old city is sacred to half the human race, and its iconic Old City walls embrace primary sites of the three great monotheistic religions. For Jews, Jerusalem has always been their spiritual focus and historical national center; the imposing Western Wall is the last remnant of the ancient Temple complex. For almost 2,000 years, Christians have venerated Jerusalem as the place where their faith was shaped—through the death, burial, and resurrection of Jesus of Nazareth—and the candlelit Church of the Holy Sepulcher is where the greater part of Christendom recognizes those events. Islamic tradition identifies Jerusalem as the *masjid al-aqsa,* the "farthermost place," from which Muhammad ascended to Heaven for his portentous meeting with God: the dazzling, gold-top Dome of the Rock marks the spot.

The Old City is far more than shrines, however. Its arches, hidden courtyards, and narrow cobblestone alleyways beckon you back in time. The streets are crowded with travelers, pilgrims, and vendors of everything from tourist trinkets and leather sandals to fresh produce, embroidered fabrics, and dubious videocassettes. Your senses are assaulted by intense colors and by the aromas of turmeric, fresh mint, wild sage, and cardamom-spiced coffee. The blare of Arabic music and the burble of languages fill the air.

Step outside the Old City and you'll be transported into the 21st century—well, at least the 20th: quaint neighborhoods, some restored, embody an earlier simplicity. West Jerusalem forms the bulk of a modern metropolis of almost 800,000, Israel's largest city. It is not as cosmopolitan as Tel Aviv, to be sure, but it does have good restaurants, fine hotels, cultural venues, vibrant markets, and high-quality stores. The Downtown triangle of Jaffa Street, King George Street, and Ben-Yehuda Street, and the elegant Mamilla Mall outside Jaffa Gate, are natural gathering places.

The city prides itself on its historical continuity. A municipal bylaw dating back to 1918 makes it mandatory to face even high-rise commercial buildings with the honey-colored "Jerusalem stone," the local limestone that has served Jerusalem's builders since, well, forever. Watch the stone walls glow at sunset—the source of the by-now clichéd but still compelling phrase "Jerusalem of Gold"—and understand the mystical hold Jerusalem has had on so many minds and hearts for so many thousands of years.

EXPLORING JERUSALEM

Immerse yourself in Jerusalem. Of course you can see the primary sights in a couple of days—some visitors claim to have done it in less!—but don't short-change yourself if you can help it. Take time to wander where the spirit takes you, to linger longer over a snack and people-watch, to follow the late Hebrew poet, Yehuda Amichai, "in the evening into the Old City / and . . . emerge from it pockets stuffed with images / and metaphors and well-constructed parables . . ." The poet struggled for breath in an atmosphere "saturated with prayers and dreams"; but the city's baggage of history and religion doesn't have to weigh you down. Decompress in the markets and eateries of the Old City, and the jewelry and art stores, coffee shops and pubs of the New.

Jerusalem beyond its ancient walls is a city of neighborhoods. Several are picturesque or quaint enough to attract the casual daytime visitor, but hold little interest once the sun sets: the upscale Talbieh-Yemin Moshe area and the lower-end Machaneh Yehuda-Nachla'ot area are good examples. Two hives of activity after dark are the Downtown complex of the Ben-Yehuda Street pedestrian mall (*midrachov*) and Nahalat Shiva, and Emek Refa'im, the main artery of the German Colony.

Let's put Jerusalem on the map. The city is built on a series of hills, part of the country's north–south watershed. To the east, the Judean Desert tumbles down to the Dead Sea, the lowest point on earth, less than an hour's drive away. The main highway to the west winds down through the pine-covered Judean Hills toward the international airport and Tel Aviv. North and south of the city—Samaria and Judea, respectively—is what is known as the West Bank. Since 1967, this contested area has been administered largely by Israel, though the major concentrations of Arab population are currently under autonomous Palestinian control.

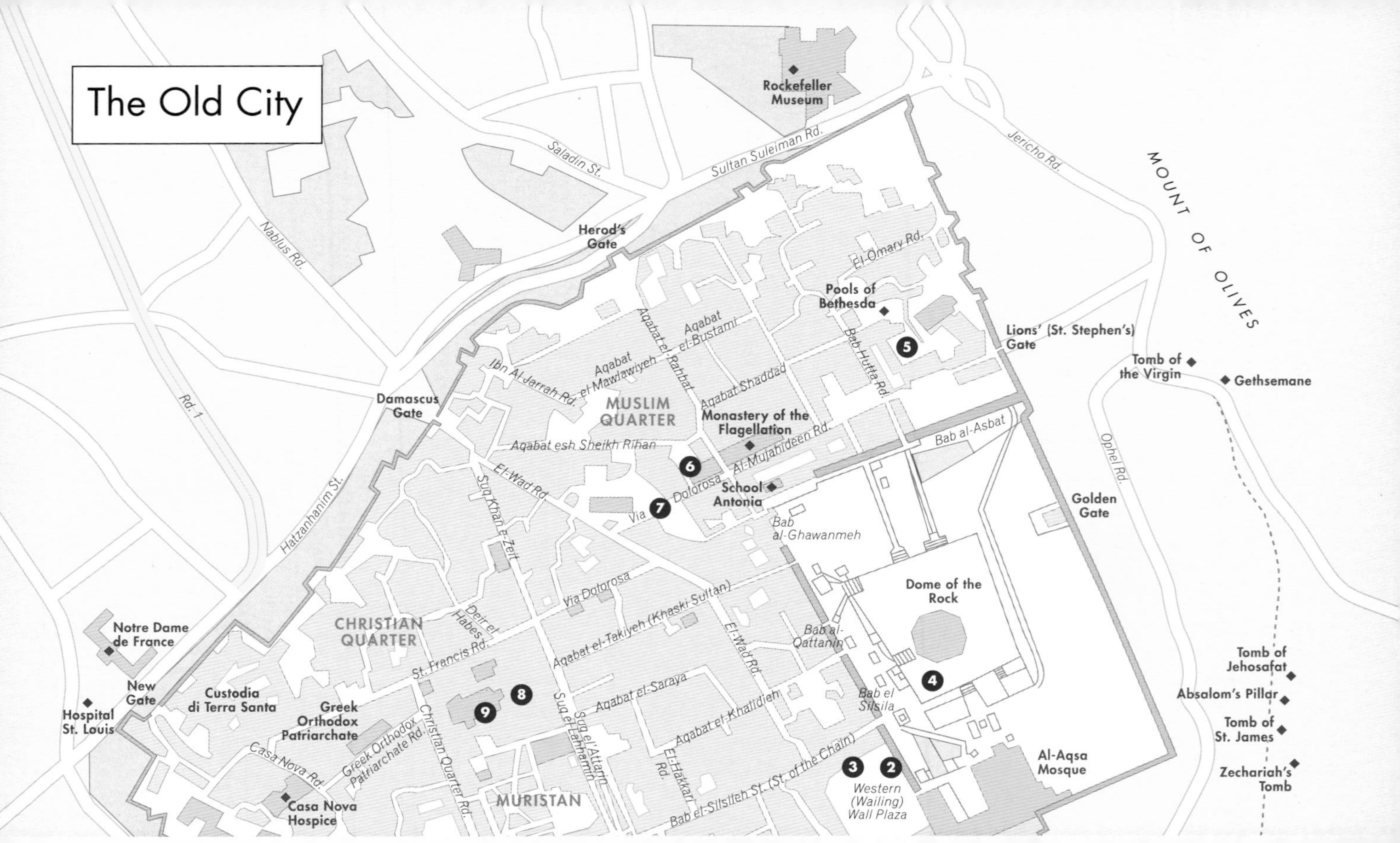

The Old City
Rockefeller Museum
Saladin St.
Sultan Suleiman Rd.
Jericho Rd.
MOUNT OF OLIVES
Nablus Rd.
Herod's Gate
El-Omary Rd.
Pools of Bethesda
Aqabat el-Bustami
Aqabat el-Rahbat
Bab Hutta Rd.
Lions' (St. Stephen's) Gate
Tomb of the Virgin
Gethsemane
Rd. 1
Ibn Al Jarrah Rd.
Aqabat el Mawlawiyeh
Aqabat Shaddad
Damascus Gate
MUSLIM QUARTER
Monastery of the Flagellation
Al-Mujahideen Rd.
Bab al-Asbat
Ophel Rd.
Aqabat esh Sheikh Rihan
El-Wad Rd.
Suq Khan e-Zeit
Via Dolorosa
School Antonia
Golden Gate
Hatzanhanim St.
Bab al-Ghawanmeh
Dome of the Rock
Via Dolorosa
Aqabat el-Takiyeh (Khaski Sultan)
Notre Dame de France
CHRISTIAN QUARTER
Deir el Habes
St. Francis Rd.
Bab al-Qattanin
Tomb of Jehosafat
Absalom's Pillar
Tomb of St. James
Zechariah's Tomb
New Gate
Hospital St. Louis
Custodia di Terra Santa
Greek Orthodox Patriarchate
Aqabat el-Saraya
Bab el Silsila
Aqabat el-Khalidieh
Suq el-Lahhamin
Suq el'Attarin
El-Hakkari Rd.
Christian Quarter Rd.
Greek Orthodox Patriarchate Rd.
Casa Nova Rd.
Bab el-Silsileh St. (St. of the Chain)
Western (Wailing) Wall Plaza
Al-Aqsa Mosque
Casa Nova Hospice
MURISTAN

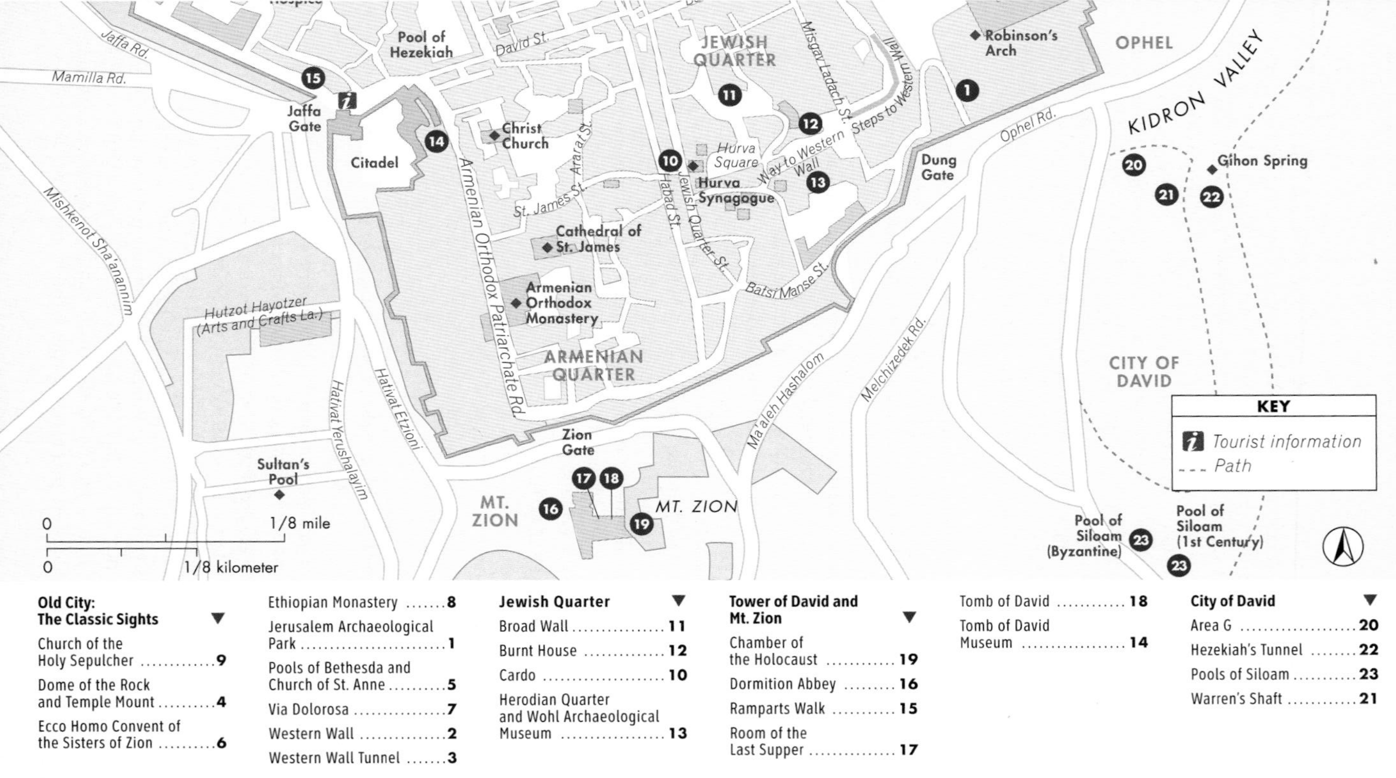

Old City: The Classic Sights ▼

Church of the Holy Sepulcher 9
Dome of the Rock and Temple Mount 4
Ecco Homo Convent of the Sisters of Zion 6
Ethiopian Monastery 8
Jerusalem Archaeological Park 1
Pools of Bethesda and Church of St. Anne 5
Via Dolorosa 7
Western Wall 2
Western Wall Tunnel 3

Jewish Quarter ▼

Broad Wall 11
Burnt House 12
Cardo 10
Herodian Quarter and Wohl Archaeological Museum 13

Tower of David and Mt. Zion ▼

Chamber of the Holocaust 19
Dormition Abbey 16
Ramparts Walk 15
Room of the Last Supper 17
Tomb of David 18
Tomb of David Museum 14

City of David ▼

Area G 20
Hezekiah's Tunnel 22
Pools of Siloam 23
Warren's Shaft 21

OLD CITY: THE CLASSIC SIGHTS

Drink in the very essence of Jerusalem as you explore the city's primary religious sites in the Muslim and Christian quarters, and at the Western Wall, and touch the different cultures that share it. The Old City's 35,000 inhabitants jostle in the cobblestone lanes with an air of ownership, at best merely tolerating the "intruders" from other quarters. Devout Jews in black and white scurry from their neighborhoods north and west of the Old City, through the Damascus Gate and the Muslim Quarter, toward the Western Wall. Arab women in long embroidered dresses flow across the Western Wall plaza to Dung Gate and the village of Silwan beyond it. It is not unusual to stand at the Western Wall, surrounded by the sounds of devotions, and hear the piercing call to prayer of the Muslim *muezzin* above you, with the more distant bells of the Christian Quarter providing a counterpoint.

Sites such as the Western Wall, Calvary, and the Haram esh-Sharif bring the thrill of recognition to ancient history. The devout cannot fail to be moved by the holy city, and its special, if sometimes dissonant, moods and modes of devotion tend to fascinate the nonbeliever as well.

GETTING HERE AND AROUND

To explore the key sites in one day, keep in mind opening times and geography, and plan accordingly. Heading to Dung Gate first thing in the morning will get the Western Wall area and the Temple Mount (Muslim shrines) off the list. Exit the northern end of the mount to the Via Dolorosa and Holy Sepulcher. Jaffa Gate will take you right to the Holy Sepulcher and on to the Western Wall but poses a problem of timing for the Temple Mount. Lions' Gate is best for beginning with the Via Dolorosa, and fine for everything else except the Temple Mount. With some initial walking through the bazaar, Damascus Gate allows you to choose your preferred sequence of sights. Of course, you can spread your visit over more than one day.

TIMING AND PRECAUTIONS

It's best to avoid the Via Dolorosa, which largely runs through the Muslim Quarter, between noon and 2 pm Fridays, the time of important weekly Muslim prayers. All the holy places demand modest dress: no shorts and no sleeveless tops.

TOP ATTRACTIONS

★ **Church of the Holy Sepulcher.** *For information about the church, see the feature Jerusalem: Keeping the Faith in this chapter.*

★ **Dome of the Rock and Temple Mount.** *For information about these sites, see the feature Jerusalem: Keeping the Faith in this chapter.*

Jerusalem Archaeological Park. Overlooked by many casual visitors, the site still often referred to as the Western and Southern Wall Excavations, or the Ophel, was a historical gold mine for Israeli archaeologists in the 1970s and '80s. Interesting Byzantine and early Arab structures came to light, but by far the most dramatic and monumental finds were from the Herodian period, the late 1st century BC. Walk down to the high corner facing you. King Herod the Great rebuilt the Second Temple on the exact site of its predecessor, where the Dome of the Rock now stands. He expanded the sacred enclosure by constructing a massive, shoebox-shaped retaining wall on the slopes of the hill, the biblical Mt. Moriah. The inside was filled with thousands of tons of rubble to create the huge plaza, the size of 27 football fields, still known today as the Temple Mount. The great stones near the corner, with their signature precision-cut borders, are not held together with mortar; their sheer weight gives the structure its stability. The original wall would have been at least one-third higher than it is today.

Exposed to the left of the corner is the white pavement of an impressive main street and commercial area from the Second Temple period. The protrusion left of the corner and high above your head is known as **Robinson's Arch.** Named for a 19th-century American explorer, it is a remnant of a monumental bridge to the Temple Mount which was reached by a staircase from the street where you now stand: look for the ancient steps. The square-cut building stones heaped on the street came from the top of the original wall, dramatic evidence of the Roman destruction of AD 70.

Return to the higher level by way of the wooden steps and turn left (east). Fifty yards over, a modern spiral staircase descends below present ground level to a partially reconstructed labyrinth of Byzantine dwellings, mosaics and all; from here you reemerge outside the present city walls. Alternatively, go straight, passing through the city wall by a small arched gate. The broad, impressive **Southern Steps** on your left, a good part of it original, once brought hordes of Jewish pilgrims through the now-blocked southern gates of the Temple Mount. The rock-hewn ritual baths near the bottom of the steps were used for the purification rites once demanded of Jews before they entered the sacred temple precincts. (On Friday, this section of the site closes at noon April through September, and at 11 am October through March.) The low-rise, air-conditioned **Davidson Visitors Center** (on your right as you enter the site) offers visual aids, some artifacts, two interesting videos (which continuously alternate between English and Hebrew), and toilet facilities. It's a good place to start your visit if you're on your own. Allow 30 minutes for the center and another 40 for the site. ✉ *Dung Gate, Western Wall* ☎ *02/627–7550* 🌐 *www.archpark.org.il* 🎫 *NIS 30* ⏲ *Sun.–Thurs. 8–5, Fri. and Jewish holiday eves 8–2.*

Via Dolorosa. The Way of Suffering—or Way of the Cross, as it's more commonly called in English—is venerated as the route Jesus walked, carrying his cross, from the place of his trial and condemnation by Pontius Pilate to the site of his crucifixion and burial. (Stations I and II are where the Antonia fortress once stood, widely regarded as the site of the "praetorium" referred to in the Gospels.) The present tradition jelled no earlier than the 18th century, but it draws on much older beliefs. Some of the incidents represented by the 14 Stations of the Cross are scriptural; others (III, IV, VI, VII, and IX) are not. Tiny chapels mark a few of the stations; the last five are inside the Church of the Holy Sepulcher. Catholic pilgrim groups, or the Franciscan-led Friday afternoon procession, take about 45 minutes to wind their way through the busy market streets of the Muslim and Christian quarters, with prayers and chants at each station.

Here are the 14 stations on the Via Dolorosa that mark the route that Jesus took, from trial and condemnation to crucifixion and burial. *For a map of the Via Dolorosa, see the feature Jerusalem: Keeping the Faith in this chap*ter.

Station I. Jesus is tried and condemned by Pontius Pilate.

Station II. Jesus is scourged and given the cross.

Station III. Jesus falls for the first time. (Soldiers of the Free Polish Forces built the chapel after World War II.)

Station IV. Mary embraces Jesus.

Station V. Simon of Cyrene picks up the cross.

Station VI. A woman wipes the face of Jesus, whose image remains on the cloth. (She is remembered as Veronica, apparently derived from the words *vera* and *icon,* meaning "true image.")

Station VII. Jesus falls for the second time. (The chapel contains one of the columns of the Byzantine Cardo, the main street of 6th-century Jerusalem.)

Station VIII. Jesus addresses the women in the crowd.

Station IX. Jesus falls for the third time.

Station X. Jesus is stripped of his garments.

Station XI. Jesus is nailed to the cross.

Station XII. Jesus dies on the cross.

Station XIII. Jesus is taken down from the cross.

Station XIV. Jesus is buried.

⊠ *Muslim and Christian Quarters.*

NEED A BREAK?

Between the sixth and seventh stations of the Via Dolorosa is the very good Holy Rock Café (⊠ *Muslim Quarter*). The name may be a little hokey, but there's nothing wrong with its freshly squeezed orange and pomegranate juice (in season), Turkish coffee, mint tea, and superb *bourma*, a round Arab confection filled with whole pistachio nuts. An Internet café is only a few steps away.

★ **Western Wall.** *For information about this sight, see the Jerusalem: Keeping the Faith feature in this chapter.*

Western Wall Tunnel. The long tunnel beyond the men's side (north of the plaza) of the Western Wall is not a rediscovered ancient thoroughfare but was deliberately dug in recent years with the purpose of exposing a strip of the Western Wall along its entire length. One course of the massive wall revealed two building stones estimated to weigh an incredible 400 tons and 570 tons, respectively. Local guided tours are available and are recommended—you can visit the site only as part of an organized tour—but the times change from week to week (some include evening hours). The tour takes about 75 minutes; among the attractions are a kinetic model of the Western Wall and some of the incredible building stones. Tours end, during daylight hours, at the beginning of the Via Dolorosa, in the Muslim Quarter. After dark, that exit is closed, and

Continued on page 82

CLOSE UP

A Walk on the Via Dolorosa

The Old City's main Jewish and Muslim sites can be visited individually, but the primary Christian shrines—the Via Dolorosa (or Way of the Cross) and the Holy Sepulcher—are best experienced in sequence. This walk will keep you oriented in the confusing marketplace through which the Via Dolorosa picks its way. (Beware of slick pickpockets.) The route takes under an hour; plan additional time if you want to linger. About 300 yards up the road from St. Anne's Church (near Lions' Gate), look for a ramp on your left leading to the dark metal door of a school. This is the site of the ancient Antonia fortress. On Friday afternoons at 4 (April to September; at 3 from October to March), the brown-robed Franciscans begin their procession of the **Via Dolorosa** outside the metal door. This is Station I; Station II is across the street. Just beyond it, on the right, is the entrance to the **Ecce Homo Convent of the Sisters of Zion,** with a Roman arch in the chapel (only open during worship). The continuation of the arch crosses the street outside, and, just beyond it, a few steps on the right take you into a small vestibule with a view of the chapel's interior.

The Via Dolorosa runs down into El-Wad Road, one of the Old City's most important thoroughfares. To the right, the street climbs toward the Damascus Gate; to the left, it passes through the heart of the Muslim Quarter and reaches the Western Wall. Arab matrons sail by; black-hatted Hasidic Jews hurry on divine missions; nimble local Muslim kids in T-shirts, jeans, and sneakers play in the street; and Christian pilgrims pace out ancient footsteps.

As you turn left onto El-Wad Road, Station III is on your left. Right next to it is Station IV and, on the next corner, 50 yards farther, Station V. There the Via Dolorosa turns right and begins its ascent toward Calvary. Halfway up the street, a brown wooden door on your left marks Station VI.

Facing you at the top of the stepped street, on the busy Suq Khan e-Zeit, is Station VII. The little chapel preserves one of the columns of the Byzantine Cardo (street). Step to the left, and walk 30 yards up the street facing you to Station VIII, marked by nothing more than an inscribed stone in the wall on the left. Return to the main street and turn right. (If you skip Station VIII, turn left as you reach Station VII from the stepped street.) One hundred yards along Suq Khan e-Zeit from Station VII, turn onto the ramp on your right that ascends parallel to the street. At the end of the lane is a column that represents Station IX.

Step through the open door to the left of the column into the courtyard of the **Ethiopian Monastery** known as Deir es-Sultan. From the monastery's upper chapel, descend through a lower one and out a small wooden door to the court of the **Church of the Holy Sepulcher.** Most Christians venerate this site as that of the death, burial, and resurrection of Jesus—you'll find Stations X, XI, XII, XIII, and XIV within the church. A good time to be here is in the late afternoon, after 4 pm, when the different denominations in turn chant their way between Calvary and the tomb. *For more information on the sights in bold type, see the listings in the Old City section; see the feature Jerusalem: Keeping the Faith for a map.*

2

JERUSALEM: KEEPING THE FAITH

Unforgotten and unforgettable, the city of Jerusalem is holy ground for the three great monotheistic religions, whose numbers embrace half the world's population. Its Old City is home to some of the most sacred sites of Judaism, Christianity, and Islam: the Western Wall, the Temple Mount/Haram esh-Sharif, the Church of the Holy Sepulcher, and the Dome of the Rock and Al-Aqsa Mosque. Some travelers visit them to find their soul, others to seek a sense of communion with ancient epochs. Whether pilgrim or tourist, you'll discover that history, faith, and culture commingle here as perhaps nowhere else on earth.

By Mike Rogoff

(right) The Western Wall, (opposite left) Dome of the Church of the Holy Sepulcher, (opposite right) The Dome of the Rock

2 IN FOCUS JERUSALEM: KEEPING THE FAITH

ONE CITY UNDER GOD

Jerusalem is a composite of three faith-civilizations: Jewish, Christian, and Muslim. They cohabit the Old City uneasily, burdened by centuries of struggle with each other for rights and real estate. But at the level of day-to-day routine, each draws its adherents to, respectively, the Western Wall, the Church of the Holy Sepulcher, and the Al-Aqsa Mosque. To the visitor, the collage of spiritual traditions is often bewildering, sometimes alien, always fascinating. The intricate choreographies of devotion have been known to move nonbelievers as well as the devout.

HISTORY AND HOLY STONES

Wander the cobblestone lanes of historical Jerusalem and you can hear in your mind's ear the echoes of King David's harp, trace the revered footsteps of Jesus of Nazareth, and sense the presence of the Prophet Muhammad. In the space of just a few hours, you can visit the tomb of Jesus at Golgotha, gaze at the shrine where Islam's founder rose to "the farthermost place," and stand before the only extant remnant of the Second Temple compound. Not without reason do some visitors imagine their fold-out atlases to be road maps leading to heaven itself.

(left) Woman praying, (top right) Miracle of Holy Fire, Church of the Holy Sepulcher, (bottom right) Men praying near the Dome of the Rock

Great dramas played out on these stones—occasionally, it is claimed, on the very same stone. The rock capped by the gold dome is the summit of Mt. Moriah, identified in Jewish tradition with the biblical site where Abraham erected an altar and prepared to sacrifice his son Isaac. It was here on the Temple Mount that the "First" and "Second" Jewish Temples stood for a total of one thousand years. In the same rock, devout Muslims point to the imprint of a foot, regarded as that of Muhammad himself, as evidence that it was here that the Prophet ascended to heaven for his meeting with God. The Dome of the Rock and the nearby Al-Aqsa Mosque enshrine that tradition.

On the one hand, Jerusalem is a layer-cake of time, each period leaving distinct strata. The biblical kings David and Solomon transformed a small and already-ancient Jebusite town into an important metropolis. The march of history proceeded through destruction and the Babylonian captivity, Hellenization, Roman rule and another destruction, Byzantine Christianity, the Muslim invasions, the 12th-century Crusades, the Muslim reconquest, European rediscovery of the Holy Land and British control, and down to Jerusalem's contemporary status as the capital (though some dispute it) of the State of Israel.

At another level—change the metaphor—Jerusalem is a complex tangle, a Gordian knot of related but competing faith traditions, historical narratives, and national dreams. The knot seems fated to be around for a while yet, with no hero in sight to slice it through with one bold stroke.

Israelites enslaved during the Babylonian Captivity after the fall of Jerusalem in 586 BC

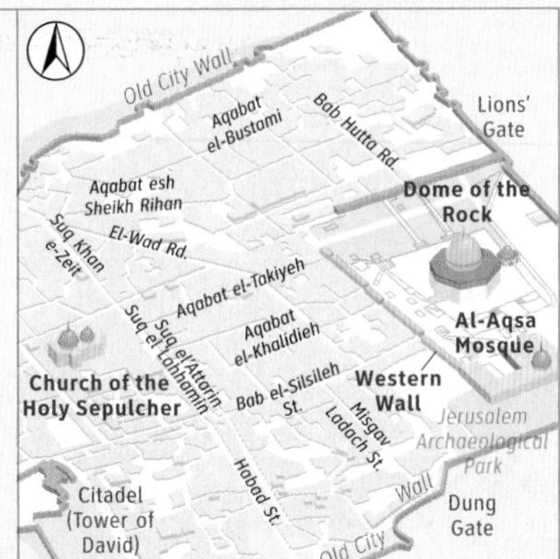

FINDING YOUR FEET

Each of the three religious sites is infused with its own unique tradition. Making a connection between these stone structures of the past and the wellsprings of religious faith or cultural identity can be uplifting. Many pilgrims focus on their own shrines; some take the time to explore the others so close at hand. The Western Wall is just steps from the Jerusalem Archaeological Park, where excavations turned up remnants of King Herod the Great's grand structures that Jesus almost certainly knew. The ramp between the Western Wall and the park leads up to the vast plaza—the Temple Mount or Haram esh-Sharif—now dominated by the Muslim shrines. Any of the gates at its far northern end will deposit you on the Via Dolorosa. A twenty-minute stroll through the bustling bazaar brings you to the Church of the Holy Sepulcher, revered as the site of Jesus' death and burial.

Whichever site you start with (this feature lists them in historical order: Wall, Church, Dome), a tour of all three unfailingly provokes a powerful appreciation of Jerusalem as an epicenter of faith.

THE WESTERN WALL

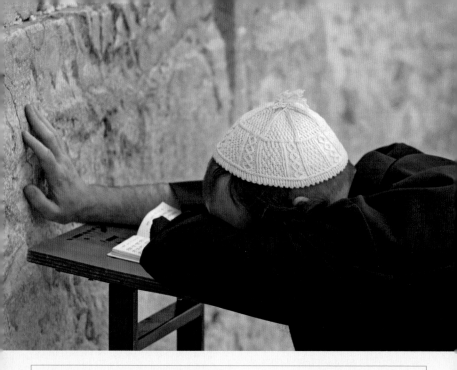

No Jewish shrine is holier than the Western Wall, the remains of the ancient Second Temple compound, whose stones are saturated with centuries of prayers and tears.

The status of the Western Wall as the most important existing Jewish shrine derives from its connection with the ancient Temple, the House of God. The 2,000-year-old Wall was not itself part of the Temple edifice, but of the massive retaining wall King Herod built to create the vast plaza now known as the Temple Mount.

After the destruction of Jerusalem by the Romans in AD 70, and especially after the dedication of a pagan town in its place 65 years later, the city became off-limits to Jews for generations. The precise location of the Temple—in the vicinity of today's Dome of the Rock—was lost. Even when access was regained, Jews avoided entering the Temple Mount out of fear of trespassing on the most sacred, and thus forbidden, areas of the ancient sanctuary. With time, the closest remnant of the period took on the aura of the Temple itself, making the Western Wall a kind of holy place by proxy.

Jewish visitors often just refer to the site as "the Wall" (*Kotel* in Hebrew); "Wailing Wall" is a Gentile term, describing the sight—once more common—of devout Jews grieving for God's House. For many Jews, the ancient Temple was as much a national site as a religious one, and its destruction as much a national trauma as a religious cataclysm.

(top) Jewish man praying at the Western Wall, (right) Western Wall

VISITING THE WALL

The swaying and praying of the devout reveal the powerful hold this place has on the hearts and minds of many Jews.

On Monday and Thursday mornings, the Wall bubbles with colorful bar-mitzvah ceremonies, when Jewish families celebrate the coming of age of their 13-year-old sons. The excitement is still greater on Friday evenings just after sunset, when the young men of a nearby yeshiva, a Jewish seminary, sometimes come dancing and singing down to the Wall to welcome in the "Sabbath bride." The fervor reaches its highest point three times a year during the three Jewish pilgrimage festivals—Passover, Sukkot (Feast of Tabernacles), and Shavuot (Feast of Weeks), when many Jews come to pray. But many people find that it's only when the crowds have gone (the Wall is floodlit at night and always open), and you share the warm, prayer-drenched stones with just a handful of bearded stalwarts or kerchiefed women, that the true spirituality of the Western Wall is palpable.

The Wall precinct functions under the aegis of the rabbinic authorities, with all the trappings of an Orthodox synagogue. Modest dress is required (men must cover their heads in the prayer area), there is segregation of men and women in prayer, and smoking and photography on the Sabbath and religious holidays are prohibited. Expect a routine check of your bags. ✉ In the southeast corner of the Old City; accessible from Dung Gate, the Jewish Quarter, and the Muslim Quarter's El-Wad St. 🌐 http://english.thekotel.org ⏲ 24 hrs daily.

NOTES IN THE WALL

The cracks between the massive stones of the Western Wall are stuffed with slips of paper bearing prayers and petitions. "They reach their destination more quickly than the Israeli postal service," it has been said, with a mixture of serious faith and light cynicism. The cracks are cleared several times a year, but the slips are never simply dumped. Since they often contain God's name, and are written from the heart, the slips are collected in a sack and buried with reverence in a Jewish cemetery.

THE TEMPLE MOUNT, OR HARAM ESH-SHARIF

The size of 27 football fields, the Temple Mount is the vast plaza constructed around the Second Temple in the late 1st century BC by King Herod.

In order to rebuild the Temple on a grand scale, and significantly expand the courts around it, Herod leveled off the top of Mt. Moriah with thousands of tons of rubble. The massive retaining walls include some of the largest building stones known. Structurally, the famous Western Wall is simply the western side of the huge shoebox-like project.

Some scholars regard the Temple Mount as perhaps the greatest religious enclosure of the ancient world, and the splendid Temple, the one Jesus knew, as an architectural wonder of its day. The Romans reduced the building to smoldering ruins in the summer of AD 70, in the last stages of the Great Revolt of the Jews (AD 66–73). Many of its treasures, including the gold menorah, were carried off to Rome as booty.

Jewish tradition identifies the great rock at the summit of the hill—now under the golden Dome of the Rock—as the foundation stone of the world, and the place where Abraham bound and almost sacrificed his son Isaac (Genesis 22). With greater probability, this was where the biblical King David made a repentance offering to the Lord (II

(top) Aerial view of the Jewish Quarter and the Temple Mount, (top left) Al-Aqsa Mosque, (top right) Drawing of a reconstruction of the First Temple

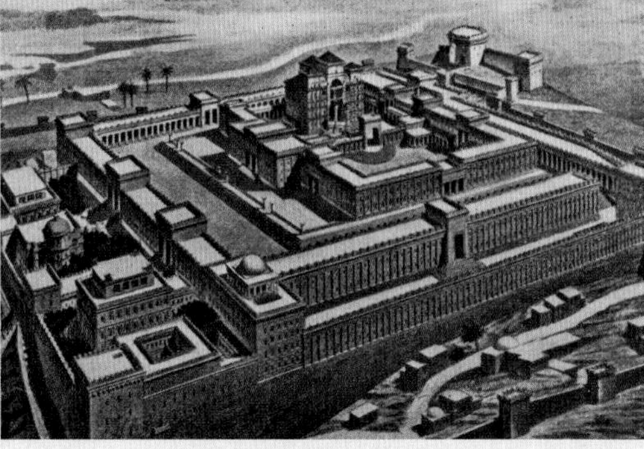

Samuel 22), and where his son Solomon built "God's House," the so-called First Temple. The Second Temple stood on the identical spot, but the precise location of its innermost holy of holies is a question that engages religious Jews and archaeologists to this day.

Christian tradition adds the New Testament dimension. Here Jesus disputed points of law with other Jewish teachers, angrily overturned the tables of money changers, and, looking down at the Temple precinct from the Mount of Olives, predicted its destruction. The Byzantines seem to have neglected the place (perhaps believing it cursed); the medieval Templars took their name from the area in which they set up their headquarters.

Muslims identify it as "the farthermost place," from which Muhammad rose to heaven, and call this area Haram esh-Sharif, the Noble Sanctuary. *(See section on the Muslim shrines in this feature.)*

✉ Access between the Western Wall and Dung Gate, Temple Mount ☎ 02/662-6250 ⏲ Apr.–Sept., Sun.–Thurs. 7:30 AM–11 AM and 1:30 PM–2:30 PM; Oct.–Mar., Sun.–Thurs. 7:30 AM–10 AM and 12:30 PM–1:30 PM, subject to change.

THE JERUSALEM ARCHAEOLOGICAL PARK

Immediately south of the Western Wall, in the shadow of the Temple Mount, is an important archaeological site, still popularly known as the Western and Southern Wall excavations. The dominant monumental structures were the work of King Herod the Great, some 2,000 years ago, though there are some Byzantine and early Arab buildings of interest. Robinson's Arch, named for a 19th-century American explorer, once supported a monumental stairway leading up to the Temple Mount. Also discovered were numerous "mikva'ot" (singular "mikveh," a Jewish ritual bath) and a Herodian street, once lined with shops. In the southern part of the site is the low-rise Davidson Visitors Center; its exhibits range from ancient artifacts to computer-animated recreations of the Second Temple. *For complete information, see the separate entry for Jerusalem Archaeological Park in this chapter.*

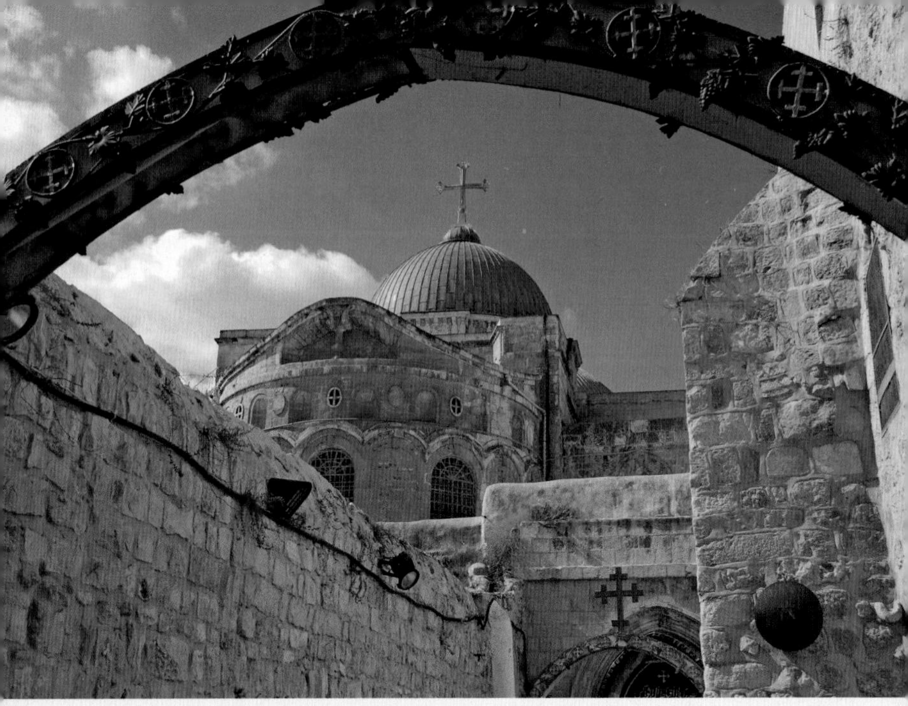

THE CHURCH OF THE HOLY SEPULCHER

Follow the footsteps of Jesus along the Via Dolorosa to the hallowed church that enshrines Golgotha—the hillside of Jesus' crucifixion, burial, and resurrection.

Vast numbers of Christians, especially adherents of the older "mainstream" churches, believe that this church marks the place where Jesus was crucified by the Romans and buried by his followers, and where he rose from the dead three days later. Some claim that the antiquity of the Holy Sepulcher tradition argues in favor of its authenticity, since the fervent early Christian community would have striven to preserve the memory of such an important site. The church is outside the city walls *of Jesus' day*—a vital point, for no executions or burials took place within Jerusalem's sacred precincts.

The site was officially consecrated, and the first church built here, following the visit in AD 326 by Helena, mother of the Byzantine emperor Constantine the Great. The present imposing structure, the fourth church on the site, was built by the Crusaders in the 12th century. Interior additions over the years have distorted the Gothic plan, but look for the Norman-style vault at the far end of the Greek Orthodox basilica (facing the tomb), and the ceiling of the dim corridor leading to the adjacent Catholic chapel. After a fire in 1808, much of the church was rebuilt in 19th-century style.

(top) Church of the Holy Sepulcher, (top right) Greek Orthodox chapel, Calvary, (bottom right) Monk kissing the Stone of Unction

HOLIEST LANDMARKS

On the floor just inside the entrance of the church is the rectangular pink **Stone of Unction**, where, it is said, the body of Jesus was cleansed and prepared for burial. Pilgrims often rub fabric or religious trinkets on the stone to absorb its sanctity, and take them home as mementos. Nearby steep steps take you up to **Golgotha**, or Calvary, meaning "the place of the skull," as the site is described in the New Testament. Up the steps, the chapel on the right is Roman Catholic: a window looks out at Station X of the Via Dolorosa, a wall mosaic at the front of the chapel depicts Jesus being nailed to the cross (Station XI), and a bust of Mary in a cabinet to the left of it represents Station XIII where Jesus was taken off the cross. The central chapel—all candlelight, oil lamps, and icons—is Greek Orthodox. Under the altar, and capping the rocky hillock on which you stand, is a silver disc with a hole, purportedly the place—Station XII—where the cross actually stood.

The **tomb** itself (Station XIV), encased in a pink marble edifice, is in the rotunda to the left of the main entrance of the church, under the great dome that dominates the Christian Quarter. The only hint of what the tomb must have been like 2,000 years ago is the ledge in the inner chamber (now covered with marble) on which Jesus' body would have been laid. You can see a more pristine example of an upscale Jewish tomb of the period in the gloomy Chapel of St. Nicodemus, opposite the Coptic chapel in the back of the sepulcher.

SHARING THE CHURCH

An astonishing peculiarity of the Holy Sepulcher is that it is shared, albeit unequally and uncomfortably, by six Christian denominations. Centuries of sometimes-violent competition for control of key Christian sites culminated in the Status Quo Agreement of 1852.

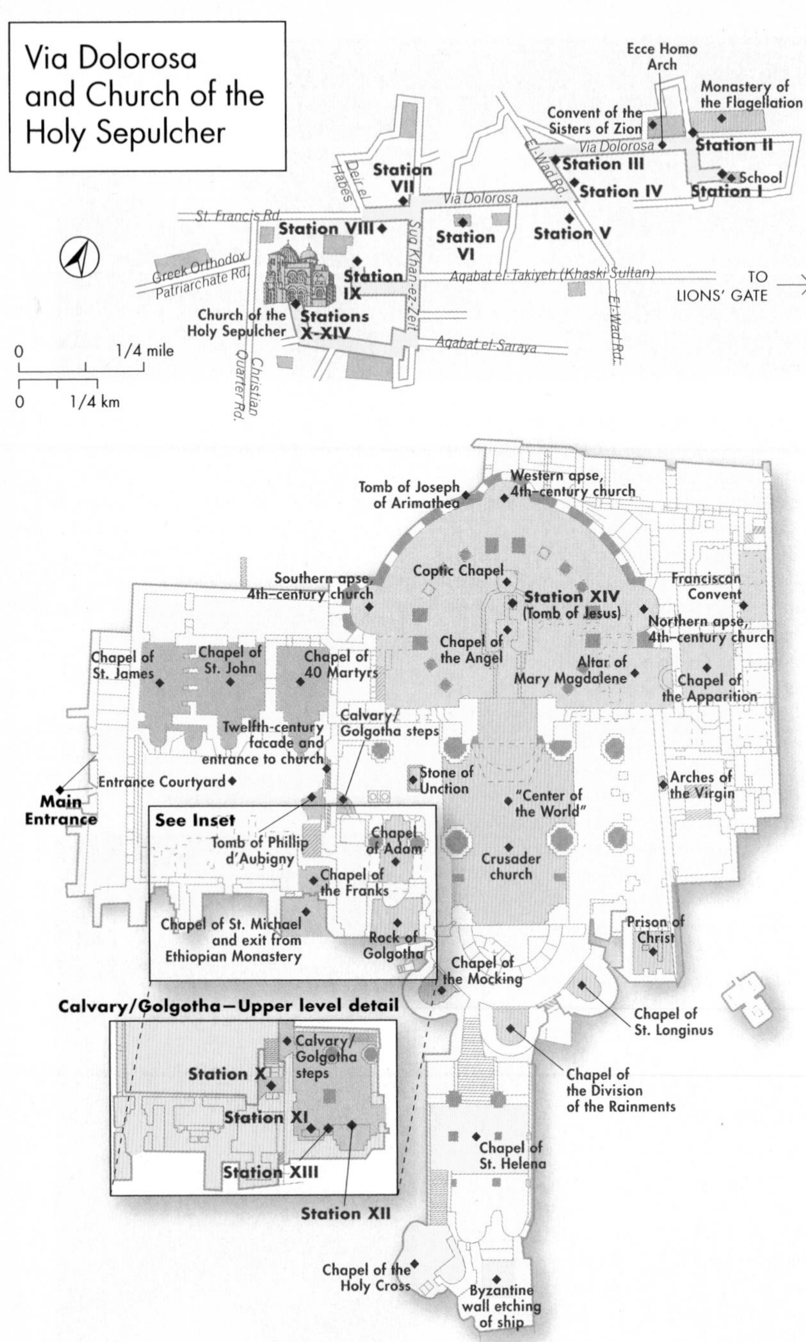
Via Dolorosa and Church of the Holy Sepulcher
Ecce Homo Arch
Monastery of the Flagellation
Convent of the Sisters of Zion
Via Dolorosa
Station II
Station III
El-Wad Rd.
School
Station IV
Station I
Station VII
Deir el Habes
Via Dolorosa
St. Francis Rd.
Station VIII
Suq Khan-ez-Zeit
Station VI
Station V
Greek Orthodox Patriarchate Rd.
Station IX
Aqabat el-Takiyeh (Khaski Sultan)
TO LIONS' GATE
Church of the Holy Sepulcher
Stations X–XIV
El-Wad Rd.
0
1/4 mile
Aqabat el-Saraya
0
1/4 km
Christian Quarter Rd.
Tomb of Joseph of Arimathea
Western apse, 4th-century church
Southern apse, 4th-century church
Coptic Chapel
Station XIV (Tomb of Jesus)
Franciscan Convent
Northern apse, 4th-century church
Chapel of St. James
Chapel of St. John
Chapel of 40 Martyrs
Chapel of the Angel
Altar of Mary Magdalene
Chapel of the Apparition
Calvary/Golgotha steps
Twelfth-century facade and entrance to church
Stone of Unction
Arches of the Virgin
Entrance Courtyard
Main Entrance
"Center of the World"
See Inset
Tomb of Phillip d'Aubigny
Chapel of Adam
Chapel of the Franks
Crusader church
Chapel of St. Michael and exit from Ethiopian Monastery
Rock of Golgotha
Prison of Christ
Chapel of the Mocking
Calvary/Golgotha—Upper level detail
Chapel of St. Longinus
Calvary/Golgotha steps
Station X
Station XI
Station XIII
Station XII
Chapel of the Division of the Rainments
Chapel of St. Helena
Chapel of the Holy Cross
Byzantine wall etching of ship

Mosaic of Jesus near the Stone of Unction

Under the pressure of Orthodox Russia, the Ottoman Turks recognized the precedence of the Greek Orthodox as on-the-ground representatives of the Eastern Rite churches.

Each denomination guards its assigned privileges, and minor infringements by one of its neighbors can flare up into open hostility. At the same time, the phenomenon gives the place much of its color. Try visiting in the late afternoon (the exact time changes with the seasons), and watch the groups in turn—Greek Orthodox, Latins (as Roman Catholics are known in the Holy Land), Armenian Orthodox, and Egyptian Copts—in procession from Calvary to the tomb. The candlelight and swinging censers are passingly similar; the robes and lusty hymn-singing are different.

A modern agreement among the Greeks, the Latins, and the Armenians on the interior restoration of the great dome was hailed as a breakthrough in ecumenical relations, and it was rededicated in January, 1997 in an unprecedented interdenominational service. ✉ Between Suq Khan e-Zeit and Christian Quarter Rd., Christian Quarter ☎ 02/627–3314 Free ⏲ Apr.–Sept., daily 5 AM–9 PM; Oct.–Mar., daily 4 AM–7 PM

SUGGESTIONS FOR YOUR VISIT

While the first nine Stations of the Cross are to be found along the Way of the Cross—the Via Dolorosa—the final and most holy ones are within the Church of the Holy Sepulcher itself. The best time to visit may be around 4PM when many denominations are found worshipping. *For more information, see the separate entry for the Via Dolorosa elsewhere in this chapter.*

As in many religious sites, modest dress and discreet behavior are required here, but it's difficult for the clergy of any particular community to assert authority. Come early or late to avoid the worst crowds; be patient, too. A small flashlight or some candles will help you explore the small tomb of St. Nicodemus, an authentic Jewish tomb of the period.

Entrance of the Church of the Holy Sepulcher

THE DOME OF THE ROCK AND AL-AQSA MOSQUE

The focal point of these sanctuaries, whose interiors are currently open only to Muslims, is the Rock—the place from which Muhammad is believed to have ascended to heaven to be given the divine precepts of Islam.

The magnificent golden **Dome of the Rock** dominates the vast 35-acre Temple Mount, the area known to Muslims as Haram esh-Sharif (the Noble Sanctuary). This is the original octagonal building, completed in AD 691. It enshrines the great rock—the summit of Mt. Moriah—from which the prophet Muhammad is said to have risen to heaven. Jerusalem is not mentioned in the Koran, but Muhammad's "Night Ride" is. Awakened by the archangel Gabriel, he was taken on the fabulous winged horse el-Burak to the *masjid al-aqsa*, the "farthermost place." From there he rose to heaven, met God face to face, received the teachings of Islam, and returned to Mecca the same night. Tradition has it that the *masjid al-aqsa* was none other than Jerusalem, and the great rock the very spot from which the prophet ascended.

(top) Eight *qanatirs* (arcades) stand by sets of steps leading to the Dome of the Rock, (top right) The rock, the Dome's central shrine

To be sure, Muhammad's triumphant successors venerated Jerusalem's biblical sanctity; but some modern scholars suggest they did not like the feeling of being Johnnies-come-lately in the

holy city of rival faiths. The impressive Dome of the Rock, built by the Ummayad caliph Abd el-Malik, was almost certainly intended to proclaim the ascendancy of the "true faith."

A SPLENDID SHRINE

Considering the original builders and craftsmen adopted the artistic traditions of their Byzantine predecessors, it's hardly surprising that the plan of the shrine resembles those of its Christian contemporaries, like the Byzantine Church of San Vitale in Ravenna, Italy. Take a close look at the bright exterior tiles in variegated shades of blue. The marvelous gold dome was restored in the 1990s, with 176 pounds of 24-carat gold electroplated on copper.

At the time of this writing, non-Muslims were denied entry to the interior of the building, with its beautiful granite columns supporting arches, some of which bear the original green-and-gold mosaics set in arabesque motifs. In obedience to Islamic religious tradition, no human or animal forms appear in the artwork. The mosaics were restored in 1027, but preserved much of the original work.

All this splendor was designed to emphasize the importance of the rock itself, directly under the great dome. The faithful reach out and touch an indentation which, they believe, was nothing less than the Prophet's footprint, left there as he ascended to heaven.

THE THIRD-HOLIEST OF ALL

At the southern end of the Haram, immediately in front of you as you enter the area from the Western Wall plaza (the only gate for non-Muslims), is the large, black-domed **Al-Aqsa Mosque**. The Dome of the Rock is a shrine, the place where a hallowed event is believed to

THE DOME'S MOSAICS

Some of the Arabic inscriptions in the mosaics are quotations from the Koran; others are dedications. One of the latter originally lauded Abd el-Malik, caliph of the Damascus-based Ummayad dynasty, who built the shrine. Some 140 years later, the caliph of a rival dynasty removed el-Malik's name and replaced it with his own, but he neglected to change the date.

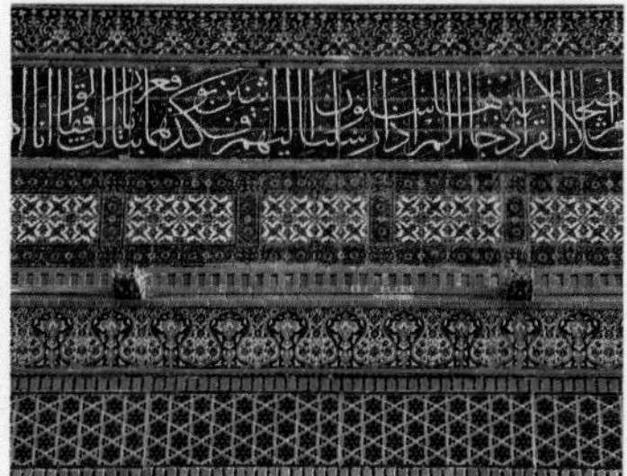

have taken place. Individuals go there to pray, but Al-Aqsa is a true mosque, attracting thousands of worshippers on Fridays and Muslim holidays. It is third in holiness for Muslims everywhere, after the great mosques of Mecca and Medina, both in Saudi Arabia.

Built by the Ummayad dynasty in the early 8th century AD, it has been destroyed and restored several times. In the 12th century, the Al-Aqsa Mosque became the headquarters of the Templars, a Crusader monastic order that took its name from the ancient temple that once stood nearby. The spot has been the setting for more recent dramas, most importantly the assassination of King Abdullah I of Jordan (the present king's great-grandfather) in 1951.

EXPLORING THE HARAM

The Haram today is a Muslim preserve, a legacy that dates back to AD 638, when the Arab caliph Omar Ibn-Khatib seized Jerusalem from the Byzantines. At the time of this writing, the Muslim shrines were closed to non-Muslims indefinitely, leaving the faithful alone to enjoy their wondrous interiors.

Even if you can't get inside, the vast plaza is visually and historically arresting, and worth a visit. Fifteenth-century Mamluk buildings line the western edge. Overlooking the plaza at its northwestern corner is a long building, today an elementary school, built on the artificial scarp that protected Herod's Antonia fortress. Christian tradition, very possibly accurate, identifies the site as the praetorium where Jesus was tried.

Security check lines to enter the Haram esh-Sharif are often long; it's best to come early. Note that the Muslim attendants prohibit Bibles in the area. ✉ Access between the Western Wall and Dung Gate, Haram esh-Sharif, Temple Mount ☎ 02/622–6250 ⏲ Apr.–Sept., Sun.–Thurs. 7:30 AM–11 AM and 1:30 PM–2:30 PM; Oct.–Mar., Sun.–Thurs. 7:30 AM–10 AM and 12:30 PM–1:30 PM, subject to change. Last entry 1 hr before closing.

(top) Parts of columns on the Haram, (right) Mosaics and arches grace the Dome's interior

the tour retraces its steps through the tunnel. The ticket office is under the arches at the northern end of the Western Wall plaza. ✉ *Western Wall* ☎ *02/627–1333* 🌐 *english.thekotel.org* 🎫 *NIS 25* ⏲ *Sun.–Thurs. 7 am–late evening (changing schedules), Fri. and Jewish holiday eves 7–noon. Call ahead for exact times.*

WORTH NOTING

Ecce Homo Convent of the Sisters of Zion. The arch that crosses the Via Dolorosa, just beyond Station II, continues into the chapel of the adjacent convent. It was thought to have been the gate of Herod's Antonia fortress, perhaps the spot where the Roman governor Pontius Pilate presented Jesus to the crowd with the words "*Ecce homo!*" ("Behold, the man!"). Recent scholarship suggests otherwise: it was a triumphal arch built by the Roman emperor Hadrian in the 2nd century AD.

The basement of the convent has two points of interest worth about 20 minutes of your time: an impressive reservoir with a barrel-vault roof, apparently built by Hadrian in the moat of Herod's older Antonia fortress, and the famous *lithostratos,* or stone pavement, etched with games played by Roman legionnaires. The origin of one such diversion—the notorious Game of the King—called for the execution of a mock king, a sequence tantalizingly reminiscent of the New Testament description of the treatment of Jesus by the Roman soldiers. Contrary to tradition, however, the pavement of large, foot-worn brown flagstones is apparently not from Jesus' day, but was laid down a century later. ✉ *Via Dolorosa, Muslim Quarter* ☎ *02/627–7292* 🌐 *www.eccehomoconvent.com* 🎫 *NIS 8* ⏲ *Daily 8:30–5.*

Ethiopian Monastery. Stand in the monastery's courtyard beneath the medieval bulge of the Church of the Holy Sepulcher, and you have views of the churches of Christendom. The adjacent Egyptian Coptic monastery peeks through the entrance gate, and a Russian Orthodox gable, a Lutheran bell tower, and the crosses of Greek Orthodox, Armenian Orthodox, and Roman Catholic churches break the skyline.

The robed Ethiopian monks live in tiny cells in the rooftop monastery. One of the modern paintings in their small, dark church depicts the visit of the Queen of Sheba to King Solomon. Ethiopian tradition holds that more passed between the two than is related in the Bible—she came to "prove" his wisdom "with hard questions" (I Kings 10)—and that their supposed union produced an heir to both royal houses. The prince was met with hostility by Solomon's legitimate offspring, says the legend, and the king was compelled to send him home—with the precious Ark of the Covenant as a gift. To this day (say the Ethiopians) it remains in a sealed crypt in their homeland. The script in the paintings is Gehz, the ecclesiastical language of the Ethiopian church. Taking in the rooftop view and the church will occupy about 15 minutes. ✉ *Roof of the Church of the Holy Sepulcher, access from Suq Khan e-Zeit, Christian Quarter* 🎫 *Free* ⏲ *Daily during daylight.*

Pools of Bethesda and Church of St. Anne. The transition is sudden and complete, from the raucous cobbled streets and persistent vendors to the pepper trees, flower patches, and birdsong of this serene Catholic cloister. The Romanesque Church of **St. Anne** was built by the Crusaders

The Via Dolorosa often teems with pilgrims but can sometimes offer a quiet path.

in 1140, and restored in the 19th century. Its austere and unadorned stone interior and extraordinarily reverberant acoustics make it one of the finest examples of medieval architecture in the country. According to local tradition, the Virgin Mary was born in the grotto over which the church is built, and the church is named for her mother. In the same compound are the excavated **Pools of Bethesda,** a large, double public reservoir in use during the 1st century BC and 1st century AD. The New Testament speaks of Jesus miraculously curing a lame man by "a pool, which is called in the Hebrew tongue Bethesda" (John 5). The actual bathing pools were the small ones, east of the reservoir, but it was over the big pools that both the Byzantines and the Crusaders built churches, now ruined, to commemorate the miracle. A visit to both sites will take no more than 30 minutes. ✉ *Al-Mujahideen Rd., near Lions' Gate, Muslim Quarter* ☎ *02/628–3285* 💳 *NIS 7* ⏲ *Apr.–Sept., daily 8–12 and 2–6; Oct.–Mar., daily 8–12 and 2–5.*

JEWISH QUARTER

This is at once the Old City's oldest quarter and its newest neighborhood. Abandoned for a generation, the quarter was restored and resettled after the Six Days' War of 1967. The subsequent archaeological excavations exposed artifacts and structures that date back 27 centuries and more. If you have a photographer's eye, get off the main streets and stroll at random. The limestone houses and alleys—often counterpointed with a shock of bougainvillea or palm fronds and ficus trees—offer pleasing compositions.

If you like to people-watch, find a shaded café table and sip a good latte while the world jitterbugs by. The population of the Jewish Quarter is almost entirely religious, roughly split between "modern" Orthodox (devout, but integrated into contemporary Israeli society at every level) and the more traditional ultra-Orthodox (men in black frock coats and black hats, in many ways a community apart). The locals, especially the women, tend to dress very conservatively. Several religious-study institutions attract a transient population of young students, many of them from abroad. Religious Jewish families tend to have lots of kids, and little ones here are given independence at an astonishingly early age. It's quite common to see three- and four-year-olds toddling home from preschool alone, or shepherded by a one-year-more-mature brother or sister. And if you see a big group of Israeli soldiers, don't assume the worst. The army maintains a center for its educational tours here, and the recruits are more likely than not boisterously kidding around with each other as they follow their guide. Shopping is good here—jewelry, Judaica, gift items—and there are decent fast-food options when hunger strikes.

A renewed landmark of the quarter is the high, white-domed Hurva Synagogue. It was built and soon destroyed in the 18th century, rebuilt in the 19th, and blown up when the Jordanian Arab Legion captured the area in the 1948 war. The current building, rededicated in spring 2010, is a faithful reconstruction of its predecessor.

GETTING HERE AND AROUND

It's best to approach the Jewish Quarter on foot. From Jaffa Gate, you can plunge into the Arab bazaar and follow David Street until it becomes a T-junction: the right turn becomes Jewish Quarter Street. Alternatively, after you enter Jaffa Gate, follow the vehicle road to the right and through a small tunnel, then turn left (on foot) onto St. James Street and down to the quarter. A third idea is to begin your tour on Mt. Zion, and then continue to the Jewish Quarter through Zion Gate.

TIMING AND PRECAUTIONS

Allow at least two hours to explore the Jewish Quarter, not counting shopping and eating. If you're pressed for time, absorb the scene over the rim of a glass or mug, and take time to visit the Herodian Quarter. Avoid visiting on Saturday, when everything is closed, and some religious locals may resent you taking pictures on their Sabbath. Sites with entrance fees close by midday Friday.

TOP ATTRACTIONS

Burnt House. "We could almost smell the burning and feel the heat of the flames," wrote archaeologist Nahman Avigad, whose team uncovered evidence of the Roman devastation of Jerusalem in AD 70 at this house site, part of a larger, unexcavated complex under the Jewish Quarter. Charred cooking pots, sooty debris, and—most arresting—the skeletal hand and arm of a woman clutching a scorched staircase recaptured the poignancy of the moment. Stone weights inscribed with the name Bar Katros—a Jewish priestly family—suggested that this might have been a basement industrial workshop, possibly for the manufacture of sacramental incense used in the Temple. A video presentation recreates the bitter civil rivalries of the period and the city's tragic end. ✉ *Tiferet Israel St., Jewish Quarter* ☎ *02/626–5922* 🎫 *NIS 20; combined ticket with Herodian Quarter NIS 25* ⏲ *Sun.–Thurs. 9–5, Fri. and Jewish holiday eves 9–noon (last entry 40 mins before closing).*

★ **Herodian Quarter and Wohl Archaeological Museum.** Excavations in the 1970s exposed the Jewish Quarter's most visually interesting site: the remains of sumptuous mansions from the aristocratic Upper City of the Second Temple period. Preserved in the basement of a modern Jewish seminary—but entered separately—the geometrically patterned mosaic floors, still-vibrant frescoes, and costly glassware, stone objects, and ceramics provide a peek into the life of the wealthy in the days of Herod and Jesus. Several small stone cisterns have been identified as private *mikvahs* (Jewish ritual baths); holograms depict their use. Large stone water jars are just like those described in the New Testament story of the wedding at Cana. Rare stone tables resemble the dining-room furniture depicted in Roman stone reliefs found in Europe. On the last of the site's three distinct levels is a mansion with an estimated original floor area of some 6,000 square feet. None of the upper stories have survived, but the fine, fashionable stucco work and the quality of the artifacts found here indicate an exceptional standard of living, leading some scholars to suggest this may have been the long-sought palace of the high priest. The charred ceiling beam and scorched mosaic floor and fresco at the southern end of the reception hall bear witness to the Roman torching of the neighborhood in the late summer of AD 70, exactly one month after the Temple itself had been destroyed. Allow about 45 minutes to explore the site. ✉ *Hakara'im Rd., Jewish Quarter* ☎ *02/626–5922* 🎫 *NIS 13; combined ticket with Burnt House NIS 25* ⏲ *Sun.–Thurs. 9–5, Fri. and Jewish holiday eves 9–noon (last entry 30 mins before closing).*

WORTH NOTING

Broad Wall. The discovery in the 1970s of the rather unobtrusive 23-foot-thick foundations of an Old Testament city wall was hailed as one of the most important archaeological finds in the Jewish Quarter. Hezekiah, King of Judah and a contemporary of the prophet Isaiah, built the wall in 701 BC to protect the city against an impending Assyrian invasion. The unearthing of the Broad Wall—a biblical name—resolved a long-running scholarly debate about the size of Old Testament Jerusalem: a large on-site map shows that the ancient city was far larger than was once thought. ✉ *Jewish Quarter St., Jewish Quarter.*

Cardo. Today it's known for shopping, but the Cardo has a long history. In AD 135, the Roman emperor Hadrian built his town of Aelia Capitolina on the ruins of Jerusalem, an urban plan essentially preserved in the Old City of today. The *cardo maximus,* the generic name for the city's main north-south street, began at the strategic Damascus Gate in the north, where sections of the pavement have been unearthed. With the Christianization of the Roman Empire in the 4th century, access to Mt. Zion and its important Christian sites became a priority, and the main street was eventually extended into today's Jewish Quarter. The original width—today you see only half—was 73 feet, about the width

CLOSE UP

Jews in the Old City

The history of Jewish life in the Old City has been marked by the trials of conflict and the joys of creating and rebuilding community. Here are some highlights from the medieval period on.

1099. Crusaders conquer Jerusalem, followed by wholesale massacre. Jews lived at the time in today's Muslim Quarter.

1267. Spanish rabbi Nachmanides ("Ramban") reestablishes Jewish community. (His synagogue is on Jewish Quarter Street.)

1517. Ottoman Turks conquer Palestine and allow Sephardic Jews (expelled from Spain a generation earlier) to resettle the country. They develop four interlinked synagogues in the quarter.

1700. A large group of Ashkenazi Jews from Eastern Europe settles in Jerusalem.

1860. The first neighborhood is established outside the walls (Mishkenot Sha'ananim). Initially, very few Old City Jews had the courage to move out.

1948. Israel's War of Independence. Jewish Quarter surrenders to Jordanian forces and is abandoned. By then, the residents of the quarter represent only a tiny percentage of Jerusalem's Jewish population.

1967. Six Days' War. The Jewish Quarter, much of it ruined, is recaptured. Archaeological excavations and restoration work begin side by side.

1980s. Section after section of the Jewish Quarter becomes active again as the restoration work progresses—apartments and educational institutions, synagogues and stores, restaurants and new archaeological sites.

of a six-lane highway. A strip of good stores (jewelry, art, Judaica, T-shirts, and souvenirs) occupies the Cardo's medieval reincarnation. ✉ *Jewish Quarter St., Jewish Quarter.*

TOWER OF DAVID AND MT. ZION

When you've "done" the main sights, take a leisurely few hours to dip into lesser-known gems on the periphery of the Old City. Most of the city walls were built in the 16th century by the Ottoman sultan Suleiman the Magnificent. According to legend, his two architects were executed by order of the sultan himself and buried behind the railings just inside the imposing Jaffa Gate. One version relates that they angered Suleiman by not including Mt. Zion and the venerated Tomb of David within the walls. Others say that the satisfied sultan wanted to make sure they would never build anything grander for anyone else.

Jaffa Gate got its name from its westerly orientation, toward the once-important Mediterranean harbor of Jaffa, now part of Tel Aviv. Its Arabic name of Bab el-Halil, Gate of the Beloved, points you south, to the city of Hebron, where the biblical Abraham, the "Beloved of God" in Muslim tradition, is buried. The vehicle entrance is newer, created by the Ottoman Turks in 1898 for the visit of the German emperor, Kaiser

Wilhelm II. The British general, Sir Edmund Allenby, took a different approach when he seized the city from the Turks in December 1917: he and his staff officers dismounted from their horses to enter the holy city with the humility befitting pilgrims.

The huge stone tower on the right as you enter Jaffa Gate is the last survivor of the strategic fortress built by King Herod 2,000 years ago. Today it is part of the so-called citadel that houses the Tower of David Museum—well worth your time as the springboard for exploring this part of the historical city. Opposite the museum entrance (once a drawbridge) is the neo-Gothic Christ Church (Anglican), built in 1849 as the first Protestant church in the Middle East. Directly ahead is the souk (Arab bazaar), a convenient route to the Christian and Jewish quarters. To reach Mt. Zion, follow the vehicle road inside the walls to Zion Gate, or take the Ramparts Walk.

GETTING HERE AND AROUND

Jaffa Gate, the logical entry point for this area and tour, is an easy walk from the Downtown or King David Street areas. City bus routes 20, 38, and 99 take you right there, but any Downtown drop-off is within striking distance.

TIMING AND PRECAUTIONS

Sunday through Thursday is when everything is open. Some sites have limited hours or are closed Friday or Saturday. Modest dress is required at shrines.

TOP ATTRACTIONS

★ **Ramparts Walk.** The narrow stone catwalks of the Old City walls provide great panoramic views and interesting perspectives of this intriguing city. But they also offer an innocent bit of voyeurism as you look down into gardens and courtyards and become, for a moment, a more intimate partner in the secret domestic life of the different quarters you pass. Across the rooftops, the domes and spires of the three religions that call Jerusalem holy compete for the skyline, just as their adherents jealously guard their territory down below. Peer through the shooting niches, just as the long-ago watchmen did. The hotels and high-rises of the new city dominate the skyline to the west and south; the bustle of East Jerusalem is almost tangible to the north; and the churches and cemeteries quietly cling to Mt. of Olives to the east. There are many high steps on this route; the railings are secure, but small children should not walk alone.

The two sections of the walk are disconnected from each other (though the same ticket covers both). The shorter southern section is accessible only from the end of the seemingly dead-end terrace outside Jaffa Gate (at the exit of the Tower of David Museum). Descent is at Zion Gate or just before Dung Gate. The longer and more varied walk begins at Jaffa Gate (up the stairs immediately on the left as you enter the Old City), with descent at New, Herod's, or Lions' gates. In terms of timing, allow 40 minutes for the shorter section, south-southeast to Zion Gate, with an extra 10 to 15 minutes to Dung Gate. For the longer section, it takes 20 minutes to walk north-northeast to New Gate, another 20 minutes east to Damascus Gate, 15 minutes from there to Herod's Gate, and about 20 minutes more to Lions' Gate. ✉ *Jaffa Gate* ☎ *02/625–4403* 🎫 *NIS 16 (for both sections); combined ticket with Ophel Archaeological Garden, Damascus Gate, and Zedekiah's Cave (good for 3 days) NIS 55* ⏲ *Apr.–Sept., Sat.–Thurs. 9–5; Oct.–Mar., Sat.–Thurs. 9–4. Short route also open Fri. 9–2, long route closed Fri. Zedekiah's Cave and Damascus Gate archaeological site are closed Fri.*

Room of the Last Supper. Tradition has enshrined this spare, 14th-century second-story room as the location of the "upper room" referred to in the New Testament (Mark 14). Two thousand years ago, when Jesus and his disciples celebrated the ceremonial Passover meal that would become known as the Last Supper, the site was *inside* the city walls. Formally known as the Cenacle or the Coenaculum, the room is also associated with a second New Testament tradition (Acts 2), as the place where Jesus' disciples, gathered on Pentecost seven weeks after his death, were "filled with the Holy Spirit," and began to speak in foreign "tongues."

A little incongruously, the chamber has the trappings of a mosque as well. There are restored stained-glass Arabic inscriptions in the Gothic windows, and one window is blocked by an ornate *mihrab* (an alcove indicating the Muslim direction of prayer, toward Mecca). There are also two Arabic plaques in the wall and a Levantine dome. The Muslims were not concerned with the site's Christian traditions but with the supposed Tomb of King David—the Prophet David in their tradition—on the level below. Allow 10 minutes to explore the site. ✉ *Mt. Zion* 🎫 *Free* ⏲ *Sat.–Thurs. 8–5, Fri. 8–1.*

★ **Tower of David Museum.** Many visitors find this museum invaluable in mapping Jerusalem's often-confusing historical byways. Housed in a series of medieval halls, known locally as the Citadel (*Hametzuda* in Hebrew), the museum tells the city's four-millennia story through models, maps, holograms, and videos. The galleries are organized by historical period around the Citadel's central courtyard, where the old stone walls and arches add an appropriately antique atmosphere. Walking on the Citadel ramparts provides unexpected panoramas. You'll need at least 90 minutes to do justice to the museum. Be sure to inquire at the ticket office about the next screening of the animated introductory film (which has English subtitles), and don't miss the spectacular view from the top of the big tower. Take the guided tour if the timing works for you. The stunning "Night Spectacular" is a high-tech sound-and-light pageant of historical images played onto the ancient stone walls and towers. The outdoor event runs throughout the year (unless it rains) on Monday, Wednesday, Thursday and Saturday nights, with anywhere from two to five shows a night. The Web site gives updates on times and extra shows. Dress warmly for this. ✉ *Jaffa Gate* ☎ *02/626–5333; 02/626–5310 for recorded info* 🌐 *www.towerofdavid.org.il* 🎫 *NIS 30 (museum), NIS 50 (night show), NIS 65 (combined ticket)* ⏲ *Sept.–June, Mon.–Thurs. 10–4, Sat. 10–2; July and Aug., Mon.–Thurs., Sat. 10–5, Fri. 10–2. Guided tour in English at 11 (included in cost of admission), Sun.–Thurs. year-round, plus Fri. in July and Aug. (not on Jewish religious holidays or holiday eves).*

A bicycle is one way anyone can avoid Jerusalem's often intense traffic.

ALSO WORTH NOTING

Chamber of the Holocaust. Not to be confused with Yad Vashem in West Jerusalem, this small museum is also dedicated to the memory of the 6 million European Jews annihilated by the Nazis in the Second World War. Among the artifacts salvaged from the Holocaust are items that the Nazis forced Jews to make out of sacred Torah scrolls (the biblical Five Books of Moses). One Jewish tailor fashioned a vest for his Nazi "customer" out of the inscribed parchment, but with grim humor he chose sections that contained the worst of the biblical curses. Plaques commemorate many of the 5,000 European Jewish communities destroyed from 1939 to 1945. ✉ *Near Tomb of David, Mt. Zion* ☎ *02/671–5105* 🌐 *www.holocaustchamber.org* 🎫 *NIS 12* 🕓 *Sun.–Thurs. 9–3:45, Fri. 9–1:30.*

Dormition Abbey. The round, black-domed Roman Catholic church, with its distinctive ornamented turrets and landmark clock tower, is a Jerusalem landmark. It was built on land given by the Turkish sultan to the German emperor, Kaiser Wilhelm II, when the latter visited Jerusalem in 1898. The German Benedictines dedicated the echoing main church, with its Byzantine-style apse and mosaic floors, in 1910. The lower-level crypt houses a cenotaph with a carved-stone figure of Mary in repose (*dormitio*), reflecting the tradition that she fell into eternal sleep. Among the adjacent little chapels is one donated by the Ivory Coast, with wooden figures and motifs inlaid with ivory. The premises include a bookstore and a coffee shop. A visit takes about 20 minutes. ✉ *Near the Room of the Last Supper, Mt. Zion* ☎ *02/565–5330* 🎫 *Free*

CLOSE UP

The Quarters of the Old City

Today the third of a square mile within the Old City walls is home to some 35,000 Jerusalemites, representing a babel of languages, a plethora of religious rites, and a potpourri of ethnicities. Different sections, or quarters, within the walls have distinct characters. Here's a brief guide to the highlights.

The Muslim Quarter, located between Damascus Gate and the Western Wall, and east to Lions' Gate, is the largest in both area and population. The famous Via Dolorosa (Way of the Cross) that winds through this quarter offers an illusory universalism: the side streets, with their busy grocery stores, neighborhood mosques, and stenciled pictures of Mecca, bespeak the real character of this residential area. The enormous Haram esh-Sharif (the Jewish Temple Mount), with the gold Dome of the Rock and the black-domed Al-Aqsa Mosque, is its natural extension.

Fragmented into a dozen denominational domains, the Christian Quarter is capped by the gray dome of the Church of the Holy Sepulcher. (The struggle for visibility in the Holy City seems to be as much about dominating the skyline as about controlling real estate.) The numerous churches and religious institutions in this quarter, which is west of the Muslim Quarter, make for low population density.

The Jewish Quarter lies to the west of the Western Wall. Shattered in the 1948 war, it was revived in aesthetic stone in the 1970s and is home largely to religious Jews. Archaeological finds and the neighborhood's contemporary tale have given the area a uniqueness all its own.

The heart of the Armenian Quarter, the Old City's smallest, is the monastery, in the southwest corner within the walls. The closed enclave perpetuates the life and faith of a far-off land, the first to embrace Christianity.

🕙 *Weekdays 8:30–11:45 and 12:40–5:30; Sat. 8:30–11:45, 12:40–2:45, and 3:30–5:30; Sun. 10:30–11:45 and 12:30–5:30.*

Tomb of David. According to the Bible, King David, the great Israelite king of the 10th century BC, was buried in "the City of David," one of the contemporary names for his capital, Jerusalem. The actual site of the city has been identified and excavated on the small ridge east of here, but medieval Jewish pilgrims erroneously placed the ancient city on this hill, where they sought—and supposedly found—the royal tomb. Its authenticity may be questionable, but a millennium of tears and prayers has sanctified the place.

A cenotaph, a massive stone marker draped with velvet cloth and embroidered with symbols and Hebrew texts traditionally associated with David, caps the tomb itself. Behind it is a stone alcove, which some scholars think may be the sole remnant of a synagogue from the 5th century AD, the oldest of its kind in Jerusalem. Regulations by Jewish religious authorities have divided the shrine, already cramped, into two tiny prayer areas to separate men and women. Modest dress is required; men must cover their heads. ✉ *Mt. Zion* ☎ *02/671–9767*

Free ⏲ Apr.–Sept., Sun.–Thurs. 8–6, Fri. and Jewish holiday eves 8–2; Oct.–Mar., Sun.–Thurs. 8–5, Fri. and Jewish holiday eves 8–1.

CITY OF DAVID

If you thrill to the thought of standing where the ancients once stood, you'll be in your element in this city of memories, from its Old Testament walls and water systems to its Second Temple streets and stones. In this archaeological adventure, you plunge underground to sense Jerusalem's primal pulse—the Spring of Gihon, the lifeblood of the ancient city and the primary reason for its settlement, over four millennia ago. The Israelite king David captured this modest ridge from the Jebusites around 1000 BC, and made it his capital. David's son Solomon, who was anointed at the spring, expanded the city northward to Mt. Moriah, where he built the Temple of God (on the site of today's Dome of the Rock). In time, Jerusalem spread farther west and north; but in recent years, the name "City of David" has been revived to describe the city's ancient core.

GETTING HERE AND AROUND

At the time of this writing, a new archaeological dig reduced even further the limited legal parking nearby. Best come by cab, or walk down from the Old City by way of Dung Gate.

TIMING AND PRECAUTIONS

Allow yourself enough time for an unhurried tour of, say, two hours, noting that the site is closed Friday afternoon and all Saturday. There is a minibus (fare NIS 5) to shuttle you from the exit up the steep hill to the Visitors Center. The site is in the heart of the predominantly Arab Silwan neighborhood, where friction between veteran Palestinians and newly ensconced Jewish settlers is not unknown. The layout of the site and the guards on duty dispel any security concerns, however. The local guides and the engaging 3-D film in the Visitors Center—both optional—betray a little of the settlers' political agenda, but not enough to detract from the fascination of discovering where Jerusalem began. Severe claustrophobes may prefer to avoid the tunnels.

TOP ATTRACTIONS

Fodor's Choice ★ **Hezekiah's Tunnel.** Wading through a 2,700-year-old tunnel that once supplied water to the city is a great adventure for those who like a little exercise with their history. The Assyrians invaded Judah in 701 BC, 20 years after they had destroyed its sister-kingdom of Israel to the north. According to the Bible, King Hezekiah attempted to protect Jerusalem's precious water supply in order to meet the imminent assault on the capital. He instructed his men to "stop the water of the springs that were outside the city" (II Chronicles 32). Racing against time, they dug a water tunnel a third of a mile long through solid rock, one team starting from the Gihon Spring and the other from a new inner-city reservoir. Miraculously, considering the serpentine course of the tunnel, the two teams met in the middle. The chisel marks, the ancient plaster, and the zigzags near the halfway point as each team sought the other by sound bear witness to the remarkable project. With the water now diverted into the city, the original opening of the spring was blocked

SIGHTSEEING TOURS

Jerusalem's guides and tour operators offer everything from orientation tours by bus to thematic walks. If your time is limited or you have a special interest, tours are useful.

ORIENTATION

Veteran nationwide tour operators Egged Tours and United Tours offer similar half-day Jerusalem orientation tours, including a panoramic view and Old City highlights. The full-day tour usually adds the Yad Vashem Holocaust memorial (except on Saturday) and/or Mt. Zion shrines and another Christian site. Some itineraries have a particular Christian orientation. One creative alternative (Egged tour No. 216) includes the Mt. of Olives panorama, Mt. Zion, Jewish Quarter sites, and the City of David.

Prices are usually quoted in U.S. dollars so that visitors are exempt from the VAT. The approximate cost is $42 for the half-day tour and $62 for the full day, though some full-day tours run $89. The price includes pickup from major hotels, but some do not return you there. Some tours (curiously) do not include entrance fees: verify. The bottom line: tours like these are worth it if you have very limited time in Jerusalem, or if the tour takes you to less-easy-to-get-to places. You can reserve directly or through your hotel concierge.

Zion Walking Tours is best known for its topic-focused Old City walking tours, but some of its seven routes venture well beyond the walls as well (biblical Jerusalem; Christian sites on Mt. of Olives; old Jewish neighborhoods).

Another option is Egged's Route 99 bus, a two-hour circle tour of Jerusalem. *See Bus Travel in Getting Here and Around in Travel Smart Israel for information.*

Tour Contacts **Egged Tours** (☎ *1700/70–75–77 or 03/527–1212* 🌐 *www.egged.co.il/Eng*). **United Tours** (☎ *03/617–3333* 🌐 *www.unitedtours.co.il*). **Zion Walking Tours** (✉ *Inside Jaffa Gate, opposite police station, Jaffa Gate* ☎ *02/628–7866* 🌐 *zionwt.dsites1.co.il*).

PERSONAL GUIDES

At this writing, the daily rate for a private guide with an air-conditioned car, limousine, or seven-passenger van was $450 to $550; add another $100 for bigger vans. Many guides will offer their services without a car for $250 to $350 per day, and $150 to $200 for a half day. For private guiding, approach Genesis 2000 or Eshcolot Tours.

Guide Contacts **Eshcolot Tours** (☎ *02/566–5555* ✉ *advantag@netmedia.net.il*).

Genesis 2000 (☎ *052/286–2650, 052/381–4484, or 02/676–5868* ✉ *genesis4@netvision.net.il*).

WALKING TOURS

Zion Walking Tours offers both classic and off-the-beaten-path itineraries. Tours last three to three-and-a-half hours and cost $30 to $40, depending on the sites visited. Both Egged Tours and United Tours do half-day walking tours of Old City highlights. *(See Orientation, above, for contact information.)*

to deny the enemy access. In the 19th century, an inscription in ancient Hebrew (since removed) was found chiseled into the tunnel wall near the exit. "This is the story of the boring through . . . ," it began, echoing the biblical account; " . . . the tunnelers hewed the rock, each man toward his fellow. And the water flowed from the spring toward the reservoir for 1,200 cubits [577 yards]."

2

If you don't want to get your feet wet, you can still view the spring and marvel at the ingenuity of the ancient engineers, and then exit the site through a narrow but dry Canaanite tunnel. If you do decide to enter the spring and wade the long narrow tunnel, you can easily imagine the digging of the ancient teams, and relive the electrifying moment when the last chunk of rock was removed, the water flowed, and the city was saved. The tunnel emerges in the Pool of Siloam, mentioned in the New Testament as the place where a blind man had his sight restored (John 9). What you see today is a modest Byzantine construction; but the current exit takes you over the large flagstones of a Second Temple street to the original, impressive 1st-century reservoir, only recently discovered and partially exposed. ✉ *Off Ophel Rd., Silwan* ☎ *02/626–8700 or *6033 toll-free in Israel* 🌐 *www.cityofdavid.org.il* 🎫 *NIS 27 for city of David sites, add NIS 10 for 3-D film, guided tour NIS 60 (includes admission and film)* ⏲ *Apr.–Sept., Sun.–Thurs. 8–7, Fri. and Jewish holiday eves 8–3; Oct.–Mar., Sun.–Thurs. 8–5, Fri. and Jewish holiday eves 8–1, last entrance 2 hrs before closing.*

★ **Warren's Shaft.** In 1867 British army engineer Charles Warren discovered this spacious, sloping access tunnel in the City of David—note the ancient chisel marks on the walls—which burrowed under the city wall to a point 40 feet above the Gihon Spring, in the valley. A narrow vertical shaft dropped into the spring, giving access to ancient water drawers. The presumption was that it was pre-Davidic, and perhaps the actual biblical *tzinnor* (gutter or water shaft) of II Samuel 5 through which David's warriors penetrated the city, circa 1000 BC. Archaeologists now believe that the space was only created in a later era; and a dig around the Gihon Spring at the bottom of the hill has uncovered a different access to the spring, protected by two towers that date back to the Middle Bronze Age, centuries before David. The biblical story remains intact for the moment, but Warren's Shaft may not have been the exact place where it occurred. ✉ *Off Ophel Rd., Silwan* ☎ *02/626–8700 or *6033 toll-free in Israel* 🌐 *www.cityofdavid.org.il* 🎫 *NIS 27 for City of David sites, add NIS 10 for 3-D film, guided tour NIS 60 (includes admission and film)* ⏲ *Apr.–Sept., Sun.–Thurs. 8–7, Fri. and Jewish holiday eves 8–3; Oct.–Mar., Sun.–Thurs. 8–5, Fri. and Jewish holiday eves 8–1, last entrance 2 hrs before closing.*

WORTH NOTING

Area G. This open-air dig site comes with the territory and your City of David ticket. Archaeologists have dug up bits of the city for well over a century—notably Charles Warren in the 1860s and Kathleen Kenyon a hundred years later. Israeli archaeologist Yigal Shiloh, however, led the most thorough expedition from 1978 to 1985. In this locale, he confirmed Kenyon's assertion that the angular pieces of the city wall, seen at the top, were indeed part of the 2nd-century BC construction that the historian Flavius Josephus dubbed the "First Wall." On the other hand, he redated the sloping "stepped structure" to at least the 10th century BC, the time of Israelite kings David and Solomon, when it apparently supported a palace or fortification on the crest of the ridge. In the 7th century BC, a house (now partially restored on a platform) was built against it.

The most intriguing artifacts found were 51 bullae, clay seals used for documents, just as hot wax might be used today, with personal names impressed on them in ancient Hebrew script. All the seals were found in one chamber, suggesting that it was used as an archive or a royal office. This idea was reinforced by the biblical name on one of the seals: Gemariah ben Shafan, the royal secretary in the days of the prophet Jeremiah. The clay seals were baked into pottery by a massive fire, apparently during the Babylonian destruction of Jerusalem in 586 BC. ✉ *Off Ophel Rd., Silwan* ☎ *02/626–8700 or *6033 toll-free in Israel* 🌐 *www.cityofdavid.org.il* 🎫 *NIS 27 for City of David sites, add NIS 10 for 3-D film, guided tour NIS 60 (includes admission and film)* 🕓 *Apr.–Sept., Sun.–Thurs. 8–7, Fri. and Jewish holiday eves 8–3; Oct.–Mar., Sun.–Thurs. 8–5, Fri. and Jewish holiday eves 8–1, last entrance 2 hrs before closing.*

Siloam Pool. The ingenious water system devised by King Hezekiah in 701 BC to protect the city's water supply (and divert it into Shilo'ach, an inner-city reservoir) was still in use in the Second Temple period, the time of King Herod and of Jesus. The New Testament (John 9) tells of the healing of a blind man. Jesus "spat on the ground and made mud of the saliva and spread the mud on the man's eyes, saying to him, 'Go, wash in the pool of Siloam'" (the Greek form of the original Hebrew name). And the man's sight was restored. The small pool at the outlet of the tunnel is 5th-century Byzantine. The small church, built at the same time to enshrine the miracle, has not survived.

In 2004, city workers repairing a sewage pipe stumbled across a few ancient steps 70 yards down the slope. Subsequent excavation revealed several rows of finely cut steps, as well as the corners where they turned to form a rectangular pool. The pool may have served as a large public mikvah, or Jewish ritual bath, for some of the out-of-towners who flocked to Jerusalem and the Temple 2,000 years ago. The assumption now is that this was the authentic Pool of Siloam of the Gospel story. An impressive city street unearthed nearby, apparently Herodian (1st century BC), is the southern extremity of a broad commercial thoroughfare that sliced down through the entire city. ✉ *Off Ophel Rd., Silwan* ☎ *02/626–2341* 🌐 *www.cityofdavid.org.il* 🎫 *Included in entrance to City of David; NIS 12 for ancient pool and street only* 🕓 *Apr.–Sept., Sun.–Thurs. 8–7, Fri. and Jewish holiday eves 8–3; Oct.–Mar., Sun.–Thurs. 8–5, Fri. and Jewish holiday eves 8–1.*

MT. OF OLIVES AND EAST JERUSALEM

Loosely speaking, East Jerusalem refers to the Arab neighborhoods controlled by Jordan in the years when the city was divided (1948–1967). That includes Mt. of Olives, the areas north of the Old City, and in

CLOSE UP

Jerusalem Through the Ages

The first known mention of Jerusalem is in Egyptian "hate texts" of the 20th century BC, but many archaeologists give the city a considerably earlier founding date. Abraham and the biblical Joshua may have been here, but it was King David, circa 1000 BC, who captured the city and made it his capital, thus propelling it onto the center stage of history.

FIRST AND SECOND TEMPLES

King David's son Solomon built the "First" Temple, giving the city a preeminence it enjoyed until its destruction by the Babylonians, and the exile of its population, in 586 BC. The Israelites returned 50 years later, rebuilt the Temple (the "Second"), and began the slow process of revival. By the 2nd century BC, Jerusalem was again a vibrant Jewish capital, albeit one with a good dose of Hellenistic cultural influence. Herod the Great (who reigned 37 BC–4 BC) revamped the Temple on a magnificent scale and expanded the city into a cosmopolis of world renown.

This was the Jerusalem Jesus knew, a city of monumental architecture, teeming—especially during the Jewish pilgrim festivals—with tens of thousands of visitors. It was here that the Romans crucified Jesus (circa AD 29), and here, too, that the Great Jewish Revolt against Rome erupted, ending in AD 70 with the destruction (once again) of the city and the Temple.

ROMANS AND OTTOMANS

The Roman emperor Hadrian redesigned Jerusalem as the pagan polis of Aelia Capitolina (AD 135), an urban plan that became the basis for the Old City of today. The Byzantines made it a Christian center, with a massive wave of church building (4th–6th centuries AD), until the Arab conquest of AD 638 brought the holy city under Muslim sway. Except during the golden age of the Ummayad Dynasty, in the late 7th and early 8th centuries, Jerusalem was no more than a provincial town under the Muslim regimes of the early Middle Ages. The Crusaders stormed it in 1099 and made it the capital of their Latin Kingdom. With the reconquest of Jerusalem by the Muslims, the city again lapsed into a languid provincialism for 700 years under the Mamluk and Ottoman empires. The British conquest in 1917 thrust the city back into the world limelight as rising rival nationalisms vied to possess it.

DIVIDED AND REUNITED

Jerusalem was divided by the 1948 war: the larger Jewish western sector became the capital of the State of Israel, while Jordan annexed the smaller, predominantly Arab eastern sector, which included the Old City. The Six Days' War of 1967 reunited the city under Israeli rule, but the concept of an Arab "East" Jerusalem and a Jewish "West" Jerusalem remains, even though new Jewish neighborhoods in the northeastern and southeastern sections have made the distinction oversimplified.

The holy city continues to engage the attention of devotees of Christianity, Islam, and Judaism. Between Jews and Arabs it remains the subject of debate and occasional violence as rival visions clash for possession of the city's past and control of its future. It is widely recognized that any peace negotiations between Israel and the Palestinians will fail unless the issue of sharing Jerusalem is resolved.

fact the Old City itself. *(The Old City sights are covered elsewhere in this chapter).*

The sights in this area are for the most part distinctly Christian. A few are a little off the beaten path, and the best way to explore them—if you're energetic enough—is on foot. If you're driving, however, you can find parking at the Seven Arches Hotel on the Mt. of Olives, and at the cluster of large hotels near the American Colony; or take a cab.

GETTING HERE AND AROUND

The Route 99 circle tour has a stop near Hebrew University's Mt. Scopus campus. If you enjoy a bit of a walk and the weather is fine, it's no more than 20 minutes across to Mt. of Olives (with a bonus of a panoramic view of the Judean Desert to the east). A cab ride is an alternative, but if you skip the top of the mountain, the rest of the sights are accessible by foot from the Old City.

TIMING AND PRECAUTIONS

Morning views are best from Mt. of Olives. Some of the sites are closed on Sundays. Watch out for pickpockets on Mt. of Olives and the road down to Gethsemane, and the Nablus Road outside the Garden Tomb.

TOP ATTRACTIONS

Garden of Gethsemane. After the Last Supper, the New Testament relates, Jesus and his disciples came to a "place" called Gethsemane. There he agonized and prayed, and there, in the end, he was betrayed and arrested. Gethsemane derives from the Aramaic or Hebrew word for "oil press," referring to the precious olive that has always flourished here. The enormous, gnarled, and still-productive olive trees on the site may be older than Christianity itself, according to some botanists. They make a fine picture, but a fence prevents pilgrims from taking home sprigs as a more tangible souvenir. The **Church of All Nations,** with its brilliantly colorful, landmark mosaic facade, was built in the garden in 1924 on the scanty remains of its Byzantine predecessor. The prolific architect, Antonio Barluzzi, filled the church's interior domes with mosaic symbols of the Catholic communities that contributed to its construction. The seal of the United States is in the first dome on the right as you enter the church; Canada is two up in the same line; and the English dome is the first, nearest the door, in the middle line. The windows are glazed with translucent alabaster in somber browns and purples, creating a mystical feeling in the dim interior. At the altar is the so-called Rock of the Agony, where Jesus is said to have endured his Passion; this is the source of the older name of the church, the **Basilica of the Agony.**

A popular approach to Gethsemane is walking down the steep road from the top of Mt. of Olives, perhaps stopping in on the way at the Dominus Flevit church where, tradition has it, Jesus wept as he foretold the destruction of the city (Luke 19). The entrance to the well-tended garden at the foot of the hill is marked by a small platoon of vendors outside. ✉ *Jericho Rd., Kidron Valley* ☎ *02/626–6444* 🎫 *Free* 🕒 *Apr.–Sept., daily 8–12 and 2–6; Oct.–Mar., daily 8–12 and 2–5.*

★ **Garden Tomb.** A beautifully tended English-style country garden makes this an island of tranquillity in the hurly-burly of East Jerusalem. What

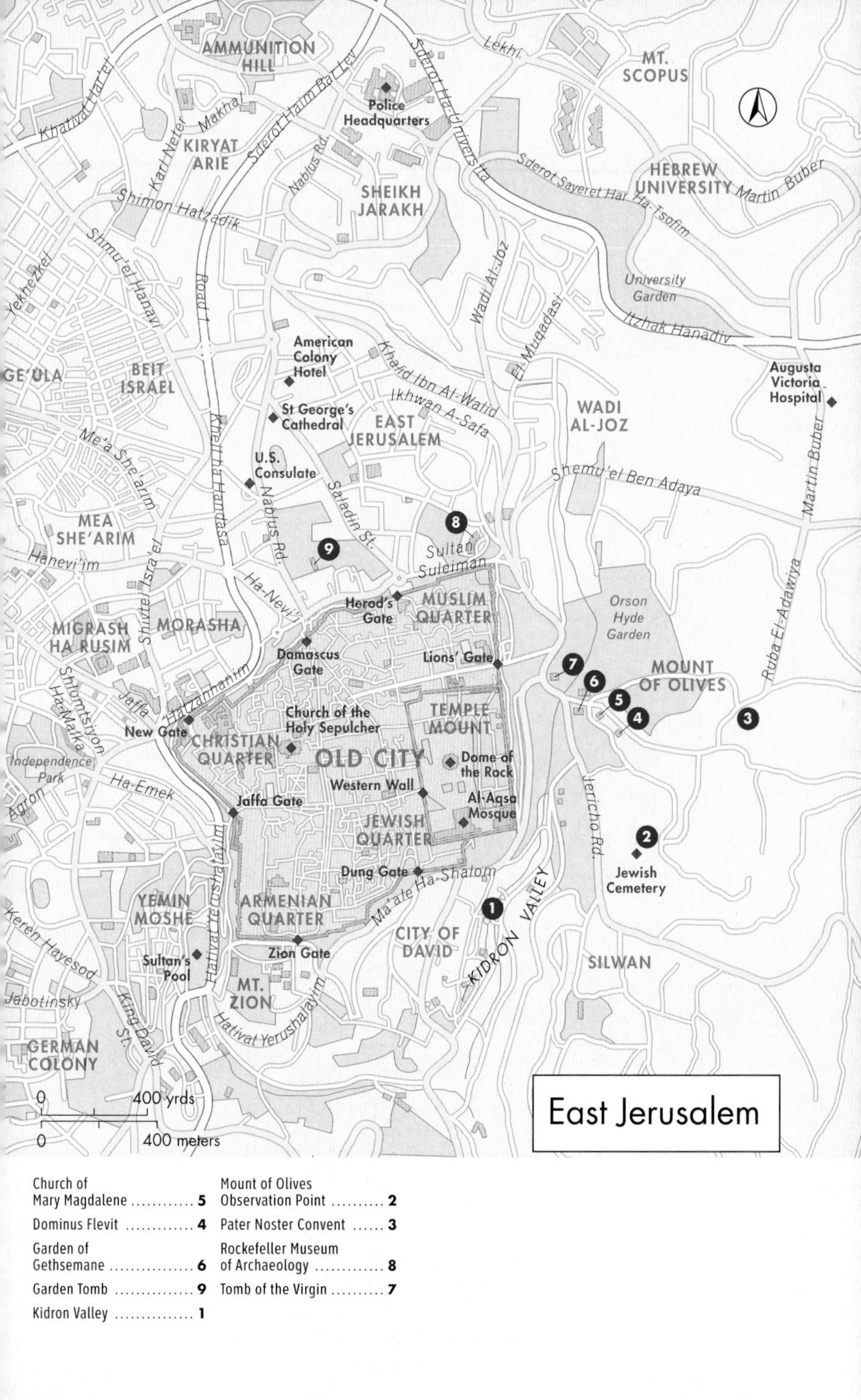

Church of Mary Magdalene **5**
Dominus Flevit **4**
Garden of Gethsemane **6**
Garden Tomb **9**
Kidron Valley **1**
Mount of Olives Observation Point **2**
Pater Noster Convent **3**
Rockefeller Museum of Archaeology **8**
Tomb of the Virgin **7**

DID YOU KNOW?

Many graves in the Jewish cemetery on the slope of the Mt. of Olives have stones placed on the marker (burial is belowground). The ancient custom indicates that the visitors have stopped and paid their respects to the deceased.

Christian pilgrims come for, however, is an empty ancient tomb, and a moving opportunity to ponder the Gospel account of the death and resurrection of Jesus. It is a favorite site for the many Protestant visitors who respond less or not at all to the ornamentation and ritual of the Holy Sepulcher.

The theory identifying this site with Calvary and Jesus' burial place goes back to 1883, when the British general Charles Gordon (of later Khartoum fame) spent several months in Jerusalem. From his window looking out over the Old City walls, the skull-like features of a cliff face north of the Damascus Gate struck Gordon. He was convinced that this, rather than the traditional Calvary in the Church of the Holy Sepulcher, was "the place of the skull" (Mark 15) where Jesus was crucified. His conviction was infectious, and after his death, a fund-raising campaign in England resulted in the purchase of the adjacent site in 1894. An ancient rock-cut tomb had already been uncovered there, and subsequent excavations exposed cisterns and a wine press, features typical of an ancient garden.

All the elements of the Gospel account of Jesus' death and burial seemed to be in evidence, and the newly formed Garden Tomb Association was jubilant. According to the New Testament, Jesus was buried in the fresh tomb of the wealthy Joseph of Arimathea, in a garden close to the execution site, and archaeologists identified the tomb as an upper-class Jewish burial place of the Second Temple period. Recent research has challenged that conclusion, however. The tomb might be from the Old Testament period, making it too old to have been that of Jesus, since his was freshly cut. The gentle guardians of the Garden Tomb do not insist on the identification of the site as that of Calvary and the tomb of Christ, but are keen to provide a contemplative setting for the pilgrim, in a place that just might have been historically significant. ✉ *Conrad Schick St., East Jerusalem* ☎ *02/627–2745* 🌐 *www.gardentomb.com* 🎫 *Free* ⏲ *Mon.–Sat. 9–noon and 2–5:30.*

NEED A BREAK?

The upscale American Colony Hotel (✉ *1 Louis Vincent St. at Nablus Rd., American Colony* ☎ *02/627–9777*) is an elegant 19th-century limestone building with cane furniture, Armenian ceramic tiles, and a delightful courtyard. The food is generally very good, and a light lunch or afternoon tea in the cool lobby lounge, at the poolside restaurant, or on the patio under the trees can make for a well-earned break.

★ **Mt. of Olives Observation Point.** This is the classic panoramic view of the Old City: looking across the Kidron Valley over the gold Dome of the Rock. It's best in the early morning, with the sun at your back, or at sunset on days with some clouds, when the golden glow can compensate for the glare.

The Mt. of Olives has been bathed in sanctity for millennia. On the slope beneath you, and off to your left, is the vast **Jewish cemetery,** reputedly the oldest still in use anywhere in the world. For more than 2,000 years, Jews have been buried here to await the coming of the Messiah and the resurrection to follow. The raised structures over the graves are merely tomb markers, not crypts; burial is belowground.

In the Old City wall facing you, and just to the right of the Dome of the Rock, is the blocked-up, double-arched Gates of Mercy, also known as the Golden Gate or the Eastern Gate. Jewish tradition holds that the Messiah will enter Jerusalem this way; Christian tradition says he already did, on Palm Sunday. To the south of the Dome of the Rock is the black-domed al-Aqsa Mosque, and behind it the stone arches and large white synagogue dome of the Jewish Quarter. Some distance behind the Dome of the Rock is the large, gray dome of the Church of the Holy Sepulcher. To the left of the Old City, the cone-roof Dormition Abbey and its adjacent clock tower mark the top of Mt. Zion, today outside the walls but within the city of the Second Temple period.

Camel and donkey drivers (usually one of each) are always pushing to give you a short ride (not cheap!), and the vendors can be persistent, but a polite "no thank you" is sometimes enough for them to go bother someone else. The frequent police presence has made the locals less aggressive, but still beware of pickpockets here and on the road down to Gethsemane. Fairly good bathrooms are a welcome addition. ✉ *E-Sheikh St., opposite Seven Arches Hotel, Mt. of Olives.*

Rockefeller Museum of Archaeology. The Rockefeller's octagonal white stone tower is an East Jerusalem landmark. Built in the 1930s, the museum has echoing stone halls and somewhat old-fashioned display techniques that recall the British Mandate period, when it was in its prime. The finds are all from this country, dating from prehistoric times to around AD 1700. Among the most important exhibits are cultic masks from Neolithic Jericho, ivories from Canaanite (Bronze Age) Megiddo, the famous Israelite "Lachish Letters" (6th century BC), Herodian inscriptions, and decorative reliefs from Hisham's Palace, in Jericho, and from the Church of the Holy Sepulcher. The Rockefeller is a branch of the Israel Museum. The museum has some parking on Saturday only. For winter visitors, note that the buildings have no heating. ✉ *27 Sultan Suleiman St., East Jerusalem* ☎ *02/670–8811* 🌐 *www.english.imjnet.org.il; follow link to Wings* 🎟 *Free* ⏲ *Sun., Mon., Wed., and Thurs. 10–3, Sat. 10–2.*

WORTH NOTING

Church of Mary Magdalene. With its sculpted white turrets and gold onion domes, this Russian Orthodox church looks like something out of a fairy tale. It was dedicated in 1888, when the competition among European powers for influence in this part of the world was at its height. The church has limited hours, but its icon-studded interior and tranquil garden are well worth a visit if your plans bring you to the area at the right time. ✉ *Above Gethsemane, Mt. of Olives* ☎ *02/628–4371* 🎟 *Free* ⏲ *Tues. and Thurs. 10–noon.*

Dominus Flevit. Designed by Antonio Barluzzi in the 1950s, the tear-shaped church—its name means "the Lord wept"—preserves the New Testament story of Jesus' sorrowful prediction of the destruction of Jerusalem (Luke 19). The remarkable feature of its simple interior is a picture window facing west, the iron cross on the altar silhouetted against a superb view of the Old City. Many small archaeological items were found here, but the tradition that holds this as the site of the

On the Mount of Olives, the stunning mosaic facade of the Church of All Nations is a city landmark.

Gospel story is no older than the Crusader period. The courtyard is a good place to enjoy the view in peace between waves of pilgrim groups. (Equally worthy of mention are the restrooms, rare in this area.) The church is about one-third of the way down the steep road that descends to Gethsemane from the Mt. of Olives observation point. Beware of pickpockets on the street outside. ✉ *Below Mt. of Olives observation point, Mt. of Olives* ☎ *02/626–6450* 🎫 *Free* ⏲ *Daily 8–11:45 and 2:30–5.*

Kidron Valley. This deep valley separates the Old City and the City of David from the high ridge of the Mt. of Olives and the Arab neighborhood of Silwan. In the cliff face below the neighborhood are the symmetrical openings of tombs from both the First Temple (Old Testament) and Second Temple (Hellenistic-Roman) periods. You can view the impressive group of 2,200-year-old funerary monuments from the lookout terrace at the southeast corner of the Old City wall, down and to your left, or wander down into the valley itself and see them close up. The huge, square, stone structure with the conical roof is known as **Absalom's Pillar.** The one crowned by a pyramidal roof, a solid block of stone cut out of the mountain, is called **Zachariah's Tomb.** The association with those Old Testament personalities was a medieval mistake, and the structures more probably mark the tombs of wealthy Jerusalemites of the Second Temple period who wished to await the coming of the Messiah and the resurrection to follow in the style to which they were accustomed. To see the structures up close, access is best from Jericho Road, just south of Gethsemane. ✉ *Kidron Valley.*

Pater Noster Convent. The focal point of this Carmelite convent is a grotto, traditionally identified as the place where Jesus taught his disciples the so-called Lord's Prayer: "Our Father [*Pater Noster*], Who art in Heaven" (Matthew 6). The site was purchased by the Princesse de la Tour d'Auvergne of France in 1868, and the convent stands on the site of earlier Byzantine and Crusader structures. The ambitious basilica, begun in the 1920s, was designed to follow the lines of a 4th-century church, but was never completed: its aisles, open to the sky, are now lined with pine trees. The real attractions of the site, however, are the many ceramic plaques adorning the cloister walls and the small church, with the Lord's Prayer in more than 100 different languages. (Look for the high wall and metal door on a bend 200 yards before the Seven Arches Hotel.) ✉ *E-Sheikh St., Mt. of Olives* ☎ *02/626–4904* 🎫 *NIS 7* ⏲ *Mon.–Sat. 8:30–noon and 2:30–4:30.*

Tomb of the Virgin. The Gothic facade of the underground Church of the Assumption, which contains this shrine, clearly dates it to the Crusader era (12th century). Nevertheless, tradition has it that this is where the Virgin Mary was interred and then "assumed" into heaven. In an otherwise gloomy church—hung with age-darkened icons and brass lamps—the marble sarcophagus, thought to date from the 12th century, remains illuminated. The Status Quo Agreement in force in the Church of the Holy Sepulcher and Bethlehem's Church of the Nativity pertains here, too: the Greek Orthodox, Armenian Orthodox, and even the Muslims control different parts of the property. The Roman Catholic Franciscans were expelled in 1757, a loss of privilege that rankles to this day. The shrine is a few steps away from the Garden of Gethsemane. ✉ *Jericho Rd., adjacent to Gethsemane, Kidron Valley* ☎ *02/628–4613* 🎫 *Free* ⏲ *Daily 6–noon and 2:30–5.*

WEST JERUSALEM

Visitors tend to focus, naturally enough, on the historical and religious sights on the eastern side of town, especially in the Old City; but West Jerusalem houses the nation's institutions, is the repository for its collective memory, and—together with the Downtown—gives more insight into contemporary life in Israel's largest city. The world-class Israel Museum and Yad Vashem are located here, as well as poignant Mt. Herzl and the picturesque neighborhood of Ein Kerem. These attractions, which are spread out, are most easily accessed by car or by a combination of buses and short cab rides.

GETTING HERE AND AROUND

There are good city bus services in this part of town (ask at each site how to get to the next), but a few cab rides (most under $10 on the meter) will be a much better use of limited time. Remember that Route 99 serves a good number of sights in this part of town.

TIMING AND PRECAUTIONS

Pay attention to the closing times of sites: several are not open on Saturdays and close early on Fridays. Some museums have evening hours on particular days—a time-efficient option. Avoid burnout by staggering visits to the museums, and combining them with different kinds of experiences.

TOP ATTRACTIONS

Bible Lands Museum. Most archaeological museums group artifacts according to their place of origin (Egyptian, Babylonian, and so on), but the curators here have abandoned this method in favor of a chronological display. The museum was the brainchild of the late Elie Borowski, whose personal collection of ancient artifacts forms its core. The display method allows a comparison of objects of neighboring cultures of the same period. Exhibits cover a period of more than 6,000 years—from the prehistoric Neolithic period to that of the Byzantine Empire—and sweep geographically from Afghanistan to Nubia (present-day Sudan). Rare clay vessels, fertility idols, cylinder seals, ivories, and sarcophagi fill the soaring, naturally lighted galleries. Look for the ancient Egyptian wooden coffin, in a stunning state of preservation.

The concept of the museum is intriguing, but some have criticized its methodology. A concept was imposed on a largely preexisting collection, rather than a collection being created item by selected item to illustrate a concept. Plan on an hour or 90 minutes to see the place; join the guided tour to get the most out of a visit. The museum runs a Saturday-night concert series, with cheese and wine served in the foyer. The NIS 75 ticket (sometimes cheaper) includes access to the exhibition areas, with the option of a free highlights tour, for one hour before and 30 minutes after the concert. ✉ *25 Granot St., Givat Ram* ☎ *02/561–1066* 🌐 *www.blmj.org* 🎫 *NIS 40* 🕓 *Sun.–Tues. and Thurs. 9:30–5:30, Wed. 9:30–9:30, Fri. and Jewish holiday eves 9:30–2, Sat. 10–3. Closed on Jewish religious holidays. Guided tours in English Sun.–Fri. at 10:30 (Wed. at 5:30 in addition); call ahead to verify.*

Chagall Windows and Hadassah Hospital. Some remarkable stained glass draws travelers to Hadassah, one of the leading general hospitals in the Middle East and the teaching hospital for Hebrew University's medical, dental, and public-health schools. When the U.S.-based Hadassah women's organization approached the Russian-born Jewish artist Marc Chagall in 1959 about designing stained-glass windows for the synagogue at the new hospital, he was delighted and contributed his work for free. Taking his inspiration from the Bible—Jacob's deathbed blessings on his sons and, to a lesser extent, Moses' valediction to the tribes of Israel—the artist created 12 vibrant windows in primary colors, with an ark full of characteristically Chagallian beasts and a bag of Jewish and esoteric symbols. The innovative techniques of the Reims glassmakers give the wafer-thin windows an astounding illusion of depth in many places. Buses 12, 19, 27 and 42 serve the hospital. The recorded explanations in the synagogue alternate languages. ✉ *Hadassah Hospital, Henrietta Szold Rd., Ein Kerem* ☎ *02/677–6271* 🌐 *www.hadassah.org.il/english* 🎫 *NIS 10* 🕓 *Sun.–Thurs. 8–1, 2–4; for holiday periods, call ahead to verify times.*

★ **Ein Kerem.** The neighborhood of Ein Kerem (sometimes Ein "Karem") still retains much of its old village character. A couple of hours is enough time to explore it, though you could spend more if you take time out

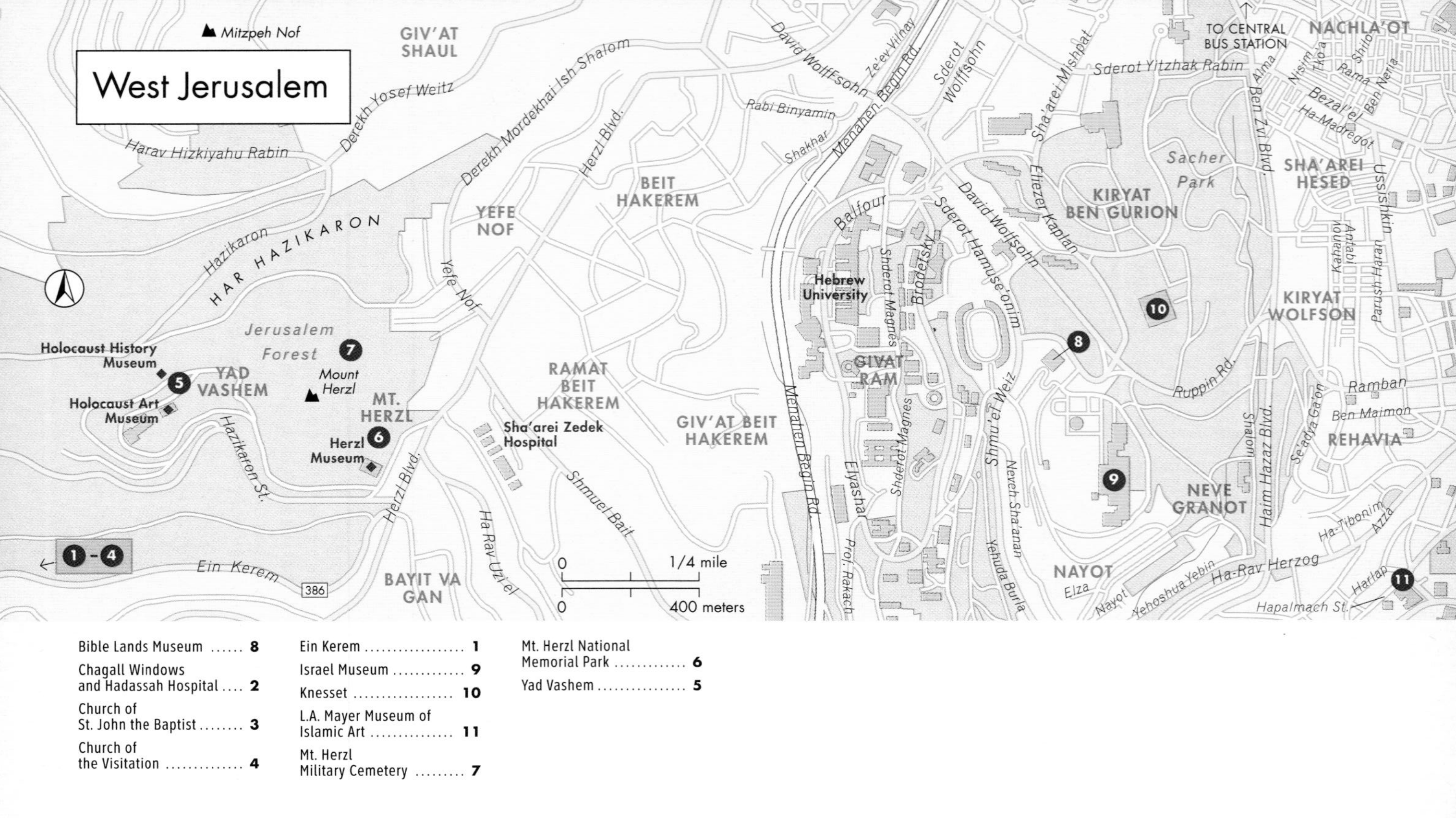

Bible Lands Museum **8**
Chagall Windows and Hadassah Hospital **2**
Church of St. John the Baptist **3**
Church of the Visitation **4**
Ein Kerem **1**
Israel Museum **9**
Knesset **10**
L.A. Mayer Museum of Islamic Art **11**
Mt. Herzl Military Cemetery **7**
Mt. Herzl National Memorial Park **6**
Yad Vashem **5**

for a coffee or a meal. Tree-framed stone houses are strewn across its hillsides with a pleasing Mediterranean nonchalance. Artists and professionals who have joined the older working-class population over the last 40 years have marvelously renovated many homes. Back alleys provide an off-the-beaten-path feel, and occasionally a serendipitous art or craft studio. Though not mentioned by name in the New Testament, Ein Kerem is identified as the home of John the Baptist, and indeed the orange-roofed **Church of St. John the Baptist** in the heart of the village, and the **Church of the Visitation** *(⇨ see below for these listings)* up the hillside above the Spring of the Virgin, are its most prominent landmarks. (The newly restored gold-domed Russian church currently has no published visiting hours.)

BRIDGE OF STRINGS

The "Bridge of Strings" (or "Cords") was designed by Spanish architect Santiago Calatrava to suspend the new light rail over the busy intersection at Jerusalem's western entrance (Tel Aviv Highway, Route 1). The commission was intended to provide the city with a contemporary icon. "What do we need it for?" complained some residents. Judge for yourself from the best angle: not as you enter the city but from the sidewalk outside the International Convention Center (✉ *Binyanei Ha'ooma, Zalman Shazar Blvd.*). At this writing, the light rail, years behind schedule and millions over budget, was slated to operate later in 2011.

The road down to the valley begins at the big Mt. Herzl intersection. Alternatively, if you're driving and you've just visited the Chagall Windows, turn right as soon as you leave the hospital grounds, and descend to where the road joins Route 386. Turn right again, reentering Jerusalem through the bottom of Ein Kerem. The neighborhood is served by city bus 17 and is 5 minutes from Mt. Herzl or Yad Vashem, and less than 10 minutes from the Hadassah hospital. ✉ *Ein Kerem.*

Fodor's Choice ★ **Israel Museum.** In 2010, this eclectic treasure trove and world-class don't-miss museum emerged like a butterfly from a lengthy renewal of its entire main complex. The three main specialties of art, archaeology, and Judaica have been much enhanced by new or rearranged exhibits, fresh ideas, and state-of-the-art presentations.

Some strategy notes: if you like museums, plan on two visits. The vegetarian/dairy café Mansfeld is a good place for a light meal or coffee—and you get live music with the Friday brunch buffet. The more expensive Modern has tempting meat and fish combinations. Both are open outside museum hours. The lockers and an ATM in the museum's entrance hall are useful additions.

The **Dead Sea Scrolls** are certainly the Israel Museum's most famous—and most important—collection. A Bedouin boy discovered the first of the 2,000-year-old scrolls in 1947 in a Judean Desert cave, overlooking the Dead Sea. All in all, nine main scrolls (one engraved on copper) and bags full of small fragments surfaced over the years: the Israel Museum possesses some of the most important and most complete of these ancient texts. *(⇨ See Masada and the Dead Sea in Chapter 3)*. The white dome of the Shrine of the Book, the separate building in which the scrolls are housed, was inspired by the lids of the clay jars in which the first ones were found.

The scrolls were written in the Second Temple period by a fundamentalist Jewish sect, conventionally identified as the Essenes, a group described by contemporary historians. Archaeological, laboratory, and textual evidence dates the earliest of the scrolls to the 2nd century BC; none could have been written later than AD 68, the year in which their home community, known today as Qumran, was destroyed by the Romans. Written on parchment, and still in an extraordinary state of preservation because of the dryness of the Dead Sea region, the scrolls contain the oldest Hebrew manuscripts of the Old Testament ever found, authenticating the almost identical Hebrew texts still in use today. Sectarian literature includes "The Rule of the Community," a sort of constitution of this ascetic group, and "The War of the Sons of Light Against the Sons of Darkness," a blow-by-blow account of a final cataclysmic conflict that would, they believed, presage the messianic age.

The medieval Aleppo Codex, on display in the small lower gallery under the white dome, is considered the most authoritative text of the Hebrew Bible in existence. If this speaks to you, the excellent Web site (🌐 *www.aleppocodex.org*) will have you impatient to see the real thing.

The quarter-acre **1:50 scale model,** adjacent to the Shrine of the Book, represents Jerusalem as it was on the eve of the Great Revolt against Rome (AD 66). Until 2006, the huge, intricate reconstruction was a popular attraction in its original home, on the grounds of the former Holyland Hotel in West Jerusalem. The outdoor model was originally designed and built in the mid-1960s by the late Professor Michael Avi-Yonah. He relied on considerable data gleaned from Roman-period historians, important Jewish texts, and even the New Testament, and based some of his generic reconstructions (villas, a theater, markets, etc.) on Roman structures that have survived across the ancient empire, from France to Turkey. Later archaeological excavations have sometimes confirmed and sometimes contradicted Avi-Yonah's sharp intuition, and the model has been updated occasionally to incorporate new knowledge. The available audio guide is a worthwhile aid in deciphering the site.

Taken together, the Dead Sea Scrolls, the huge model, and certain Roman-period exhibits in the Archaeology Wing evoke the turbulent and historically momentous Second Temple period. That was the era from which Christianity emerged; and when the Romans razed the Temple in Jerusalem, it compelled a slow revolution in Jewish life and religious practice that has defined Judaism to this day.

The **Archaeology Wing** has been reorganized to highlight particular treasures in galleries that follow a historical sequence. (Well, "historical" may be too limiting a term, given the global uniqueness of several of its prehistorical finds.) If you know a bit of Bible, many artifacts in the Canaanite, Israelite, and Hellenistic-Roman sections offer evocative illustrations of familiar texts. Don't miss the small side rooms devoted to glass, coins, and the Hebrew script.

The Shrine of the Book at the Israel Museum dramatically displays delicate sections of the Dead Sea Scrolls.

Jewish Art and Life is the new name for the wing made up mostly of finely wrought Jewish ceremonial objects (Judaica) from widely disparate communities. The "synagogue route" with its reconstructed old synagogues from Cochin (India), Germany, and Venice (Italy) has acquired an addition from the Caribbean community of Suriname.

The **Art Wing** is a confusing maze spread over different levels, but if you have patience and time, the payoff is great. Older European art rubs shoulders with modern works, contemporary Israeli, design, and photography. The flyer available at the museum entrance lists new and temporary exhibitions. Landscape architect Isamu Noguchi designed the open-air **Art Garden.** Crunch over the gravel amid works by Daumier, Rodin, Moore, Picasso, and a number of less-legendary local luminaries.

The **Youth Wing** mounts one new exhibition a year, delightfully interactive and often adult-friendly, designed to encourage children to appreciate the arts and the world around them, or be creative in a crafts workshop. Parents with restless kids will also be grateful for the outdoor play areas. ✉ *Ruppin Rd., Givat Ram* ☎ *02/670–8811* 🌐 *www.imj.org.il* 🎫 *NIS 48 (includes audio guide); half price for return visit within 3 months (keep your ticket)* 🕒 *Sun., Mon., Wed., Thurs., Sat., and Jewish holidays 10–5, Tues. 4–9, Fri. and Jewish holiday eves 10–2.*

Knesset. Both the name of Israel's one-chamber parliament and its number of seats (120) were taken from *Haknesset Hagedolah*, the Great Assembly of the Second Temple period, some 2,000 years ago. The 40-minute public tour held on Sunday and Thursday includes the session hall as well as three enormous, brilliantly colored tapestries designed by Marc Chagall on the subjects of the Creation, the Exodus, and Jerusalem. On other days, when in session, the Knesset is open to the public—call ahead to verify but note that all the proceedings are of course conducted in Hebrew. Arrive at least 30 minutes before the tour (especially in summer, when the lines are longer), and be sure to bring your passport. Bags and cameras have to be deposited with security.

Across the road from the Knesset main gate is a 15-foot-high bronze menorah, based on the one that once graced the ancient temple in Jerusalem. The seven-branch candelabrum was adopted soon after independence as the official symbol of the modern State of Israel. This one, designed by artist Bruno Elkin, and given as a gift by the British Parliament to the Knesset in 1956, is decorated with bas-relief depictions of events and personages in Jewish history, from biblical times to the modern day. Behind the menorah is the Wohl Rose Garden (enter from outside the Knesset security barrier), which has hundreds of varieties of roses, many lawns for children to romp on, and adult-friendly nooks in its upper section. ✉ *Kiryat Ben-Gurion, Givat Ram* ☎ *02/675–3416* 🌐 *www.knesset.gov.il* 🎫 *Free* 🕓 *Guided tours in English (45 mins) Sun. and Thurs. at 8:30, noon and 1:45.*

Mt. Herzl National Memorial Park. Cedars of Lebanon and native pine and cypress trees surround the entrance to the memorial and cemetery, which has a section with the graves of Zionist visionary Theodor Herzl and many Israeli leaders. The **Herzl Museum** (✉ *Mt. Herzl* ☎ *02/632–1515* 🌐 *www.herzl.org* 🕓 *Sun.–Thurs. 8:45–3:15, Fri. 8:45–12:15, closed eve of Jewish religious holidays*), immediately to the left as you enter the memorial park, is a strongly engaging, interactive introduction to the life, times, and legacy of Israel's spiritual forebear. Tours take 50 minutes and cost NIS 25. Call ahead to verify times of tours in English. In 1894, the Budapest-born Theodor Herzl was the Paris correspondent for a Vienna newspaper when the Dreyfus treason trial hit the headlines. The anti-Semitic outbursts that Herzl encountered in cosmopolitan Paris shocked him. Dreyfus, a Jewish officer in the French army, had actually been framed and was later exonerated. Herzl devoted himself to the problem of Jewish vulnerability in "foreign" host countries and to the need for a Jewish state. The result of his activity was the first World Zionist Congress, held in Basel, Switzerland, in 1897. That year Herzl wrote in his diary: "If not in five years, then in 50, [a Jewish state] will become reality." True to his prediction, the United Nations approved the idea exactly 50 years later, in November 1947. Herzl died in 1904, and his remains were brought to Israel in 1949. His simple grave marker, inscribed in Hebrew with just his last name, caps the hill.

To the left (west) of the grave site, a gravel path leads down to a section containing the graves of Israeli national leaders, among them prime ministers Levi Eshkol, Golda Meir, and Yitzhak Rabin, and presidents Zalman Shazar and Chaim Herzog. Bear down and right through the military cemetery, exiting back on Herzl Boulevard, about 250 yards below the parking lot where you entered. The main gate closes at set times; the exit via the military cemetery is always open. ✉ *Herzl Blvd., Mt. Herzl* ☎ *02/643–3266* 🎫 *Free* 🕓 *Apr.–Sept., Sun.–Thurs. 8–6:45, Fri. and Jewish holiday eves 8–12:45; Oct.–Mar., Sun.–Thurs. 8–4:45, Fri. and Jewish holiday eves 8–12:45.*

CLOSE UP

Israel's Electoral System

"Take two Israelis," runs the old quip, "and you've got three political parties!" The saying is not without a kernel of truth in a nation where everyone has a strong opinion, and usually will not hesitate to express it. The Knesset, Israel's parliament, reflects this rambunctious spirit, sometimes to the point of paralyzing the parliamentary process and driving the public to distraction.

Israel's electoral system is based on proportional representation. In contrast with the winner-takes-all approach of the constituency system, any Israeli party that wins 2% of the national vote gets the number of seats in the 120-member Knesset to which its share of the ballot entitles it. The system is a legacy of the dangerous but heady days of Israel's War of Independence, in 1948–49. To avoid an acrimonious and divisive election while the fledgling state was still fighting for its life, the founding fathers developed a one-body parliamentary system that gave representation to rival ideological factions in proportion to their comparative strength in the country's *pre*-State institutions.

The good news is that it's wildly democratic: even relatively small fringe groups can have their voices heard. The bad news is that the system spawns a plethora of political parties, making it virtually impossible for one party to get the majority needed to govern alone. (The past phenomenon of single-member parties was curbed by the introduction of the threshold: a party that wins that share of the vote automatically gets two seats, and more often than not a third one as well.) Consequently, Israeli governments have always consisted of a coalition of parties, inevitably making them governments of compromise. The smaller coalition partners have been able to demand a price for their crucial parliamentary support—influential political positions, budgets for pet projects, and so on—that is often beyond what a minor party deserves, and sometimes at odds with the good of the nation at large.

Israel also has a president—citizen No. 1 but not a political leader—chosen by the members of the Knesset for one term of seven years. After the Knesset elections, the president consults with every party that made the 2% cut, and entrusts the party leader who seems to have the best coalition options with the job of forming a government. If successful within a designated period, he or she becomes prime minister.

OFF THE BEATEN PATH

Tisch Family Zoological Gardens. Spread over a scenic 62-acre ridge in the Judean Hills, this zoo has many of the usual species that delight zoo visitors everywhere: monkeys, snakes, and birds, for example. But it goes much further, focusing on two groups of wildlife. The first is creatures mentioned in the Bible that have become locally extinct, some as late as the 20th century. Among these are Asian lions, bears, cheetahs, the Nile crocodile, and the Persian fallow deer. Plaques on the enclosures give biblical references and modern information. The second focus is on endangered species worldwide, among them the Asian elephant and rare macaws. This is a wonderful place to let kids expend some energy (and adults to have some downtime from regular touring). Early morning or late afternoon are the best hours in summer; budget 2½ hours for a really full visit. A wagon train does the rounds of the zoo, at a nominal fee of NIS 2 (not on Saturdays and Jewish holidays). The Noah's Ark Visitors Center has a movie and computer programs. The zoo is served by the Circle Tour bus (line 99), and by city routes 26 (from Central Bus Station) and 33 (from Mt. Herzl). The ride is about 30 minutes; a cab would take 15 minutes from Downtown hotels. ✉ *Near the Jerusalem (Malcha) Mall, Malcha* ☎ *02/675–0111* 🌐 *www.jerusalemzoo.org.il* 🎫 *NIS 46* ⏲ *June–Aug., Sun.–Thurs. 9–7, Fri. 9–4:30, Sat. 10–6; May, Sun.–Thurs. 9–6, Fri. and Jewish holiday eves 9–4:30, Sat. 10–6; Sept.–Apr., Sun.–Thurs. 9–5, Fri. and Jewish holiday eves 9–4:30, Sat. 10–5. Closing times in Apr. and Sept. are sometimes late; call ahead. Last entrance 1 hr before closing.*

★ **Yad Vashem.** The experience of the Holocaust—the annihilation of 6 million Jews by the Nazis during World War II—is so deeply seared into the Jewish national psyche that understanding it goes a long way toward understanding Israelis themselves. The institution of Yad Vashem, created in 1953 by an act of the Knesset, was charged with preserving a record of those times. The name Yad Vashem—"a memorial and a name (a memory)"—comes from the biblical book of Isaiah (56:5). The Israeli government has made a tradition of bringing almost all high-ranking official foreign guests to visit the place.

The riveting **Holocaust History Museum**—a well-lit, 200-yard-long triangular concrete "prism"—is the centerpiece of the site. Powerful visual and audiovisual techniques in a series of galleries document Jewish life in Europe before the catastrophe and follow the escalation of persecution and internment to the hideous climax of the Nazi's "Final Solution." Video interviews and personal artifacts individualize the experience.

The sequence of the galleries reflects the phases of the Sho'ah (as the Holocaust is also known); yet the theme of a particular gallery can be elusive at first, especially when crowds get in the way. Browse Yad Vashem's Web site before you come, to "walk" through its succinct description of each gallery.

Note that children under 10 are not admitted; large bags have to be checked.

Near the exit of the museum are a film center, a computer center, and an art museum. In the basement of an older wing nearby (look for the Auditorium) is a permanent, very poignant exhibition called "No Child's Play," about children's activities during the Holocaust.

The small **Children's Memorial** is dedicated to the 1.5 million Jewish children murdered by the Nazis. Architect Moshe Safdie wanted to convey the enormity of the crime without numbing the visitor's emotions or losing sight of the victims' individuality. The result is a single dark room, lit by five candles infinitely reflected in some 500 mirrors. (The reason for the numbers is technical, not symbolic.) Recorded narrators intone the names, ages, and countries of origin of known victims. The

In Yad Vashem's Holocaust History Museum, the Hall of Names includes 600 photos of Jews who perished.

effect is electrifying. There are no steps to watch for, and guide rails are provided throughout.

The **Avenue of the Righteous** encircles Yad Vashem with several thousand trees marked with the names of Gentiles in Europe who risked and sometimes lost their lives trying to save Jews from the Nazis. Raoul Wallenberg, King Christian X of Denmark, Corrie ten Boom, Oskar Schindler, and American journalist Varian Fry are among the more famous honorees. The **Hall of Remembrance** is a heavy basalt-and-concrete building that houses an eternal flame, with the names of the death camps and concentration camps in relief on the floor.

At the bottom of the hill, large rough-hewn limestone boulders divide the **Valley of the Communities** into a series of small, man-made canyons. Each clearing represents a region of Nazi Europe, laid out geographically. The names of some 5,000 destroyed Jewish communities are inscribed in the stone walls, with very large letters highlighting those that were particularly important in prewar Europe.

There is an information booth (be sure to buy the inexpensive map of the site), a bookstore, and a cafeteria at the entrance to Yad Vashem. Photography is not permitted within the exhibition areas. Allow about two hours to see the Holocaust History Museum, more if you rent an audio guide. If your time is short, be sure to see the Children's Memorial and the Avenue of the Righteous in addition to the museum. To avoid the biggest crowds, come first thing in the morning or during lunch (noon to 2). The site is an easy 10-minute walk or a quick free shuttle from the Mt. Herzl intersection, which in turn is served by many city bus lines. The Egged sightseeing bus 99 takes you right into Yad

Vashem. ✉ *Hazikaron St., near Herzl Blvd., Mt. Herzl* ☎ *02/644–3565* 🌐 *www.yadvashem.org* 🎫 *Free* ⏲ *Sun.–Wed. 9–5, Thurs. 9–8 (late closing for History Museum only), Fri. and Jewish holiday eves 9–2. Last entrance 1 hr before closing.*

WORTH NOTING

Bloomfield Science Museum. For kids, this may be the city's best rainy-day option, but don't wait for a rainy day (and you don't have to be a kid) to enjoy the museum. Along with the expected range of intriguing, please-touch interactive equipment that demonstrates scientific principles in an engagingly fun environment (staff talk about average visits of two hours), there is lots of innovation and creativity—not least of all in the changing exhibits. Explanations are in English, and Hebrew University science students, as many as 20 at a time on busy weekends, are on hand to explain stuff. ✉ *Museum Blvd., Givat Ram* ☎ *02/654–4888* 🌐 *www.mada.org.il; Hebrew only* 🎫 *NIS 34* ⏲ *Mon.–Thurs. 10–6; Fri. and holiday eve 10–2; Sat. 10–3 (10–4 Apr.–Sept.). Last entrance 30 mins before closing.*

Church of St. John the Baptist. Apart from the grotto where John the Baptist is said to have been born, the church's old paintings and glazed tiles alone make it worth a visit. The orange tile roof of this large, late-17th-century Franciscan church is a landmark in Ein Kerem. Though not mentioned by name in the New Testament, the village has long been identified as the birthplace of John the Baptist, a tradition that apparently goes back to the Byzantine period (5th century AD). ✉ *Ein Kerem St., Ein Kerem* ☎ *02/632–3000* 🎫 *Free* ⏲ *Apr.–Sept., daily 8–noon and 2:30–6; Oct.–Mar., daily 8–noon and 2:30–5.*

Church of the Visitation. Built over what is thought to have been the home of John the Baptist's parents, Zechariah and Elizabeth, this church sits high up the hillside in Ein Kerem, with a wonderful view of the valley and the surrounding wooded hills. It is a short but stiff walk up from the spring at the center of the village. When Mary, pregnant with Jesus, came to visit her cousin, the aging Elizabeth, who was also with child, "the babe leaped in [Elizabeth's] womb" with joy at recognizing the unborn Jesus. Mary thereupon pronounced the paean to God known as the Magnificat ("My soul doth magnify the Lord" [Luke 1]). One wall of the church courtyard is covered with ceramic tiles quoting the Magnificat in 41 languages. The upper church is adorned with large wall paintings depicting the mantles with which Mary has been endowed—Mother of God, Refuge of Sinners, Dispenser of All Grace, Help of Christians—as well as the Immaculate Conception. Other frescoes depict Hebrew women of the Bible also known for their "hymns and canticles," as the Franciscan guide puts it. ✉ *Above Spring of the Virgin, Ein Kerem* ☎ *02/641–7291* 🎫 *Free* ⏲ *Apr.–Sept., daily 8–11:45 and 2:30–6; Oct.–Mar., daily 8–11:45 and 2:30–5. Gates closed Sat., ring bell.*

L. A. Mayer Museum for Islamic Art. The institution prides itself on being a private Jewish initiative (opened 1974) that showcases the considerable and diverse artistic achievements of Islamic culture worldwide. Its rich collections—ceramics, glass, carpets, fabrics, jewelry, metalwork, and painting—reflect a creativity that spanned half a hemisphere, from Spain to India, and from the 7th century to modern times. Unconnected to the main theme is a unique collection of rare (some priceless) antique European clocks and watches, the pride of the founder's family. ✉ *2 Hapalmach St., Hapalmach* ☎ *02/566–1291* 🌐 *www.islamicart.co.il/en* 🎫 *NIS 40* 🕘 *Sun., Mon., Wed. 10–3; Tues., Thurs. 10–7; Fri. and Jewish holiday eves 10–2; Sat. and Jewish holidays, 10–4.*

Mt. Herzl Military Cemetery. The tranquillity and well-tended greenery of Israel's largest military cemetery almost belie its somber purpose. Different sections are reserved for the casualties of each of the wars the nation has fought. The large number of headstones, all identical, is a sobering reminder of the price Israel has paid for its national independence and security. Note that officers and privates are buried alongside one another—lost lives are mourned equally, regardless of rank. ✉ *Herzl Blvd., Mt. Herzl* ☎ *02/643–7257* 🎫 *Free* 🕘 *Daily.*

CENTER CITY

West Jerusalem's Downtown and near-Downtown areas, just west of the Old City, are a mix of old neighborhoods, new limestone edifices, monuments, and markets. There are plenty of hotels and restaurants here, too. Few of the attractions appear on a Jerusalem don't-miss checklist, but you'll rub shoulders with the locals in the Machaneh Yehuda produce market, breathe the atmosphere of day-to-day life on Ben-Yehuda and Jaffa streets, get a feel for the city's more recent history in Nahalat Shiva and Yemin Moshe—in short, for a few brief hours be a bit less of a tourist.

GETTING HERE AND AROUND

Avoid driving into the center city, at least until the new light rail starts running and the dust on the attendant chaotic roadwork has settled. Walk if you can; otherwise use cabs or ride city buses: lines 18, 20, 21, and 23 from Mt. Herzl via the Central Bus Station (where other lines join the route); 4, 18, and 21 from the German Colony and Talbieh; 9 from the Knesset and the Israel Museum.

TIMING AND PRECAUTIONS

Jaffa Street, Ben-Yehuda Street, and Machaneh Yehuda are ghostly quiet from Friday afternoon until Saturday night because of the Jewish Sabbath. Morning through midday Friday is the most bustling, as Jerusalemites meet friends for coffee or lunch, and do their weekend shopping.

TOP ATTRACTIONS

Ben-Yehuda Street. Most of the street is an open-air pedestrian mall, in the heart of the Downtown, forming a triangle with King George Street and Jaffa Street. It is known locally as the **Midrachov,** a term concocted from two Hebrew words: *midracha* (sidewalk) and *rechov* (street). The street is named after the brilliant linguist Eliezer Ben-Yehuda, who in the late 19th century almost single-handedly revived Hebrew as a modern spoken language; he would have liked the clever new word. Cafés have tables out on the cobblestones; vendors display cheap, arty items like funky jewelry and prints; and buskers are usually out in good weather, playing tunes old and new. It's a great place to sip coffee or munch

Ben-Yehuda Street 8
Bet Ticho 7
Hinnom Valley ... 4
Independence Park 5
Machaneh Yehuda 9
Montefiore's Windmill 1
Nahalat Shiva ... 6
Yemin Moshe 3
YMCA 2

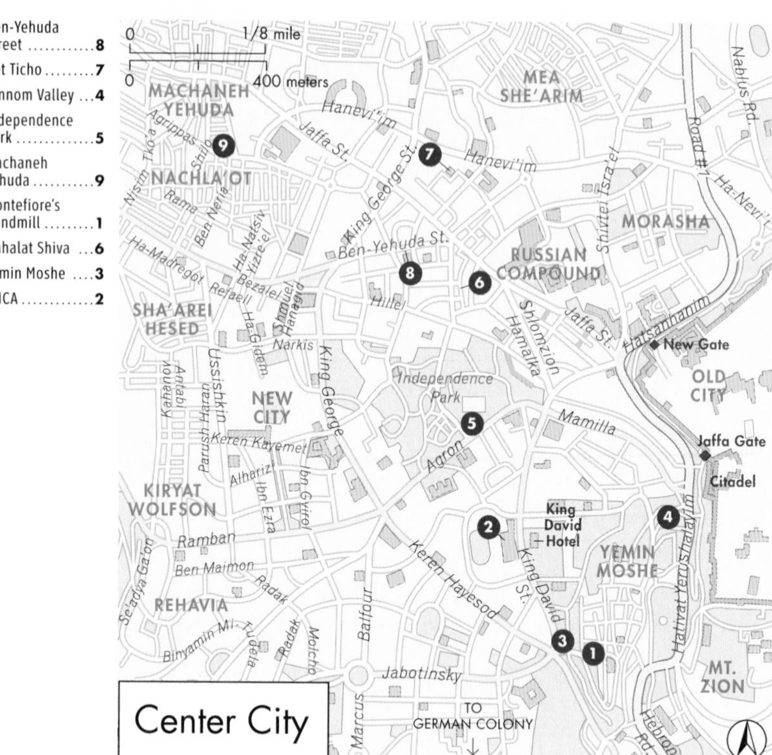

falafel and watch the passing crowd. ✉ *Downtown* ⊙ *A few restaurants but nothing else open Sat. and Jewish holidays.*

Fodor's Choice ★ **Machaneh Yehuda.** For a unique local experience, head to this block-long alley and a parallel wider street filled with the brilliant colors of the city's best-quality and lowest-priced fruit, vegetables, cheeses, confection stalls, falafel stands, fresh fish, and poultry. It's fun to elbow your way through this decidedly unslick market anytime, but it's riotously busy on Thursday and Friday in particular, when Jewish Jerusalem shops for the Sabbath, and the hawkers' cries get more passionate as closing time approaches. Look for the excellent coffee shop called Mizrachi/Hakol le'ofeh Ve'gam Kafeh (sign in Hebrew only), on Shazif Street, the third lane on the left as you enter from the Agrippas Street end. The market links Jaffa Street and Agrippas Street, parallel to and just a five-minute walk up from King George Street (as you go west). Many of the Downtown bus lines stop on Jaffa Street or King George, and a few on Agrippas itself while the light rail on Jaffa Street is under construction. There is paid parking close to the market. ✉ *Machaneh Yehuda* ⊙ *Sun.–Thurs. 8 am–sunset, Fri. and Jewish holiday eves 8 am–2 hrs before sunset.*

Montefiore's Windmill. Sir Moses Montefiore had this limestone windmill built in 1857 to provide a source of income for his planned

GERMAN COLONY

Israelis have discovered the old-world charms of "the Moshava" (the Colony), and so should you. This isn't the place to go for big sights; instead, take in the pleasant eateries, cafés, and stores proliferate in this neighborhood south of Downtown. It's a good place to relax along with the residents. Come during daytime Friday or on warm evenings (except Friday). Look for the (irregular) Friday food and flea market at the Adam School on the main drag (✉ *22 Emek Refai'm Street*).

German inscriptions on 19th-century stone houses along the same street recall the Templers (not medieval, spelled with an *e*), breakaway Lutherans who believed their presence in the Holy Land would hasten the Second Coming. Jerusalem's German Colony was one of half a dozen communities established in the 1860s and '70s under extremely trying conditions.

Feelings of German patriotism ran high in World War I, and many were interned as enemy aliens in 1918, in the wake of the British conquest of Palestine. Some of their pro-Nazi descendants were exiled during World War II.

2

neighborhood of Mishkenot Sha'ananim, but it was poorly located for harnessing the prevailing winds, and anyway soon newfangled steam-driven mills superseded it. The restored carriage in which Montefiore once traveled the country was on display until torched by vandals in the 1980s; the one you see now is an exact replica. He was a prominent figure in the financial circles of mid-19th-century London—a rare phenomenon for a Jew at the time. It didn't harm his fortunes that he married into the legendary Rothschild family, and became the stockbroker of its London branch. The larger-than-life philanthropist—he stood a remarkable 6 feet 3 inches, or 1.90 meters—devoted much of his long life, and his wealth, to aiding fellow Jews in distress, wherever they might be. To this end he visited Palestine, as this district of the Ottoman Empire was then known, seven times. ✉ *Yemin Moshe St., Yemin Moshe*.

★ **Nahalat Shiva.** This small Downtown neighborhood has a funky feel, with worn flagstones, wrought-iron banisters, and defunct water cisterns. Its name translates roughly as "the Estate of the Seven," so called by the seven Jewish families that founded the quarter, only the second to be established outside the Old City walls, in 1869. The parallel narrow arteries of Salomon and Rivlin streets stretch from Jaffa Street to Hillel Street. Their in-between alleys and courtyards have been refashioned as a pedestrian district, offering equal opportunities to the keen photographer, the eager shopper, and the gastronome. An eclectic variety of eateries, from Israeli to Italian, Asian to Arabic, tempt you to take a break from the jewelry and ceramics. ✉ *Nahalat Shiva* ⏲ *Many establishments closed Sat. and Jewish holidays*.

YMCA. The high-domed landmark bell tower thrusts out of the palatial white-limestone facade of the YMCA, offering superb, long-range views in all directions. For NIS 5 you can ride the small elevator to the balconies, 150 feet aboveground, and get an unsurpassed view over the roof of the famous King David Hotel toward the Old City and farther east. The complex often surprises visitors who associate the YMCA with modest buildings and sports facilities. The Jerusalem Y has those, too, as well as an auditorium with a Levantine-inspired dome and excellent acoustics, a hotel, and a bilingual Arabic-Hebrew preschool. A bit of trivia: the building, dedicated in 1933, was designed by Arthur Loomis Harmon, one of the architects of New York City's Empire State Building. ✉ *26 King David St., Downtown.* ☎ *02/569–2692* 🌐 *www.jerusalemymca.org* 🎫 *Free; elevator NIS 10* ⏲ *Tower: Sun.–Thurs. 8–8, Fri.–Sat. 8–5.*

WORTH NOTING

Bet Ticho *(Ticho House).* Set among pine trees, just a few steps off the busy Downtown streets, this handsome two-story historical building is part museum, part restaurant, and part concert venue. Dr. A. A. Ticho was a renowned Jewish ophthalmologist who immigrated to Jerusalem from Austria in 1912. His cousin, Anna Ticho, a trained nurse, followed the same year, to assist him in his pioneering struggle against the endemic scourge of trachoma. They were soon married, and in 1924 bought and renovated this fine 19th-century stone house. Anna's artistic talent gradually earned her a reputation as a brilliant chronicler—in charcoal, pen, and brush—of the landscape around Jerusalem. Bet Ticho displays a selection of her works, offers changing intimate art and photography exhibitions, and has a very good nonmeat restaurant. Chamber music concerts are held regularly on Friday mornings, in the upper gallery. ✉ *Ticho La., at 9 Harav Kook St., Downtown* ☎ *02/624–5068* 🌐 *www.imj.org.il* 🎫 *Free* ⏲ *Sun., Mon., Wed., and Thurs. 10–5, Tues. 10–10, Fri. and Jewish holiday eves 10–2 (upper gallery closed for concert Fri. 10:30–12:15 pm).*

OFF THE BEATEN PATH

Haas Promenade. Get your bearings in Jerusalem by taking in the panorama from the Haas Promenade, an attractive 1-km (2/3-mi) promenade (*tayelet* in Hebrew) along one of the city's highest ridges. Hidden behind a grove of trees to the east (your right as you pan the view) is a turreted limestone building, the residence of the British High Commissioner for Palestine in the 1930s and '40s. In Hebrew, the whole ridge is known as Armon Hanatziv, the Commissioner's Palace. The building became the headquarters of the U.N. Truce Supervision Organization (UNTSO), charged with monitoring the 1949 armistice line that divided the city. It remained a neutral enclave between Israeli West Jerusalem and Jordanian-controlled East Jerusalem until the reunification of the city in the Six Days' War of 1967. West Jerusalem is off to your left, its Downtown area easily distinguishable by the high-rises. The walls of the Old City and the golden Dome of the Rock are directly in front of you. To the right of it is the ridge of Mt. Scopus–Mt. of Olives, with its three towers (from left to right, Hebrew University, Augusta Victoria Hospital, and Russian Church of the Ascension), separated from the Old City by the deep Kidron Valley. South of the Old City walls (between your location and the black-domed al-Aqsa Mosque) is a blade-shaped strip of land, between the valley and a steep asphalt road. That was the original nucleus of ancient Jerusalem, established over 4,000 years ago, and captured by King David circa 1000 BC (whence came the biblical name "the City of David"). You can reach the promenade by car from Hebron Road—consult a map, and look for signs to East Talpiot and the Haas Promenade—by Bus 8, or of course by cab. If the traffic flows well, it's a 10-minute drive from Downtown, 5 minutes from the German Colony. ✉ *Daniel Yanovsky St., East Talpiot.*

Hinnom Valley. The Hinnom Valley achieved notoriety in the 7th century BC during the long reign of the Israelite king Menasseh (697–640 BC). He was an idolater, the Bible relates, who supported a cult of child sacrifice by fire in the Valley of the Son of Hinnom. Over time, the biblical Hebrew name of the valley—Gei Ben Hinnom, contracted to Gehennom or Gehenna—became a synonym for hell in both Hebrew and New Testament Greek.

In the late 1970s, Israeli archaeologist Gabriel Barkai discovered a series of Old Testament-period rock tombs at the bend in the valley, below the fortresslike St. Andrew's Scots Church. A miraculously unplundered pit yielded "grave goods" like miniature clay vessels and jewelry. The most spectacular finds, however, were two tiny rolled strips of silver designed to be worn around the neck as amulets. When unrolled, the fragile pieces revealed a slightly condensed version of the biblical priestly benediction, inscribed in the ancient Hebrew script. (The original, in Numbers 6, reads: "The Lord bless you and keep you; the Lord make his face to shine upon you and be gracious to you; the Lord lift up his countenance upon you and give you peace.") The 7th-century BC text is the oldest biblical passage ever found. The tombs are an open site, behind the Menachem Begin Heritage Center. Access is through the center, but only when it's open for business. ✉ *6 Nahon St. (below St. Andrew's Scots Church), Hinnom Valley* ☎ *02/565-2020* 💵 *Free* 🕒 *Sun., Mon., Wed., Thurs. 9–5; Tues. 9–7; Fri. and Jewish holiday eves 9–12:30).*

Independence Park. This is a great area for lounging around, throwing Frisbees, or eating a picnic lunch in warm weather. Some of the Muslim graves at the bottom of the park date from the 13th century. The large defunct reservoir nearby, known as the Mamilla Pool, is probably late medieval, though it may have much earlier Roman origins. ✉ *Between Agron and Hillel sts., Downtown* 🕒 *Daily.*

★ **Yemin Moshe.** This now-affluent neighborhood, with its attractive old stone buildings, bursts of greenery and bougainvillea, and well-kept cobblestone streets, grew up a century ago alongside the older Mishkenot Sha'ananim, and was named for that project's founder, Sir Moses (*Moshe* in Hebrew) Montefiore. In the 1950s and '60s, the area overlooked the jittery armistice line that gashed through the city, and was dangerously exposed to Jordanian sniper positions on the nearby Old City walls. Most families sought safer lodgings elsewhere, leaving only those who couldn't afford to move, and the neighborhood ran to seed. The reunification of Jerusalem under Israeli rule after the Six Days' War in 1967 changed all that. Developers bought up the area, renovated old buildings, and built new and spacious homes in a compatible style. Yemin Moshe is now a place to wander at random, offering joy to photographers and quiet nooks for meditation. A couple of restaurants are added bonuses. ✉ *Yemin Moshe.*

CLOSE UP

Me'a She'arim

The name of this neighborhood just north of Downtown is the biblical "hundredfold," describing the bountiful blessing God gave Isaac (Genesis 26). The appearance of that verse in the cyclical Torah reading the very week the neighborhood was founded, in 1874, was regarded as a good omen. This is 24/7 ultra-Orthodox Judaism. The community is insular and uncompromising—residents have no TVs; some reject the legitimacy of modern Israel; people speak Yiddish rather than the "sacred" Hebrew as the conversational language—and clings to an old-world lifestyle.

Modesty in dress and behavior is imperative for anyone entering the neighborhood. Visitors (best in tiny groups) must avoid male-female contact; women should wear long skirts, long sleeves, and nothing exposed below the neck. It's a voyeuristic experience, but avoid the Sabbath and photograph discreetly at other times if you choose to go.

Me'a She'arim is traversed by Me'a She'arim Street, and most of the historic neighborhood is on the slope above it (in the direction of Hanevi'im Street and the Downtown area). To the west it is more or less bounded by Strauss Street; to the east it almost touches Road No. 1.

WHERE TO EAT

Jerusalem is less chic and cosmopolitan than Tel Aviv—no question about it—but you can still eat very well in the holy city. Inexpensive eateries serving Middle Eastern standards, fast-food favorites, or sandwiches and salads remain popular; but travel abroad by Israelis has whetted the appetite of both cooks and customers for more interesting food. The excellence of local produce that is still, by and large, eaten seasonally, and the endurance of ethnic or family culinary traditions have been fertilized by imported new ideas and individual inspiration.

The result—common enough to sniff a trend in it—is a joyfully rich menu of palate pleasers. Some of the new restaurants clearly identify themselves by cuisine—French or Spanish, for example—while others defy easy labeling. Not quite Mediterranean, not quite European (though clearly influenced by both), they are, well, Israeli enough to deserve a new sobriquet: modern Israeli. How groundbreaking the trend is remains to be seen—categorizing cuisines is not an exact science—but there is no doubt that the new restaurants have markedly changed the culinary map of Jerusalem.

Some cuisine designations are self-explanatory, but other terms may be less so. A restaurant advertising itself as "dairy" will serve meals without meat; many such places do fish, in addition to pasta, soup, and salads. "Oriental" on a sign is usually a literal translation of *mizrachi*, suggesting Middle Eastern (in contrast to Western).

The term *kosher* does not imply a particular style of cooking, only that certain religious restrictions are adhered to in the selection and preparation of the food. In Jerusalem, where there are many kosher standards from which to choose, the selection can be dizzying. But unless specific kosher standards apply to your eating habits, don't worry. You can find plenty of fine steaks and some fish fillets. Remember that most kosher restaurants are closed for Friday dinner and Saturday lunch in observation of the Jewish Sabbath. A generous handful of kosher cafés, bars and restaurants remain open, and most nonkosher establishments remain open all weekend.

Dress codes are pretty much nonexistent in Jerusalem's restaurants (as in the rest of Israel). People tend to dress very casually—jeans are perfectly appropriate almost everywhere anytime. A modicum of neatness and modesty (trousers instead of jeans, a button-down shirt instead of a T-shirt) might be expected in the more exclusive establishments. If you brought the kids, you're in luck: nearly every Israeli restaurant is kid-friendly, and many have special menus and high chairs.

Use the coordinates at the end of each listing (⊕ 2A) to locate a site on the corresponding map.

WHAT IT COSTS IN ISRAELI SHEKELS

	¢	$	$$	$$$	$$$$
AT DINNER	under NIS 32	NIS 32–NIS 49	NIS 50–NIS 75	NIS 76–NIS 100	over NIS 100

Prices are for a main course at dinner.

CENTER CITY

The area extends from the Machaneh Yehuda market and Nachla'ot neighborhood, through the central Downtown triangle, to Nahalat Shiva and the junction with King David Street (which is a stone's throw from the Old City), a walk of 15 minutes from end to end. The range is vast, from funky budget or takeaway joints to upscale fine-dining specialists, from Middle Eastern food to European cuisine, and several surprises in between. Nonkosher restaurants do a roaring trade on Friday night, after the Sabbath begins, when their kosher counterparts are closed and the city streets quiet.

$$$
MODERN ISRAELI
Fodor's Choice ★

Angelica. The proprietor-chef trained in fine dining, and it shows; wonderfully fresh and perfectly cooked ingredients add the dimension of texture to an explosion of great flavors. The clean lines and aqua tints of Angelica's modern decor add an extra touch of class, as does the excellent service. Try not to fill up on the wonderfully crusty bread as you sample starters of homemade merguez sausage, beef fillet tartare, or foie gras tortellini. Main courses are carnivore heaven: superb lamb shoulder osso buco, tender top-quality steaks, and goose confit with apples and chestnuts. If that's not your style, choose one of the tempting fish or pasta dishes. An array of fruit tarts is the house dessert specialty. ✉ *7 Shatz St., Downtown* ☎ *02/623–0056* 🌐 *www.angelica.rest-e.co.il* *Reservations essential* 💳 *AE, MC, V* ⏲ *Closed Fri. No lunch Sat.* ⊕ *2A.*

$$ MIDDLE EASTERN ✕ **Barood.** Tenth-generation Jerusalemite Daniella Lerer fiercely preserves her family's Sephardic culinary traditions: casserole dishes; *pastilla* filled with beef, pine nuts, and grilled eggplant; *sufrito* (braised dumplings cooked with Jerusalem artichokes); and a beef and leek dish in lemon juice. For dessert, look for the traditional *sutlach,* a cold rice pudding topped with cinnamon, nuts, and jam. Barood's other face is its well-stocked bar serving more familiar fare like spareribs and sausages. Reservations are a must for dinner Friday night. ✉ *Feingold Courtyard, 31 Jaffa St., Downtown* ☎ *02/625–9081* ▭ *AE, MC, V* ⏲ *Closed Sun.* ✣ *2C.*

$$ AMERICAN ✕ **Black Burger & Bar.** This trendy chain establishment—black and crimson upholstery, a mirrored ceiling, and a warm glow illuminating the liquor bottles—serves hamburgers, but the resemblance to fast-food joints ends there. Apart from the wide selection of burgers including beef, lamb, chicken, and veggie, the menu lists entrées such as steak and schnitzel (panfried slices of turkey or chicken). Gluten-free options are available, as is a takeout option. The bar, with its good range of drinks, exudes youthful cool. ✉ *18 Shlomzion Hamalka St., Downtown* ☎ *02/624–6767* ▭ *AE, DC, MC, V* ⏲ *No dinner Fri. No lunch Sat.* ✣ *2C.*

$ FAST FOOD ✕ **Burgers Bar.** The menu bears a passing resemblance to that of the big hamburger chains, but the product is a different creature altogether. Hamburgers of different weight are more like cakes than patties, come with tasty sauces, and all are made to order. Lamb wraps and robust salads reflect Israeli tastes. Even those who generally oppose fast food have been happy here. The traditional sandwich averages NIS 30, the meal version closer to NIS 50. ✉ *12 Shammai St., Downtown* ☎ *02/622–1555* ▭ *MC, V* ⏲ *No dinner Fri. No lunch Sat.* ✣ *1B.*

¢ CAFÉ Fodor's Choice ★ ✕ **Café Mizrachi.** Established by Eli Mizrachi, who sold dried beans in a stall at Machaneh Yehuda, Café Mizrachi was created to add a more sophisticated flavor to the beloved market. Expanded to the size of three market stalls, Mizrachi is known for its excellent local fare, including laffa flatbread stuffed with feta, chopped tomatoes, and salty olives; french toast served with creamy goat cheese and fresh fruit; and the wondrously sinful ricotta and raisin brioche. The coffee is also excellent. This is a worthwhile stop on summer evenings, when Mizrachi stays open late to serve tapas, drinks, and sometimes jazz. ✉ *12 HaShezif St., Machaneh Yehuda* ☎ *02/624–2103* ▭ *AE, DC, MC, V* ✣ *3D.*

$$$$ FRENCH ✕ **Canela.** The parquet flooring, upholstered chairs, diaphanous drapes, and flower arrangements hint at class, not trendiness; the cream-colored baby grand confirms it. The restaurant sees itself as a pioneer in kosher fine dining (no contradiction anymore). That will hardly affect your meal, but your fellow diners may include religiously observant Jews celebrating a night out. Great starters include the sauteed mushrooms, the carpaccio of veal fillet, and the foie gras terrine. The deliberately restrained entrée menu offers a pasta dish and a couple of interesting

BEST BETS FOR JERUSALEM DINING

With hundreds of restaurants to choose from, how will you decide where to eat? Fodor's writers and editors have selected their favorite restaurants by price, cuisine, and experience in the lists below. In the first column, Fodor's Choice properties represent the "best of the best" across price categories. You can also search by area for excellent eats—just check out our complete reviews in the following pages.

Fodor's Choice★

Angelica, $$$, p. 119
Café Mizrachi, $, p. 120
Chakra, $$$, p. 126
Eucalyptus, $$, p. 127
HaChazer, $$$, p. 132
Ima, $$$, p. 128
Little Jerusalem, $$, p. 128
Mahneyuda, $$, p. 129
Mona, $$$, p. 129

By Price

¢

Abu Shukri, p. 133
Pinati, p. 130

$

Baba Israeli Kitchen, p. 132
Café Mizrachi, p. 120
Focaccia, p. 128
Spaghettim, p. 130
Te'enim, p. 136
Village Green, p. 131

$$

Eucalyptus, p. 127
Ima, p. 128
Little Jerusalem, p. 128
Paradiso, p. 134
Sakura, p. 130
T'mol Shilshom, p. 131

$$$

Angelica, p. 119
Chakra, p. 126
Dolphin Yam, p. 127
HaChazer, p. 132
Ima, p. 128
Mahneyuda, p. 129
Mona, p. 129

$$$$

Canela, p. 120
Darna, p. 126

By Cuisine

MEAT LOVERS

Angelica, $$$, p. 119
Black Burger & Bar, $$, p. 120
Burgers Bar, $, p. 120
El Gaucho, $$$, p. 127
HaChazer, $$$, p. 132
Joy Grill, $$$, p. 133
Mahneyuda, $$, p. 129
Olive, $$$, p. 133

MIDDLE EASTERN

Baba Israeli Kitchen, $, p. 132
Ima, $$$, p. 128
Nafoura, $$, p. 134

MODERN ISRAELI

Angelica, $$$, p. 119
Chakra, $$$, p. 126
HaChazer, $$$, p. 132
Mona, $$$, p. 129
Scala, $$$$, p. 136

DAIRY AND FISH

Little Jerusalem, $$, p. 128
T'mol Shilshom, $$, p. 131

VEGETARIAN

Te'enim, $, p. 136
Village Green, $, p. 131

By Experience

CHILD-FRIENDLY

Baba Israeli Kitchen, $, p. 132
Burgers Bar, $, p. 120
Keshet, $, p. 134
Luciana, 133
Little Jerusalem, $$, p. 128
Spaghettim, $, p. 130

OUTSIDE DINING

Barood, $$, p. 120
Chakra, $$$, p. 126
Colony, $$, p. 132
Keshet, $, p. 134
Little Jerusalem, $$, p. 128
Nafoura, $, p. 134
Village Green, $, p. 131

LOCAL FAVORITES

Abu Shukri, ¢, p. 133
Caffit, $$, p. 132
Focaccia, $, p. 128
Ima, $$$, p. 128
Joy, $$$, p. 133
Pinati, ¢, p. 130

GREAT VIEWS

Chakra, $$$, p. 126
Lavan, $$, p. 136
Rooftop, $$, p. 130
Te'enim, $, p. 136

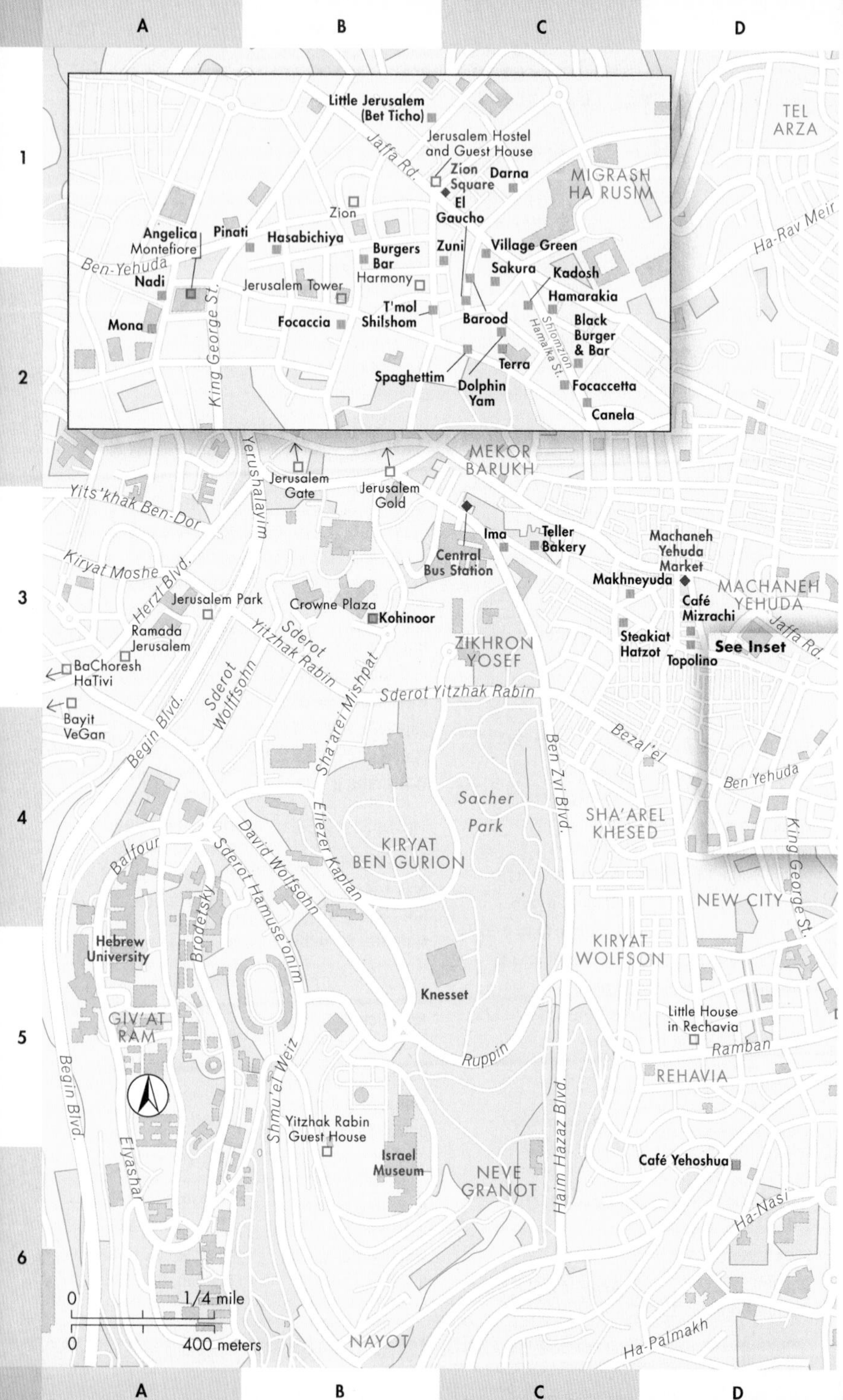
A
B
C
D
1
2
3
4
5
6
Little Jerusalem (Bet Ticho)
Jaffa Rd.
Jerusalem Hostel and Guest House
Zion Square
Darna
MIGRASH HA RUSIM
El Gaucho
Zion
Angelica
Montefiore
Pinati
Hasabichiya
Burgers Bar
Zuni
Village Green
Ben-Yehuda
Nadi
Harmony
Sakura
Kadosh
Jerusalem Tower
Hamarakia
T'mol Shilshom
Mona
Focaccia
Barood
Black Burger & Bar
Shlomzion Hamalka St.
King George St.
Terra
Spaghettim
Dolphin Yam
Focaccetta
Canela
TEL ARZA
Ha-Rav Meir
MEKOR BARUKH
Yerushalayim
Jerusalem Gate
Jerusalem Gold
Yits'khak Ben-Dor
Ima
Teller Bakery
Central Bus Station
Machaneh Yehuda Market
Kiryat Moshe
Herzl Blvd.
Makhneyuda
MACHANEH YEHUDA
Jerusalem Park
Crowne Plaza
Kohinoor
Café Mizrachi
Jaffa Rd.
Ramada Jerusalem
Sderot Yitzhak Rabin
ZIKHRON YOSEF
Steakiat Hatzot
Topolino
See Inset
BaChoresh HaTivi
Sderot Wolffsohn
Sderot Yitzhak Rabin
Bayit VeGan
Begin Blvd.
Sha'arei Mishpat
Bezal'el
Ben Zvi Blvd.
Ben Yehuda
Sacher Park
Eliezer Kaplan
SHA'AREI KHESED
King George St.
David Wolfsohn
Balfour
KIRYAT BEN GURION
Sderot Hamuse'onim
NEW CITY
Brodetsky
Hebrew University
KIRYAT WOLFSON
Knesset
Little House in Rechavia
GIV'AT RAM
Ramban
Ruppin
Begin Blvd.
REHAVIA
Shmu'el Weiz
Haim Hazaz Blvd.
Yitzhak Rabin Guest House
Elyashar
Israel Museum
Café Yehoshua
NEVE GRANOT
Ha-Nasi
0
1/4 mile
0
400 meters
NAYOT
Ha-Palmakh

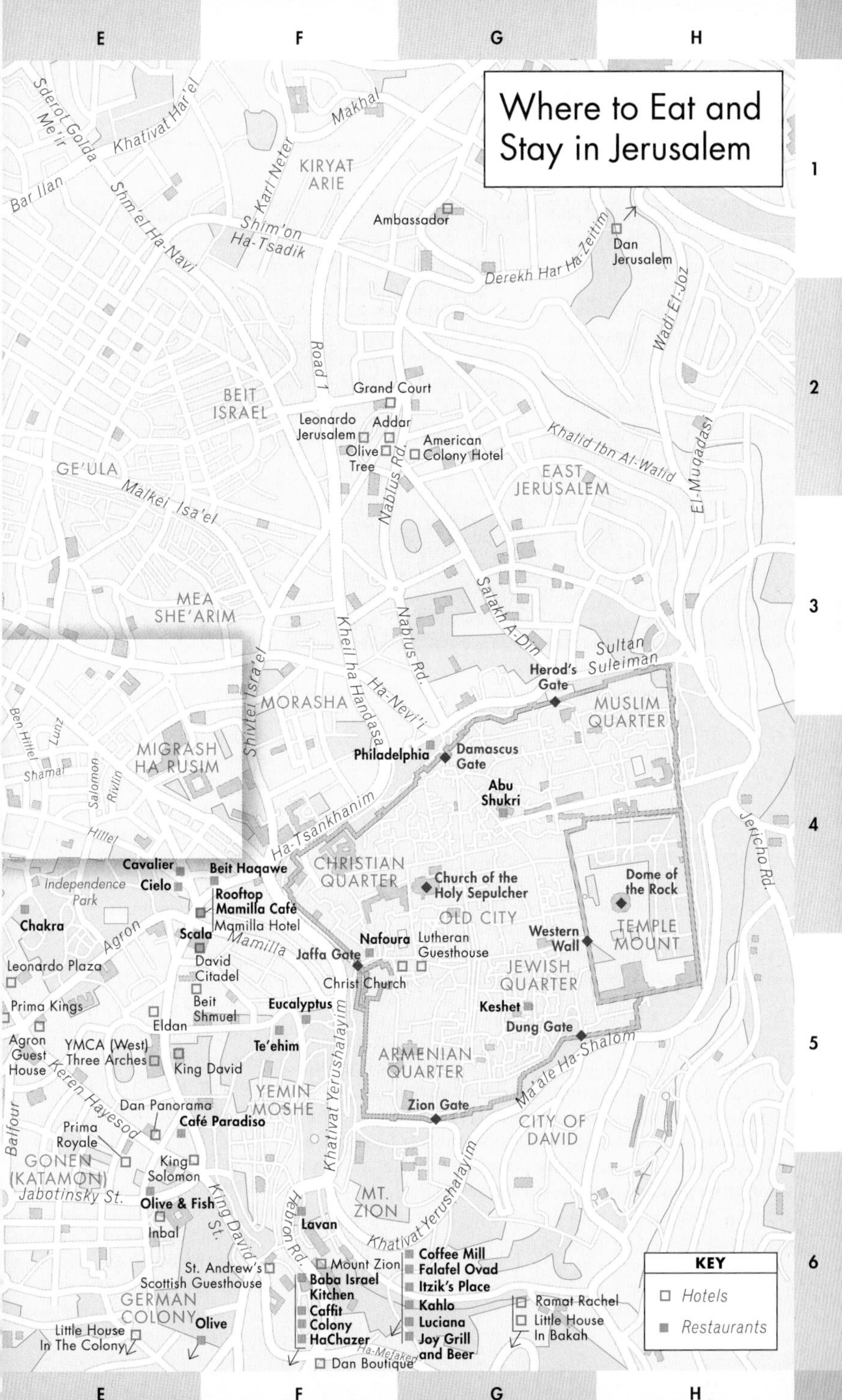
Where to Eat and Stay in Jerusalem
E
F
G
H
1
2
3
4
5
6
KIRYAT ARIE
Ambassador
Dan Jerusalem
Grand Court
Leonardo Jerusalem
Addar
Olive Tree
American Colony Hotel
BEIT ISRAEL
GE'ULA
EAST JERUSALEM
MEA SHE'ARIM
MORASHA
MIGRASH HA RUSIM
Herod's Gate
MUSLIM QUARTER
Philadelphia
Damascus Gate
Abu Shukri
CHRISTIAN QUARTER
Church of the Holy Sepulcher
Dome of the Rock
TEMPLE MOUNT
OLD CITY
Western Wall
Nafoura
Lutheran Guesthouse
Jaffa Gate
Christ Church
JEWISH QUARTER
Keshet
Dung Gate
ARMENIAN QUARTER
Zion Gate
CITY OF DAVID
MT. ZION
Cavalier
Cielo
Beit Haqawe
Independence Park
Rooftop Mamilla Café
Mamilla Hotel
Chakra
Scala
Leonardo Plaza
David Citadel
Beit Shmuel
Prima Kings
Eldan
Eucalyptus
Te'ehim
Agron Guest House
YMCA (West) Three Arches
King David
YEMIN MOSHE
Dan Panorama
Café Paradiso
Prima Royale
GONEN (KATAMON)
King Solomon
Olive & Fish
Inbal
Lavan
St. Andrew's Scottish Guesthouse
Mount Zion
Baba Israel Kitchen
Caffit Colony
HaChazer
Coffee Mill
Falafel Ovad
Itzik's Place
Kahlo
Luciana
Joy Grill and Beer
Ramat Rachel
Little House In Bakah
GERMAN COLONY
Olive
Little House In The Colony
Dan Boutique
KEY
Hotels
Restaurants
Sderot Golda Me'ir
Bar Ilan
Khativat Har'el
Makhal
Karl Neter
Shim'on Ha-Tsadik
Shm'el Ha-Navi
Derekh Har Ha-Zeitim
Wadi El-Joz
Road 1
Khalid Ibn Al-Walid
El-Muqadasi
Nablus Rd.
Malkei Isra'el
Salakh A-Din
Sultan Suleiman
Kheil ha Handasa
Ha-Nevi'i
Shivtei Isra'el
Ben Hillel
Lunz
Shamai
Salomon
Rivlin
Hillel
Ha-Tsankhanim
Jericho Rd.
Agron
Mamilla
Khativat Yerushalayim
Ma'ale Ha-Shalom
Keren Hayesod
Balfour
Jabotinsky St.
King David St.
Hebron Rd.
Ha-Mefaked

HOLIDAY FOODS IN ISRAEL

You know it's a holiday when special treats suddenly appear in bakeries, street stalls, supermarkets, and restaurants. Round doughnuts dabbed with jelly at Hanukkah, cheese blintzes bursting with raisins at Shavuot, or triangles of filled pastry at Purim: foods symbolize each holiday's historical event or theme.

On holidays, families and friends sit down to festive meals of favorite foods eaten in time-honored tradition. Tu b'Shevat, the winter New Year of Trees celebration, has everyone munching juicy dried fruit such as tart apricots, golden raisins, and sweet dates and figs, accompanied by nuts and pumpkin or sunflower seeds. On Independence Day in spring, people barbecue, and the scent of sizzling meat wafts throughout Israel.

Shabbat, the Jewish Sabbath, is observed each Friday night and Saturday. Pride of place goes to a golden-crusted, braided, soft *challah* bread; look for these in bakeries each week.

PASSOVER MATZOH

The journey from slavery in Egypt to freedom, remembered during the weeklong Passover holiday each spring, inspires the preparation of unleavened bread called matzoh. Why unleavened? The Hebrew people left Egypt in a hurry and had no time for bread to rise. Today it is rare to find bread or any foods made with leavening agents for sale during Passover, especially in Jerusalem. Matzoh is a flat, crisp—and bland on its own—square of crunchiness. Modern times have produced matzoh flavored with onion and made richer with eggs. Cooks get creative with fried matzoh and baked treats.

ROSH HASHANAH

During the New Year holiday each fall, *sweet* is the byword, indicating wishes for a sweet year: apple slices dipped in honey are nibbled, and ruby-red pomegranate seeds decorate salads and are eaten with the hope that good deeds performed in the coming year will be as plentiful as the seeds of this fruit. Plump dates hang in bunches at markets; Sephardic Jews end the holiday meal with them. Bakeries and restaurants feature dark honey cake enhanced with ginger and cinnamon.

HANUKKAH

As winter approaches, Hanukkah celebrates a 2nd-century BC victory over the Greeks; the story includes a miraculous amount of oil for the Temple menorah, or candelabrum. Foods fried in oil are the order of the day. Round, deep-fried jelly doughnuts called *sufganiyot*—browned to a crisp on the outside and pillowy soft inside—appear all over town. Fillings get more creative every year, from caramel or chocolate to lemon cream or halvah.

PURIM

This early spring holiday commemorates a victory in which food helped win the day, the 6th-century BC triumph over the evil Haman. On Purim, everyone eats triangular pastries called hamantaschen or, in Hebrew, *oznai Haman*—Haman's ears. The treats are

filled with jam, poppy seeds, dates, or chocolate. It's a tradition, known as *mishloach manot*, to exchange gifts of foods, and you'll see children on the streets carrying little baskets of goodies as well as the ubiquitous "ears."

SHAVUOT

The Feast of Weeks, a spring holiday, marks the giving of the Torah at Mt. Sinai. Explanations for the connection with eating dairy foods are many; one is that just as milk sustains the body, so the Torah provides spiritual nourishment for the soul. Look for rich, creamy cheesecakes with sour-cream toppings and cheese blintzes with raisins. Try cheeses from Israel's goat and sheep farms, from cottage cheese to sharp blue and chunky tom (a goat cheese).

RAMADAN

The holiest month of the Islamic year is Ramadan, when believers fast from sunrise to sunset every day. Special sweets are enjoyed at family meals in the evening and at the feast of Eid el-Fitr, at the end of Ramadan. A favorite delicacy is *attayif*, puffy little pancakes folded over a filling of cheese or nuts and doused in syrup. Look for these at bakeries or on outdoor griddles in the Old City of Jerusalem, Nazareth, Haifa, and Akko's Old City.

—by Judy Stacey Goldman

fish dishes, but more variety for meat eaters. The beef tongue in mushroom sauce is quite creative, as is the pullet steak with sweet chili, mango, and coconut cream. ✉ *8 Shlomzion Hamalka St., Downtown* ☎ *02/622–2293* 🌐 *www.canela.rest-e.co.il* ▭ *AE, DC, MC, V* ⏲ *Closed Fri. No lunch Sat.* ✣ *2C.*

$$$$ FRENCH

✕ **Cavalier.** Stone balconies overhung with wisteria, gently lit yellow and cream walls, wood beams, and alcoves filled with racks of wine offer a warm welcome. The predominantly French menu is modified by Mediterranean influences. Don't fill up on the great crusty whole-wheat bread; look for starters like goose liver crème brûlée made with truffles, apples, and caramel. There is a tempting range of fish and shrimp dishes, and several steak and veal options. A standout is the lamb sirloin served on couscous with pine nuts, a light curry, and sweet sauce. Top it off with a fruit tart or the red-fruit (mostly berries) *vacherin* (based on a meringue core). ✉ *1 Ben Sira St., Downtown* ☎ *02/624–2945* ✍ *Reservations essential* ▭ *AE, DC, MC, V* ✣ *4E.*

$$$ MODERN ISRAELI Fodor's Choice ★

✕ **Chakra.** Despite a central location and sophisticated ambience, Chakra still pretends to anonymity: the name of the restaurant is nowhere in sight. It draws a lively thirtysomething crowd of hip Jerusalemites that appreciate the tasty fare coming out of the open kitchen. The bistro-bar layout includes a large semicircular counter but plenty of table seating, some on comfy sofas. The patio, perfect for fine-weather dining, enjoys a park view. Daily specials enhance the expansive menu, and some good starters are beef or red-tuna carpaccio, grilled eggplant, or shrimp; ask for bread and baba ghanoush dip. Fish and beef dishes are excellent, the beef medallions in particular. The tasting menu is a tempting way to go. Share a dessert of ice cream in tahini and date honey sauce. Reservations are essential for dinner Thursday and Friday. ✉ *41 King George St., Downtown* ☎ *02/625–2733* 🌐 *www.chakra-rest.com* ▭ *AE, DC, MC, V* ✣ *4E.*

$$$ ITALIAN

✕ **Cielo.** Chef Adi Cohen maintains his family's tradition of good Italian fare. The soft lighting is easy on the eye, and the lack of decoration is not a shortcoming in the very intimate setting: large, tastefully framed wall mirrors add depth to the room. The service is professional and friendly. A starter menu includes great traditional dishes like ravioli (the stuffings change: look for seafood or truffles), and a superb lasagna and cannelloni combination. Especially interesting among the entrées—beef, chicken, and fish are also options—are the tender *piccatina con funghi* (thinly sliced veal with lemon and mushrooms), and the succulent veal Marsala. ✉ *18 Ben Sira St., Downtown* ☎ *02/625–1132* 🌐 *www.cielo.rest-e.co.il* ✍ *Reservations essential* ▭ *AE, DC, MC, V* ⏲ *No lunch Fri.* ✣ *4E.*

$$$$ MOROCCAN

✕ **Darna.** A vaulted tunnel sets you down in a corner of Morocco, complete with imported floor tiles and inlaid chairs. The high-end fixed-price menus (NIS 175 and NIS 240 per person, respectively) are a veritable banquet; ordering à la carte, though, offers more flexibility. The salads are quite different from the local Arab meze, but don't miss the *harira* soup of meat, chickpeas, and lentils, flavored with cumin, or the *pastilla fassia,* phyllo pastry stuffed with almonds, cinnamon, and Cornish hen (nonmeat versions are usually available). The *tagines,* or Moroccan stews, are excellent entrées, but the house specialty is the more expensive roast baby lamb shoulder with almonds, served on couscous. Finish with refreshing mint tea (served with fine ceremony) and the wonderful *toubkal* delight, sweet phyllo layers in cinnamon and (nondairy) almond milk. ✉ *3 Horkonos St., Downtown* ☎ *02/624–5406* 🌐 *www.darna.co.il* ▭ *AE, DC, MC, V* ⏲ *Closed Fri. No lunch Sat.* ✥ *1C.*

$$$ SEAFOOD ✕ **Dolphin Yam.** Known in translation as Sea Dolphin, this eatery serves some of the city's best seafood. The decor is pleasant enough—pale yellow stucco, recessed wine racks, stone-arched windows, a central wooden counter—but it's not a place for intimacy. Food is what draws the mixed clientele, including families. Start with a meze of refillable dishes; the green salad and the eggplant in tomato sauce are excellent. Try the shrimp in cream and mushroom sauce or the *musar baladi* (drum fish) with ginger and black olives. Beef, poultry, and pasta are other options. ✉ *9 Ben Shetach St., Downtown* ☎ *02/623–2272* ✍ *Reservations essential* ▭ *AE, DC, MC, V* ✥ *2C.*

$$$$ ARGENTINE ✕ **El Gaucho.** Red meat reigns at this Argentinian grill in the Downtown Nahalat Shiva neighborhood. The stone building with interior arches and a flagstone floor has wooden tables and ceiling beams. Nibble on great chicken wings while you wait for your steak: try the entrecôte or the chorizo (don't confuse this sirloin with the sausage of the same name, which is also available) with a parsley-based *chimichurri* sauce. A house specialty is the slow-cooked *asado*, a boneless rib. There are chicken options, a kids' menu, and salads, pastas, and a vegetarian platter. ✉ *22 Rivlin St., Nahalat Shiva* ☎ *02/624–2227* 🌐 *www.elgaucho.co.il* ▭ *AE, DC, MC, V* ⏲ *Closed Fri. No lunch Sat.* ✥ *2C.*

$$ MEDITERRANEAN Fodor's Choice ★ ✕ **Eucalyptus.** Soft-spoken owner-chef Moshe Basson, repeated winner of international couscous contests, has explored the kitchens and fields of older Jewish and Arab women to revive antique recipes and unfashionable ingredients. The result is a delicious and intriguing feast. Appetizers are all tasty, but try the figs stuffed with chicken breast in a tamarind sauce and the extraordinary stuffed mallow leaves (instead of conventional dolmades). Two exquisite mains are the sweet and sour beef on eggplant and the clay-baked lamb with okra, herbs, and tomato gravy. If you're in the mood, ask Moshe to share his culinary lore at your table. Finish with unusual desserts and herbal tea. Good company and one of the two "celebration" taster menus will make a memorable evening. ✉ *14 Hativat Jerusalem St., Hutzot Hayotzer* ☎ *02/624–4331* 🌐 *www.the-eucalyptus.com* ✍ *Reservations essential* ▭ *AE, DC, MC, V* ⏲ *No lunch Sat.* ✥ *5F*

$$ ITALIAN ✕ **Focaccetta.** This bar-restaurant is quiet at midday, but the clubby atmosphere comes alive in the evening. Focaccia, with an extraordinary variety of toppings to choose from, is the house specialty, and the earth oven seems to give it and the pizza options a special flavor. The Italian influence is felt as well in the seafood fettuccine with cream sauce, and other saltwater delectables. Mexican dishes—try the chicken fajita—are part of Focaccetta's eclecticism. Reservations are essential on weekends. ✉ *4 Shlomzion Hamalka, Downtown* ☎ *02/624–3222* ▭ *AE, DC, MC, V* ✥ *2C.*

$$ ITALIAN

Focaccia. The smallish interior in an old stone building is pleasant enough, but the spacious patio just off the street is much livelier. A popular haunt for twenty- and thirtysomethings (and also popular with families), this restaurant has the feel of a neighborhood brasserie. There are many toppings (don't miss the black olive spread), and some tasty starters (try the fried mushrooms stuffed with sheep's cheese). Chicken livers stir-fried with apples, shallots, and nuts are delicious. There are great sandwich options, like sirloin strips, and several salads and pasta dishes. It's worth making a reservation on weekends, when it is packed with regulars. ✉ *4 Rabbi Akiva St., Downtown* ☎ *02/625–6428* 🌐 *www.fucaccia-bar.rest-e.co.il* ▬ *AE, DC, MC, V* ✥ *2B.*

¢ ISRAELI

Hamarakia. Housed in a slightly dilapidated old building, this funky hangout draws young, impecunious students. The name means "soup pot," and a changing menu of hearty soups and stews, served with half loaves of crusty bread, butter, and pesto make it a satisfying alternative to the conventional three-course meal. *Shakshuka* (a tangy simmering dish of eggs, tomatoes, and onions) and a dessert pie complete the menu. There's a piano in the corner, a box of old records, and a chandelier made of spoons. Late-evening drinkers can hear jazz two nights a week, usually Mondays and Wednesdays. When the weather permits, you can sprawl on the couches and pillows arranged out back. ✉ *4 Koresh St., Downtown* ☎ *02/625–7797* ⏲ *No lunch. Closed Fri.* ✥ *2C.*

$$$ MIDDLE EASTERN Fodor's Choice ★

Ima. It's pronounced "*ee*-mah," means "mom," and is named for Miriam, the owner's Kurdish-Jewish mother, who still cooks some of the excellent traditional Middle Eastern food. In the Nachla'ot neighborhood, walking distance from Machaneh Yehuda, the restaurant has a more diverse clientele than the fast-food places up the street. The floor plan of the century-old stone house, with its arched doorways and niched windows (what locals call "very Jerusalemite"), create different-size dining areas that create a feeling of intimacy. First courses include a modest but quality meze of some half-dozen salads, such as hummus and baba ghanoush, as well as the wonderful *kibbeh* (seasoned ground meat deep fried in a jacket of bulgur wheat) and stuffed grape leaves. The selection of stuffed vegetables is an excellent choice if you're sharing. Try one of the tangy kibbeh soups, full of dumplings—it's almost a meal in itself. Entrées, like shashlik, chicken or a Jerusalem mixed grill, are often accompanied by *majadra* (rice and lentils). ✉ *189 Agrippas St., Nachla'ot* ☎ *02/624–6860* ▬ *AE, DC, MC, V* ⏲ *No dinner Fri. Closed Sat.* ✥ *3C.*

$$ ISRAELI Fodor's Choice ★

Little Jerusalem (Bet Ticho). This imposing old stone building, in a tranquil rustic setting, was once the home of artist Anna Ticho, whose evocative drawings of Jerusalem adorn its walls. House specialties include excellent salmon blintzes, quiches, onion soup served inside a crusty loaf of bread, and sea bream in fresh ginger sauce. The generous portions are often large enough to share, particularly the salads, and desserts are sinful. On Tuesday night, there is a wine-and-cheese buffet accompanied by jazz music. Friday morning you can hear a chamber-music concert in the upstairs gallery for a separate fee. Angle for a table on the patio in good weather. ✉ *9 Harav Kook St., Downtown* ☎ *02/624–4186*

2

FAST FOODS TO TRY

Falafel and hummus are ubiquitous in Jerusalem, as is the **sabich,** a pita stuffed with deep-fried eggplant and hard-boiled eggs. Tasty **shawarma** is grilled lamb or turkey, also served in pita bread. Try the stands in the Ben-Yehuda Street open-air mall, and near the Machaneh Yehuda produce market.

If you crave meat, **me'oorav yerushalmi** (Jerusalem-style mixed grill) is a specialty of the eateries on Agrippas Street, near the Machaneh Yehuda market. It's a deliciously seasoned meal of pitas stuffed with grilled chicken hearts and other organ meats.

The line is often long at **Falafel Ovad** (✉ *78 Bethlehem Rd., Baka* ☎ *No phone*), but it's worth the wait for Ovad's crisp falafel balls paired with fresh salads and tangy sauces. They are tasty stuffed in pitas or wrapped up in a flat laffa bread.

The sign is only in Hebrew at **Hasabichiya** (✉ *9 Shamai St., Downtown* ☎ *No phone*), a hole-in-the-wall stand featuring what many say is the best sabich in the city. Thin slices of fried eggplant are combined with a mix of salads and wrapped in a laffa or stuffed into a pita. The hours? Until the eggplant runs out.

www.go-out.com/ticho *Reservations essential* *AE, DC, MC, V* *No dinner Fri. No lunch Sat.* *1B.*

$$ ISRAELI Fodor's Choice ★ **Mahneyuda.** This hot spot is named for the way Israelis pronounce the name of Machaneh Yehuda. In the middle of its namesake market, this restaurant is considered one of the best in Jerusalem, possibly the country. With ample seating at the busy kitchen bar and at the rustic tables scattered throughout the two-level dining room, there's plenty of opportunity to watch the efficiently exuberant chefs slice, dice, and sauté your meal. The menu—composed of fresh, seasonal ingredients—changes daily, but nearly always includes *chamshuka*, a fusion of chopped meat and hummus; a dreamily creamy polenta topped with crisp asparagus, mushroom ragout, and shaved Parmesan; and a flavorful bouillabaisse. Reserve at least two weeks in advance. ✉ *10 Beit Yaakov St., Machaneh Yehuda* ☎ *02/533–3442* *Reservations essential* *AE, DC, MC, V* *No dinner Fri. No lunch Sat.* *3C.*

$ CAFÉ **Mamilla Café.** The Mamilla Hotel has added more than one option to the Jerusalem dining scene, and this café on Mamilla Avenue is the latest. With a dining room with long marble tabletops and a spacious outdoor patio, it's an appealing space. The tapas-style menu is geared toward sharing. The bulgur salad is delicious, as are the pumpkin and anchovy pizza and the ricotta ravioli with tomatoes and capers. The fruit tart is worth the calories. ✉ *Mamilla Hotel, Mamilla Ave., Mamilla* ☎ *02/548–2230* *www.mamillahotel.com/mamillacafe* *AE, DC, MC, V* *No dinner Fri. No lunch Sat.* *4E.*

$$$ MODERN ISRAELI Fodor's Choice ★ **Mona.** You cross the austere stone hall of the Artists' House to get here: but it's another world inside. The atmosphere envelops you at the door—flagstone floors, an open fire in winter, yesteryear artifacts, and a great bar. Start your exploration of modern Israeli fare with the sublime cream of root vegetable soup or the tasty carpaccio. Meat eaters

and piscatorians have plenty to choose from; vegetarians have a variety of large salads (perfect to share) and a couple of pasta dishes (try the ravioli). Wonderful mains are the richly flavored butcher's cut stew with chestnuts and red wine, and the well-blended spiciness of the calamari and shrimp in ginger, chili pepper, and sesame oil. The apple strudel and strawberry mascarpone is the house dessert of choice. ✉ *12 Shmuel Hanagid, Downtown* ☎ *02/622–2283* 🌐 *www.monas.co.il* ✍ *Reservations essential* ▭ *AE, DC, MC, V* ✥ *2A.*

¢ MIDDLE EASTERN ✕ **Pinati.** When aficionados of local standards like hummus, skewered shish kebab, schnitzel and bean soup argue hotly about the merits of *their* favorite eateries, Pinati comes up as a leading contender. In the very heart of the Downtown, this is the original location of Pinati, which means "corner" in Hebrew. It's now a chain, but this simple spot remains a convenient place to take the weight off your feet and rub shoulders with the locals. Not for long, though: your table will soon be in demand. ✉ *13 King George St., Downtown* ☎ *02/625–4540* 🌐 *www.pinati.rest-e.co.il* ✍ *Reservations not accepted* ▭ *No credit cards* ⏲ *No dinner Fri. Closed Sat.* ✥ *1B.*

$$$ MODERN ISRAELI ✕ **Rooftop.** The rooftop of the Mamilla Hotel lays claim to one of the best views of Jerusalem, and you can enjoy it from a cushioned chair as you dine on spiked iced tea and roast beef focaccia. The brasserie-style menu isn't perfect, so you might want to opt for a hamburger rather than spending your shekels on a beef fillet. But the atmosphere is lovely and the view is unbeatable, so reservations are a must. ✉ *11 King Solomon St., Mamilla* ☎ *02/548–2230* 🌐 *www.mamillahotel.com/rooftop* ✍ *Reservations essential* ▭ *AE, DC, MC, V* ✥ *2C.*

$$ JAPANESE ✕ **Sakura.** Many consider Jerusalem's veteran Japanese restaurant the best of its kind in the country, with its specially imported ingredients and high standard of food and presentation. The sushi/sashimi combination is a must for fish enthusiasts, as is the salmon teriyaki and jumbo shrimp tempura. Vegetarian options are also available. Cleverly renovated, the old structure preserves and illuminates its honey limestone through a glass facade by day and soft lighting by night. An intimate loftlike upstairs room, a sushi bar, and a few tables in the entrance courtyard give a range of options. ✉ *Finegold Courtyard, 31 Jaffa St., Downtown* ☎ *02/623–5464* ✍ *Reservations essential* ▭ *AE, DC, MC, V* ✥ *2C.*

$ ITALIAN ✕ **Spaghettim.** Although pizza and other pasta dishes are available, spaghetti is the thing here—the name weds the Italian term to a Hebrew plural form—with more than 40 sauces using olive oil, tomato, cream, and butter. Look for traditional combinations as well as variations like the carbonara, a tempting mixture of smoked meat, sausage, white wine, butter, nutmeg, ground pepper, and cream. Among the reasonably priced meat and fish options, try the salmon grilled in a brick oven with garlic confit and sun-dried tomatoes. Whole-wheat pasta and tofu substitutes are available, as are simple pastas for kids. The high ceiling and sleek metallic lines are trendy elements; the clientele here is a mix of families and young patrons. ✉ *35 Hillel St., Downtown* ☎ *02/623–5547* 🌐 *www.spaghettim.co.il* ▭ *AE, DC, MC, V* ✥ *2C.*

$$ MIDDLE EASTERN FAST FOOD **Steakiat Hatzot.** Agrippas Street, down the block from the Machaneh Yehuda produce market, has some of Jerusalem's best-known blue-collar *mizrahi* (Middle Eastern) diners. Loyalists claim that Steakiat Hatzot, which means "midnight grill," actually pioneered the *me'oorav yerushalmi*—Jerusalem mixed grill—a substantial and delicious meal-in-a-pita of cumin-flavored bits of chicken hearts and other organ meats. For a late-night snack, there's no equal to a sandwich eaten on the sidewalk in front of the streetside grill. Make sure of prices before you order to avoid unasked-for side dishes. ✉ *123 Agrippas St., Machaneh Yehuda* ☎ *02/624–4014* *Reservations not accepted* ▭ *No credit cards* ⌚ *Closed Fri. and Sat.* ✢ *3C.*

$$ ISRAELI **T'mol Shilshom.** The name—a Hebrew literary phrase that translates roughly as "yesteryear"—is a clue to the character of the place. This funky restaurant and bookstore occupies two separate rooms on the upper floor of a mid-19th-century house. Hosting Hebrew (and occasionally English) poetry readings and modest book launches, it's long been a popular spot with intellectuals and folks who just enjoy lingering over a novel. No meat is served, but choose from a tempting selection of salads, pasta, and fish dishes such as salmon fillet in white wine and fig sauce. Desserts have taken a serious turn for the better, and the array of hot drinks is always welcome on a cold, rainy day. ✉ *5 Yoel Salomon St., Nahalat Shiva* ☎ *02/623–2758* 🌐 *www.tmol-shilshom.co.il* ▭ *AE, DC, MC, V* ⌚ *No dinner Fri. No lunch Sat.* ✢ *2B.*

$ ITALIAN **Topolino.** Israelis love anything Italian, so it's not surprising that on Agrippas Street you'll find this cozy trattoria offering a well-honed selection of traditional fare. Try the smattering of seats outside for a quick espresso or plate of homemade pasta after buying your fruits and vegetables in the nearby Machaneh Yehuda market. In the evening, be prepared to wait for one of the closely grouped tables inside, where house specialties include figs baked in goat cheese, sardine bruschetta, or creamy chestnut gnocchi, all made with fresh ingredients from the market stalls. ✉ *62 Agrippas St., Machaneh Yehuda* ☎ *02/622–3466* ▭ *AE, DC, MC, V* ✢ *3D.*

$ VEGETARIAN **Village Green.** Near Zion Square, this airy vegetarian restaurant prides itself on the quality of its offerings. There are a good variety of soups, quiches, and salads. Many ingredients are organic, and this is a great choice for vegans as well. Salads and the hot buffet are self-service (charged by weight); every meal comes with a choice of homemade rolls. For a coffee-time option, take a fine latte and a slice of home-baked cake or pie (gluten-free and sugar-free options available) out to a table on the shaded sidewalk. ✉ *33 Jaffa St., Downtown* ☎ *02/625–3065* 🌐 *www.2eat.co.il/eng/village* ▭ *AE, DC, MC, V* ⌚ *No dinner Fri. Closed Sat.* ✢ *1C.*

$$$ AMERICAN **Zuni.** In this elegantly clubby version of the 24-hour diner, you can enjoy cappucino and croissants in the morning (or opt for the classic Israeli breakfast of eggs, cheeses, and fresh vegetables), a BLT for lunch, or grilled lamb with a beet and pomegranate sauce for dinner. Bring your laptop and take advantage of the free Wi-Fi over a cup of coffee. The vibe is more of a gentleman's (or lady's) club than café. ✉ *15 Yoel Salomon St., Nahalat Shiva* ☎ *02/625–7776* ▭ *AE, DC, MC, V* ✢ *1C.*

GERMAN COLONY AND BAKA

South of Downtown, the German Colony is a hot spot for eateries, cafés, and little shops. It's a fun spot to pass a morning, afternoon, or evening. Cross the nearby railway tracks (being converted into a bike path) to reach the neighborhood of Baka. With its own set of quirky cafés, it's worth the 10-minute walk.

$ MIDDLE EASTERN ✕ **Baba Israeli Kitchen.** This popular *chummousiya*, as restaurants serving hummus-based dishes are called, is a worthwhile stop for a quick lunch or dinner. Try the hallmark dish with minced lamb, grilled tomato, and roasted pine nuts; with marinated slices of boneless chicken thighs; or with spicey merguez sausage. If you're not in the mood for hummus, there's also grilled chicken and finely chopped salad served on a grilled half pita. ✉ *31 Emek Refaim St., German Colony* ☎ *02/671–9922* ▭ *AE, DC, MC, V* ⊗ *No dinner Fri. Closed Sat.* ✣ *1C.*

$$ CAFÉ ✕ **Caffit.** This German Colony institution is known as much for its famed Oreganatto salad (made with sweet potatoes) as for the sweet potato pancakes and salmon burgers. One of the few local cafés serving a Friday morning breakfast buffet—although you may want to order the usual eggs, cheeses and salad—it's a warm, welcoming place with a personable staff. It's the favorite spot for locals, both for the excellent coffee and the full meals. The newer branch at the Botanical Gardens has the same menu, but a different view: lily pads, birds, and flowers rather than Emek Refa'im pedestrians. ✉ *31 Emek Refa'im St., German Colony* ☎ *02/671–9922* ✉ *1 Burla St., Nayot* ☎ *02/648–0003* ▭ *AE, DC, MC, V* ⊗ *No dinner Fri. Closed Sat.* ✣ *1C.*

$$$ ECLECTIC ✕ **Colony.** Once used by the British Railroad Company, this hanger has been transformed into a spacious restaurant with dining areas and party rooms both inside and on the balcony. There's a lengthy bar with comfortable couches and chairs for those seeking more of a salon vibe. A hangout for foreign journalists, diplomatic corps, and in-the-know locals, Colony offers a familiar but tasty menu of steaks, pastas, and salads, including a highly recommended roasted eggplant and marinated chicken. The extensive drink menu is worth a gander, especially the sabra cactus cocktail. Be sure to order dessert, which usually includes a divine strawberry cassata and flavorful tahini ice cream. ✉ *7 Bethlehem Rd., Baka* ☎ *02/671–9922* 🌐 *www.2eat.co.il/colony* ▭ *AE, DC, MC, V* ✣ *1C.*

$$$$ MODERN ISRAELI Fodor's Choice ★ ✕ **HaChazer.** In a former train station in Baka, this spacious eatery's dark-wood tables and white cloth napkins might be unremarkable, but the food more than makes up for it. Known for such specialties as sweetbreads, HaChazer takes meat eating seriously, adding Mediterranean, South American, and Asian touches to the menu. There's a fine selection of house stews, including an oxtail tagine and veal asado, and a selection of juicy steaks. Don't pass up the worthwhile pasta dishes, including the feathery tortellini in a sauce of Jerusalem artichokes. Starters include a divine salad of some seven different types of tomato, or sweetbreads with borlotti beans and smoked goose breast. The desserts are eminently worthwhile, particularly the *kadaif* pastry with sabra cactus and figs in a red wine sauce served with coconut sorbet.

✉ 7 Bethlehem Rd., Baka ☎ 02/671–9922 🌐 www.2eat.co.il/engl/hachazer ▭ AE, DC, MC, V ⏲ No dinner Fri. Closed Sat. ✣ 1C.

$$$ ECLECTIC ✕ **Joy Grill and Beer.** In the heart of busy Emek Refa'im, the main drag of the German Colony, this is an easy spot for a family meal, quiet time for two, or a get-together with a large group. The menu emphasizes meat dishes, so be sure to try the tangy chicken wings, beef carpaccio with garlic fries, or savory sweet potato fries before digging into one of the excellent hamburgers or lamb kebabs. For the diet-conscious diner, there's the classic Joy salad with chicken slices and grilled chicken liver. There's a solid bar, including some excellent beers on tap. *✉ 24 Emek Refa'im St., German Colony ☎ 02/625–3065 🌐 www.joy.rest-e.co.il ▭ AE, DC, MC, V ⏲ No dinner Fri. Closed Sat. ✣ 1C.*

$$$ ITALIAN ✕ **Luciana.** With the same owners as the neighboring Joy Grill, this fairly new addition to the busy Emek Refa'im restaurant scene has a spacious deck with a good view of the sidewalk. Late at night you'll spot locals here sipping glasses of wine and nibbling at eggplant rolls. In the dining room, the glass walls offer ample light and a feeling of spaciousness. With a meatless Italian menu, Luciana offers flavorful pastas, including beetroot tortellini. Luciana is also a good choice if you have kids in tow, as it offers plenty of pizzas and simple pasta dishes. *✉ 27 Emek Refa'im St., German Colony ☎ 02/563–0111 🌐 www.luciana.rest-e.co.il ▭ AE, DC, MC, V ⏲ No dinner Fri. Closed Sat. ✣ 1C.*

$$$ STEAK ✕ **Olive.** A German Colony landmark, Olive attracts a more mature crowd that seems to prefer the glass-enclosed, bilevel front yard to the Templar-period dining room and its arched windows and stronger acoustics. At this happy hunting ground for carnivores, beef and lamb kebabs are superb, as are the chicken livers. Vegetarians can keep starvation at bay with a hearty soup (try the tomato-based lentil, if available) or salad. Save room for a dessert pie or the delicious passion fruit sorbet. A full taster's menu is available by prior arrangement. *✉ 36 Emek Refa'im St., German Colony ☎ 02/561–1102 ✍ Reservations essential ▭ AE, DC, MC, V ⏲ No dinner Fri. No lunch Sat. ✣ 6F.*

OLD CITY

The walled Old City pretty much shuts down at night, so most watering holes cater to the lunch customer. There are several falafel-and-shawarma places and Middle Eastern eateries in the Muristan area of the Christian Quarter, very few in the Muslim Quarter, and a more numerous and broader range of stands and restaurants (falafel, pizza, sandwiches, burgers, and some fuller-menu options) in and near the Jewish Quarter's Hurva Square, and on the route to the Western Wall.

¢ MIDDLE EASTERN ✕ **Abu Shukri.** In the heart of the Old City, at Station V on the Via Dolorosa, this place has an extraordinary and well-deserved reputation for the best hummus in town. Don't expect much in the way of decor. This is a neighborhood eatery, and a look at the clientele—Palestinian Arabs and Jewish Israeli insiders—confirms that you have gone local. Enjoy the excellent fresh falafel balls, baba ghanoush, tahini, and *labaneh* (a slightly sour cheese served with olive oil and *za'atar* [spice mixture]); no meat is served. Eat family style, and don't over-order: you can get additional portions on the spot. ✉ *63 El-Wad Rd. (Hagai St.), Muslim Quarter* ☎ *02/627–1538* *Reservations not accepted* ▬ *No credit cards* ⊙ *No dinner* ✣ *4G.*

$ CAFÉ ✕ **Keshet.** With wooden tables in the cool dining room and under the trees in the nearby square, this daytime-only eatery is a very good lunch option. It's also a place to take the weight off your feet and sip a beer, or grab a latte and a crêpe. The menu offers a modest variety of soups, pasta, lasagna, quiches, latkes, and salads—try the deliciously fresh (and virtuously healthy) earth salad. ✉ *2 Tiferet Israel St., Jewish Quarter* ☎ *02/628–7515* ⊕ *www.keshethahurva.com* ▬ *MC, V* ⊙ *Closed Sat. No dinner* ✣ *5G.*

$$ MIDDLE EASTERN ✕ **Nafoura.** Just inside the Jaffa Gate (up the first street on the left), Nafoura offers a tranquil courtyard for alfresco lunchtime dining. Your table might lean against the Old City's 16th-century wall. The pleasant if unremarkable interior is a comfortable refuge in inclement weather. Start with the traditional meze, an array of salads: the smaller version is enough for two people. Insist on the excellent local dishes only (hummus, eggplant dip, tahini, carrots, and so on) and skip the mushrooms and corn. Ask for the *kibbeh,* delicacies of cracked wheat and ground beef, or the *lahmajun,* the meat-topped "Armenian pizza." From the typical selection of entrées, try the lamb cutlets or the sea bream. The NIS 50 buffet (chicken, kebab, side dishes, and fruit) is an excellent value. ✉ *18 Latin Patriarch Rd., Christian Quarter* ☎ *02/626–0034* ▬ *AE, DC, MC, V* ⊙ *No dinner* ✣ *5F.*

$$ MIDDLE EASTERN ✕ **Philadelphia.** Just outside the Old City's Damascus Gate sits the curiously named Philadelphia, where the traditional fare includes local favorites such as lamb or chicken on a bed of rice, St. Peter's fish or red snapper, and stuffed vegetables. Having been around for more than a quarter century, the place knows how to make you feel very comfortable in the Ottoman-style domed dining rooms. ✉ *9 El Azhara St., Damascus Gate* ☎ *02/628–9770* ▬ *AE, DC, MC, V* ✣ *5F.*

REHAVIA, TALBIEH, KING DAVID STREET, AND YEMIN MOSHE

These upscale, classic Jerusalem neighborhoods, some of them an easy walk south from Downtown, are home to a good number of the city's hotels, and most of the top ones. While that fact explains the presence of at least some of the restaurants, don't write them off as tourist traps: some have a very good local reputation. Pay particular attention to Aza Street, Rehavia's main drag, where a number of solid restaurants and cafés are patronized all day and evening by locals of all ages.

$$ MEDITERRANEAN ✕ **Café Paradiso.** You may be suspicious of its strategic location near the major hotels, but the food is excellent and much of the clientele local. Although the white stucco and dark-wood touches are pleasant, the decor is not the big attraction. The menu tempts with unusually flavored appetizers (dolmades and stuffed vegetables; a seasonal salad of fresh figs, blue cheese, and greens), grilled steaks and imaginative meat combinations and tasty pasta dishes. Mullet baked with rosemary, olive oil, and white wine is recommended, but ask about other seafood dishes

JERUSALEM'S CAFÉS

Sitting down for coffee and cake in one of Jerusalem's fine cafés is something of a tradition. Yeast cakes and strudels recall the past, but today's palate craves flaky brioches and savory tarts. Italian coffee machines have driven a rise in quality and a demand for the perfect *hafuch*, the strong Israeli version of a cappuccino.

Two Jerusalem coffee chains have proven so popular that they have expanded across the country. Aroma has excellent coffee and fresh sandwiches and salads made on the premises. Hillel is a favorite with locals for breakfast, with its good food and good prices. You'll find branches in most neighborhoods.

In Jerusalem, the open-air mall of Ben-Yehuda Street has several venerable hangouts, but the newer cafés along the bars and restaurants of Shlomzion Hamalka Street offer more sophisticated menus—and better coffee. The Mamilla strip mall, outside Jaffa Gate, is known for its coffee places, but don't overlook Emek Refa'im Street in the German Colony or Bethlehem Road in Baka.

Most popular watering holes serve decent light, affordable meals for lunch and dinner as well, and courtyard seating gets full in fine weather and on summer evenings. Coffee and a pastry are about NIS 30 to NIS 40; sandwiches, salads, quiche, and pasta will cost NIS 16 to NIS 46. If you're not a coffee drinker, consider trying a *gazoz*, a fizzy drink mixed with fruit-flavored syrups.

Beit Haqawe (✉ *3 Yanai St., Downtown* ☎ *02/566–1665*), billed as a boutique café, is just down the block from the Mamilla Hotel. Owner Hili Klatchko offers extremely tasty cakes, salads and coffee, as well as drinks for the after-work crowd.

Coffee Mill (✉ *23 Emek Refa'im St., German Colony* ☎ *02/566–1665*) is a must for coffee devotees, with its dizzying selection of blends. You can opt for a light meal, too.

Itzik's Place (✉ *33 Bethlehem Rd., Baka* ☎ *02/561–2054*), in the middle of the Bethlehem Road shopping district, is a tiny shop known for its coffee, sandwiches, and salads.

Kadosh (✉ *6 Shlomzion Hamalka St., Downtown* ☎ *02/625–4210*) is one place locals are reluctant to share, lest it lose its "Jerusalemite" character. Home-baked goods, generous breakfasts, and '30s-style decor are part of the draw. The place is always packed.

Kahlo (✉ *31 Bethlehem Rd., Baka* ☎ *02/673-6365*) is popular with locals and tourists alike for its shabby chic decor. Generous sandwiches named for the nearby streets are great with icy cold *limonana* (lemonade with crushed mint).

Modus (✉ *31 King George St., Downtown* ☎ *02/624–4215*) has a loyal following for the homemade sandwiches, apple strudel, and bourekas.

Nadi (✉ *10 Shatz St., Downtown* ☎ *02/624–4215*) is popular with older folks in the morning, business types at lunch and hipsters in the evening. The solid menu focuses on artisanal Israeli cheeses and fabulous sourdough bread.

Teller Bakery (✉ *74 Agrippas St., Machaneh Yehuda* ☎ *02/622-3227*) has decent coffee and pastries, but don't miss the sourdough breads.

on the constantly changing menu. There are child-friendly options, too. For fine-weather dining, there is a small deck over the sidewalk. Reservations are essential Friday night but are not accepted otherwise. ✉ *36 Keren Hayesod St., Talbieh* ☎ *02/563–4805* ▭ *AE, DC, MC, V* ✥ *5E.*

$$ AMERICAN ✕ **Café Yehoshua.** One of the restaurants that locals flock to for breakfast, lunch, or dinner, Café Yehoshua offers an Israeli take on American diner meals. The menu includes everything from french toast to Philly steaks to shrimp cocktail. Grab a seat in one of the booths and linger over comfort food, particularly the Roquefort schnitzel. Evening is a great time to stop by for a drink and a bite-sized burger. ✉ *17 Aza St., Rehavia* ☎ *02/563–2898* 🌐 *www.yehoshua.rest-e.co.il* ▭ *AE, DC, MC, V* ✥ *6D.*

$$ CAFÉ ✕ **Lavan.** At the renovated in-house eatery of the popular Cinematheque, coffee and other beverages satisfy film buffs. The superb view of Old City walls from the glassed-in patio makes this a destination for locals as well as tourists. (The fact that it's open Saturday is another plus.) The fare is light: fresh fish of the day, pizza, and salads. The chef's more inventive dishes have mixed success, but one winner is gnocchi with chestnuts and sautéed onions. Do try the unusual ice cream made with tahini and halva. ✉ *11 Hebron Rd., Yemin Moshe* ☎ *02/673–7393* ▭ *AE, MC, V* ✥ *6F.*

$$$$ MEDITERRANEAN ✕ **Olive & Fish.** Its location near major hotels is part of its appeal, but Olive & Fish pleases locals on its own merits. With no trendy pretensions, the restaurant draws an older crowd. The glass-enclosed front porch is popular; the interior, with pale yellow walls, framed prints, and unintrusive lighting, is warm and inviting. For starters, try the tasty grilled eggplant with tahini or the excellent sirloin salad. Great fish options include sea bass or St. Peter's fish with artichokes, sun-dried tomatoes, white wine, and lemon. Other temptations are delectable lamb and beef kebabs, or tender *pargiyot* (spring chicken chunks) in a date-honey sauce. Save room for one of the pies or chocolate creations. ✉ *2 Jabotinsky St., Talbieh* ☎ *02/566–5020* ⚠ *Reservations essential* 🌐 *www.2eat.co.il/eng/oliveandfish* ▭ *AE, DC, MC, V* ⏲ *Closed Fri. No lunch Sat.* ✥ *6E.*

$$$$ MODERN ISRAELI ✕ **Scala.** Instead of a selection of appetizers followed by a full main-course menu, Scala has created intriguing dishes in middle-size portions. For two people, the way to go is to choose three or four and share. Creations are not equally successful, but worth trying are the confit of tomatoes, seared artichoke and okra; stuffed vegetables with lamb and pine nuts; and the duck leg confit and lamb chops with garlic and rosemary. The bar menu is also worth a look. The chocolate desserts are delicious (but skip the nondairy ice cream). The service at this kosher hotel restaurant is informed and attentive. Dark wood, thoughtful lighting, and jazzy background music enhance the sophisticated atmosphere. ✉ *David Citadel Hotel, 7 King David St., King David St.* ☎ *02/621–1111* 🌐 *www.scala-rest.com* ⚠ *Reservations essential* ▭ *AE, DC, MC, V* ⏲ *No lunch. Closed Fri. and Sat.* ✥ *5E.*

$ VEGETARIAN ✕ **Te'enim.** In the classic limestone Confederation House—with stone arches, flagstones, and tantalizing views (from the couple of window tables) of the Old City walls—Te'enim finds a delicate balance between traditional and innovative in its vegetarian fare. Great choices include the spinach salad with ricotta or the endive salad with grilled goat cheese and roasted almonds. Standard main dishes include a mushroom, polenta, olive, garlic, and red wine bake; and the successful *Maharajah majadra,* with bulgur, onion, ginger chutney, and yogurt. Daily specials at Te'enim ("figs" in Hebrew) include such unusual offerings as Mexican chili. The homemade sorbets and unusually flavored ice creams are excellent, but try the surprising mini eggplant in date honey and almonds. ✉ *12 Emile Botta St., Yemin Moshe* ☎ *02/625–1967* 🌐 *www.teenim.rest-e.co.il* 💳 *AE, DC, MC, V* ⏲ *No dinner Fri. Closed Sat.* ✥ *5F.*

2

WEST JERUSALEM

The "cultural mile" in West Jerusalem is not known for fine dining—lunch-time cafeterias is the best you can hope for—but one superb Indian restaurant is a shining exception.

$$ INDIAN ✕ **Kohinoor.** Moghul-influenced decor immediately sets a tone of quiet, informal elegance at this hotel restaurant. Naan breads, piquant dips, and slightly spicy lamb samosas are great starters. The cuisine is the less-fiery northern Indian: among the best entrées are the superb lamb *rogan gosht* and the subtle, tender, tandoori-baked chicken tikka. Curries or the flavorsome *dhal makham* (beans, lentils, and onions in a spicy sauce) are vegetarian options. Finish with fragrant *kulfi* ice cream or the exotic *elaichi kheer* rice pudding. The lunch buffet is an excellent value. ✉ *Crowne Plaza Hotel, 1 Ha'aliyah St., Givat Ram* ☎ *02/658–8867* 🌐 *www.tandoori.co.il* ✍ *Reservations essential* 💳 *AE, DC, MC, V* ⏲ *No dinner Fri. No lunch Sat.* ✥ *3B.*

WHERE TO STAY

Some travelers insist on a hotel in a central location; others prefer to retreat to a haven at the end of the day, with ambience more important than accessibility. Jerusalem has more of the first kind than the second, and even hotels once considered remote are really no more than 10 minutes by cab from the city center. Most hotels are contemporary and modern, but a few have retained an old-world charm. There are also guesthouses, B&Bs and other lodgings that offer more of the local charm coupled with often-cheaper prices.

The majority of Jerusalem's better hotels are in West Jerusalem, the Jewish/Israeli side of the old Green Line that divided the city between 1948 and 1967. Some Israelis still avoid Arab East Jerusalem, but the term is as much a matter of perception as of political geography: three large Israeli-run hotels (Olive Tree, Grand Court, and Leonardo Jerusalem) are just over the old line, sharing the seam where East meets West with the Palestinian-run American Colony and Addar.

The less-expensive hotels in East Jerusalem were seriously affected by Palestinian street violence in the late 1980s and early '90s, and again in the early 2000s. The ensuing shrinkage of hotel occupancy led to a widespread decline in standards as well.

Defining high season is not an exact science. Some hotels may talk about peak periods in addition to or instead of high season, typically the weeklong Jewish holiday of Passover (March–April), and a similar period over the Sukkoth (Tabernacles) holiday in October. Depending on the hotel, rates may go up during other Jewish holidays, as well as Christmas. Because of variations in hotel policy, and because the dates of Jewish holidays shift annually in accordance with the Hebrew calendar, the difference in room rates can be significant. Shop around and check online for the best deals.

New construction in Jerusalem tends to be high-end (the Harmony Hotel is a refreshing exception). A new development for late 2011 is the luxury Waldorf Astoria, built in the shell of a historic building, at the bottom of Agron Street.

All West Jerusalem hotels, with the exception of the YMCA, are kosher.

Use the coordinates at the end of each listing (⊕ 2A) to locate a site on the corresponding map.

WHAT IT COSTS IN U.S. DOLLARS

	¢	$	$$	$$$	$$$$
FOR TWO PEOPLE	under $120	$120–$200	$201–$300	$301–$400	over $400

Prices are for two people in a standard double room in high season. Non-Israeli citizens paying in foreign currency are exempt from the 16% VAT on hotel rooms.

CENTER CITY

This section embraces an area from the Rehavia neighborhood northeast down to Zion Square in the heart of Downtown. It's more about central locations than leafy retreats. Parking is at a premium: this is discouraging territory for rental cars.

¢ **Agron Guest House.** The Israel Youth Hostel Association has reinvented itself in the last couple of decades, upgrading its properties to simple but comfortable and well-designed guesthouses, and Agron is no exception. The hostel is all light and limestone, with ground-floor courtyards and a large second-floor pergola-covered patio that offers a great city view. Its location is excellent: a less than 10-minute walk from Downtown, and just 15 minutes from the Old City. **Pros:** strategic touring location; free Internet access; near late-night supermarket. **Cons:** sometimes noisy; most rooms only available February to August. ✉ *6 Agron St., Downtown* ☎ *02/594–5522* 🌐 *www.iyha.org.il* *55 rooms* *In-room:* a/c, *refrigerator, Internet. In-hotel: restaurant, laundry facilities, Internet terminal, parking (free)* *AE, DC, MC, V* *Sept.–Jan.* *BP* ⊕ *5E.*

$$ Fodor's Choice ★ **Harmony Hotel.** The appearance of a boutique hotel in the historic Nahalat Shiva neighborhood, in the heart of Downtown Jerusalem, created a buzz in tourism circles. The cleverly arranged furniture and ceilings covered with silk-screened historical Jerusalem photos make for a comfortable intimacy; full-length mirrors on the walls enhance the sense of space. The modern feel is carried over into the guest rooms,

2

BEST BETS FOR JERUSALEM LODGING

Fodor's writers and editors have selected their favorites hotels and other lodgings by price and experience. Fodor's Choice properties represent the "best of the best" across price categories. You can also search by area for excellent places to stay—just check out our complete reviews on the following pages.

Fodor's Choice ★

David Citadel, $$$$, p. 142
Harmony Hotel, $$, p. 138
Inbal, $$$, p. 143
Mamilla Hotel, $$$$, p. 144
Mount Zion, $$$, p. 149
Ramat Rachel, $$, p. 150

By Price

¢

Lutheran Guesthouse, p. 151
Yitzhak Rabin Guest House, p. 148
Zion, p. 141

$

Addar, p. 151
Ambassador, p. 151
Little House in the Colony, p. 149
Dan Jerusalem, p. 152
St. Andrew's Scottish Guesthouse, p. 150

$$

Crowne Plaza, p. 147
Dan Boutique, p. 149
Dan Panorama, p. 142
Harmony Hotel, p. 138
Ramada Jerusalem, p. 148
Ramat Rachel, p. 150

$$$

Inbal, p. 143
Mount Zion, p. 149
Prima Royale, p. 145

$$$$

American Colony Hotel, p. 152
David Citadel, p. 142
King David, p. 143
Mamilla Hotel, p. 144

By Experience

BEST ISRAELI BREAKFAST

American Colony Hotel, $$$$, p. 152
Inbal, $$$, p. 143
King David, $$$$, p. 143
Mamilla Hotel, $$$$, p. 144
Leonardo Plaza, $$$$, p. 140

BEST SPA

David Citadel, $$$$, p. 142
Inbal, $$$, p. 143
Ramada Jerusalem, $$, p. 148
Dan Jerusalem, $, p. 152

BEST FOR KIDS

David Citadel, $$$$, p. 142
Inbal, $$$, p. 143
Ramada Jerusalem, $$, p. 148
Ramat Rachel, $$, p. 150
Yitzhak Rabin Guest House, ¢, p. 148
YMCA (West)—Three Arches, $, p. 145

BEST VIEWS

Crowne Plaza, $$, p. 147
Mamilla Hotel, $$$$, p. 144
Ramat Rachel, $$, p. 150
Dan Jerusalem, $, p. 152
Leonardo Plaza, $$$$, p. 140

BEST POOL

King David, $$$$, p. 143
Mount Zion, $$$, p. 149
Ramada Jerusalem, $$, p. 148
Ramat Rachel, $$, p. 150

BEST FOR HISTORY BUFFS

American Colony Hotel, $$$$, p. 152
Christ Church, $, p. 150
King David, $$$$, p. 143

BEST HOTEL BAR

American Colony Hotel, $$$$, p. 152
King David, $$$$, p. 143
Mamilla Hotel, $$$$, p. 144

BEST ROOF DECK

Dan Boutique, $$, p. 149
Lutheran Guesthouse, ¢, p. 151
Mamilla Hotel, $$$$, p. 144

BEST FOR ROMANCE

American Colony Hotel, $$$$, p. 152
Little House in the Colony, $, p. 149
Mamilla Hotel, $$$$, p. 144
Mount Zion, $$$, p. 149

with off-white, dove-gray, red, and blue accents. The daily happy hour (5–7 pm) includes free glasses of wine, hot drinks, fruit, and cookies. **Pros:** free Internet access; heart of where it's happening; free leaflets for self-guided tours. **Cons:** parking difficult and/or expensive; Downtown noise when you open windows. ✉ *6 Yoel Salomon St., Downtown* ☎ *02/621–9999* 🌐 *www.atlas.co.il* *50 rooms* *In-room: a/c, safe, refrigerator, Wi-Fi. In-hotel: laundry service, Internet terminal, Wi-Fi hotspot* ▭ *AE, DC, MC, V* *BP* ✥ *2B.*

¢ **Jerusalem Hostel and Guest House.** Overlooking Zion Square, this is as Downtown as you can get. Don't look for frills—this is for the budget traveler—but you do get double-glazed windows and (somewhat frayed) wall-to-wall carpeting, keeping the noise level down. Dormitory beds (eight in a room) are $21 a night; larger private rooms with a balcony sleep parents and two kids; children under 12 are free. There's air-conditioning at certain hours. **Pros:** good value; free Internet access. **Cons:** noisy street; a bit down at the heel. ✉ *44 Jaffa St., Downtown* ☎ *02/623–6102* 🌐 *www.jerusalem-hostel.com* *20 rooms, 3 dormitories* *In-room: a/c, no phone. In-hotel: laundry facilities, Internet terminal, Wi-Fi hotspot, some pets allowed* ▭ *AE, DC, MC, V* ✥ *1B.*

$ **Jerusalem Tower.** The choice location, right in the center of Downtown, makes this hotel a great option for those who enjoy being close to the action. Guest rooms are smallish and somewhat worn, but have large wall mirrors above the wood-panel headboards to enhance the sense of space. Furnishings are a pleasing blend of beige, gold, and dark blue. Ask for an east-facing room above the sixth floor to guarantee a view. The dining room, which has private seating nooks and arched stained-glass windows, is an unexpected attraction. **Pros:** in the heart of things; free Wi-Fi. **Cons:** guest rooms ready for renovation; rooms not spacious. ✉ *23 Hillel St., Downtown* ☎ *02/620–9209* 🌐 *www.jthotels.com* *120 rooms* *In-room: a/c, safe. In-hotel: restaurant, bar, laundry service, Internet terminal, Wi-Fi hotspot, parking (free)* ▭ *AE, DC, MC, V* *BP* ✥ *2B.*

$$$$ **Leonardo Plaza.** On a hill near the lively Downtown area, the 22-story Leonardo Plaza is a Jerusalem landmark. The terrific views, especially from upper floors (the top two have balconies) remind you where you are. The hotel is popular with high-end religious Jewish clientele. All guest rooms have been recently renovated, in gold and dark blue hues. Primavera, the nonmeat Italian restaurant presided over by acclaimed chef Shalom Kadosh, has won kudos locally for its good food and elegance. In addition, an outdoor barbecue is offered Sunday through Thursday in summer. The small pool, surrounded by unaesthetic concrete, encourages quick dips, not prolonged relaxation. **Pros:** minutes away from Downtown; plenty to eat; new gym. **Cons:** business hotel feel; pricey. ✉ *47 King George St., Downtown* ☎ *02/629–8666* 🌐 *www.leonardo-hotels.com* *300 rooms* *In-room: a/c, safe, Wi-Fi. In-hotel: 4 restaurants, room service, bar, pool, laundry service, Internet terminal, Wi-Fi hotspot, parking (paid)* ▭ *AE, DC, MC, V* *BP* ✥ *5E.*

$$ **Montefiore.** The side-street location smack in the center of town—shops and restaurants abound within yards of the front door—doesn't seem to trouble the hotel's serenity. The lobby is an aesthetic blend of

Ancient arches and minarets are both part of the distinctive landscape of the Old City.

rough limestone walls, parquet and flagstone floors, and faux-leather sofas. Renovations spiffed up the modestly sized rooms with flat-screen TVs and dark-wood furnishings. Off-white bedcovers and large mirrors enhance light and space in the rooms (those facing the street are larger; windows are double-glazed). After breakfast, the dining room is transformed into Angelica, the excellent fine-dining restaurant, with independent access from the street. **Pros:** easy walking distance from Old City. **Cons:** no in-house restaurant serving lighter fare. ✉ *7 Shatz St., Downtown* ☎ *02/622–1111* 🌐 *www.montefiorehotel.com* *47 rooms, 1 suite* *In-room: a/c, Wi-Fi (some). In-hotel: restaurant, laundry service, Internet terminal, Wi-Fi hotspot* 💳 *AE, DC, MC, V* 🍽 *BP* ✥ *2A.*

$ **Zion.** With little balconies overlooking a pedestrian street off the Downtown Ben-Yehuda mall, this 19th-century stone building has an old-world feel. Front rooms get some street noise until late hours, though air-conditioning and double-glazed windows ease the problem. Furnishings are simple; ask for a superior room if you want a balcony, flat-screen TV, and slightly less minimalistic surroundings. The lobby, reception area, and a few rooms are up a single flight of stairs (other rooms are up farther still—there is no elevator). Breakfast can be included, and there is also a good coffee shop downstairs. The manager speaks five languages, not including English. **Pros:** fun Downtown location; inexpensive; European character. **Cons:** slightly dingy; not for guests with physical disabilities. ✉ *10 Dorot Rishonim St., Downtown* ☎ *02/623–2367* 🌐 *www.hotelzion.com* *25 rooms* *In-room: a/c, refrigerator. In-hotel: laundry service, Wi-Fi hotspot* 💳 *AE, MC, V* ✥ *1B.*

REHAVIA, TALBIEH, AND KING DAVID STREET

These are desirable residential neighborhoods (good for jogging and after-dinner strolls), their prime locations just 10 to 20 minutes' walk from both the Old City and Downtown. Alongside the city's high-end hotels are several budget-friendly options.

$ **Beit Shmuel.** This is a limestone complex, with cool inner courtyards and fabulous Old City views from the roof. The new wing has better-grade hotel rooms: ask for one facing the private inner courtyard and lawn; the Old City view is somewhat obstructed. The guesthouse (superior hostel) rooms are bright and pleasant, if utilitarian. They can sleep six when bunk beds are lowered from the walls. Request a street-facing room to avoid the noise of fine-weather evening events in the inner courtyard. The location is excellent: only 5 minutes' walk to Jaffa Gate, 10 minutes to Downtown. **Pros:** free Internet; great coffee in the snack bar. **Cons:** no frills; only street parking. ✉ *13 King David St. (entrance on Sham'a St.), King David St.* ☎ *02/620–3456* 🌐 *www.beitshmuel.com* *41 rooms* *In-room: a/c, refrigerator, no phone, Wi-Fi. In-hotel: restaurant, laundry service, Internet terminal, Wi-Fi hotspot* *AE, DC, MC, V* *BP* ✣ *5E.*

$$$ **Dan Panorama.** The recently renovated lobby and dining room have perked up this landmark in the middle of the hotel district. The newer guest rooms are a bit compact, but thoughtful lighting and interesting old prints on the walls make a difference; the similarly smallish bathrooms have pleasing sand-colored tiles. Rooms in the older wing are larger but less well appointed; depending on availability, the front desk is usually happy to accommodate your preference. **Pros:** excellent location; pleasant staff. **Cons:** wannabe deluxe hotel. ✉ *39 Keren Hayesod St., Talbieh* ☎ *02/569–5695* 🌐 *www.danhotels.com* *283 rooms, 8 suites* *In-room: a/c, safe, refrigerator (some), Wi-Fi. In-hotel: 2 restaurants, room service, bar, pool, gym, spa, laundry service, Internet terminal, Wi-Fi hotspot, parking (free)* *AE, DC, MC, V* *BP* ✣ *5E.*

$$$$ Fodor'sChoice ★ **David Citadel.** Stonework and arches at this hotel, just five minutes from Jaffa Gate and 10 minutes from Downtown, make a powerful first impression. The recently renovated lobby—by noted Italian architect Piero Lissoni—is elegant and welcoming, as is the soothingly decorated lounge and terrace one floor above. Views of the Old City walls from many rooms and public areas remind you that this is more than a good business hotel. The aesthetics are carried over into the spacious guest rooms, with furnishings in soft tones of beige and cream, decorative old-style mosaic wall pieces, and well-appointed bathrooms. Scala may tempt guests to stay in for dinner, particularly if preceded by a treatment at the hotel's expansive spa. There's also a children's corner, complete with games and computers. **Pros:** friendly staff; great location; welcomes families; year-round outdoor pool. **Cons:** feel of a large business hotel; events sometimes intrusive. ✉ *7 King David St., King David St.* ☎ *02/621–1111* 🌐 *www.thedavidcitadel.com* *381 rooms* *In-room: a/c, safe, Internet, Wi-Fi. In-hotel: 3 restaurants, room service, bar, pool, gym, spa, laundry service, Internet terminal, Wi-Fi hotspot, parking (paid)* *AE, DC, MC, V* *BP* ✣ *5E.*

$$ **Eldan.** Its central location in the heart of a prestigious hotel district—just a 10-minute walk from Downtown or from Jaffa Gate—is a major draw. Rooms are bright and decorated in cheerful colors. Those over the side-street main entrance are smaller but quieter. Rooms facing King David Street (from some you can see the Old City) are more spacious, but expect traffic noise when the double-glazed windows are open. The rental-car company that owns the property often offers good deals. **Pros:** prime location; cheerful. **Cons:** few frills; busy street. ✉ *24 King David St., King David St.* ☎ *02/567–9777* 🌐 *www.eldanhotel.com* *76 rooms* *In-room: a/c, safe, refrigerator, Wi-Fi. In-hotel: 2 restaurants, laundry service, Internet terminal, Wi-Fi hotspot, parking (free)* *AE, DC, MC, V* *BP* ✣ *5E.*

$$$ Fodor's Choice ★ **Inbal.** The low-rise building of Jerusalem stone wrapped around a central courtyard and atrium makes an eye-pleasing first impression; and the Inbal's energetic spirit complements the picture. In warm weather, an excellent outdoor breakfast in the shaded courtyard makes a great start to the day. The well-maintained guest rooms, decorated in shades of brown and beige, are comfortable; bathrooms are compact. Many deluxe rooms have balconies and fine views of a park next door as well as the Old City, and the heated pool in winter is an added bonus. The hotel's location next to the playgrounds of Liberty Bell Garden is convenient for families. **Pros:** near restaurants; business center. **Cons:** smallish bathrooms; not for guests seeking quiet intimacy. ✉ *3 Jabotinsky St., Talbieh* ☎ *02/675–6666* 🌐 *www.inbal-hotel.co.il* *282 rooms, 26 suites* *In-room: a/c, safe, refrigerator, DVD (some), Internet, Wi-Fi. In-hotel: 3 restaurants, room service, bar, pool, gym, spa, laundry service, Wi-Fi hotspot, parking (paid)* *AE, DC, MC, V* *BP* ✣ *6E.*

$$$$ **King David.** The grande dame of Israeli luxury hotels opened in 1931 and has successfully (and self-importantly) defended its title ever since. The ceilings, columns, and walls of the bustling lobby-lounge are decorated in "ancient Mesopotamian" geometrics. Airy guest rooms are elegantly orchestrated in cream and gold, with old-fashioned writing tables a gracious addition. Pricier rooms have views of the Old City, and suites have balconies facing the same direction. Recent changes include two additional executive floors and high-tech suites, as well as an updated gym, sauna, and spa. The landscaped pool area is a winner. An in-house French-style restaurant, La Régence, completes the picture. **Pros:** great pool and garden; terrific location; historic building. **Cons:** reputation for snobbish staff; limited parking. ✉ *23 King David St., King David St.* ☎ *02/620–8888* 🌐 *www.danhotels.com* *240 rooms, 35 suites* *In-room: a/c, safe, kitchen (some), refrigerator (some), DVD (some), Wi-Fi. In-hotel: 4 restaurants, room service, bar, tennis court, pool, gym, spa, laundry service, Internet terminal, Wi-Fi hotspot, parking (free), some pets allowed* *AE, DC, MC, V* *BP* ✣ *5E.*

$ **King Solomon.** The centerpiece of the lobby is a huge, spherical sculpture of Jerusalem by renowned sculptor Frank Meisler. A split-level atrium reveals shops half a floor down and the dining room a floor below that. The standard guest rooms are average-sized, but the more deluxe ones are quite large. The decor is attractive, with matching drapes and bedcovers, dark wood, translucent glass tabletops, and prints above the beds. The small pool (on an upper floor) offers a stunning view of southeast Jerusalem. The hotel has a large religious clientele, especially on Friday, Saturday and Jewish holidays. Over the weeks of Passover (spring) and Sukkoth (October), room rates soar. **Pros:** restaurants close by; comfortable lobby-bar area; great views. **Cons:** ripe for renovation; reception sometimes understaffed. ✉ *32 King David St., Talbieh* ☎ *02/569–5555* 🌐 *www.kingsolomon-hotel.com* *142 rooms, 6 suites* *In-room: a/c, safe, refrigerator, Wi-Fi. In-hotel: 2 restaurants, room service, bar, pool, laundry service, Internet terminal, Wi-Fi hotspot, parking (free)* *AE, DC, MC, V* *BP* ✥ *6E.*

$ **Little House in Rechavia.** For quick walks to the Old City, lots of green space, and pleasant strolling, Rechavia is a good choice. The hotel makes no pretensions about being a full-service facility, but it is comfortable and a good value. There is some street noise, but double-glazed windows help. Some of the rooms are more spacious, especially the quads and family units. **Pros:** nice location; neighborhood feel. **Cons:** only breakfast available. ✉ *20 Ibn Ezra St., Rehavia* ☎ *02/563–3344* 🌐 *www.o-niv.com/rechavia* *27 rooms* *In-room: a/c, Wi-Fi. In-hotel: Wi-Fi hotspot* *AE, DC, MC, V* *BP* ✥ *5D.*

$$$$ **Mamilla Hotel.** The latest addition to the luxury hotel scene, the Mamilla has a clever and soaring architectural design by Moshe Safdie. The restrained yet luxe style of interior designer Piero Lissoni makes this a sleek and comfortable haven. All rooms include wood floors, raw-metal headboards, and richly textured drapes, while the übercontemporary bathrooms boast deep rectangular bathtubs and clear walls that can frost over for privacy. The dining establishments—the Winery, the Mirror Bar, Mamilla Rooftop, and the Mamilla Café—are a draw for both guests and locals, offering posh surroundings as well as appealing menus. Be sure to try a "wine flight" with the head sommelier, and take a dip in the underused underground pool, tiled in navy blue mosaics. Don't skip the in-house breakfast, as Mamilla takes the Israeli morning repast of eggs, cheeses, and salads to a whole new level. ✉ *11 King Solomon St., Mamilla* ☎ *02/548–2222* 🌐 *www.mamillahotel.com* *194 rooms, 33 suites* *In-room: a/c, safe, Wi-Fi. In-hotel: 2 restaurants, room service, 2 bars, tennis court, pool, gym, spa, laundry service, Wi-Fi hotspot, parking (free)* *AE, DC, MC, V* *BP* ✥ *5E.*

Fodor's Choice ★

$$ **Prima Kings.** The Kings—the name by which it's still known—is on a busy intersection, less than a 10-minute walk from the city center. Cane furniture and deep sofas create comfortable, if not particularly intimate, public areas. The hotel is popular with religious Jews, especially on weekends and Jewish holidays. Most of the guest rooms are fairly large; the deluxe ones are done in tones of burgundy and green, with touches of leather. If your budget allows, upgrade to a junior suite with a balcony. Especially large family rooms are also available. The entrance is on Ramban Street. **Pros:** 15 minutes from Old City; adjacent late-night supermarket. **Cons:** a bit overpriced; traffic noise when windows are open. ✉ *60 King George St., Rehavia* ☎ *02/620–1201* 🌐 *www.prima.co.il* *217 rooms* *In-room: a/c, safe, Wi-Fi (some). In-hotel: 2 restaurants, room service, bar, laundry service, Internet terminal, Wi-Fi hotspot, parking (paid)* *AE, DC, MC, V* *BP* ✥ *5E.*

2

$$$ **Prima Royale.** The landmark Windmill Hotel was gutted and reinvented in admirable taste. The golden-marble lobby—with potted palms, brightly colored armchairs and cushions, and touches of leather—augurs well. Guest rooms are very compact, but burgundy drapes and cushions and colorful accents in the bathrooms offer some compensation. Ask for a room with a view. The chain has designated the Royale as its cultural flagship: Chopin and champagne for breakfast, art in the dining room, live jazz, and more. The location is good, too: a 15- to 20-minute walk from the center city or the Old City. **Pros:** free culture and drinks; tasteful decor. **Cons:** small rooms; pricey for what it is. ✉ *3 Mendele St., off Keren Hayesod, Talbieh* ☎ *02/560–7111* 🌐 *www.prima.co.il* *126 rooms, 7 suites* *In-room: a/c, safe, refrigerator, DVD (some), Wi-Fi (some). In-hotel: 2 restaurants, room service, bar, gym, spa, laundry service, Internet terminal, Wi-Fi hotspot, parking (free)* 💳 *AE, DC, MC, V* *BP* ✥ *6E.*

$$ **YMCA Three Arches.** Built in 1933, this limestone building with its famous domed bell tower is a Jerusalem landmark. Stone arches, exotic murals, latticed cupboards, Armenian tiles, and the front patio give the place charm and character. The guest rooms are comfortably spacious for this grade, and attractively fitted in beige with patterned burgundy touches and prints of landscape artist Anna Ticho on the walls. Recent room renovations include new carpeting and bathroom upgrades. The atmosphere, the excellent sports facilities, and a great location make the Y an attractive deal. **Pros:** great location; free sports facilities. **Cons:** poor restaurant. ✉ *26 King David St., Box 294, King David St.* ☎ *02/569–2692* 🌐 *www.ymca3arch.co.il* *52 rooms, 4 suites* *In-room: a/c, refrigerator (some). In-hotel: restaurant, bar, pool, gym, laundry service, Internet terminal, Wi-Fi hotspot, parking (free)* 💳 *AE, DC, MC, V* *BP* ✥ *5E.*

WEST JERUSALEM

This cluster of hotels in Givat Ram and Romema is near the point where the Tel Aviv Highway (Route 1) enters Jerusalem. Some properties are right at the Central Bus Station, others closer to the Israel Museum and the Knesset. Ein Kerem, a leafy enclave, is included here, too, along with Mt. Herzl. Downtown is some distance away, the Old City even farther—a long walk, but 10 to 15 minutes by cab or bus, and bus lines are plentiful. If it's hotel deals you're after or if other places in town are booked, this area makes a great option.

$$ **BaChoresh HaTivi.** The exuberantly lush garden and sweeping view of the valley are your first hint that you've found the perfect hideaway; the well-appointed pine-and-tile suites with kitchenettes confirm it. Two of the three units are of superior standard, one with a kid-friendly loft. Private patios and garden furniture extend the living area into the outdoors. Wine and a classical guitarist can be booked for warm evenings. **Pros:** whirlpool baths in suites; massage available. **Cons:** parking can be remote; 60 steps to the place; far from the rest of Jerusalem. ✉ *Ein Kerem St. G/7, Ein Kerem* ☎ *02/643–6586* 🌐 *www.bachti.co.il* *3*

Fodor's Choice ★

The Inbal Jerusalem Hotel

Mamilla Hotel

The David Citadel Hotel

suites ♂ *In-room: a/c, no phone, DVD. In-hotel: parking (free)* ▭ *No credit cards* 🍴 *BP* ⊕ *3A.*

¢ **Bayit VeGan.** The setting, opposite Mt. Herzl in West Jerusalem, has sweeping views of the Judean Hills, yet is only a 15-minute cab ride or a 25-minute bus ride from Downtown. Upgraded from a youth hostel to a guesthouse, it offers two levels of accommodations. The new wing is essentially an economy hotel: 78 spacious, well-laid-out rooms (light-wood furnishings; most with tubs, some shower only) that comfortably sleep four. The 53 older hostel rooms (some sleep six) are simpler, though still with carpets and en-suite bathrooms. Always ask for a view. Meals are substantial and cheap. **Pros:** free Internet access; good falafel stand nearby. **Cons:** remote location; sometimes noisy. ✉ *8 Hapisgah St., Bayit VeGan, Box 16350, Mt. Herzl* ☎ *02/642–0990* ⊕ *www.bvh.co.il* ⇆ *115 rooms* ♂ *In-room: a/c, no phone, safe, no TV. In-hotel: restaurants, Wi-Fi hotspot, parking (free)* ▭ *AE, DC, MC, V* 🍴 *BP* ⊕ *3A.*

$$ **Crowne Plaza.** Although this landmark building with sweeping city views is a classic business hotel, it's also a comfortable vacation option. Renovated rooms with white duvets make a pleasing combination in guest rooms; bathrooms, though aesthetic, are small. The lobby-level bar–coffee shop is well laid out, with discreet alcoves, and the Kohinoor Indian restaurant is a real treat. The pool, and its adjacent lawns and playground, provide a welcome refuge for all ages at the end of a hot day. **Pros:** away from city noise; spa and sports facilities. **Cons:** few attractions within walking distance; limited parking. ✉ *1 Ha'aliyah St., Givat Ram* ☎ *02/658–8888* ⊕ *www.crowneplaza.com* ⇆ *375 rooms, 21 suites* ♂ *In-room: a/c, safe, Wi-Fi. In-hotel: 3 restaurants, room service, bar, tennis courts, pool, gym, spa, laundry service, Internet terminal, Wi-Fi hotspot, parking (paid)* ▭ *AE, DC, MC, V* 🍴 *BP* ⊕ *3B.*

$ **Jerusalem Gate.** Its main clientele is tour groups, but the good value of this hotel attracts individual tourists and budget-minded families as well. The location near the Central Bus Station makes transportation simple. The comfortable and well-cared-for guest rooms have solid-wood furniture and duvets; ask for a high floor with a cityscape view. An attractive bar with a reflective copper ceiling looks down onto the open and airy lobby from an unobtrusive mezzanine. **Pros:** a spacious place to stay; direct access to mall; on major bus routes. **Cons:** far from Downtown; attracts large groups. ✉ *43 Yirmiyahu St., Romema* ☎ *02/500–8500* ⊕ *www.jerusalemgatehotel.com* ⇆ *294 rooms, 4 suites* ♂ *In-room: a/c, refrigerator (some), Wi-Fi. In-hotel: 2 restaurants, room service, bar, children's programs (summer), laundry service, Internet terminal, Wi-Fi hotspot, parking (paid)* ▭ *AE, DC, MC, V* 🍴 *BP* ⊕ *2B.*

$ **Jerusalem Gold.** Owner-manager Ariella Shmida Doron's homemaker's touch is felt in the well-coordinated guest-room decor: some rooms are done in burgundy, others in bottle green. Bathrooms are small, but very light cream tiles enhance the sense of space. Double-glazed windows allow guests to ignore the very urban surroundings. **Pros:** bus lines to everywhere; mall conveniently close. **Cons:** crowded seating in lounge; grungy neighborhood; few attractions nearby. ✉ *234 Jaffa St., Romema* ☎ *02/501–3333* ⊕ *www.jerusalemgold.com* ⇆ *163 rooms, 35 suites* ♂ *In-room: a/c, safe, kitchen (some), refrigerator, Wi-Fi. In-hotel:*

2

2 restaurants, room service, bar, laundry service, Internet terminal, Wi-Fi hotspot, parking (paid) ▭ *AE, DC, MC, V* 🍽 *BP* ✥ *2B.*

$$ **Jerusalem Park.** This West Jerusalem hotel clings to its good local reputation. The bar-lounge offers comfortable sofas, deeply upholstered in burgundy or bottle green. Guest rooms are better than adequate, with pastel duvets and dark carpets; a tasteful touch in the small bathrooms is aqua accents on the light tiles. One designated business floor was recently renovated and the other is to follow in 2011. Breakfast is served in a roofed stone courtyard. Guests have free access to Hebrew University's sports center, with tennis, squash, and a year-round pool. **Pros:** friendly; intimate atmosphere. **Cons:** sports facilities not on-site; small rooms. ✉ *2 Vilnai St., Givat Ram* ☎ *02/658–2222* 🌐 *parkplazajerusalem.co.il* *210 rooms, 7 suites* *In-room: a/c, refrigerator, Wi-Fi. In-hotel: 2 restaurants, room service, bar, tennis courts, pool, gym, laundry service, Internet terminal, Wi-Fi hotspot, parking (free)* ▭ *AE, DC, MC, V* 🍽 *BP* ✥ *3A.*

$$ **Ramada Jerusalem.** The marble lobby, with its reflecting copper ceiling and potted palms, is elegant in a grand sense. Nicely renovated rooms are comfortably large and warmly designed with duvets, beige wallpaper, and navy drapes; the bathrooms are small but freshly redone. Most have fine city views and open spaces, some with small balconies—insist on one from the fifth floor up. The well-landscaped pool area with kids' playground equipment is a great asset. **Pros:** good value; great spa and gym; wonderful kiddie spaces. **Cons:** a ride from Downtown. ✉ *Ruppin Bridge at Herzl Blvd., Givat Ram* ☎ *02/659–9999* 🌐 *www.ramada.com* *350 rooms, 10 suites* *In-room: a/c, safe, refrigerator, Wi-Fi. In-hotel: 3 restaurants, room service, bar, tennis court, pools, gym, spa, laundry service, Internet terminal, Wi-Fi hotspot, parking (free)* ▭ *AE, DC, MC, V* 🍽 *BP* ✥ *3A.*

¢ **Yitzhak Rabin Guest House.** Part of the official Youth Hostel Association, this place is an example of how good budget accommodations can get. The large, airy, stone-and-aluminum lobby is a gathering place that opens out to flower-filled patios, with a view of Hebrew University. Guest rooms are spacious (they sleep from two to five, two in fold-up bunks), with private showers and toilets making this a budget family option; furnishings are functional. The Israel Museum is a short walk away, and there is a bus route to Downtown and the Central Bus Station. Meals are substantial and good. **Pros:** big on aesthetics; great place to meet fellow travelers; snack bar. **Cons:** no-frills rooms; closest bus line a bit infrequent. ✉ *1 Nahman Avigad St., Givat Ram* ☎ *02/594–5511* 🌐 *www.iyha.org.il/eng* *77 rooms* *In-room: a/c, no phone, refrigerator. In-hotel: restaurant, laundry service, Internet terminal, Wi-Fi hotspot, parking (free)* ▭ *AE, DC, MC, V* 🍽 *BP* ✥ *6B.*

GERMAN COLONY, HEBRON ROAD, AND ENVIRONS

This area lies in Jerusalem's southeast quadrant, due south of Jaffa Gate. Baka is some distance away, but all other listed properties are a fairly easy walk from the Old City. The German Colony has become a popular leisure-time neighborhood, with numerous restaurants and coffee shops.

The slightly rustic kibbutz location of Ramat Rachel is technically south of the city limits, but geographically part of Jerusalem—enjoying the best of both worlds, as locals would say.

$$ **Dan Boutique.** An onyx, red, and copper reception area and bright lobby lounge welcome you to this contemporary lodging. Room decor is a tasteful balance, done up in a similar color scheme. About a quarter of the rooms are classified as "deluxe," regardless of size: you pay for the excellent views of Mt. Zion and the more distant Mt. of Olives. A third-floor sundeck offers a 180-degree panorama. **Pros:** inviting public area; close to restaurants and bars. **Cons:** not to everyone's taste; video screens in public areas intrusive. ✉ *31 Hebron Rd., Hebron Rd.* ☎ *02/568–9999* 🌐 *www.danhotels.com* *123 rooms, 6 suites* *In-room: a/c, safe, refrigerator, DVD, Wi-Fi. In-hotel: 2 restaurants, room service, bar, gym, laundry service, Internet terminal, Wi-Fi hotspot, parking (free)* ▭ *AE, DC, MC, V* *BP* ✥ *6F.*

2

$ **Little House in Bakah.** An attractive, stone-arched building on the edge of a residential neighborhood, with good bus lines and many eateries and shops just a short walk away, is not a bad recipe for the budget-conscious. Some rooms are a little cramped, others feel less so: ask for an upper floor if stairs don't bother you. The renovated rooms have homey wood floors. Family units, with refrigerator and a balcony, sleep five. A sunken room with vaulted ceiling and wooden floor serves as an inviting bar, coffee shop, and Italian restaurant, spilling out into a shaded courtyard. **Pros:** intimacy; good value; nice neighborhood. **Cons:** a bit dowdy; no elevator. ✉ *1 Yehuda St., corner of 80 Hebron Rd., Bakah* ☎ *02/673–7944* 🌐 *www.o-niv.com/bakah* *34 rooms* *In-room: a/c, refrigerator (some), Wi-Fi. In-hotel: restaurant, bar, Internet terminal, Wi-Fi hotspot, parking (free)* ▭ *AE, DC, MC, V* *BP* ✥ *6G.*

$ **Little House in the Colony.** Billed as the "smallest hotel in Jerusalem," this lodging is on a quiet street just steps away from the German Colony's bubbling main drag. It shares its historic setting with the landmark Smadar Cinema and a restaurant. Room decor is simple but aesthetically pleasing (wood headboards; bathrooms tiled in a tranquil beige), and wood floors add to the charm. **Pros:** quiet and intimate; shops and eateries nearby. **Cons:** a bit expensive for what you get; only breakfast provided. ✉ *4a Lloyd George St., German Colony* ☎ *02/566–2424* 🌐 *www.o-niv.com/melonit* *22 rooms* *In-room: a/c, Wi-Fi. In-hotel: restaurant* ▭ *AE, DC, MC, V* *BP* ✥ *6E.*

Fodor's Choice ★ $$$ **Mount Zion.** Columns, arched doorways, and windows in Jerusalem stone frame this hotel's ethereal views of the Hinnom Valley. The core of the hotel is a 19th-century building that once served as a British hospital. A new wing was added in the 1970s, but the older Citadel rooms are more interesting and roomy. While the architectural adaptations are inspired, the Moroccan decor in some rooms needs updating. The beautiful pool area has sprawling views, and the lush gardens are redolent with rosemary, honesuckle, and olive trees. The Turkish steam bath spa complex, decorated with traditional blue tiles, is a great addition. **Pros:** wonderful aesthetics in public areas; inviting pool area; easy walk to Old City. **Cons:** staff could be cheerier; pricey. ✉ *17 Hebron Rd., Hebron Rd.* ☎ *02/568–9555* 🌐 *www.mountzion.co.il* *116 rooms, 14* *suites* *In-room: a/c, safe, refrigerator, DVD (some), Wi-Fi. In-hotel: 2 restaurants, room service, bar, pool, gym, spa, laundry service, Internet terminal, Wi-Fi hotspot, parking (free)* *AE, DC, MC, V* *BP* *6F.*

$$ **Ramat Rachel.** The relaxed, informal atmosphere is a big part of this hotel's appeal. Rooms in the older South Wing have stunning views of Bethlehem and the Judean Desert. Recent renovations have introduced light-colored wood furniture offset by colorful throw cushions and bedcovers. Long sofas hugging the rooms' picture windows can be folded out to sleep up to three kids. Updated bathrooms are very compact but well appointed. West Wing guest rooms, facing the pool, are decorated in tasteful aquamarines. With its fine pool (including a giant waterslide) and other sports facilities, all free to guests, Ramat Rachel feels like an isolated resort. Cheaper hostel rooms are also available. **Pros:** rustic location; tennis courts; children's playground and petting farm. **Cons:** remote location; sometimes crowded with tour groups. *Kibbutz Ramat Rachel, Ramat Rachel* *02/670–2555* *www.ramatrachel.co.il* *164 rooms* *In-room: a/c, safe, refrigerator, Wi-Fi (some). In-hotel: 2 restaurants, bar, tennis courts, pool, gym, spa, laundry service, Internet terminal, Wi-Fi hotspot, parking (free)* *AE, DC, MC, V* *BP* *6G.*

Fodor's Choice ★

$ **St. Andrew's Scottish Guesthouse.** Built in the early 1930s as part of the St. Andrew's Church complex, the guesthouse is as much a retreat as a place to stay overnight—"feeling like you're home," is the way they like to put it. The comfortable library, the garden, and the lounge with stuffed chairs and stone arches framing Old City views define the character of the place. Some of the guest rooms—tiled floors, gold-and-orange bedcovers and curtains—have tubs, others showers only. Bigger rooms have less of a view; some rooms have balconies. **Pros:** serene; close to German Colony; interesting gift shop. **Cons:** no meals other than breakfast; steps to climb. *1 David Remez St., Hebron Rd.* *02/673–2401* *www.scotsguesthouse.com* *17 rooms, 1 suite, 1 apartment* *In-room: a/c, kitchen (some), no TV, Wi-Fi. In-hotel: Wi-Fi hotspot, parking (free)* *AE, DC, MC, V* *BP* *6F.*

OLD CITY

The Old City, the historic walled heart of Jerusalem, includes the Armenian Quarter, the Christian Quarter, the Jewish Quarter, and the Muslim Quarter. Lodging options here are limited.

$ **Christ Church.** This is the guesthouse of the adjacent Anglican church, the oldest Protestant church (1849) in the Middle East. Pinkish limestone floors and light furnishings in the guest rooms make for a pleasing aesthetic. Rooms in the newer Nicolayson Block are air-conditioned. The courtyard is a good retreat, and there is a library and a comfortable common room with cane chairs and cable TV. The location, in the Old City just inside Jaffa Gate, is excellent for sightseeing. **Pros:** tranquil haven; Internet cafés and convenience stores close by. **Cons:** not always comfortable for non-Christian guests. *Armenian Patriarchate St., Jaffa Gate* *02/627–7727* *christch@netvision.net.il* *32 rooms*

In-room: a/c (some), no TV, Wi-Fi. In-hotel: laundry service, Wi-Fi hotspot, parking (free) ▭ *AE, MC, V* ¦◎¦ *BP* ⊕ *5G.*

$ **Lutheran Guesthouse.** Tucked into an Old City alley, between Jaffa Gate and the Jewish Quarter, the guesthouse is a maze of stone buildings and courtyards. The tranquil roof garden offers sweeping views of Jerusalem's holy places. Single rooms are very small; triples are ample. Angle for double room No. 25 with its own balcony. The top-floor addition includes an indoor-outdoor coffee shop. **Pros:** free Internet access; leaf-framed panoramas; free hot drinks. **Cons:** Old City atmosphere not for everyone. ✉ *St. Mark's Rd., Old City* ☎ *02/626–6888* 🌐 *www.evangelisch-in-jerusalem.org/guesthouse* *34 rooms* *In-room: a/c, Wi-Fi. In-hotel: restaurant, Internet terminal, Wi-Fi hotspot* ▭ *AE, MC, V* ¦◎¦ *BP* ⊕ *5G.*

2

EAST JERUSALEM AND THE "SEAM LINE"

The cluster of hotels here, some Israeli-run, some Palestinian, are within yards of each other, and of the old "seam" (as it's sometimes called) that once divided Jerusalem into East and West. At some levels, the old divisions remain, but the seam area itself has become a comfortable middle ground.

In splendid isolation on the northeast side of town, with long views southwest toward the Old City, Mt. Scopus is home to the original Hebrew University and Hadassah Hospital campuses. The Regency Jerusalem hotel here abuts the French Hill neighborhood, at the northern end of the ridge.

$ **Addar.** Elegantly intimate, this well-kept boutique hotel is on the seam between East and West Jerusalem. The red marble floor, gilded columns, wooden lattices, wrought-iron work, and plush burgundy upholstery of the lobby suggest other eras, and somehow manage to avoid gaudiness. The suites were freshly renovated in 2008; in-room whirlpool tubs are standard in the marble bathrooms. **Pros:** personable, English-speaking manager; reasonable à la carte meals. **Cons:** not an inviting neighborhood to stroll; dead area at night. ✉ *10 St. George Rd., Seam Line* ☎ *02/626–3111* 🌐 *www.addar-hotel.com* *7 rooms, 23 suites* *In-room: a/c, safe, kitchen (some), refrigerator, DVD, Internet, Wi-Fi. In-hotel: restaurant, room service, gym, laundry service, Internet terminal, parking (free), some pets allowed* ▭ *AE, DC, MC, V* ¦◎¦ *BP* ⊕ *2F.*

$ **Ambassador.** One of East Jerusalem's veteran hotels, the Ambassador has been transformed by thorough, tasteful renovations, and the use throughout of Jerusalem limestone. Rooms are airy and well appointed; for extra space, upgrade to a junior guest room, and ask for an Old City view. In fine weather, the somewhat eclectic but charming Al-Diwan à la carte restaurant—Middle Eastern and Italian, mostly—expands to the patio where there is a summer bar and Bedouin tent for more relaxed dining in the inviting garden. **Pros:** in-house patisserie; comfortable rooms. **Cons:** far from attractions; staff lack warmth. ✉ *80 Nablus Rd., Sheikh Jarrah, East Jerusalem* ☎ *02/541–2222* 🌐 *www.jerusalemambassador.com* *120 rooms* *In-room: a/c, safe, refrig-*

erator, Wi-Fi. In-hotel: 2 restaurants, room service, bar, gym, laundry service, Internet terminal, parking (free) ▭ *AE, DC, MC, V* 🍽 *BP* ✢ *1E.*

$$$$ **American Colony Hotel.** Once a pasha's palace, this cool limestone oasis with its flower-filled inner courtyard has been a hotel for more than a century. It's a 10-minute walk from the Damascus Gate, in East Jerusalem, but worlds away from the hubbub of the Old City. A favorite haunt of American and British expats, foreign journalists, and diplomats, the Swiss-run hotel is famous for its ambience: turquoise-and-blue tilework, Damascene wood inlay, potted palms. The best, exceptionally large rooms breathe elegance, with rug-strewn flagstone floors and vaulted or antique painted-wood ceilings. The hotel is being renovated in sections, with most guest rooms redesigned in an antique style. **Pros:** international atmosphere; sparkling pool; good English bookstore. **Cons:** dead neighborhood at night; a cab ride from most attractions. ✉ *1 Louis Vincent St. at Nablus Rd., Seam Line* ☎ *02/627–9777* 🌐 *www.americancolony.com* *73 rooms, 13 suites* *In-room: a/c, safe, DVD (some), Internet, Wi-Fi. In-hotel: 3 restaurants, room service, bar, pool, gym, spa, laundry service, Internet terminal, parking (free)* ▭ *AE, DC, MC, V* 🍽 *BP* ✢ *2G.*

$$ **Dan Jerusalem.** Cascading down Mt. Scopus, the Dan Jerusalem has a dramatic setting and a bold design. The lobby is a stylish combination of stone and greenery; one-third of the guest rooms have Old City views; and the pool area, with an adjacent playground, is a cool enclave of palms and plants. The large, sophisticated spa, popular among Jerusalemites, includes an authentic marble Turkish bath, imported piece by piece. **Pros:** impressive architecture; great panoramic view. **Cons:** needs renovation; remote location. ✉ *32 Lehi St., Mt. Scopus* ☎ *02/533–1234* 🌐 *www.danhotels.com* *455 rooms, 50 suites* *In-room: a/c, safe, refrigerator, Wi-Fi, Wi-Fi (some). In-hotel: 2 restaurants, room service, bar, pool, gym, spa, laundry service, Internet terminal, parking (free)* ▭ *AE, DC, MC, V* 🍽 *BP* ✢ *1H.*

$$ **Grand Court.** This huge hotel is a celebration of light and space: from the large, airy lobby, with its limestone walls and marble arches, to the well-lighted, comfortable guest rooms, with their soft-color decor and light-tile bathrooms. The suites are impressively large. Guests have free access to Hebrew University's excellent sports center. **Pros:** cheerful natural lighting; well-decorated rooms. **Cons:** remote location; neighborhood dead at night. ✉ *15 St. George St., Seam Line* ☎ *02/591–7777* 🌐 *www.grandcourt.co.il* *427 rooms, 15 suites* *In-room: a/c, safe, refrigerator, Wi-Fi. In-hotel: 3 restaurants, room service, bar, tennis courts, pool, gym, laundry service, Internet terminal, parking (free)* ▭ *AE, DC, MC, V* 🍽 *BP* ✢ *2F.*

$ **Leonardo Hotel Jerusalem.** The huge skylit atrium in the middle of the lobby has a comfortable if not intimate coffee shop. The blues in the decor offset the light-colored guest-room furniture and parquet floors. "Superior" is the house term for standard rooms; the better "deluxe" rooms are on the eighth floor and have balconies. **Pros:** a sense of spaciousness. **Cons:** a drive from most places; neighborhood dead at night; no distinctive character. ✉ *9 St. George St., Seam Line* ☎ *02/532–0000* *www.leonardo-hotels.com 382 rooms, 18 suites In-room: a/c, safe, refrigerator, Wi-Fi. In-hotel: 2 restaurants, room service, bar, pool, gym, laundry service, Internet terminal, parking (free) AE, DC, MC, V BP 2F.*

$$ **Olive Tree.** Aesthetics are the strong point of this property. Stone arches, wood latticework, and bronze ornaments in the reception area, old flagstones in the skylit atrium, and polished floorboards in the comfortable lounge all combine to create a distinctly regional ambience. Guest rooms are not huge, but are comfortable. Black and gold touches, and framed old prints, give them some class. **Pros:** superior sports facilities. **Cons:** neighborhood is dead at night. *23 St. George St., Seam Line 02/541–0410 www.olivetreehotel.com 300 rooms, 4 suites In-room: a/c, safe, refrigerator, Internet, Wi-Fi. In-hotel: 2 restaurants, room service, bar, tennis courts, pool, gym, spa, laundry service, Internet terminal, parking (free) AE, DC, MC, V BP 2F.*

2

NIGHTLIFE AND THE ARTS

The holy city is not as staid as you might think, even though over half its residents—ultra-Orthodox Jews and the Arab community—do not partake in Western-style entertainment and arts. You can combine a great meal or tasty snack with a concert, pub, or dance bar for a lively evening out on the town. Thursday and Friday nights are the hot times for bars and clubs and late-night shows; classical music and dance performances tend to avoid Friday nights, and take place over the rest of the week. Check out listings in English-language publications and free booklets, which you can find in hotels.

NIGHTLIFE

Although Jerusalem can't compete with Tel Aviv in terms of the number of nightlife attractions, what the city lacks in quantity it more than makes up for in quality. Pubs, bars, and nightclubs in Jerusalem tend to be more relaxed than those in Tel Aviv—they're friendlier, more informal, and often less expensive. As in Tel Aviv, the nightlife scene in Jerusalem starts very late: some places only begin to fill up after midnight, and most pubs are open until the early hours of the morning. Given the university presence in the city, there is often a younger crowd at many places.

BARS AND PUBS

With a mayor who's encouraging Jerusalem's after-dark scene, there's been a rash of new bars and pubs. There's now a bar for every type of music lover and drink imbiber.

The **Cellar Bar** (*American Colony Hotel, 1 Louis Vincent St. at Nablus Rd., East Jerusalem 02/627-9777 www.americancolony.com*) has the feel of an intimate wine cellar, with small tables, quiet corners and a mix of languages that makes one feel far away from all the political problems of the holy city.

Ha'taklit (✉ *7 Helene Hamalka St., Downtown* ☎ *02/624–4073*) means "The Record," a nostalgic tribute by the three young, musically-inclined owners to the vinyl predecessor to CDs and MP3s. This is a great place for beer and music, with frequent live acts, occasional dance parties, and a back room where international soccer games are screened.

Mia Bar (✉ *18 Hillel St., Downtown* ☎ *02/625–9491*), named for the character in *Pulp Fiction*, offers an impressive selection of beers, whiskeys, and cocktails mixed and served by a well-trained bartending staff.

Mirror Bar (✉ *Mamilla Hotel,11 King Solomon St., Mamilla* ☎ *02/548–2222*) is a chic hotel bar appealing to a cross section of travelers, locals, and expats. The intimate space is perfect for a nightcap or a full meal of excellent tapas.

★ The long-standing **Stardust** (✉ *6 Rivlin St., Nahalat Shiva* ☎ *02/622–2196*) occupies a 19th-century stone building, has a warm, intimate atmosphere, and is open until 5 am.

Tuvia (✉ *6 Shushan St., Downtown* ☎ *02/624–0949*) offers a wide variety of imported beers, good bar food, and good background music to a slightly older crowd.

As a sort of inside joke, **Uganda** (✉ *4 Aristobulus St., Downtown* ☎ *02/623–6087*) is named for the African country once proposed as an alternative home for the Jewish state, and alternative is what the pub is all about. It also sells comic books and vinyl records, hosts live music, and is quite popular with art students.

Yudaleh (✉ *Beit Yaacov St., Machaneh Yehuda* ☎ *02/533–3442*) is a wine and tapas bar that's good for a predinner drink or a light meal.

RESTAURANT BARS

More mature customers who find the pubs too loud or frenetic can retreat to one of several good restaurants where latecomers are welcome to order just drinks.

Adom (✉ *Feingold Courtyard, off 31 Jaffa St., Downtown* ☎ *02/624–6242*) has a reputation for good shrimp and other seafood.

Barood (✉ *Feingold Courtyard, 31 Jaffa St., Downtown* ☎ *02/625–9081*) serves a unique variety of meat dishes and has a pub atmosphere and a good bar.

Chakra (✉ *41 King George St., Downtown* ☎ *02/625–2733*) has a large, diverse menu as well as soft lighting and good background music.

Jan's (✉ *20 Marcus St., Talbieh* ☎ *02/561–2054*), under the plaza of the Jerusalem Theatre, is an intimate spot with low lighting, colorful pillows and rugs, and a dated but good vegetarian menu.

Link (✉ *3 Hama'a lot St., Downtown* ☎ *02/625–3446*) is popular with legal and other professionals. The deck's a great spot on warm evenings and the grilled chicken wings are terrific.

Mona (✉ *12 Shmuel Hanagid St., Downtown* ☎ *02/622–2283*), in the old stone Artists' House, is a place to see and be seen. The food is excellent, but you must wait until late in the evening if you want to order just drinks.

You can join Jerusalemites as they unwind at the movies at the popular Jerusalem Cinematheque.

Restobar (⊠ *1 Ben Maimon St., Rehavia* ☎ *02/622–2283*) is popular with locals all day, especially for a glass of wine on the lovely deck.

Selina (⊠ *24 Emek Refa'im St., German Colony* ☎ *02/567–2049*) is a solid option if you're in the German Colony and are looking for a place for a postdinner drink.

Zuni (⊠ *15 Yoel Salomon St., Nahalat Shiva* ☎ *02/625–7776*), the Jerusalem version of a gentleman's club, fills up with a young crowd after midnight.

DANCE CLUBS

Discos have declined; for young partiers, dance bars are where it's at.

★ **Bar Shva-esray** (⊠ *17 Ha'oman St., Talpiot Industrial Zone* ☎ *02/678–1658*) means "Bar 17"—the establishment's street number. The place has reinvented itself as a hip, nicely styled mega dance bar, with a different genre of music each night of the week (closed Sunday; private events Wednesday). Hum along with Israeli hits Tuesday, break loose to house and disco on Thursday, enjoy a more freestyle atmosphere Saturday.

Bass Dance Club (⊠ *1 Habistadrut St., Downtown* ☎ *077/512–3056*) is quickly becoming one of the hottest spots in Jerusalem, while maintaining its underground appeal. It specializes in techno/electro/drum and bass, but other styles of music are played as well. Admission is often waived for premidnight early arrivals.

Hakatzeh (⊠ *4 Shushan St., Downtown*), which means "The Edge," is a drink-and-dance pub. Music styles vary considerably from night to night, but the atmosphere is always lively. It operates as a gay bar one night a week.

HaTza'atzua (✉ *6 Dhu Nuwas St., Downtown* ☎ *02/623-6666*), or "The Toy," is named for a beloved store that previously occupied this space. The multilevel space has an extensive bar and cozy couches for drinking and nibbling, massive flat-screen televisions for keeping an eye on the game, and a great selection of local DJs.

★ **Sira** (✉ *4 Ben-Sira St., Downtown* ☎ *02/624–2298*) is a great watering hole and the small dance floor, variety of music spun by DJs, and late hours make this one of the most fun places in the city to dance. Here you'll find a Bohemian hodgepodge of students and internationals.

JAZZ CLUBS

Apart from performances in auditoriums and other more conservative venues, you can sometimes find jazz at smaller places around town.

Both international and local musicians play at **The Lab** (*The Jerusalem Performing Arts Laboratory or, in Hebrew, Hama'abada* ✉ *28 Hebron Rd., Hebron Rd.* ☎ *02/629–2000*). You can sit at the bar and just enjoy the DJ's offerings, or pay extra for a specific performance. Check listings ahead of time.

Yellow Submarine (✉ *13 Ha'rechavim St., Talpiot Industrial Zone* ☎ *02/679–4040*) is a not-for-profit music center, and jazz is one of its strong suits. Occasional festivals and individual gigs by both international and local artists make it a venue worth checking.

THE ARTS

Classical music is the capital's strong suit: it's worth checking schedules of ensembles and main venues ahead of time. Artists in other musical genres pass through from time to time, but Jerusalem is seldom their main focus. Dance performances are more infrequent, and professional English theater is very rare, although amateurs are often worthwhile.

For English-language schedules of performances and other cultural events, consult the Friday weekend section of the *Jerusalem Post* and its insert *In Jerusalem*; Friday's "The Guide" of *Haaretz*'s English edition; *Time Out Jerusalem*; and the free weekly and monthly booklets available at hotels and information bureaus.

Bimot (✉ *8 Shammai St., Downtown* ☎ *02/623–7000* 🌐 *www.bimot.co.il/eng*) is the main ticket agency for performances in Jerusalem. Student discounts are sometimes available; present your card at the ticket office.

DANCE

The better-known Tel Aviv–based troupes seldom make it to Jerusalem, but you can watch the listings and hope. Look out for two excellent Jerusalem contemporary dance companies: **Vertigo** (🌐 *www.vertigo.org.il*), and the more innovative **Kolben** (🌐 *www.kolbendance.com*), which are both based at the **Gerard Behar Center** (✉ *11 Bezalel St., Downtown* ☎ *02/625–1139*).

2

FESTIVALS

Top Israeli and international orchestras, choirs, singers, theater companies, dance troupes, and street entertainers participate in the **Israel Festival** (☎ *02/623–7000* 🌐 *www.israel-festival.org.il*), usually held in late May or early June. All the performing arts are represented, and offerings range from the classical to the avant-garde. The Jerusalem Theatre is the main venue, but a dozen secondary locations around the city get some of the smaller, more "fringe" acts.

Fodor's Choice ★ The fine crafts and lively concerts of August's **Hutzot Hayotzer Arts and Crafts Festival** (☎ *02/629–7481* 🌐 *www.artfair.jerusalem.muni.il*), is a highlight of the summer. Located in the Sultan's Pool, an ancient reservoir in the Hinnom Valley across from the walls of the Old City, the 10-day event showcases crafts by Israeli and international artisans and features open-air concerts by Israeli singers.

★ The **Oud Festival** (☎ *02/624–5206* 🌐 *www.confederationhouse.org/english*), held each November, pays homage to the Arabic lute and presents a range of ethnic music from Turkey, Iraq, India, and a host of other cultures, often including Israeli rock. The festival is held at various concert halls around town. Like many Jerusalem festivals, it's an occasion for Jerusalemites and their out of town friends.

August's **Wine Festival** (☎ *02/670–8811* 🌐 *www.imj.org.il*) presents the latest vintages for the country's vineyards. For the price of a wine glass, you can sample all you want. The Israel Museum is the main venue, and it's very pleasant to wander through the sculpture garden with a glass of fine wine.

★ The **Puppet Festival** (☎ *02/561–8514* 🌐 *www.traintheater.co.il*), the creation of Jerusalem's Train Theater, is dedicated to the art of puppeteering. Each August, puppeteers from around the globe bring their productions to theaters around Jerusalem. Shows are generally geared toward youngsters, although there are also shows appropriate for the whole family.

FILM

Many new films, American and otherwise, reach Israel screens very quickly, while some are mysteriously delayed. Israeli films have been garnering international praise in recent years; they and other non-English-speaking movies are almost always subtitled in English. Check newspaper listings for showtimes.

★ **Jerusalem Cinematheque** (✉ *11 Hebron Rd., Hinnom Valley* ☎ *02/565–4333* 🌐 *www.jer-cin.org.il*) specializes in old, rare, and art films, but its many programs often include recent offerings. Its monthly programs focus on specific directors, actors, or subjects, and its annual **Jerusalem Film Festival,** held in July, is a must for film buffs. December's **Jewish Film Festival** is a smaller but no less enjoyable experience. The theater is open Friday night.

The venerable **Jerusalem Theatre** (✉ *20 Marcus St., Talbieh* ☎ *02/560–5755* 🌐 *http://www.jerusalem-theatre.co.il*) screens films in several theaters within the complex, many of them from abroad.

The veteran **Lev Smadar** (✉ *4 Lloyd George St., German Colony* ☎ *02/561–8168* 🌐 *www.lev.co.il*), in the German Colony, is a bit of a throwback to yesteryear's movie atmosphere. It's a single cinema in an older building on a narrow lane, with its own café and bar and a local following.

Rav Chen (✉ *19 Ha'oman St., Talpiot Industrial Zone* ☎ *02/679–2799*) is a multiauditorium cinema group that shares a building with a large supermarket.

MUSIC

Classical music abounds in Jerusalem, with Israeli orchestras and chamber ensembles performing year-round and a trickle of international artists passing through. There's other interesting programming around town, too.

The **International Convention Center** (✉ *1 Zalman Shazar Blvd., Givat Ram* ☎ *02/655–8558* 🌐 *www.iccjer.co.il/en*), opposite the Central Bus Station, is the local venue for the subscription series of the world-renowned Israel Philharmonic Orchestra.

The **Jerusalem Theatre** (✉ *20 Marcus St., Talbieh* ☎ *02/560–5755*) houses four auditoriums of different sizes. It's officially named the Jerusalem Centre for the Performing Arts, though nobody calls it that. The 750-seat Henry Crown Auditorium is the home base of the Jerusalem Symphony Orchestra, and the venue for the popular **Etnachta** series of free concerts produced by Israel Radio's classical station and broadcast live Monday at 5 pm, generally from October through June.

Beit Avi Chai (✉ *44 King George St., Downtown* ☎ *02/621–5300* 🌐 *www.bac.org.il*) explores Jewish culture, thought, and creativity. Its 270-seat auditorium hosts lectures, concerts, and theater in Hebrew and English throughout the year.

The musical and theatrical performances at **Beit Shmuel** (✉ *6 Eliyahu Shama'a St., King David St.* ☎ *02/620–3455* 🌐 *www.beitshmuel.com*) are usually in Hebrew, but the music often speaks a universal language.

Bet Ticho (✉ *9 Harav Kook St., near Zion Sq., Downtown* ☎ *02/624–5068*) holds intimate recitals on Friday mornings in a serene setting.

Next to the Israel Museum, the **Bible Lands Museum** (✉ *25 Granot St., Givat Ram* ☎ *02/561–1066* 🌐 *www.blmj.org*) offers Saturday-evening classical, jazz, gospel, and folk music concerts for most of the year. Each concert is preceded by cheese and wine in the foyer.

The 500-seat **YMCA Concert Hall** (✉ *26 King David St., King David St.* ☎ *02/569–2692* 🌐 *www.jcmf.*

MUSIC IN CHURCHES

Hearing music in one of Jerusalem's many churches can be a moving experience. The **Church of the Redeemer** (✉ *Muristan, Christian Quarter* ☎ *02/626–6800* 🌐 *www.elcjhl.org/cong/jerusalem*) is a favorite venue. **Dormition Abbey** (✉ *Mt. Zion* ☎ *02/565–5330* 🌐 *www.dormitio.net*) offers concerts, mostly on Saturday, late morning. The **Mormon campus** (✉ *Mt. Scopus* ☎ *02/626–5666* 🌐 *www.ce.byu.edu/jc*) hosts a Sunday evening classical concert series in its fine auditorium.

org.il/EN) is the main venue for the much-acclaimed **Jerusalem International Chamber Music Festival** in late August. It hosts a rousing Israeli folklore performance—mostly singing and folk dancing—usually on Monday, Thursday, and Saturday evenings. Reservations are advised; arrive early, as seats are unnumbered. The cost is about NIS 100.

THEATER

The **Israel Festival,** held in May or June in the Jerusalem Theatre, is your best bet for quality English-language productions.

The **Khan Theater** (✉ *2 David Remez Sq., Hebron Rd.* ☎ *02/671–8281*) has mostly Hebrew productions, but there are a few in English. **The Lab** (✉ *28 Hebron Rd., Hebron Rd.* ☎ *02/629–2000 or 02/629–2001* 🌐 *www.maabada.org.il*) is a place to call about possible English productions.

SPORTS AND THE OUTDOORS

Most visitors who like to exercise regularly, or want to atone for eating their way through Israel, make do with the hotel gym or a jog through the neighborhood. You might also want to try joining an informal soccer or basketball game in Sacher Park, on Ben-Zvi Boulevard, on Friday afternoons and Saturday mornings.

BIKING

The **Jerusalem Bicycling Club** (☎ *052/253–1667*) leads mountain-bike rides on Saturday morning at 7 am, starting from the International Convention Center, Binyanei Ha'ooma (opposite the Central Bus Station). This informal club is a good source for information on bike rentals and can recommend routes within the city.

Ofnei Nitzan (✉ *137 Jaffa St., Downtown* ☎ *02/625–2741*) is a good place to rent bicycles. The shop is closed Saturday.

Fodor's Choice ★ Tour guide Moshe Gold runs **Midnight Biking Through Jerusalem** (✉ *Haas Promenade parking lot, Yanovsky St., Talpiot Industrial Zone* ☎ *054/636–2884* 🌐 *www.jerusalembiking.com*), a three-hour tour through the streets of Jerusalem. The ride, which begins at 10 pm, is for riders ages 12 and up. Led by licensed English and Hebrew-speaking guides, they can be customized according to your interests.

SWIMMING

The enthusiast can swim year-round at several hotel pools, including those at the Dan Jerusalem, the Ramada Jerusalem, and Ramat Rachel. There are also public pools. Check opening hours, as some pools provide specific hours for mixed or single-sex swimming.

The **Jerusalem Pool** (✉ *43 Emek Refa'im St., German Colony* ☎ *02/563–2092*) has a public Olympic-sized pool that is covered in winter. It gets very crowded in July and August, and the locker rooms are cramped, but it's one of the most reasonable places around, with admission at NIS 45 for the day.

TENNIS

Tennis has become increasingly popular in Israel. In addition to the courts below, a few major hotels have their own courts, but may restrict usage to guests or club members. Ask your concierge to make inquiries if you want to play at a particular hotel. At all venues, advance reservations are always required.

The **Hebrew University at Mt. Scopus** (✉ *1 Churchill St., Mt. Scopus* ☎ *02/588–2796* 🌐 *www.cosell.co.il*) has 10 lighted courts and rental equipment. Courts go for NIS 20 an hour during the day and NIS 25 an hour in the evening. You can rent a racket for NIS 20, and buy three balls for NIS 30. Call ahead to book, especially during campus recess.

The **Israel Tennis Center** (✉ *5 Almaliach St., Katamon Tet* ☎ *02/679–1866* 🌐 *www.israeltenniscenter.com*) has 18 lighted courts, available for NIS 45 per hour during the day, NIS 60 at night. Equipment rental is sometimes available.

SHOPPING

Jerusalem offers distinctive ideas for gifts—for yourself or others—from jewelry and art to traditional crafts, items of a religious nature, and souvenirs. The several shopping areas make it easy to plan expeditions. Prices are generally fixed in the center city and the Jewish Quarter of the Old City, though you can sometimes negotiate for significant discounts on expensive art and jewelry. Shopping in the Old City's colorful Arab bazaar, or souk (pronounced "shook" in Israel—rhymes with "book"), is fascinating but can be a trap for the unwary.

Young fashion designers, often graduates of Jerusalem's Bezalel Academy of Arts and Design, have opened a stream of shops and boutiques. They are scattered throughout the city.

Stores generally open by 8:30 am or 9 am, and some close between 1 pm and 4 pm. A few still close on Tuesday afternoon, a traditional but less and less observed half day. Jewish-owned stores (that is, all of West Jerusalem—the "New City"—and the Old City's Jewish Quarter) close on Friday afternoon by 2 pm or 3 pm, depending on the season and the kind of store (food and souvenir shops tend to stay open later), and reopen on Sunday morning. Some stores geared to the tourist trade, particularly Downtown, reopen on Saturday night after the Jewish Sabbath ends, especially in summer. Arab-owned stores in the Old City and East Jerusalem are busiest on Saturday and quietest on Sunday, when many (but not all) Christian storekeepers close for the day.

SHOPPING STREETS AND MALLS

Arts and Crafts Lane (*Hutzot Hayotzer,* ✉ *Hinnom Valley*), opposite and downhill from the Jaffa Gate, is home to goldsmiths and silversmiths specializing in jewelry, fine art, and Judaica, generally done in an ultramodern, minimalist style. The work is of extremely high quality and priced accordingly. Look for the exquisite designs of **Sari Sru-**

lovitch (✉ *Hutzot Hayotzer, Hinnom Valley* ☎ *02/628–6699* 🌐 *www.sarisrulovitch.com*).

The **Cardo** (✉ *Jewish Quarter St., Jewish Quarter*), in the Old City's Jewish Quarter, began life as the main thoroughfare of Byzantine Jerusalem, was a commercial street during the Crusader era, and has now been converted into an attractive shopping area. Beyond discovering souvenirs and Judaica, you'll find good-quality jewelry and art here.

Emek Refa'im (✉ *German Colony*) has become a popular area in which to shop, eat, and people-watch from early morning to late at night. Gifts and jewelry are easy to find in a rainbow of styles and tastes to meet different budgets.

King David Street (✉ *King David St.*) is lined with prestigious stores and galleries, most with an emphasis on art, Judaica, antiquities, or high-end jewelry.

Malcha Mall (✉ *Malcha* ☎ *02/679–1333*), known locally as Kenyon Malcha, is—at 500,000 square feet, not counting parking—one of the largest in the Middle East. It includes a department store, a supermarket, and almost 200 shops and eateries. The interior is an attractive mix of arched skylights and wrought-iron banisters in a quasi–art deco style.

Mamilla Avenue (✉ *King Solomon St.*), a new addition to the shopping scene, is bordered on one end by the upscale Mamilla Hotel and at the other by Old City's Jaffa Gate. Besides the selection of familiar clothing chains such as Ralph Lauren and Tommy Hilfiger, and some more unique choices, there's a growing handful of restaurants and cafés.

The pedestrian-only **Midrachov** (✉ *Downtown*) is simply Downtown Ben-Yehuda Street, the heartbeat of West Jerusalem. The selection of clothing, shoes, jewelry, souvenirs, T-shirts, and street food here makes for a fun shopping experience. Street musicians serenade the passersby, and the human parade is best appreciated from one of the many outdoor cafés. Summer evenings are lively, as the mall fills with peddlers of cheap jewelry and crafts, and young admiring shoppers.

Yoel Salomon Street (✉ *Nahalat Shiva*), in the old neighborhood of Nahalat Shiva, just off Zion Square, has also been developed as a pedestrian mall. Between the restaurants, you'll find several crafts galleries and arty jewelry and clothing shops, both on the main drag and in the adjacent alleys and courtyards.

STREET MARKETS

★ Jerusalem's main market is the **souk** (✉ *Christian and Muslim Quarters*) in the Old City, spread over a warren of intersecting streets. This is where much of Arab Jerusalem shops. It's awash with color and redolent with the clashing scents of exotic spices. Village women's baskets of produce vie for attention with hanging shanks of lamb, fresh fish on ice, and fresh-baked delicacies. Food stalls are interspersed with purveyors of fabrics and shoes. The baubles and trinkets of the tourist trade often seem secondary, except along the well-trodden paths of the Via Dolorosa, David Street, and Christian Quarter Road.

Stores along the narrow streets of the souk in the Old City tempt passersby with food, fabrics, and ceramics.

Haggling with merchants in the Arab market—a time-honored tradition—is not always the good-natured experience it once was. It is not always easy to identify the honest merchants among the many whose jewelry, antiquities, leather, and embroidery are often not what they claim. Unless you know what you want, know how much it's *really* worth, and enjoy the sometimes aggressive give-and-take of bargaining, you're better off just enjoying the local color and doing your shopping in the less crowded New City. Note that women should watch their purses and dress discreetly.

Fodor's Choice ★

Near the commercial Clal Center is the produce market **Machaneh Yehuda** (✉ *Off Jaffa St., Machaneh Yehuda*), a block-long alleyway that becomes a blur of brilliant primary colors as the city's best-quality fruit and vegetables, pickles and cheeses, fresh fish and poultry, confections, and falafel await inspection. The busiest days are Thursday and Friday, when Jews shop for the Sabbath; the market is closed on Saturday along with the rest of Jewish West Jerusalem. Combine your visit with lunch or a snack at one of the many Middle Eastern restaurants in the neighborhood, or grab a cup of excellent coffee at a Western-style café. And before you fill your baskets and bags, stop in at the wonderful boutiques and shops scattered throughout the market.

SPECIALTY STORES

ART GALLERIES

Several galleries representing Israeli artists are close to the city's premier hotels, on King David Street.

Udi Merioz, the artist and owner of **Blue and White Art Gallery** (✉ *1 Cardo St., Jewish Quarter* ☎ *02/628–8464* 🌐 *www.blueandwhiteart.com*), does "soft painting," a special appliqué technique that uses cloth on cloth. The gallery also represents Israeli artist Yaacov Agam.

On Arts and Crafts Lane, **Motke Blum** (✉ *Hutzot Hayotzer, Hinnom Valley* ☎ *02/623–4002* 🌐 *www.motke.com*) does fine soft-colored oils and minimalist landscapes.

BEAUTY PRODUCTS

The **Ahava Center** (✉ *5 Ben-Yehuda St., Downtown* ☎ *02/625–2592*) stocks all the Ahava products that use minerals from the Dead Sea, but at less attractive prices than elsewhere.

The **Dead Sea Gallery** (✉ *17 Jaffa St., corner of King Solomon St., Downtown* ☎ *02/622–1451*) stocks Ahava skincare products. Their Dermud line with Dead Sea minerals is particularly worth trying. The helpful staff and the competitive prices make this visit a particular pleasure. Mail-order service is also available.

Laline (✉ *Mamilla Ave., Mamilla* ☎ *02/622–1451*) in the Mamilla Mall is known for its trademark white-and-black setting for luxe creams and soaps.

Sabon Shel Paam (✉ *21 Emek Refa'im St., German Colony* ☎ *02/622–1451*) sells herb-infused soaps, creams, lotions, and scrubs.

CLOTHING

Clothing can be expensive in Israel, but Jerusalem is now home to the boutiques of a collection of relatively affordable Israeli designers. Once, it seemed, you could only find clothes for impossibly thin teenagers or full-figured women, but the new stores offer classy and fashionable items for in-between sizes as well. Another unsuspected innovation: if you're looking for that special wedding gown, you may well find it in the holy city.

A.B.C. (✉ *25 King George St., Downtown* ☎ *02/624–2549*) is a homegrown label that has developed popular, well-made women's lines.

Comme il faut (✉ *24 Hillel St., Downtown* ☎ *03/717–1534* 🌐 *www.comme-il-faut.com*) is the Jerusalem outpost of this Tel Aviv collection of hip, loose clothing made for and by women.

With well-chosen pieces by local designers, **Elsa** (✉ *53 Bethlehem Rd., Baka* ☎ *077/550–2878*) is a small but well-stocked boutique with a friendly staff that knows its wares.

Gilgul (✉ *8 Emek Refa'im, German Colony* ☎ *02/566–0555*) has a wonderful selection of both imported and Israeli clothing for babies, toddlers, and preschoolers.

Haegoz (✉ *30 Haegoz, Machaneh Yehuda* ☎ *02/623–2467*) offers a monochromatic selection of Israeli designer clothing and offbeat accessories, chosen by the owner who knows what looks good on her customers.

Hemp Shop (✉ *27 Ben-Yehuda St., Downtown* ☎ *02/623–0668*) brings you items made from, well, hemp. The fabrics are both gentle on your skin and environmentally friendly. It's pricey but worth a look.

Him with the Shirts (✉ *3 Ben Sira St., Downtown* ☎ *077/783–3499*) has a great array of T-shirts with clever sayings and designs, primarily in Hebrew.

Lord Kitsch (✉ *42 Jaffa St., Downtown* ☎ *02/625–2595* ✉ *Jerusalem Mall, Malcha* ☎ *02/678–0576* ✉ *Achim Yisrael Mall, 18 Yad Harutzim, Talpiot Industrial Zone* ☎ *02/673–3106*) stocks a range of casual clothes, including T-shirts in a full range of colors.

Israeli fashion designer **Kedem Sasson** (✉ *21 King George St., Downtown* ☎ *02/625–2602* 🌐 *www.kedem-sasson.com*) caters to the fuller figure, with clothes in soft fabrics, some of them in decidedly quirky styles.

Naama Bezalel (✉ *27 King George St., Downtown* ☎ *02/625–5611* ✉ *26 King George St., Downtown* ☎ *02/622–3479*) specializes in decidedly feminine lines for a range of ages, as well as a selection of distinctly beautiful bridal dresses. The second store across the street carries discounted leftovers from past seasons.

Pashmina (✉ *4 HaMelitz St., German Colony* ☎ *02/561–0567*) offers a wonderful selection of Israeli-designed clothing, jewelry, shoes, belts, and bags. Let the owner, Michal, or her skilled assistants advise you; they know their inventory and are helpful without being pushy.

Poenta (✉ *21-23 Yoel Salomon St., Nahalat Shiva* ☎ *02/624–5677* ✉ *6 Shatz St., Downtown* ☎ *02/500–1106*) now has three locations in Jerusalem. Two stores sit side by side in Nahalat Shiva, one selling unique bags, jewelry and crafts, the other a distinctive selection of Israeli designer clothing. The Downtown store offers a more upscale offering, as well as bags and jewelry.

Ronen Chen (✉ *Alrov Mamilla Ave., Mamilla* ☎ *02/624–2881* 🌐 *ronenchen.com*) designs simple, classic styles in very comfortable fabrics.

Shoofra (✉ *5 Hillel St., Downtown* ☎ *02/623–4414* 🌐 *www.shoofra.co.il*) carries hip shoes from Europe, Israel, and the United States.

Sigal Dekel (✉ *Alrov Mamilla Ave., Mamilla* ☎ *0732/150–115* 🌐 *www.sigaldekel.com*) is trendy and expensive, with clothes in interesting fabrics others don't use.

Sofia (✉ *2 Bezalel St., Downtown* ☎ *02/625–2765*) offers a well-honed selection of Israeli designer clothing and accessories, chosen by owner Miri Ashur Zuta.

Sweet (✉ *2 Ben-Yehuda St., Downtown* ☎ *02/625–4835*) has a good selection of T-shirts ready for custom decoration.

Tali Imbar (✉ *Jerusalem Mall, Malcha* ☎ *02/679–3890* 🌐 *www.talimbar.com*) creates casually elegant clothes that are a pleasure to wear.

Tashtari (✉ *25 King George St., Downtown* ☎ *02/625–3282*) is an exclusive boutique that features imported handmade evening bags (including a line made of recycled materials), owner Amos Sadan's own outstanding "wearable art"—much of which is influenced by Japanese aesthetics—as well as hats, scarves, and shawls.

Ceramic creations large and small are among the many lovely crafts worth seeking out around Jerusalem.

CRAFTS

Australian immigrant **Barbara Shaw** (✉ *2 Bezalel St., Downtown* ☎ *02/625–7474* ✉ *Harmony Hotel, 6 Yoel Salomon St., Downtown* ☎ *02/623–3350* 🌐 *www.barbarashawgifts.com*) has put her colorful, contemporary stamp on a selection of household gifts, from crisp dishtowels and whimsical aprons to pillows and tote bags.

Charlotte (✉ *4 Coresh St., Downtown* ☎ *02/625–1632*) carries colorful items of high quality: ceramics, weavings, painted silks, jewelry, and fashion accessories.

Danny Azoulay (✉ *5 Yoel Salomon St., Nahalat Shiva* ☎ *02/623–3918*) offers delicate items in fine porcelain, all hand-painted in rich shades of blue, red, and gold. Many are traditional Jewish ritual objects—some pricey—but you can also find less expensive items, such as napkin rings and bottle stoppers.

Hoshen (✉ *32 Emek Refa'im, German Colony* ☎ *02/563–0966* 🌐 *www.hoshenshop.com*) offers attractive items in wood, ceramics, fabric, and jewelry.

Gans (✉ *8 Rivlin St., Nahalat Shiva* ☎ *02/625–1159* 🌐 *www.gans.co.il*) proudly sells art and crafts made only in Israel. Choose from good-quality Judaica, glassware, weaving, jewelry, painted silk, wood, and ceramic ornaments; there are many moderately priced options.

Klein (✉ *3 Ziv St., off Bar Ilan St., Tel Arza* ☎ *02/538–8784*) produces some of the highest-quality olive-wood objects in Israel. This is the factory showroom, off the tourist route. It stocks everything they make, from bowls and yo-yos to attractive trays of Armenian pottery tiles set in olive wood, picture frames, boxes, and desktop paraphernalia.

Jerusalem Experience (✉ *17 Jaffa St., opposite Safra Square, Downtown* ☎ *02/622–3030*) is the place for items of Christian interest and handmade Judaica. The friendly staff is happy to show you Israeli perfumes, skincare products, ceramics, glassware, and textiles, but also books about Jerusalem and other aspects of the Holy Land.

The **Jerusalem House of Quality** (✉ *12 Hebron Rd., Hebron Rd.* ☎ *02/671–7430* 🌐 *www.art-jerusalem.com*) showcases the work of some excellent Israeli craftspeople in the media of ceramics, glass, jewelry, sculpture, wooden ornaments, and ritual objects. You can often see them at work in their studios on the second floor.

Nisha (✉ *31 Bethlehem Rd., Baka* ☎ *02/672–5630*) displays an ample selection of well-priced Israeli crafts, from clay jewelry to whimsical pottery.

Ruth Havilio (✉ *Ein Kerem St. D/4, Ein Kerem* ☎ *02/641–7912*) makes hand-painted tiles with a more modern feel, for both decorative and practical purposes. Her sense of color and fun (whimsical clay animals, for instance) plays alongside more traditional styles. You can have tiles personalized, but keep in mind that this cannot be done on the spot. To get there, take the alley to the left of St. John's Church. Part of the charm of the gallery is its evocative setting in a courtyard.

Set (✉ *34 Emek Refa'im, German Colony* ☎ *02/566–3366*) can solve your gift problems with an array of different objects, from jewelry to handbags, in both traditional and modern styles.

ARMENIAN POTTERY

Armenian hand-painted pottery—geometric or stylized natural motifs, in blues and greens, with somewhat non-Western brown, yellow, or mauve accents—is a good and well-priced idea for gifts.

Darian Armenian Ceramics (✉ *12 Shlomzion Hamalka, Downtown* ☎ *02/623–4802*) is the only Armenian gallery in West Jerusalem. Besides pieces with Jewish themes, it makes tables and mirrors to order and has a plentiful selection of bargain-priced seconds.

The standouts in Armenian **Hagop Antreassian's** studio (✉ *near Zion Gate, Armenian Quarter* ☎ *02/627–2584*) are his wonderful large bowls. They won't fit in your carry-ons, but Hagop ships. You can often catch him painting or firing his clay creations in his studio just inside Zion Gate.

Jerusalem Pottery (✉ *15 Via Dolorosa, Muslim Quarter* ☎ *02/626–1587* 🌐 *www.jerusalempottery.biz*), at the VI Station of the Cross, is the store of one of the best local artisans: Stefan Karakashian. His particularly high-quality work includes plates, bowls, tiles, and plaques.

Sandrouni (✉ *Armenian Orthodox Patriarchate Rd., Armenian Quarter* ☎ *02/628–3567* 🌐 *www.sandrouni.com*) stocks a variety of utilitarian pieces in many colors and styles.

COOPERATIVE STORES

Whether you like the unpredictable shapes of contemporary ceramics or more conservative items, local artists present a rich choice at three cooperative stores, all on the same street.

Cadim (✉ *4 Yoel Salomon St., Nahalat Shiva* ☎ *02/623–4869*) presents a decidedly contemporary selection.

The **Guild of Ceramicists** (✉ *27 Yoel Salomon St., Nahalat Shiva* ☎ *02/624–4065*) beckons with its delightful serendipity of colorful tiled steps. Some of the functional and ornamental pottery is made by Russian-Israeli artists, and it looks more whimsical that usual.

Shemonah Beyachad (✉ *11 Yoel Salomon St., Nahalat Shiva* ☎ *02/624–7250*) has grown to become a group of 11 individual ceramicists (even though the name means "Eight Together"), one of whom is usually on duty in the store.

PAPERCUTS

Papercutting is a traditional and well-established Jewish art form. These pieces make unusual gifts—to say nothing of being both light and easy to pack.

Archie Granot (✉ *1 Agron St., Downtown* ☎ *02/625–2210* 🌐 *www.archiegranot.com*) has evolved his own complex, multilayered style of papercut Judaica inspired by traditional motifs. Some of his high-end creations are displayed in museum collections around the world.

Judaicut (✉ *21 Yoel Salomon St., Nahalat Shiva* ☎ *02/623–3634* 🌐 *www.judaicut.co.il*) sells more traditional and affordable papercuts, which can be customized with your name.

HARPS

The **House of Harrari** (✉ *Ramat Raziel* ☎ *02/570–9075* 🌐 *www.harrariharps.com*) is in the village of Ramat Raziel, a 25-minute drive from Downtown Jerusalem, west of Ein Kerem. The Bible (the makers say) inspired the small decorative door harps and graceful 10- and 22-string folk instruments. The workshop displays the instruments in different stages of production. There are many kinds of ornamentation, and the door harps can be decorated with an inscription. The gallery will ship your purchase home. Call for directions.

JEWELRY

Jewelry in Israel is of a high international standard. You can choose between conservative styles; sleek, modern pieces inspired by different ethnicities; and the increasingly popular bead jewelry of Michal Negrin and other current Israeli stars of both the local and international scene.

Adipaz (✉ *20 Pierre Koenig St., Talpiot Industrial Zone* ☎ *02/678–3887*) cuts diamonds and makes its own jewelry, much of it without precious stones.

★ **Dan Alsberg** (✉ *Hinnom Valley* ☎ *02/627–1430* 🌐 *www.studioalsberg.com*), in the Arts and Crafts Lane (Hutzot Hayotzer), outside Jaffa Gate, is a particularly outstanding and original craftsman of modern pieces, mostly in gold and silver.

Hedya (✉ *23 Hillel St., Downtown* ☎ *02/622–1151*) carries the collections of both Ze'ev and Sharon Tammuz: necklaces and earrings made from antique silver, amber, and other materials that retain a feel of the past.

H. Stern (✉ *7 King David St., King David St.* ☎ *02/624–3606*) is an international company that offers high-quality, expensive pieces.

Idit (✉ *23 King George St., Downtown* ☎ *02/622–1911* 🌐 *www.iditjewelry.com*) offers an intriguing range of in-house designs. The family business is still run by veteran craftsman Chaim Paz.

Keo (✉ *25 Emek Refa'im, German Colony* ☎ *02/563–7026*) specializes in delicate, modern pieces at reasonable prices.

Lia (✉ *42 Emek Refa'im, German Colony* ☎ *02/563–0830*) displays the work of Israeli designers, with a special emphasis on bold, modern creations out of precious and semiprecious metals. There's a workshop downstairs for those who'd like to learn for themselves.

Michal Negrin (✉ *Alrov Mamilla Ave., Mamilla* ☎ *02/624–2112* ✉ *Jerusalem Mall, Malcha* ☎ *02/648–0067* ✉ *12 Yoel Salomon St., Nahalat Shiva, Downtown* ☎ *02/622–3573* 🌐 *www.michalnegrin.com*) has become a remarkable success story with her whimsical, vintage-inspired jewelry and fashion accessories.

Sheshet (✉ *34 Emek Refa'im, German Colony* ☎ *02/566–2261*) has a solid selection of contemporary Israeli gold and silver pieces, as well as locally designed leather bags, belts, and wallets.

Stav (✉ *40 Emek Refa'im, German Colony* ☎ *02/563–7059* 🌐 *www.stavjewelry.com*) offers exquisite (and expensive) pieces in a graceful mix of both ethnic and modern influences.

Around Jerusalem and the Dead Sea

WITH MASADA AND BETHLEHEM

WORD OF MOUTH

"This was taken on my trip to Israel and the Dead Sea. There were only a few of us on this stretch of beach, and I captured this lone paddler, with Jordan visible in the distance."

—photo by markdewd, Fodors.com member

WELCOME TO AROUND JERUSALEM AND THE DEAD SEA

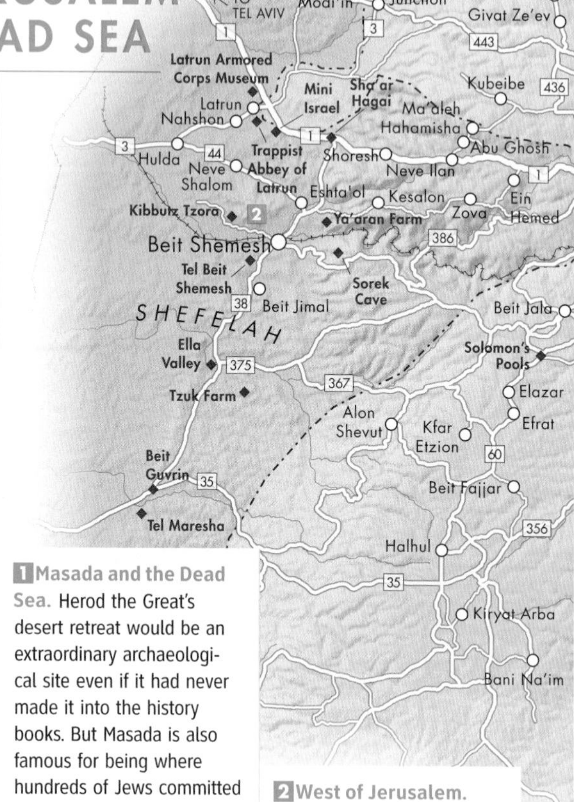

TOP REASONS TO GO

★ **Ein Gedi:** This oasis rich in flora, fauna, and archaeology—praised in the Bible for its beauty and today one of Israel's most impressive national parks—offers spectacular hiking near waterfalls and canyons.

★ **Masada:** The spectacular remains of this mountaintop palace overlooking the Dead Sea recall its history as a retreat for Herod the Great and the site of the last stand of the Jewish rebels against Rome in AD 73.

★ **Dead Sea:** At the lowest point on Earth, float effortlessly on one of the world's saltiest bodies of water, renowned for its therapeutic qualities. In Ein Bokek, cover yourself with the mud, exported as a beauty treatment.

★ **Bethlehem:** The location of Jesus' manger is believed to be beneath the Byzantine-era Church of the Nativity.

★ **Judean Hills wineries:** Close to Jerusalem, this area is home to more than two-dozen wineries that produce some excellent and highly prized wines.

1 Masada and the Dead Sea. Herod the Great's desert retreat would be an extraordinary archaeological site even if it had never made it into the history books. But Masada is also famous for being where hundreds of Jews committed suicide rather than surrender to Rome. Hike (or take the cable car) to the top of the plateau for sunrise over the Dead Sea then take a relaxing dip in this saltiest of all lakes. Combine a visit with a trip to Ein Gedi or Ein Bokek, both near the Dead Sea, for unforgettable desert adventures.

Ein Gedi oasis

2 West of Jerusalem. The Judean Hills west of Jerusalem are dotted with natural springs, forested nature reserves, and picturesque villages—as well as some excellent wineries. Pack a picnic and take the winding road to visit Soreq Cave and Beit Guvrin National Park.

3 Bethlehem. Just a few miles south of Jerusalem in the West Bank, visit the birthplace of Jesus, today marked by the Church of the Nativity on Manger Square.

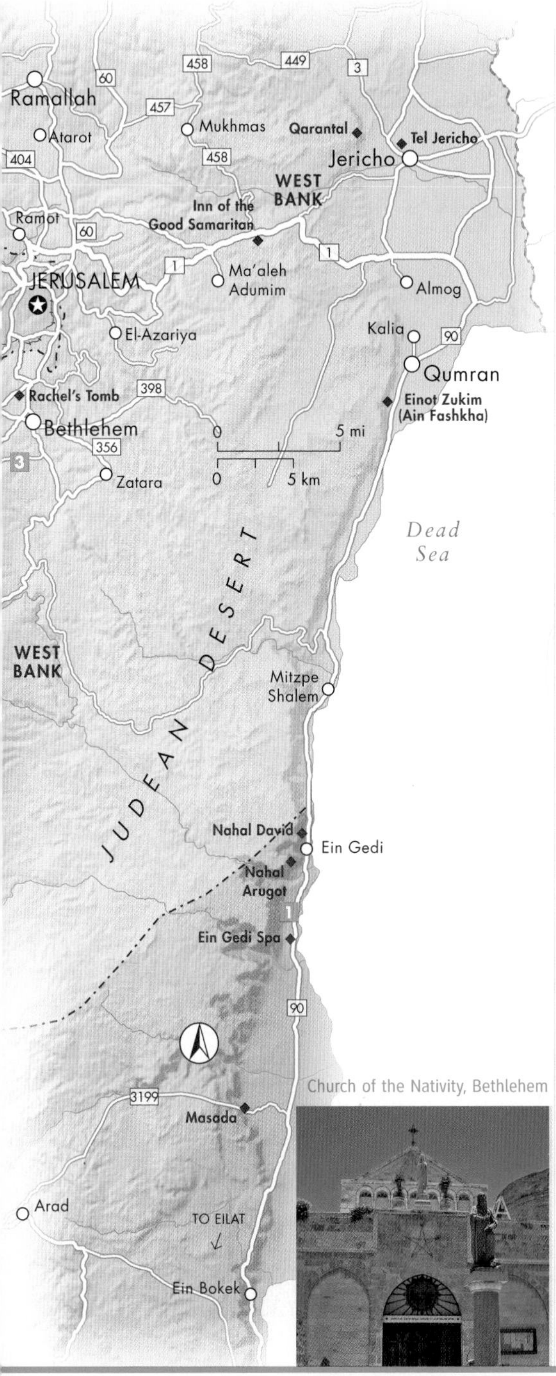

GETTING ORIENTED

The wealth of beautiful landscapes, historical treasures, and biblical sites within an easy drive of Jerusalem makes a number of good day trips. To the west lie the Judean Hills, covered with vineyards and farms. To the south is Bethlehem, an age-old pilgrimage site for Christians. And to the east is the Judean Desert, graced with fertile oases like Jericho and Ein Gedi. Descending from Jerusalem's peaks, you quickly arrive at the Dead Sea—the lowest point on the face of Earth. Ein Bokek, near the Dead Sea's southern end, is a good place to float in its warm, salty water.

Church of the Nativity, Bethlehem

סכנת טביעה
خطر الغرق
DANGER OF
DROWNING

Near the Dead Sea

AROUND JERUSALEM AND THE DEAD SEA PLANNER

When To Go

The Dead Sea region is pleasant between October and April, but suffers from searing dry heat during the summer. Beginning the day with a tour of Masada can help beat the heat and the crowds. Ein Bokek, with its unique hotels and spas by the Dead Sea, attracts visitors even in broiling hot summer. Bethlehem is best early or late in the day if you want to avoid the crowds. Before you set out, check the hours for the Church of the Nativity. The area to the west of Jerusalem is agreeable any time of the year.

Some advanced planning pays off if you want to visit this region during a religious holiday, since transportation can be difficult during Jewish holidays like Yom Kippur and the Muslim observance of Ramadan. Similarly, Christmas is celebrated three times in Jerusalem and Bethlehem, according to the Western, Orthodox, and Armenian rites.

Getting Here and Around

Bus Travel: Egged buses are modern, air-conditioned, and reasonably priced. Service is dependable on main routes but infrequent to outlying rural districts. Egged buses do not run sunset Friday to sunset Saturday.

From the Beer Sheva Central Bus Station, buses depart four times a day for Arad, Ein Bokek, and other southern points. For Ein Bokek, there's also a daily 8:30 am bus from Tel Aviv's Central Bus Station (a three-hour ride) and several buses, departing on the hour, from Jerusalem (a two-hour journey). Buses can be crowded, especially on Friday and Sunday. You cannot buy tickets *or* reserve seats by phone for the above routes; go to the bus station, and arrive early.

Car Travel: Driving is preferable to relying on public transportation here, as some sights are on secondary roads where bus service is scarce. Highway conditions are good, and most destinations are signposted in both Hebrew and English. The steep road between Arad and Ein Bokek has one hairpin turn after another. Unless otherwise posted, stick to the intercity speed of 90 kph (56 mph). Budget extra time for leaving Jerusalem during rush hours. Gas stations are plentiful; some are open 24 hours but play it safe and keep the tank at least half full. If you plan to drive to areas controlled by the Palestinian Authority, there are two additional things to check in advance: whether your rental company allows its cars into the West Bank, and whether there is any political unrest that makes the roads unsafe.

Sherut Travel: *Sheruts,* or shared taxis seating up to 10 passengers, run set routes (usually along major bus routes) and charge a nominally more expensive fare. Arab sheruts to Bethlehem and Jericho are available from East Jerusalem's Damascus Gate, though an Arab taxi may be delayed at military checkpoints.

Train Travel: Israel Railways has regular—but slow—train service between Jerusalem and Tel Aviv, hourly from 6 am to 8 pm, from the southern neighborhood of Malcha; there are occasional departures from the Jerusalem Biblical Zoo. The beautiful 40-minute ride through forested hills to the Judean lowlands is spectacular for the scenery alone.

For more information on getting here and around, see Travel Smart Israel.

Dining

Some Judean Hills wineries offer fancy meals along with their tastings, but these should be reserved in advance. Abu Ghosh, on the way to Latrun, is known for its hummus and kebab restaurants. There are also some passable cafeterias west of Jerusalem, but few really tempting restaurants for dinner. An alternative is to take a packed lunch or have a picnic west of Jerusalem with wine and cheese. At the Dead Sea, it's always a good idea to make reservations in Ein Bokek restaurants, especially on Friday and Saturday night.

Lodging

Visitors, both national and international, who come to "take the waters" and enjoy the serene desert scenery, heavily use the lodgings in the Dead Sea region. On the northern shore, facilities range from youth hostels to kibbutz inns. Although they might conjure up visions of spartan plainness, the kibbutz inns are surprisingly comfortable. They also offer a chance to see life on the communal settlements firsthand.

Along the southern shore, hotels in sunny Ein Bokek run from family-style simplicity to pampering luxury. Shuttle buses link hotels with each other and the center of town. A beautiful and luxurious spa with a wide range of facilities is an important feature of each large hotel, and many smaller hotels as well. The high seasons are mid-March to mid-June, and mid-September to the end of November.

Since visitors typically explore the area west of Jerusalem on a day trip, lodgings are few and far between. The exceptions are some fine bed-and-breakfast–style guesthouses known as *zimmers*.

WHAT IT COSTS

	¢	$	$$	$$$	$$$$
Restaurants	under NIS 32	NIS 32–NIS 49	NIS 50–NIS 75	NIS 76–NIS 100	over NIS 100
Hotels	under $120	$120–$200	$201–$300	$301–$400	over $400

Restaurant prices are per person for a main course at dinner in NIS (Israeli shekels). Hotel prices are in U.S. dollars, for two people in a standard double room in high season. Non-Israeli citizens paying in foreign currency are exempt from the 16% VAT tax on hotel rooms.

Planning Your Time

The Dead Sea can be a great day trip from Jerusalem but you'll have a richer experience if you spend a few nights in Ein Bokek. An ideal itinerary might be: On the first morning, climb Masada and marvel at the views then head to your Ein Bokek hotel for an afternoon at the Dead Sea; watch the hills of Jordan redden as the sun sets. On the second day, drive to Ein Gedi (1/2 hour north of Ein Bokek) for the waterfalls and a dip in the pools. On the third day, stop in Jericho on the way back to Jerusalem.

When traveling to Bethlehem, Jericho, and other areas under Palestinian control, you'll need to present your passport at the checkpoint. This usually just takes a minute. There can be traffic crossing back from Bethlehem to Jerusalem, so allow extra time.

Sightseeing Tours

Bus tours pick you up and return you to your hotel in Jerusalem: very convenient. Egged and United have full-day tours of Masada, the Dead Sea, and Ein Gedi, daily for about $70 per person from Jerusalem. The Jerusalem-based Eshcolot runs private tours.

Egged Tours (☎ *03/694–8888* 🌐 *www.egged.co.il/Eng*).

Eshcolot Tours (☎ *02/566–5555*). **United Tours** (☎ *03/617–3315* 🌐 *www.unitedtours.co.il*).

Updated by Benjamin Balint

The Judean Hills that encircle Jerusalem, together with the wilderness that slopes precipitously eastward to the Dead Sea, offer an astonishing range of scenery: springs and oases, forests and fields, hiking trails, and impressive archaeological sites such as Masada. West of the city, nature reserves and wineries offer other worthwhile excursions. Don't miss Soreq Cave, full of fantastic stalagmites and stalactites, or the extraordinary man-made caverns of Beit Guvrin and Maresha. The area is becoming more popular with a wide range of travelers, thanks to its thriving wineries and cheese and olive oil producers.

The Judean Desert–Dead Sea area—little changed from when Abraham wandered here with his flocks—contrasts sharply with the lush greenery of the oases of Ein Gedi, Ain Fashkha, and the verdant fields of Jericho. Nomadic Bedouin still cling to their ancestral way of life, herding sheep and goats, though you'll notice some concessions to modernity: pickup trucks are parked beside camels.

The route along the Dead Sea shore is hemmed in by towering brown cliffs fractured by *wadis*, or dry riverbeds. Ein Gedi has two of the most spectacular of these wadis, Nahal David and Nahal Arugot. In Ein Bokek, near the southern end of the Dead Sea, you can settle into one of the numerous health and beauty spas that make use of the Dead Sea's saline waters and medicinal mud.

Just to the north is Masada, Herod the Great's mountaintop palace-fortress built over 2,000 years ago, named a UNESCO World Heritage Site in 2001. Overlooking the Dead Sea, the king's extravagant architectural feat still displays ingenious water systems, elaborate frescoes and mosaic floors, and bathhouses. Add the human drama of the last Jewish stand against Rome during the Great Revolt, and it is easy to understand why this is one of the most visited sights in Israel.

Just south of Jerusalem, Bethlehem is a major site of Christian pilgrimage. The Church of the Nativity, the oldest church in the country, erected in the 4th century, is built over the grotto where Christian tradition holds Jesus was born. The West Bank Arab city of almost 40,000 sits on the ancient highway through the rocky Judean Hills.

MASADA AND THE DEAD SEA

The 4,000-foot descent from Jerusalem to the Dead Sea is only 24 km (15 mi), but takes you on a journey from one climate to another. Annual precipitation plummets from 22 inches in Jerusalem to 2 inches at the Dead Sea. Still, the desert's proximity has always made it part of that city's consciousness. Refugees fled here, hermits sought its solitude; and when the Temple stood, on the Day of Atonement a scapegoat bearing the sins of the Jewish people was symbolically driven off its stark precipices.

INN OF THE GOOD SAMARITAN

20 km (13 mi) east of Jerusalem on Route 1 and 500 yards east of the junction with Route 458.

GETTING HERE AND AROUND

Follow Route 1 east from Jerusalem for 20 km (13 mi). The site is clearly signposted on the south side of the road. You'll need your own car, as buses do not stop here.

EXPLORING

Inn of the Good Samaritan. This one-story building sits on the strategic spot that marks the halfway point between Jerusalem and Jericho, as well as the border between the biblical Israelite tribes of Benjamin, to the north, and Judah, to the south. Although no 1st-century remains have been found, the restored Ottoman-period *caravansary* (inn) likely sits in the same place as the inn mentioned in the New Testament (*Luke 10*) parable of a man ambushed on the Jericho road and helped by an altruistic Samaritan traveler. Also part of this site, the **Museum of the Good Samaritian** has indoor and open-air displays of mosaics and archaeological findings from Jewish and Samaritan synagogues as well as a Byzantine church.

If you're energetic, turn away from the inn, cross the highway *very, very* carefully, and climb the dirt track to the top of the hill opposite. Amid the scanty ruins of the small 12th-century Crusader fort of Maldoim—from which the outskirts of Jerusalem and Jericho are visible—the Gospel passage comes alive. ✉ *Rte 1.* 🎫 *Free.*

JERICHO

35 km (22 mi) east of Jerusalem on Route 1 and 5 km (3 mi) north on Route 90.

The sleepy oasis of Jericho—adorned with date palms, orange groves, banana plantations, bougainvillea bushes, and papaya trees—is aptly called Arikha, or "fragrant," in Arabic. This oldest continuously

Masada and the Dead Sea
WEST BANK
JORDAN
Jordan River
Dead Sea
JUDEAN DESERT
Ramallah
Bira
Horon Junction
Bet Horon
Givat Ze'ev
Atarot
Mukhmas
Qarantal
Hisham's Palace
Tel Jericho
Jericho
Kubeibe
Ma'aleh Hahamisha
Neve Ilan
Kiryat Anavim
Ramot
Inn of the Good Samaritan
TO TEL AVIV
Zova
Ein Hemed
Kesalon
JERUSALEM
Ma'aleh Adumim
Almog
Kalia
El-Azariya
Nes Harim
Rachel's Tomb
Bet Jala
Marsabah
Qumran
Einot Zukim (Ain Fashkha)
Kalia Beach
Bethlehem
see detail map
Solomon's Pools
Zatara
Elazar
Efrat
Kfar Etzion
Taqu
Beit Fajjar
Halhul
Kiryat Arba
Hebron
Bani Na'im
Mitzpe Shalem
Mineral Beach
Synagogue
Nahal David
Ein Gedi
Nahal Arugot
Ein Gedi Spa
Yatta
Karmel
Samu
Mezadot Yehuda
Masada
Tel Arad
Arad
Kuseifa
TO EILAT
Ein Bokek
0
5 mi
0
5 km
466
455
463
60
458
449
3
90
457
443
404
436
1
386
398
356
35
3269
316
80
3199
31

inhabited city in the world, Jericho is immortalized as the place where "the walls came tumblin' down" at the sound of Joshua's trumpets. Those ramparts haven't been found, but the ruins of Hisham's Palace will give you an idea of the devastating power of an earthquake at a time when cities were built of mud, wood, and stone.

The Arab population of about 25,000 is mostly Muslim, but the tiny Christian minority is well represented by a number of landmark churches and monasteries. These biblical and archaeological sites are what draw most tourists today.

GETTING HERE AND AROUND

Follow Route 1 east from Jerusalem for 35 km (13 mi), then turn north on Old Route 90. Jericho is clearly signposted. Egged bus drivers will drop you off at the side of Route 1, but it's still 5 km (3 mi) to Jericho.

TIMING

Jericho is very pleasant during the winter months, but swelteringly hot in the summer.

SAFETY AND PRECAUTIONS

As always, it's wise to check on the political situation before venturing into the Palestinian Authority. There are seldom problems in Jericho, however. Although there are no restrictions on tourists in private cars visiting the town, you will need to present your foreign passport to reenter Israeli-controlled territory. Your car rental insurance won't cover visits to this area, so you might prefer to hire a driver or visit with a tour group.

EXPLORING

TOP ATTRACTIONS

Hisham's Palace. Known as Khirbet al-Mafjar in Arabic, the recently restored Hisham's Palace has exquisite stonework and a spectacular mosaic floor. Hisham was a scion of the Ummayad dynasty, which built the Dome of the Rock and al-Aqsa Mosque in Jerusalem. Although the palace was severely damaged by the great earthquake of AD 749 while still under construction, the surviving mosaics and stone and plaster reliefs are evidence of its splendor.

A small gatehouse leads into a wide courtyard dominated by a star-shape stone window that once graced an upper floor. Several sections of the fine geometric mosaics have been left exposed; others are covered by sand. The most impressive part of the complex is the reception room, off the plaza. Its intricate mosaic floor, depicting a lion hunting gazelles, is one of the most beautiful in the country. The balustrade of an ornamental pool reflects the artistic influences of both East and West. Fragments of ornate stucco reliefs are still visible on some of the walls.

To get here go north from the traffic circle that constitutes downtown Jericho, follow Hisham's Palace Road for 4 km (2½ mi), turn right at the sign to Hisham's Palace after the Police Intelligence Building, and then take an immediate left down a 1 km (½ mi) access road. ✉ *Hisham's Palace Rd.* ☎ *02/232–2522* 🎫 *NIS 10* ⏲ *Daily 8–5.*

Tel Jericho. Also called Tel es-Sultan (Sultan's Hill), Tel Jericho is the mound of accumulated strata that entombs the legendary ancient city.

From the top you'll see a sweeping view of Jericho, the biblical "City of Palms." Although Tel Jericho has been extensively excavated, archaeologists have not found the walls that fell to the blast of Israelite rams' horns when Joshua stormed the city in the mid-13th century BC. The most impressive ruins that have been unearthed are a massive tower and a wall, remains of the world's oldest walled city, which predates the invention of pottery. Carbon-14 tests have placed human skulls and bones found here in the Neolithic period (Late Stone Age) between 7800 and 6500 BC. Little is known about these early urbanites, or why they needed such fortifications thousands of years before they became common in the region, but a wealth of artifacts, displayed in the Israel and Rockefeller museums in Jerusalem, helps us imagine their domestic life and customs. Across the road, capped by a pump house, is **Ain as-Sultan,** or the Sultan's Spring. The name comes from the prophet Elijah's miracle of sweetening the water with a bowl of salt (*II Kings 2:19–22*), and the waters are still eminently drinkable if you wish to refill your bottles. To the east in Jordan are the mountains of the biblical kingdoms of Ammon and Moab, among them the peak of Mt. Nebo, from which Moses viewed the Promised Land before dying at the ripe old age of 120.

To the south, among the banana trees some 3 km (2 mi) away and not far from the checkpoint at the south end of Jericho, are a number of small but distinctive mounds on both banks of Wadi Kelt. This is **Telul Abu 'Alayiq,** where the remains of the royal palace of the Hasmonean dynasty (2nd–1st centuries BC) have been uncovered. In the 1st century BC, Mark Antony gave the valuable oasis of Jericho to his beloved Cleopatra; the humiliated King Herod, Antony's local vassal, was then forced to lease the property back from the Egyptian queen. Herod the Great expanded and improved the palace, turning it into a winter retreat. He died there in 4 BC. The site is not developed; there is no entrance fee and you can wander here during daylight.

To the west is the **Mount of Temptation,** identified by tradition as the "exceedingly high mountain" from which Satan tempted Jesus with dominion over "all the kingdoms of the world" (Matthew 4). Halfway down the mountain sits the remarkable Greek Orthodox monastery of Qarantal, the name being a corruption of *quarantena*—a period of 40 days (the source of the English word *quarantine*)—the period of Jesus' temptation. Built into the cliff face in 1895 on Byzantine and Crusader remains, it is flanked by caves that once housed hermits. From a ticket booth facing Tel Jericho, a **cable car** offers round-trip rides up the mountain for NIS 55. The Jericho Heights Restaurant, with a spectacular view to the east, serves the cable car's upper station from which stairs lead up to the monastery.

To get to the tell by car, drive along Old Route 90, the main road through Jericho, and turn left at the traffic circle onto Ain as-Sultan Street. The parking lot is about 2 km (1 mi) down the road. ✉ *Ain as-Sultan St.* ☎ *02/232–1590 or 02/232–2240* 🌐 *www.jericho-cablecar.com* 🎫 *NIS 10* ⏲ *Oct.–Mar., daily 8:30–5; Apr.–Sept., daily 8:30–6.*

Tree of Zacchaeus. As you enter Jericho from Route 1, take the left fork at the traffic island. A few hundred yards farther, the road swings sharply to the left. To the right of the bend and one block down a no-entry street is a fenced-off, wide-girthed sycamore tree, which tradition (and the postcard vendors) identifies as the very one Zacchaeus, the chief tax collector, climbed to get a better look at Jesus (Luke 19:1–4).

WORTH NOTING

Banana Land. About 4 km (2½ mi) north of Tel Jericho along Canaanite Dulok Street, Banana Land is the only water park in the West Bank. Around the swimming pools you'll encounter Palestinian families enjoying a day off. ✉ *Canaanite Dulok St.* ☎ *02/232–0445* *NIS 10* *Daily 8:30–noon.*

WHERE TO EAT AND STAY

$$ MIDDLE EASTERN ✕ **Jericho Heights.** Reachable by cable car, this small hilltop restaurant offers tasty Middle Eastern cuisine, delicious Turkish coffee, and spectacular views of the oasis below. The pleasant dining room, perched on a terrace, has blissfully cool air-conditioning. ✉ *Qarantal St.* ☎ *02/232–1590* *AE, MC, V.*

$ MIDDLE EASTERN ✕ **Temptation.** The closest restaurant to Tel Jericho (they share a parking lot), Temptation offers excellent *bourma,* a honey-rolled pastry filled with whole pistachio nuts. The lunches are a good value, with tasty meat dishes and *mezzes* (Middle Eastern salads). ✉ *Ain as-Sultan St.* ☎ *02/232–2614* *AE, MC, V.*

$$ **Intercontinental Jericho.** On the southern edge of the city, the Intercontinental Jericho is the only major hotel in town. A pleasant blend of modern and traditional, rooms are comfortably appointed. The main attractions, however, are the two pools (and poolside restaurant and bar), open-air hot tub, and tennis courts. There's tasty Middle Eastern cuisine at the ninth-floor Lemon Grove restaurant. **Pros:** sparkling pool; plenty of amenities. **Cons:** not within walking distance of downtown. ✉ *Jerusalem-Jericho Rd.* ☎ *02/231–1200* *www.intercontinental.com* *181 rooms, 14 suites* *In-room: a/c, safe. In-hotel: restaurant, room service, bar, tennis court, pool, gym, spa, children's programs (ages 3–10), Internet terminal, Wi-Fi hotspot* *AE, DC, MC, V* *CP.*

QUMRAN

13 km (8 mi) south of the Almog Junction on Route 90, 20 km (13 mi) south of Jericho, 50 km (31 mi) east of Jerusalem.

GETTING HERE AND AROUND

Follow Route 1 east from Jerusalem for 50 km (31 mi), turning south on Route 90. Qumran is on the right. Not far from Qumran are some Dead Sea beaches worth a stop if you have a car, including Mineral Beach. Qumran is in the West Bank, but cars are routinely waved through the checkpoints.

SAFETY AND PRECAUTIONS

Check the weather forecast before hiking in the winter. On rare occasion, flash floods cause closures on Route 90.

The dryness of Qumran helped preserve the Dead Sea Scrolls stored in caves in the sculpted rock.

EXPLORING

Qumran. Although the remains of Qumran (the name comes from the Arabic word meaning "crescent moon") are not visually impressive, caves in the cliffs along the northwest shore of the Dead Sea yielded the most significant archaeological find ever made in Israel: the Dead Sea Scrolls. (Some are on display at the Israel Museum in Jerusalem.) These biblical, apocryphal, and sectarian religious texts were found under extraordinary circumstances in 1947 when a young Bedouin goatherd stumbled on a cave containing scrolls in earthen jars. Because the scrolls were made from animal hide, he first went to a shoemaker to turn them into sandals. The shoemaker alerted a local antiquities dealer, who brought them to the attention of Professor Eliezer Sukenik of the Hebrew University of Jerusalem. Six other major scrolls and hundreds of fragments have since been discovered in 11 of the caves.

Most scholars believe that the Essenes, a Jewish separatist sect that set up a monastic community here in the late 2nd century BC, wrote the scrolls. During the Great (Jewish) Revolt against Rome (AD 66–73), they apparently hid their precious scrolls in the caves in the cliffs before the site was destroyed in AD 68. Others contend the texts were brought from libraries in Jerusalem, possibly even the library of the Jewish Temple.

Almost all books of the Hebrew Bible were discovered here, many of them virtually identical to the texts still used in Jewish communities today. Sectarian texts were also found, including the constitution or "Community Rule," a description of an end-of-days battle ("The War of the Sons of Light Against the Sons of Darkness"), and the "Thanksgiving Scroll," containing hymns reminiscent of biblical psalms.

A short film at the visitor's center introduces the mysterious sect that once lived here. Climb the tower for a good view, and note the elaborate system of channels and cisterns that gathered precious floodwater from the cliffs. Just below the tower (looking toward the Dead Sea) is a long room some scholars have identified as the **scriptorium.** A plaster writing table and bronze and ceramic inkwells found here suggest that this may have been where the scrolls were written. Other archaeologists dispute this interpretation, arguing that before Qumran was taken over by rebels during the Great Revolt against Rome in 66 to 73, the site was a plantation for the now-extinct balsam tree. Like frankincense and myrrh, the expensive balsam perfume was greatly prized in Rome. Thus the scriptorium was, in this view, a business office. You shouldn't need more than an hour to tour this site.

3

⊠ *Rte. 90, 13 km (8 mi) south of Almog Junction* ☎ *02/994–2235* 🌐 *www.parks.org.il* 🎟 *NIS 20* ⏲ *Apr.–Sept., daily 8–5; Oct.–Mar., daily 8–4.*

BEACHES AND POOLS

Qumran is conveniently located near some beaches on the Dead Sea. You can't actually swim in the briny water; you take a leisurely float in its incredible salinity, about 10 times that of the ocean. Anyone can enjoy the benefits of the mineral concentration in the Dead Sea water and mud, and the oxygen-rich atmosphere at the lowest point on Earth. Beach shoes or rubber sandals are a must, as the salt in the hypersaturated water builds up into sharp ridges that are hard to walk on. Any open cuts on your body will sting when they encounter the briny water.

Beautiful **Biankini Beach** has a spa offering mineral treatments and massages, and a Moroccan restaurant featuring couscous and other traditional dishes. There are restrooms, showers, wheelchair access, changing rooms, and a freshwater wading pool for kids. ⊠ *Off Rte. 90, 3 km (2 mi) north of Qumran* ☎ *02/940–0266* 🌐 *www.biankini.co.il* 🎟 *NIS 50* ⏲ *Oct.–Mar., daily 8–5; Apr.–Sept., daily 8–6.*

Known for its freshwater springs, **Einot Zukim** (also called Ein Fashkha) is a nature reserve with many species of trees and reeds not often found in the arid Judean Desert. You can swim in two shallow spring-fed pools and visit an archaeological site from the Second Temple period and a manor from the Herodian period. Picnic and changing facilities are also available. ⊠ *Rte. 90, 3 km (2 mi) south of Qumran* ☎ *02/994–2355* 🌐 *www.parks.org.il* 🎟 *NIS 25* ⏲ *Oct.–Mar., daily 8–4; Apr.–Sept., daily 8–5.*

On the Dead Sea, **Kalia Beach** (the name derives from *kalium*, the Latin name for potassium, which is found in abundance here) is the place to go for a free mud bath. Slather your whole body with the mineral-rich mud and let it dry before showering; you'll enjoy the rejuvenating properties of this spalike experience. The beach, adjacent to a kibbutz, also has chair and towel rentals, a gift shop, and a snack bar. ⊠ *3 km (2 mi) north of Qumran off Rte. 90* ☎ *02/994–2391* 🎟 *NIS 35* ⏲ *Oct.–Mar., daily 8–5; Apr.–Sept., daily 8–6:30.*

Less touristy and more serene than some of the other beaches, **Mineral Beach** is a good place to mix and mingle with Israelis. There are restrooms, showers, a pool fed by a nearby thermal spring, a freshwater wading pool for kids, and a snack shop. It also offers massages (reserve in advance). ✉ *Rte. 90, 20 km (12½ mi) south of Qumran* ☎ *02/994–4888* 🌐 *www.dead-sea.co.il* 🎫 *Sun.–Thurs. NIS 45; Fri. and Sat. NIS 55* ⏲ *Sun.–Thurs. 9–6, Fri. and Sat. 8–6.*

Neve Midbar Beach, south of Biankini Beach, has restrooms, showers, changing rooms, and a restaurant. The beach here is popular with boisterous Israeli young people, especially at night. ✉ *Rte. 90, 3 km (2 mi) north of Qumran* ☎ *02/994–2781* 🌐 *www.nevemidbar-beach.com* 🎫 *NIS 40* ⏲ *Oct.–Mar., daily 8–5; Apr.–Sept., daily 8–7.*

EN ROUTE

Kibbutz Mitzpe Shalem (✉ *Rte. 90* ☎ *02/994–5117*) manufactures the excellent Ahava skin- and hair-care products based on (but not smelling like) the Dead Sea minerals. The factory outlet here is open Sunday to Thursday 8 to 5, Friday 8 to 4, and Saturday 8:30 to 5. It's 20 km (12½ mi) south of Qumran.

EIN GEDI

★ *33 km (21 mi) south of Qumran, 20 km (12½ mi) north of Masada, 83 km (52 mi) southeast of Jerusalem.*

After miles of burnt brown and beige desert rock, the green lushness of the Ein Gedi oasis leaps out in vivid and unexpected contrast. This nature reserve is one of the most beautiful places in Israel—with everything from hiking trails to ancient ruins. Settled for thousands of years, it inspired the writer of the *Song of Songs* to describe his beloved "as a cluster of henna in the vineyards of Ein Gedi."

GETTING HERE AND AROUND

Follow Route 1 east from Jerusalem for 50 km (31 mi), turning south on Route 90. Ein Gedi is on the right. Egged bus drivers will drop you off at the side of Route 90. From there it's a short walk to the gate of the national park.

SAFETY AND PRECAUTIONS

Check the weather forecast before hiking in the winter. Flash floods are an occasional danger.

EXPLORING

Ein Gedi Nature Reserve. The beautiful Ein Gedi Nature Reserve features two year-round streams, **Nahal David** (David's Stream) to the north and the **Nahal Arugot** to the south. Nahal David is believed to be the place where David hid from the wrath of Saul (I Samuel 24:1–22) 3,000 years ago, cutting the edge of the king's robe rather than killing his monarch. The clearly marked trail rises past several pools and small waterfalls to the beautiful upper waterfall. There are many steps, but it's not too daunting. Allow at least 1¼ hours to include a refreshing dip under one of the lower waterfalls. Look out for ibex (wild goats), especially in the afternoon, and for the small, furry hyrax, often seen on tree branches. Leopards here face extinction because of breeding problems; they're seldom seen nowadays.

If you're a more serious hiker who is interested in further adventure, don't miss the trail that breaks off to the right 50 yards down the return

Waterfalls, pools, and desert landscapes are among the pleasures awaiting hikers in Ein Gedi's nature reserve.

path from the top waterfall. It passes the remains of Byzantine irrigation systems and offers breathtaking views of the Dead Sea. The trail doubles back on itself toward the source of Nahal David. Near the top, a short side path climbs to the remains of a 4th-millennium BC Chalcolithic temple, the treasures of which can be seen in Jerusalem's Israel Museum. The main path leads on to the streambed, again turns east, and reaches **Dudim Cave,** formed by boulders and filled with crystal-clear spring water. Swimming in "Lover's Cave" is one of the most refreshing and romantic experiences in Israel. You are directly above the waterfall of Nahal David (don't throw stones—there are people below). Since this trail involves a considerable climb (and hikers invariably take time to bathe in the "cave"), access to the trail is permitted only up to 3½ hours before closing time. Reaching Ein Gedi from the north, the first turnoff to the right is the parking lot at the entrance to Nahal David. ✉ *Rte. 90, Ein Gedi* ☎ *08/658–4285* 🌐 *www.parks.org.il* 🎫 *NIS 25, includes admission to Nahal Arugot and the ancient synagogue* ⏲ *Sat.–Thurs. 8–4, Fri. 8–3; last admission 1 hr before closing.*

Nahal Arugot. Although not as lush as Nahal David, the deep canyon of Nahal Arugot is perhaps more spectacular. Enormous boulders and slabs of stone on the opposite cliff face seem poised in midcataclysm. The hour-long hike to the **Hidden Waterfall** (not too difficult) passes by beautiful spots where the stream bubbles over rock shelves and shallow pools offer relief from the heat. If you're adventurous and have water shoes, you can return through the greenery of the streambed, leaping the boulders and wading the pools. Experienced hikers can ascend the Tsafit Trail to Mapal Hachalon, or the Window Waterfall. It offers stunning views over the Dead Sea. To get here from the Nahal David parking lot, continue south through the date orchards of the kibbutz and follow signs to Nahal Arugot. ✉ *Off Rte. 90, Ein Gedi* ☎ *08/658–4285* 🌐 *www.parks.org.il* 🎫 *NIS 25, includes admission to Nahal David and the synagogue* ⏲ *Sat.–Thurs. 8–4, Fri. 8–3; last admission 2 hrs before closing.*

WORD OF MOUTH

"Dipping in the Dead Sea is such a unique experience. Your kids will love it! Ein Gedi has its own beach (across the road from the kibbutz), and the whole kibbutz is considered a botanical garden. In the morning you could take an easy hike in the beautiful natural reserve of Ein Gedi. If you are lucky (and we usually are), you will encounter small herds of ibexes, which is, of course, an exciting sight." —eri

Synagogue. A Jewish community lived in Ein Gedi for more than 1,200 years, beginning in the 7th century BC. In the 3rd century AD, they built a synagogue nestled between Nahal David and Nahal Arugot whose beautiful mosaic floor is a highlight worth seeing. The mosaic includes an inscription in Hebrew and Aramaic invoking the wrath of heaven on various troublemakers, including "whoever reveals the secret of the town." The secret is believed to refer to a method of cultivating a now-extinct balsam tree, which was used to make the prized perfume for which Ein Gedi was once famous. To get here from Nahal David parking lot, continue south a few hundred yards through the date orchards. ✉ *Off Rte. 90, Ein Gedi* ☎ *08/658–4285* 🌐 *www.parks.org.il* 🎫 *NIS 13; NIS 25 includes admission to Nahal Arugot and Nahal David* ⏲ *Sat.–Thurs. 8–4, Fri. 8–3.*

BEACHES AND POOLS

With access to the Dead Sea, **Ein Gedi Spa** lets you soak in one of six covered pools whose water is rich in sulfur, magnesium, calcium, sodium and potassium. You can also relax in a freshwater pool or slather yourself in mud. The place has good facilities, including indoor showers, lockers, and changing rooms. Massages (NIS 200 for 50 minutes) and treatments are available; advance reservation recommended. A snack bar and restaurant are here, too. ✉ *Rte. 90* ☎ *08/659–4813* 🎫 *Sun.–Fri. NIS 65, Sat. NIS 70* ⏲ *Oct.–Mar., daily 8–5; Apr.–Sept., daily 8–6.*

The somewhat rocky **Ein Gedi Public Beach** gives you free access to the Dead Sea. Freshwater showers (absolutely essential) by the water's edge and basic changing facilities are NIS 8. There are also an air-conditioned restaurant and a gift shop. Don't leave valuables unguarded. ✉ *Rte. 90* ☎ *08/659–4761* 🎫 *Free* ⏲ *Oct.–Mar., daily 8–5; Apr.–Sept., daily 8–6.*

SPORTS AND THE OUTDOORS

There is no problem hiking the area alone, on well-marked trails. Be sure to ask for a trail map at the admission booth to the national park.

WHERE TO EAT AND STAY

$$ FAST FOOD ✕ **Pundak Ein Gedi.** The nondescript entrance to the restaurant can be somewhat misleading. In addition to offering a blissfully air-conditioned respite from the blistering desert sun, this self-service restaurant has a large salad bar, as well as assorted cooked entrées. It's nothing fancy, but

the food is wholesome. The outdoor kiosk is open 24 hours a day and serves sandwiches, ice cream, and espresso. ✉ *Rte. 90* ☎ *08/659–4761* ▭ *AE, MC, V* ⊙ *No dinner.*

¢–$ **Ein Gedi Guest House.** Surrounded by a spectacular botanical garden with baobab trees, rare cacti, and hundreds of species of topical flora, this inn is nestled between 1,600-foot-high cliffs and the Dead Sea. Accommodations range from simple rooms to deluxe suites with terraces overlooking Nahal Arugot. Rates include breakfast, another full meal, and unlimited entry to the nearby Ein Gedi Spa, to which there's a free shuttle throughout the day. Sitting by the large swimming pool in the adjoining kibbutz, you're likely to meet some gregarious members or volunteers who have come from all over the world. **Pros:** informative staff; serene oasis atmosphere. **Cons:** some dingy rooms. ✉ *Rte. 90* ☎ *08/659–4220 or 08/659–4221* ⊕ *www.ein-gedi.co.il/en* *148 rooms* *In-room: no phone (some), kitchen. In-hotel: tennis courts, pool* ▭ *AE, DC, MC, V* *MAP.*

ARAD

20 km (12½ mi) west of Masada, 25 km (15½ mi) west of Ein Bokek and the Dead Sea, 45 km (28 mi) east of Beersheva.

Breathe deeply: Arad sits 2,000 feet above sea level and is famous for its dry, pollution-free air and mild climate, ideal for asthma sufferers. The modern town was established by ex-kibbutzniks as a planned community in 1962. Its population of nearly 25,000 now includes immigrants from Russia and Ethiopia, as well as the acclaimed Israeli writer Amos Oz.

Arad is often used as a base for excursions to sites in the Dead Sea area. It has an archaeological site and is also near Yatir, one of the country's finest desert wineries. You can also take a stroll through the galleries and workshops of Eshet Lot, the artist's quarter.

GETTING HERE AND AROUND

Arad is accessible by Route 31; the city is 45 km (28 mi) east of Beersheva. Driving from Jerusalem by Route 40 will take about 2½ hours; avoid Route 60 and Hebron in the West Bank. Egged bus lines run to Arad from Beersheva and Tel Aviv. The tourist office is behind the Paz gas station opposite the entrance to Arad; you'll see a yellow sign with the "i" for Information on it. A small supply of maps, brochures, and hiking information is available; a simple 24/7 café called Yellow is next to the gas pumps.

ESSENTIALS

Visitor Information **Arad Tourist Information Center** (☎ *08/995–1622*).

EXPLORING

The **Glass Art Museum.** This gallery displays the exciting creations of artist Gideon Fridman, who uses recycled glass in his personally developed fusing methods to create "talking glass" sculptures in ovens he built himself. Works by other artists working in glass are also on display. The gallery is on the road to the tourist information center. Pass the gas station on your left, turn right at the roundabout, take the second

Continued on page 192

DID YOU KNOW?

King Herod built a dam in the valley so that reservoir water could be carried to cisterns atop Masada. His engineers also created channels, visible today, that guided water from streams into cisterns hewn into the mountainside.

MASADA: DESERT FORTRESS

The isolated flattop rock of Masada commands the surrounding desert, its ancient remains bearing witness to long-ago power and conflict. One of Israel's most stunning archaeological sites, Masada earned fame and a place in history first as one of King Herod's opulent palace-fortresses and later as the site of the last stand of Jewish rebels against the legions of Rome, almost 2,000 years ago.

A KING'S PALACE

Surrounded by steep cliffs and with spectacular views of the Dead Sea and the desert, the Masada plateau offers nearly impregnable natural protection.

Herod the Great, the brilliant builder and paranoid leader who reigned over Israel as king of the Jews by the grace of the Roman Empire in the 1st century BC, developed the 18-acre site. Both for his relaxation and as a possible refuge from his enemies (including Cleopatra) and hostile subjects, Herod built atop Masada a fantastic, state-of-the-art complex of palaces, storehouses, and water systems.

THE REVOLT OF THE JEWS

Herod died around 4 BC, and the Jews rebelled against Rome in AD 66. By AD 70, the Roman Empire had destroyed Jerusalem and crushed the Jewish revolt there. Around AD 72, the last Jewish rebels took refuge at Masada. For at least a year, 960 Israelite men, women, and children lived here, protected from thousands of Roman soldiers by cliffs more than 1,400 feet high.

The Roman general and governor Flavius Silva, determined to end the rebellion, built eight legionnaire camps around the mountain. Silva's forces gradually erected an assault ramp on Masada's western side.

THE REBELS' "TERRIBLE RESOLVE"

According to a few survivors who related the story to the 1st-century historian Flavius Josephus, the night before the Romans reached Masada's walls, the rebel leader Elazar Ben-Yair gave a rallying speech. He reminded his community that they had resolved "neither to serve the Romans nor any other save God." After discussion, the Jews agreed to commit suicide rather than be taken captive.

The men drew lots to choose the ten who would kill the others. Those ten, having carried out "their terrible resolve," Josephus wrote, drew additional lots to select the one who would kill the other nine and then himself. When the Romans breached the walls the next morning, they found hundreds of corpses. The zealots' final action made the Roman victory at Masada a hollow one.

Although Josephus' physical description of Masada is accurate, some historians doubt his narrative. Several artifacts, including pottery shards bearing names (the lots, perhaps?), support the accuracy of Josephus' text, but no one can be sure what happened at the end. Masada continues to inspire debate.

TOURING MASADA'S TOP SIGHTS

Ride the cable car up Masada, or walk the Snake Path or easier Ramp Path. Take in these highlights of Herod's buildings and the Jewish rebels' presence—and awesome desert views.

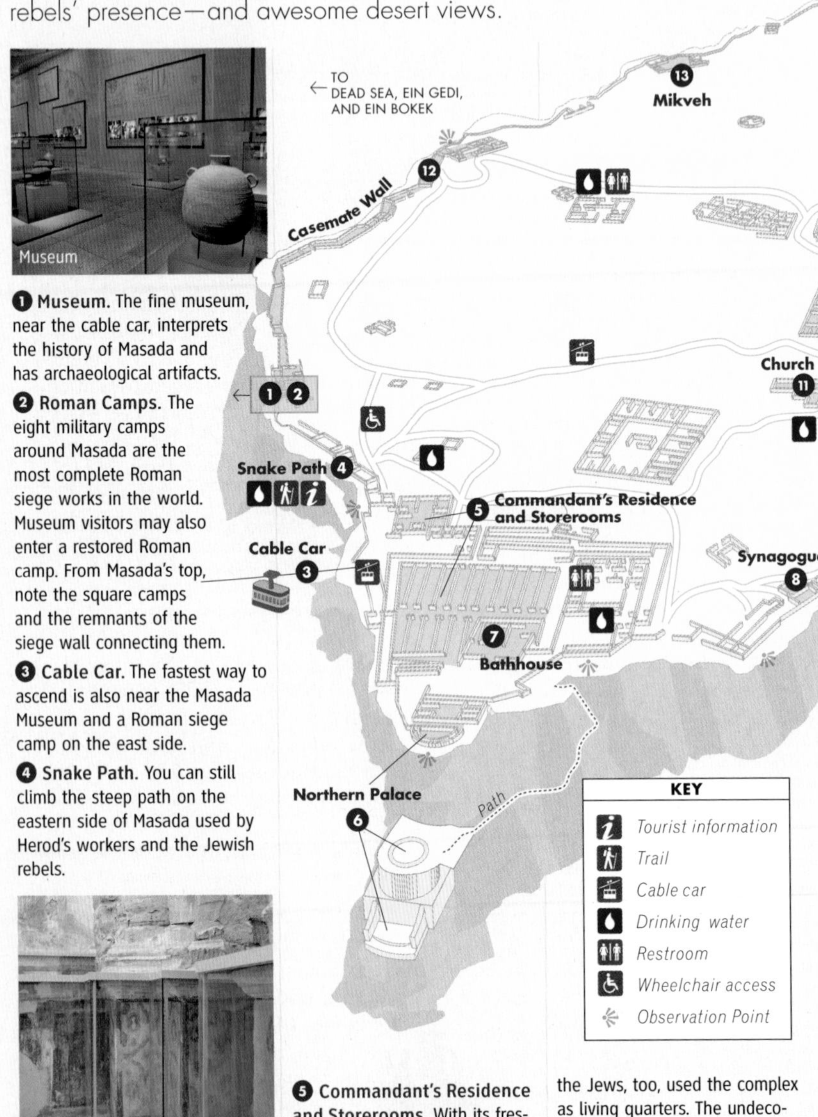

Museum

❶ Museum. The fine museum, near the cable car, interprets the history of Masada and has archaeological artifacts.

❷ Roman Camps. The eight military camps around Masada are the most complete Roman siege works in the world. Museum visitors may also enter a restored Roman camp. From Masada's top, note the square camps and the remnants of the siege wall connecting them.

❸ Cable Car. The fastest way to ascend is also near the Masada Museum and a Roman siege camp on the east side.

❹ Snake Path. You can still climb the steep path on the eastern side of Masada used by Herod's workers and the Jewish rebels.

Frescoed walls

❺ Commandant's Residence and Storerooms. With its frescoed walls, this area may have housed Herod's commanders. Simple ovens here indicate that the Jews, too, used the complex as living quarters. The undecorated rooms stored grain, dry fruit, and wine.

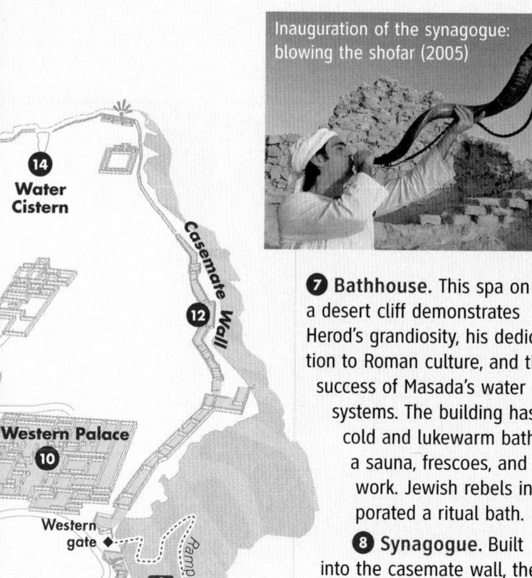

Inauguration of the synagogue: blowing the shofar (2005)

Bathhouse

Roman Ramp on the western slopes of Masada

Northern Palace

6 Northern Palace. Herod's personal living quarters is an extraordinary three-tiered structure that seems to hang from the cliffs. The amazing, terraced buildings feature colorful frescoes, Greek-inspired architecture, and Herod's personal bathhouse.

7 Bathhouse. This spa on a desert cliff demonstrates Herod's grandiosity, his dedication to Roman culture, and the success of Masada's water systems. The building has cold and lukewarm baths, a sauna, frescoes, and tile work. Jewish rebels incorporated a ritual bath.

8 Synagogue. Built into the casemate wall, the synagogue is oddly shaped, but its benches and geniza (space for damaged scrolls) indicate its function. Here, perhaps, the rebels agreed to die at their own hands. Today the synagogue is used for bar and bat mitzvahs.

9 Roman Ramp. You can stand on the western edge where Romans breached Masada's defenses. The original ramp is below, as well as a modern path for walkers.

10 Western Palace. Believed to have been an administrative base and a guest house, this palace retains frescoed walls and mosaics in Greek style; unusual for Herodian mosaics, one has a fruit motif.

11 Church. During the 5th to 7th centuries, monks lived at Masada, choosing it for its isolation. This 5th-century chapel is Byzantine in design, with mosaic floors.

12 Casemate Wall. Despite Masada's strategic advantages, Herod built a casemate (double-layered) wall around the oblong flattop rock, including offices and storerooms. The Jewish rebels used these rooms as dwellings.

13 Mikveh. In Jewish culture, the mikveh, or ritual bath, is a symbol of life and hope. Two found on Masada were built in accordance with Jewish laws still followed today. The presence of mikvehs indicates the rebels' religious piety.

14 Water Cistern. Like other cisterns at Masada, the southern cistern—into which you may descend—was built underground to prevent evaporation. Also make your way to see the spectacular canyon view to the south, and test the echoes.

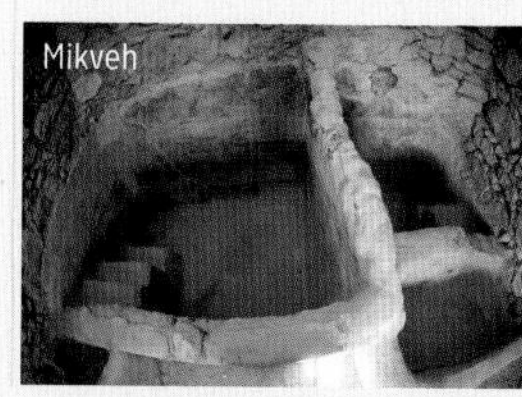
Mikveh

MASADA FROM JERUSALEM

Masada lookout

BY CAR

For Masada's eastern side, take Route 1 east to Route 90 south along the Dead Sea. Masada is off Route 90, about 15 minutes south of Ein Gedi (it's also near Ein Bokek). One-way driving time is about 80 minutes; add time to get out of Jerusalem.

For Masada's western side and the Roman Path entrance, head to Route 6 south, which merges with Route 40; continue on Route 31 to Arad and Route 3199/ Masada. It takes about 2.5 hours one way from southern Jerusalem. Avoid Route 60 and Hebron, and take a good map.

Note: There is no direct car access from the west side of Masada to the east. Those wishing to ascend on one side and descend on the other must arrange for their car to meet them on the other side; the drive is about 30 minutes.

BY GUIDED TOUR OR BUS

Your hotel can help you join a group tour to Masada, or contact **United Tours** (☎ 02/625–2187, 🌐 www.unitedtours.co.il) for daily, English-language trips from Jerusalem to Masada and other sites in the Judean Desert and the Dead Sea.

Egged Bus Lines (☎ 03/694–8888) runs buses for the two-hour trip from Jerusalem's Central Bus Station to Masada approximately every hour Sunday through Thursday between 8:45 AM and 1 PM; return buses leave 8:30 AM to 7:50 PM. Friday service is limited.

THREE WAYS TO GET UP AND DOWN MASADA

On Masada's east side, the cable car takes only three minutes. The quickest way up, the **cable car** is convenient to the Masada Museum and a restored Roman siege camp. The long, steep **Snake Path** up the east side is an arduous but rewarding one-hour hike, recommended for visitors who are fit or determined to ascend Masada the same way the Jewish rebels did. Accessible from Arad on the west side, the **Ramp Path** is less grueling and takes fifteen to thirty minutes to ascend; it's equivalent to climbing about twenty flights of stairs.

MAKING THE MOST OF YOUR VISIT

WHEN TO VISIT

The weather at Masada is fairly consistent year-round; it's hot during the day. Visit in the early morning or late afternoon, when the sun is weakest. ■ TIP➔ It's popular to hike up before dawn via the Snake or Ramp Path, and watch the sun rise from behind Jordan and the Dead Sea. After 9 or 10 AM, extreme heat may dictate that you use the cable car.

WHAT TO WEAR AND BRING

Layered clothing is recommended, as cool early-morning temperatures rise to uncomfortable heat. Good walking shoes and hats or bandanas are musts. Free drinking water is available at Masada, but bring plenty to start with. Food is not sold atop the site. The museum cafeteria sells lunch after 11 AM. Sunscreen and a camera are essential.

TIMING AND HIGHLIGHTS

Visiting Masada, a UNESCO World Heritage Site, can take three to seven hours, depending on your interest. The museum takes about an hour. Going up can take from three minutes (cable car) to sixty minutes (Snake Path). Your tour at the top might take ninety minutes or up to three hours.

The **Masada Museum**, near the cable car, offers an excellent combination of life-size scenes depicting the history of Masada; archaeological artifacts; and audio guide (available in English). Watch the short English-language film near the cable-car entrance. Atop Masada, many highlights such as Herod's **Northern Palace** and the **bathhouse** are toward the site's northern end. On the sparser southern side, the views and echo point near the southern **water cistern** are notable.

Cooking pots at Masada

Cable car heading down from Masada

OTHER THINGS TO DO

If you're traveling or staying overnight on the Dead Sea side, combine your excursion with a hike in **Ein Gedi** or a visit to a spa in **Ein Bokek.** If you're staying in Arad, check out the Masada **Sound-and-Light Show** (☎ 08/995–9333) Tuesday and Thursday evenings at 8:30 PM from March through October. To arrange a bar mitzvah at Masada, contact the **Israel Parks Service** at ✉ info@parks.org.il.

VISITOR INFORMATION

Masada National Park: Off Rte. 90 (east) or Rte 3199 (west), ☎ 08/658–4207, ⊕ www.parks.org.il **Note:** Most of Masada is wheelchair accessible.

⏲ **Park and cable car hours:** Apr.–Sept., Sun.–Fri. 8-5; Oct.–Mar., Sun.–Fri. 8–4; closes 1 hour earlier on Fri. and Jewish holiday eves. Closed Yom Kippur.

⏲ **Pre-dawn entrance for walkers:** Snake Path opens 1 hour before sunrise; Ramp Path opens 45 minutes before sunrise.

🎫 **Admission:** NIS 25 park, via Snake or Roman paths; NIS 49 park plus cable car one-way; NIS 67 park plus round-trip cable car; NIS 20 museum (includes audio guides for museum and site); NIS 20 audio guide to park (includes museum entrance).

A DRIVE TO THE DEAD SEA

From Arad, you can make the steep, 24-km (15-mi) descent to the Dead Sea and on to Ein Bokek via the sharp curves of Route 31. The stunning canyons and clefts that unfold on every side enhance the drama of the drive.

On the way out of town, you can pause at the Moav observation point, which features an impressive sculpture by the artist Yigal Tumarkin. Watch for the sign on the right indicating that you've reached sea level. Two more observation points soon appear on the left. You can't cross to the first—Metsad Zohar—from your side of the road. The second—Nahal Zohar—looks down on an ancient, dry riverbed, the last vestige of an eons-old body of water that once covered this area. The Dead Sea lies directly east, with the Edom Mountains of Jordan on the other side. To the right (south) is Mt. Sodom. You'll soon see, from above, the southern end of the Dead Sea, sectioned off into the huge evaporation pools of the Dead Sea Works, where potash, bromine, and magnesium are extracted.

The road ends where it joins Route 90; once there, you are at 1,292 feet below sea level, the lowest point on Earth.

right onto Sadan Street, go to the end of the street, and it's on the left. A trip here is worth the effort. ✉ *11 Sadan St.* ☎ *08/995–3388* 🌐 *www.warmglassil.com/english* ⏲ *Sun.–Wed. 10–1, Thurs. and Sat. 10–2.*

Tel Arad. The 250-acre site of the biblical city of Arad (to the northwest of the modern city) contains the remains of a major metropolis from the Bronze Age and the Israelite period. The lower city, with its meticulously planned streets and plazas, was inhabited in the Early Bronze Age (3150–2200 BC), when it was one of the largest cities in this region. (The city's name appears on the Temple of Amon in Karnak, Egypt.) Here you can walk around a walled urban community and enter the carefully reconstructed dwellings, whose style became known as the "Arad house."

After the Early Bronze Age, Arad was abandoned. The book of Numbers (21:1–3) relates that the Canaanite king of Arad battled the Israelites during the exodus from Egypt, but that his cities were "utterly destroyed." The upper city was first settled in the Israelite period (1200 BC). It's worth the trek up the somewhat steep path to see the Israelite temple, a miniature version of Solomon's Temple in Jerusalem.

At the entrance, pick up the Israel Nature and Parks Authority pamphlet, which explains the ongoing excavations, and purchase (for NIS 8) the plan of the Canaanite city of Arad, with a map, recommended walking tour, and diagrams of a typical Arad house. Tel Arad is 8 km (5 mi) west of Arad. At the Tel Arad Junction on Route 31, turn north on Route 80 for 3 km (2 mi). ✉ *Rte. 80* ☎ *057/776–2170* 🌐 *www.parks.org.il* 🎟 *NIS 13* ⏲ *Apr.–Sept., Sun.–Thurs. 8–5, Fri. and Jewish holiday eves 8–2; Oct.–Mar., Sun.–Thurs. 8–4, Fri. and Jewish holidays eves 8–2.*

Yatir Winery. At the foot of the ancient Tel Arad, you might stop to check out the modern Yatir Winery, a boutique vineyard established in 2000. Yatir Forest (Cabernet Sauvignon blend) is the premier label. The adjacent Yatir Forest, after which the winery is named, is the largest planted forest in Israel. Call ahead for a visit and tasting. ✉ *Rte. 80* ☎ *08/995–9090* 🌐 *www.yatir.net.*

3

WHERE TO EAT AND STAY

$ MIDDLE EASTERN ★ ✕ **Muza.** With chunky wood furniture, soccer scarves draped along one wall, and a bar lined with beer bottles, this is a classic pub. It's on Route 31, at the entrance to Arad. The place is warm and cozy, staffed by smiling servers and filled with locals and travelers enjoying meat on skewers, hummus, and *malawach* (a flaky Yemenite pastry). Here you can also indulge your yen for an American-style tuna melt: request "toast," the Israeli term for a grilled cheese sandwich, with tuna salad, accompanied by Muza's home-cut "chips" (french fries). A big-screen TV shows soccer matches, and the covered terrace with a billiard table at one end allows for alfresco dining. ✉ *Rte. 31* ☎ *08/997–5555* 🌐 *www.muza-arad.co.il* *Reservations not accepted* *AE, DC, MC, V.*

$$ **Inbar.** At the entrance to Arad, the five-story Inbar is unmissable because of its facade of white stone with orange trim. The upstairs lobby is inviting with its blue and yellow ceiling lamps; there's a sculpted-metal divider with birds on it at the entrance to the dining room, which overlooks the street. Rooms are petite, done in beige and olive. **Pros:** welcoming staff; nice saltwater pool. **Cons:** straddles a noisy intersection; nothing much within walking distance. ✉ *38 Yehuda St.* ☎ *08/997–3303* 🌐 *www.hotel-inbar.com* *103 rooms, 7 suites* *In-room: a/c, safe. In-hotel: restaurant, pool* *AE, DC, MC, V* *CP.*

EIN BOKEK

Fodor's Choice ★ *40 km (25 mi) east of Arad, 8 km (5 mi) north of Zohar–Arad Junction on Route 90.*

The sudden and startling sight, in this bare landscape, of gleaming, ultramodern hotels surrounded by waving palm trees signals your arrival at the spa-resort area of Ein Bokek, near the southern tip of the Dead Sea. According to the Bible, it was along these shores that the Lord rained fire and brimstone on the people of Sodom and Gomorrah (Genesis 19:24) and turned Lot's wife into a pillar of salt (Genesis 26). Here, at the lowest point on Earth, the hot, sulfur-pungent air hangs heavy, and a haze often shimmers over the water. You can float, but you cannot sink, in the warm, salty water.

Once upon a time, Ein Bokek comprised a handful of hotels, each with a small "spa," with a pebbly beach out front. Today, it's a collection of large and luxurious hotels with curvy pools and landscaped outdoor areas; each has a rooftop solarium and a state-of-the-art spa equipped to provide beauty and health treatments, and some have private beaches. Each hotel has a decent restaurant. There are no full-service restaurants outside the hotels, although a few casual eating places are set along the beach and in the two tiny shopping centers. The central cluster of hotels is linked by a promenade to two hotels at the very southern end of the area.

GETTING HERE AND AROUND

To drive to Ein Bokek from Jerusalem, take Route 1 eastbound, marked Jericho–Dead Sea. At the Dead Sea, Take Route 90 south, passing Qumran, Ein Gedi, and Masada, until you reach Ein Bokek. Egged buses run between Jerusalem and Ein Bokek several times a day. The trip is 1½ hours.

WORD OF MOUTH

"We stayed in Ein Bokek by the Dead Sea. We were in need of some downtime and pampering. We booked for one night and stayed for three. It was the relaxing/vacation part of our trip. Swimming in the large pool, the Dead Sea, massages, etc." —ljane

WHERE TO STAY

Some of Ein Bokek's hotels are more lavish than others, but you can always check out the restaurants and spas at different establishments. If you want to make the predawn climb up the Snake Path at Masada, the budget Masada Guest House is an option.

$$ **Crowne Plaza.** This 12-story hotel may not be as flashy as some of its neighbors, but its spa facilities are first-rate and its beachfront location is ideal. A third of the rooms offer direct panoramic views of the Dead Sea, while the others have balconies facing the sea. Carpets, curtains, and bedspreads please the eye with their taupe-and-navy color scheme. The Sato Bistro, a restaurant serving Asian fusion cuisine, is a treat in an area with a dearth of good eateries. The pool has a central island reached by a bridge, and one section is marked off for swimming laps. **Pros:** private beach; perfect location. **Cons:** main dining room can be noisy, especially on weekends. ✉ *Off Rte. 9086930* ☎ *08/659–1919* 🌐 *www.crowneplaza.com* *304 rooms, 15 suites* *In-room: a/c, safe, Wi-Fi. In-hotel: 2 restaurants, room service, bar, pool, gym, spa, beachfront, children's programs (ages 3–10), laundry service* *AE, DC, MC, V* *CP.*

$$$ **Daniel Dead Sea.** The Daniel features an undulating front wall that swirls around a huge flower-shaped pool. The public rooms are on the plain side, but the guest accommodations are well appointed, most with a sofa that opens into an additional bed. The dining room serves several styles of cuisine each evening. There's a shuttle to the beach across the street. Request a room on the Club Floor. **Pros:** bowling alley; excellent spa with 20 treatment rooms. **Cons:** drab decor; staff can be brusque. ✉ *Off Rte. 9086930* ☎ *08/668–9999* 🌐 *www.tamareshotels.co.il/e/daniel_dead_sea* *302 rooms, 12 suites* *In-room: a/c, safe. In-hotel: restaurant, room service, bar, tennis court, pool, gym, spa, children's programs (ages 3–10), Internet terminal* *AE, DC, MC, V* *CP.*

$$$ **Isrotel Dead Sea.** Gleaming white inside and out, the nine-story Isrotel sits across the road from the beach. Two towering silver urns furnish the lofty lobby, and glass elevators add to the airy feel. Each room has a balcony; suites also have whirlpool baths. The wooden wall at the entrance to the dining room is carved in a distinctive bas-relief with date palms, fish, flowers, and fruit. The gracious spa features hydrotherapy for two with an underwater aromatic-oil massage, and two sulfur pools. The

Dead Sea–water pool starts inside the hotel and ends outside. A motorized trolley transports guests to the private beach. **Pros:** sparkling pool; convenient information center. **Cons:** one Internet terminal; in summer overrun with kids. ✉ *Off Rte. 9086930* ☎ *08/668–9666* 🌐 *www.isrotel.co.il* *298 rooms, 18 suites* *In-room: a/c, safe, refrigerator. In-hotel: restaurant, room service, bar, pools, spa, children's programs (ages 3–10), Internet terminal* ▭ *AE, DC, MC, V* 🍴 *CP.*

$$ ★ **Le Meridien.** This chain hotel stands out for its inviting parquet-floor lobby filled with paintings and sculptures by Israeli artists. The hotel is set against a backdrop of small palm trees and gurgling waterfalls. Treatments in the spacious, sparkling spa include the use of therapeutic mud. The comfortable rooms, all of which face the water, are decorated in shades of calm brown. A shuttle zips guests to the hotel's private beach. The 16th and 17th floors are perfect for business travelers. Pros: the area's largest outdoor pools; air-conditioned squash court. **Cons:** set back from the beach; very crowded weekends; occasional poor service. ✉ *Off Rte. 90 86930* ☎ *08/659–1234* 🌐 *www.fattal.co.il* *510 rooms, 68 suites* *In-room: a/c, Internet, Wi-Fi (some). In-hotel: restaurant, room service, bar, tennis courts, pool, gym, spa, children's programs (ages 3–12), laundry service, Internet terminal* ▭ *AE, DC, MC, V* 🍴 *CP.*

$$ **Leonardo Club.** You might consider bringing the whole family to this all-inclusive property, where adults can enjoy a midnight supper and kids can have Popsicles around the clock. The hotel, at the southern end of the promenade, has huge windows in the reception lobby that look out on the dolphin-shaped pool and the lagoon with umbrellas in the water. Suites have hot tubs on the balconies. The hotel offers several children's clubs classified by age group (ages 1 to 4, 4 to 9, and 9 to 12) as well as a miniature golf course, two kiddie pools, computer games, and supervised day care. **Pros:** the area's only all-inclusive hotel; excellent kids' programs. **Cons:** plain rooms. ✉ *Off Rte. 9086930* ☎ *08/668–9444* 🌐 *www.fattal.co.il* *388 rooms, 12 suites* *In-room: a/c, safe, refrigerator, Internet. In-hotel: restaurant, bar, pool, spa, beachfront, children's programs (ages 1–12)* ▭ *AE, DC, MC, V* 🍴 *FAP.*

¢ **Masada Guest House.** Here's an option for those combining a trip to Ein Bokek with Masada, 15 km (9 mi) to the north. This moderately priced guesthouse at the foot of Masada is the most convenient lodging for those intent on watching the spectacular sunrise over the Dead Sea and mountains of Moab. It has single, double, and family rooms, each with private bath. **Pros:** convenient to Masada; swimming pool; air-conditioning. **Cons:** rowdy teenage groups; no evening entertainment. ✉ *Off Rte. 90, at the entrance to Masada* ☎ *08/995–3222* 🌐 *www.youth-hostels.org.il* *88 rooms* *In-room: a/c, no phone. In-hotel: pool, Internet terminal* ▭ *AE, DC, MC, V* 🍴 *BP.*

$$$$ **Royal.** A crown topped with the letter R sits perched atop this 18-story tower, the largest of the Dead Sea hotels. The hotel has a spare, minimalist entrance, unlike the impressive indoor pool area where striped lounge chairs face windows that soar two floors high and overlook the sand-colored mountains. The pool, with hot tub, is immense. At the lavish spa with 52 treatment rooms, you can enjoy the fitness room and

3

A DRIVE ON THE ARAVA ROAD

The **Arava Road** (Route 90) traverses the Arava Valley south from Ein Bokek to Eilat 177 km (111 mi) and parallels the Israel-Jordan border, almost touching it at some points. To the east rise the spiky, red-brown mountains of Moab, in Jordan. The road follows an ancient route mentioned in biblical descriptions of the journeys of the Children of Israel.

The Arava (meaning "wilderness") is part of the Great Rift Valley, the deep fissure in the earth stretching from Turkey to East Africa, the result of an ancient shift of landmasses. Just south of Ein Bokek, you'll pass signs for the settlements **Neot HaKikar** and **Ein Tamar** (home to many craftspeople), whose date palms draw water from underground springs rather than irrigation.

With the Edom Mountains rising in the east, the road continues along the southern Dead Sea valley. You'll cross one of the largest dry riverbeds in the Negev, Nahal Zin, and you'll pass several kibbutzim, including Yahel (founded by the Reform movement), Ketura (home of the Arava Institute for Environmental Studies), and Yotvata (known for its dairy products).

soak in individual sulfur and therapeutic baths. Rust-colored curtains and bedcovers set off the peach walls in the guest rooms. The hotel's Triton's Choice restaurant serves seafood. The beach is across the street. **Pros:** large and luxurious spa facilities; plentiful buffet; wheelchair accessible. **Cons:** on a steep hill. ✉ *Off Rte. 90 86930* ☎ *08/668–8555* *394 rooms, 26 suites* *In-room: a/c safe, refrigerator. In-hotel: 2 restaurants, room service, bar, pool, spa, children's programs (ages 3–10), laundry service* *AE, DC, MC, V* *CP.*

$$$ ★ **Spa Club.** This haven of tranquility—no cell phones or other distractions allowed—centers on a deluxe spa decorated in Moroccan style. It offers a heated indoor pool, Finnish sauna, Turkish hammam, and elegant spa suites with private whirlpool tubs big enough for couples. The decor, in the rooms and lobbies, is gleaming white set off by calming earth tones. **Pros:** excellent service; extraordinary spa treatments. **Cons:** beach is across the road. ✉ *Off Rte. 9086930* ☎ *08/668–8000* 🌐 *www.prima.co.il* *98 rooms* *In-room: a/c, television, safe. In-hotel: restaurant, room service, pool, gym, spa* *AE, DC, MC, V* *CP.*

OUTDOOR ACTIVITIES

The Tamar Local Council has beautified the beaches of Ein Bokek. They're free to the public and are usually fairly crowded. Regrettably, most do not have facilities for changing; the only option is to have a bite at the Tapuah Sodom restaurant and use its restrooms to change. A lifeguard is on duty year-round, and there's ample parking alongside the promenade. The only water sport in the Dead Sea is floating!

SHOPPING

Several companies manufacture excellent Dead Sea skin and beauty products made from mud, salts, and minerals; the actual mud is sold in squishy, leak-proof packages. Ahava and Jericho are popular brands sold at the shopping centers of Ein Bokek and at the shops in most hotels.

Diamonds and unique handcrafted jewelry by Israeli designers are sold at the **Dead Sea Diamond Center** (✉ *Rte. 90* ☎ *08/995–8777*). Call for a shuttle to pick you up.

Petra Kanion (✉ *near Le Meridien, Rte. 90*) shopping center contains a minimarket that sells wine and liquor, a currency exchange kiosk, and two swimwear and resort wear boutiques.

WEST OF JERUSALEM

The rugged Judean Hills tumble down from Jerusalem to the west, eventually easing into the gentler terrain of the coastal lowlands (known in Hebrew as the Shfela). This is a region of forests, springs, monasteries, battlefields, national parks, and archaeological treasures. It's the fastest-growing wine-producing area in the country, encompassing more than two-dozen vineyards. A number of local farmers also produce goat and sheep cheese. For Jerusalemites, the Judean Hills are a place to hike and picnic. For visitors, this sparsely populated region with its ancient terraced hills evokes the landscape of the Bible with none of the distractions of a big city.

LATRUN

25 km (16 mi) west of Jerusalem on Route 1.

Latrun is the ridge that projects into and dominates the western side of the Ayalon Valley. A natural passage between the coastal plain and the Judean Hills, the strategic valley has served as a battleground throughout history, from the conquests of the biblical Israelite leader Joshua in the 13th century BC, through the Hasmonean campaigns of the 2nd century BC, to the bloody defeat of the newly established Israel Defense Force by Jordan's Arab Legion in 1948. Today, the Trappist monastery is known for its olive oil and wine, and Mini Israel is a favorite for children of all ages.

GETTING HERE AND AROUND

Coming from Jerusalem on Route 1, exit onto Route 3 (the Modi'in and Ashkelon–Be'er Sheva road), about 5 km (3 mi) west of the Sha'ar Hagai gas station. At the T-junction, turn left for the Trappist Abbey of Latrun, the Latrun Armored Corps Museum, and Mini Israel. There are no good public transportation options.

EXPLORING

Trappist Abbey of Latrun. This 19th-century abbey belongs to the Trappist Order. The monks have been producing wine here since the 1890s. The interior of the church is an odd mix of round neo-Byzantine arches and apses and the soaring ceiling that seems Gothic in inspiration. Survivors of the Cistercian Order suppressed in the French Revolution, the Trappists keep a vow of silence. But you needn't worry about making a faux pas by talking; the staff selling Domaine de Latroun wines and olive oil in the shop will address you—in English, French, Hebrew, or Arabic.

Continued on page 203

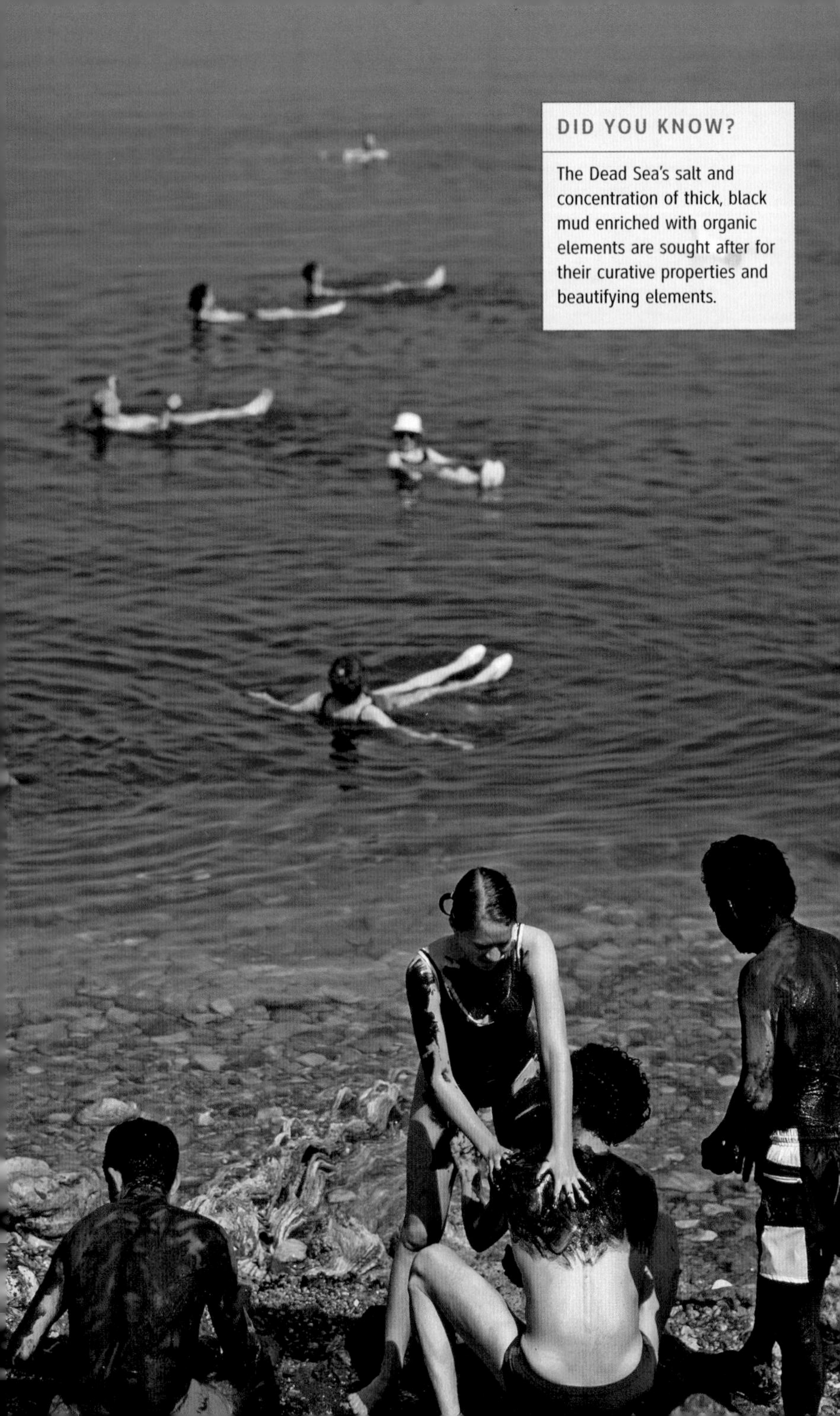

DID YOU KNOW?

The Dead Sea's salt and concentration of thick, black mud enriched with organic elements are sought after for their curative properties and beautifying elements.

THE DEAD SEA
A NATURAL WONDER

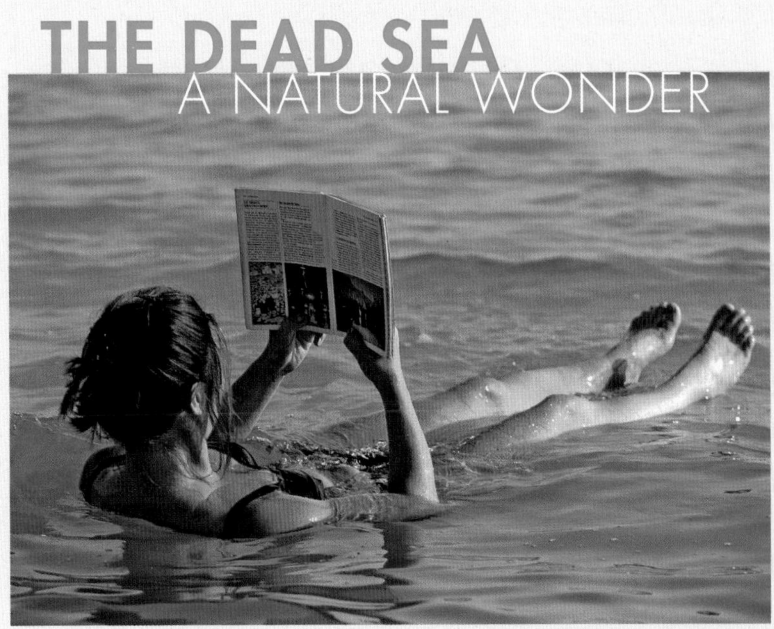

The Dead Sea at Ein Bokek

Taking a dip in the Dead Sea is a must-do experience in Israel. This unique body of water—the shores of which are the lowest point of dry land on Earth—was a resort for King Herod in the 1st century BC and the site of Queen Cleopatra's cosmetics empire.

It remains to be seen if the Dead Sea will be around centuries from now. A combination of less rainfall in the region and human interaction has caused its waters to recede at a rapid rate, threatening the area's ecology.

Israel started developing the Dead Sea as a tourist destination in the 1950s. Today, more than a dozen hotels in the area take advantage of the Dead Sea's mineral-rich mud and waters, known for nourishing, cleansing, and stimulating the skin, as well as for therapeutic benefits for treating medical conditions. Spas offer an array of services: body wraps, mud massages, facial peels, and the like, in addition to general amenities such as Jacuzzis and saunas.

It's an easy day-trip from Jerusalem, but spending the night allows you to watch the sun rise over Jordan. After a day on the beach, you can head back to your hotel for lunch and a spa treatment, followed by a Turkish bath or a dip in a warm sulfur pool.

by Sarah Bronson

THE DEAD SEA: PAST AND PRESENT

The stark, beautiful shores of the Dead Sea are literally the lowest point of dry land on Earth, at 1,373 feet below sea level. It's called the Dead Sea because virtually nothing can live in it; with a salt concentration of about 32%, the water is almost 9 times saltier than the ocean.

WHY IS THE DEAD SEA SALTY?

The Dead Sea is salty because water flows in from the Jordan River and other sources, but has no way of flowing out. Evaporation leaves a massive amount of salt behind. Beaches here aren't sandy—they're caked with hardened crystals of salt. The consistently dry air surrounding the Dead Sea has a high oxygen content, low pollution and allergen levels, and weakened ultraviolet radiation.

HOW DID THE DEAD SEA FORM?

The high mesas of the Judean desert nearby, also below sea level, bear testimony to the millions of years of geological changes that created this unique place. The Dead Sea was formed by fault lines shifting in the Earth's crust, a process that began about 15 million years ago and created the basin where the Dead Sea is now located.

WHY IS THE DEAD SEA IN DANGER?

Since it receives a maximum of 2 to 4 inches of rain per year, the Dead Sea's main source of water is the Jordan River, and by extension, the Sea of Galilee to the north.

The Dead Sea's water levels have fluctuated greatly over the last 10,000 years. However, its shores have significantly receded in the past few decades—about one meter per year—due to the lack of rainfall in Israel's north and human activity. Israel, Jordan, and Syria all divert water away from the Jordan River for drinking and irrigation. Less than 7% of the river's original flow reaches the Dead Sea.

WHAT'S BEING DONE TO STOP IT?

Israel and Jordan have been in talks for years to seek a solution to this pressing environmental problem. Currently the countries hope to build a canal to pump water into the Dead Sea from the Red Sea. Environmentalists are concerned about the possible negative impacts of such a canal both on the Dead Sea and on the Arava region. In any case, no firm plans to move forward have been announced.

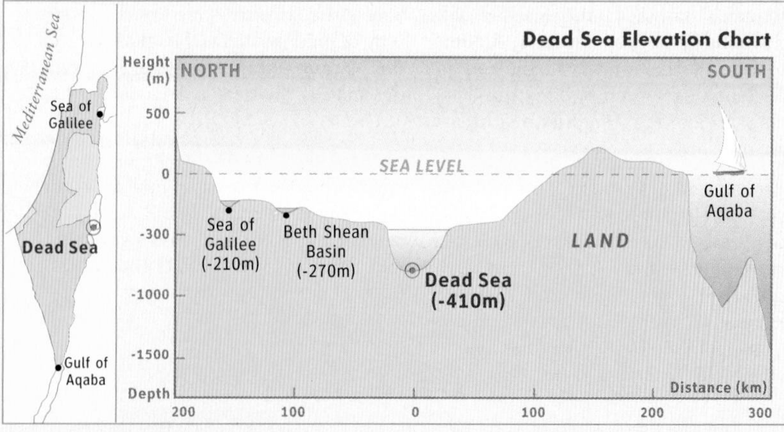

EXPERIENCING THE SPAS AND BEACHES

Before booking at a hotel or spa, carefully check what services it offers and whether any particular areas are closed for the season or for repairs. Quality of treatments at the spas can vary widely.

ENJOYING THE WATER

When entering the Dead Sea, wear flip flops or waterproof sandals, as the sea's floor has a rough, rock salt surface. Before getting in the water, check for the nearest source of fresh water, in case you get painful salt water in your eyes. (Note: The Ein Gedi spa provides freshwater spigots in the Dead Sea itself, floating on buoys). Lean back slowly and rise gently, and be careful not to splash water toward yourself or others.

Small wounds such as scratches will burn for a few moments, but avoid getting salt water in any deep or open wounds. Don't stay in the Dead Sea (or in the spas' warmed mineral pools) for more than 15 minutes at a time, and drink plenty of water afterward.

GETTING MUDDY

It can be surprisingly difficult to find free Dead Sea mud. Some hotels pump the mud to their grounds, or provide vats of it at their beach. You can also purchase more refined mud in packets and apply it at the beach for your photos.

(top) People sunbathing on the shores of the Dead Sea. (bottom) Covered in Dead Sea mud

Bring a friend to the mudbaths so that you can help each other slather the dark goo on every inch of exposed skin. Cake it on evenly but thinly, so that it will dry within 15-20 minutes in the sun. You might need a third person to take pictures, unless you want mud on your camera!

Dead Sea products, including salts and mud, make great gifts and are available at all the spas, but note that similar items may be available at your local health food store at home.

PLANNING YOUR VISIT

(left) Dead Sea. (right) Artist creating salt sculptures in the Dead Sea

GETTING HERE FROM JERUSALEM

By car: Take Route 1 east past Jericho to Route 90 south along the Dead Sea shore. Continue about an hour to reach Ein Gedi or Ein Bokek. Total driving time is about 90 minutes.

By public transportation: Egged Bus Lines run buses from Jerusalem's Central Bus Station along the Dead Sea shore every hour or so Sun.–Thurs. from 8:45 AM to 1 PM, and return buses from 8:30 AM – 7:50 PM. Just tell your driver which hotel or spa you're visiting. On Fridays bus service is more limited. To check schedule updates, call Egged at 03/694-8888.

By guided tour: Hotel staff can help you join a group tour to the Dead Sea. Or contact United Tours (02/625-2187 www.unitedtours.co.il) for daily, English-language trips from Jerusalem.

WHEN TO GO

In fall (Oct.-Nov.) and spring (Mar.–May) it's almost always sunny and pleasant. In winter temperatures are 68°–74°, and there's consistent sun. In summer it's usually an uncomfortable 90°–102° and scorching.

BEACH AND SPA TIPS

- The Dead Sea has several public beaches, sometimes with a token fee for use of the showers or for lawn chair rental. "Private" hotel beaches are, by law, open to anyone, though only hotel guests will receive amenities.
- Inquire carefully when booking your hotel if the cost of meals is included. There are few restaurants in the area.
- For non-guests, most hotels offer day rates of about NIS 80 to use their spas, pools, saunas, and fitness rooms. Extra charges apply for meals, facials, and massages.

WHAT ELSE IS NEARBY

- Combine a visit to Ein Bokek with visits to Ein Gedi and Qumran, which also have Dead Sea beaches and nature reserves.
- To arrange a Dead Sea cruise, desert hike, overnight camping trip, or group event, call the Dead Sea Tourist Information Center at 08/997-5010.
- Ask your concierge about visiting the tiny town of Ein Tamar, just south of Ein Bokek, home to many artists and craftspeople.

You can explore the gardens here; the setting in the foothills is lovely. ✉ *Rte. 3, 2 km (1.5 mi) off Rte. 1* ☎ *08/922–0065* 🎫 *Free* 🕐 *Church: Apr.–Sept., Mon.–Sat. 8:30–noon and 3:30–5; Oct.–Mar., Mon.–Sat. 8:30–11 and 2:30–4. Wine shop: Apr.–Sept., Mon.–Sat. 8:30–6; Oct.–Mar., Mon.–Sat. 8:30–5:30.*

MINERALS AND MUD

The Dead Sea's salt content (six times denser than that of the Mediterranean), concentrations of special minerals, and thick, black mud, enriched with organic elements, are sought out for their curative and beautifying properties. They are found nowhere else in the world. Ein Bokek also features sulfur-rich hot springs with a temperature of 31°C (88°F). Many hotels have tapped into these for their spas; the water is used along with Dead Sea water and mud to treat rheumatic and arthritic problems. The combination of sunshine (it's sunny 320 days a year), Dead Sea water, and mineral-rich mud works wonders on skin ailments.

3

Latrun Armored Corps Museum. The name "Latrun" is thought to derive from "La Toron de Chevaliers" (the Tower of the Knights), the French name of the Crusader castle that occupied the crest of the hill in the 12th century. Eight centuries later, in 1940, the British erected the concrete fortress that today holds the museum. In the 1948 War of Independence, Israeli forces attempted five times to capture the fortress from Jordanian soldiers. The names of 142 Israeli soldiers who fell in these unsuccessful attempts are engraved on the walls. There are more than 100 assorted antique tanks on which children love to climb. The museum has a decent restaurant, offering salads and hot meals. ✉ *Rte. 3, 1 km (½ mi) south of Rte. 1* ☎ *08/978–4315* 🌐 *www.yadlashiryon.com* 🎫 *NIS 30* 🕐 *Sun.–Thurs. 8:30–4:30, Fri. 8:30 am–12:30 pm, Sat. and holidays 9–4.*

Mini Israel. One of the most popular attractions in Israel, this theme park is designed in the shape of the Star of David. The world's largest miniature city spreads over 13 acres and contains nearly 400 models of the most important historical, national, religious, and natural sites in the country. Worth an hour's visit, the site is especially fun for children. About 25,000 miniature "residents" have been meticulously created to present not just the physical, but also the cultural, religious, and social aspects of contemporary Israel. A walk through the park allows visitors to see and hear the people of different faiths and cultures that make up the country's human landscape. ✉ *Rte. 424, 1 km (½ mi) south of Latrun* ☎ *700/559–559* 🌐 *www.minisrael.co.il* 🎫 *NIS 79, audio guide NIS 10* 🕐 *Sun.–Thurs. and Sat. 10–7, Fri. 10–2.*

OFF THE BEATEN PATH

Neot Kedumim (Oases of Antiquity). About 20 km (12 mi) north of Latrun, this 625-acre "Biblical landscape reserve" re-creates the ancient landscape. Ancient terraces and wine and oil presses were excavated and restored, thousands of trees and shrubs were planted, and pools and cisterns were dug. A network of roads and walking paths (most of them paved and wheelchair accessible) allows for a leisurely exploration of the site. Take one of the self-guided tours (brochures and maps in English provided) or inquire ahead of time about guided tours in English. Allow two hours minimum for the visit. ✉ *Rte. 443, 40 km*

(25 mi) west of Jerusalem ☎ *08/977–0777* 🌐 *www.neot-kedumim.org.il* 🎫 *NIS 25* 🕒 *Sun.–Thurs. 8:30–4, Fri. 8:30–1.*

WHERE TO EAT

On the way to Latrun and its sights, take a detour onto Route 425 to reach the picturesque village of Abu Ghosh. This village of 7,000 is renowned for its hummus, the tasty blend of chickpeas, sesame paste, olive oil, lemon juice, and garlic. In 2010, 50 chefs prepared over four tons of hummus, beating the world record set the month before in Lebanon. A number of excellent Middle Eastern restaurants line its main street.

$$ AMERICAN ✕ **Elvis Inn.** At the far western end of the village of Abu Ghosh—11 km (7 mi) east of Latrun—is this American-style diner with the largest collection of Elvis memorabilia this side of Graceland. This kitschy place is probably the only Elvis souvenir shop in the world where you can get *shawarma* (spit-grilled meat). Don't worry, there's also traditional roadhouse fare that the King would love. Serious fans should come on his birthday (August 16) or his *yahrzeit* (anniversary of his death, January 8), when Israel's Elvis impersonators come to get all shook up. ✉ *Rd. 4115, Abu Ghosh village* ☎ *02/534–1275* 💳 *No credit cards.*

$$ FAST FOOD ✕ **Nof Latrun.** At this self-service cafeteria with indoor seating and outdoor picnic tables, indulge in one of the fish or meat dishes or partake

of the salad bar. It's a good place to try schnitzel and chips (breaded and fried chicken or turkey breast served with french fries). Sandwiches and ice cream are available at the takeout window. The cafeteria is across the parking lot from the Latrun Armored Corps Museum. ✉ *Rte. 3, 1 km (½ mi) south of Rte. 1* ☎ *08/920–1670* ▭ *AE, MC, V* ⌚ *No dinner Fri. Closed Sat.*

SOREQ CAVE

25 km (17 mi) southwest of Jerusalem on Rtes. 386 and 3866, 12 km (7½ mi) east of Beit Shemesh on Route 3855.

GETTING HERE AND AROUND

Follow Route 1 west from Jerusalem, then head south on Route 38 and east on Route 3855. Turn northwest on Route 3866, continuing up the mountain for about 5 km (3 mi) to a junction with a large sculpture commemorating the Challenger spacecraft. Turn left and continue for about 2 km (1 mi) to the parking lot.

EXPLORING

★ **Soreq Cave.** At the heart of the Avshalom Nature Reserve on the western slopes of the Judean hills, the Soreq Cave contains a wondrous variety of stalactites and stalagmites. Some formations are at least 300,000 years old and allow scientists to track climate changes over the millennia. It was discovered in 1968 when a routine blast in the nearby Har-Tuv quarry tore away the rock face, revealing a subterranean wonderland.

Colored lights are used to highlight the natural whites and honey browns of the stones. Local guides have given the stalactite forms nicknames like "macaroni," "curtains," and "sombreros." In a series of "interfaith" images, some find rocky evocations of Moses, the Madonna and Child, Buddha, and the Ayatollah Khomeini. Photography is allowed only on Friday morning, when there are no guided tours. Despite the high humidity, the temperature in the cave is comfortable year-round.

The 150 steps down to the cave mean it's not ideal for visitors with mobility concerns. Local guides take groups as they arrive into the cave every 15 minutes for a 30-minute tour (English tours on request). An English-language video explains how the cave was formed. ✉ *Rte. 3866* ☎ *02/991–1117* 🌐 *www.parks.org.il* 🎫 *NIS 25* ⌚ *Apr.–Sept., Sat.–Thurs. 8–5, Fri. 8–3; Oct.–Mar., Sat.–Thurs. 8–4, Fri. 8–1; last entry 1¼ hr before closing.*

WHERE TO STAY

There are some very good kibbutz guesthouses in wooded enclaves of the Judean Hills, a 15- to 20-minute drive west of Jerusalem. All have commanding hilltop views, quiet surroundings, very comfortable if not luxurious accommodations, and good swimming pools.

$ **Hotel Tzuba.** Fun family activities are the specialty of this kibbutz hotel. On the premises are a children's entertainment park called Keftziba (one of the country's most popular), tennis courts, a swimming pool, and a sports center. Hikes to the Cave of John the Baptist, which he is said to have used for ritual water immersions, are popular. Suites can accommodate up to five people and include separate bedrooms, kitchens, and porches with magnificent views of the Judean Hills. Arrive on Friday to sample cheeses, fish, and salads as part of the hotel's unique Friday brunch. **Pros:** great place for young children; interesting tours; panoramic views. **Cons:** no evening entertainment; meals eaten in the kibbutz dining hall. ✉ *Rte. 39, 12 km (7½ mi) west of Jerusalem* ☎ *02/534–7000* 🌐 *www.belmont.co.il* *64 suites* *In-room: a/c, kitchen. In-hotel: tennis courts, pool, gym* *AE, DC, MC, V* *BP.*

$ **Ma'aleh Hahamisha.** This large guesthouse, spread over beautiful landscaped gardens, is ideal for nature lovers. It has a health club, including an indoor heated lap pool, gym, saunas, and whirlpool baths. Some rooms lead to a garden patio. **Pros:** panoramic views; indoor pool; parklike setting. **Cons:** no evening entertainment; mountaintop location gets chilly. ✉ *Rte. 1, 14 km (9 mi) west of Jerusalem* ☎ *02/533–1331* 🌐 *www.inisrael.com/maale5* *230 rooms* *In-room: a/c. In-hotel: pool, gym* *AE, DC, MC, V* *BP.*

¢ **Neve Ilan.** A cut above its neighbors, this recently renovated hotel has large, nicely furnished rooms. Suites with their own whirlpool baths are available. The pool is covered year-round and heated in winter, and there is a well-equipped exercise room. **Pros:** panoramic views; beautiful swimming pool. **Cons:** no evening entertainment. ✉ *North of Rte. 1, 15 km (10 mi) west of Jerusalem* ☎ *02/533–9339* 🌐 *www.c-hotels.co.il* *160 rooms, 4 suites* *In-room: a/c, Wi-Fi. In-hotel: pool, gym* *AE, DC, MC, V* *BP.*

SHOPPING

The small but popular **Ya'aran Farm,** run by Yavshi and Bar Ya'aran, produces more than 10 types of hard and soft goat cheese. It's best to come on a Saturday, when they bake their own bread. If Bar isn't too busy, she'll explain to you her vision of living off the land, using only rainwater, and solar power and windmills for energy. The Jewish National Fund hired the couple in 1995 as firewatchers for the newly replanted forest. Since grazing animals keep down the brush, the Ya'arans began herding goats. ✉ *On Rte. 3866, near Soreq Cave* ☎ *02/999–7811* *Call for hrs.*

BEIT SHEMESH

12 km (7½ mi) west of Soreq Cave on Rtes. 3855 and 38, 35 km (22 mi) west of Jerusalem.

The modern town of Beit Shemesh, Hebrew for "House of the Sun," takes its name from an ancient city now entombed by the tell on a rise on Route 38, 2 km (1 mi) south of the main entrance.

This is Samson country. Samson, one of the judges of Old Testament Israel, is better known for his physical prowess and lust for Philistine women than for his shining spiritual qualities, but it was here, "between Tzorah and Eshta'ol," that "the Spirit of the Lord began to stir him" (Judges 13). Today, Eshta'ol is a *moshav* (a cooperative settlement composed of individual farms) a few minutes' drive north, and Tzora is the wine-producing kibbutz immediately to the west.

WINERIES IN THE JUDEAN HILLS

For years, good Israeli wine was an oxymoron, but the days of producing only sweet sacramental wines are long gone. In the past few decades, a viniculture revolution has yielded an abundance of wines that easily compete against those from older vineyards. The Judean Hills area is now home to more than two-dozen vineyards, the majority of them close to Route 38, north and south of Beit Shemesh. Since most vineyards are "boutique"—producing fewer than 100,000 bottles per year—few have visitor centers that encourage drop-in visits or have regularly scheduled tours, so call ahead. The wineries are convenient to Tel Aviv (40 minutes away) as well as Jerusalem (about 20 minutes). Every October, the area's 27 wineries sponsor a wine festival at Ein Hemed National Park.

Domaine du Castel consistently produces some of the country's best wines. The small winery—and its exquisite cellar—is open by appointment to groups no larger than six people. ✉ *Rte. 395,* Moshav Ramat Raziel ☎ 02/534–2249 🌐 *www.castel.co.il.*

In Kibbutz Netiv Halamed Hey, **Ella Valley Vineyards** is a "stone's throw" from where David slew Goliath (I Samuel 17). Under the supervision of French-trained winemaker Doron Rav Hon, this young winery produced its first harvest in 2002, but ancient winepresses from the Byzantine Period attest to the region's historical wine production. Their top-quality wines include Cabernet, Merlot, Chardonnay, and Muscat. ✉ *Rte. 38, 10 km (6½ mi) south of Beit Shemesh* ☎ *02/999–4885* 🌐 *www.ellavalley.com* ⏲ *Sun.–Thurs. 8:30–4:30, Fri. 8:30–12:30; by appointment only.*

Overlooking the Soreq Valley, **Kibbutz Tzora** produces some excellent reds, as well as homemade olive oil, honey, and cheese. Breakfast lunch are served in the garden. You can also buy a picnic basket—complete with tablecloth, plates, wine, cheeses, and salad. ✉ *Rte. 38, 300 yds south of Beit Shemesh* ☎ *02/990–8261* 🌐 *www.tzorawines.com* ⏲ *Sun.–Thurs. 10–5, Fri. 10–2.*

Mony Wines, on the grounds of the Deir Raffat monastery, is family-run but supervised by Sam Soroka, one of the most experienced winemakers in Israel. The shop sells their wines, mostly reds, but also Chardonnay and Muscat, as well as olives and olive oil. ✉ *Rte. 3856, 4 km (2½ mi) west of Kibbutz Tzora* ☎ *02/991–6629* ⏲ *Daily 9:30–5:30.*

A kibbutz that produces tasty hard and soft sheep's cheese runs the **Nachshon Winery**, near Latrun. The shop sells red wine and close to a dozen different cheeses. Drop in to the shop or call in advance to arrange a tour of the winery, vineyard, and ancient winepress. ✉ *Kibbutz Nachshon, 2 km (1¼ mi) south of Latrun, off Rte. 3* ☎ *08/927–8641* 🌐 *www.nachshon.org.il* ⏲ *Sun.–Fri. 8–4, Sat. 10–sunset.*

Tzuba Vineyard, part of the eponymous kibbutz, prroduces excellent red dessert wines as well as a blend of Cabernet Sauvignon and Cabernet Franc. ✉ *Rte. 395, 12 km (7½ mi) west of Jerusalem* ☎ *02/534–7678* 🌐 *www.tzubawinery.co.il* ⏲ *Daily 8–2.*

GETTING HERE AND AROUND

Follow Route 1 west from Jerusalem, then head south on Route 38 to Beit Shemesh. Israel Railways provides regular train service between Jerusalem and Tel Aviv via Beit Shemesh on an hourly basis from 6 am to 8 pm.

EXPLORING

Tel Beit Shemesh. This low-profile archaeological site has fine views of the fields of Nahal Soreq, where Samson dallied with Delilah (Judges 16). When the Philistines captured the Israelite Ark of the Covenant in battle (11th century BC), they found that their prize brought divine retribution with it, destroying their idol Dagon and afflicting their bodies with tumors and their cities with rats (I Samuel 5). The Philistines rid themselves of the jinxed ark by sending it back to the Israelites at Beit Shemesh. This is a nice spot to pull out the Bible, but the stone ruins of the tell—including the oldest iron workshop in the world—are hard to interpret without an archaeologist on hand. ✉ *Rte. 38, 2 km (1 mi) from Tzora turnoff.*

ELLA VALLEY

10 km (6 mi) south of Beit Shemesh, 42 km (26 mi) west of Jerusalem.

The Ella Valley is one of those delightful places—not uncommon in Israel—where you can relate the scenery to a specific biblical text and confirm the maxim that once you've visited this country, you'll never read the Bible in quite the same way again. Beyond the junction of Route 38 with Route 383, and up to the right above the pinewood slopes of Park Britannia, is a distinctively bald flattop hill, **Tel Azekah,** the site of an ancient Israelite town. The hills are especially delightful in March and April when the wildflowers are out, and hiking paths are plentiful.

In the Ella Valley, the southernmost of the great valleys that cut from the Judean highlands toward the coast, Route 38 crosses a usually dry streambed; 200 yards beyond it is a place to pull off and park. If you have a Bible, open it to I Samuel 17 and read about the dramatic duel between Israelite shepherd David and the Philistine champion Goliath. The battle probably took place close to where you're standing:

And Saul and the men of Israel were gathered, and encamped in the valley of Ella, and drew up in line of battle against the Philistines. And the Philistines stood on the mountain on the one side, and Israel stood on the mountain on the other side, with a valley between them.

Look east up the valley to the mountains of Judah in the distance and the road from Bethlehem—the same road by which David reached the battlefield. The white northern ridge, a spur of the mountains of Judah, may have been the camp of the Israelite army. The southern ridge (where the gas station is today) is where the Philistines gathered. The creek, the only one in the valley, is where David "chose five smooth stones." The rest, as they say, is history: Goliath was slain, the Philistines were routed, and David went on to become the darling of the nation and eventually its king.

Beit Guvrin and Tel Maresha national park preserves ancient caves used for storage, industry, and tombs.

GETTING HERE AND AROUND

Follow Route 1 west from Jerusalem, then head south on Route 38, passing Beit Shemesh on your left.

EXPLORING

★ **Tzuk Farm.** Nestled in the hills south of the Ella Valley, this tranquil farm produces fabulous goat cheese, wine, olives, olive oil, and pomegranates. Reservations are essential for meals, which include a platter of cheeses, fresh bread, and seasonal salads. Picnic baskets with wine, tablecloth, cheese, and salads are available for NIS 170. The farm also has a shop in Tel Aviv. ✉ *Take eastern turn off south of Ella Valley Junction (Rtes. 38 and 375), 2 km (1 mi) down dirt road* ☎ 054/523–9117 ⏲ *Thurs.–Sat., call for hrs.*

BEIT GUVRIN

21 km (13 mi) south of Beit Shemesh, 52 km (33 mi) southwest of Jerusalem.

GETTING HERE AND AROUND

Follow Route 1 west from Jerusalem, then head south on Route 38 through Beit Shemesh until the end of the road. At Nehushga Junction turn west on Route 35. The park is off Route 35 opposite Kibbutz Beit Guvrin.

EXPLORING

★ **Beit Guvrin.** This national park encompasses some 1,250 acres of rolling hills in the Judean lowlands. For thousands of years people here have been digging quarries, burial caves, storerooms, hideouts, and dovecotes—a subterranean labyrinth of unparalleled complexity. In the Second Temple Period millions of pilgrims ascended to Jerusalem to offer animal sacrifices. At Bet Guvrin, doves were raised on a vast scale to supply the pilgrims' need. Unlike many ruins, this national park allows you to readily envision life 2,000 years ago.

Beit Guvrin is a wonderland, both under the ground and above it. The antiquities sprawl around the kibbutz of Bet Guvrin, just beyond the junction of Routes 38 and 35. These are bits and pieces of the 2nd- to 3rd-century AD Beit Guvrin, renamed (around the year 200) Eleuthropolis, "the city of free men." The amphitheater—an arena for Roman blood sports and mock sea battles—is one of only a few discovered in Israel.

After entering the park, drive toward the flattop mound of ancient Maresha, known today as **Tel Maresha.** King Rehoboam of Judah fortified it, but it was during the Hellenistic period (4th–2nd centuries BC) that the city reached its height and that the endless complexes of chalk caves were dug. Maresha was finally destroyed by the Parthians in 40 BC, and replaced by the nearby Roman city of Beit Guvrin. The view from the tell is worth the short climb.

Ancient Mareshans excavated thousands of underground chambers to extract soft chalk bricks, with which they built their homes aboveground. Residents then turned their "basement" quarries into industrial complexes, including water cisterns, olive oil presses, and **columbaria** (derived from the Latin word *columba,* meaning dove or pigeon). The birds were used in ritual sacrifice, and as food, producers of fertilizer, and message carriers.

The most interesting and extensive cave system is just off the road on the opposite side of the tell (the trail begins at a parking lot). It includes water cisterns, storerooms, and a restored ancient olive press. The excitement of exploration makes this site a must for kids (with close parental supervision, though the safety features are good), but the many steps are physically demanding.

The great "bell caves" of **Beit Guvrin** date from the Late Roman, Byzantine, and even Early Arab periods (2nd–7th century AD), when the locals created a quarry to extract lime for cement. At the top of each bell-shaped space is a hole through the four-foot-thick stone crust of the ground. When the ancient diggers reached the soft chalk below, they began reaming out their quarry in the structurally secure bell shape, each bell eventually cutting into the one adjacent to it. Although not built to be inhabited, the caves may have been used as refuges by early Christians. In the North Cave, a cross high on the wall, at the same level as an Arabic inscription, suggests a degree of coexistence even after the Arab conquest of the area in AD 636.

After leaving this system, make sure to continue walking down the hill to visit the **Sidonian Burial Caves.** These magnificent 3rd- to 2nd-century BC tombs—adorned with colorful, restored frescoes and inscriptions—offer important archaeological evidence as to the nature of the town's ancient Phoenician colonists.

3

DIG AT BEIT GUVRIN

Archaeological Seminars, in Jerusalem, runs a program at Beit Guvrin called **Dig for a Day** (☎ *02/586-2011* 🌐 *www.archesem.com* 🎫 *US$30*).

The three-hour activity includes supervised digging in a real excavation inside a cave, into which local inhabitants dumped earth and artifacts 21 centuries ago. Participants then sift the buckets of dirt they have hauled out of the cave, looking for finds. Some museum-quality artifacts of the 3rd to 2nd centuries BC (Hellenistic Period) have been uncovered here. (No, you can't take home what you find!)

The participants are then led on a fun 30-minute exploration through caves not yet open to the public. This involves some crawling, because some spaces are too tight or too low for walking upright. Those who prefer to pass on that experience can just wait for the last component—a short talk in the pottery shed about how clay vessels are reconstructed.

The undeveloped complexes of caves near the tell are off-limits to visitors. Keep to the marked sites only. The brochure at the entrance has a good map of the site. ✉ *Off Rte. 35, 21 km (13 mi) south of Beit Shemesh* ☎ *08/681–1020* 🌐 *www.parks.org.il* 🎫 *NIS 25, includes entrance to Beit Guvrin* ⏲ *Apr.–Sept., Sat.–Thurs. 8–5, Fri. 8–4; Oct.–Mar., Sat.–Thurs. 8–4, Fri. 8–3.*

EN ROUTE

Instead of the Tel Aviv–Jerusalem expressway, an attractive alternative route back to Jerusalem is Route 375 through the Ella Valley, past Israel's main satellite communications receiver, and up through wooded hill country to Tzur Hadassah (look out for the rock-hewn Roman road on the right). Route 386 heads off to the left and runs north to Jerusalem through rugged mountain scenery, emerging in the Ein Kerem neighborhood on the city's western edge.

BETHLEHEM

Fodor's Choice ★

8 km (5 mi) south of Jerusalem.

Even from a distance, it's easy to identify the minarets and steeples that symbolically vie for control of the skyline of Bethlehem, home to one of the oldest Christian communities in the world. Although a few decades ago most residents were Christians, today the great majority of Bethlehem's 38,000 residents are Muslim, as elsewhere in the West Bank.

For Christians the world over, the city is synonymous with the birth of Jesus, and the many shrines that celebrate that event. Bethlehem is also the site of the Tomb of Rachel, Jacob's wife, who died in childbirth here. Rachel's Tomb today lies in Israeli-controlled territory, immediately to the north of the wall that divides the area.

GETTING HERE AND AROUND

The birthplace of Jesus is 15 minutes south of Jerusalem. Bethlehem is part of the Palestinian Authority, and is set off from Jerusalem by the controversial security wall that snakes through the Judean hills.

The wall is especially intimidating around the Bethlehem border crossing, as it stands taller than most of the surrounding buildings and is constructed of solid concrete. On the Bethlehem side it has been sprayed with graffiti, much of it in English, demanding rights for Palestinians. As daunting as it seems, tourists with a foreign passport will have no difficulty visiting Bethlehem. Simply show the cover of your passport and you'll be whisked through, usually without a single question.

At the moment, Israelis are not allowed across the border. Your tour guide or the concierge at your hotel will be able to arrange for Palestinian guides to meet you across the border. If you're a more independent traveler, you can take one of the Palestinian taxis at the border. If taking a taxi, *sherut* (shared taxi), or bus from East Jerusalem, you must take a local bus or taxi from the Bethlehem side of the terminal to Manger Square. Because your rental agreement almost always forbids it, driving yourself is not recommended.

CHRISTMAS IN BETHLEHEM

In Bethlehem, Christmas is celebrated three times: December 25 by the Roman Catholics and Protestants; January 6 by the Greek, Coptic, and Russian Orthodox; and January 19 by the Armenian Orthodox. For nearly a month, Manger Square is brilliantly illuminated and bursting with life. On December 24, choirs from around the world perform carols and sacred music in the square between 8:30 pm and 11:30 pm, and at midnight at the Franciscan Church of St. Catherine. That mass is relayed on closed-circuit television onto a large screen in Manger Square and, via satellite, to all parts of the globe.

TIMING

Allow at least two hours for a visit to the Church of the Nativity and Manger Square.

SAFETY AND PRECAUTIONS

Tourists can travel to Bethlehem as political and security conditions permit. At press time, Israeli citizens are prohibited from entering areas under full Palestinian Authority control. Tourists are unlikely to be bothered in Bethlehem, but ask your hotel concierge if there have been any recent issues.

ESSENTIALS

Visitor Information **Tourist Information Office** (✉ *Peace Center, Manger Sq., Bethlehem* ☎ *02/276–6677* 🌐 *www.travelpalestine.ps*).

EXPLORING

★ **Church of the Nativity.** At this church marking the traditional site of the birth of Jesus, the stone exterior is crowned by the crosses of the three denominations sharing it: the Greek Orthodox, the Latins (Roman Catholic, represented by the Franciscan order), and the Armenian Orthodox. The blocked square entranceway dates from the time of the Byzantine emperor Justinian (6th century), the arched entrance (also blocked) within the Byzantine one is 12th-century Crusader, and the

Christmas in Bethlehem includes a colorful Greek Orthodox procession in Manger Square.

current low entrance was designed in the 16th century to protect the worshippers from attack by hostile Muslim neighbors.

The church interior is vast and gloomy. In the central nave, a large wooden trapdoor reveals a remnant of a striking mosaic floor from the original basilica, built in the 4th century by Helena, mother of Constantine the Great, the Roman emperor who first embraced Christianity. Emperor Justinian's rebuilding two centuries later enlarged the church, creating its present-day plan and structure, including the 44 red stone columns with Corinthian capitals that run the length of the nave in two paired lines.

This is the oldest standing church in the country. When the Persians invaded in 614, they destroyed every Christian church and monastery in the land except this one. Legend holds that the church was adorned with a wall painting depicting the Nativity tale, including the visit to the infant Jesus by the Three Wise Men of the East. For the local artist, "east" meant Persia, and he dressed his wise men in Persian garb. The Persian conquerors did not understand the picture's significance, but "recognized" themselves in the painting and so spared the church. In the 8th century, the church was pillaged by the Muslims and was later renovated by the Crusaders. Patches of 12th-century mosaics high on the walls, the medieval oak ceiling beams, and the figures of saints on the Corinthian pillars hint at its medieval splendor.

The elaborately ornamented front of the church serves as the parish church of Bethlehem's Greek Orthodox community. The right transept is theirs, too, but the left transept belongs to the Armenian Orthodox. The altar in the left transept is known as the altar of the kings, because

CLOSE UP

The West Bank

The West Bank is that part of the onetime British Mandate of Palestine, west of the Jordan River, that was occupied by the Kingdom of Transjordan in its war with the nascent State of Israel in 1948 and annexed shortly afterward. That country then changed its name to the Hashemite Kingdom of Jordan to reflect its new geopolitical reality. The territory was lost to Israel in the Six-Day War of 1967.

Following the Oslo Accords in 1993, much of the West Bank has been turned over to the Palestinian Authority. In Israel itself, the region is often referred to as "the territories," "over the Green Line" (a term denoting the 1949 armistice line between the West Bank and Israel), or by its biblical names of Judea (the area south of Jerusalem) and Samaria (the much larger area north of Jerusalem).

The West Bank is a kidney-shape area, a bit larger than the U.S. state of Delaware. The large majority of the approximately 2 million Arabs are Muslim, with the Christian minority living mostly in the greater Bethlehem area and Ramallah, and a tiny community of Samaritans living on Mt. Gerizim near Nablus.

While the Oslo Accords promised peace and final status discussions, a comprehensive agreement has proven elusive due to seemingly irreconcilable differences on the thorny issues of land, refugees, and Jerusalem. In late 2000, the simmering crisis exploded with lethal ferocity as young Palestinians took to the streets in riots known as the Second Intifada. In 2005, Israel unilaterally withdrew from the Gaza Strip and four remote settlements in northern Samaria. Although violence has subsided significantly, many visitors still avoid the West Bank. Others, while exercising caution, visit such worthwhile West Bank sites as Bethlehem and Jericho.

In addition to the 2 million Arabs in the West Bank, half a million Israelis also live there in hundreds of small settlements and a number of cities. Although the cities and bigger towns are really suburbs of Jerusalem and Tel Aviv, nationalist Israelis who see the region as an integral and inalienable part of the biblical homeland set up other settlements.

With its prime location within 14 km (9 mi) of the Mediterranean Sea, and its mountain heights—dominating Israel's main population centers—the West Bank has a strategic value that has convinced even many Israelis that it would be folly to relinquish it to potentially hostile Arab control. Other Israelis favor some kind of two-state solution.

A person's attitude toward the questions of continuing settlement in the West Bank and the ultimate status of the region is an important touchstone of political affiliation in Israel. The country remains completely divided on these issues.

Tourists can travel to Bethlehem and Jericho as security conditions permit; they need to take passports with them. At this writing, Israeli citizens are prohibited from entering areas under full Palestinian control. Please check your government's travel advisory before visiting these areas.

Church of the Nativity 3
Chuch of St. Catherine 4
Manger Square ...2
Rachel's Tomb 1

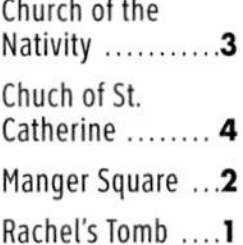

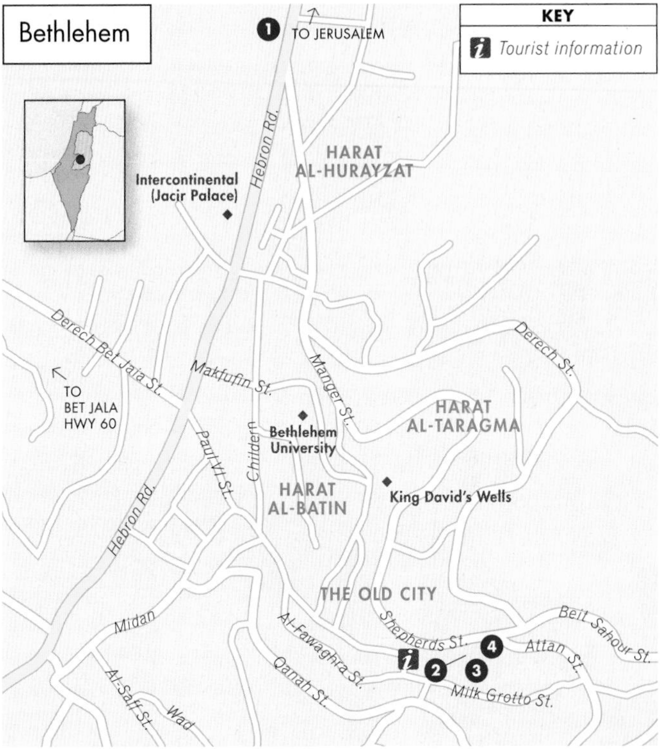

tradition holds this to be the place where the three magi dismounted. For centuries, all three "shareholders" in the church have vied for control of the holiest Christian sites in the Holy Land. The 19th-century Status Quo Agreement that froze their respective rights and privileges in Jerusalem's Church of the Holy Sepulcher and the Tomb of the Virgin pertains here, too: ownership, the timing of ceremonies, the number of oil lamps, and so on are all clearly defined.

From the right transept at the front of the church, descend to the **Grotto of the Nativity,** encased in white marble. Long lines can form at the entrance to the grotto, making the suggestion of spending just an hour to see the church an impossibility. Once a cave—precisely the kind of place that might have been used as a barn—the grotto has been reamed, plastered, and decorated beyond recognition. Immediately on the right is a small altar, and on the floor below it is the focal point of the entire site: a 14-point **silver star** with the Latin inscription "hic de virgine maria jesus christus natus est" (Here of the Virgin Mary, Jesus Christ was born). The Latins placed the original star here in 1717 but lost control of the altar 40 years later to the more influential Greek Orthodox. In 1847 the star mysteriously disappeared, and pressure from the Turkish sultan compelled the Greeks to allow the present Latin replacement to be installed in 1853. The Franciscan guardians do have

DID YOU KNOW?

Bethlehem is a magnet for Christian pilgrims, but it's also a center of Palestinian culture. The city is known for handicrafts such as olive-wood carvings, embroidery, and mother-of-pearl items.

possession, however, of the little alcove a few steps down on the left at the entrance to the grotto, said to be the manger where the infant Jesus was laid. ✉ *Manger Sq.* ☎ *02/274–1020* 🎟 *Free* ⏲ *Church: Apr.–Sept., daily 6:30 am–7:30 pm; Oct.–Mar., daily 5:30–5:30. Grotto: Apr.–Sept., Mon.–Sat. 9–7:30, Sun. noon–7:30; Oct.–Mar., Mon.–Sat. 9–5:30, Sun. noon–5:30.*

Church of St. Catherine. Adjacent to the Church of the Nativity, and accessible by a passage from its Armenian chapel, is Bethlehem's Roman Catholic parish church. Built by Franciscans in 1882, the church incorporates remnants of its 12th-century Crusader predecessor. Note the bronze doors with reliefs of St. Jerome, St. Paula, and St. Eustochium. From this church, the midnight Catholic Christmas mass is broadcast around the world. Steps descend from within the church to a series of dim grottoes, clearly once used as living quarters. Chapels here are dedicated to Joseph; to the Innocents killed by Herod the Great; and to the 4th-century St. Jerome, who wrote the Vulgate, the Latin translation of the Bible, supposedly right here. Adjacent to the church is a lovely cloister, restored in 1949. A small wooden door (kept locked) connects the complex with the Grotto of the Nativity. ✉ *Manger Sq.* ☎ *02/274–2425* ⏲ *Apr.–Sept., daily 6–noon and 2–7; Oct.–Mar., daily 5:30–5:30.*

Manger Square. Bethlehem's central plaza and the site of the Church of the Nativity, Manger Square is built over the grotto thought to be the birthplace of Jesus. The end of the square opposite the church is the Mosque of Omar, the city's largest Muslim house of worship. The square occupies the center of Bethlehem's old city. It has a tourist-information office, a few restaurants, and several good souvenir shops.

Rachel's Tomb. This Israeli enclave in a Palestinian area is on the right shortly after passing through the border. The Bible relates that the matriarch Rachel, second and favorite wife of Jacob, died in childbirth on the outskirts of Bethlehem, "and Jacob set up a pillar upon her grave" (Genesis 35:19–20). There is no vestige of Jacob's original pillar, but observant Jews for centuries have hallowed the velvet-draped cenotaph inside the building as the site of Rachel's tomb. People come to pray here for good health, fertility, and a safe birth. Some pilgrims wind a red thread seven times around the tomb, and give away snippets of it as talismans to cure all ills. Note that men and women are segregated here and have different entrances. The historic white dome is now hidden behind fortifications, as the Palestinians attacked the tomb in 1996 and again during the Second Intifada beginning in late 2000. The area is now safe for travel and was opened to private cars in 2008.

Islam as well venerates Rachel. Next to the tomb is a Muslim cemetery, reflecting the Middle Eastern tradition that it is a special privilege to be buried near a great personage. ✉ *Rte. 60* 🎟 *Free* ⏲ *Sun.–Thurs., open 24 hrs.*

Shepherds' Fields. As you approach Bethlehem, you'll see the fields of the adjacent town of Beit Sahour, to the east of the city, traditionally identified with the biblical story of Ruth the Moabite, daughter-in-law of Naomi, who "gleaned in the field" (Ruth 2:2) of Boaz, Naomi's kinsman. The same fields are identified by Christian tradition as those where bewildered shepherds "keeping watch over their flock by night" received "tidings of great joy"—word of the birth of Jesus in Bethlehem (Luke 2). Two chapels—the Greek Orthodox Der El Rawat and the Catholic El Ghanem—commemorate the event.

WHERE TO EAT AND STAY

$ MIDDLE EASTERN **Ka'bar.** In the village just west of Bethlehem, this is the proverbial hole in the wall where the cognoscenti come to enjoy scrumptious grilled chicken. There's no menu; the restaurant only serves chicken grilled on charcoal on the outdoor grill. The set menu includes five side dishes, among them an excellent house-made hummus. Make sure to sample the hot chili sauce and the restaurant's signature condiment, garlic and olive oil whipped into a mayonnaise-like dip for your chicken. End your meal with refreshing mint tea. Taxi drivers can take you here from Manger Square. ✉ *Derech Beit Jala, near Municipality Bldg., Beit Jala* ☎ *02/274–1419* ▭ *No credit cards* ⏲ *Closed Sun.*

$ **Intercontinental Bethlehem.** Known to locals as Jacir Palace, this luxurious lodging is like something out of *One Thousand and One Nights.* In 1910, Mayor Suleiman Jacir built the mansion, intending that his entire extended family would live here. The main building, an arabesque fantasy, is now home to restaurants including Baidar, with international buffets and garden views; the Riwaq, in the elegant courtyard; and the Rozana Terrace, set against the view of the Judean Hills. Two wings hold the guest rooms, which are some of the most comfortable in the area. Even if you don't stay here, stop by for a drink after a visit to the Church of the Nativity. **Pros:** amazing architectural atmosphere; convenient to Bethlehem; relatively inexpensive. **Cons:** difficult to reach by taxi from Jerusalem. ✉ *Jerusalem-Hebron Rd.* ☎ *02/276–6777* 🌐 *www.ichotelsgroup.com* *250 rooms; 5 suites* *In-room: a/c, refrigerator. In-hotel: 4 restaurants, room service, bars, tennis courts, pool, gym, spa, laundry service* ▭ *AE, DC, MC.*

SHOPPING

In the city's 300 workshops, Bethlehem craftspeople make carved olivewood and mother-of-pearl objects, mostly of a religious nature, but the many stores along the tourist route in town sell jewelry and trinkets. For quality and reliability, most of the large establishments on Manger Street are worth investigating, but some of the merchants near the Church of the Nativity, on Manger Square, have good-quality items as well.

4

Tel Aviv

WORD OF MOUTH

"Tel Aviv is full of life, and immersing oneself in the buzz of modern Israel helps illuminate the historical sites and landscapes you'll encounter subsequently. Go to Jaffa, go to the beach, go to the Carmel Market, the Neveh Tzedek district, and see why Tel Aviv is a World Heritage Site for its Bauhaus architecture."

—Gardyloo

WELCOME TO TEL AVIV

TOP REASONS TO GO

★ **Exploring the neighborhoods:** Check out Neveh Tzedek's pastel-colored homes and boutiques, Jaffa's jumble of a flea market, Tel Aviv Port's undulating boardwalk, and Florentine's urban hipster feel.

★ **Mediterranean beaches:** Hit the sand, walk along the promenade, or watch the sun dip into the Mediterranean with the locals in the evening.

★ **Bauhaus architecture:** Tel Aviv is also known as "The White City" because it is home to the largest concentration of Bauhaus architecture in the world. Explore it on a walking tour.

★ **Nahalat Binyamin Pedestrian Mall:** Stalls of this twice-weekly street fair offer a range of handmade crafts from pottery to jewelry at reasonable prices.

★ **Israel's best modern cuisine:** Inventive chefs have put the city on the gastronomic map—all good news for the hungry traveling gourmet.

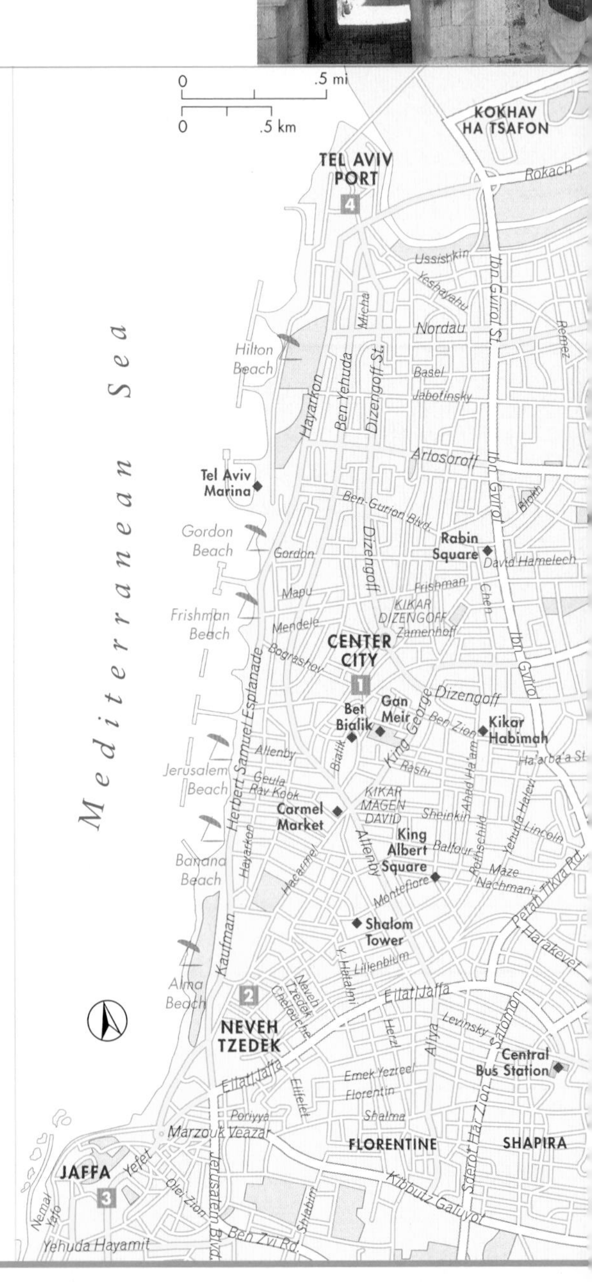

Azrieli Center

1 Center City. Most of Tel Aviv's major sites can be found in this warren of small side streets and hidden parks. Look for Rothschild Boulevard brimming with Bauhaus buildings, Carmel Market, and the Nahalat Binyamin Pedestrian Mall.

2 Neveh Tzedek. Restoration has meant a renaissance for this neighborhood of narrow roads lined with boutiques, galleries, and cafés. The Suzanne Dellal Centre for Dance and Theatre, with its orange-tree-studded square, is magical.

3 Jaffa. The port here—where a certain whale is said to have swallowed Jonah—is one of the oldest in the world. Here you'll find a flea market crammed with antique furniture and a growing number of trendy boutiques and restaurants.

4 The Tel Aviv Port and Northern Tel Aviv. The abandoned warehouses of the Tel Aviv Port have been transformed into upscale restaurants, cafés and clubs. Cyclists and strolling families pack the undulating boardwalk.

GETTING ORIENTED

Tel Aviv's compact size and flat landscape make it easy to get around on foot. The city's main north–south thoroughfares of Hayarkon, Ben Yehuda (which becomes Allenby), Dizengoff, and Ibn Gvirol streets run more or less parallel to the Mediterranean shoreline. Closest to the water is Hayarkon and the beachfront Tayelet (promenade). At the northern end of Hayarkon is the Tel Aviv Port. Most hotels are on the beachfront along Hayarkon.

Sheinkin Street

TEL AVIV PLANNER

Getting Here

From the airport, the fastest and easiest way into the city is by taxi, and costs NIS 140. During rush hour, allow 45 minutes for a trip that would otherwise be 20 minutes. The train is a money saver for NIS 14 and takes about 25 minutes.

Driving in Tel Aviv is not for the fainthearted. Major highways lead in and out of Tel Aviv: Route 1 from Jerusalem, Route 4 from the northern coast, and Route 5 from the east. Take advantage of Tel Aviv's belt road, the Ayalon Freeway, to access various parts of the city.

When to Go

Tel Aviv's mild Mediterranean climate means that any time is a good time to visit. However, midday summer temperatures in the 90s may mean choosing museums and other air-conditioned sites until the sun dips and the sea breeze stirs. Weekends (in Israel this means Thursday nights, Fridays, and Saturdays) are the busiest times, but also the most fun in terms of people-watching and special events.

Getting Around

Bus Travel: Buses are run primarily by Dan, and also by Egged. The fare is a fixed NIS 5.80 within the city center, and you buy your tickets on the bus. There is a small discount for a 10-ride card. Combined train-and-bus tickets are also available. Privately run minibuses also service two of the major lines: Bus 4 (Ben Yehuda and Allenby streets) and Bus 5 (Dizengoff Street and Rothschild Boulevard). You can flag these down and ask to get off at any point along their routes; the fare is the same as on regular buses. Minibuses also run on Saturday, when regular buses do not. Buses leave for Jerusalem every 15 minutes throughout most of the day.

Taxi Travel: Taxis here can be any car model or color and have lighted signs on top. They're plentiful, even in bad weather; drivers honk to catch your attention, even if you're not trying to catch theirs. If traveling within the metropolitan area, make sure the driver turns the meter on when you get in. Rates are NIS 11.10 for the first 18 seconds and 30 agorot in increments thereafter. *Sherut* taxis consist mainly of a fleet of vans at the Central Bus Station that run the same routes as the buses, at comparable one-way prices. They run on Saturday at a higher charge.

Train Travel: The train is an excellent way to travel between Tel Aviv and cities and towns to the north, such as Netanya, Hadera, Haifa, and Nahariya. The northbound train leaves from the Central Railway Station and the Azrieli station. The information office is open Sunday to Thursday 6 am to 11 pm and Friday 6 to 3. Trains run roughly every hour on weekdays from between 5 am and 6 am to between 10 pm and 11 pm depending on the destination; there are fewer trains on Friday and Jewish holiday eves and no service on Saturday or on holidays. There is also a line to Beersheva.

Contacts **Dan** (*03/639–4444* *www.dan.co.il*). **Egged** (*03/694–8888* *www.egged.co.il*). **Central Railway Station** (*Arlosoroff St.* *03/611–7000* *www.rail.co.il/en*).

For more information on getting here and around, see Travel Smart Israel.

Planning Your Time

With two to four days, you can explore most of Tel Aviv and still have time for the beach. Although it's not a huge area to cover, see the city in geographical order. Start with old Jaffa in the south, and amble through the art galleries, flea market, and fishing port. Jaffa's a good choice in the evening for strolling, low-key restaurants, and wine bars. From here, it's a quick walk north to see Neveh Tzedek. Check out the well-restored buildings, and catch a performance at the Suzanne Dellal Centre at night. In the center of town, don't miss the Bauhaus buildings of the White City or the Nahalat Benyamin market (on Tuesday or Friday). With more time, explore the north, and see the Diaspora, the Palmach, and the Eretz Israel museums, as well as Hayarkon Park for boating or cycling. The Tel Aviv Port is a good place for trendy dining and nightlife.

Dining

Tel Aviv is very much a café society. Locals of all ages love their morning, afternoon, and evening coffee time—so much so that it's often hard to get a seat. The city's cosmopolitan character is reflected in its restaurants, which offer cuisines from around the world. Still occupying many street corners are stands selling delicious Middle Eastern fast food—such as *falafel* (patties made from chickpeas) and *shawarma* (spit-grilled meat).

Lodging

The major hotels along Hayarkon Street are right on the Tayelet next to the beach. Staying at a boutique hotel in restored historic buildings adds a wonderful accent to the Tel Aviv experience. Most of the city's hotels are only a short distance from most major attractions.

WHAT IT COSTS

	¢	$	$$	$$$	$$$$
Restaurants	Under NIS 32	NIS 32–49	NIS 50–75	NIS 76–100	Over NIS 100
Hotels	Under $120	$120–$200	$201–$300	$301–$400	Over $400

Restaurant prices are per person for a main course at dinner in NIS (Israeli shekels). Hotel prices are in U.S. dollars, for two people in a standard double room in high season. Non-Israeli citizens paying in foreign currency are exempt from the 16% VAT on hotel rooms.

Tours

The Tel-Aviv–Jaffa Municipality has laid out three self-guided tours. The White Route relates Tel Aviv's history, the Blue Route its coastline, and the Green Route its natural wonders. Free, city-sponsored walking tours sponsored by the Tel-Aviv–Jaffa Municipality are available as follows: Old Jaffa, beginning at the clock tower on Wednesday at 9 am; neighborhood evening historical tour beginning at the corner of Rothschild Boulevard and Herzl Street, Tuesday 8 pm; the Bauhaus White City, Saturday 11 am beginning at 46 Rothschild Boulevard. No prior registration is required.

Information Tel Aviv–Jaffa Municipality (☎ *599/588–888* 🌐 *www.tel-aviv.gov.il*).

Visitor Information

The Israeli Government Tourist Office operates a 24-hour information desk in the Arrivals hall at Ben Gurion Airport that will make same-day reservations. The city tourist office, which stocks maps of walking tours around the city, is open Sunday to Thursday 9:30 to 5:30, Friday 9:30 to 1. It's on the oceanfront promenade.

Information Israel Government Tourist Office (☎ *03/975–4260* 🌐 *www.goisrael.com*). **Tel Aviv Tourist Information Office** (✉ *46 Herbert Samuel St.* ☎ *03/516–6188* 🌐 *www.visit-tlv.com*.

4

BAUHAUS STYLE IN TEL AVIV

The rounded corner balconies, rooftop garden, and staircase with windows are classic Bauhaus elements in this restored building at 17 Emile Zola Street.

One great way to explore Tel Aviv is through the Bauhaus architecture that is its defining style. The geometric forms and pastel colors of this modern design ethos, transplanted in the 1930s by Jewish architects fleeing Europe, fit both the landscape and Zionist notions of a socialist Utopia.

The so-called "White City," the central part of Tel Aviv that is home to the largest concentration of Bauhaus buildings, was named a World Cultural Heritage Site by UNESCO in 2003. Bauhaus-inspired architecture, more accurately referred to as the Modern or International style, was based on the idea that art should serve society and that form should also have function. For example, balconies were not designed to be merely decorative but to serve as a source of shade, fresh air, and a place from which to interact with neighbors. Today conservation efforts are making headway, but many classic buildings need repair, their beauty lost under peeling paint. It's a work in progress as the city offers incentives to owners to restore their properties.

STYLE ELEMENTS

Signature **vertical staircases** offset the predominance of horizontal lines and are recognizable by the steel-frame windows that provide light. **Roof gardens**, identifiable by pergolas of beams and columns, were designed with the expectation that neighbors would socialize on their rooftops. Simple and well-proportioned, **balconies** can be curved or square or rectangular in shape, and are often overhung with ledges that provide shade.

A BAUHAUS WALK

The city's Bauhaus bounty is best discovered by foot. A good place to stroll is along **Rothschild Boulevard** and its side streets, which also have pleasant cafés and restaurants. A walking tour can begin at **No. 90**, corner of Balfour Street. Here a three-story mustard-colored building, with the clean lines that are a trademark of the style, stands in contrast to the highly decorated building next door. Note the front door with horizontal strips of wood inlaid in the glass. Its wooden shutters are not necessarily an element that would be seen in European Bauhaus examples, but here became a necessity because of the sun. Walk to **Nos. 89 and 91**, twin buildings in need of renovation, and see the small vertical windows indicating the placement of a central staircase and the two main styles of balcony, rounded and rectangular.

Walk back across boulevard and look for **Engel Street**, a pedestrian-friendly lane lined with Bauhaus buildings. **No. 7** features horizontal bands of balconies and windows. The front door has an asymmetrical overhang and canopy. For an example of the city's restoration efforts, look up to its top floor, which continues the horizontal theme.

Returning to Rothschild Boulevard, walk to **Nos. 113/115**; note the "thermometer" staircase and its small, elegant windows. On the right-hand side the balconies wrap around the building, mimicking the corner of the street; on the left-hand side the balconies are aligned with the side of the building.

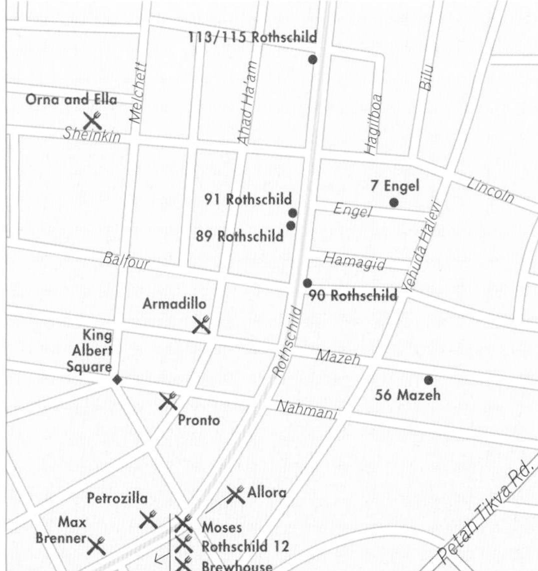

SEEING MORE

Check the **city tourist office** for free Bauhaus walking tours. The **Bauhaus Center** at 99 Dizengoff Street sells books and more, and offers excellent walking tours.

Another resource is the **Bauhaus Foundation Museum** at 21 Bialik Street, open Wednesday and Friday. Bialik Street has many attractive older buildings.

Exploring on your own? Here are a few key buildings around the city.

9 Gordon St., 1935. One of the first Bauhaus buildings to be refurbished in the city; take in its elegant cube within a cube design, wooden shutters, and rooftop pergola.

Haaretz Print Works, 56 Mazeh St., 1934. The building where *Haaretz* newspaper was once printed has steel-framed glass windows and balconies with rounded railings and cantilevered roofs.

25 Idelson St., 1931. Designed as a family villa: note a mix of balconies, the asymmetric form, and the mix of small horizontal and vertical windows.

4

Updated by Dina Kraft

Tel Aviv, Israel's ever-growing metropolis, would be unrecognizable to its founders, a small group of Jewish immigrant families in what was then Ottoman-ruled Palestine. A skyline of shimmering skyscrapers has replaced the towering sand dunes of just over a century ago. The city is now known for its boxy Bauhaus buildings, theaters, and concert halls, as well as its legions of sidewalk cafés that host overflow crowds every night of the week.

The city manages to pull off the seemingly impossible task of being both hip and homey: witness the happy mix of wine bars, clothing boutiques, hardware shops, and greengrocers—often on the same block. High-end restaurants mingle with old-school eateries where elderly men hold noisy court about the issues of the day over black coffee and apple turnovers.

Sometime described as an urban village, Tel Aviv is made for walking (or biking, now that it has an extensive network of 62 miles of bike paths). From most parts of the city the sea is never more than a 20-minute walk. In this combination beach town, business center, and arts mecca, people spend Friday afternoons bumping into friends, wandering from café to café, and pausing to hear live jazz trios, all the while strolling with their dogs down boulevards lined with 1940s-era newspaper kiosks that have been transformed into gourmet sandwich stands.

Tel Aviv is not the most beautiful of cities, although its charms have a way of making you forgive its aesthetic shortcomings. It was declared a UNESCO World Cultural Heritage Site in 2003 because its collection of International-style architecture, known more commonly as Bauhaus, is the largest in the world. Although restoration efforts are moving along, many of these buildings are in need of a facelift. It might take an hour or two of wandering on the tree-lined side streets for you to appreciate their graceful lines and subtle architectural flourishes.

There is a spirit of freedom in Tel Aviv, where it's possible to escape from the difficult political realities that are closer to the surface in places like Jerusalem. After all, the city's nickname among Israelis is "the Bubble." Residents tend to be politically and socially liberal. The gay scene is thriving, as are the arts and music communities. It's an exciting city, one that newcomers, returning visitors, and longtime residents all find captivating.

EXPLORING TEL AVIV

From the city center, it's easy to head south to Jaffa and its ancient port and lively flea market—to get there the scenic way, saunter along the seaside promenade overlooking the beach—and the other southern neighborhoods like the gentrified Neveh Tzedek and the more urbane Florentine.

Even further north at the edge of Tel Aviv proper lies the sprawling green lung of Tel Aviv, Hayarkon Park. You'll also discover the city's recently renovated port area, an ideal setting for a seaside breakfast or a toast at sunset with which to usher in Tel Aviv's infamous inexhaustible nightlife.

CENTER CITY

Think of downtown Tel Aviv as a cat's cradle of boulevards and side streets leading to all the city's great sights. These few square miles are the heart and soul of the city. Swirling around you might be surfers heading up from the beach, film crews shooting commercials, couples walking their dogs along leafy boulevards, and students stopping for sandwiches at newspaper kiosks that have been transformed into cafés. At Hayarkon Park, a welcome swath of green on the Yarkon River, families picnic not far from joggers and bikers on well-paved paths.

GETTING HERE AND AROUND

Most of the main bus lines travel through the center of the city, but two in particular are of interest to travelers: Bus 4 on Ben Yehuda Street and Bus 5 on Dizengoff Street. Both run at frequent intervals. Both of these thoroughfares also have minibuses that can be hailed like taxis and are often an even faster option for getting around. The flat landscape makes strolling along streets like Dizengoff, King George, Rothschild and Ibn Gvirol very easy.

TIMING AND PRECAUTIONS

Give yourself the better part of a day to savor this part of the city, as there is a lot to see. It's well lighted at night and is considered safe for evening strolls.

TOP ATTRACTIONS

Bauhaus Foundation Museum. Those who love architecture won't want to miss this one-room museum on historic Bialik Street. It occupies the ground floor of an original Bauhaus building, built in 1934 and home to the Bauhaus Foundation. Visitors discover that the pristine lines and basic geometric forms typical of the Bauhaus school extend to everyday

Center City and Neveh Tzedek

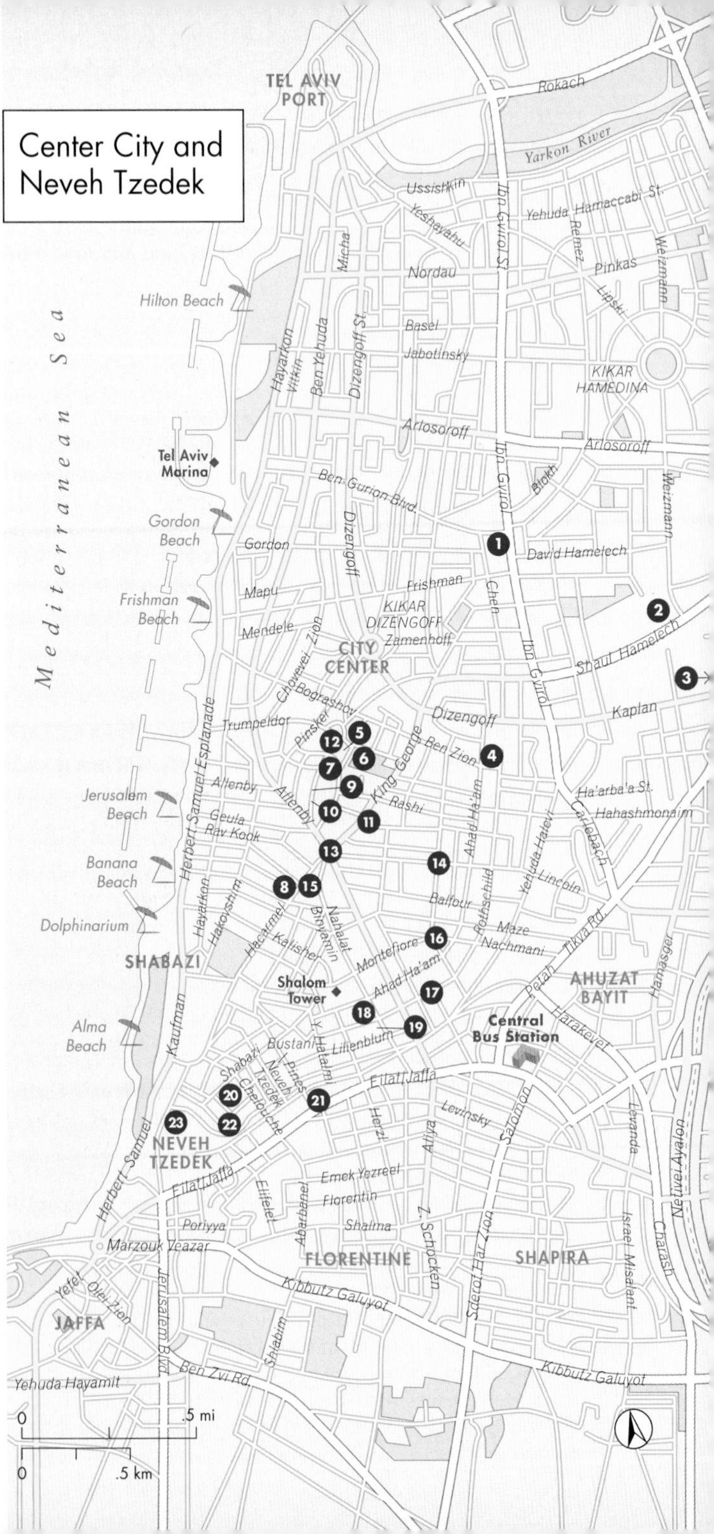

Azrieli Towers ... **3**
Bauhaus Foundation Museum **12**
Beit Ha'ir **5**
Beit Bialik **7**
Bialik Street ... **10**
Carmel Market **8**
Founders' Monument and Fountain **18**
Gan Meir **6**
Gutman Museum **22**
HaTachana **23**
Helena Rubinstein Pavilion **4**
Independence Hall Museum .. **19**
Kikar Magen David **13**
King Albert Square **16**
Nahalat Binyamin Pedestrian Mall **15**
Rabin Square **1**
Rokach House **21**
Rothschild Boulevard **17**
Rubin Museum **9**
Sheinkin Street **14**
Simtat Plonit .. **11**
Suzanne Dellal Centre for Dance and Theater **20**
Tel Aviv Museum of Art **2**

objects as well, from furniture to light fixtures to glazed stoneware. There's even a door handle designed by Walter Gropius (1883–1969), founder and first director of the Bauhaus. ✉ *21 Bialik St., Center City* ☎ *03/620–4664* 🎟 *Free* ⏲ *Wed. 11–5, Fri. 10–2.*

★ **Beit Ha'ir.** Catch up on Tel Aviv's remarkable history at this historical museum in the original 1924 municipal building, an architectural masterpiece that has been lovingly restored. Among the exhibits highlighting the progress of the last century is a brief film tracing the city's development from huts in the sand to gleaming apartment towers. There's also a pretty patchwork floor made up of colorful tiles typical of vintage Tel Aviv buildings and the restored office of the city's first mayor, Meir Dizengoff, with the original map of Tel Aviv hanging on a wall. ✉ *27 Bialik St., Center City* ☎ *03/525–3403* 🌐 *www.beithair.org* 🎟 *NIS 20* ⏲ *Mon. and Tues. 9–5, Fri. and Sat. 10-2.*

4

★ **Carmel Market.** The first section of Carmel Market (commonly referred to as the *shuk*) consists of cheap clothing, but a little farther down, in the fruit and vegetable section, is where the real local color begins. Vendors loudly hawk their fresh produce, and crowded aisles reveal Israel's incredible ethnic mix. It's a great sight to see particularly on Tuesdays or Fridays, when it can be combined with a visit to the Nahalat Binyamin Pedestrian Mall's crafts fair. ✉ *Along Hacarmel St., Center City.*

NEED A BREAK?

The Carmel Market and Allenby Road border the Yemenite Quarter, which hides several cheap and satisfying little eateries (closed Friday night and Saturday) offering shawarma and barbecued skewered meats, all kosher. Wash it down with a beer as you gaze out onto the neighborhood's warren of cobblestone lanes. Some streets that are nice to stroll include Nahliel and Haim Havshush, both known for restaurants serving tasty hummus and Yemenite flatbread. Although it's gotten a lot of press lately, the Yemenite Quarter still feels a bit down at heel.

Independence Hall Museum. This impressive building was originally the home of the city's first mayor, Meir Dizengoff; he donated it to the city in 1930 to be used as Tel Aviv's first art museum. More significantly, the country's leaders assembled here on May 14, 1948, to announce to the world the establishment of the State of Israel. Today the museum's **Hall of Declaration** stands as it did on that dramatic day, with the original microphones on the long table where the dignitaries sat. Behind the table is a portrait of the Zionist leader Theodor Herzl. ✉ *16 Rothschild Blvd., Center City* ☎ *03/517–3942* 🎟 *NIS 20* ⏲ *Sun.–Fri. 9–2.*

Fodor's Choice ★ **Nahalat Binyamin Pedestrian Mall.** The selection at this street market, open Tuesday and Friday, is broad—ranging from plastic trinkets to sophisticated crafts such as hand-carved wooden boxes, attractive glassware, and handmade silver jewelry. Nahalat Binyamin is further enlivened by a profusion of buskers. For a finishing touch of local color, cafés serving cakes and light meals line the street. At the end of the fair is a large Bedouin tent, where you can treat yourself to a *laffa* with *labaneh* and *za'atar* (large pita bread with tangy sour cream, sprinkled with hyssop, a mintlike herb). ✉ *Nahalat Binyamin St., off Allenby St., Center City* ⏲ *Tues. and Fri. until sundown.*

★ **Rothschild Boulevard.** Half a century ago, this magnificent tree-lined boulevard was one of the most exclusive streets in the city. Today, this is quintessential urban Tel Aviv, and the central stretch of the boulevard is once again what its designers at the beginning of the 20th century meant it to be—a place for people to meet, stroll, and relax. Along it are some of the city's best restaurants and bars, and many Bauhaus gems are on or just off the street.

Rubin Museum. Recognized as one of Israel's major painters, Reuven Rubin (1893–1974) bequeathed his house to Tel Aviv along with 45 of his works, which make up the permanent collection. The house, built in 1930, is now an art gallery, with changing exhibits by Israeli artists in addition to the great Rubin's work. Upstairs is a small but well-stocked art library where you can pore over press clippings and browse through art books. A moving audiovisual presentation tells the story of Rubin's life, with many fascinating segments in his own voice. His original studio can still be seen on the third floor. ✉ *14 Bialik St., Center City* ☎ *03/525–5961* 🌐 *www.rubinmuseum.org.il* 🎫 *NIS 20* ⏲ *Mon., Wed., and Thurs. 10–3, Tues. 10–8, Sat. 11–2.*

Tel Aviv Museum of Art. This museum houses a fine collection of Israeli and international art, including works by prominent Jewish artists like Marc Chagall and Roy Lichtenstein. There's also an impressive French Impressionist collection and many sculptures by Aleksandr Archipenko. A lavish new wing, scheduled to open 2011, will double its exhibition space. ✉ *27 Shaul Hamelech Blvd., Center City* ☎ *03/607–7020* 🌐 *www.tamuseum.com* 🎫 *NIS 42* ⏲ *Mon., Wed., and Sat. 10–4, Tues. and Thurs. 10–10, Fri. 10–2.*

WORTH NOTING

Azrieli Towers. A spectacular 360-degree view of Tel Aviv and beyond awaits on the 49th-floor observatory of this office building and mall complex, which consists of three buildings—one triangular, one circular, and one square. The observatory is sometimes closed for private events, so call ahead. ✉ *Hashalom exit west, Ayalon Fwy., Center City* ☎ *03/608–1179* 🌐 *www.mitzpe49.co.il* 🎫 *NIS 22 for observatory.*

Beit Bialik *(Bialik House)*. Spiffed up for the city's centennial, Bialik House is the charming two-story home of Chaim Nachman Bialik (1873–1934), considered the father of Hebrew poetry. The original bold colors were restored, as were many of the original furnishings. Bialik was already a respected poet and publisher by the time he moved to Tel Aviv from Russia in 1924; in the remaining 10 years of his life, his house, built in 1927, became the intellectual center of Tel Aviv. It's said that when Bialik lived here, the street was closed to traffic in the afternoon in order to let him write in peace and quiet. English-language tours can be arranged in advance. ✉ *22 Bialik St., Center City* ☎ *03/525–3403.*

Bialik Street. This area has been more successful than many other Tel Aviv neighborhoods in maintaining its older buildings. Bialik has long been a popular address with many of the city's artists and literati, so it's not surprising that some of the houses have been converted into small museums, including Beit Ha'ir, Beit Bialik, the Rubin Museum, and the Bauhaus Foundation Museum. Here you'll find a **mosaic,** designed by artist Nahum Gutman, which depicts the history of the city from the ancient days of Jaffa to the rise of Tel Aviv. Gutman was among the elite group of Tel Aviv's first artists.

Founders' Monument and Fountain. Dedicated in 1949, the Founders' Monument names those who founded Tel Aviv. This large slab of stone also encapsulates the city's past in three copper bas-relief panels representing the earliest pioneer days of planting and building as well as modern architecture. ✉ *Rothschild Blvd., on the traffic divider at Nahalat Binyamin St., Center City.*

4

Gan Meir. You're virtually guaranteed a traffic jam on this section of King George Street not far from Dizengoff Center, but you can get a respite by sitting on one of Gan Meir's benches, shaded by beautiful old trees. The first trees were planted in 1936 when the city offered to name the park after its first mayor, Meir Dizengoff, in honor of his 70th birthday. The feisty Dizengoff objected, so the park only got its official name in 1944, years after he passed away. There's a large playground for kids and an enclosed dog run. ✉ *King George and Hashmonim sts., Center City.*

Helena Rubinstein Pavilion. This annex of the Tel Aviv Museum of Art houses changing contemporary art exhibitions of contemporary Israeli art in an intimate space that is a particularly effective venue for one-person exhibitions. It's a great escape from the midday sun. ✉ *6 Tarsat St., Center City* ☎ *03/528–7196* 🌐 *www.tamuseum.com* 🎟 *Free* ⏲ *Mon., Wed., and Sat. 10–4, Tues. and Thurs. 10–10, Fri. 10–2.*

Kikar Magen David. This meeting point of six streets is named for the six-point Magen David, or Star of David. Faded historic buildings flank it on one side, shops and eateries on the other. Most important, it's the gateway to the Carmel Market, the open-air fruit and vegetable market. The intersection gives you an all-too-close look at how locals drive; if you're crossing the street here, use the underpass. ✉ *King George and Allenby sts., Center City.*

King Albert Square. Named after the Belgian monarch who was a personal friend of Mayor Dizengoff, this prominent square is surrounded by some interesting monuments. The Bauhaus-style Pagoda House, now made over as a luxury apartment building, was built in 1924 as a private home. The rooftop ornament gives the building its name. Inside the elegant stairwell of the Shifrin House, at 2 Melchett Street, are crumbling remnants of frescoes of the Western Wall and Rachel's Tomb. ✉ *Nahmani and Montefiore sts., Center City.*

Rabin Square. The square was renamed for Prime Minister Yitzhak Rabin after he was assassinated here on November 4, 1995. Passersby often pause at the small monument of black stones, rippled and uneven as if after an earthquake. This quiet memorial is the work of Israeli artist Danny Karavan. ✉ *Ibn Gvirol St., Center City.*

Sheinkin Street. This popular thoroughfare, off Allenby Street, has plenty of cafés and restaurants where you can watch passersby. This is where

CLOSE UP

A Focus on the Arts

For a tiny nation, Israel has a thriving and abundant arts scene. The country is home to thousands of classical musicians—many of whom immigrated from the former Soviet states—and the Israel Philharmonic Orchestra has a world-class reputation.

A number of music festivals are held annually, drawing international crowds—from the Red Sea Jazz Festival, in the south, to the Voice of Music chamber music event and Jacob's Ladder Folk Festival, in the north.

Israeli theater, too, enjoys a significant following. There are six professional repertory theaters—including the Habmiah and the Cameri in Tel Aviv—and dozens of regional and amateur companies performing throughout the country. They perform almost exclusively in Hebrew.

Professional dance companies also abound in Israel today. The Suzanne Dellal Centre for Dance and Theatre in Tel Aviv is the primary venue and home to the Bat Sheva Dance Company, the national dance troupe.

Folk dancing has always been popular in Israel—in fact, it's an evolving art form. As well as "Israeli" folk dancing (really a blend of Jewish and non-Jewish folk dance forms from around the world), some of Israel's different ethnic groups have preserved their traditional dances.

Enthusiasm for the visual arts can be seen in all walks of Israeli life. A wide range of Israeli art can be viewed at the Israel Museum in Jerusalem, the Tel Aviv Museum of Art, and for modern Israeli art, the Ramat Gan Art Museum. Small art galleries abound; a large concentration can be found on Gordon Street in Tel Aviv.

young people shop for the latest fashions; the sizes are tiny, the favored color is black, and some of the boutiques are so miniscule you'll think you walked straight into the dressing room. Street performances add to the boisterous fun (though it's hard to see much through the crowds).

Simtat Plonit. Wander down this alley to see old Tel Aviv decorative architecture at its best. Two plaster obelisks at the entrance mark the city's first "gated" community. Note the stucco lion in front of **Number 7**, which used to have glowing eyes fitted with lightbulbs. The original apartment house is painted pale yellow with a garish orange trim. An outspoken builder named Meir Getzel Shapira bought Simtat Plonit in the 1920s and insisted that this pint-size street be named after him. Tel Aviv's first mayor, Meir Dizengoff, argued that another street already had that name. The mayór emerged victorious and named it Simtat Plonit, meaning "John Doe Street."

NEVEH TZEDEK

Neveh Tzedek is a prime tourist destination because of its restaurants, cafés, cultural life, and historic buildings. Not surprisingly, it's where you'll find the fantastic dance and theater complex, the Suzanne Dellal Centre, as well as a growing number of trendy galleries and gift shops. Though bordered on three sides by major thoroughfares (Eilat Road to

A crowd enjoys the folk music and the sunshine on the Promenade Tayelet.

the south, Herzl Street to the west, and Kaufman Street along the sea), this quarter is very tranquil.

Made up of about a dozen tiny streets crammed with one- and two-story dwellings in various stages of renovation, Neveh Tzedek is rich with history. This is where the saga of Tel Aviv began, when a small group of Jewish families from Jaffa laid the cornerstone for their new neighborhood, naming it Neveh Tzedek (Dwellings of Justice). When Tel Aviv was busy expanding to the north and the east in the early days of the state, Neveh Tzedek was allowed to deteriorate. But in recent years the beautiful old buildings were rediscovered, and the lovingly restored homes here are now among the most prestigious addresses in the city.

GETTING HERE AND AROUND

The spine of Neveh Tzedek is Shabazi Street, which runs the length of the neighborhood. Most shops and restaurants are either on or near Shabazi Street. The roads here are notoriously narrow, and pedestrians have the right of way.

TIMING AND PRECAUTIONS

Neveh Tzedek is the perfect place to spend a few leisurely hours exploring the interesting shops and tasty eateries. The neighborhood can get pretty crowded on weekends, so if you are looking for a more tranquil vibe try to visit during the week. At night the streets can feel a bit deserted.

TOP ATTRACTIONS

HaTachana. On the edge of Neveh Tzedek, this Turkish-era train station is where travelers once embarked to Jerusalem on the first piece of railroad in the Middle East. Even Theodor Herzl, founder of modern

Aside from colorful buildings, Sheinkin Street is packed with buskers, restaurants, and cafés.

Zionism, passed through here. Dubbed HaTachana, Hebrew for "The Station," it recently reopened to the public after a NIS 100 million renovation. Situated on 49 acres, the complex includes 22 different buildings, among them the former station that now houses art exhibits. A pair of restored train cars tells the story of the station's days as a major travel hub in the region. You'll also find restaurants, cafés, and boutiques peddling handcrafted jewelry and homegrown designer clothes. ✉ *Koifman and Ha'Mered sts., Neveh Tzedek* ☎ *No phone* 🌐 *www.hatachana.co.il* 🎫 *Free* 🕒 *Sat.–Thurs. 10–10; Fri. 10–5.*

★ **Suzanne Dellal Centre for Dance and Theatre.** The large whitewashed buildings, one built in 1892 and the other in 1908, make up this attractive complex. The square, designed by foremost landscape designer Shlomo Aronson, has hints of a medieval Middle Eastern courtyard in its scattering of orange trees connected by water channels. One side of the square is decorated with a tile triptych, which illustrates the neighborhood's history and famous people who lived here in the early years, including S.Y. Agnon, who went on to win the Nobel Prize in Literature. There's a café-bar on the premises. ✉ *6 Yehieli St., Neveh Tzedek* ☎ *03/510–5656* 🌐 *www.suzannedellal.org.il.*

WORTH NOTING

Gutman Museum. In the 1920s, a number of Tel Aviv's most famous writers lived in this building, whose renovations have somewhat obscured its original look. One of the first houses in Neveh Tzedek, the building now displays the art of Nahum Gutman, colorful chronicler of early Tel Aviv. Tours in English are available by prearrangement. ✉ *21 Rokach St., Neveh Tzedek* ☎ *03/510–8554* 🌐 *www.gutmanmuseum.co.il* 🎫 *NIS*

If you're looking for a "bird's-eye" view of the city, it doesn't get better than from the top of the Azrieli Towers.

24 ⏲ Sun.–Thurs. 10–4, Thurs. 10–10, Fri. and Jewish holiday eves 10–2, Sat. 10–3.

Rokach House. The founder of Neveh Tzedek, Shimon Rokach, built this mansion, now a museum. It had fallen into disrepair and was slated for demolition before being reclaimed and restored by the Rokachs' granddaughter, artist Leah Majaro-Mintz. It now houses an exhibit of items from the quarter's early days, as well as pieces of her own art. Guided tours in English are available by calling ahead. A dramatization (in Hebrew) of Neveh Tzedek's history, preceded by tastings of the period's cuisine, is offered on Thursday and Friday evening at 8:30. *✉ 36 Rokach St., Neveh Tzedek ☎ 03/516–8042 🌐 www.rokach-house.co.il 🎫 NIS 10 ⏲ Sun.–Thurs. 10–4, Fri. and Sat. 10–2.*

JAFFA

Part of the sprawling municipality of Tel Aviv, the ancient port city of Jaffa is a mix of Jews, Christians, and Muslims. It's an ideal place for strolling down cobblestone streets and for dining at one of the no-frills fish restaurants that line the quay. Don't miss the Old City, where art galleries and shops occupy the centuries-old buildings along the narrow roads. At the Jaffa Flea Market, you can be part of the trading and bargaining for treasures—real and perceived—that are a hallmark of the Middle East.

The streets around Clock Tower Square bustle on weekday afternoons, when schoolchildren stop by the open-air eateries for flaky pastries, and weekend evenings, when the bars empty out and their patrons are in search of a late-night bite. An oceanfront promenade, completed in 2009, connects Tel Aviv with Jaffa. The sprawling park that runs parallel to the promenade was once a landfill, but is now one of the city's greenest areas. Kids love the playgrounds and vast stretches of grass.

South of Jaffa are two worthwhile excursions. Design Museum Holon, in the suburb of that name, is an exciting contemporary art museum. A bit farther south, in Rehovot, is the Weizmann Institute of Science.

Some historians claim that Jaffa was named after its founder, Japhet, son of Noah; others think its name is from the Hebrew *yafeh* (beautiful). What is certain is its status as one of the world's oldest ports—perhaps the oldest. The Bible says the cedars used in the construction of the Holy Temple passed through Jaffa on their way to Jerusalem; the prophet Jonah set off from Jaffa before being swallowed by the whale; and St. Peter raised Tabitha from the dead here. Napoléon was but one of a succession of invaders who brought the city walls down; these walls were rebuilt for the last time in the early 19th century by the Turks and torn down yet again as recently as 1879.

GETTING HERE AND AROUND

From central Tel Aviv, Dan buses 18 and 10 take you to Jaffa. You can also walk or bike along the seafront promenade to get here.

TIMING AND PRECAUTIONS

Jaffa can feel deserted at night. Stay away from dark streets and avoid walking alone.

TOP ATTRACTIONS

★ **Jaffa Flea Market.** Originally one of many small bazaars surrounding the clock tower in the mid-19th century, the Jaffa Flea Market is the only survivor of that era. Along the newly paved cobblestone streets, you can find everything from European antiques to Israeli memorabilia. Clothing designers have opened boutiques on its alleys. The market's main street is **Olei Zion,** but there are a number of smaller streets and arcades to explore at your leisure, so take your time. While you're probably not going to lug a 19th-century sideboard home, you can watch the locals shop and bargain, and do what they do: never agree to the first price a seller demands.

★ **Jaffa Port.** With a recently refurbished promenade, this small, intimate-feeling marina (one of the most ancient ports in the world) is home to bobbing wooden fishing boats, and a waterfront of restaurants, cafés, boutiques, and a small number of art galleries. Some of its warehouses have now been converted into public space for rotating art exhibits. From here, enjoy a fish lunch and then hop on a boat for a cruise along the city's coastline. ✉ *Retsef Aliyah Ha'Shniyah, Jaffa.*

Kedumim Square. Old Jaffa is indisputably charming and should not be missed. The focus of Kedumim Square is an archaeological site that exposes 3rd-century BC catacombs; the site has been converted into a free underground visitor center with large, vivid, illustrated descriptions of Jaffa's history. A labyrinthine network of tiny alleys snakes in all directions from Kedumim Square down to the fishing port; a good selection of galleries and jewelry stores can be found south of the square around Mazal Dagim Street. ✉ *Kedumim Square St., Jaffa.*

Jaffa

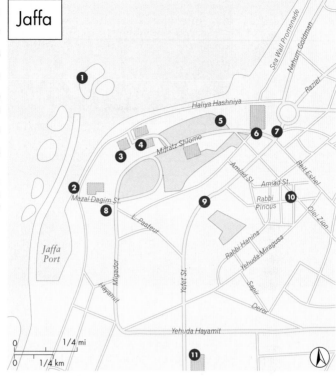

St. Peter's Monastery. Jaffa is famous as a meeting point of East and West, and as soon as you step into this century-old Franciscan church, you'll find yourself steeped in a European atmosphere. St. Peter's was built over the ruins of a citadel dating from the Seventh Crusade, which was led by King Louis IX of France. A monument to King Louis stands at the entrance to the friary. Napoléon is rumored to have stayed here during his Jaffa campaign of 1799. To enter, ring the bell on the right side of the door; you will probably be greeted by one of the custodians, most of whom speak Spanish and some English. ⌧ *Kedumim Sq., Jaffa* ☎ *03/682–2871.*

Summit Park. Newlyweds come here to be photographed at sunset against the backdrop of the sea and the ancient buildings. Seven archaeological layers have been unearthed in a part of the park called Ramses II Garden. The oldest sections of wall (20 feet thick) have been identified as part of a Hyksos city dating from the 17th century BC. Other remains include part of a 13th-century BC city gate inscribed with the name of Ramses II; a Canaanite city; a Jewish city from the time of Ezra and Nehemiah; Hasmonean ruins from the 2nd century BC; and traces of Roman occupation. At the summit is a stone sculpture called Faith, in the shape of a gateway, which depicts biblical stories. ⌧ *Kedumim Square St., Jaffa.*

Old Town Jaffa.

WORTH NOTING

Andromeda's Rock. From Kedumim Square, a number of large boulders can be seen out at sea not far from shore. Greek mythology says one of these (pick your own, everyone does) is where the people of Jaffa tied the virgin Andromeda to sacrifice her to a sea monster to appease Poseidon, god of the sea. But Perseus, riding the winged horse Pegasus, soared down from the sky to behead the monster, rescue Andromeda, and promptly marry her.

Clock Tower Square. The clock tower is the focus of Jaffa's newly renovated central square. The clock tower was completed in 1906, in time to mark the 30th anniversary of the reign of Sultan Abdul Hamid II; similar clock towers were built for the same occasion in Akko, Jerusalem, and other cities. The modern (1965) stained-glass windows in the old tower depict events in Jaffa's history. The centuries-old buildings have been carefully restored, preserving their ornate facades. Since Jaffa was a major port in Turkish times, it's not surprising to find the Turkish Cultural Center here. ⊠ *Clock Tower Square, Yefet St., Jaffa.*

OFF THE BEATEN PATH

Design Museum Holon. Israeli-born architect Ron Arad designed this striking, much-acclaimed structure made of rounded ribbons of orange and red steel that rise off a drab street like a modernist mirage. Inside is a two-story space with changing exhibits on contemporary design, including fashion, jewelry, and textiles. It's a nice change of pace from historical sights. English language recorded tours are available for free. A good café known for tasty pastries and cakes is located at the entrance. The museum is in Holon, a suburb south of Tel Aviv that is easily reachable by Egged buses 90 or 97 or Dan bus 3. ⊠ *8 Pinhas Eilon*

St., Holon ☎ 73/215–1515 🌐 www.dmh.org.il 💰 NIS 35 ⏲ Mon. and Wed. 10–4, Tues. and Thurs. 10–8, Friday 10–2, Saturday 10–4.

El-Mahmoudiye Mosque. When Turkish governor Muhammed Abu Najat Aja built the fountain here in the early 19th century, it had six pillars and an arched roof, providing shade as well as water. The fountain's foundation is still visible in the parking lot west of the minaret. It's closed to the public, as is the rest of the mosque, but if its ornate carved doors on the western side are open, you can peek into the spacious restored courtyard surrounded by arches. The archway on the south side formed the entrance to the hammam, or old Turkish bath. In the late 19th century, a separate entrance was built into the east wall to save the governor and other dignitaries the bother of having to push through the market-square crowds at the main entrance, on the south wall. ✉ *Yefet St., at Mifratz Shlomo St., Jaffa.*

TEL AVIV TOURS

PERSONAL GUIDES

Twelve Tribes provides personal guides, usually with a car, who will take you anywhere in the city and even around the country. Personal guides can also be arranged through most hotels.

BOAT TOURS

Kefland runs a half-hour boat tour on Saturday year-round, from the Jaffa Port along the Tel Aviv waterfront and back. The fare is NIS 20.

Contacts **Kefland** (✉ *Jaffa Port* ☎ *03/682–9070*). **Twelve Tribes** (✉ *29 Hamered St.* ☎ *03/510–1911* 🌐 *www.twelve-tribes.co.il*).

NEED A BREAK?

There's always a line outside Abulafia Bakery (✉ *7 Yefet St., Jaffa*), south of the clock tower. For a simple snack with an exquisite flavor, order a pita topped with *za'atar* (a mixture of herbs, spices, and seeds), or stuffed with salty cheese, calzone-style. In the winter, Abulafia is a good place to try *sachlab*, a warm drink sprinkled with coconut and cinnamon.

Ilana Goor Museum. The veteran Israeli artist Ilana Goor works and resides in this restored 18th-century house with its romantic stone arches and high ceilings. She's turned part of it into a museum of her sculptures in wood, stone, and metal, some reminiscent of the "found-art" genre, and of local crafts. A gift shop also occupies part of the complex. ✉ *4 Mazal Dagim St., Jaffa* ☎ *03/683–7676* 🌐 *www.ilanagoor.com* 💰 *NIS* 32 ⏲ *Sun.–Fri. 10–4, Sat. and Jewish holidays 10–6.*

San Antonio Roman Catholic Church. Although its white bricks look new, this church actually dates from 1932, when it was built to accommodate the growing needs of Jaffa's Roman Catholic community. The church is named for St. Anthony of Padua, friend and disciple of St. Francis of Assisi. ✉ *51 Yefet St., Jaffa* ☎ *03/513–3800.*

OFF THE BEATEN PATH

Weizmann Institute of Science. On the grounds of one of Israel's finest science centers, the Weizmann Institute is educational and fun for kids of all ages. A highlight is the open-air Clore Garden of Science, where you can experience how it feels to walk on the moon, and climb on or through dozens of other interactive exhibits that explain various scientific phenomenon. Also worth a visit is the Solar Complex, a research center that screens a brief film about the institute and its storied accomplishments. A new addition is a glass-and-steel dome called the Eco-Sphere, which houses educational exhibits on the environment. Call ahead for reservations. ✉ *1 Herzl St., Rehovot* ☎ *08/934–4500* 🌐 *www.weizmann.ac.il* 🎟 *NIS 35* ⏲ *Museum, Sun.–Thurs. 9–4. Clore Garden of Science, Sun.–Thurs. 9–4, Fri. 10–2.*

Yefet Street. Think of Yefet as a sort of thread between eras: beneath it is the old market area, while all around you stand schools and churches of the 19th and 20th centuries. Several deserve mention. At Number 21 is the Tabitha School, established by the Presbyterian Church of Scotland in 1863. Behind the school is a small cemetery where some fairly prominent figures are buried, including Dr. Thomas Hodgkin, the first to define Hodgkin's disease. Number 23 was once a French Catholic school, and it still carries the sign "collège des frères." At Number 25, the fortresslike Urim School was set up as a girls' school in 1882.

THE TEL AVIV PORT AND NORTHERN TEL AVIV

While still considered center city, from the east–west cross street of Arlozoroff north, Tel Aviv flows into blocks of tranquil residential streets of small apartment houses, up to the banks of the Yarkon River and its beautiful park. The Tel Aviv Port is one of the city's hottest places to eat, shop, and stroll. Just north of the river are three important museums. The Eretz Israel Museum is close to Tel Aviv University; the Palmach Museum is next door to it; and the Diaspora Museum is farther north.

GETTING HERE AND AROUND

Dan Bus Company's Route 4 is an easy way to reach the port. The museums are about 8 km (5 mi) from the downtown hotels; Dan buses 7, 25, and 45 will take you to the area, as will the Kavim company's buses 94, 95, and 137. Allow at least two hours to visit each. The train's University station will bring you within a short distance of all three, as well.

TIMING AND PRECAUTIONS

The port area can feel a bit overrun on the weekends, especially with families and young children. Northern Tel Aviv tends to be bustling by day, sleepy at night.

TOP ATTRACTIONS

★ **Diaspora Museum.** Presented here are 2,500 years of Jewish life in the Diaspora (the settling of Jews outside Israel), beginning with the destruction of the First Temple in Jerusalem and chronicling such major events as the exile to Babylon and the expulsion from Spain in 1492. Photographs and text labels provide the narrative, and films and music enhance the experience. One highlight is a replica collection of miniature synagogues throughout the world, both those destroyed and those still functioning. Another is the computerized genealogy section, where it's possible to look up Jewish family names to determine their origins. In addition, there's a music center containing a large listening library of Jewish music from around the world. At this writing, a children's gallery with interactive exhibits was scheduled to open in late 2011. ✉ *Tel Aviv University Campus, Klausner St., Ramat Aviv* ☎ *03/745–7800* 🌐 *www.bh.org.il* 🎟 *NIS 35* ⏲ *Sun.–Tues. and Thurs. 10–4, Wed. 10–6, Fri. 9–1.*

Tel Aviv Port and Northern Tel Aviv

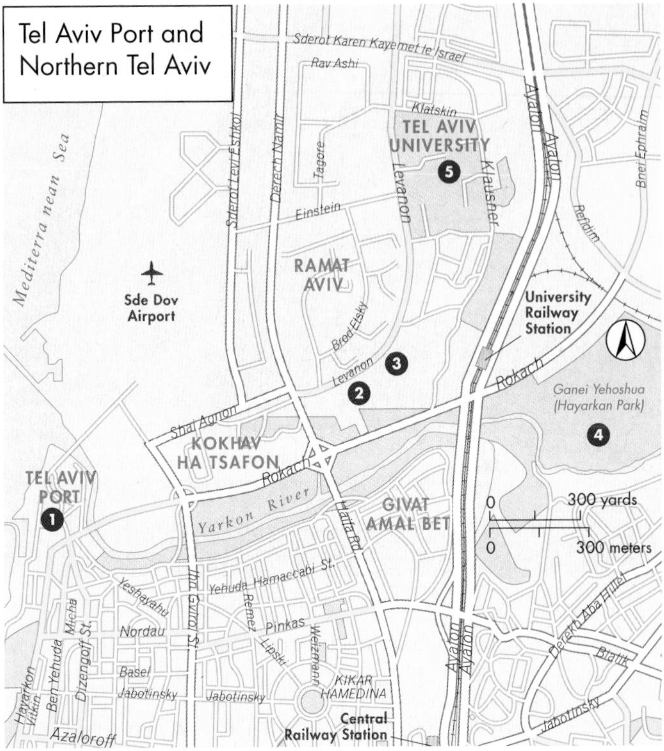

★ **Eretz Israel Museum.** This museum's eight pavilions span 3,000 years of Israeli life, covering such topics as ethnography and folklore, ceramics and other handicrafts, and coinage. In the center of the complex is the ancient site of Tel Kassile, where archaeological digs have so far uncovered 12 layers of settlements. There is also a daily sound-and-light show in the adjacent planetarium with Hebrew narration (call to verify hours). ✉ *2 Levanon St., Northern Tel Aviv* ☎ *03/641–5244* 🌐 *www.eretzmuseum.org.il* 🎫 *Museum NIS 35, planetarium NIS 58* ⏲ *Sun.–Thurs. 9–3, Fri. and Sat. 10–2.*

Ganei Yehoshua *(Hayarkon Park).* This park is a strip of emerald tranquility in the midst of the hustle and bustle of the city. Located in the northern part of town, it's the place where Tel Avivians go to stretch out on the grass for a picnic or a nap in the shade. For those seeking more activity, a bike ride on one of its paths can be combined with a visit to the tropical garden and the rock garden (open Sunday–Thursday 10 to 2:30, Friday 10 to 1:30, Saturday 10 to 3:30). Or you can rent a pedal boat, rowboat, or motorboat to ply Yarkon Stream. There's even a pleasure boat, which takes up to 80 people for 20-minute rides. ✉ *Rokach Blvd., Northern Tel Aviv* ☎ *03/642–2828* 🌐 *www.park.co.il.*

Tel Aviv Port. The port, which a little over a decade ago was a cluster of decrepit warehouses, is now buzzing with cafés and restaurants in its

The colorful Design Museum Holon hosts changing exhibits that explore the importance of design in daily life.

southern and northern sections. It ends where the pavement gives way to a wooden platform designed with moderate dips and curves, pleasing to the eye and fun for roller skaters. Also here is Bayit Banamal, a small mall with eclectic boutiques. It's one of Tel Aviv's most popular attractions for locals. On weekends, when restaurants are all packed by 1 pm, there's a farmer's market and a small swap meet good for finding handmade jewelry, old books, and Israeli memorabilia. ✉ *Hayarkon and Dizengoff sts., Northern Tel Aviv.*

WORTH NOTING

Palmach Museum. This museum makes you feel as if you were back in the days of the Palmach, the pre-state underground, with a group of young defenders. Visitors are led through rooms, each of which encompasses one part of the Palmach experience. There's the "forest," which has real-looking trees; a room with a falling bridge and faux explosions; and a chilling mock-up of an illegal-immigrants' ship. Call ahead for reservations. ✉ *10 Haim Levanon St., Ramat Aviv* ☎ *03/643–6393* 🌐 *www.palmach.org.il* 🎟 *NIS 30* ⏲ *Sun. and Mon., 9–4:30, Tues. 9–8, Wed. 9–1:30, Thurs. 9–4, Fri. 9–11:30.*

WHERE TO EAT

The city's cosmopolitan character is happily represented in its food, although stands selling Middle Eastern fast food for which this part of the world is famous—such as falafel and shawarma—still occupy countless street corners. You'll find restaurants serving everything from American-style burgers to sushi and chili con carne. In contrast to Jerusalem, diners who keep kosher have to search for a kosher restaurant, aside from those in the hotels. A spate of new kosher establishments caters to a significant slice of the discerning dining market, but with the fairly rapid turnover of some Tel Aviv eateries, the concierge is still the best person to ask about the latest in kosher restaurants.

Most Tel Aviv restaurants, except those that keep kosher, are open seven days a week. Many serve business lunches at reasonable prices, making them less-expensive options than the price categories suggest. As elsewhere in the Mediterranean, Israelis dine late; chances are there will be no trouble getting a table at 7 pm, whereas past 10, diners may face a long line. Casual attire is always acceptable in Tel Aviv, even in the poshest restaurants.

Tel Aviv's restaurants are concentrated in a few areas: Sheinkin and Rothschild streets, Basel, Ibn Gvirol Street, and the Tel Aviv Port. Herzliya Pituach, a seaside suburb north of Tel Aviv, has a cluster of good restaurants in the upscale Arena Mall at the marina, with a picturesque view of the yachts at anchor.

Use the coordinate (⊕ A1) at the end of each listing to locate a site on the corresponding map.

WHAT IT COSTS IN ISRAELI SHEKELS

	¢	$	$$	$$$	$$$$
Restaurants	under NIS 32	NIS 32–NIS 49	NIS 50–NIS 75	NIS 76–NIS 100	over NIS 100

Prices are for a main course at dinner.

CENTER CITY

$$ ISRAELI Fodor's Choice ★ ✕ **Abraxus North.** For one of the best meals in the city, take your place at one of the tables spilling out onto the sidewalk or alongside the small, chic bar. The menu changes daily, depending on what Eyal Shani, its celebrity chef, finds to be the freshest produce or catch of the day. A couple of delectable dishes are often featured, including lamb shawarma marinated overnight in wine grapes from the Judean Hills, and cold shrimp with green onions and tomatoes served in piping hot homemade pita. If you arrive without reservations, you can usually take a seat at the bar. ✉ *40 Lilienblum St., Center City* ☎ *054/678–6560* ✍ *Reservations essential* ▭ *DC, MC, V* ⊕ *5B.*

$$ ITALIAN ✕ **Allora.** The well-stocked wooden bar is the centerpiece of this tiny, 10-table eatery, where the roaring brick oven and pizza-dough kneaders are in full view. The focaccia makes a great starter, served with a variety of dips including Clemente-olive spread, garlic confit, and, for

BEST BETS FOR TEL AVIV DINING

With hundreds of restaurants to choose from, how will you decide where to eat? Fodor's writers and editors have selected their favorite restaurants by price, cuisine, and experience in the lists below. In the first column, Fodor's Choice properties represent the "best of the best" across price categories. You can also search by area for excellent eats—just check out our complete reviews in the following pages.

Fodor's Choice ★

Abraxus North, $$, p. 243
Herbert Samuel, $$$, p. 253
Messa, $$$$, p. 250
Orna and Ella, $$, p. 251
Shalvata, p. 258

Best By Price

¢

Café Mersand, p. 249
Sabich, p. 252
Sonya Getzel Shapira, p. 253

$

Panini Lilush, p. 252
Shalvata, p. 258
Yaffo Caffe, p. 257

$$

Abdu Hadayag, p. 254
Abraxus North, p. 243
Moses, p. 251
Orna and Ella, p. 251

$$$

Charcuterie, p. 254
Herbert Samuel, p. 253
Montifiore, p. 251
NG, p. 254

$$$$

Messa, p. 250
Mul-Yam, p. 257

Best By Cuisine

ITALIAN

Belini's, $$$, p. 253
Pronto, $$$, p. 252

MEDITERRANEAN

Abraxus North, $$, p. 243
Herbert Samuel, $$$, p. 253
Suzanna, $$, p. 254

MIDDLE EASTERN

Dr. Shakshuka, $, p. 256
Sabich, ¢, p. 249

Best By Experience

BRUNCH

Brasserie, $$, p. 248
Puaa, $, p. 257
Yaffo Caffe, $, p. 257

HOT SPOTS

Charcuterie, $$$, p. 254
Herbert Samuel, $$$, p. 253
Orna and Ella, $$, p. 251

CHILD-FRIENDLY

Dr. Shakshuka, $, p. 256
Max Brenner, $, p. 250
Shalvata, $, p. 258
Sonya Getzel Shapira, ¢, p. 253
Yaffo Caffe, $, p. 257

OUTSIDE DINING

Café Metzada, $$, p. 249
Ha'Basta, $$$, p. 250
Manta Ray, $$$, p. 256
Margaret Tayar, $$$, p. 256
Shalvata, $, p. 258
Sus Etz, $$, p. 253

MOST ROMANTIC

The Container, $$, p. 254
Montefiori, $$$$, p. 251
Mul-Yam, $$$$, p. 257
NG, $$$, p. 254

SEAFOOD

Abdo Hadayag, $$, p. 254
The Container, $$, p. 254
Margaret Tayar, $$$, p. 256
Mul-Yam, $$$$, p. 257
Shtsupak, $$, p. 252

VIEWS

Allora, $$, 243
comme il faut, $$, p. 257
Manta Ray, $$$, p. 256
Margaret Tayar, $$$, p. 256
Raphael, $$$, p. 252

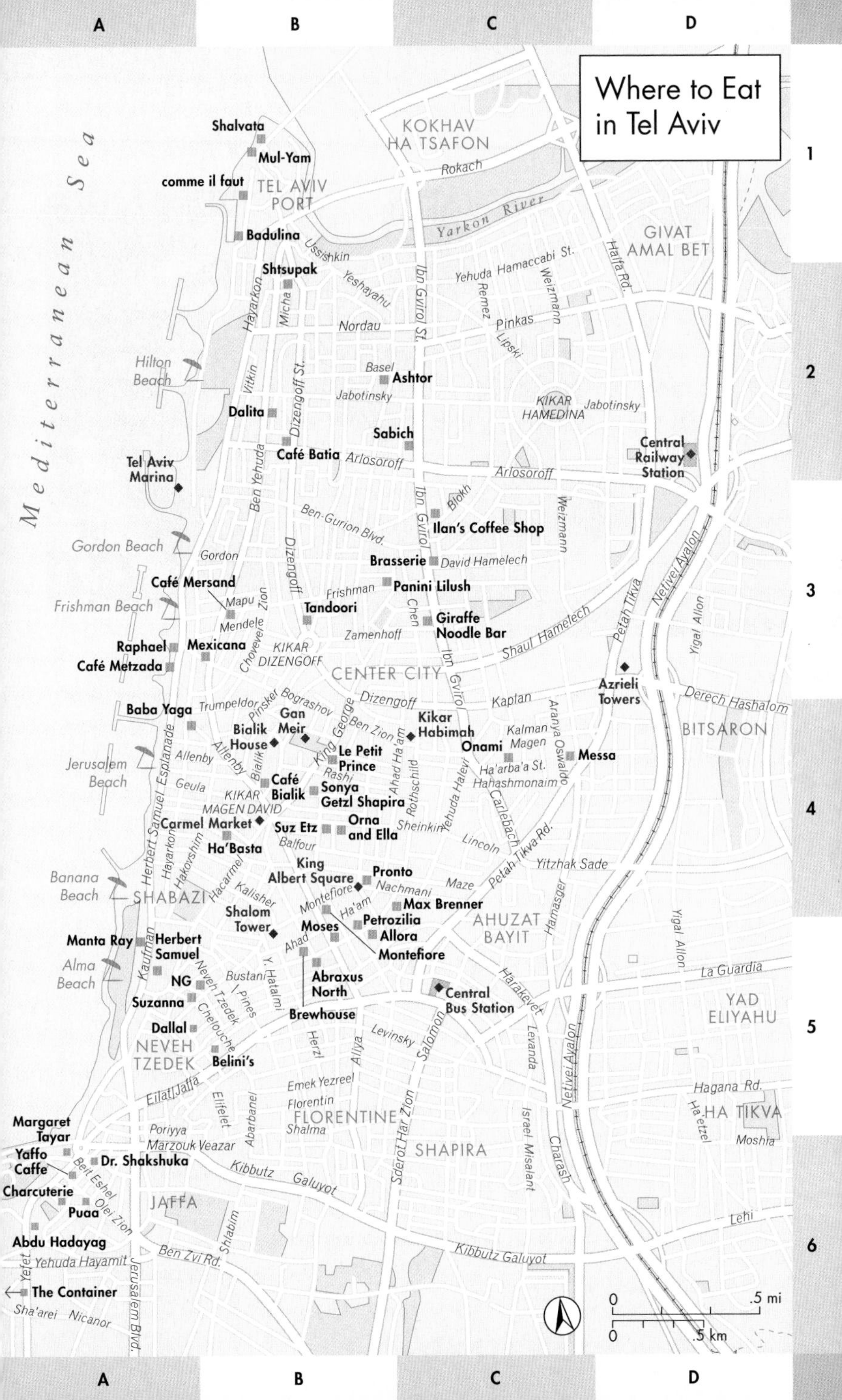
Where to Eat in Tel Aviv
A
B
C
D
1
2
3
4
5
6
Mediterranean Sea
Shalvata
Mul-Yam
comme il faut
TEL AVIV PORT
Badulina
Shtsupak
KOKHAV HA TSAFON
Rokach
Yarkon River
GIVAT AMAL BET
Ashtor
Dalita
Café Batia
Sabich
Tel Aviv Marina
Central Railway Station
KIKAR HAMEDINA
Hilton Beach
Gordon Beach
Frishman Beach
Jerusalem Beach
Banana Beach
Alma Beach
Ilan's Coffee Shop
Brasserie
Panini Lilush
Café Mersand
Tandoori
Giraffe Noodle Bar
Raphael
Mexicana
Café Metzada
KIKAR DIZENGOFF
CENTER CITY
Azrieli Towers
Baba Yaga
Gan Meir
Bialik House
Kikar Habimah
Le Petit Prince
Onami
Messa
BITSARON
Café Bialik
Sonya Getzl Shapira
KIKAR MAGEN DAVID
Carmel Market
Suz Etz
Orna and Ella
Ha'Basta
King Albert Square
Pronto
Max Brenner
SHABAZI
Shalom Tower
Moses
Petrozilia
Allora
Montefiore
AHUZAT BAYIT
Manta Ray
Herbert Samuel
NG
Suzanna
Abraxus North
Brewhouse
Central Bus Station
YAD ELIYAHU
Dallal
NEVEH TZEDEK
Belini's
FLORENTINE
SHAPIRA
HA TIKVA
Margaret Tayar
Yaffo Caffe
Dr. Shakshuka
Charcuterie
Puaa
JAFFA
Abdu Hadayag
The Container
Ussishkin
Yeshayahu
Hayarkon
Micha
Nordau
Ibn Gvirol St.
Yehuda Hamaccabi St.
Remez
Weizmann
Haifa Rd.
Pinkas
Lipski
Basel
Jabotinsky
Vitkin
Dizengoff St.
Ben Yehuda
Arlosoroff
Blokh
Ben-Gurion Blvd.
Gordon
Dizengoff
David Hamelech
Frishman
Mapu
Zion
Chen
Mendele
Zamenhoff
Chovevei Zion
Shaul Hamelech
Petah Tikva
Netivei Ayalon
Yigal Allon
Trumpeldor
Pinsker
Bograshov
King George
Ben Zion
Dizengoff
Kaplan
Kalman Magen
Aranya Oswaldo
Derech Hashalom
Allenby
Herbert Samuel Esplanade
Geula
Bialik
Rashi
Ahad Ha'am
Rothschild
Yehuda Halevi
Ha'arba'a St.
Hahashmonaim
Carlebach
Sheinkin
Lincoln
Balfour
Petah Tikva Rd.
Yitzhak Sade
Hakovshim
Hacarmel
Kalisher
Nachmani
Maze
Hamasger
Montefiore
Ha'am
Ahad
Kaufman
Neveh Tzedek
Bustani
Y. Hatalmi
Pines
Chelouche
Harakevet
La Guardia
Herzl
Levinsky
Aliya
Salomon
Levanda
Netivei Ayalon
Eilat/Jaffa
Elifelet
Abarbanel
Emek Yezreel
Florentin
Shalma
Sderot Har Zion
Israel Misalant
Charash
Hagana Rd.
Ha'etzel
Moshia
Poriyya
Marzouk Veazar
Kibbutz Galuyot
Beit Eshel
Olei Zion
Shlabim
Lehi
Ben Zvi Rd.
Yehuda Hayamit
Jerusalem Blvd.
Yefet
Sha'arei Nicanor
0
.5 mi
0
.5 km

STREET FOOD IN ISRAEL

Fast, faster, fastest! If you're hungry right now, the streets of the Holy Land await your eating pleasure. Israel has a refined culture of noshing on the run, since everyone is always in a hurry and apparently hungry most of the time. Put food and drink in hand and join the locals.

To find the goods from falafel to fresh papayas, look for the food stalls and kiosks that line Israel's main city streets and shopping areas. Fruit and vegetable markets, notably Carmel Market in Tel Aviv and Machaneh Yehuda in Jerusalem, offer snack opportunities. In Tel Aviv, Rothschild Boulevard and Ben-Gurion Boulevard have popular food kiosks offering made-to-order sandwiches and fresh-squeezed juices. In Jerusalem, try the Old City's hummus spots or home-style restaurants. Most fast-food stalls serve lunch only. The outdoor markets in Tel Aviv and Jerusalem close in late afternoon and on Shabbat. In Jerusalem, no food stalls open on Shabbat, but in the Old City (except the Jewish Quarter) hummus and falafel joints do business.

GRAB IT AND GO

Some street fare is substantial, whether it's falafel or the sandwiches on five-nut artisanal breads that are edging out traditional favorites in Tel Aviv. Other choices are lighter. Sold in markets, in bakeries, and on street stands are sweet pastries called rugelach: these two-bite-size twists are rolled up with cinnamon or oozing with chocolate. Just-roasted nuts or sunflower seeds are a quick pick-me-up; or sip fresh-squeezed fruit juices such as pomegranate or carrot. Frosty frozen yogurt and rich ice creams are perfect on hot days. A frothy cappuccino is always good; in winter, try a cup of hot custard-like sahlab, perhaps sprinkled with cinnamon.

FALAFEL

The region's ultimate fast-food snack consists of deep-fried chickpea balls—the best are crispy outside with soft centers. *Falafel* also refers to the whole production of the balls served in pita pockets with an array of chopped vegetable salads plus hummus, tahini, and pickles that you add yourself and then eat (watch for drips!) with a waxed paper napkin for further refinement. Vendors compete with extra touches such as free salads. It's filling, nutritious, and cheap.

HUMMUS

Ubiquitous in the Middle East, *hummus* is a creamy paste made from mashed chickpeas, olive oil, garlic, and *tahini* (a sesame sauce). You eat it in a pita or scoop it up from a plate with the same. In Hebrew, there's a verb for this action specifically related to hummus: *lenagev*, which means "to wipe." Heartfelt arguments prevail among Israelis over where to find the best hummus, but eat it at a Middle Eastern specialty place; some of the best are on market alleys and side streets—even at gas stations.

SHAWARMA

For this fast-food favorite, marinated lamb or turkey slices are stacked and grilled on a vertical spit, then sliced off and stuffed into a pita. Accompaniments are usually the same choice as for falafel, though onion rings and french fries are other extras. Jerusalem mixed grill (*me'oorav Yerushalmi*) is unique to the Holy City; look for it on Agrippas Street, alongside the outdoor fruit and vegetable market. It's a well-seasoned meal of grilled chicken hearts and other organ meats eaten in a pita with grilled onions.

TAHINI

Silky in texture, this sauce with a nutty, slightly sweet taste is made from ground sesame seeds, fresh lemon juice, and sometimes garlic. The tasty green variety has parsley chopped in. Tahini is used as a sauce and is the main ingredient in halva, the famous Middle Eastern sweet. A popular dessert—among non-dieters—is a dish of vanilla ice cream topped with tahini and crumbled halva and flooded with date syrup.

BOUREKAS

From the Balkans comes Israel's favorite snack: flaky, crispy, golden-brown *bourekas*. Best eaten warm, they're pastry triangles, squares, or crescents deliciously filled with tangy cheese or mashed potato or creamy spinach and sometimes mushrooms. Small (two bites) or large (four bites), they can be made of several kinds of dough: puff pastry, phyllo, and short pastry. Bourekas are especially fine when topped with toasted sesame seeds.

—By Judy Stacey Goldman

4

Middle Eastern good measure, *labaneh* (yogurt cheese). The Balkan pizza, topped with grilled eggplant, peppers, and feta cheese, is especially tasty. The narrow porch is your perch to watch the people strolling and cycling along the tree-lined center of Rothschild Boulevard. Come here for happy hour, weekdays from 5 to 8. ✉ *60 Rothschild Blvd., Center City* ☎ *03/566–5655* ▭ *AE, DC, MC, V* ✣ *5B.*

$ CAFÉ ✕ **Ashtor.** This small corner café, a neighborhood favorite, is where you can catch a glimpse of the beauty of European café culture. Coffee is the main event, over which you can linger for hours along with your newspaper, computer, and best of all, friends from the neighborhood. Because it's in the heart of the upscale Basel area, the patrons include the entertainment celebrities that live nearby. The menu includes everything from sandwiches and salads to pastas and shnitzel. ✉ *37 Basel St., Center City* ☎ *03/546–5318* ▭ *AE, DC, MC, V* ✣ *2B.*

$$$$ EASTERN EUROPEAN ✕ **Baba Yaga.** A pleasant lawn and wooden deck front this small restaurant at the slightly shabbier end of Hayarkon Street. Black tablecloths, high-backed chairs, old-fashioned light fixtures, and beige-and-white wallpaper give the place a touch of elegance to complement its high-end prices. Baba Yaga is a notorious witch in Russian folk tales, and there's a collection of witch dolls behind the bar. There are small but delicious seafood dishes, including a tasty cocktail of shrimp, calamari, mussels, octopus, and crab. Look for European classics and Russian favorites like borscht and Stroganoff (made with sweet cream rather than sour). There's a good selection of Israeli boutique wines, along with an interesting mix of foreign beers. ✉ *12 Hayarkon St., Center City* ☎ *03/516–7305* ▭ *AE, DC, MC, V* ✣ *4B.*

$$ FRENCH ✕ **Brasserie.** The dark upholstery, mustard-colored walls, and menu in French (in addition to Hebrew and English) are all meant to recall Paris, and the wide selection of excellently prepared food is a credit to French cuisine. It's open around the clock, and always seems to have a crowd. Brunch is popular, with dishes like eggs Creole and eggs Norwegian style (poached, on toast, with salmon and spinach), as well as pancakes and club sandwiches. For lunch or dinner, try the ravioli with crab, steak tartare, or the salade Nicoise. ✉ *70 Ibn Gvirol, Center City* ☎ *03/696–7111* 🌐 *www.hotelmontifiore.co.il/brasserie.html* ▭ *AE, DC, MC, V* ✣ *3C.*

$$$ AMERICAN ✕ **Brewhouse.** One of Rothschild Boulevard's original mansions, the Brewhouse has been restored to house a working boutique brewery. Copper vats and pipes add a gleaming accent to the interior, and beer is a highlight of the menu. The focus is grilled meat, so don't pass up the spareribs. The service is excellent and the prices are moderate for this area. ✉ *11 Rothschild Blvd., Center City* ☎ *03/516–8666* ▭ *AE, DC, MC, V* ✣ *5B.*

$ EASTERN EUROPEAN ✕ **Café Batia.** The plain decor of this Dizengoff Street institution hasn't been changed in decades, and the menu is filled with old-fashioned Eastern European favorites. Try a bowl of matzoh-ball soup, leg of goose, or stuffed cabbage for a taste of what Grandma used to prepare. If you're adventurous, try some of the less well-known dishes such as pupiks, which is Yiddish for gizzards. You can also eat outside. ✉ *197 Dizengoff St., Center City* ☎ *03/522–1335* ▭ *AE, DC, MC, V* ✣ *2B.*

Most Israeli food is kid friendly. This little one is trying pita and hummus. —photo by rooneyroo, Fodors.com member

$ CAFÉ ✕ **Café Bialik.** This veteran of Tel Aviv café culture is the perfect complement to a stroll down this historic street. Plenty of restaurants serve more or less the same menu as Café Bialik—an "Israeli breakfast," which is a wide selection of chopped salads with eggs done in a variety of ways, toast, coffee and juice, and sometimes smoked salmon and small sandwiches. But it's the neighborhood-hangout feel and the old-fashioned chrome bar stools, wooden tables, and Lenong style that make this place stand out. ✉ *2 Bialik St., Center City* ☎ *03/620–0832* ▭ *AE, DC, MC, V* ✣ *4B.*

¢ CAFÉ ✕ **Café Mersand.** For a taste of the best of the local hipster scene, score a table in the wood-paneled dining room or on the sunny sidewalk. The older customers, some of whom have been coming since the place opened its doors in 1955, mingle unusually well with the younger crowd. Everyone enjoys the specials from the original menu, including poppy seed cake and plum kuchen, a sweet pastry. In the morning try the Turkish breakfast, which includes couscous, cheese, a hard-boiled egg, and halva. ✉ *18 Frishman St., Center City* ☎ *03/523–4318* ▭ *AE, DC, MC, V* ✣ *3B.*

$$ CAFÉ ✕ **Café Metzada.** A varied but simple menu—including steak, salads, sandwiches, and pasta—makes this a good place to recharge after a day at the beach or a nice spot to relax with a glass of wine at sunset. There's a fabulous Mediterranean view and the option of indoor or outdoor seating. ✉ *83 Hayarkon St., Center City* ☎ *03/510–3353* ▭ *AE, DC, MC, V* ✣ *3A.*

$$ BAKERY ✕ **Dalita.** A bit off the beaten path, Dalita is a lovely place to rest your tired feet after exploring the Dizengoff area. The Austrian and

Hungarian pastries in this sweetshop filled with white wrought-iron tables and chairs are prepared on-site by owner Dalit Golan. They will definitely spoil your dinner, but during the summer try the *gumbotz* (dumplings filled with apricots) and the *bienenstich* (literally meaning "bee sting," these sweetbreads are topped with honeyed almonds). Another favorite is *lebkuchen*, a cake filled with homemade plum jam and coated in chocolate. ✉ *146 Ben Yehuda St., Center City* ☎ *03/529–2649* ▭ *AE, MC, V* ✣ *2B.*

$$ PAN-ASIAN ✕ **Giraffe Noodle Bar.** Generous portions of noodles in a variety of Japanese, Thai, and other Asian styles attract a loyal clientele to this often-packed restaurant. There's a selection of soups and sushi for starters. Save room for the meringue-based, berry-topped pavlova. Lunch is a particularly good bargain. ✉ *49 Ibn Gvirol St., Center City* ☎ *03/691–6294* 🌐 *www.giraffe.co.il* ▭ *AE, DC, MC, V* ✣ *3C.*

$$$ MEDITERRANEAN ✕ **Ha'Basta.** This tiny restaurant and wine bar, just a clutch of round tables on an alley just off Carmel Market, draws its inspiration from the market's fresh offerings. (The name is Hebrew for market stall.) The kitchen has a decidedly Mediterranean flair, turning out such delights as grilled calamari and artichoke flavored with lemon and tomato or ravioli stuffed with almonds and feta cheese. The paella with bacon, sausage, shrimp, and mussels is about as nonkosher as it gets for a place whose chef refers to the nearby market as the "Holy of Holies," a Biblical reference to where the Ark of the Covenant was kept. ✉ *4 Ha'Shomer St., Center City* ☎ *03/516–9234* ▭ *AE, DC, MC, V* ✣ *4B.*

$ CAFÉ ✕ **Ilan's Coffee Shop.** The 20 types of coffee, including those from Brazil, Papua New Guinea, Colombia, and Ethiopia, are not the only attraction at Ilan's. The coffee shop is also a pioneer in importing products that adhere to international Fair Trade Standards, which ensures a fair price to the farmers producing the product. A selection of teas and tea blends, specialty sandwiches, and luscious desserts are also on hand. ✉ *90 Ibn Gvirol St., Center City* ☎ *03/523–5334* 🌐 *www.ilans.co.il* ▭ *AE, DC, MC, V* ✣ *3C.*

$ VEGETARIAN ✕ **Le Petit Prince.** You'll think you've walked into someone's circa-1920s fixer-upper when you see this "living room," lined floor to ceiling with books. In addition to serving light vegetarian meals, coffee, and tea, Le Petit Prince, near the end of the cul-de-sac of Simtat Plonit, sells everything on its shelves. ✉ *3 Simtat Plonit, Center City* ☎ *03/629–9387* ▭ *MC, V* ✣ *4B.*

$ ECLECTIC ✕ **Max Brenner.** Chocolate lovers should run, not walk, to this eatery for a mouthwatering, Charlie and the Chocolate Factory experience. Beneath pipes of imaginary chocolate crisscrossing the ceiling, children of all ages can order the likes of chocolate pizza—topped with chocolate chips, of course—or chocolate fondue for dipping toasted marshmallows and fruit like melon, dates, and bananas. There's even chocolate soup! For a souvenir, take home some hand-stenciled pralines in artfully designed tins. And yes, there are nonchocolate options, including pastas and salads. ✉ *45 Rothschild Blvd., Center City* ☎ *03/560–4570* 🌐 *www.max-brenner.co.il* ▭ *AE, V, MC, DC* ⊗ *Closed Mon.* ✣ *4B.*

$$$$ MODERN ISRAELI Fodor's Choice ★ ✕ **Messa.** Chef Aviv Moshe serves traditional dishes like the shredded-wheat type of pastry called kadaif, but his method of preparation is in

a class of its own. His Mediterranean–Middle Eastern haute cuisine is enlivened with French and Italian touches. White is the dominant color in the lavish dining room, with marble floors and tented ceiling lamps on which video art is projected. A long, central table with stylish high-back chairs is the room's centerpiece, perfect for mingling with fellow diners while the attentive staff serves dishes such as goat cheese and eggplant accented with shrimp and citrus butter for a starter, followed by a main course of sea bass on shallot ravioli. Adjacent to the restaurant is the bar, a much more chaotic affair done in stark black. ✉ *19 Ha'arbaa St., Center City* ☎ *03/685–8001* 🌐 *www.messa.co.il* ✍ *Reservations essential* ▭ *AE, DC, MC, V* ✥ *4C.*

4

$$ MEXICAN ✕ **Mexicana.** It's easy to miss this place as you head up Bograshov Street, but it's worth watching for if you're hankering after Mexican food. Spices are toned down for the Israeli palate, but tell the kitchen if you prefer some kick and they'll ratchet up the jalapeños. A specialty is sombrella, strips of chicken or steak stir-fried with vegetables and served in a confit of red peppers and chipotle. The business lunch saves you a lot of pesos. ✉ *7 Bograshov St., Center City* ☎ *03/527–9911* ▭ *AE, MC, V* ✥ *3A.*

$$$$ FRENCH ✕ **Montefiore.** The restaurant at Hotel Montefiore serves modern brasserie fare, throwing in a few Vietnamese touches for good measure. Main dishes include baked fish with tomatoes and olive oil, grilled lamb chops, and sirloin steak with wild mushrooms. The dining room is in a lovingly restored home on Montefiori Street in the heart of historic Tel Aviv. The white walls, potted plants, and slatted wooden blinds—even the silver-plated sugar servers selected by co-owner Ruthie Brouda—evoke old-world colonial days. The impeccable service, well-prepared food, and interesting wine list compare very favorably with the city's more expensive restaurants. ✉ *36 Montefiori St., Center City* ☎ *03/564–6100* 🌐 *www.hotelmontifiore.co.il/restaurant* ▭ *AE, DC, MC, V* ✥ *4B.*

$$ AMERICAN ✕ **Moses.** This bar and grill at the western end of Rothschild Boulevard has a vibe that is part retro lounge, part bistro. The extensive menu has everything from shish kebabs to calamari and quesadillas. It's good for the whole family, with children's dishes like hamburgers and, for the adults, an interesting selection of cocktails. The ribs in molasses are a real treat, as is the chicken Caesar salad. Drop by after midnight, when the prices can't be beat. ✉ *35 Rothschild Blvd., Center City* ☎ *03/566–4949* ▭ *AE, DC, MC, V* ✥ *4B.*

$$ JAPANESE ✕ **Onami.** Located along the row of Tel Aviv's trendiest restaurants, Onami presents a large variety of tastefully presented Japanese dishes. The expansive bar is the restaurant's centerpiece, and the tables are filled with all sorts of locals, from three-generational families to groups of young people who arrive in clusters later in the evening. A choice of five different kinds of *zosui* (rice-based soup) can be a whole meal, combined with sushi or sashimi as a first course, making this a relatively economical option among Tel Aviv's better restaurants. ✉ *18 Ha'arba'a, Center City* ☎ *03/562–1172* 🌐 *www.onami.co.il* ▭ *AE, DC, MC* ✥ *4C.*

$$ MODERN ISRAELI Fodor's Choice ★ ✕ **Orna and Ella.** As the loyal clientele will attest, Orna and Ella is worth the trips because of its comfort-food-with-a-twist menu. Entrées might be anything from moussaka to pasta in butternut-squash sauce, or a

tomato and cucumber salad piled high with feta cheese and topped with yogurt mint dressing. The house specialty, a pile of sweet-potato pancakes, is not to be missed. Desserts include a scrumptious pear and almond cream tarte. There's often a long wait, especially Friday afternoons and weekday evenings. ✉ *33 Sheinkin St., Center City* ☎ *03/620–4753* ▭ *AE, DC, MC, V* ✢ *4B.*

$ MEDITERRANEAN ✕ **Panini Lilush.** At this cozy neighborhood bistro, the portions are generous, the prices extremely reasonable, and the atmosphere a friendly hubbub of clattering dishes and animated conversations. Tables are packed close together both in the small dining room and on the sidewalk. The thick menu is filled with pastas, quiches, and meat dishes alongside the paninis that lend the restaurant its name. In the warmer months there are creative daily specials like tasty risotto. During the winter there's a daily selection of 12 soups. ✉ *73 Frishman St., Center City* ☎ *03/529–1852* ▭ *AE, MC, V* ⊙ *Closed Sun.* ✢ *B3.*

$$ MIDDLE EASTERN ✕ **Petrozilia.** The only kosher restaurant on Rothschild Boulevard, this eatery, in one of the boulevard's original brick buildings, has a good selection of Israeli favorites, including the ubiquitous breaded chicken breasts and a typical array of Middle Eastern salads. The garrulous chefs prepare the food at a front-and-center counter. ✉ *47 Rothschild Blvd., Center City* ☎ *03/516–2468* ▭ *AE, DC, MC, V* ⊙ *No dinner Fri. No lunch Sat.* ✢ *5B.*

$$$ ITALIAN ✕ **Pronto.** Pronto's owner was made a "knight of the Italian republic" for his contribution to Italian culture outside Italy with this small oasis of Roman cuisine tucked away on a side street in the historic district. Dishes are imaginative, and although quality may vary, the grilled pullets *cento erbe* (one hundred herbs) are a treat. Among the favorites are the cold antipasti platter appetizer and the lamb osso bucco. ✉ *26 Nahmani St., Center City* ☎ *03/566–0915* ▭ *AE, DC, MC, V* ✢ *4B.*

$$$$ MEDITERRANEAN ✕ **Raphael.** This place bills itself as a bistro (to be exact, a "resto-bistro"). Diners can expect an exceptional meal, albeit not in the intimate surroundings the term *bistro* might conjure up. Raphael's elegant setting has touches of the Far East, and the Mediterranean (framed by picture windows) is also present in the seasonings used in many dishes. Try a sophisticated first course such as market vegetables stuffed with lamb, goat cheese, and basmati rice, and move on to main dishes like swordfish accented with white Madagascar pepper and tomato confit. Service is particularly attentive and pleasant. ✉ *87 Hayarkon St., Center City* ☎ *03/522–6464* ✍ *Reservations essential* ▭ *AE, DC, MC, V* ✢ *3A.*

¢ MIDDLE EASTERN ✕ **Sabich.** This hole-in-the-wall eatery on Ibn Gvirol Street specializes in *sabich*, a Middle Eastern meal-in-a-pita. It's considered a breakfast (the word comes from the Arabic for "morning") because it includes a hard-boiled egg, in addition to hummus, tomatoes, peppers, and spices. It's a filling snack any time of day, however. Another popular menu item is the plater of meatballs served in a light tomato sauce. The indoor dining area has three or four stools at a counter, and there are a few tables outside as well. ✉ *99 Ibn Gvirol, Center City* ☎ *03/523–1810* ▭ *No credit cards* ✢ *2C.*

$$ SEAFOOD ✕ **Shtsupak.** Diners crowd the tables inside and out at this unadorned fish restaurant. They've been doing so for years, despite the fact that the

much more scenic and trendier Tel Aviv Port, with several fish places of its own, is a few steps away. Locals agree the food is reasonably priced, well prepared, and always fresh. For the main course, there's a daily catch of the day, which may include whole trout, fried calamari, or oysters in cream sauce. All entrées come with an assortment of salads and spreads for starters. ✉ *256 Ben Yehuda St., Center City* ☎ *03/544–1973* 💳 *AE, DC, MC, V* ✥ *2B.*

$ CAFÉ ✕ **Sonya Getzel Shapira.** This quirky café, decorated with antique glass lamps and other flea market finds, has a refreshingly relaxed feel. A black-and-white checkered floor adds to the retro vibe. Regulars ask for the *shakshuka*, a North African dish of panfried tomatoes and spices topped with an egg, as well as the market salad with sweet potato, feta cheese, and roasted pepper dressing. If the weather is pleasant, you can sit in the garden and let the kids roam. ✉ *1 Simta Almonit St., Center City* ☎ *077/526–1234* 🌐 *www.cafesonya.co.il* 💳 *AE, MC, V* ✥ *4B.*

4

$$ CAFÉ ✕ **Sus Etz.** If you're hungry after shopping on Sheinkin, keep an eye out for this eatery's landmark—an old-fashioned wooden horse. (There's no sign in English.) The menu is extensive, including a tempting array of sandwiches served alongside generous salads, breast of chicken with rosemary, and pastas. Average folks as well as lunching ladies come here, and the people-watching in the dining room and at sidewalk tables is part of the fun. ✉ *20 Sheinkin St., Center City* ☎ *03/528–7955* 💳 *AE, DC, MC, V* ✥ *4B.*

$$ INDIAN ✕ **Tandoori.** This veteran restaurant—which introduced Israelis to fine Indian cuisine—has maintained the high quality of its food and service over the years. There are all the standard curries, but tandoori chicken is the specialty. It comes to the table sizzling hot, and finger bowls of rose water mean you can dig in with abandon. A luncheon buffet offers a good selection from the menu. ✉ *2 Zamenhoff St., Center City* ☎ *03/629–6185* 💳 *AE, DC, MC, V* ✥ *3B.*

NEVEH TZEDEK

$$$ ITALIAN ✕ **Belini's.** With indoor and outdoor seating, this Tuscan-style establishment facing the open square across from the Suzanne Dellal Centre is perfect for a pre- or postperformance nosh. For a special treat, try the gnocchi with truffle oil. The service is friendly and helpful, and the Italian house wine is a break from the usual. ✉ *6 Yechieli St., Neveh Tzedek* ☎ *03/517–8486* 🌐 *www.belini.co.il* 💳 *AE, DC, MC, V* ✥ *5B.*

$$$ MEDITERRANEAN ✕ **Dallal.** The main reasons to come to this bistro inside a beautiful restored historic building are the rarified atmosphere and the on-premises bakery that turns out a luscious array of mainly French-style pastries. The enclosed patio, with its wrought-iron tables and chairs, is a lovely place to sit and enjoy a late afternoon coffee. The setting fully compensates for a somewhat unexciting selection of meat, fish, poultry, and pasta dishes. ✉ *10 Shabazi, Neveh Tzedek* ☎ *03/510–9292* 💳 *AE, DC, MC, V* ✥ *5B.*

$$$ MEDITERRANEAN Fodor's Choice ★ ✕ **Herbert Samuel.** Walking through the door of this understated but elegant dining room, you hear the energetic hum of good conversation. The upscale but very accessible menu has a strong Mediterranean influence and changes every season, but chestnut gnocchi and Jerusalem

artichoke soup are always good picks. A glass-enclosed kitchen is on full view for those seated upstairs. If you're seeking a cool vibe, a seat downstairs, especially at the bar, is preferable. The extensive wine list is another plus. ✉ *6 Koifman St., Neveh Tzedek* ☎ *03/516–6516* 🌐 *www.herbertsamuel.co.il* *Reservations essential* ▭ *AE, DC, MC, V* ⏲ *Closed Mon. and Tues.* ✥ *5A.*

$$$ CONTEMPORARY ✕ **NG.** Tucked away in a quiet corner of the city, this small, elegant bistro specializes in fine cuts of meat expertly prepared. It's purported to be the only place in Israel where you can enjoy a real porterhouse steak. And for dessert? That depends on the time of year. Tangy strawberry-vanilla pie is a winter specialty, and fig-vanilla pie is a summer favorite. The building is historic, but the interior is contemporary, complementing the Mediterranean tile floors with geometric patterns. ✉ *6 Ahad Ha'am St., Neveh Tzedek* ☎ *03/516–7888* ▭ *AE, MC, V* ⏲ *No lunch Sun., Mon., Wed., and Thurs.* ✥ *5B.*

$$ MEDITERRANEAN ✕ **Suzanna.** This restaurant, which occupies a century-old building near the Suzanne Dellal Centre for Dance and Theatre, bustles day and night. Sample their Kurdish *kubbeh* (meat-filled semolina dumplings) and pumpkin soup, or the Moroccan *harira*, a thick soup with chickpeas, veal, and coriander. To start things off, the savory antipasti platter is a welcome sight for the hungry traveler. Opt for a table on the terrace beneath the massive branches of an old ficus tree. ✉ *9 Shabazi St., Neveh Tzedek* ☎ *03/517–7580* ▭ *AE, DC, MC, V* ✥ *4B.*

JAFFA

$$ SEAFOOD ✕ **Abdu Hadayag.** According to neighborhood lore, Abdu, who will usually be on hand to greet you at the door, was a fisherman in his early years. His simple establishment has long been a fixture of Jaffa's main street. The fishnets, lanterns, and other marine accoutrements are refreshingly down-to-earth in a city where the interior design of restaurants has sometimes become as important as the flavors and seasonings. The day's catch varies; the menu includes grouper, red snapper, gray mullet, and mackerel, as well as melita, an Israeli breed from the barracuda family. ✉ *37 Yefet, Jaffa* ☎ *03/518–2595* ▭ *AE, DC, MC, V* ✥ *6A.*

$$$ FRENCH ✕ **Charcuterie.** In an alley at the edge of Jaffa's flea market, this is one of the city's best culinary finds, especially for carnivorous gourmands. The Swiss-born chef specializes in the sausages and smoked meats he creates daily in the restaurant's kitchen, as well as a variety of freshly made pastas. A popular dish is squid-ink spaghetti topped with steaming seafood. The bread, as everything else served, is homemade and scrumptious. ✉ *3 Rabbi Hanina St., Jaffa* ☎ *03/682–8843* ▭ *AE, MC, V* ⏲ *No lunch Sun.* ✥ *6A.*

$$ SEAFOOD ✕ **The Container.** Jaffa Port's surprises include this waterfront eatery, whose name and decor are inspired by the shipping containers once unloaded along this dock. In fact, its sleek bar is fashioned from the metal shell of one discarded container. Steps away from bobbing fishing boats, diners feast on a mostly fish and seafood menu on high tables fashioned from wooden crates. The menu varies, but red snapper with horseradish, seviche with mango, and Jerusalem artichokes with truffles are among its delights. Local art graces the walls, and live music

DID YOU KNOW?

The bountiful spread that is the traditional Israeli breakfast can include everything from salads to omelets to baked goods. But not all are served alfresco!

If you visit Jaffa, sit at the old port and watch the sun dip down into the Mediterranean.

reverberates Friday night. ✉ *Jaffa Port, Warehouse 2, Jaffa* ☎ *03/683-6321* 🌐 *www.container.org.il* ▭ *AE, MC, V, DC* ✣ *6A.*

$ MEDITERRANEAN ✕ **Dr. Shakshuka.** For quick, simple, and tasty kosher North African fare, visit this eatery on the edge of Jaffa's flea market. Seating is along one of the long communal tables set up in rows that fill an airy courtyard between two stone buildings. Sample the namesake dish, *shakshuka*, a sizzling mixture of tomatoes, peppers, and spices topped off with a sunny-side-up egg and served in a metal pan. Also on offer are chicken and lamb kebabs and large bowls of couscous served with rich, chunky vegetable or meat soups and small plates of Middle Eastern salads. ✉ *3 Beit Eshel, Jaffa* ☎ *057/944–4193* ▭ *No credit cards* ✣ *6A.*

$$$ SEAFOOD ✕ **Manta Ray.** This large restaurant has a relaxed atmosphere, a great beach view, and indoor and outdoor dining, but tends to get noisy. It appeals to a cross section of diners from families to couples looking for romance, and attracts a loyal clientele from as far away as Jerusalem. The filling, imaginative appetizers are perhaps Manta Ray's finest features. These vary from day to day; some standards include shrimp with spinach, mango, and cracked wheat, and goat cheese with beets. The baked sea bream with rosemary and olive oil is simple Mediterranean fare at its best, especially with a spicy chili and pepper sauce on the side. ✉ *Alma Beach, near the Dolphinarium, Jaffa* ☎ *03/517–4773* 🌐 *www.mantaray.co.il* ✍ *Reservations essential* ▭ *AE, DC, MC, V* ✣ *5A.*

$$$ SEAFOOD ✕ **Margaret Tayar.** A Jaffa institution, this slightly ramshackle spot treats you to a view of the city's coastline. Mediterranean grilled fish is the specialty here, but the menu also includes favorites like fried sardines stuffed with caviar. Owner Margaret Tayar is a gregarious presence, serving up steaming plates from her tiny kitchen off a small wooden bar

topped with bell jars of pickling red peppers and kumquats. The snug interior is fine for cold winter days, but when the weather is fine, opt for a spot on the garden patio overlooking the sea. ✉ *8 Razif Ha'Aliyah Ha'Shnia, Jaffa* ☎ *03/682–4741* ▭ *No credit cards* ✣ *6A.*

$ BISTRO ✕ **Puaa.** In the heart of the Jaffa Flea Market, Puaa's lumpy sofas and bargain-basement-style tables and chairs make for a kick-your-shoes-off atmosphere—and some patrons oblige. It's a popular gathering place for thirtysomething Tel Avivians, as well as young families. At Puaa, all the cakes, cookies, and croissants are baked fresh on the premises. There's a good selection of vegetarian dishes, including the Middle Eastern favorite *majadarah* (rice with lentils), served with salad and yogurt. One of the prize meat dishes is sautéed chicken breast with mushrooms, onions, garlic, shatta pepper, and pieces of apple, served on a bed of whole-grain rice. ✉ *8 Rabbi Yohanan St., Jaffa* ☎ *03/682–3821* 🌐 *www.puaa.co.il* ▭ *AE, MC, V, DC* ✣ *6A.*

$$ CAFÉ ✕ **Yaffo Caffe.** The Italian-style ice creams and sorbets prepared daily by chef Ronnie Rivlin are the highlight of this light, airy corner café in the middle of the Jaffa Flea Market. Apple pie and berry frozen yogurt are among the most popular choices. The Italian menu also includes an extensive list of pastas and pizzas, making it a good choice for families when the little ones begin to clamor for lunch or a break. The sushi stand—the only one in Jaffa—thrills locals. ✉ *11 Olei Tzion St., Jaffa* ☎ *03/518–1988* ▭ *AE, DC, MC, V* ✣ *6A.*

TEL AVIV PORT AND NORTHERN TEL AVIV

$$ CAFÉ ✕ **Badulina.** Quite unassuming, this kosher establishment in the Tel Aviv Port is squeezed in along a row of splashier neon-lit restaurants. The main dishes (fish is their specialty) come with a choice of two sides, including salad and home-fried potatoes or rice. This is a good stop for coffee and dessert, prepared on-site by the expert pastry chef and appetizingly displayed in a refrigerator up front. ✉ *2 Yordei Hasira St., Tel Aviv Port* ☎ *03/544–9449* ▭ *AE, DC, MC, V* ✣ *1B.*

$$ CAFÉ ✕ **comme il faut.** This trendy eatery opens onto the Tel Aviv Port boardwalk on one side and the high-end Bayit Banamal shopping center on the other. Enjoy the cool of a sea breeze over coffee or a glass of wine. Entrées include such specialties as calamari *mesabakha* (with warm chickpeas and tahini sauce). Breakfast for two includes a morning cocktail and fresh Israeli cheeses. ✉ *1 Bayit Banamal, Tel Aviv Port* ☎ *03/717–1550* ▭ *AE, DC, MC, V* ✣ *1B.*

$$$$ SEAFOOD ✕ **Mul-Yam.** The main attractions at this high-end seafood bar are flown in fresh from abroad—including Nova Scotia lobsters, purple-hued rice from China, red snapper from New Zealand, turbot from the North Sea, clams from Brittany, and wild berries from Provence. An extensive list of fine wines the owners have personally selected from Israel and around the world complement dishes whose complex seasonings and presentation put Mul-Yam in a class of its own. Diners can watch a slice of life at the trendy Tel Aviv Port through a glass wall. Summer lunchtimes are a chance to sample some of its gastronomic delights at lower prices. ✉ *Hangar 24, Tel Aviv Port* ☎ *03/546–9920* 🌐 *www.mulyam.com* ▭ *AE, DC, MC, V* ✣ *1B.*

4

$ MIDDLE EASTERN Fodor's Choice ★ **Shalvata.** By day this Middle Eastern favorite is where trendy Tel Aviv parents take their kids to run around while they eat, but by night it's one of the city's better-known watering holes. (Monday's Latin Night features include salsa dancing.) Come winter, the fireplace offers a cozy escape from the cold. Menu favorites include crispy calmari, as well as a Greek salad with squares of tangy feta drizzled with olive oil and fresh herbs. ✉ *Near Hangar 25, Tel Aviv Port* ☎ *03/544–1279* ▭ *AE, DC, MC, V* ✣ *1B.*

WHERE TO STAY

Nothing stands between Tel Aviv's luxury hotels and the Mediterranean Sea except the golden beach and the Tayelet (promenade), outfitted with chairs and gazebos. Even most of the small hotels are only short walks from the water. Tel Aviv's hotel row is on Hayarkon Street, which becomes Herbert Samuel Esplanade as you proceed south between the Tel Aviv Port area and Jaffa. Across the street from the luxury hotels are a number of more economical ones. Boutique hotels are becoming more popular and are also centrally located. This means that no matter where you stay, you're never far from the main thoroughfares of Ben Yehuda and Dizengoff streets, with their shops and outdoor cafés, or the city's major concert hall, museums, art galleries, and open-air Carmel Market.

Don't want to stay in a city? Herzliya Pituach is a resort area 12 km (7½ mi) up the coast from Tel Aviv. It has a number of beachfront hotels, a public square with outdoor cafés that is a short walk from the beach, and a marina and adjacent Arena Mall with a selection of high-end shops, restaurants, and pubs. The area has a cosmopolitan air, as affluent suburbanites live here, as do diplomats and foreign journalists.

Hotel reservations are essential during all Jewish holidays and are advised throughout the year. In winter, Tel Aviv hotels close their outdoor pools, and the lifeguards at the public beaches take a break as well. Some hotels have parking lots, but a few rely on public lots that can be at least a short walk away.

Use the coordinate (✣ A1) at the end of each listing to locate a site on the corresponding map.

	WHAT IT COSTS IN U.S. DOLLARS				
	¢	$	$$	$$$	$$$$
Hotels	Under $120	$120–$200	$201–$300	$301–$400	over $400

Prices are for two people in a standard double room in high season. Non-Israeli citizens paying in foreign currency are exempt from the 16% VAT on hotel rooms.

CENTER CITY

$ **Adiv.** This amiable five-story hotel is on a side street between Hayarkon Street and Ben-Yehuda, which means it's a short walk from the beach and a growing crop of cafés and restaurants. Rooms have pleasing modern furnishings and pastel-print bedspreads and curtains. The four fifth-floor suites, with kitchen facilities, are good for traveling families. **Pros:** affordable rates. **Cons:** no sea views; limited parking. *5 Mendele St., Center City 03/522–9141 www.adivhotel.com 78 rooms In-room: a/c, safe, kitchen (some). In-hotel: Internet terminal, parking (paid) AE, DC, MC, V BP 3B.*

$ Fodor's Choice ★ **Art + Hotel Tel Aviv.** Designed as a showcase of modern Israeli art, this boutique hotel manages to pull off the look of a gallery and the feel of a homey oasis. Each floor includes a mural by a different Tel Aviv artist, and art books line the bookshelves of the retro-style lobby and surround the long wooden table of the dining room. A lovely roof deck with white couches is a good place to unwind. **Pros:** a fun happy hour for guests; chic but accessible style. **Cons:** small rooms; on a slightly rundown section of Ben-Yehuda Street. *35 Ben-Yehuda St., Center City 03/797–1700 www.atlas.co.il 62 rooms In-room: a/c, safe, refrigerator, Internet, Wi-Fi (some). In-hotel: laundry service, Internet terminal, Wi-Fi hotspot, some pets allowed AE, D, DC, MC, V BP 3B.*

$ Fodor's Choice ★ **Brown TLV.** Newly opened and uber-hip, this welcoming boutique hotel offers luxurious pampering at a remarkably reasonable price, making it one of the best finds in the city. Here guests lounge in a softly lighted, gold and brown hued lobby area called "the living room," sitting on chocolate colored leather couches and vintage chairs. It's like a retro 70s bachelor's paradise, a theme carried upstairs to the spa treatment rooms on every floor and the glorious roof sundeck with outdoor showers and even a sleek white bathtub. Decadent extras to wash down the gourmet breakfasts include port chasers. **Pros:** as hip as the city; great value; fun amenities. **Cons:** smallish rooms. *25 Kalisher St., Center City 03/717-0200 www.brownhotel.co.il 30 rooms In-room: a/c, safe. In-hotel: Wi-Fi, bar, spa, gym AE, DC, MC, V BP 4B.*

$$$ **Carlton.** The lobby of this massive hotel has intimate sitting areas, each of which features the work of a different artist. The hotel's friendly service and casual atmosphere make it a favorite with tour groups, while corporate travelers enjoy its business lounge. Bowls of fruit and feather duvets are welcome pampering touches, as are the fresh juice and newspapers in the morning and the complimentary milk and cookies delivered to your room at night. The accommodations, with double-glazed windows that help muffle traffic noise, are designed in pleasant muted colors. The hotel also has a rooftop pool, a glass-enclosed gym, and gives guests the option of breakfast on a deck facing the beach. **Pros:** homey feeling despite size; close to public beach. **Cons:** location near Atarim Square, which is rather shabby. *10 Eliezer Peri St., Center City 03/520–1818 www.carlton.co.il 280 rooms In-room: a/c, Wi-Fi. In-hotel: restaurant, room service, bar, pool, gym, children's*

BEST BETS FOR TEL AVIV LODGING

Fodor's writers and editors have selected their favorite hotels and other lodgings by price and experience. Fodor's Choice properties represent the "best of the best" across price categories. You can also search by area for excellent places to stay—just check out our complete reviews on the following pages.

Fodor's Choice ★

Art + Hotel Tel Aviv, $, p. 259

Brown TLV, $, p. 259

David Intercontinental, $$$, p. 267

Hotel Montefiore, $$$$, p. 263

Sheraton Tel Aviv Hotel and Towers, $$$$, p. 266

Best By Price

$

Art + Hotel Tel Aviv, p. 259

Brown TLV, p. 259

Gordon Inn, p. 263

Maxim, p. 264

$$

Center, p. 262

Cinema, p. 262

$$$

Basel, p. 264

Carlton, p. 259

Renaissance, p. 264

$$$$

Daniel, p. 268

Hotel Montefiore, p. 263

Sheraton Tel Aviv Hotel and Towers, p. 266

Best By Experience

BEST CONCIERGE

Carlton, $$$, p. 259

David Intercontinental, $$$, p. 267

Hilton Tel Aviv, $$$, p. 263

BEST ISRAELI BREAKFAST

Dan Tel Aviv, $$$, p. 262

Hilton Tel Aviv, $$$, p. 263

BEST HOTEL BAR

Hilton Tel Aviv, $$$, p. 263

Maxim, $, p. 264

Sheraton Tel Aviv Hotel and Towers, $$$$, p. 266

BEST ROOF DECK

Art + Hotel Tel Aviv, $, p. 259

Brown TLV, $, p. 259

Carlton, $$$, p. 259

Grand Beach, $$, p. 263

BEST HOTEL SPA

Dan Accadia, $$$$, p. 267

Hilton Tel Aviv, $$$, p. 263

Sheraton Tel Aviv Hotel and Towers, $$$$, p. 266

BEST FOR KIDS

Dan Accadia, $$$$, p. 267

Sharon, $$$, p. 268

Regency Suites, $$, p. 264

BEST FOR ROMANCE

David Intercontinental, $$$, p. 267

Hotel Montefiore, $$$$, p. 263

Neve Tzedek Hotel, $$$$, p. 267

BEST VIEWS

Dan Panorama, $$, p. 267

David Intercontinental, $$$, p. 267

Sheraton Tel Aviv Hotel and Towers, $$$$, p. 266

BEST BEACH

Dan Tel Aviv, $$$, p. 262

Hilton Tel Aviv, $$$, p. 263

Renaissance Tel Aviv, $$$, p. 264

BEST HISTORICAL BUILDING

Cinema, $$, p. 262

Hotel Montefiore, $$$$, p. 263

Neve Tzedek Hotel, $$$$, p. 267

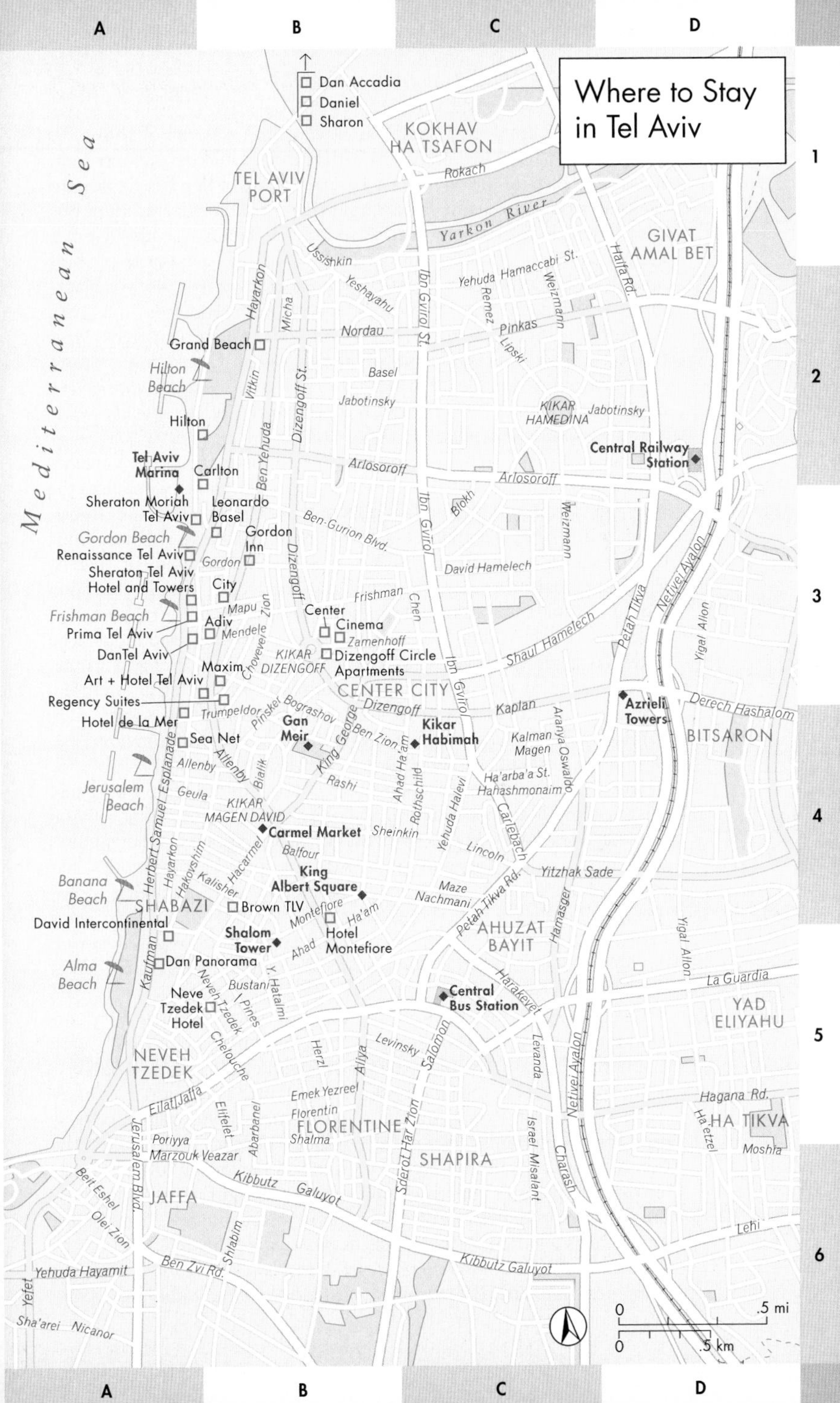

Where to Stay in Tel Aviv
A
B
C
D
1
2
3
4
5
6
Mediterranean Sea
Dan Accadia
Daniel
Sharon
KOKHAV HA TSAFON
TEL AVIV PORT
Rokach
Yarkon River
GIVAT AMAL BET
Ussishkin
Yeshayahu
Hayarkon
Micha
Ibn Gvirol St.
Yehuda Hamaccabi St.
Weizmann
Haifa Rd.
Remez
Pinkas
Lipski
Nordau
Grand Beach
Hilton Beach
Vitkin
Dizengoff St.
Basel
Jabotinsky
KIKAR HAMEDINA
Jabotinsky
Hilton
Ben Yehuda
Central Railway Station
Tel Aviv Marina
Carlton
Arlosoroff
Arlosoroff
Sheraton Moriah Tel Aviv
Leonardo Basel
Ben-Gurion Blvd.
Blokh
Gordon Beach
Gordon Inn
Ibn Gvirol
Weizmann
Renaissance Tel Aviv
Gordon
Dizengoff
David Hamelech
Sheraton Tel Aviv Hotel and Towers
City
Frishman
Chen
Netivei Ayalon
Frishman Beach
Mapu
Zion
Center Cinema
Petah Tikva
Adiv
Prima Tel Aviv
Mendele
Zamenhoff
Shaul Hamelech
Yigal Allon
DanTel Aviv
KIKAR DIZENGOFF
Dizengoff Circle Apartments
Chovevei
Maxim
Art + Hotel Tel Aviv
CENTER CITY
Ibn Gvirol
Regency Suites
Trumpeldor
Bograshov
Dizengoff
Kaplan
Azrieli Towers
Derech Hashalom
Hotel de la Mer
Pinsker
Ben Zion
Kikar Habimah
BITSARON
Sea Net
Gan Meir
King George
Kalman Magen
Aranya Oswaldo
Allenby
Allenby
Bialik
Rashi
Ahad Ha'am
Rothschild
Jerusalem Beach
Geula
Ha'arba'a St.
Hahashmonaim
Herbert Samuel Esplanade
KIKAR MAGEN DAVID
Yehuda Halevi
Carlebach
Carmel Market
Sheinkin
Balfour
Lincoln
Hayarkon
Hakovshim
Hacarmel
King Albert Square
Yitzhak Sade
Banana Beach
Kalisher
Maze
Nachmani
Petah Tikva Rd.
SHABAZI
Brown TLV
Montefiore
Ha'am
David Intercontinental
Hotel Montefiore
AHUZAT BAYIT
Hamasger
Yigal Allon
Shalom Tower
Ahad
Alma Beach
Kaufman
Dan Panorama
Y. Hatalmi
Harakevet
Neve Tzedek Hotel
Neveh Tzedek
Bustani
Pines
Central Bus Station
La Guardia
YAD ELIYAHU
Levinsky
NEVEH TZEDEK
Chelouche
Herzl
Aliya
Salomon
Levanda
Netivei Ayalon
Eilat/Jaffa
Emek Yezreel
Florentin
Hagana Rd.
Elifelet
Abarbanel
FLORENTINE
Shalma
Ha'etzel
HA TIKVA
Poriyya
Marzouk Veazar
Sderot Har Zion
Israel Misalant
Charash
Moshe
Jerusalem Blvd.
SHAPIRA
Beit Eshel
Kibbutz
Galuyot
JAFFA
Olei Zion
Lehi
Shlabim
Yehuda Hayamit
Ben Zvi Rd.
Kibbutz Galuyot
Yefet
Sha'arei
Nicanor
0
.5 mi
0
.5 km

programs (ages 5–12), laundry service, Wi-Fi hotspot, parking (paid), some pets allowed ▭ *AE, DC, MC, V* 🍴 *BP* ⊕ *2B.*

$$ **Center.** This hotel has a cozy lobby (which has a library of books and albums about Tel Aviv) and rooms with balconies looking out over some interesting slices of life on historic Dizengoff Circle. You'll recognize the building from the outside by its larger-than-life colorful statues of two people astride the balcony wall "talking" by means of empty vintage cottage-cheese containers connected by a string—a favorite pastime among Israeli kids in the 1950s. A lounge area screens vintage black-and-white films about Tel Aviv. Breakfast is served across the street at the fascinating Cinema Hotel, worth a visit in its own right. **Pros:** free bicycles for guests; trendy Bauhaus design. **Cons:** small rooms. ✉ *2 Zamenhoff St., Center City* ☎ *03/526–6100* 🌐 *www.atlashotels.co.il* *56 rooms* *In-room: a/c, refrigerator, Wi-Fi. In-hotel: bicycles, Wi-Fi hotspot* ▭ *AE, DC, MC, V* 🍴 *BP* ⊕ *3B.*

$$ **Cinema.** Hotel Cinema began life in the 1930s as the Esther Cinema, one of the first movie theaters in Tel Aviv. Skip the elevator and take the original, elegant winding staircase from the lobby to the various floors: when restoring it, the architect left the depressions made by thousands of moviegoers over the decades. Vintage projection equipment, tickets, showbills, and other paraphernalia give the feel of a truly charming museum, while the comfortable guest rooms also recall the movies, with black decor and reading lamps that look like tiny stage spotlights. The hotel has a sunny terrace with a wonderful view of Dizengoff Circle. **Pros:** a sense of history and style; complimentary afternoon coffee. **Cons:** outside the main tourist area. ✉ *1 Zamenhoff St., Center City* ☎ *03/526–7100* 🌐 *www.atlashotels.co.il* *82 rooms* *In-room: a/c. In-hotel: restaurant, bar, Wi-Fi hotspot* ▭ *AE, DC, MC, V* 🍴 *BP* ⊕ *3B.*

$$ **City.** On a street of small apartment houses a block from the beach, this six-story hotel has a light, airy lobby with a small sitting area on one side and a cozy restaurant on the other. Rooms are in colorful hues of blue and yellow, inspired by the sea, and some have balconies that offer a glimpse of the real thing. **Pros:** friendly staff; adjoining rooms great for families. **Cons:** rooms are a bit small. ✉ *9 Mapu St., Center City* ☎ *03/524–6253* 🌐 *www.atlashotels.co.il* *96 rooms* *In-room: a/c, Wi-Fi (some). In-hotel: restaurant, Wi-Fi hotspot* ▭ *AE, DC, MC, V* 🍴 *BP* ⊕ *3B.*

$$$ **Dan Tel Aviv.** Return visitors say they love the sense of history surrounding them at the Dan, built in 1953 and billed as Tel Aviv's very first hotel. The rainbow-painted rear of the hotel, facing the Mediterranean, contributes to the landmark status—famed Israeli artist Ya'akov Agam designed it. Rooms in the luxurious King David wing have panoramic sea views and double-glazed windows to muffle city noise. The leisure complex includes a gym and an indoor and outdoor saltwater pool. A popular stretch of public beach is right across the street. **Pros:** historic premises; deluxe suites have stereo systems. **Cons:** guest lounge bans children. ✉ *99 Hayarkon St., Center City* ☎ *03/520–2525* 🌐 *www.danhotels.com/Deluxe-Hotel-Tel-Aviv* *280 rooms, 49 suites* *In-room: a/c, safe, DVD (some), Wi-Fi. In-hotel: 2 restaurants, room*

service, bar, pools, gym, spa, children's programs (ages 6–12), laundry service, Wi-Fi hotspot, parking (paid) ▭ AE, DC, MC, V ⊙ BP ✥ 3A.

$ **Gordon Inn.** You'll find basic, hostel-style accommodations at a good location here, a block or so from the beach, with lots of art galleries in the vicinity, and midway between the attractions in north and south Tel Aviv. Guests in standard rooms are served a light breakfast in the small lobby, which is dominated by a pool table. **Pros:** close to the beach. **Cons:** some standard rooms share bathrooms and showers. ✉ *17 Gordon St., Center City* ☎ *03/523–8239* ⊕ *www.hosteltelaviv.com* *30 rooms* *In-room: a/c, refrigerator, Wi-Fi. In-hotel: Wi-Fi hotspot* ▭ *AE, DC, MC, V* ⊙ *BP* ✥ *3B.*

$$ **Grand Beach.** This basic hotel near the northern entrance to the city is less than five minutes from the beach. Its rooms are tastefully decorated in red and beige tones. It caters mainly to business travelers but also sees a good deal of tourist traffic, mainly tour groups from South America, Europe, and Russia. The buffet restaurant's food is unremarkable meat-and-potatoes fare, but it does have an interesting view of life bustling along Nordau and Hayarkon streets. There's a small but inviting rooftop pool and sundeck. **Pros:** close to many restaurants; comfortable lobby bar and business center. **Cons:** many tour groups. ✉ *250 Hayarkon St., Center City* ☎ *03/543–3333* ⊕ *www.grandbeach.co.il* *212 rooms* *In-room: a/c, safe, Wi-Fi. In-hotel: restaurant, room service, bar, Wi-Fi hotspot* ▭ *AE, DC, MC, V* ⊙ *BP* ✥ *2B.*

$$$ **Hilton Tel Aviv.** Perched on a cliff, this sprawling hotel is buffered on three sides by the green spaces of Independence Park. It has direct access to the beach, and for lovers of saltwater but not sand, the large seawater pool is another option. In addition to enjoying the excellent, eclectic cuisine at the intimate King Solomon Restaurant, serving everything from panfried duck breast to sea bream with olive tapenade, you can grab a bite at the Café Med or at the sushi bar. Business travelers will find a particularly good array of services, especially its two lounges with beautiful, uninterrupted views of the Mediterranean. **Pros:** separate shower stalls in many rooms; the lap of luxury. **Cons:** at the end of the hotel strip, somewhat detached from the city. ✉ *Hayarkon St., Center City* ☎ *03/520–2222* ⊕ *www.hilton.com* *584 rooms* *In-room: a/c, safe, Wi-Fi. In-hotel: 5 restaurants, room service, bars, gym, spa, beachfront, laundry service, Internet terminal, Wi-Fi hotspot, parking (paid)* ▭ *AE, DC, MC, V* ⊙ *BP* ✥ *2B.*

$$ **Hotel de la Mer.** A historic 1930s Bauhaus building a block from the beach is now a boutique hotel. The establishment prides itself on its personalized service and adherence to the design principles of Feng Shui—both in color scheme and furnishings. Its cheerful yellow lobby is small but cozy, and the rooftop terrace has a view of the ocean. **Pros:** warm service; 24-hours-a-day tea and coffee service. **Cons:** rooms on the small side; on an unattractive side street; overlooks parking lot. ✉ *62 Hayarkon, off Nes Tziona St., Center City* ☎ *03/510–0011* ⊕ *www.delamer.co.il* *26 rooms, 1 suite* *In-room: a/c, safe, Wi-Fi. In-hotel: Wi-Fi hotspot* ▭ *AE, DC, MC, V* ⊙ *BP* ✥ *4B.*

$$$$ Fodor's Choice ★ **Hotel Montefiore.** This boutique hotel shows off what restoration can bring to Tel Aviv. The two-story building stands out because of its

lovely salmon-hued exterior. Its light-colored walls, hardwood floors, and wrought-iron banisters evoke times gone by. Each of the 12 beautifully appointed rooms has the nice touch of a library filled with art books, and Persian rugs accent the interiors. **Pros:** historic building; fine restaurant; excellent breakfast. **Cons:** in a congested area. ✉ *36 Montefiore St., Center City* ☎ *03/564–6100* 🌐 *www.hotelmontefiore.co.il* *12 rooms* *In-room: a/c, Wi-Fi. In-hotel: restaurant, bar, Wi-Fi hotspot, parking (paid)* *AE, DC, MC, V* *BP* *4B.*

$ **Leonardo Basel.** Several rooms on each floor of this seven-story hotel have either sea views or views of the small swimming pool. Available at no extra charge, these spacious and airy rooms are worth requesting in advance. A pleasant corner bar and coffee shop are open all day in the lobby and look out onto a sunny deck by the pool. **Pros:** a good deal. **Cons:** not near the beach. ✉ *156 Hayarkon St., Center City* ☎ *03/520–7711* 🌐 *www.atlashotels.co.il* *120 rooms* *In-room: a/c, safe, refrigerator, Wi-Fi. In-hotel: restaurant, bar, pool, Internet terminal, Wi-Fi hotspot, parking (paid), some pets allowed* *AE, DC, MC, V* *BP* *3B.*

$ **Maxim.** This hotel is a good value, especially considering that it's across from the beach. Most rooms have sea views. Europeans like to stay here, and there is a Continental feel about the place, owing in part to the many languages heard in the lobby when guests come in after a day at the beach. **Pros:** complimentary coffee and cake in lobby. **Cons:** drab rooms. ✉ *86 Hayarkon St., Center City* ☎ *03/517–3721* 🌐 *www.maxim-htl-ta.co.il* *71 rooms* *In-room: a/c, Wi-Fi. In-hotel: restaurant, room service, bar, Internet terminal, Wi-Fi hotspot, parking (free)* *AE, DC, MC, V* *BP* *3B.*

$$ **Prima Tel Aviv.** On the corner of Frishman and Hayarkon streets, the Prima has an excellent view of the sea from many of its rooms. Table lamps and soft lighting make the tiny lobby feel homey. The hallways and rooms display artwork highlighting Tel Aviv vintage cityscapes. The independently owned dairy restaurant, the Prima Vera, has a beautiful canopied terrace lined with flowers. There's also a coffee bar. **Pros:** kosher restaurant on the premises. **Cons:** Wi-fi is not free. ✉ *105 Hayarkon St., Center City* ☎ *03/520–6666* 🌐 *www.prima.co.il* *55 rooms* *In-room: a/c, Wi-Fi. In-hotel: restaurant, room service, bars, laundry service, Wi-Fi hotspot* *AE, DC, MC, V* *BP* *3A.*

$$ **Regency Suites.** This Best Western hotel is made up entirely of well-equipped one-bedroom suites, each of which comes with a small living area and kitchenette. The best have sea views. There's a lovely breakfast room, although breakfast isn't included. **Pros:** suites are good for groups; no charge for parking. **Cons:** a buzz-in policy to an otherwise locked lobby. ✉ *80 Hayarkon St., Center City* ☎ *03/517–3939* 🌐 *www.regencysuitestelaviv.com* *30 suites* *In-room: a/c, safe, kitchen, Wi-Fi. In-hotel: restaurant, Wi-Fi hotspot, parking (free)* *AE, DC, MC, V* *4B.*

$$$ **Renaissance Tel Aviv.** All rooms have sea-facing balconies at this comfortable luxury hotel, part of the Marriott chain. Restaurants include the Jaffa Terrace, which serves a selection of dairy dishes and pastas, and the Sabres Brasserie, with buffet and à la carte menus. The hotel is

Fodor's Choice ★

Hotel Montefiore

Sheraton

David Intercontinental

Brown TLV

See art that reflects aspects of Jewish life, past and present, at the Diaspora Museum on the Tel Aviv University campus.

rare in its direct access to the beach and one of the few indoor heated swimming pools in Tel Aviv. **Pros:** pretty sun decks; beautiful indoor pool. **Cons:** business lounge closes at midnight. ✉ *121 Hayarkon St., Center City* ☎ *03/521–5555* 🌐 *www.marriott.com* *342 rooms, 4 suites* *In-room: a/c, safe, Wi-Fi. In-hotel: 2 restaurants, room service, bars, pool, gym, spa, laundry service, Internet terminal, Wi-Fi hotspot, parking (paid)* *AE, DC, MC, V* *BP* ✣ *3B.*

$ **Sea Net.** Offering simple, clean rooms, this hotel has an informal atmosphere that appeals to European travelers—French and German are frequently heard in the small lobby. Upper rooms have sea views (the hotel is a block from the real thing), as does the rooftop terrace. The location, at the southern end of the city, offers good access to the Carmel Market, Jaffa, and Neveh Tzedek. **Pros:** warm service. **Cons:** rooms are a bit worn; roof terrace can be noisy. ✉ *6 Nes Tsiona St., Center City* ☎ *03/517–1655* 🌐 *www.seanethotel.com* *70 rooms* *In-room: a/c, safe, refrigerator (some), Internet. In-hotel: restaurant, bar, parking (paid), some pets allowed* *AE, DC, MC, V* *BP* ✣ *4B.*

$$$$ Fodor's Choice ★ **Sheraton Tel Aviv Hotel and Towers.** Combining a personal touch with the efficiency and experience of an international chain, this hotel is one of the most attractive lodging options in Tel Aviv. The marble-tiled lobby is striking; it's contemporary and elegant, with opulent flower arrangements by the in-house florist and sea views through massive windows. The hotel is home to Cielo, an independently owned spa with 14 treatment rooms. **Pros:** fine restaurant; espresso machines in every room; dog beds for visiting canines. **Cons:** pool area needs updating. ✉ *115 Hayarkon St., Center City* ☎ *03/521–1111* 🌐 *www.sheratontelaviv.com* *313 rooms, 24 suites* *In-room: a/c, Wi-Fi.*

In-hotel: 2 restaurants, room service, bar, pool, gym, spa, children's programs (ages 5–12), laundry facilities, laundry service, Internet terminal, Wi-Fi hotspot, parking (paid), some pets allowed ▭ *AE, DC, MC, V* 🍽 *BP* ✥ *3B.*

NEVEH TZEDEK

$$ **Dan Panorama.** This high-rise hotel, located at the southern end of the beachfront, is a short walk to Jaffa and Neveh Tzedek. Each room has a balcony, many with sea views. Poolside barbecues in the summer are a plus. Interior is a bit drab, but the hotel is undergoing renovations as of this writing. **Pros:** across the street from the beach; efficient service. **Cons:** staid atmosphere; feels more business hotel than luxury vacation spot. ✉ *10 Y. Kaufman St., Neveh Tzedek* ☎ *03/519–0190* 🌐 *www.danhotels.com* ➪ *500 rooms* ◌ *In-room: a/c, Wi-Fi. In-hotel: restaurant, bar, pool, gym, parking (paid)* ▭ *AE, DC, MC, V* 🍽 *BP* ✥ *5A.*

4

$$$ Fodor's Choice ★ **David Intercontinental.** At the southern end of the coastline, this luxurious hotel is a top choice for celebrities. The atrium lobby is massive and elegant, with soaring ceilings, marble floors, and a high-end shopping arcade. Most rooms overlook the sea. Some rooms have a hint of Spanish style, with warm colors accented by brick-hued pillows that complement the red-tile roofs of Neveh Tzedek's buildings below. The hotel's restaurant, Aubergine, specializes in Mediterranean cuisine, such as the sea bass in lemon and olive oil. An extensive menu of Israeli wines from the major wineries is another attraction. **Pros:** near Neveh Tzedek. **Cons:** beach is across a busy avenue. ✉ *12 Kaufman St., Neveh Tzedek* ☎ *03/795–1111* 🌐 *www.ichotelsgroup.com* ➪ *516 rooms, 39 suites* ◌ *In-room: a/c, safe, Wi-Fi. In-hotel: restaurant, room service, bar, gym, spa, children's programs (ages 3–12), laundry service, Internet terminal, Wi-Fi hotspot, parking (paid)* ▭ *AE, DC, MC, V* 🍽 *BP* ✥ *5A.*

$$$$ **Neve Tzedek Hotel.** Brothers Golan Dor and Tomi Ben-David came up with the plan to restore the faded elegance of this historic building and transform it into these five luxury apartments. Wooden doors and cabinets are among some of the appointments that were hunted down in flea markets, and the sinks are constructed out of halved old wine barrels. The lacy finishing on sheets and pillowcases adds a sense of luxurious comfort. This lodging is for more independent travelers longing for a sense of living in Tel Aviv. **Pros:** innovative design; free Wi-Fi. **Cons:** no lobby; on a slightly shabby street; uninspiring views. ✉ *4 Degania St., Neveh Tzedek* ☎ *054/207–0706* 🌐 *www.nevetzedekhotel.com* ➪ *5 rooms* ◌ *In-room: a/c, kitchen, DVD, Wi-Fi. In-hotel: restaurant, room service, Wi-Fi hotspot* ▭ *AE, DC, MC, V* 🍽 *BP* ✥ *5B.*

HERZLIYA PITUACH

$$$$ **Dan Accadia.** The three buildings of this seaside hotel are surrounded by plant-filled lawns, which in turn surround a pool overlooking the sea. The standard rooms in the older part of the hotel are tastefully decorated in gold and aquamarine and have balconies with sea views. The newer section has rooms facing either the pool, with its direct access to the beach, or the marina. Garden rooms on the ground floor have

their own outdoor whirlpools. Organized activities keep children and teenagers amused on Friday and Saturday, with midweek activities for kids in summer. **Pros:** dinner buffets on summer nights. **Cons:** little local atmosphere. ✉ *22 Ramat Yam St., Herzliya Pituach* ☎ *09/959–7070* 🌐 *www.danhotels.com* *209 rooms* *In-room: a/c, DVD (some), Wi-Fi. In-hotel: 2 restaurants, room service, bar, tennis courts, pool, gym, beachfront, children's programs (ages 5–12), Wi-Fi hotspot, parking (free), some pets allowed* ▭ *AE, DC, MC, V* *BP* ✣ *1B.*

$$$$ **Daniel.** The high-ceilinged lobby has a glass wall that lets you gaze out at the Mediterranean; the rooms have even better views. The decor is a tasteful mix of sea-blue and mustard hues. Business-club floors offer office services and access to a plush lounge that serves a light buffet breakfast, lunch, and dinner. **Pros:** in-house spa. **Cons:** some rooms are small and plain; public parking is first-come, first-served. ✉ *60 Ramot Yam, Herzliya Pituach* ☎ *09/952–8282* 🌐 *www.danielhotel.com* *200 rooms* *In-room: a/c, safe, Wi-Fi. In-hotel: 2 restaurants, room service, bar, tennis courts, pools, gym, spa, beachfront, diving, water sports, bicycles, children's programs (ages 5–12), laundry service, Wi-Fi hotspot, parking (free)* ▭ *AE, DC, MC, V* *BP* ✣ *1B.*

$$$ **Sharon.** The northernmost hotel on the strip overlooking the water is close to numerous shopping and dining options. Rooms here are cozy and decorated in earth tones, and several face the garden near the outdoor seawater pool. The hotel caters to a wide variety of guests, including tour groups. An activities club for kids runs during the summer months. **Pros:** homey atmosphere; sense of local color. **Cons:** rooms on lower floors have uninspiring views; noisy lobby. ✉ *5 Ramat Yam, Herzliya Pituach* ☎ *09/957–5777* 🌐 *www.sharon.co.il* *173 rooms* *In-room: a/c. In-hotel: restaurant, room service, bar, gym, children's programs (ages 5–12), Internet terminal, Wi-Fi hotspot, parking (paid)* ▭ *AE, DC, MC, V* *BP* ✣ *1C.*

NIGHTLIFE AND THE ARTS

"When do they sleep?" That's what visitors tend to ask about Tel Avivians because they always seem to be out and about, coming or going from a bar, restaurant, or a performance. Tel Aviv's reputation for having the country's best nightlife is well deserved, and the city is also Israel's cultural center.

NIGHTLIFE

On Lilienblum and Allenby streets, and in Florentine, where many of the pubs and bars are clustered, things don't really get started until at least 10 pm, especially on Friday night. Most places stay open "until the last customer," which means at least 3 am when things finally begin to wind down, although on Allenby and in Florentine, clubs are still crowded at 5 am.

For those who want to start and finish the evening early, some nightspots open before the night owls descend; typically, they offer either full

Continued on page 273

The Bat Sheva Dance Company from Tel Aviv is well known for exceptional modern dance.

TEL AVIV AFTER DARK

Settling in at your hotel after dinner isn't an option if you want to truly experience Tel Aviv like a local. In this city famous for its nightlife, dusk is the catalyst that propels the day's steady buzz of activity into high gear. Restaurants fill to max capacity, bars become packed, and people rush to dance and musical performances. Generally speaking, southern Tel Aviv—where you'll find Florentine and Jaffa—has a mellow, low-key vibe with a bohemian flavor. Areas farther north, along Rothschild Boulevard and the Tel Aviv Port, tend to have pricier places frequented by movers and shakers. In the middle is newly hip Neveh Tzedek, where everyone mixes.

JAFFA

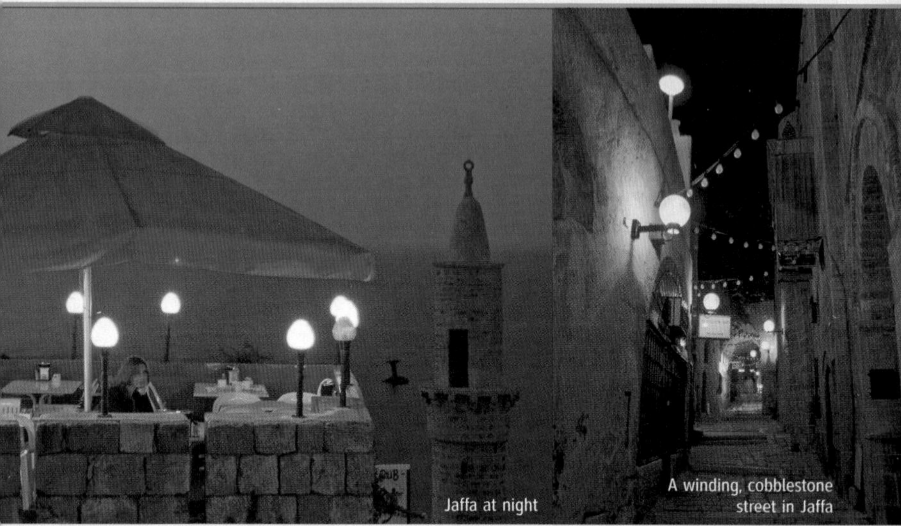
Jaffa at night

A winding, cobblestone street in Jaffa

An ancient port, mentioned in the Bible, this is one of the few examples of Jewish and Arab citizens living side-by-side. Like the Old City in Jerusalem, this area of winding stone alleyways retains its historic feel, and is today a serene spot perched on a hill in the southern end of Tel Aviv with promenades that afford alluring nighttime views of the twinkling coastline.

THE SCENE

With its tranquil vibe, Jaffa is the city's least fast-paced night spot. It's preeminently a romantic place to spend the evening to stroll, eat, and shop, where you'll find a relatively mature crowd of tourists and locals alike.

LOCATION LOWDOWN

Amble along the streets of the artist's quarter to Kedumim Plaza, and you'll find yourself at the top of the hill in the heart of Jaffa. There's live music offered here on Saturday evenings. Or catch a classical quartet at the Franciscan Church of St. Peter, a 17th-century building where Napoleon stayed after capturing the city.

NEIGHBORHOOD KNOW-HOW

If you're in the mood to learn something before going out, the Association for Tourism–Tel-Aviv-Jaffa (☎ 03/516–6188 ⊕ www.visit-TLV.co.il) offers free evening walking tours every Wednesday at 9:30 PM.

TOP PICKS

Try the candlelit **Yoezer Wine Bar** (2 Yoezer Ish HaBira St., ☎ 03/683–9115), in a beautiful arched Ottoman building next to Jaffa's landmark Clock Tower.

Jaffa Bar (Yeffet 30, ☎ 03/518–4668) draws an older, sophisticated clientele.

Saloona (Tirza 17, in the Noga Compound, ☎ 03/518–1719) is Jaffa's sexiest lounge-bar with a hip, artistic feel.

La Charcuterie (3 Rabbi Hanina St., ☎ 03/683–6321) is a hipster bar and restaurant that specializes in cured meats.

NEVEH TZEDEK

The Mann Auditorium

After many years of neglect, Neveh Tzedek has been rediscovered, becoming Tel Aviv's most popular neighborhood day or night. It brims with laid-back wine bars, galleries, boutiques, and restored two-storey houses painted in warm pastels.

THE SCENE

The first Jewish neighborhood outside of Jaffa was once home to Israeli artists and writers, and still attracts a trendy, avant-garde crowd mixed with nouveau-riche locals.

LOCATION LOWDOWN

The most scenic way to reach Neveh Tzedek is to walk from Jaffa, past the Valhalla neighborhood, across the Shlush Bridge. Neveh Tzedek centers around the Suzanne Dellal Center, Tel Aviv's modern dance hub and headquarters of internationally acclaimed dance companies such as Bat-Sheva, Inbal, and Vertigo.

NEIGHBORHOOD KNOW-HOW

After watching a contemporary dance performance, walk through the Dellal Center's beautiful piazza, with its burbling fountains and orange trees, to the neighborhood's main thoroughfare, Shabazi Street, which intersects Neveh Tzedek's charming smaller lanes.

TOP PICKS

Chill at one of the neighborhood's tiny but classy wine bars, like **Jajo** (Shabazi 47), or on the terrace at **Suzanna** (Shabazi 9).

Neveh Tzedek also happens to be a short walk from **Manta Ray** (☎ 03/517–4773, 🌐 www.mantaray.co.il), the quintessential Tel Aviv restaurant, and the perfect place to sip an aperitif on the curving terrace overlooking Alma Beach.

TEL AVIV PORT

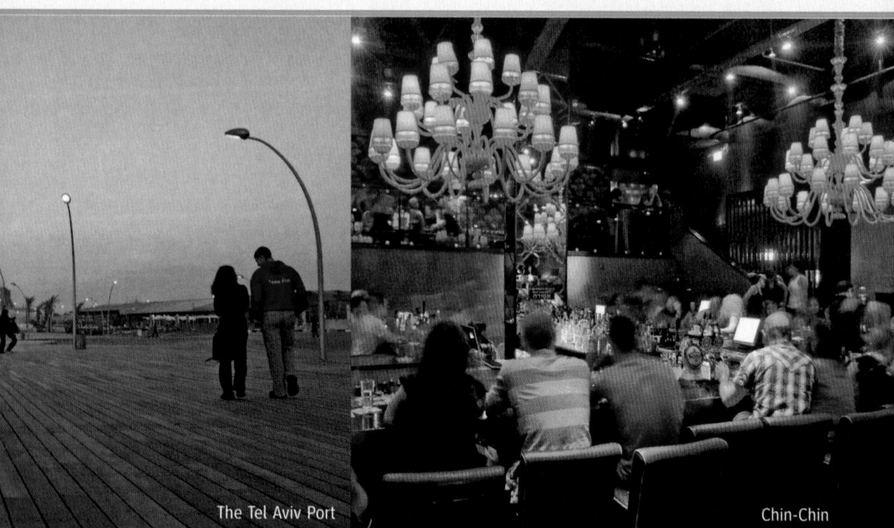

The Tel Aviv Port

Chin-Chin

Tel Aviv's hottest, loudest, most throbbing nightlife spot is the Tel Aviv Port (in Hebrew, the *Namal*) in the city's northern reaches (www.namal.co.il). With its cutting edge music, DJ-spun grooves, and raucous crowds, the Port has contributed in no small measure to Tel Aviv's newly-acquired fame as a major player in the clubbing world.

THE SCENE

Luckily for some, clubs here come alive only on weekends, when they house churning thickets of stylish club crawlers. During the week, it's all about trying the latest trendy restaurant.

LOCATION LOWDOWN

Restaurants and clubs here were built above a small, artificial harbor which stands beside the Yarkon River's estuary. Over the last decade, the port was transformed into a chic waterfront area that includes a wooden boardwalk, the largest in Israel, its undulating shape inspired by the sand dunes of Tel Aviv's early days.

NEIGHBORHOOD KNOW-HOW

Long, disorganized lines form at club entrances, so do your best to catch the doorman's eye. Speaking English sometimes helps. The Port's clubs only warm up at 2 AM, so fortify yourself with a disco nap. And most clubs won't take plastic for cover charges or drinks.

TOP PICKS

Two of the Port's most flamboyant clubs are the **TLV** (☎ 03/541–0222), with a state of the art speaker system, and the split-level **Chin-Chin** (☎ 03/544–0633), where willowy women dance on the bar.

If clubs aren't your scene, satisfy your musical appetite and catch a trio at the first-rate **Shablul Jazz Club** (🌐 www.shabluljazz.com), housed in spacious quarters at the Port's Hangar 13.

dinners, beer and fries, or at the very least the coffee and cake they've been serving throughout the afternoon.

BARS AND CLUBS

Abraksas (✉ *40 Lilienblum St., Center City* ☎ *03/510–4435*) is considered very "in" because it's frequented by local celebrities. There's live music every Sunday, and on weekends it gets a little wild when it becomes a dance bar popular with students.

At **Armadillo** (✉ *51 Ahad Ha'am St., Center City* ☎ *03/620–5573*) is billed as one of Tel Aviv's first neighborhood bars; the beer is cold and the vibe is friendly. It's a good choice if you are not looking for a party crowd.

★ **Barbunia** (✉ *192 Ben-Yehudah St., Center City* ☎ *03/524–0961*) is routinely called one of the best bars in the country. Aptly named for a small fish that's a staple of the city's old-time restaurants, Barbunia's restaurant and bar draw an unusual crowd from the mature set, from fishermen to financial planners. It manages to be both mellow and cheerful, and the music tends toward classics from the '70s.

Cafe Noga (✉ *4 Pinsker St., Center City* ☎ *03/629–6457*) is a bar that doubles as a pool hall, with 19 pool tables. And if darts is your sport, make sure to stop in on Wednesday nights for the contest. Music runs from oldies to hip-hop, depending on which waitress or bartender is working.

Chin-Chin (✉ *3 Hataarucha Street, Tel Aviv Port* ☎ *03/544–0633*) is a massive dance club where the crowds groove to house music. There's lots of dancing on the bar and in every corner.

Evita (✉ *31 Yavne St., Center City* ☎ *03/566–9559*), one of Tel Aviv's best gay bars, is a small, classy place with good food. The long line outside in the later hours attests to its popularity.

★ **HaMaoz** (✉ *32 King George St., Center City* ☎ *03/620–9458*) resembles someone's apartment, down to the black-and-white family photos on the walls. There's even a refrigerator in the kitchen and a working shower in the bathroom. There's always a crowd in the living room, where there's a flat-screen TV and a collection of DVDs. More for the twenty- or early thirtysomething crowd.

Haminzar (✉ *60 Allenby St., Center City* ☎ *03/517–3015*) has a gritty, down-to-earth feel. It's popular with a slightly older after-work crowd, as well as with students later in the evening and on weekends. Happy hour runs until 8 pm. And the kitchen serves up some fine food, too.

Hashoftim (✉ *39 Ibn Gvirol at Hashoftim St., Center City* ☎ *03/695–1153*) means "neighborhood bars," and this is the real deal. The crowd tends to be older and mellow. Groups of friends settle in at a table or the small bar while enjoying jazz or blues.

Hudna (✉ *13 Abarbanel St., Florentine* ☎ *03/518–4558*) attracts students and young professionals who lean toward the political left. The bar is split in two, with an alley down the middle ideal for kicking back and enjoying a pint. Gobble up a burger and fries, or try some of the excellent homemade hummus.

Jaffa Bar (✉ *Yeffet 30, Jaffa* ☎ *03/518–4668*) is a good choice if you're looking for space to breathe and lower decibel levels. The bar, which tends to attract an older, more sophisticated clientele, is spacious, with a sleek bar and an eclectic decor.

Jajo (✉ *47 Shabazi St., Neveh Tzedek* ☎ *03/510–0620*) seats only 20 people or so, but this dimly lit jewel of a place is as chic as it could be. The elegant chandelier dropping from the high ceiling, the flickering candles on the tables, the gracefully arched windows, and the oh-so-hip clientele all make Jajo an ideal place for quiet conversation.

★ **Levontin 7** (✉ *7 Levontin St., Center City* ☎ *03/560–5084* ⊕ *www.levontin7.com*) is a great place to experience the local music scene. The two shows each night feature the widest possible mix of musical offerings, from solo singers to bands blasting indy rock in Arabic. There's a cozy bar upstairs.

The unpretentious dance bar **Lima** (✉ *42 Lilienblum St., Center City* ☎ *03/560–0924*) gets going every night around the stroke of midnight, when both local revelers and tourists suddenly pack the cavernous space. Monday, one of its most popular nights, attracts a gay crowd. The outdoor patio offers fresh air and more merriment.

M.A.S.H. (✉ *275 Dizengoff St., Center City* ☎ *03/605–1007*) focuses squarely on sports. For soccer and rugby (that is, mostly Brits and Aussies), M.A.S.H. is the place to go, showing events that are hardly seen elsewhere, thanks to satellite TV.

Metushelah (✉ *16 Uriel Acosta St., Florentine* ☎ *03/510–2923*) is an intimate wine bar on the edge of the funky Florentine neighborhood that draws a crowd of mixed ages. Named for the Biblical Noah's grandfather, a winemaker of note, Metushelah stocks some 140 wines, the majority of them Israeli.

Mike's Place (✉ *81 Hayarkon St., Center City* ☎ *03/516–8619*) is a well-stocked bar with music that appeals to the over-30 crowd. Its location, on the promenade facing the beach, is popular with tourists.

★ **Mishmish** (✉ *17 Lilienblum St., Center City* ☎ *03/516–8178*) is a classy cocktail lounge that's a favorite with locals. A wide-ranging menu of finger foods (potato croquettes with Parmesan cheese, skewered sirloin chunks) goes well with the drinks.

Molly Bloom (✉ *32 Mendele St., Center City* ☎ *03/522–1558*) is the country's most authentic Irish pub—no surprise, as it's run by Irishman Robert Segal. Live music reverberates on Monday, Wednesday, and Friday afternoon. There's a full menu, including such Emerald Isle favorites as shepherd's pie and beef stew.

Norma Jean (✉ *23 Elipelet St., Florentine* ☎ *03/683–7383*) is a bistro-bar with an attractive brick front on the edge of the Florentine quarter. Behind the 14-seat bar are more than 130 kinds of whiskey, which Norma Jean brags is the biggest collection in the country. The kitchen also serves full meals, with a focus on pleasing the carnivorous.

Fodor's Choice ★ **Nanutchka** (✉ *30 Lilienblum St., Neveh Tzedek* ☎ *03/516–2254*) is an ornate bistro-bar occupying a courtyard and a large two-story building adorned with wall tapestries and paintings. Drinks include specialties

Bistro-bars, such as Nanutchka, are all the rage in Tel Aviv. Many have DJs and dancing nightly.

of the house—a selection of sweet but light wines from the country of Georgia. The menu is truly delicious, featuring divine appetizers like *tinakali* (cheese dumplings with yogurt).

Pas de Derriere (✉ *4 King George St., Center City* ☎ *03/629–2111*) is on an obscure passageway just off Allenby Street. Customers engage in close conversation over candlelit tables in a romantic courtyard. The Parisian-born owner has stocked the bar with an array of top wines from Israel and elsewhere. Tapas, such as delectable carpaccio topped with thin slices of Parmesan, are perfect.

Rothschild 12 (✉ *12 Rothschild St., Center City* ☎ *03/510–6430*) is a hipster café-bar with live music most nights. Things can get very loud under the exposed concrete ceiling, so you may want to escape to the cozy courtyard. This place is open all day and serves breakfast.

Fodor's Choice ★ **Saloona** (✉ *17 Tirza St., Jaffa* ☎ *03/518–1719*) is swank, but retains the hip, artistic feel that draws people to Jaffa. Enjoy a drink under the gigantic chandeliers as you listen to live music.

At **Shesek** (✉ *17 Lilienblum St., Center City* ☎ *03/516–9520*), you'll instantly feel enveloped by the cool vibe even on the hottest nights. The range of alternative music changes nightly, sometimes veering toward hip-hop, funk, or even swing. The young regulars—many of them musicians, journalists, and film-industry types—sit under retro orange light fixtures at the bar or slide into beige leather booths.

Tassa D'oro (✉ *6 Ahad Ha'am St., Neveh Tzedek* ☎ *03/516–6329*), in the heart of trendy Neveh Tsedek, serves such a wide selection of aperitifs and liquors that it makes you wonder why the place is better known as a restaurant. It's actually one of only a few spots in this city where you can enjoy a quiet drink.

TLV (✉ *Tel Aviv Port* ☎ *03/544–4194*) doesn't start jumping until around 2 am. The state-of-the-art speaker system really gets the crowds moving.

Fodor's Choice ★ **Yoezer Wine Bar** (✉ *2 Yoezar Ish Habira, Jaffa* ☎ *03/683–9115*) is a posh wine bar set under the evocative stone arches of an old Jaffa house. The wine list is said to be one of the largest in the country and includes a selection from Burgundy imported especially for Yoezer.

Zippy Trippo (✉ *7 Carlebach, Center City* ☎ *03/561–1597*) is one of the city's trendiest bars and dance clubs. The focus is on dancing, but some quiet corners can be found. Bartenders wave their hands in the air to the beat of the music, adding to the feel of escapist abandon.

THE ARTS

Tel Aviv is Israel's cultural capital, and it fulfills this role with relish. The Tel Aviv Museum of Art, the city's major artistic venue (for concerts and lectures as well as the fine arts) is complemented by a host of galleries, especially along Gordon Street. The Israeli Opera has the finest local and foreign talents in classical and modern works. Tel Aviv is also home to the Israel Philharmonic Orchestra and a dynamic dance scene, including the iconic Batsheva Dance Company for modern dance, the Israel Ballet for classical, and two percussion troupes—Mayumana and Sheketak. The Friday editions of the English-language *Jerusalem Post* and *Haaretz* contain extensive entertainment listings for the entire country.

There are three **main ticket agencies** for performances in Tel Aviv. All accept major credit cards. You must pick up your tickets in person and have your credit card with you: **Hadran** (✉ *90 Ibn Gvirol St., Center City* ☎ *03/521–5200*), **Castel** (✉ *153 Ibn Gvirol St., Center City* ☎ *03/604–5000*), and **Le'an** (✉ *101 Dizengoff St., Center City* ☎ *03/524–7373*).

DANCE

Fodor's Choice ★ Most of Israel's dance groups, including the contemporary Bat Sheva Dance Company, perform in the **Suzanne Dellal Centre for Dance and Theatre** (✉ *5 Yehieli St., Neveh Tzedek* ☎ *03/510–5656*). The complex itself is an example of new Israeli architectural styles used to restore some of the oldest buildings in Tel Aviv.

MUSIC

The **Enav Cultural Center** (✉ *71 Ibn Gvirol St., Center City* ☎ *03/521–7766 or 03/521–7763*) is a 300-seat, city-run venue offering an eclectic fare of music and theater.

Gold Star Zappa Club (✉ *24 Raoul Wallenberg St., Ramat HaChayal* ☎ *03/767–4646*) is one of Tel Aviv's best venues for live music. It's in the Ramat HaHayal neighborhood, just a short cab ride away from downtown.

Mann Auditorium (✉ *1 Huberman St., Center City* ☎ *03/528–9163* 🌐 *www.hatarbut.co.il*), Israel's largest concert hall, is the home of the Israel Philharmonic Orchestra, led by maestro Zubin Mehta. The low-slung gray building, among the most architecturally sophisticated cultural buildings in the country when it was completed in 1957, has excellent acoustics and a seating capacity of 3,000. It also hosts pop and rock concerts.

★ **Mayumana** (✉ *15 Louis Pasteur St., Jaffa* ☎ *03/681–1787* 🌐 *www.mayumana.com*) is an exciting troupe of drummers who bang in perfect synchronicity on anything from garbage pails to the floor to actual drums from cultures all over the world.

★ **Shablul Jazz Club** (✉ *Hangar 13, Tel Aviv Port* ☎ *03/546–1891* 🌐 *www.shabluljazz.com*) is an intimate jazz club, presenting everything from hip-hop to bebop to Latin and ethno-jazz Monday through Saturday nights. Performers include veteran jazz artists and up-and-coming young talents.

4

OPERA

The **Tel Aviv Performing Arts Center** (✉ *19 Shaul Hamelech St., Center City* ☎ *03/692–7777* 🌐 *www.israel-opera.co.il*) is home to the Israeli Opera, as well as the Israel Ballet and the Cameri Theatre.

THEATER

While there are a few exceptions, theater performances are almost always in Hebrew, so inquire before booking.

Most of the plays at **Beit Lessin** Theatre (✉ *101 Dizengoff St. at Frishman, Center City* ☎ *03/725–5333*) are by Israeli playwrights and are in Hebrew.

Fodor's Choice ★ The **Cameri Theatre of Tel Aviv** (✉ *19 Shaul Hamelech St., Center City* ☎ *03/606–1900* 🌐 *www.cameri.co.il*) sometimes offers screened English translations.

Habima National Theater (✉ *Habima Sq., Center City* ☎ *03/629–5555* 🌐 *www.habima.co.il*) is rooted in the Russian Revolution, when a group of young Jewish actors and artists in Russia established a theater company that performed in Hebrew—this at a time when Hebrew was barely a living language. Subsequent tours through Europe and the United States in the 1920s won wide acclaim. In the late 1920s and '30s, many of the group's members moved to Israel and helped to establish the theater.

Hasimta Theatre (✉ *8 Mazal Dagim St., Jaffa* ☎ *03/681–2126* 🌐 *www.simta.com*), in Old Jaffa, features avant-garde and fringe performances, in Hebrew only (or sometimes without words).

SPORTS AND THE OUTDOORS

Almost all outdoorsy activity in Tel Aviv centers on its gorgeous beaches, from boating to scuba diving to spreading out a towel in the sand to get some sun.

BEACHES

Tel Aviv's western border, an idyllic stretch of Mediterranean sand, has miles of beaches and a beachfront promenade. Just after dawn, it's the territory of joggers. As the sun rises, so do the number of beachgoers, from groups of bikini-clad young women to middle-aged men playing the ever-popular ball-and-paddle game called matcot. Sunsets here are spectacular.

The city beaches have many of the same amenities: restrooms, changing areas, towel and umbrella rentals, and restaurants or cafés. Beaches are generally named after something nearby—a street or a hotel, for example. They are hugely popular, especially on weekends. If you'd rather not battle the crowds, come during the week. The lapping of gentle waves offers respite and relaxation for most of the year. There's a strong undertow on these beaches, so exercise caution.

Starting from north of Tel Aviv is the **Herzliya Pituach Beach,** an especially clean slice of beach lined by well-manicured green stretches of lawn near restaurants, cafés and a handful of luxury high-rise hotels. For central Tel Aviv, Dan's Bus 90 heads to this beach.

Tel Baruch Beach, at the end of Propes Street in the northern reaches of Tel Aviv, is popular for families with young children because it has a breakwater that creates a quiet stretch of surf. Because it's the furthest from the downtown stretch, it can be less crowded. The adjacent promenade has an unsavory reputation after dark.

Hilton Beach, in front of the hotel of that name, is very popular. South of Hilton Beach is a gay-friendly area known as "Gay Beach," and beyond that is "Dog Beach" where pampered pooches are let off their leashes.

One stretch of sand that attracts a younger crowd is **Hametzizim Beach,** near the outlet of the Yarkon River. Many people buy a beer at the nearby pub and watch the sunset. It's an especially good choice for families because it has a long sandbar that keeps the waves gentle. South of Hametzizim Beach, the city has set up a private area for Orthodox Jews who prefer gender-separated swimming. The days alternate for men and for women, beginning with women's day on Sunday. On Saturday, the Sabbath, it's open for all.

Gordon Beach, at the end of Gordon Street, is popular with local families for its calm water and tidal pool.

Frischman Beach abuts a strip of restaurants and cafés on the seaside promenade. Saturday morning it attracts Israeli dancing circles. But watch out for the flying volleyballs.

Dolphinarum Beach, at the southern end of Hayarkon Street, has a festive atmosphere on Friday around sunset. Young people, many of whom have returned from post-army trips to Asia, gather for drumming circles.

Surfers line the beach in Herzliya, a resort area less than ten miles up the coast from downtown Tel Aviv.

A good place for Friday-night beach is **Jerusalem Beach,** at the bottom of Allenby Road. The beachside café features Brazilian bands that get the crowd dancing.

BIKING

EcoBike (✉ *9 Hebron Street, Ramat Gan* ☎ *077/450–1650* 🌐 *www.ecobike.co.il*) offers fun bike tours of Tel Aviv on Thursday afternoon. The "Bikes and Beer" tour includes a stop at a bar for a frosty cold one at the end.

BOATING

Ganei Yehoshua (Hayarkon Park) (✉ *Rokach Blvd., Center City* ☎ *03/642–0541*), in the northern part of the city, rents pedal boats and rowboats (NIS 60 per hour) and motorboats (NIS 80 per half hour). Pleasure boats take up to 100 people for 20-minute rides (NIS 12 per person).

Sea Kayak Club (✉ *Jaffa Port, Jaffa* ☎ *03/681–4732* 🌐 *www.kayak4all.com*) offers two-hour sea kayaking tours of the coastline year-round. Beginners are welcome if conditions are calm. The cost is NIS 150.

SAILING

You can charter a yacht with a skipper at **Ofek Yachts** (✉ *14 Pri Eliezer St.* ☎ *03/529–9988* 🌐 *www.ofek-yacht.co.il*) at the Tel Aviv Marina. At Herzliya Marina, **Derech Hayam** (✉ *1 Yordei Hayam, Herzliya* ☎ *09/957–8811* 🌐 *www.yamclub.co.il*) is the place to charter a sailboat or other vessel.

Jaffa is the place to browse in shops and galleries, as the neighborhood has a slow-paced, mellow vibe.

SCUBA DIVING

Dugit Diving Center (✉ *250 Ben-Yehuda St., Center City* ☎ *03/604–5034* 🌐 *www.dugit.co.il*) is a popular meeting place for veteran divers. Although the view beneath the surface of the Mediterranean Sea doesn't offer as breathtaking an array of fish and coral as the Red Sea, it's a good place to start. Dugit can also make arrangements for diving courses in Herzliya.

SWIMMING

Memadiyon (✉ *Ganei Yehoshua, North Tel Aviv* ☎ *03/642–2777*), open from June to September, is a 25-acre water park featuring a half-size Olympic swimming pool, water slides, a wave pool, a toddlers pool, and lawns with plastic easy chairs and sunshades.

SHOPPING

The Tel Aviv shopping scene is the most varied in the country. It's Israel's fashion capital, with boutiques galore, and you'll find styles quite different from what you might see back home in terms of design and color. The real pleasure of shopping in Tel Aviv is access to the exciting creations of its cadre of young designers that have made waves around the world. Dizengoff Street, north of Arlozoroff Street, is where you'll find the shops of many of Israel's best-known designers.

If it's crafts and jewelry you're shopping for, Neveh Tzedek is the place to go, especially along the main drag of Shabazi Street. Crafts and jewelry also star in the Tuesday and Friday Nahalat Benyamin Pedestrian Mall, where prices can be lower than at regular stores and you can almost always meet the artist who made them. As for Judaica, Jerusalem and Safed are much more famous for this than Tel Aviv, but there are still a number of stores here that are fun to browse on Ben-Yehuda and Dizengoff streets.

DEPARTMENT STORES

Hamashbir (✉ *Dizengoff Center, Dizengoff and King George sts., Center City* ☎ *03/622–7444*) is a great place to shop for women's clothing by local designers, many of whom also have boutiques at the northern end of Dizengoff Street. Sample the range here, and then ask for the address if you'd like to see more of a particular designer's line.

MARKETS

Carmel Market, beginning at Allenby Road, is the city's primary produce market, but also has stalls with clothes and housewares. The **Indoor Farmer's Market** in the Tel Aviv Port is both a place to shop for local organic produce, fresh pasta, and novelties like purple carrots, and to sample the freshest offerings at eateries like the in-house tapas bar. Try the freshly squeeezed pomegranate juice. **Jaffa Flea Market** is a mix of junk, fine antique furniture, and designer clothing The flea market has a wide selection of reasonably priced Middle Eastern–style jewelry that uses chains of small silver coins and imitation stones. **Levinsky Market,** in the up-and-coming but still gritty Florentine area, is known as a spice and herb market but also has wonderful Mediterranean delicacies; nearby are good Persian eateries. At the **Nahalat Binyamin Pedestrian Mall** street fair, held Tuesday and Friday, local crafts ranging from handmade puppets to olive-wood sculptures and silver jewelry attract throngs of shoppers and browsers.

SPECIALTY STORES

CLOTHING

Bingo (✉ *24 Hey B'Iyar St., Kimar Hamedina, Center City* ☎ *03/641–4915*) specializes in high-end Italian and Spanish brands.

Couple Of (✉ *144 Dizengoff St., Center City* ☎ *03/529–1098*) is known for making beautiful and comfortable shoes for hard-to-fit narrow feet.

Ido Recanati (✉ *13 Malchei Yisrael St., Center City* ☎ *03/529–8481* 🌐 *www.idorecanti.com*) offers tailored but casual clothes for women. The designer has a talent for creating clothing that is flattering for all, including fuller figures.

Mandinka (✉ *105 King George, Center City* ☎ *03/624–1431* 🌐 *www.mandinka.co.il*) is the place for modern, sophisticated clothing in light fabrics that are perfect for Tel Aviv's steamy climate.

Rina Zin (✉ *216 Dizengoff St., Center City* ☎ *03/523–5746*) is a designer whose chic styles with a European cut appeal to older women.

CRAFTS

Homer Tov Ceramics Gallery (✉ *27 Shabazi St., Neveh Tzedek* ☎ *03/516–6229* 🌐 *www.homertov.co.il*) is a great ceramics gallery on Neveh Tzedek's main drag. It's a cooperative of 14 artists.

Olia (✉ *73 Frishman St., Center City* ☎ *03/522–3235* 🌐 *www.olia.co.il*) is a boutique specializing in olive oil. Look for Israeli-made olive oils, pomegranate- or date-flavored vinaigrettes, and herbs from the Galilee.

One of the most pleasant memento-shopping experiences in Tel Aviv, and in a good location—two long blocks east of the main hotels on Yarkon Street—is at **Raphael** (✉ *94 Ben Yehuda St., Center City* ☎ *03/527–3619*), which carries a large selection of Judaica, jewelry, and handcrafts by some of the best Israeli artists.

Shlushshloshim Ceramics Gallery (✉ *30 Shlush St., Neveh Tzedek* ☎ *03/510–6067*) is a cooperative of 11 ceramicists who display a pleasingly eclectic mix of both decorative and practical items in a variety of colors, shapes, and textures. One of the outside walls, covered with colorful ceramic pieces, has become a landmark.

JEWELRY

★ **Ayala Bar** (✉ *36 Shabazi St., Neveh Tzedek* ☎ *03/510–0082* 🌐 *www.ayalabar.com*) is the sparkling, multicolored creation of Israeli designer Ayala Bar. Her bracelets, earrings, and necklaces, now famous around the world, can be seen from time to time in shops throughout the country, but the best selection is at this flagship store.

JUDAICA

Dar-Fez (✉ *23 Raziel St., Clock Tower Sq., Jaffa* ☎ *03/518–1417*) has an extensive and colorful selection of ceramics, fabrics, silver and copper repoussé-adorned and mother-of-pearl inlayed Judaica, and furnishings.

Specializing in Judaica, and with a particularly wide selection of silver items, but also home to a good selection of jewelry in general is **Miller** (✉ *157 Dizengoff St., Center City* ☎ *03/524–9383*).

LOCAL SPECIALTIES

★ **The Bauhaus Center** (✉ *99 Dizengoff St., Center City* ☎ *03/522–0249*), with its display of books, maps, posters, furnishings, dishes, and even Judaica, all inspired by Bauhaus design, reminds visitors that this school of design embraced more than buildings.

Galilee's (✉ *Bait Banamal, Hangar 26, Tel Aviv Port* ☎ *03/544–2834* 🌐 *www.galilees.com.il*), located in the Bait Banamal retail space, features agricultural and artistic products made in the north, among them wines, olives, herbs and spices, health and beauty products, and pottery.

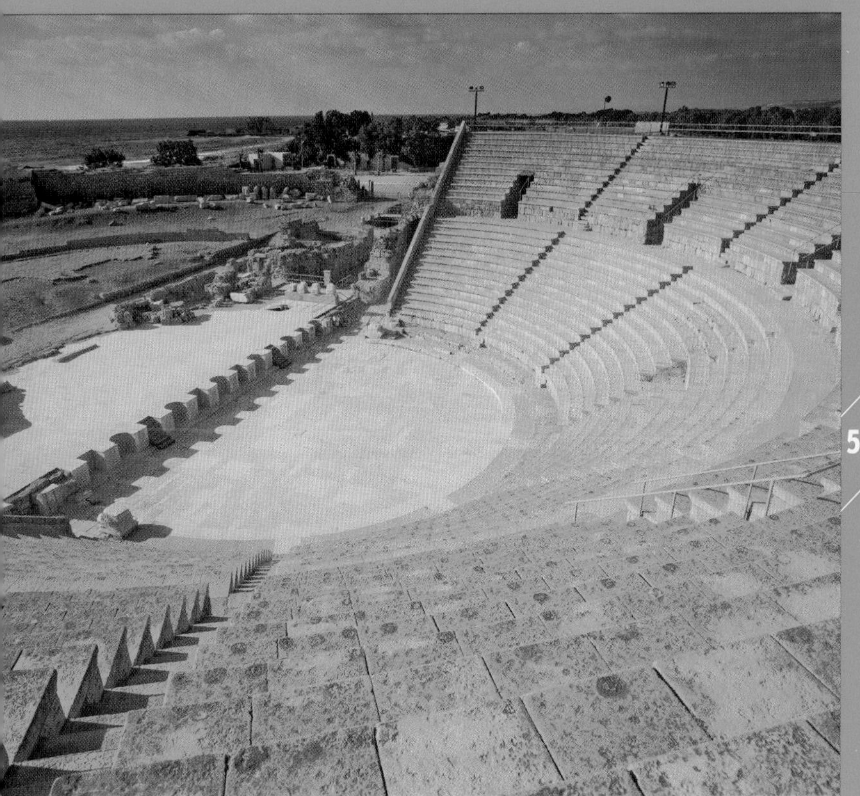

5

Haifa and the Northern Coast

WITH CAESAREA, AKKO, AND ROSH HANIKRA

WORD OF MOUTH

"We headed to Caesarea, with a beautiful location right on the ocean. The site was well preserved and restored. It did seem a bit more 'commercial' than other archaeological sites—it would be cool to see a concert in the amphitheater."

—igg

WELCOME TO HAIFA AND THE NORTHERN COAST

TOP REASONS TO GO

★ **Caesarea:** Originally built by Herod the Great, these 2,000-year-old ruins occupy a strategic spot on the sea. They include Byzantine bathhouses and Crusader moats.

★ **Baha'i Gardens:** In the middle of Haifa, this unforgettable series of gardens tumbles down from the mountaintop. The 18 jewel-like terraces enclose a shimmering gold-domed shrine.

★ **Underground Akko:** At this fascinating archaeological site, see how the Crusaders built numerous halls lined with huge pillars. There's a secret tunnel and a Turkish bathhouse.

★ **Glorious beaches:** The coast means beaches, and this is Israel's finest stretch of golden sand. Haifa's beaches are particularly beautiful. Whether you're into scuba diving or paragliding, there's plenty to keep you busy.

★ **Great wine:** Taste and toast internationally known wines at the Shomron wineries, in the hillsides of the northern coast. Tishbi and Carmel are worth visiting.

Rosh Hanikra

Baha'i Gardens, Haifa

GETTING ORIENTED

Two seaside cities anchor this stretch of coastline. Haifa, a hilltop city on a peninsula jutting into the Mediterranean, offers the magnificent Baha'i Shrine and Gardens, the bustling German Colony, fine restaurants, the Carmelite Monastery, and more. The ancient port city of Akko has underground ruins dating from the era of the Crusaders. Many people come to this area for the beaches, but the coastal Route 2 and the slightly more inland Route 4 can whisk you to such sites as King Herod's port city of Caesarea, the 19th-century town of Zichron Ya'akov, and the artists' colony of Ein Hod. Far to the north are the cliffs and grottoes of Rosh Hanikra.

1 Haifa. This is a city of fairly steep slopes, which reward you not only with sights to see amid pine trees and blossoming foliage but also with vistas of the Mediterranean at every turn, all accompanied by hillside breezes. At the base of the hill are the beaches, some of the area's best.

2 The Northern Coast. The Mediterranean is especially lovely at this string of beaches south of Haifa. Besides the stretches of sand, you'll find wonderfully preserved archaeological sites at Caesarea and Nahsholim-Dor.

3 The Wine Country and Mt Carmel. The quality of Israeli wines has risen to heady heights on the international scene. One of the country's very first wineries is here, along with two others of equal stature. They're in or near the main towns such as Zichron Ya'akov, making access as easy as saying "l'chaim."

4 Akko to Rosh Hanikra. The northern coast is known for its fine-sand beaches and nature reserves. You'll also find upscale bed-and-breakfast lodgings tucked away in long-established rural agricultural settlements. The sea-battered caves at Rosh Hanikra are worth the trip north.

Crusader halls, Akko

HAIFA AND THE NORTHERN COAST PLANNER

When To Go

There's really no bad time to visit this region. Spring (April and May) and fall (October and November) are balmy and crisp, making them the most pleasant seasons for travelers. Summer (June to September) is hot, but there's no humidity, and soft sea and mountain breezes cool things down. Winter (December to March) brings cold weather (sun interspersed with rain), while the sea makes the wind chilly.

As in the rest of Israel, hotels and other lodgings are often booked solid on weekends. On Saturdays and national holidays, Israelis hit the road, so it's best to avoid north-to-south travel out of Tel Aviv or Jerusalem. If you're taking a few days to explore the region, traveling Sunday to Thursday will guarantee you plenty of peace and quiet. If you can only go on Friday and Saturday, make reservations well in advance. Prepare for big crowds at the beaches and tourist sights.

Getting Here and Around

Air Travel: Ben Gurion International Airport, the country's main gateway, is 105 km (65 mi) south of Haifa, about a 90-minute drive. A convenient *sherut* (shared taxi) to Haifa costs NIS 30. You can also catch Bus 5 and transfer to Bus 947. The price for the journey is NIS 36.

Bus Travel: Egged serves the coastal area from Jerusalem Central Bus Station to Tel Aviv Central Station. There's service to Netanya, Hadera, Zichron Ya'akov, and Haifa from both cities. From Jerusalem, a direct bus to Haifa takes one hour 40 minutes. Getting to Caesarea requires a change at Hadera. To get to Akko, change at Haifa. Crowds are heavy at bus stations on Thursday night and Sunday morning. Buses usually do not operate from Friday evening to Saturday evening; in Haifa, some buses run on Saturday.

Car Travel: Driving can be the most comfortable and convenient way to tour this region.

You can take Route 2 (the coastal road) or Route 4 (parallel to Route 2, but slightly inland) north along the coast from Tel Aviv to Haifa, continuing on Route 4 up to the Lebanese border. From Jerusalem follow Route 1 to Tel Aviv; connect via the Ayalon Highway to Herzliya and Route 2.

Taxi Travel: In towns, taxis can be hailed on the street day or night. Ask the driver to turn on the meter (*moneh*).

Train Travel: The northern coast is one part of Israel where train travel is fairly practical. As always, remember that service is interrupted Friday evening to Saturday evening. Israel Railways trains from Jerusalem and Tel Aviv travel at least twice a day to Netanya, Benyamina, Caesarea, Haifa, Atlit, Akko, and Nahariya. You might have to change trains in Tel Aviv when coming from Jerusalem.

The train line from Ben Gurion Airport travels to Tel Aviv, Benyamina, Atlit, Haifa, Akko, and Nahariya. The trip from Tel Aviv to Haifa takes about one hour. Sunday to Thursday, trains depart every 20 minutes from 6:20 am until 9:30 pm; on Friday they run from 6 am until 3:20 pm. On Saturday there are four departures after 7:30 pm. Train travel from Jerusalem to Haifa is feasible only if you have plenty of time, as you have to change in Tel Aviv.

For more information on getting here and around, see Travel Smart Israel.

Dining

You won't have to look hard for a restaurant, whether simple or fancy, with a striking view of the Mediterranean. Fish, served with a variety of sauces, is usually grilled or baked. The most common types are *locus* (grouper), *mulit* (red mullet), *churi* (red snapper), and *farida* (sea bream). Also fresh, but from commercial ponds and the Sea of Galilee, are the ubiquitous tilapia, *buri* (gray mullet), and *iltit* (a hybrid of salmon and trout). Fresh seafood, such as shrimp and calamari, is also found along the coast. Many casual restaurants serve schnitzel (breaded and fried chicken cutlets) with french fries, which kids often love.

Until recently, coastal restaurants weren't as refined as those in Tel Aviv. No longer. Hilly Haifa has several interesting restaurants with creative chefs. The artists' village of Ein Hod has sumptuous Argentinean dining, and there's locally famous falafel in the Druze village of Daliyat el Carmel. Netanya has the region's highest concentration of kosher establishments. Dress is always informal.

Lodging

Options range from small inns to luxury hotels, though the selection and quality of accommodations doesn't equal that of, say, Tel Aviv. Gracious bed-and-breakfasts (known in Israel as *zimmers*) are tucked into coastal rural settlements, mostly north of Nahariya. The splendid spa hotel in the Carmel Forest near Haifa deserves its reputation. In some places, such as Zichron Ya'akov, pickings are slim; but because this region is so compact, you can cover many coastal sights from one base, such as Haifa.

The chart below lists peak-season prices—July, August, and the main Jewish holidays. Many hotels are less expensive—sometimes 40% less—from November through February.

WHAT IT COSTS

	¢	$	$$	$$$	$$$$
Restaurants	under NIS 32	NIS 32–NIS 49	NIS 50–NIS 75	NIS 76–NIS 100	over NIS 100
Hotels	under $120	$120–$200	$201–$300	$301–$400	over $400

Restaurant prices are per person for a main course at dinner in NIS (Israeli shekels). Hotel prices are in U.S. dollars, for two people in a standard double room in high season. Non-Israeli citizens paying in foreign currency are exempt from the 16% VAT on hotel rooms.

Planning Your Time

Haifa, the country's third-largest city, can be a useful base for seeing top sights to the south (Caesarea and the wine country) and north (the Crusader city in historic Akko and the coast up to Rosh Hanikra). Ein Hod, an artists' colony, and the Carmel Caves are also nearby. Haifa itself is notable for the Baha'i Gardens and Germany Colony. However, the coast's southern sights can also be seen easily if you're staying in Tel Aviv. Both United and Egged tours have day tours to Caesarea and Akko from Jerusalem, Tel Aviv, and Netanya; this may be a useful option.

Not counting time in Haifa, you could see the area's highlights in a couple of days, starting with King Herod's port city, Caesarea, and the wine country in the Carmel Hills. Check tour information for the wineries in Benyamina and Zichron Ya'akov. The Druze villages of Daliyat el Carmel and Isfiya are worth a visit, too. You can also spend a half or a full day exploring Akko, to the north; the grottoes at Rosh Hanikra are lovely, but far north. Plan time for swimming or hiking; the Mediterranean coast has great beaches and scenic trails.

By Judy Stacey Goldman

Stretched taut on a narrow coastal strip between Tel Aviv and the Lebanese border, this region offers more than balmy beaches. Historical sights line the shore along with the dunes, fertile fields, and citrus groves of the Sharon Plain. The ancient port of Caesarea has spectacular restored Roman, Byzantine, and Crusader ruins, and vast Crusader halls beckon from underground in seaside Akko. In Haifa, the sea surrounds a modern city on a promontory.

It was in the softly contoured foothills and valleys at the base of Mt. Carmel that the philanthropic Baron Edmond de Rothschild came to the Jews' aid in helping Israel create a wine industry, now one of the region's most successful enterprises. The Carmel range rises dramatically to its pine-covered heights over the coast of Haifa, a friendly, hardworking, and thoroughly modern port city. To the north across the sweeping arc of Haifa Bay lies Akko, a jewel of a Crusader city that combines Romanesque ruins, Muslim domes and minarets, and swaying palms. To the north, the resort town of Nahariya draws droves of vacationing Israelis. And south of the Lebanese border, don't miss the amazing seaside caves at Rosh Hanikra, which have been scooped from the cliffs by the pounding surf.

As the scenery changes, so does the ethnic mix of the residents and their ancestors: Druze, Carmelite monks, Ottomans, Baha'is, Christian and Muslim Arabs, and Jews. Paleontologists continue to study on-site the artifacts of the most ancient natives of all, the prehistoric people of the caves of Nahal Me'arot, on Mt. Carmel. The Baha'is, whose Universalist religion embraces the teachings of many others, dominate Haifa's mountainside. Their golden-domed shrine gleams, and the terraced gardens spill down the slope like bright jewels. Robed Carmelite monks preside quietly over their monasteries in Haifa and in Mukhraka, on Mt. Carmel, next door to the Druze villages. Although the north-coast Druze consider themselves an integral part of Israeli society, they maintain a unique cultural and religious enclave on Mt. Carmel, with the secret rites and rituals of their faith and the distinctive handlebar moustaches and white head scarves favored by the older men. Akko's vast subterranean Crusader vaults and halls, Ottoman skyline of domes and minarets, and outdoor *shuk* (market) are enchanting.

As you drive north, you'll enjoy long stretches of unimpeded views of the sparkling blue Mediterranean. Beautiful beaches lie beside Netanya, Haifa, and Achziv (and in between), with soft sand, no-frills hummus joints, and seaside restaurants. You can learn to scuba dive or explore underwater shipwrecks, and then visit ancient Caesarea and Akko, listening to the crash of the surf all the while. Other great pleasures of the region include hiking the slopes of pine-scented Mt. Carmel, treading the winding lanes of Ein Hod artists' village, and tasting local wines and tangy cheeses at some excellent wineries.

HAIFA

Spilling down from the pine-covered heights of Mt. Carmel, Haifa is a city with a vertiginous setting that has led to comparisons with San Francisco. The most striking landmark on the mountainside is the gleaming golden dome of the Baha'i Shrine, set amid utterly beautiful circular grass terraces that fill the slope from top to bottom. The city is the world center for the Baha'i faith, and its members provide informative walking tours of the flower-edged terraces. At the top of the hill you'll find some small but interesting museums, while at the bottom is the lovingly restored German Colony.

Israel's largest port and third-largest city, Haifa was ruled for four centuries by the Ottomans and gradually grew up the mountainside into a cosmopolitan city whose port served the entire Middle East. The climate is gentle, the beaches are beautiful, and the downtown area is perfect for strolling.

You won't see the religious garb of Jerusalem or the tattoos and piercings of Tel Aviv in this diverse but fairly conservative city. In fact, you can't always tell at a glance who is part of an Arab or Jewish Israeli family, or if someone is a more recent immigrant from the former Soviet Union.

GETTING HERE AND AROUND

A direct bus operated by Egged leaves Tel Aviv for Haifa every 20 minutes between 5:20 am and 11 pm; travel time is one hour. Trains from Tel Aviv to Haifa also take one hour and cost NIS 25. Trains depart every half hour from 6 am until 10:30 pm; on Friday from 6 am until 3:20. During the day on Saturdays trains do not run, but there are four departures after 7:30 pm.

A car is a must for getting to, and around, the city of Haifa, mostly because it's built on a steep hill. There are plenty of nice walks in the city, but to see the sights, a car or a taxi is required; another option is the local buses.

New in 2010 were the Carmel Tunnels, which bypass the most congested parts of Haifa by boring below Carmel Mountain. This underground highway is mostly used by commuters avoiding downtown

CLOSE UP

Haifa's History

First mentioned in the Talmud, the area around Haifa had two settlements in ancient times. To the east, in what is today a congested industrial zone in the port, lay Zalmona, and 5 km (3 mi) west around the cape was Shiqmona.

The Crusaders conquered Haifa when it was an important Arab town and maintained it as a fortress along the coastal road to Akko for 200 years; it was lost and repeatedly regained by the Christians. During this period, in 1154, the Order of Our Lady of Mount Carmel (the Carmelite order) was founded on the slopes of Mt. Carmel by a group of hermits following the principles of the prophet Elijah and the rules of poverty, vegetarianism, and solitude.

After Akko and Haifa succumbed to the Mamluk Sultan Baybars in 1265, Haifa was destroyed and left derelict. It was a sleepy fishing village for centuries.

The city reawakened under the rule of Bedouin sheikh Dahr el-Omar, who had rebelled against direct Ottoman rule in the mid-18th century and independently governed Akko and the Galilee. In 1761 Dahr ordered the city to be demolished and moved about 3 km (2 mi) to the south. The new town was fortified by walls and protected by a castle, and its port began to compete with that of Akko across the bay.

Napoléon, too, came to Haifa, though only briefly, and en route to ignominious defeat at Akko during his Eastern Campaign. Napoléon left his wounded at the Carmelite Monastery when he beat a retreat in 1799, but the French soldiers there were killed and the monks driven out by Ahmed el-Jazzar, the victorious pasha of Akko.

The religious reform movement known as the Templers founded Haifa's German Colony in 1868; the area has been lovingly restored. The city became the center of the Baha'i faith in the early 20th century. With the creation of a deep-water port in 1929, Haifa's development as a modern city began. By the time the state of Israel was declared in 1948, Haifa had a population of more than 100,000. Today it's the country's third-largest city, home to 265,000 Jews and Arabs.

streets, as it cuts a 30- to 45-minute trip down to less than 10. The toll is NIS 11.40, and can be paid with cash or credit card. The tunnels aren't much use to visitors, but if you're just passing through, they could save you time. Coming north from Tel Aviv, the entrance is at the end of Route 2. From the north, it's off Route 4 near the Checkpoint Interchange.

Haifa has the five-station Carmelit subway—actually a funicular railway—that runs from Gan Ha'em Park on Hanassi Boulevard (opposite the Dan Panorama) in Central Carmel down to Kikar Paris in the port area in six minutes. The fare is NIS 6, and the train operates Sunday to Thursday 6 am to 10 pm, Friday 6 to 3, and Saturday 7 pm to midnight. Though the Carmelit doesn't serve the tourist sites, children enjoy this ride (it's so short you just travel both ways).

TOURS

Three times a week, Carmelit Cruiser offers boat tours of Haifa Bay. The ride lasts one hour and costs NIS 30. Call ahead for departures.

ESSENTIALS

Banks and Exchange Services **Panorama Change** (✉ *Panorama Center, 109 Hanassi Blvd., Merkaz Carmel* ☎ *04/836–2019*).

Boat Contact **Carmelit Cruiser** (☎ *04/841–8765*).

Bus Contact **Egged** (☎ *03/694–8888* 🌐 *www.egged.co.il*).

Internet **Viva Cafe** (✉ *25 Nordeau St., Hadar* ☎ *04/867–2645*).

Taxi Contacts **Carmel-Ahuza** (☎ *04/838–2727*). **Mercaz Mitzpe** (☎ *04/866–2525*).

Train Contact **Israel Railways** (☎ *03/611–7000* 🌐 *www.israrail.org.il*).

Visitor Information **Haifa Tourist Board** (✉ *48 Ben Gurion Blvd., German Colony* ☎ *04/853–5606* 🌐 *www.tour-haifa.co.il*).

5

EXPLORING HAIFA

The metropolis is divided into three main levels, each crisscrossed by parks and gardens: the port down below; Hadar, a rather unappealing commercial shopping area in the middle; and Merkaz Carmel (known as "the Merkaz"), with the posher hotels and many restaurants, on the crest of Mt. Carmel.

Thanks to the beneficence of the Baha'is, you can enjoy a walking tour that takes you through the stunning terraces that lie like multicolored jewels from the crest of the city at Mt. Carmel to the German Colony below.

TOP ATTRACTIONS

Fodor's Choice ★ **Baha'i Shrine and Gardens.** The most striking feature of the stunning gardens that form the centerpiece of Haifa is the Shrine of the Bab, whose brilliantly gilded dome dominates—and illuminates—the city's skyline. The renovated shrine of the Bab, unveiled in April 2011, gleams magnificently with 11,790 gold-glazed porcelain tiles.

Haifa is the world center for the Baha'i faith, founded in Iran in the 19th century. It holds as its central belief the unity of mankind. Religious truth for Baha'is is not doctrinaire; rather, it consists of progressive revelations of a universal faith. Thus the Baha'is teach that great prophets have appeared throughout history to reveal divine truths, among them Moses, Zoroaster, Buddha, Jesus, Muhammad, and most recently, the founder of the Baha'i faith, Mirza Husayn Ali, known as Baha'u'llah—the Glory of God. The Shah and then the Ottomans exiled Baha'u'llah (1817–92) from his native Persia to Akko, where he lived as a prisoner for almost 25 years. The Baha'is' holiest shrine is on the grounds of Baha'u'llah's home, where he lived after his release from prison and where he is now buried, just north of Akko.

Here in Haifa, at the center of the shrine's pristinely manicured garden terraces, is the mausoleum built for the Bab (literally, the "Gate"), the forerunner of this religion, who heralded the coming of a new faith to be revealed by Baha'u'llah. The Persian authorities martyred Bab in 1850. Baha'u'llah's son and successor built the gardens and shrine and had the Bab's remains reburied here in 1909. The building, made of Italian stone and rising 128 feet, gracefully combines the canons of classical European architecture with elements of Eastern design and also houses the remains of Baha'u'llah's son. The dome glistens with some 12,000 gilded tiles imported from the Netherlands. Inside, the floor is covered with rich Oriental carpets, and a filigree veil divides the public area from the inner shrine.

WORD OF MOUTH

"I assume you will be getting to Haifa just in time to sleep, but I recommend eating in one of the restaurants on Ben Gurion Boulevard, in the German Colony. It's below the beautifully lit Baha'i shrine and gardens." –KatPen

The magnificent gardens are a sight to behold: 19 stunningly landscaped circular terraces extend from Yefe Nof Street for 1 km (½ mi) down the hillside to Ben Gurion Boulevard, at the German Colony. The terraces are a harmony of color and form—pale pink-and-gray-stone flights of stairs and carved urns overflowing with red geraniums set off the perfect cutouts of emerald green grass and floral borders, dark green trees, and wildflowers, with not a leaf out of place anywhere. The gardens are one of Israel's 11 UNESCO World Heritage sites.

Three areas are open to the public year-round, except on Baha'i holidays: the shrine and surrounding gardens (Hatziyonut Avenue, near Shifra Street); the upper terrace and observation point (Yefe Nof Street); and the entry at the lower terrace (Hagefen Square, at the end of Ben Gurion Boulevard). Tours are offered at noon every day except Wednesday. These depart from 45 Yefe Nof Street, near the top of the hill. Note: the Shrine of the Bab is a pilgrimage site for the worldwide Baha'i community; visitors to the shrine are asked to dress modestly (no shorts). ✉ *16 Golomb St., Merkaz Carmel* ☎ *04/835–8358* 🌐 *www.bahai.org* 🎫 *Free* ⏲ *Shrine daily 9–noon; gardens daily 9–5.*

Fodor's Choice ★ **German Colony.** It is only one street—actually a broad boulevard—but "The Colony" packs in history (with explanatory placards), interesting architecture, great restaurants, and wonderful spots for people-watching. Ben Gurion Boulevard was the heart of a late-19th-century colony established by the German Templer religious reform movement. Along either side are robust one- and two-story stone houses with pointed red-tile roofs. Many bear German names, dates from the 1800s, biblical inscriptions above the doors, and old wooden shutters framing narrow windows.

Neglected for years, the German Colony is now one of the city's loveliest (and flattest) strolls. It's best to start your exploration around Yaffo (Jaffa) Street so that you're walking toward the stunning Baha'i Gardens. Along the way you can have a meal or a cup of coffee, explore the shops in the City Centre Mall, and learn about the history of the German Templers. Any time of day is pleasant, but evening, when the cafés and restaurants are brimming with people, is best.

WORD OF MOUTH

"Shrine of the Bab is one of many holy sites in Israel. Perched on the slopes of Mt. Carmel, the Baha'i Gardens pay homage to Baha'i's founders." —photo by GeneZ, Fodors.com member

Haifa
BAT GALIM
Hasharon
Ha'aliya
Hashnia
Sderot Hahagana
Elijah's Cave
Haf Carmel Train & Bus Station
Heyl Hayam St.
EIN HAYAM
Sderot Hahagana
Hatoren St.
KIRYAT ELIEZER
Allenby Road
Zahal St.
Yaffo
Stella Maris Rd.
Tel Aviv St.
KIRYAT ELIAHU
Deror
Sderot James de Rothchild
Derekh Zorfat
FRENCH CARMEL
Shaul Tshernikhovski
Sha'ar Ha'aliqa St.
Yeshayahu
Allenby Rd.
Yizhaq Sade St.
Hagefen Blvd.
Ezel St.
RAMAT HATISHBI
Shomrom
Yefe Nof St.
Sderot Hatziyonut
NEVE DAVID
Hayam
WESTERN CARMEL
Hanassi Blvd.
Hacarmel St.
Eliyahu Golumb St.
Hayam
Kabirim St.
Hahashmona'im St.
KABABIR
MERKAZ CARMEL (THE TOP OF THE MOUNTAIN)
Kadima St.
Sderot Wedgewood
KEY
Rail Lines
Carmelit Funicular

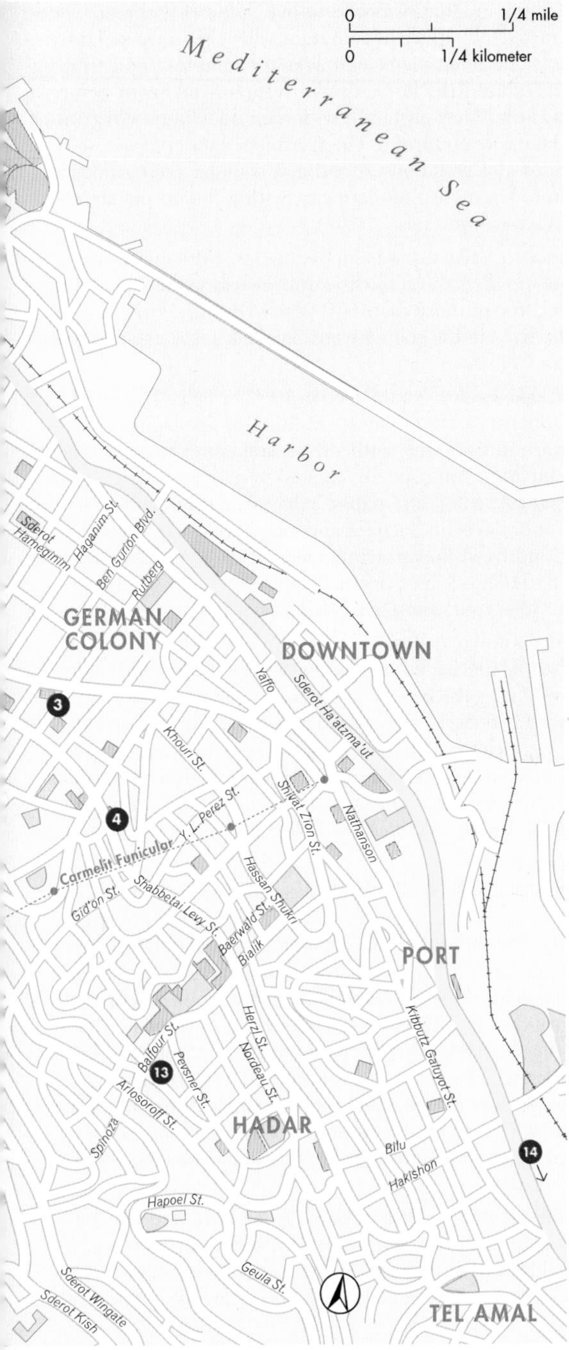

Baha'i Shrine and Gardens	1
Carmelite Monastery and Stella Maris Church	5
Clandestine Immigration and Naval Museum	6
German Colony	3
Haifa Museum of Art	4
Haifa Zoo	9
Hecht Museum	12
Mané Katz Museum	10
National Maritime Museum	7
National Museum of Science and Technology	13
Technion	14
Tikotin Museum of Japanese Art	11
Vista of Peace Sculpture Garden	2
Yefe Nof Street	8

The Templers' colony in Haifa was one of five in the Holy Land. The early settlers formed a self-sufficient community; by 1883 they had built nearly 100 houses and filled them with as many families. Industrious workers, they introduced the horse-drawn wagon—unknown before their arrival—to Haifa. They also built with their own funds a pilgrimage road from Haifa to Nazareth. The Germans' labors gave rise to modern workshops and warehouses, and it was under their influence that Haifa began to resemble a modern city, with well-laid-out streets, gardens, and attractive homes.

Haifa's importance to Germany was highlighted in 1898, when Kaiser Wilhelm II sailed into the bay, on the first official visit to the Holy Land by a German emperor in more than 600 years. During World War II, the Germans who lived in the colony were expelled, suspected of being Nazis. ✉ *German Colony.*

★ **Tikotin Museum of Japanese Art.** Established in 1957 by Felix Tikotin, this graceful venue adheres to the Japanese tradition of displaying beautiful objects that are in harmony with the season, so exhibits change frequently. The Japanese atmosphere, created in part by sliding doors and partitions made of wood and paper, enhances a display of scrolls, screens, pottery and porcelain, lacquer and metalwork, paintings from several schools, and fresh-flower arrangements. ✉ *88 Hanassi Blvd., Merkaz Carmel* ☎ *04/838–3554* 🌐 *www.hms.org.il* 🎫 *NIS 30* 🕒 *Mon.–Thurs. 10–4, Fri. 10–1, Sat. and Jewish holidays 10–3.*

★ **Yefe Nof Street.** Also known as Panorama Road, this curving street high above the city skirts the backs of Haifa's biggest hotels, providing remarkable views. Enjoy the beauty of the lushly planted Louis Promenade, with shaded benches along the way, beginning behind the Dan Carmel Hotel. On a clear day, from any of several lookouts you can see the port below, Akko across the bay, and the cliffs of Rosh Hanikra, with Lebanon in the distance. Panorama Road is beautiful during the day and at night. ✉ *Merkaz Carmel.*

WORTH NOTING

Carmelite Monastery and Stella Maris Church. Perched high up on the hillside is this imposing church. The wall paintings bring to life the dramatic story of the prophet Elijah, the patron of the Carmelite order. During the Crusader period, certain hermits emulating the ascetic life of the prophet Elijah lived in caves on this steep mountain slope. In the early 13th century they united under the leadership of Saint Berthold, who petitioned the patriarch of Jerusalem for a charter. Thus was born the Carmelite order, which spread across Europe. The Carmelite monks were forced to leave their settlements on Mt. Carmel at the end of the 13th century, and they did not return until nearly four centuries later. When they found Elijah's cave inhabited by Muslim dervishes, they set up a monastery nearby.

The church of the present monastery dates from 1836 and was built with the munificence of the French monarchy, hence the name of the surrounding neighborhood: French Carmel. A small pyramid, topped with an iron cross, that stands outside explains the French connection.

Haifa's restored, 19th-century German Colony is a relaxing place to dine or spend an evening.

The monument commemorates those French who were slaughtered here by the Turks in 1799 after the retreating Napoléon left his ailing troops behind at the monastery. Inside, the academic paintings in the dome depict Elijah in the chariot of fire in which he ascended to heaven, and other biblical prophets. The small cave a few steps down at the end of the nave is traditionally associated with Elijah and his pupil, Elisha. ✉ *Carmelite Monastery, Stella Maris Rd., French Carmel* ☎ *04/833-7758* 🎫 *Free* ⏲ *Daily 8–12:30 and 3–6.*

Clandestine Immigration and Naval Museum. The rather dull name of this museum belies the dramatic nature of what's inside: the museum tells the story of the often-heroic efforts to bring Jewish immigrants to Palestine from war-torn Europe in defiance of British policy.

In 1939, on the eve of World War II, the British issued the so-called White Paper, which effectively strangled Jewish immigration to Palestine. Out of 63 clandestine ships that tried to run the blockade after the war's end, all but five were intercepted, and their passengers were deported to Cyprus. The museum is full of moving stories of courage, tenacity, and disaster. A photomural of the celebrated ship the *Exodus* recalls the story of the 4,530 refugees aboard who were forcibly transferred back to Germany in 1947, but not before the British forces opened fire on the ship. ✉ *204 Allenby Rd., Kiryat Eliezer* ☎ *04/853-6249* 🌐 *www.amutayam.org.il* 🎫 *NIS 15* ⏲ *Sun.–Thurs. 8:30–4.*

Elijah's Cave. This site is considered sacred by Jews, Christians, and Muslims; an early Byzantine tradition identified it as the cave in which Elijah found refuge from the wrath of Ahab, king of Israel from 871 to

The blue Mediterranean, Haifa's hills, and the rolling green of the Baha'i Gardens make irresistible photos.

853 BC. Graffiti from pilgrims of various faiths and different centuries are scrawled on the right wall, and written prayers are often stuffed into crevices. Modest dress is required. The cave is a pretty 20-minute walk down the fairly steep path across from the entrance to the Carmelite Monastery and church. ✉ *Allenby Rd., Ein Hayam* 🎫 *Free* ⏲ *Sun.–Thurs. 8–5, Fri. and Jewish holiday eves 8–1.*

Haifa Museum of Art. Displayed here are works from all over the world, dating from the mid-18th century to the present. It's an excellent venue to learn about contemporary Israeli art: included are 20th-century graphics and contemporary paintings, sculptures, and photographs. The print collection is of special note. ✉ *26 Shabbtai Levy St., Hadar* ☎ *04/852–3255* 🌐 *www.hms.org.il* 🎫 *NIS 30* ⏲ *Sun.–Wed. 10–4, Thurs. 4–7, Fri. 10–1, Sat. 10–3.*

NEED A BREAK?

In a city known for its falafel, check out the falafel joints called Michel and Haskenim at 18 and 21 Wadi Street, the circular street in the Wadi Nisnas market. You'll get plenty of fresh steaming chickpea balls stuffed into warm pita bread.

Haifa Zoo. Amid masses of trees and foliage is a seemingly happy collection of roaring lions and tigers, big brown bears, chattering monkeys, stripe-tailed lemurs, a placid camel, lots of snakes, one croc, and fierce-eyed eagles and owls—plus a bat cave and a waterbird pond. It's a hilly place, but there's a tram to take visitors up the steepest terrain. ✉ *Hanassi Blvd., Merkaz Carmel* ☎ *04/837–2886* 🎫 *NIS 30* ⏲ *Apr.–June, Sun.–Thurs. 8–5; July and Aug., Sun.–Thurs. 8–6; Sept.–Mar., Sun.–Thurs. 8–4.*

Hecht Museum. It's worth the trip to Haifa University to see this museum's archaeological treasures. At the summit of Mt. Carmel, in the main campus tower, the collection spans the millennia from the Chalcolithic era to the Roman and Byzantine periods, concentrating on "The People of Israel in Eretz Israel." The artifacts range from religious altars and lamps to two coffins and figurines from the Early Bronze Age. Featured prominently are finds from the excavations of Jerusalem's Temple Mount. A separate wing displays a small collection of paintings, mostly Impressionist works by Monet, Soutine, and Pissarro, among others. The roof observation deck, on the 27th floor, affords spectacular views. To get here, take Bus 37 from the Nof Hotel. ✉ *Abu Hushi St., Har Carmel* ☎ *04/824–0577* 🌐 *www.mushecht.haifa.ac.il* 🎫 *Free* 🕐 *Sun., Mon., Wed., and Thurs. 10–4; Tues. 10–7; Fri. and holiday eves 10–1; Sat. 10–2.*

5

Mané Katz Museum. This is the house and studio where the Expressionist painter Emmanuel Katz (1894–1962) lived and worked for the last four years of his life. Katz spent the 1920s in Paris, where he exhibited with a group of Jewish artists from the École de Paris. As in the canvases of fellow members Marc Chagall and Chaim Soutine, a recurring theme in his work is the village life of Jews in Eastern Europe. A whitewashed building, it contains Katz's paintings, drawings, and sculptures. You'll also find the Ukrainian-born artist's collection of rugs, 17th-century antiques from Spain and Germany, and Judaica. ✉ *89 Yefe Nof St., Merkaz Carmel* ☎ *04/838–3482* 🎫 *Free* 🕐 *Sun., Mon., Wed., and Thurs. 10–4, Tues. 2–6, Fri. 10–1, Sat. 10–2.*

National Maritime Museum. About 5,000 years of maritime history are told with model ships, archaeological finds, coins minted with nautical symbols, navigational instruments, and other artifacts. There are also intriguing underwater finds from nearby excavations and shipwrecks. The ancient-art collection is one of the finest in the country; it comprises mostly Greek and Roman stone and marble sculpture, Egyptian textiles, Greek pottery, and encaustic grave portraits from Fayyum, in Lower Egypt. Particularly rare are the figures of fishermen from the Hellenistic period. ✉ *198 Allenby Rd., Kiryat Eliezer* ☎ *04/853–6622* 🌐 *www.hms.org.il* 🎫 *NIS 30* 🕐 *Mon.–Thurs. 10–4, Fri. 10–1, Sat. 10–3.*

National Museum of Science and Technology (Technoda). Both children and adults are captivated by the hands-on chemistry and physics exhibits in this beautifully designed building. ✉ *12 Balfour St., Hadar* ☎ *04/861–4444* 🌐 *www.mustsee.org.il* 🎫 *NIS 74* 🕐 *Mon.–Wed. 10–4, Thurs. 4–9, Fri. 10–1, Sat. 10–3.*

Technion. Israel's top institute for science and technology, the 300-acre Israeli Institute of Technology is highly fertile ground for research in such fields as engineering, medicine, architecture, and city planning. There's a virtual tour of the institute and an interactive film about the 2004 Nobel Prize in Chemistry. To get here, take Bus 31 from the Nof Hotel or the Dan Panorama Hotel. ✉ *Kiryat Ha-Technion, Neve Sha'anan* ☎ *04/829–3863* 🌐 *www.technion.ac.il* 🎫 *Free* 🕐 *Sun.–Thurs. 8:30–3.*

Vista of Peace Sculpture Garden. You can contemplate the life-size bronzes of people and animals from a bench on the winding path through this garden, which has views of Haifa Bay beyond. Sculptor Ursula Malbin, who came to Israel as a refugee from Nazi Germany, created this oasis. The garden, west of Baha'i Shrine, opens at sunrise and closes at 6. ✉ *112 Zionism Ave., Bahai* 🌐 *www.malbin-sculpture.com.*

WHERE TO EAT

There are plenty of restaurants near the large hotels at the top of the city in Merkaz Carmel. Another popular place to eat is along Ben Gurion Boulevard in the German Colony, where the evening hours are whiled away at sidewalk terraces. The port area is being gentrified, so there are always new restaurants opening up. Dress is casual, Israeli style.

Use the coordinate (✣ A1) at the end of each listing to locate a site on the corresponding map.

$$ VEGETARIAN

✕ **Café Louise.** At this vegetarian eatery, breakfast, lunch and dinner are served in the cheerful dining room or on the glass-enclosed patio. Grains are the mains here: choose from among such creative dishes as red quinoa salad with sweet-carrot vinaigrette, or vegetable curry stew graced with cashews. If you prefer fish, try the filet of salmon in a lemongrass sauce with whole-wheat couscous. For dessert, there's tapioca in coconut milk with seasonal fruit. Consider indulging in an Israeli-style Bellini—arak and fresh-squeezed red grapefruit juice. Many Israeli wines are also on offer, as is organic coffee. ✉ *58 Moriah St., Merkaz Carmel* ☎ *04/834–9950* ▭ *AE, MC, V.* ✣ *6B*

$$ MEDITERRANEAN

✕ **Douzan.** Inside this old German Templer building with a pleasant outdoor terrace, a huge metal lamp studded with colored glass casts lacy designs on the walls. The food, much of it prepared by the owner's mother, is an intriguing combination of French and local Arabic cuisines. Her specialty is *kibbeh,* deep-fried torpedoes of cracked wheat kneaded with minced beef, pine nuts, onions, and exotic spices. A variation on it is *sfeeha,* puff pastry topped with delicately spiced beef, onions, and pine nuts. ✉ *35 Ben Gurion Blvd., German Colony* ☎ *04/852–5444* 🌐 *www.rest.co.il* ▭ *AE, DC, MC, V.* ✣ *4B*

$$ MIDDLE EASTERN

✕ **Fattoush.** Olive trees hung with blue and green lights set the tone for the elaborate interior, which contains several intimate rooms. One is a "cave" with Arabic script on the walls, low banquettes, wooden stools, and filigree lamps; another is modern with leather seats, embroidered cushions, and a changing art exhibit set against burnt orange walls. And now for the food: Fattoush salad is a favorite, consisting of chopped tomato, cucumber, onion, and mint and sprinkled with crisp toasted pita pieces. You might follow it with *emsakhan,* roast chicken topped with pieces of sumac and served on oven-baked pita. For a daring dessert, try Arabic *knaffe,* consisting of crispy noodles with soft cheese and honey. ✉ *40 Ben Gurion Blvd., German Colony* ☎ *04/852–4930* 🌐 *www.rest.co.il* ▭ *AE, DC, MC, V.* ✣ *4B*

$$ ASIAN

✕ **Giraffe.** Here's a welcome combination of jolly atmosphere and tasty food. There's some culinary combining going on here, too: Asian cuisine precedes French desserts. It's sort of a New York lounge–style

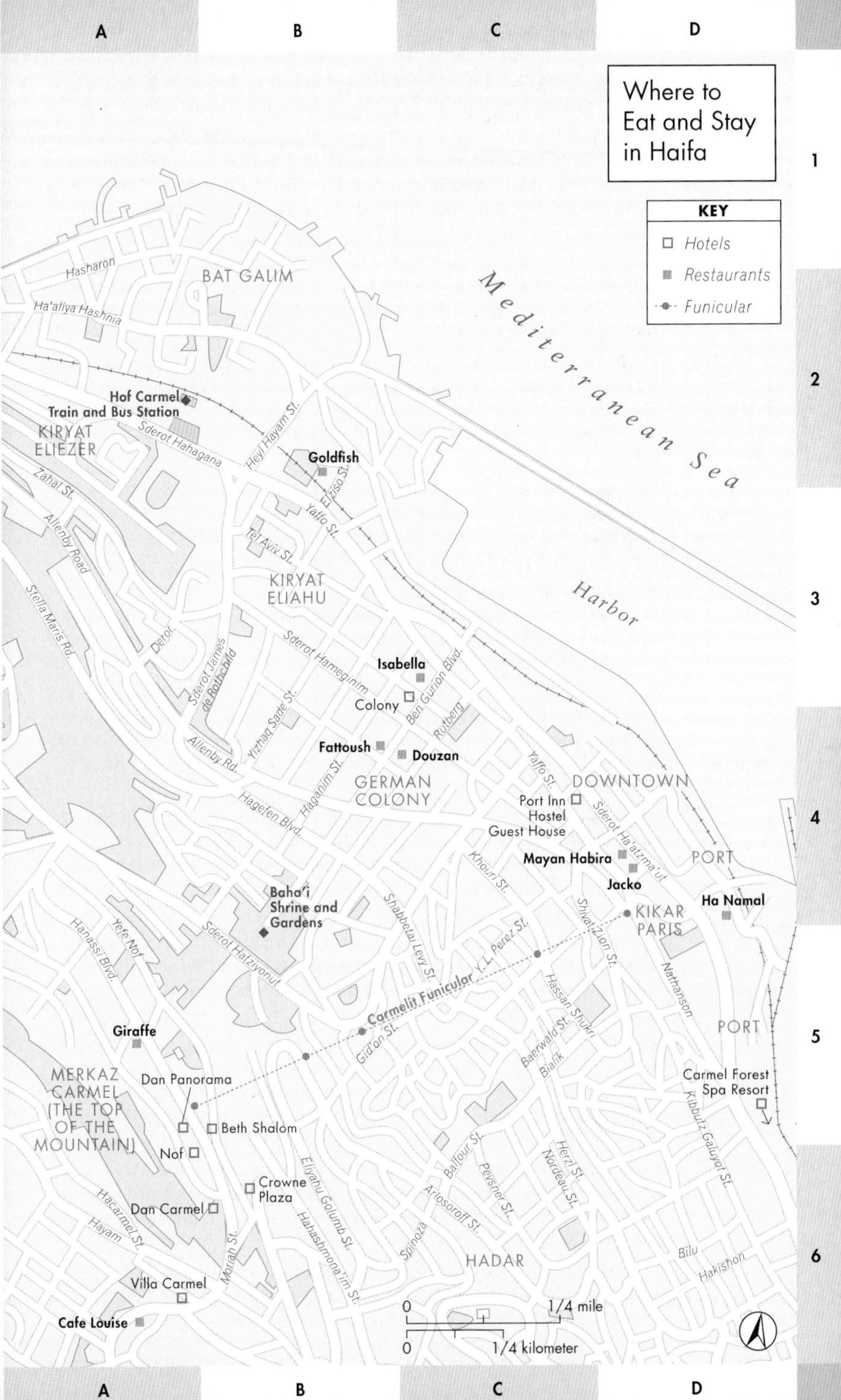

A
B
C
D
Where to Eat and Stay in Haifa
KEY
Hotels
Restaurants
Funicular
1
2
3
4
5
6
Mediterranean Sea
Harbor
Hasharon
BAT GALIM
Ha'aliya Hashnia
Hof Carmel
Train and Bus Station
KIRYAT ELIEZER
Sderot Hahagana
Heyl Hayam St.
Goldfish
Elziso St.
Yaffo St.
Zahal St.
Allenby Road
Tel Aviv St.
KIRYAT ELIAHU
Stella Maris Rd.
Deror
Sderot James de Rothchild
Sderot Hameginim
Isabella
Colony
Ben Gurion Blvd.
Yizhaq Sade St.
Rutberg
Allenby Rd.
Fattoush
Douzan
Haganim St.
GERMAN COLONY
Yaffo St.
DOWNTOWN
Port Inn Hostel Guest House
Hagefen Blvd.
Sderot Ha'atzma'ut
Khouri St.
Mayan Habira
Jacko
PORT
Ha Namal
Baha'i Shrine and Gardens
Shabbetai Levy St.
Y. L. Perez St.
KIKAR PARIS
Hanassi Blvd.
Yefe Nof
Sderot Hatziyonut
Shivat Zion St.
Nathanson
Carmelit Funicular
Hassan Shukri
Giraffe
Gid'on St.
Baerwald St.
Bialik
PORT
Carmel Forest Spa Resort
MERKAZ CARMEL (THE TOP OF THE MOUNTAIN)
Dan Panorama
Beth Shalom
Nof
Balfour St.
Herzl St.
Nordeau St.
Kibbutz Galuyot St.
Crowne Plaza
Elīyahu Golumb St.
Pevsner St.
Hacarmel St.
Dan Carmel
Arlosoroff St.
Hayam
Hahashmona'im St.
Spinoza
Moriah St.
HADAR
Bilu
Hakishon
Villa Carmel
Cafe Louise
0
1/4 mile
0
1/4 kilometer
A
B
C
D

hangout: stainless-steel open kitchen, black tables and chairs, black bar and stools, silver photography-studio ceiling lights, and a staff in bright white T-shirts, jeans, and long black aprons. Noodles are the specialty, and most dishes are prepared in a wok. You might start with a crispy Thai salad in peanut sauce; then feast on spicy Philippine egg noodles with chicken, roast goose, and chopped shrimp in a hot chili sauce. ✉ *131 Hanassi Blvd., Merkaz Carmel* ☎ *04/810–4012* 🌐 *www.restaurants-in-israel.co.il* ▭ *AE, DC, MC, V.* ✣ *5A*

$ SEAFOOD **Goldfish.** Over the shabby doorway, a crooked sign announces that the fish is "fresh every day." That's all you need to know about Goldfish, a bare-bones seafood restaurant. Take a seat at one of the six tables, each covered with rough white paper, and you'll be treated to lots of what Israelis call *salatim*, or little dishes of salads. These delicious nibbles of roast eggplant, fish roe, and hummus come first before the selected main dish. There's no menu in English, and no need for one as only three dishes are offered: shrimp, seafood, and fish. There's no dessert, just jangling-strong espresso. ✉ *26 Elziso St., Downtown* ☎ *04/855-2663* ▭ *No credit cards* ⊙ *Closed Sun.* ✣ *2B*

$$$ MODERN ISRAELI ✕ **Ha Namal.** Careful renovations have transformed this old wheat and corn warehouse in Haifa's rather rundown port into an elegant Tuscan country inn. Climbing the stairs you arrive at five rooms of various sizes (one's the bar, with leather sofas) with original stone floors, brick walls, and lofty ceilings. The inventive chef offers starters such as cream of onion soup with truffle cream and bok choy leaves and entrées such as lamb sirloin in a cashew-pesto crust, or fillet of mullet on cashew risotto, tomato confit, and whipped chive cream. There's a fixed-price lunch and a children's menu. ✉ *24 Hanamal St., off Sha'ar Palmer St., the Port* ☎ *04/862–8899* 🌐 *www.namal24.co.il* ▭ *AE, MC, V* ⊙ *Closed Sun.* ✣ *4D*

$$ ITALIAN ✕ **Isabella.** With walls in muted gray tones, a brushed-cement floor, and dark-wood tables with leather chairs, Isabella is a suitable setting for modern Italian cuisine. Among the appetizers, try the eggplant carpaccio in garlic-lemon tahini sauce or the excellent "stuffed" pizza (filled with, among other choices, ham, mozzarella cheese, grilled eggplant, and tomatoes). Street side on the patio, or inside with the crowd, you can enjoy hearty dishes such as pasta with bacon and forest mushrooms or lamb with rosemary and lemon sauce. Families will be happy with the attentive service. ✉ *6 Ben Gurion Blvd., City Center Mall, German Colony* ☎ *04/855–2201* ✍ *Reservations essential* ▭ *AE, DC, MC, V.* ✣ *3C*

$$ SEAFOOD ✕ **Jacko.** If ever there was a beloved eating place in Haifa, Jacko is it. Give the name to your taxi driver, he'll nod approvingly, gun the motor, and drop you at a nondescript building with a Hebrew sign. Since 1976, this family-run restaurant has been serving delicious food in a rowdy, informal setting with shared tables. The specialties here are fish and seafood served grilled or fried. There are piles of crab, mussels, and calamari served with a variety of sauces, large shrimp grilled in their shells, and Mediterranean lobster (in summer). For dessert try the Turkish cookies or semolina and coconut cake. ✉ *12 Kehilat Saloniki St.,*

Downtown ☎ *04/866–8813* 🌐 *www.asiarooms.com* ✍ *Reservations essential* ▭ *AE, DC, MC, V* ⊙ *No dinner.* ⊕ *4D*

$$ EASTERN EUROPEAN ✕ **Mayan Habira.** If you're looking for meat with a capital *M*, you've found the place. The decor is informal: beer kegs are piled up in a corner; the walls are covered with photos of glowing restaurant reviews and a mural of the customers painted by an art student in 1989. The family-run business has been around since 1962; today Reuven and his son do the excellent cooking. To start, savor chopped liver, jellied calf's foot, gefilte fish, or oxtail soup. Then go to work on delectable pork spareribs or goose or beef pastrami, which they smoke themselves. In the summer, diners sit outside and enjoy live music. It's usually a lunch place, but Tuesday night it's open for dinner. ✉ *4 Nathanson St., Downtown* ☎ *04/862–3193* ▭ *AE, DC, MC, V* ⊙ *Closed Sat. No dinner Wed.–Mon.* ⊕ *4D*

WHERE TO STAY

Haifa's best-known hotels are at the top of the city in the Merkaz Carmel area. The Colony Hotel, one of the city's newest lodgings, is in the downtown area, as is the Port Inn hostel-guesthouse; both offer more affordable stays. Within easy reach of the city, the Carmel Forest Resort Spa is quiet and pampering.

Use the coordinate (⊕ A1) at the end of each listing to locate a site on the corresponding map.

¢ **Beth Shalom.** Plain but pleasant, this Christian-run lodging has three floors of small rooms. Each has wicker furniture, beds with fluffy duvets, and good reading lights. A healthy breakfast is served cafeteria-style, and you can enjoy it on the patio. Beth Shalom is on a busy street, but the front rooms are quiet thanks to the double-glazed windows. **Pros:** central location; modest price. **Cons:** no restaurant; basic decor. ✉ *110 Hanassi Blvd., Merkaz Carmel* ☎ *04/837–7481* 🌐 *www.beth-shalom.co.il* *30 rooms* *In-room: a/c, refrigerator, Wi-Fi. In-hotel: bar, parking (free)* ▭ *AE, DC, MC, V* 🍽 *CP.* ⊕ *5B*

$$$$ Fodor's Choice ★ **Carmel Forest Spa Resort.** Set off by itself in the Carmel Forest, this spa-resort lies 25 km (15 mi) from Haifa. It's the ultimate escape: a handsome, top-of-the-line spa with a tastefully appointed lodging designed to pamper guests in a calm and healthful setting (no cell phones or children under 16). The hotel is on a hillside, with stunning views of pine trees and the Mediterranean. Treatment rooms offer a variety of massages, including aromatherapy, body peels, and seaweed wraps. Green wicker chaises let you relax with a cup of herbal tea as you contemplate nature through the solarium windows. A sample day? Consult the nutritionist, strike out on a forest walk, have a sesame-oil massage, and then sit down to a meal prepared with all-natural ingredients. Day guests are welcome. **Pros:** peaceful setting; lovely forest walks. **Cons:** no public transportation; rather pricey. ✉ *Carmel Forest* ☎ *04/830–7888* 🌐 *www.isrotel.co.il* *126 rooms* *In-room: a/c, safe, Wi-Fi. In-hotel: restaurant, bar, tennis court, pools, gym, spa, bicycles, Internet terminal, parking (free), no kids under 16* ▭ *AE, DC, MC, V* 🍽 *BP.* ⊕ *5D*

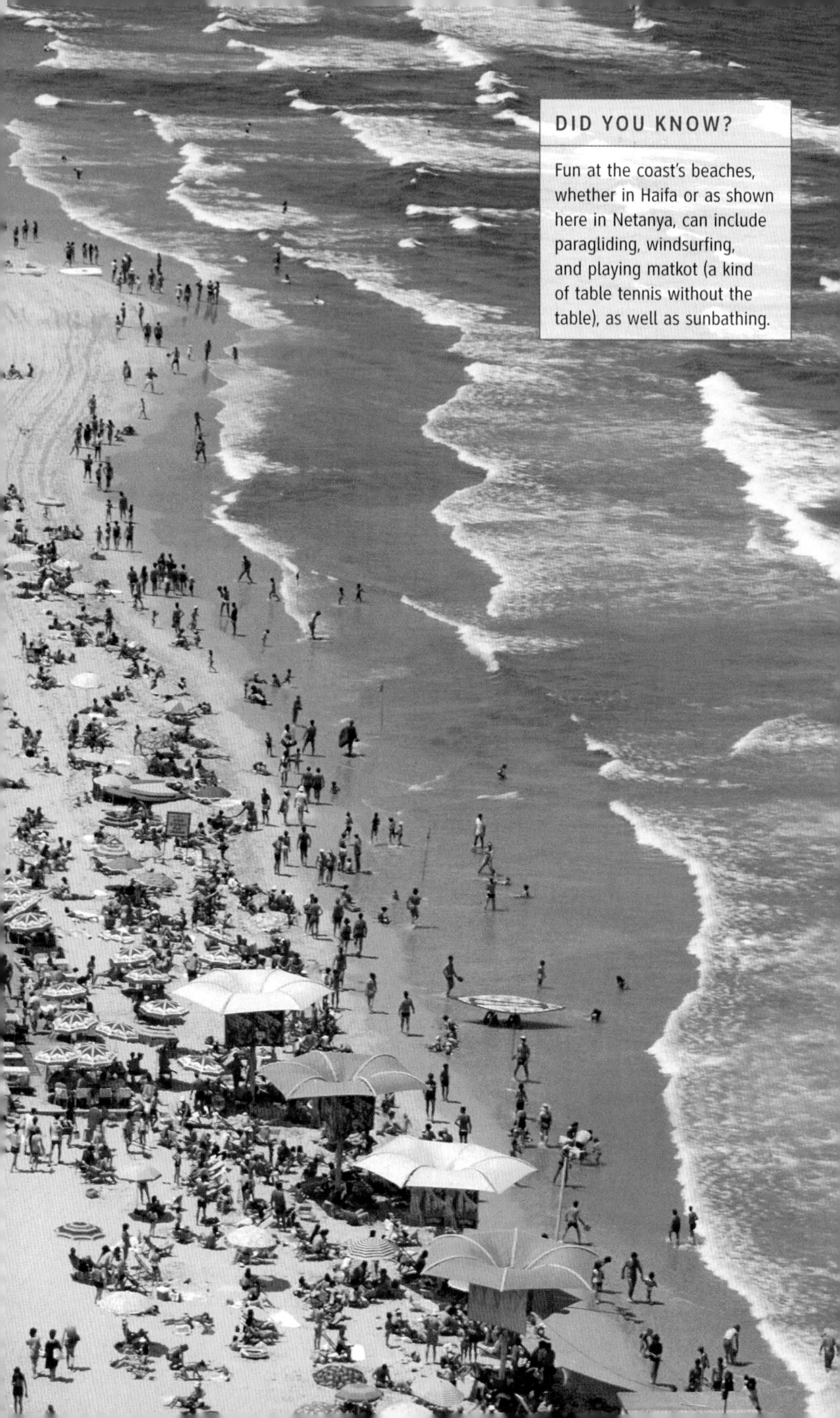

DID YOU KNOW?

Fun at the coast's beaches, whether in Haifa or as shown here in Netanya, can include paragliding, windsurfing, and playing matkot (a kind of table tennis without the table), as well as sunbathing.

$ **Colony.** Step into this palm-shaded courtyard and you're in the world of the German Templers. The five-story lodging is in the center of the German Colony, set amid the neighborhood's carefully restored red-roofed homes. Lovingly renovated in 2009, the hotel's 40 rooms have the original geometric tile floors and other graceful touches. Ask for a room with a gorgeous view of the Baha'i terraces. A dozen rooms have hot tubs, and all have freestanding bathtubs in spacious bathrooms. The rooftop terrace has eye-popping views of the thriving port. Room service is delivered from a nearby restaurant, and breakfast is served in the charming dining room. **Pros:** unique setting; discounts to local restaurants. **Cons:** no pool; no restaurant. ✉ *23 Ben Gurion Blvd., German Colony* ☎ *04/851–3344* 🌐 *www.colony-hotel.co.il* *40 rooms* *In-room: a/c, safe, refrigerator, DVD (some), Wi-Fi. In-hotel: room service, bar, laundry service, Internet terminal, some pets allowed* ▭ *AE, D, DC, MC, V* *BP.* ✥ *3C*

5

$$ **Crowne Plaza.** Catering to a business crowd, this well-designed hotel is built into a pine-shaded slope. The glass-domed lobby has mauve and silver couches set off by floral arrangements in clay pots. The executive floor has a fully equipped 24-hour business center and rooms with fax machines, Internet connections, and trouser presses to keep you looking spiffy. Views from the guest rooms are gorgeous, especially the ones on the sixth floor with balconies. **Pros:** pleasant atmosphere; quiet setting. **Cons:** dark dining room. ✉ *111 Yefe Nof St., Merkaz Carmel* ☎ *04/835–0835* 🌐 *www.holiday-inn.com/haifaisrael* *100 rooms* *In-room: a/c, safe, refrigerator, Internet, WiFi (some). In-hotel: restaurant, room service, bar, pool, gym, spa, Internet terminal, Wi-Fi hotspot, parking (paid)* ▭ *AE, DC, MC, V* *BP.* ✥ *6B*

$$$ **Dan Carmel.** The Dan is beautifully situated on the heights of Merkaz Carmel. One of Haifa's first hotels, this longtime favorite has a stately charm and a devoted staff. The premises could use a renovator's touch, but the deluxe rooms on the upper floors are nicely furnished, with wooden bureaus and satin bedspreads. Other rooms are less luxurious, but they're cheerfully decorated in pastels. All guest rooms have balconies with stunning views over the city or the bay below. The large garden around the pool, with potted geraniums and many trees, is always breezy and pleasant. **Pros:** great views; doting staff. **Cons:** outdated decor; pricey for what you get. ✉ *87 Hanassi Blvd., Merkaz Carmel* ☎ *04/830–6211* 🌐 *www.danhotels.co.il* *204 rooms, 18 suites* *In-room: a/c, safe (some), refrigerator. In-hotel: restaurant, room service, bar, pool, gym, Internet terminal, Wi-Fi hotspot, parking (paid)* ▭ *AE, DC, MC, V* *BP.* ✥ *6B*

$$ **Dan Panorama.** A member of the Dan hotel chain, this one is somewhat glitzier than its sister, the Dan Carmel, up the road. Popular with business executives (especially the comfortable second-floor lobby with its circular bar), the hotel has an established, clubby feel. The rooms are spacious with blue-and-yellow color schemes and pale-wood furnishings. Some look out onto the gold-topped Baha'i Shrine and the bay, while the rest have lovely city views. The hotel is connected to the Panorama Center mall, with casual eateries and boutiques. **Pros:** helpful staff; good reading lights; large fitness center. **Cons:** no balconies; dated decor. ✉ *107 Hanassi Blvd., Merkaz Carmel* ☎ *04/835–2222* 🌐 *www.danhotels.co.il* *266 rooms* *In-room: a/c, safe, refrigerator, Internet, Wi-Fi. In-hotel: restaurant, room service, bar, pool, gym, Internet terminal, parking (paid)* *AE, DC, MC, V* *BP.* *5A*

$ **Nof.** On Merkaz Carmel, these modest guest rooms take full advantage of the setting, with large windows facing the sea. Ask for a room on the fourth, sixth, or seventh floor; they've all been nicely renovated. The lobby lounge, which opens onto the promenade, also has superb views. The friendly front-desk staff is welcoming; the on-site kosher Chinese restaurant makes for a convenient and rewarding dining experience. **Pros:** central location; modest prices. **Cons:** basic rooms; lobby can be noisy; no pool. ✉ *101 Hanassi Blvd., Merkaz Carmel* ☎ *04/835–4311* 🌐 *www.inisrael.com/nof* *80 rooms, 6 suites* *In-room: a/c, refrigerator, safe, Internet (some), Wi-Fi. In-hotel: restaurant, room service, bar, Internet terminal, parking (free)* *AE, DC, MC, V* *BP.* *6A*

¢ **Port Inn Hostel Guest House.** A haven for budget travelers, this inn is in a neighborhood filled with interesting shops. It occupies a beautifully renovated house painted quiet shades of pale yellow. The dormitories mainly interest backpackers (one is for women, one for men, and two are co-ed), but there are 10 double rooms with private bath, and one that has a shared bath. **Pros:** cheerful; good for single travelers. **Cons:** far from tourist sites; not a lot of privacy. ✉ *34 Yaffo St., Downtown* ☎ *04/852–4401* 🌐 *www.portinn.co.il* *10 rooms, 9 with bath* *In-room: a/c, Wi-Fi. In-hotel: bar, laundry service, Internet terminal* *AE, DC, MC, V* *CP.* *4C*

$ **Villa Carmel.** The facade may look ordinary, but this boutique hotel's interior is unlike anything else you'll find in Haifa. The ultramodern rooms are sleek and stylish, with dove gray curtains, gleaming chrome lamps, and black leather hassocks. Many have whirlpool tubs, and some have balconies. A tufted-leather sofa adds a homey touch to the small lobby, while white leather chairs distinguish the glass-enclosed dining room. There's a hot tub and sauna on the rooftop terrace, as well as a pleasant garden outside. The location is ideal, putting you within easy walking distance of shops and restaurants. **Pros:** chic ambience; attention to detail; on a quiet street. **Cons:** no pool; no room service. ✉ *2 Heinrich Heine, Merkaz Carmel* ☎ *04/837–5777* 🌐 *www.villacarmel.co.il* *15 rooms* *In-room: a/c, safe, refrigerator, DVD (some), Wi-Fi. In-hotel: restaurant, bar, laundry service, Internet terminal, parking (free), some pets allowed* *AE, D, DC, MC, V* *BP.* *6A*

NIGHTLIFE AND THE ARTS

Haifa isn't Tel Aviv, but there are a few interesting things to do after dark. For information on performances and other special events in and around Haifa, check Friday's *Jerusalem Post* or the *Haaretz* newspaper; both publish separate weekend entertainment guides. In balmy weather, a stroll along the Louis Promenade and then along Panorama Road, with lovely views of nighttime Haifa, is a relaxing way to end the day.

NIGHTLIFE

For a festive evening, try the restaurants and cafés-cum-pubs in the German Colony. Nightspots in Haifa come and go, and some open only on certain evenings, so call ahead if possible.

The bar at **Barbarossa** (✉ *8 Pica St., Horev* ☎ *04/811–4010*) is on the balcony, where you can enjoy happy hour while soaking up the great view from 6:30 to 9. The bar swings all night.

The lovely **Duke** (✉ *107 Moriah Blvd., Merkaz Carmel* ☎ *04/834–7282*) is old-world European and offers entertainment from noon on.

With the unlikely name of **Frangelico** (✉ *132 Moriah Blvd., Merkaz Carmel* ☎ *04/824–8839*), this bar not only serves every kind of drink imaginable, but dishes up sushi as well.

In the Haifa tradition, **Mydlar's** (✉ *126 Moriah Blvd., Merkaz Carmel* ☎ *04/824–8754*) serves particularly tasty food at the bar. Attracting a younger crowd, this is a warm and inviting place for a drink.

★ One of Haifa's oldest and most reliable bars, the cozy **Pundak Ha Dov** (✉ *135 Hanassi Blvd., Merkaz Carmel* ☎ *04/838–1703*) has live music weekly and tends to fill up with enthusiastic revelers.

BEACH BASICS

Between Tel Aviv and the Lebanese border are miles of beautiful sandy beaches, most of them public and attended by lifeguards from early May to mid-October. Many Israeli beaches are left untended off-season and get pretty grubby, but they're generally cleaned up and well maintained once warm weather returns. Beachside restaurants can make for rough-and-tumble eating because of loud music, but it's fun to eat fresh food by the beach. *Never* swim in the absence of a lifeguard, as the currents and undertows can be dangerous.

THE ARTS

The **Haifa Symphony Orchestra** (✉ *6 Eliyahu Hakim St., French Carmel* ☎ *04/859–9499*) performs at the Haifa Auditorium four to five times a month from October through July. For ticket and performance information, contact the box office.

The **Israel Philharmonic Orchestra** (✉ *138 Hanassi Blvd., Merkaz Carmel* ☎ *04/810–1558*) gives 20 concerts at the Haifa Auditorium from October through July.

SPORTS AND THE OUTDOORS

BEACHES

Haifa's coastline is one fine, sandy public beach after another. They span 5 km (3 mi) of coast and have lifeguard stations, changing rooms, showers, toilets, refreshment stands, sports areas, restaurants, and a winding stone promenade. To be on the safe side, never swim when a lifeguard is not on duty. There is parking at every beach, and all are free. All city beaches are reachable by local buses.

Carmel Beach (✉ *David Elazar St., South Haifa*) sits in front of the Leonardo Hotel at the southern entrance to Haifa. Although there's a lifeguard, it doesn't have the amenities of Dado and Zamir.

On Saturday at **Dado Beach** (✉ *David Elazar St., South Haifa*), Israelis of all ages come and folk dance, to the delight of onlookers. You'll also find exercise equipment near the water and a small bathing pool for young children.

North of the Leonardo Hotel, **Hof HaShaket** (✉ *David Elazar St., South Haifa*) offers separate gender days: Sunday, Tuesday, and Thursday for women; Monday, Wednesday, and Friday for men; Saturday for whomever.

Zamir Beach (✉ *David Elazar St., South Haifa*), near Dado Beach, is regarded as one of the best Haifa beaches, with fine golden sand and many amenities, including coffeehouses and restaurants.

DIVING

At **Ze'ev Ha Yam** (✉ *Kishon Fishing Harbor and Marina, Kishon Park, Haifa Port* ☎ *04/832–3911*), which means "Wolf of the Sea," you can sign up for a half-day introductory class or rent equipment and sail out to a dive site where you'll see underwater caves and a shipwreck. The staff is happy to pick you up at your hotel.

SHOPPING

Haifa is studded with modern shopping malls with boutiques, eateries, and movie theaters plus drugstores, photography stores, and money-exchange desks.

SHOPPING CENTERS

Near the Hof Carmel railway station, a popular mall called **Castra** (✉ *8 Fliman St., South Haifa* ☎ *04/859–0000*) sells local art and is filled with jewelry and clothing stores.

Near the hotels on Mt. Carmel is the **Panorama Center** (✉ *109 Hanassi Blvd., Merkaz Carmel* ☎ *04/837–5011*). Travelers will find everything from a pharmacy and newspaper stand to a wine outlet and clothing shops.

SPECIALTY STORES

Amira's IOS Gallery (✉ *55 Ben Gurion Blvd., opposite the tourism office, German Colony* ☎ *04/850–7504*) has lovely glass art, jewelry, and souvenirs; Amira's workshop is behind the shop.

★ **Sara's Gift Shop** (✉ *Dan Carmel Hotel, 85–87 Hanassi Blvd., Merkaz Carmel* ☎ *04/830–6238*) is crammed with jewelry made exclusively for this boutique; the silver and Roman glass pieces are unique. Other choices are Judaica and gifts for Baha'i visitors.

THE NORTHERN COAST

Beaches abound, the sea sparkles, and skies are sunny most of the year in this area of the northern coast that lies south of Haifa. Archaeological sites, such as the outstanding Roman, Byzantine, and Crusader ruins at Caesarea, are not just dusty old ruins but rather beautiful restored treasures, and historical museums are fun and not fusty. Netanya and Nahsholim-Dor have plenty for the sun and fun seeker, including paragliding and other adventures. Fresh fish, seafood, and good local wine please every palate.

NAHSHOLIM-DOR

29 km (19 mi) south of Haifa.

The beautiful beach at Dor is fit for a king—not surprising since it has a royal history. Founded 3,500 years ago, biblical Dor was once the maritime capital of the Carmel coast. Its small bay made it the best harbor between Jaffa and Akko and thus a target for many imperial ambitions, from the ancient Egyptians and the "Sea Peoples" through to King Solomon and on down. It was renowned in antiquity for its precious purple dye; reserved for royalty, this hue was extracted from a mollusk that was abundant along the coast.

GETTING HERE AND AROUND

Take Route 2, getting off at the Zichron Ya'akov exit. At the Fureidis Junction, travel north about 1 km (½ mi) until you reach the small sign for Nahsholim-Dor. There is no public transportation to this place.

EXPLORING

★ **Nahsholim-Dor Museum.** Well worth a visit, this museum holds a rich trove of finds from both local nautical digs and excavations at nearby Tel Dor. It's in the partly restored former glass factory opened by Baron Edmond de Rothschild in 1891 to serve the wineries of nearby Zichron Ya'akov. The sequence of peoples who settled, conquered, or passed through Dor—from the Canaanites to Napoléon—can be traced through these artifacts. Of particular interest is the bronze cannon that Napoléon's vanquished troops dumped into the sea during their retreat from Akko to Egypt in May 1799. An interesting film in English illuminates the history of the ancient city of Dor. ✉ *Kibbutz Nahsholim, Rd. 7011* ☎ *04/639–0950* *NIS 20* ⏲ *Sun.–Thurs. 9–2, Fri. 9–1, Sat. 10:30–3.*

WHERE TO EAT AND STAY

$ ISRAELI ✕ **Pikalily–Sahara.** Grab a table on the deck at this raucous beach bar and you'll soon be enjoying cool ocean breezes. Israeli beach fare is on offer here, so order a tasty melted cheese on a seeded roll (called "cheese toast"), fresh fillet of salmon, or a meaty kebab. Polish off your meal with a glass of wine or knock back a beer at the bar. ✉ *Dor Beach* ☎ *No phone* *AE, DC, MC, V.*

$$ **Nahsholim Hotel.** You'd have to travel quite a distance to find a prettier beach than this one. Low-slung buildings contain standard rooms (many with sea views) and apartments with room for up to five people. Breakfast is included in the rate; for other meals you can enjoy seaside eating at the restaurant at nearby Dor Beach. Small islets just off the

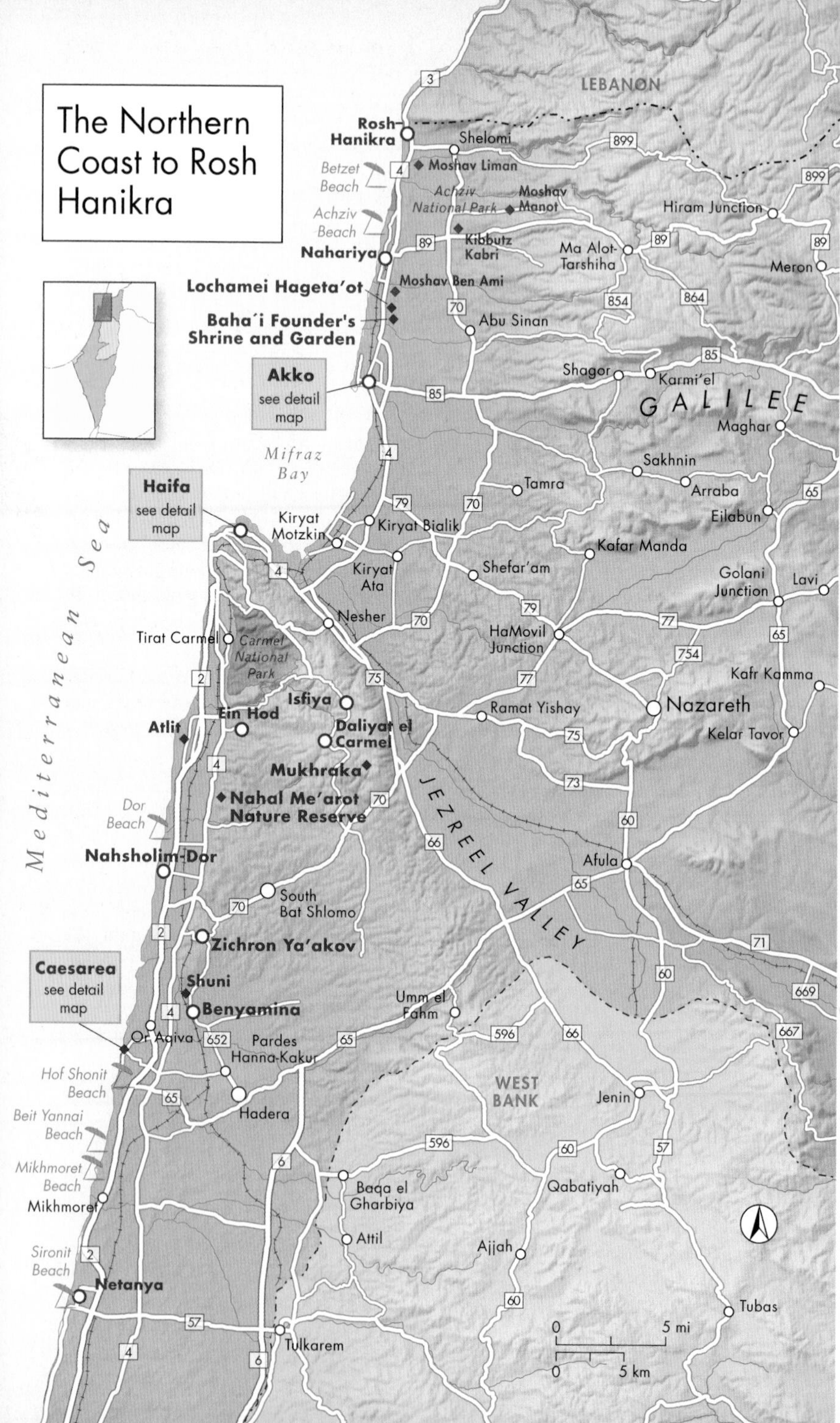

The Northern Coast to Rosh Hanikra
LEBANON
Rosh Hanikra
Shelomi
Betzet Beach
Moshav Liman
Achziv National Park
Moshav Manot
Achziv Beach
Kibbutz Kabri
Hiram Junction
Nahariya
Ma Alot-Tarshiha
Meron
Lochamei Hageta'ot
Moshav Ben Ami
Baha'i Founder's Shrine and Garden
Abu Sinan
Akko
see detail map
Shagor
Karmi'el
GALILEE
Maghar
Mifraz Bay
Sakhnin
Tamra
Arraba
Haifa
see detail map
Eilabun
Kiryat Motzkin
Kiryat Bialik
Kafar Manda
Kiryat Ata
Shefar'am
Golani Junction
Lavi
Mediterranean Sea
Nesher
Tirat Carmel
Carmel National Park
HaMovil Junction
Kafr Kamma
Isfiya
Ramat Yishay
Nazareth
Ein Hod
Atlit
Daliyat el Carmel
Kelar Tavor
Mukhraka
Nahal Me'arot Nature Reserve
Dor Beach
JEZREEL VALLEY
Nahsholim-Dor
Afula
South Bat Shlomo
Zichron Ya'akov
Caesarea
see detail map
Shuni
Benyamina
Umm el Fahm
Or Aqiva
Pardes Hanna-Kakur
Hof Shonit Beach
WEST BANK
Jenin
Hadera
Beit Yannai Beach
Mikhmoret Beach
Mikhmoret
Baqa el Gharbiya
Qabatiyah
Attil
Sironit Beach
Ajjah
Netanya
Tubas
Tulkarem
0
5 mi
0
5 km

coast attract nesting birds and give nature watchers plenty to see in spring and fall. **Pros:** fabulous beach; family-friendly vibe. **Cons:** expensive for what you get. ✉ *Kibbutz Nahsholim, Rd. 7011* ☎ *04/639–9533* 🌐 *www.nahsholim.co.il* *41 rooms, 48 apartments* *In-room: refrigerator, Wi-Fi (some). In-hotel: restaurant, tennis court, Internet terminal, Wi-Fi hotspot* *AE, DC, MC, V* *BP.*

SPORTS AND THE OUTDOORS

★ **Dor Beach** (✉ *Off Rte. 4*), also known as Tantura Beach, is a dreamy stretch of beige sand. Rocky islets form breakwaters that provide calm seas for happy bathers. Amenities are ample: lifeguards in season, chair and umbrella rentals, a first-aid station, a restaurant, parking, and changing rooms and showers. The beach, beside Kibbutz Nahsholim, gets crowded on summer weekends and holidays.

Paradive (✉ *Habonim Beach, off Rte. 4* ☎ *04/639–1068* 🌐 *www.paradive.co.il*) offers thrills and chills with tandem skydives over the Mediterranean. It's about 3 km (2 mi) north of Kibbutz Nahsholim.

★ Kurt Raveh, a diver-archaeologist and resident of Kibbutz Nahsholim, runs the **Underwater Archaeological Center** (☎ *052/279–6695* 🌐 *www.northern-wind.com*). Raveh conducts underwater expeditions and "dives into history" where divers (even those without experience) get to tour ancient shipwrecks under his experienced eye. You can also arrange kayaking trips along the coast.

EN ROUTE

Atlit is a peninsula with the jagged remains of an important Crusader castle. Of more recent vintage, to the west (about 1,500 feet from the highway), is the **Atlit detention camp.** It was used by the British to house refugees smuggled in during and after World War II. The reconstructed barracks, fences, and watchtowers stand as reminders of how Jewish immigration was practically outlawed under the British Mandate after the publication of the infamous White Paper in 1939. More than a third of the 120,000 illegal immigrants to Palestine passed through the camp from 1934 to 1948. The authenticity of the exhibit is striking: it was re-created from accounts of actual detainees and their contemporaries; you'll see the living quarters, complete with laundry hanging from the rafters. The camp is 15 km (9 mi) south of Haifa. ✉ *Rte. 2* ☎ *04/984–1980* *NIS 17* *Sun.–Thurs. 9–4, Fri. 9–12:30.*

CAESAREA

49 km (29½ mi) south of Haifa.

Caesarea is most famous for its sprawling archaeological site full of intriguing Roman, Byzantine, and Crusader ruins. Near the archaeological site is the modern community of Caesarea, a group of homes on the sea. Here you'll find the Ralli Museum and the famed Roman aqueduct.

GETTING HERE AND AROUND

A car is your best option for reaching Caesarea. It's off Route 2, about one hour by car from Tel Aviv or Haifa. You can also opt for a guided bus tour with Egged Tours or United Tours, two well-regarded companies.

5

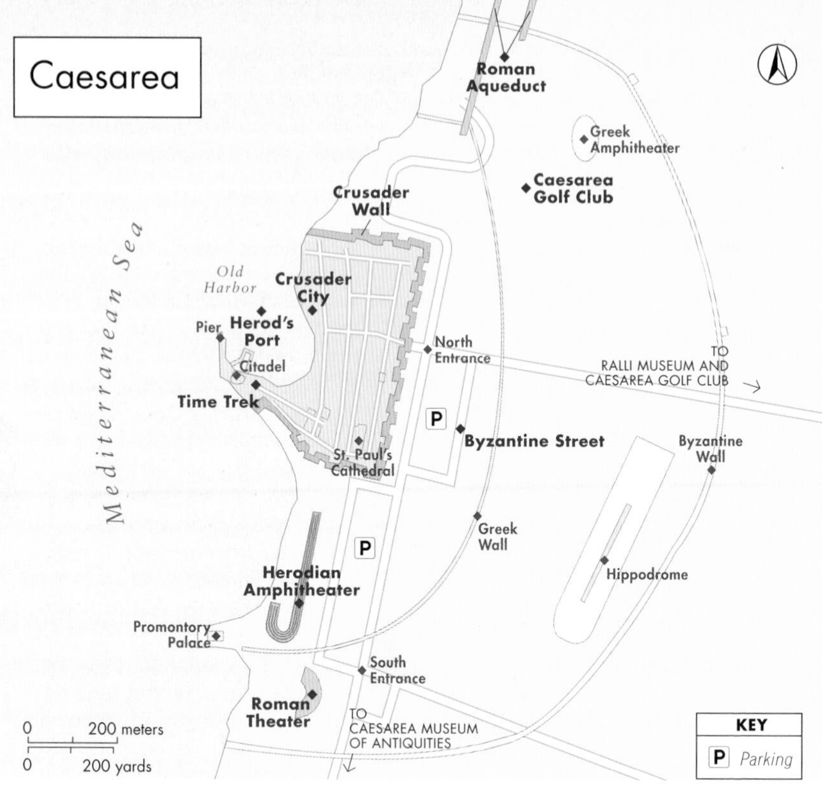

ESSENTIALS

Tour Contacts **Egged Tours** (☎ *03/920–3919* 🌐 *www.eggedtours.com*). **United Tours** (☎ *03/617–3315* 🌐 *www.unitedtours.co.il*).

EXPLORING

Fodor'sChoice ★ **Caesarea.** By turns an ancient Roman port city, a Byzantine capital, and a Crusader stronghold, Caesarea is one of the country's major archaeological sites. There's no need to think of this as "dusty piles of stones." It is a delightful place to spend up to a day of leisurely sightseeing among the fascinating ruins. You can browse in souvenir shops and art galleries, swim at the beach, snorkel or dive around a submerged port, or enjoy a seaside meal. Caesarea is an easy day trip from Tel Aviv and Haifa, or even Jerusalem.

There are two entrances to this intriguing site. A good strategy is to start at the Roman Theater, at the southern entrance. After exploring, you can then leave through the northern entrance. If you're short on time, enter through the northern entrance and take a quicker tour of the site. At either entrance, pick up the free brochure and map.

Entry to the **Roman Theater** is through one of the vomitoria (arched tunnels that served as entrances for the public). Herod's theaters—here and elsewhere in Israel—were the first of their kind in the ancient Near East. The theater today seats 3,600 and is a spectacular venue for

CLOSE UP

Herod's Amazing Port at Caesarea

The port's construction at Caesarea was an unprecedented challenge—there was no artificial harbor of this size anywhere in the world. During preliminary underwater digs in 1978, archaeologists were stunned to discover concrete blocks near the breakwater offshore, indicating the sophisticated use of hydraulic concrete (which hardens underwater).

Historians knew that the Romans had developed such techniques, but before the discoveries at Caesarea, they never knew hydraulic concrete to have been used on such a massive scale. The main ingredient in the concrete, volcanic ash, was probably imported from Italy's Mt. Vesuvius, as were the wooden forms. Teams of professional divers actually did much of the trickiest work, laying the foundations hundreds of yards offshore.

Once finished, two massive breakwaters—one stretching west and then north from the Citadel restaurant some 1,800 feet and the other 600 feet long, both now submerged—sheltered an area of about 3½ acres from the waves and tides.

Two towers, each mounted by three colossal statues, marked the entrance to the port; and although neither the towers nor the statues have been found, a tiny medal bearing their image was discovered in the first underwater excavations here, in 1960. The finished harbor also contained the dominating temple to Emperor Augustus and cavernous storage facilities along the shore.

summer concerts and performances. What you see today is predominantly a reconstruction. Only a few of the seats of the *cavea* (where the audience sat) near the orchestra are original, in addition to some of the stairs and the decorative wall at the front of the stage.

The huge **Herodian Amphitheater** is a horseshoe-shape stadium with sloping sides filled with rows of stone seats. It's most likely the one mentioned by 1st-century AD historian Josephus Flavius in *The Jewish War.* A crowd of 10,000 watched horse and chariot races and various sporting events here some 2,000 years ago. Up the wooden steps, you'll see the street's beautiful and imaginative mosaic floors in the bathhouse complex of the Roman-Byzantine administrative area.

King Louis IX of France built the walls that surround the **Crusader City.** The bulk of what you see today—the moat, escarpment, citadel, and walls, which once contained 16 towers—dates from 1251, when the French king actually spent a year pitching in with his own two hands to help restore the existing fortifications. As you enter the southern wall gate of the Crusader city, you'll see the remains of an unfinished cathedral; the three graceful curves of its apses stand out.

At the observation point you can gaze out over the remains of **Herod's Port,** once a magnificent sight that writers of the day compared to Athens's port of Piraeus. An earthquake devastated the harbor in AD 130, which is why the Crusaders utilized only a small section of it when they conquered the city in 1101.

Caesarea. "We stumbled upon this field of flowers by the ruins." —photo by mgplessner, Fodors.com member

When you're exploring the harbor area, don't miss the **Time Trek.** Inside, you'll meet Caesarea's fascinating historic personages—among them Herod the Great, Rabbi Akiva, and St. Paul. These realistic-looking, larger-than-life figures can answer all kinds of questions you might have about their long-ago lives in Caesarea. Now climb the stairs of the nearby squarish stone tower with glass windows, on the pier sticking out into the harbor. Here you can view an intriguing three-dimensional animation on giant screens that explains the amazing construction of the port.

East of the northern entrance to the site, a fenced-in area encloses Caesarea's **Byzantine Street.** It was during the Byzantine period and in late Roman times that Caesarea thrived as a center of Christian scholarship. In the 7th century, Caesarea had a famous library of some 30,000 volumes that originated with the collection of the Christian philosopher Origen (185–254), who lived in Caesarea for two decades. Towering over the street are two headless marble statues, probably carted here from nearby Roman temples. The provenance of the milky white statue is unknown; Emperor Hadrian might have commissioned the reddish figure facing it when he visited Caesarea.

A wonderful finale to your trip to Caesarea, especially at sunset, is the beachfront **Roman Aqueduct.** The chain of arches tumbling northward until they disappear beneath the sand is a captivating sight. During Roman times, the demand for a steady water supply was considerable, but the source was a spring about 13 km (8 mi) away in the foothills of Mt. Carmel. Workers had to cut a channel approximately 6½ km (4 mi) long through solid rock before the water was piped into the aqueduct. In the 2nd century, Hadrian doubled its capacity by adding a new channel. Today you can walk along the aqueduct and see marble plaques dedicated to support the troops of various legions who toiled here. ☎ *04/636–1010* 🌐 *www.parks.org.il* 🎫 *NIS 36* ⏲ *Oct.–Mar., daily 8–4; Apr.–Sept., daily 8–5.*

Caesarea Museum of Antiquities. Just outside Caesarea, this excellent museum houses many of the artifacts found by kibbutz members as they plowed their fields in the 1940s. The small museum has arguably the best collection of late-Roman sculpture in Israel; impressive holdings of rare Roman and Byzantine gemstones; and a large variety of coins minted in Caesarea over the ages, as well as oil lamps, urns excavated from the sea floor, and fragments of jewelry. ✉ *Kibbutz Sdot Yam, near southern entrance to Caesarea* ☎ *04/636–4367* 🌐 *www.parks.org.il* 🎫 *NIS 13* ⏲ *Tues.–Thurs. 10–4, Fri. 10–1.*

Ralli Museum. Once you've entered Caesarea's villa area you can't miss the two Spanish-style buildings of the Ralli Museum, with their red-tiled roofs and expansive terraces. One of these dazzlingly white buildings houses an exhibit on the ancient city's history. The second building examines Spanish Jewry in the Middle Ages. It's a pleasure to wander along the walls of the courtyard and gaze at the sculptures of various dignitaries such as Maimonides and Nostradamus. Inside are paintings with biblical themes by European artists of the 16th to 18th centuries. ✉ *Rothschild Blvd.* ☎ *04/626–1013* 🎫 *Free* ⏲ *Mar.–Dec., Mon., Tues., Thurs., and Fri. 10:30–3; Jan. and Feb., Fri. and Sat. 10:30–3.*

WHERE TO EAT

$ AMERICAN ✕ **Agenda.** If you're one of those people who could eat breakfast three times a day, Agenda is for you. Try *shakshuka*, a local dish in which eggs are poached in a sharp tomato sauce. For lunch and dinner there are also sandwiches, salads, pizzas, and other light fare, plus cocktails and wine. The staff is friendly, the ambience casual. ✉ *Off Rte. 2* ☎ *04/626–2092* 💳 *AE, DC, MC, V* ⏲ *No dinner Fri. No lunch Sat.*

$$$ SEAFOOD ✕ **Crusaders' Restaurant.** You can depend on satisfying, tasty fare at this cavernous seaside restaurant. Expect the menu to include plenty of fresh seafood, caught right from the sea below, as well as juicy steaks and kebabs. An excellent starter is the salad of grilled eggplant, hummus, and fried cauliflower, with crunchy pita rounds toasted with olive oil and local spices served alongside. House specialties include baked red snapper topped with chopped vegetables, or black mussels sautéed in garlic, butter, and wine. Still hungry? Creamy cheesecake or warm apple pie with ice cream does the trick. ✉ *Northern end of the port* ☎ *04/636–1679* 💳 *AE, DC, MC, V.*

$$$ MEDITERRANEAN Fodor's Choice ★ ✕ **Helena.** Two of Israel's best-known culinary personalities opened this restaurant, aiming to create a first-rate yet affordable dining experience. It occupies a beautifully restored stone building in the ancient port. Large windows everywhere maximize the sea view under a wooden pergola. The chef specializes in Mediterranean-style cooking, turning out such tantalizing appetizers as calamari with lemon and hyssop leaves on sheep's milk yogurt, and sliced sirloin in aged balsamic vinegar with Cambozola cheese and pistachios. Main dishes include an aromatic fish stew made of red mullet, spinach, and Swiss chard, and grilled *barbuni*

CLOSE UP

Caesarea: Roman City

Herod the Great gave Caesarea its name, dedicating the magnificent Roman city he built to his patron, Augustus Caesar. It was the Roman emperor who had crowned Herod—born to an Idumean family that had converted to Judaism—King of the Jews around 30 BC.

Construction began in 22 BC; Herod spared nothing in his elaborate designs for the port and the city itself, which included palaces, temples, a theater, a marketplace, a hippodrome, and water and sewage systems. When Caesarea was completed 12 years later, only Jerusalem outshined it. Its population under Herod grew to around 100,000, and the city covered some 164 acres.

In AD 6, a decade after Herod died, Caesarea became the seat of the Roman procurators, one of whom was Pontius Pilate, governor of Judea when Jesus was crucified. With Jerusalem predominantly Jewish, the Romans preferred the Hellenistic Caesarea, with its Jewish minority, as the seat of their administration.

Religious harmony did not prevail. The mixed population of Jews and Gentiles (mainly Greeks and Syrians) repeatedly clashed, with hostilities exploding during the Jewish revolt of AD 66. Vespasian, proclaimed emperor by his legions in AD 69, squelched the first Jewish rebellion. A year later, his son and coruler, Titus, captured and razed Jerusalem and celebrated his suppression of the Jewish revolt.

Henceforth Caesarea was a Roman colony and the local Roman capital of Palestine for nearly 600 years. It was here that Peter converted the Roman centurion Cornelius to Christianity—a milestone in the spread of the new faith—and Paul preached and was imprisoned for two years. In the 2nd century, Rabbi Akiva, the spiritual mentor of the Bar Kochba revolt, was tortured to death here.

(sardine-sized fish). The wine room holds the chef's private collection. A children's menu is available. ✉ *Southern end of the port* ☎ *04/610–1018* ▭ *AE, DC, MC, V.*

$$ JAPANESE ✕ **Minato.** With a name that means "port" in Japanese, Minato is perfect for beachgoers craving sushi. The restaurant does a brisk takeout business, serving sashimi and nigiri as well as a variety of tempura dishes. You can also eat in at the long sushi bar and watch the knives flash in front of you. ✉ *Rte. 2* ☎ *04/636–0812* ▭ *AE, DC, MC, V* ⊙ *No dinner Fri. No lunch Sat.*

WHERE TO STAY

$$ **Dan Caesarea.** Equidistant from Tel Aviv and Haifa, this chain hotel suits business executives and vacationers alike. The 15 acres of rolling green lawns, the sparkling swimming pool, and the nearby golf course make it great for families. All the guest rooms in this four-story hotel have balconies overlooking the sea or the countryside. Especially recommended are the comfortable deluxe doubles, with marble bathrooms and modern decor in cheerful hues. The hotel is a short drive to the beach and Caesarea. Bikes are on hand for riding around in the conveniently flat countryside. **Pros:** beautiful grounds; family-friendly

vibe; helpful staff. **Cons:** no public transportation; far from restaurants. ✉ *1 Rothschild St., Caesarea* ☎ *04/626–9111* 🌐 *www.danhotels.com* *111 rooms, 3 suites* *In-room: a/c, safe, refrigerator, Wi-Fi. In-hotel: restaurant, room service, bar, tennis courts, pool, gym, spa, Internet terminal, parking (free)* *AE, DC, MC.*

SPORTS AND THE OUTDOORS

BEACHES

★ In a calm, sandy cove in Caesarea's ancient harbor, the **Caesarea Beach Club** (✉ *Northern entrance to archaeological site*) has chairs, umbrellas, and showers. A lifeguard is on duty in season, and the restaurant sells sandwiches and other light fare. Admission is NIS 25.

The largest and most popular beach in the area is **Hof Shonit** (✉ *South of archaeological site*). There are lifeguards in season, a refreshment stand, and a restaurant, as well as restrooms and cold showers. Parking is NIS 15.

At the **Roman Aqueduct** (✉ *North of archaeological site*) is a spacious beach with the dramatic backdrop of arches disappearing into the sand. The amenities, however, are limited to restrooms. There is no entrance fee, and there's plenty of parking. The beach and swimming area have been cleared of rocks and debris, but swimming outside the designated area is prohibited. Never swim unless the seasonal lifeguard is on duty.

GOLF

The country's only 18-hole golf course is the **Caesarea Golf Club** (✉ *Off Rte. 2* ☎ *04/617–4444* 🌐 *www.caesarea.com*), adjacent to the Dan Caesarea. Noted golf course architect Pete Dye remodeled the course to high standards in 2009. Greens fees are NIS 460 on weekdays, NIS 520 on weekends. There's also a shop and a restaurant.

At the nine-hole **Ga'ash Golf Club** (✉ *Off Rte. 2* ☎ *09/951–5111* 🌐 *www.golfgaash.co.il*), you can play a second time from alternative tees to make for an 18-hole experience. Greens fees are NIS 300 for nine holes on weekdays and NIS 375 on weekends. There's a shop and a restaurant here, too.

SCUBA DIVING

★ **Old Caesarea Diving Center** (✉ *Caesarea harbor, behind Time Trek* ☎ *04/626–5898* 🌐 *www.caesarea-diving.com*) runs a full range of diving courses for novices, experts, and everyone in between. Snorkelers are welcome, and divers can use a plastic map to follow a route of numbered artifacts in the submerged port built by King Herod 2,000 years ago. Introductory dives range from NIS 210 to NIS 350.

NETANYA

65 km (43 mi) south of Haifa, 30 km (18 mi) north of Tel Aviv.

Netanya has a pretty seaside promenade along the cliffs, endless sandy beaches, a pleasant town square, and plenty of cafés and restaurants. Once a sleepy place surrounded by orange groves, the town—named after Jewish philanthropist Nathan Strauss—has steadily grown from a few settlers in 1929 to some 200,000 residents today.

5

Though citrus farming is still evident on Netanya's outskirts, there are few traces of small-town charm. Tracts of residential development during the past five years or so can be seen all along the southern approach to the city following the shoreline, with high-rise towers dotting the landscape, many of the apartment units bought by vacationers from abroad.

GETTING HERE AND AROUND

To get here by car from Tel Aviv or Haifa, take coastal Route 2. Trains from Haifa depart on the hour and take about 25 minutes. Egged buses from Haifa leave at least every 30 minutes and take 1 hour 40 minutes.

ESSENTIALS

Vistor Information **Netanya Tourist Information Office** (✉ *12 Ha'atzmaut Sq.* ☎ *09/882–7286* 🌐 *www.gonetanya.com*).

EXPLORING

Ha'atzmaut Square. Benches set among the palm trees surround a large fountain at this lively square. Its open-air cafés and restaurants are crowded from the morning until late into the evening. Netanya attracts droves of French visitors, and in summer their lilting tones float above the café au lait and croissants. Saturday night is enlivened by folk dancing, and the amphitheater hosts free concerts in summer and an arts-and-crafts fair on Friday morning.

NEED A BREAK?

Cool off at Tony's Ice Café (✉ *Ha'atzmaut Sq., near Dizengoff St.*) with divine authentic gelati in a huge array of flavors, all made by hand by a family of immigrants from Italy. Tony's also has a wide selection of coffees, milkshakes, and pastries.

★ **Seaside Promenade.** Also known as "the boulevard," the seaside promenade extends north and south of the city for a total of about 6 km (4 mi). This beautifully landscaped walkway winds around the contours of the cliffs overlooking the sea; at every angle there's a different gorgeous view. It's dotted with pergola-shaded benches, colorful playground areas on soft groundcover, and waving palm trees. An elevator at the center of the promenade eases the climb up and down the seaside cliff, and a bridge offers a bird's-eye view of the coastline.

WHERE TO EAT

$$$ STEAK ✕ **El Gaucho.** Tucked into the Carmel Hotel, El Gaucho is one of Israel's best kosher steak houses. Decorated in a rustic style, the restaurant is dominated by a dramatic view of the sea. South American–style meat specialties, among them thick slabs of beef, are cooked over embers on a giant grill. Juicy steaks, grilled fish, and chicken (often done on a spit) are highlights, and the wine list is extensive. ✉ *Carmel Hotel, Oved ben Ami St.* ☎ *09/884–1264* 🌐 *www.el-gaucho.co.il* *Reservations essential* 💳 *AE, DC, MC, V* ⊗ *No dinner Fri. No lunch Sat.*

$$ FRENCH ✕ **Mul Hayam.** On a cliff overlooking the sea, this eatery has a wonderful view from every table. Its menu has a French accent: trout amandine in butter and herbs, for example, and mushroom or spinach quiches. There's also an extensive wine menu. Seating is available in an outdoor plaza or in the dining room with its comfortable upholstered banquettes.

During the Jewish holiday of Purim, revelers in Netanya and around the country dress up in costume.

✉ *1 King David Plaza, Gan Hamelech* ☎ *09/884–5885* 🌐 *www.mulhayam.com* 💳 *AE, DC, MC, V* ⏲ *No dinner Fri. Closed Sat.*

$$ MEDITERRANEAN ✕ **Myriam's Grill.** A stone's throw from the main approach to the beach, this eatery on Ha'atzmaut Square faces a bubbling fountain. Moroccan-style grilled fish and lamb dishes are served both indoors and outdoors. Appetites sharpened by sea breezes and splashes in the surf will be rewarded with appetizers like creamy hummus, tasty couscous, or shakshuka. Main dishes are served with crispy fries or green salads. Wine and beer are provided. ✉ *7 Ha'atzmaut Sq.* ☎ *09/834–1376* 💳 *AE, DC, MC, V* ⏲ *No dinner Fri. No lunch Sat..*

$$ SEAFOOD ✕ **Rosemarine.** At this unpretentious heaven for fish lovers, you can enjoy fresh and tasty fare as you sit indoors or on the terrace overlooking the famous promenade. The kitchen serves a wide range of fish dishes, such as tilapia and gray mullet, which are grilled, baked, or sautéed. Entrées come with salad or roasted potatoes. ✉ *8 Nitza Blvd.* ☎ *09/832–3322* 🌐 *www.restaurants-in-israel.co.il* 💳 *AE, DC, MC, V* ⏲ *Closed weekends.*

WHERE TO STAY

$ **Mizpeh Yam.** Don't expect luxury at this family-owned hotel. What you can count on is good value and a warm welcome. The rooms are compact but have modern furnishings; the entrance has pleasant sitting areas on an attractive veranda. There's no pool, though the beach is a few minutes away. There's a sundeck on the roof, and self-service coffee machines are in the hallways. **Pros:** near the promenade; near the beach. **Cons:** no sea views; basic decor. ✉ *1 Jabotinsky St.* ☎ *09/862–3730* *www.mizpe-yam.co.il* *30 rooms* *In-room: a/c, safe, refrigerator. In-hotel: restaurant, Wi-Fi hotspot* *AE, DC, MC, V* *BP.*

$$$$ **Seasons Netanya.** Consistently good service is the hallmark of this hotel. Guest rooms are spacious, with private terraces and sea views; the bathrooms are luxurious. Eight garden rooms surround the pool, and suites are big enough to accommodate couples with three or four children. The pool (open all year, but not heated in winter) overlooks the sea and is surrounded by colorful gardens and yellow chaise lounges. A nicely furnished lobby features live piano music in the evening. **Pros:** plenty for kids to do; sea views. **Cons:** not for those seeking peace and quiet. *1 Nice Blvd.* *09/860–1555* *www.seasons.co.il* *103 rooms, 45 suites* *In-room: a/c, safe, refrigerator. In-hotel: 2 restaurants, room service, bar, tennis court, pool, gym, children's programs (ages 3–11), laundry service, Internet terminal, Wi-Fi hotspot* *AE, DC, MC, V.*

SPORTS AND THE OUTDOORS

BEACHES

Showers, restrooms and changing rooms, lifeguards, and first-aid stations are available free at all of Netanya's beaches, which cover 14 km (8½ mi) of soft, sandy coastline. Most beaches rent beach chairs and umbrellas.

★ The main beach, **Sironit** (*Gad Machness St.*), is the largest stretch of sand on the Netanya coast. An elevator takes you down the seaside cliff to this beach. There are two cafés and two drink kiosks with seating inside and out. The parking lot is on the beach, just south of Ha'atzmaut Square. It costs NIS 15 per car.

North of town is the Orthodox beach **Kiryat Sanz** (*Nitza Blvd.*), where men and women have different bathing days and hours.

Herzl (*Ha'atzmaut Square*) has a broad staircase that leads down to the beach. For fitness nuts there's a shaded exercise area with all sorts of equipment and a paved basketball court. You can rent kayaks and windsurfing gear in the summer. There's also a café and two lifeguard stations.

About 5 km (3 mi) north of Netanya is lovely **Beit Yannai.** Amenities include barbecue grills, picnic tables, restrooms with showers, chair and umbrella rentals, and seasonal lifeguards. There's a seafood restaurant right on the beach. Parking is NIS 20 on weekdays and NIS 30 on Saturday.

The beach at **Mikhmoret,** 7½ km (4½ mi) north of Netanya, is popular with swimmers as well as those who laze away the day under an umbrella. The huge dirt parking lot, which charges NIS 30 per car, is 1 km (½ mi) after the turnoff from Route 2. There are three lifeguard stations, a restaurant, a café, and chair and umbrella rentals.

HORSEBACK RIDING

In northern Netanya, **Ha Hava** (*Havatzelet Hasharon St.* *09/866–3525*) has horseback riding for NIS 120 per hour. It's wise to reserve well ahead for weekend trips or for sunset rides along the beach.

PARAGLIDING

Netanya's cliffs make for exciting paragliding. Under the guidance of experienced instructors, you take off from a specially designed field along the promenade about half a mile south of the city center.

Dvir Paragliding (☏ *09/899–0277* 🌐 *www.tourplanisrael.com*) is an established company that offers thrilling adventures throughout the year.

Sky Paragliding School (☏ *09/884–1981* 🌐 *www.paragliding.co.il*) offers a one-time guided experience plus equipment rental.

Udi Paragliding (☏ *052/803–3824* 🌐 *www.paragliding.co.il*) offers paragliding instruction as well as a video of you soaring through the air.

THE WINE COUNTRY AND MT. CARMEL

5

This route south of Haifa wanders through the foothills and up the spine of Mt. Carmel. It's a major wine region, and three of the country's most famous vineyards are here: Carmel, Benyamina, and Tishbi. Druze villages are another attraction. The Druze are known for their hospitable ways; a meal in one of the towns will not only be a tasty experience, but also a warmly welcoming one.

Though wine has been produced in Israel for thousands of years, and the Rothschilds updated viniculture around Zichron Ya'akov some 120 years ago, truly high-quality wines have appeared on the market only in the last decade or so. This is one of the country's prime wine-growing areas (its classification is Shomron). After a tour of the winery it's delightful to sit under the grapevines and sample the vintages along with fresh salad, warm bread, and good local cheese.

Route 4 is smooth sailing, with Mt. Carmel looming to the east beyond cultivated fields and banana plantations (though you may not see the bananas, as they're usually bagged in blue or gray plastic to protect them from bugs). The road leads through undulating countryside dotted with cypresses, palms, and vineyards.

In December 2010, a forest fire—the most severe in Israel's history—raged for several days on Mount Carmel. It was all the more devastating due to dry conditions following many years of drought. The area damaged was estimated at about one third of the entire forested area of the Carmel mountain range. As a result, you may notice bare swathes along the mountainside when traveling along Route 2 or Route 4. In the aftermath of the fire replanting was initiated, and many areas will show bright green new growth, along with the gradual natural regeneration of oak, pistachio, and pine trees.

EIN HOD

★ *15 km (10 mi) south of Haifa, 5 km (3 mi) west of Isfiya.*

A charming little village, Ein Hod is home to around 135 families, most of them sculptors, painters, and other types of artists. The setting is an idyllic one, with rough-hewn stone houses built on the hillside and sweeping views down to the Mediterranean. The Dadaist painter Marcel Janco (1895–1984) wrote upon his first visit in 1950: "The beauty of the place was staggering."

Parking is across the road, opposite the entrance to the village. Climbing up the hill, you soon come to a winding street on the left that starts a lovely walk through the small village. Signs along the way indicate studios and workshops where artists paint, sculpt, and make jewelry, pottery, silkscreen prints, and clothing. You can continue straight to the town square, bordered by a restaurant and a large gallery where works by Ein Hod artists are exhibited.

GETTING HERE AND AROUND

Your best option is to get here by car via Route 4, since buses are few and far between. The village itself is small and very walkable.

EXPLORING

Janco-Dada Museum. On the village square is this museum dedicated to one of the founders of the Dada movement. The Romanian-born Marcel Janco had already established a considerable professional reputation by the time he moved here in 1941. The museum houses a permanent collection of the artist's works in various media, reflecting Janco's 70-year output both in Europe and Israel. A 20-minute slide show chronicles the life of the artist and the Dada movement. Don't miss the view from the roof. ✉ *Near village square* ☎ *04984–2350* 🎫 *NIS 20* ⏲ *Sun.–Thurs. 9:30–3:30, Fri. 9:30–2, Sat. 10–4.*

★ **Nahal Me'arot Nature Reserve.** The prehistoric Carmel Caves are a highlight of the Nahal Me'arot Nature Reserve, 3 km (2 mi) south of Ein Hod. The three excavated caves are up a steep flight of stairs, on a fossil reef that was covered by the sea 100 million years ago. The first discoveries of prehistoric remains were made when this area was being scoured for stones to build the Haifa port. In the late 1920s, Dorothy Garrod of England headed the first archaeological expedition, receiving assistance from a British feminist group on condition that exclusively women carry out the dig.

In the Tannur cave, the first on the tour, the strata Garrod's team excavated are clearly marked, spanning about 150,000 years in the life of early humans. The most exciting discovery made in the area was that of both Homo sapiens and Neanderthal skeletons; evidence that both lived here has raised fascinating questions about the relationship between the two and whether they lived side by side. A display on the daily life of early man as hunter and food gatherer occupies the Gamal cave. The last cave you'll visit, called the Nahal, is the largest—it cuts deep into the mountain—and was actually the first discovered. A burial place with 84 skeletons was found outside the mouth of the cave.

The bone artifacts and stone tools discovered in the Nahal cave suggest that people who settled here, about 12,000 years ago, were the forebears of early farmers, with a social structure more developed than that of hunters and gatherers. There is also evidence that the Crusaders once used the cave to guard the coastal road. Inside, an audiovisual show sheds light on how early man lived here. There's a snack bar at this site. ✉ *Off Rte. 4* ☎ *04/984–1750* 🌐 *www.parks.org.il* 🎫 *NIS 20* ⏲ *Oct.–Mar., Sat.–Thurs. and holidays 8–4, Fri. and Jewish holiday eves 8–1; Apr.–Sept., Sat.–Thurs. 8–5, Fri. 8–2.*

Nisco Museum of Mechanical Music. When is the last time you've seen a hurdy-gurdy? Nisan Cohen, a colorful and charming character who knows everything there is to know about old mechanical musical instruments, has amassed music boxes, hand-operated automatic pianos, antique gramophones on which to play his collection of old Yiddish records, and more musical marvels. Cohen will be pleased to give you a guided tour, then treat you to a personal concert. His sense of humor and gift of the gab make for a touching and intriguing experience. Before the entrance to Ein Hod, watch for a brown wooden sign with yellow letters. ✉ *Off Rte. 7111* ☎ *052/475–5313* 🌐 *www.nisco.com* 🎫 *NIS 30* ⏲ *Mon.–Sat. 10–5.*

NEED A BREAK?

Enjoy a homemade beer or a slice of delicious pizza (call ahead to order) in the garden at Danny and Analia's ArtBar (✉ *South of Ein Hod village square* ☎ *050/982-6313*). While you're here, have a look at Analia's unusual sculptures and paintings.

WHERE TO EAT

$ ISRAELI

Abu Yakov. You reach Abu Yakov's by climbing the stone seats of Ein Hod's amphitheater, or through nearby Café Ein Hod. There are a few seats inside—most people head outside to the blue plastic chairs beneath a ragged plastic tarp. It feels a bit makeshift, but the fresh food counts for everything. Dine on what locals often called "Oriental" (meaning Middle Eastern) food: hummus, fluffy pita bread, chopped vegetable salad, and grilled meat on skewers. Call ahead for oven-roasted lamb. ✉ *Near village square* ☎ *04/984–3377* 💳 *No credit cards* ⏲ *Closed Sun.*

$ CAFÉ

Café Ein Hod. Climb up the stairs beside the Dona Rosa restaurant and keep an eye out for this two-level collection of mismatched chairs and odd tables surrounded by potted plants—there's often a cat sunning himself on a stool. Inside the old stone building, handmade handbags and clothes are for sale. You can sit outside to sip coffee or fruit smoothies or chow down on homemade *bourekas* (filled pastry triangles), carrot cake, or apple pie. If you're hungry, nosh on grilled cheese sandwiches with salad. You can stop for a beer or a glass of wine, too. ✉ *Near village square* ☎ *054/667–6089* 💳 *No credit cards* ⏲ *Closed Mon.*

$$$ ARGENTINEAN

Dona Rosa. If you can't read the restaurant's sign in Hebrew, just follow the tantalizing aroma up the steps of this wooden building on the town square. Dona Rosa's grandsons, Uri and Doron, import meat and special charcoal from Argentina and roast the food in the true Argentinean style. The bar is decorated with a drawing of a hefty cow that illustrates each cut of meat. Highlights include grilled pork spareribs; seafood simmered with fragrant yellow rice; and *assado*, delicious, chunky ribs (available only on Saturday). There's beer and Chilean and Argentinean wine, too. ✉ *Near village square* ☎ *04/954–3777* 🌐 *www.donarosa.co.il* 💳 *AE, DC, MC, V* ⏲ *Closed Sun.*

WHERE TO STAY

$ **Jancourt B&B.** Batia and Claude's bed-and-breakfast is quiet and private, hidden behind masses of hot-pink bougainvillea. There are two units to choose from: the "Provence" is a ground-level apartment with a little garden and patio. Furnished in antique French provincial style, you'll find armchairs and a pullout sofa in the large living area, plus a good-size bedroom and kitchenette. The two-level "Green Room" is a studio furnished with art-deco touches. Olives from the yard, local cheeses, and homemade bread and jam make breakfast special. **Pros:** pretty, private building; fun shop. **Cons:** often gets booked in advance. ✉ *Second entrance to Ein Hod* ☎ *04/984–1648* 🌐 *www.eisenwasser-jancourt.co.il* *2 rooms* *In-room: a/c. In-hotel: kitchen, DVD, Wi-Fi* *No credit cards* *BP.*

$ **Yakir Ein Hod.** Care for a dip in a pool ringed by olive trees while you gaze at the blue Mediterranean? That's what you can do at this delightful lodging. Host Yakir offers three delightful suites, each with a hot tub and a stunning view of the sea. Each unit has a sitting area for reading or watching television and a kitchenette. A bountiful brunchlike breakfast for two costs NIS 100. **Pros:** quiet location; pool; lovely views. **Cons:** minimum stay required on weekends. ✉ *Second entrance to Ein Hod* ☎ *050/554–3982* 🌐 *www.yakireinhod.co.il* *3 rooms* *In-room: kitchen. In-hotel: pool* *AE, DC, MC, V.*

NIGHTLIFE AND THE ARTS

Just off the main square, **Gertrud Kraus House** (✉ *Village square* ☎ *052/645–6072*) features chamber music concerts. Admission is NIS 50, which often includes coffee and cake.

SHOPPING

Many of the artists who live in the winding lanes of Ein Hod throw open their workshops to visitors, who are welcome to browse and buy. Between the olive trees and behind painted gates, look for signs on homes that indicate the sale of jewelry, gold metalwork, sculptures, paintings, ceramics, stained glass, hand-painted clothing, and artistic photography. Either start at the entrance to the village where signs point to the left, or head for the village square straight ahead.

★ **Central Gallery** (✉ *Village square* ☎ *04/984–2548*) carries a wide selection of handicrafts and art by resident artists at its space on Ein Hod's main square. Displayed in the front room are ceramics, enamel, and silver and gold jewelry while through the arch into another room are paintings, sculptures, and graphic works. The gallery is open Sunday to Thursday and Saturday 11 to 4, Friday 10 to 2.

Silver Print (✉ *Ein Hod* ☎ *04/954–1673*) is a lovely little studio holding Vivienne Silver-Brody's collection of works by Israel's best photographers. The emphasis is on the building of the State of Israel. There's also a wide range of 19th-century photos of the Holy Land. A digital print costs NIS 150. Call ahead for hours.

DALIYAT EL CARMEL AND ISFIYA

16 km (11 mi) south of Haifa.

Daliyat el Carmel is Israel's largest Druze village, and well worth exploring. Though most of the younger generation wears jeans and T-shirts, most older people wear traditional garb. Head coverings indicate the degree of religious belief, from the high white turban resembling a fez to the white kerchief covering the head and shoulders. Many men sport a bushy moustache, a hallmark of the Druze, and some older ones wear dark robes and black pantaloons.

Very similar to neighboring Daliyat el Carmel, Isfiya is a village of flat-roof homes built closely together into the hillside, many of them raised on pillars and cut with arched windows. Hospitality is second nature to the Druze who live here; you may be able to visit a village home and eat pita bread with yogurt cheese and spices while hearing about Druze life. The village is about 1 km (½ mi) from Daliyat el Carmel.

GETTING HERE AND AROUND

Coming from Haifa, drive south on Route 672.

To really get to know Isfiya, arrange a tour through Druze Hospitality in Isfiya. Your guide will take you to visit their place of prayer, an olive oil press, and then to a private home where the matriarch bakes pita bread in a *tabun* (oven). You will hear about the distinctive Druze way of life. It's best to call a few days ahead. The price is NIS 120 per person.

ESSENTIALS

Tour Information **Druze Hospitality** (☎ *04/839-0125*).

EXPLORING

Daliyat el Carmel Marketplace. About 1 km (½ mi) inside town, take a right turn into the marketplace, a colorful jumble of shops lining the street. You can be assured of eating excellent falafel at any of the roadside stands or restaurants.

WHERE TO EAT

$ MIDDLE EASTERN ✕ **Halabi Brothers.** At this storefront eatery, brothers Fouad and Ahmad Halabi greet you with a handshake and a "Hello, my cousin!" The delicious falafel and shwarma, wrapped in thin, lightly browned Druze-style pitas, are a nice change from the fluffy ones served at most other places in the country. A refreshing splash of lemon tips the platter of salads. Watch everything being prepared in the glass-front kitchen that opens onto a series of tile-floor dining rooms. The adjoining gift shop, also run by the siblings, displays locally woven tablecloths and pillowcases. ✉ *14 Commercial Center Str., Daliyat el Carmel* ☎ *052/477–6048* ▭ *MC, V.*

$$ MIDDLE EASTERN ✕ **House of Druze Heritage.** The Druze are famous for their hospitality. Here you get not only a warm welcome from Fadal, the congenial owner, but if you call ahead you can enjoy a traditional meal in his own home. Fadal explains the Druze way of life and shows you displays of Druze farm implements, household objects, and handicrafts. If you choose to dine à la Druze, the meal may include skewers of grilled lamb or steak and big, flat pita bread. Baklava and Turkish coffee provide

CLOSE UP

The Druze

The Druze are an Arabic-speaking people who practice a secret religion; they form one of the most intriguing entities in the mosaic of Israel's population, of which they number about 118,000, or 2%. They live in areas from Mt. Carmel to the Upper Galilee and the Golan Heights. Larger kindred communities exist in Syria and Lebanon.

So exclusive is this sect that only a fraction of the community is initiated into its religious doctrine, one tenet of which is a belief in continuous reincarnation. The Druze broke away from Islam about 1,000 years ago, incorporating other traditions and also believing in the divinity of their founder, al-Hâkim bi-Amr Allâh, the Caliph of the Egyptian Fatimid dynasty from AD 996 to 1021. They do not permit gambling or the use of alcohol.

The Druze who live in the two existing villages on Mt. Carmel (Daliyat el Carmel and Isfiya) serve in the Israeli Army, a sign of their loyalty to Israel.

the finishing touch. ✉ *4 Ahat St., Daliyat el Carmel* ☎ *04/839–3242* ▭ *AE, DC, MC, V.*

$$ MIDDLE EASTERN ✕ **Nof Carmel.** To find this very good Druze restaurant, drive to the northern edge of the village. The eatery is on your left; look for a few tables outside under the trees. People come from all over for the fine Middle Eastern fare, especially the homemade hummus with pine nuts, olive oil, garlic, and lemon juice, and the well-seasoned kebab on skewers. Those with a sweet tooth should sample the *sahlab* (a warm, custardlike pudding of crushed orchid bulb with thickened milk and sugar). ✉ *Rte. 672, Isfiya* ☎ *04/839–1718* ✍ *Reservations not accepted* ▭ *AE, MC, V.*

SHOPPING

Along a brief stretch of the main road that winds through Daliyat el Carmel are shops selling lightweight throw rugs, handwoven baskets, brightly colored pottery, brass dishes, characteristic woven wall hangings, and embroidered skullcaps worn by men. Bargaining is expected. Some shops close on Friday; the strip is crowded on Saturday.

The trunks of olive trees outside indicate that something unusual is happening at **Shorashim** (✉ *Rte. 672, Isfiya* ☎ *04/839–2279*). Shachar Amasha and his workers fashion art out of gnarled pieces of olive wood. He will offer you strong Druze coffee and show you around the workshop and the beautiful benches, chairs, and decorative pieces fashioned there. The store fronts on the main street running through Isfiya.

MUKHRAKA

18 km (12 mi) south of Haifa, 2 km (1 1/3 mi) west of Daliyat el Carmel.

You can't miss Mukhraka, marked by a tall white statue of Elijah the Prophet with his sword raised on high. Just beyond is the graceful Carmelite Monastery with a sweeping rooftop view.

GETTING HERE AND AROUND

Mukhraka is an interesting stop if you're on the way to Isfiya and Daliyat el Carmel on Route 70. It's not accessible for those without a car.

EXPLORING

★ **Carmelite Monastery.** Past open, uncultivated fields and a goatherd's rickety shack, Mukhraka's Carmelite Monastery stands on the spur of the Carmel range, at an altitude of 1,580 feet, on or near the site where the struggle between Elijah and the priests of Ba'al is believed to have taken place. Climb to the roof for an unforgettable panorama: to the east stretches the Jezreel Valley and the hills of Nazareth, Moreh, and Gilboa. On a clear day you can even see Jordan's Gilead Mountains beyond the Jordan River and Mt. Hermon.

Mukhraka is the Arabic word for a place of burning, referring to the fire that consumed the offering on Elijah's altar. The conflict developed because the people of Israel had been seduced by the pagan cults introduced by King Ahab's wife, Jezebel. Elijah demanded a contest with the priests of Ba'al in which each would erect an altar with a butchered ox as an offering and see which divinity sent down fire. Elijah drenched his altar with water, yet it burst into flames. On his orders, the priests were taken down to the Brook of Kishon and executed.

The stark stone monastery was built in 1883 over Byzantine ruins. There's a small gift shop in the monastery, but no place to buy drinks or snacks. ☎ *No phone* 🎫 *NIS 4* ⏲ *Mon.–Sat. 8–1:30 and 2:30–5.*

5

ZICHRON YA'AKOV

★ *35 km (22 mi) south of Haifa, 61 km (40 mi) north of Tel Aviv.*

A visit to the charming town of Zichron Ya'akov should start on its main street, Hameyasdim. Residents have made every effort to maintain the original appearance of this short thoroughfare, and the cobblestone street is lined, for the most part, with small, restored, red-roof 19th-century homes. Pick up a town map in the tourist office at the entrance to the town.

GETTING HERE AND AROUND

If you're driving from Haifa or Tel Aviv, take Route 2 to the Zichron Ya'akov exit. Buses run from Haifa and Tel Aviv.

ESSENTIALS

Vistor Information **Zichron Ya'akov Tourist Office** (✉ *Southern entrance to town, opposite the cemetery* ☎ *04/639–8811*).

EXPLORING

TOP ATTRACTIONS

★ **Carmel Winery.** Rare among Israel's many wineries are Carmel Winery's underground vaulted-ceiling wine cellars. Dating from 1892, the huge old, chilly rooms are a contrast to the state-of-the art facility aboveground, where the winery's top wines are produced. Founder Baron Edmond de Rothschild, owner of France's famous Château Lafite, would be pleased at the success of his viniculture venture, now the country's largest winery. A guided one-hour tour outlines the stages of

Continued on page 335

In a land where grapes have been grown and enjoyed since biblical times, a modern winemaking revolution has taken hold. Whether the vintage is from big producers or boutique up-and-comers, the improved quality of Israeli wine has catapulted all things oenological into the spotlight. This tiny country is now home to over 200 wineries large and small. It was Baron Edmond de Rothschild—the proprietor of France's prestigious Château Lafite winery and an early Zionist—who jumpstarted the modern Israeli wine industry by providing money to found wineries in the 1880s. After a few false starts, Carmel Mizrachi, which his funds helped support, flourished; to this day it is Israel's most prolific wine producer.

by Adeena Sussman

(top) Ancient floor mosaic depicting wine vase at Eretz Israel Museum, Tel Aviv. (right) Golan Heights Winery

The Wines of Israel

WINEMAKING IN ISRAEL

(top left) Winemaking barrel shop in Zichron Ya'akov, 1890s. (bottom left) Golan Heights Winery. (right) Wine fair in Tel Aviv.

Israel manufactured mostly mediocre wines until the late 1970s, when the first *moshavim* and *kibbutzim* (living cooperatives) planted vines in the Golan Heights on the advice of scientists from California, who saw a grape-growing diamond in the rough amid the mountain ranges of this northern region. Soon thereafter Golan Heights Winery was born, and awards and accolades were uncorked almost immediately.

GROWTH AND CHALLENGE

Besides two dozen or so larger operations, more than 150 smaller wineries now operate, many less than 15 years old and some producing just a few thousand bottles per year. Five large wineries account for 75 percent of production. Winemaking is a relatively young industry, sparked by a new crop of winemakers with experience at outstanding wineries. Though top wine writers have given some Israeli wines high marks, confirming internationally that these are vintages worth seeking out, there is still room for improvement in the ongoing, so-called "quality revolution."

Per capita wine consumption in Israel has nearly doubled since the late 1990s but remains low. A culture of wine appreciation is gradually fomenting, although the lion's share of bottles are exported to the United States and Europe. Despite challenges, winemakers continue to experiment: up-and-coming regions include the Judean Hills outside Jerusalem and even the Negev desert.

KOSHER & MEVUSHAL: MESSAGE ON A BOTTLE

For a wine to be certified kosher, as many Israeli wines are, a religious supervisor must oversee the process to ensure that no non-kosher tools or ingredients are used. Only rigorously observant Jews can handle equipment. Critics agree that these regulations don't affect the quality of wine. *Mevushal* wines, with more stringent kosher requirements, are flash-pasteurized, and then rapidly chilled; this can affect quality. However, many top-tier Israeli wines today are non-Mevushal, or are unsupervised altogether.

WINE REGIONS AND GRAPES

Sea Horse winery

GRAPE EXPECTATIONS

After commercial vines were first planted in the 19th century, Israeli winemakers focused on a small group of grape varietals that seemed to take well to Israeli terrain. The country has no indigenous grapes. With the help of technology, experience, and trial and error, a wide range of grapes are now raised with success.

Some of Israel's red wines are world-class, notably those that blend Cabernet Sauvignon grapes with Merlot, Cabernet Franc, and Petit Verdot. Chardonnays also do well here—the warm days and cool nights of the northern region seem particularly advantageous for this varietal.

Winemakers consistently push the envelope, introducing exciting new wines into the market. Two recent examples? Viognier, which has been one of the darlings of the current Israeli wine market, and Syrah, a grape that flourishes amid the country's hot days and cool, breezy nights.

Israel's wine-growing areas are typically divided into five regions, although no official, European-style government-regulated classification system exists. Since the country is so small—about the size of New Jersey—grapes are often shared among the regions. This is especially true of the northern plains, which provide grapes to many of the country's best wineries. Still, each area is geographically unique.

GALILEE Actually two regions, this area covers a lot of geographical ground in the north. The Galilee is a rocky area, and the Golan Heights, which borders Syria, sees winter snowfall at its highest altitudes. With cool climes and rich soil, the Galilee and Golan still claim bragging rights as home to many of the country's premier grapes.

SHOMRON/CARMEL The advantageous growing conditions of the lush Carmel Mountains make this coastal plain south of Haifa the most prolific grape-growing region in Israel, if not the most prestigious. The climate and soil variety make it the most traditionally Mediterranean of the regions.

SAMSON/CENTRAL COAST Situated west of Jerusalem and stretching north toward Tel Aviv and south toward Ashkelon, this region has hot, humid summers and mellow winters that make for good growing conditions. If you're in Tel Aviv, this is an easy region for accessing great wineries.

JUDEAN HILLS Ten years ago, barely a winery or tasting room existed here, though ancient winemaking equipment has been unearthed. Thin limey or rocky soil, sunny days, and breezy nights have helped this region's wines shine. With its winding roads, and lush, shallow mountainsides, the region west and south of Jerusalem is day-trip perfect from Jerusalem and Tel Aviv.

THE NEGEV Thanks to drip-irrigation technology, grapes are thriving in the desert. Since there are relatively few wineries in the southern part of the Negev, they're best included in a trip to Eilat or Mitzpe Ramon; call to schedule a visit.

Clos de Gat Winery in the Judean Hills

WINE TOURING AND TASTING

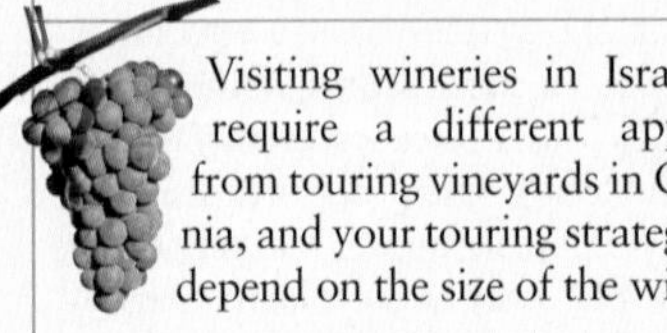

Visiting wineries in Israel can require a different approach from touring vineyards in California, and your touring strategy may depend on the size of the winery.

Most of the **bigger players,** including Golan Heights, Carmel, and Barkan/Segal, offer tasting rooms. You can simply stop by and visit to sample and purchase wines, though generally it's good to call in advance if you want to include a winery tour. Many **medium- and smaller-sized wineries** are often happy to accommodate visitors, but always call ahead to ensure that English-speaking staff will be on hand and to confirm hours.

A few **boutique** wineries welcome tourists, but many of the best aren't equipped for a regular onslaught of visitors. While you can call yourself, this is where private tour guides come in handy. Often, these individuals have the connections to get you inside wineries you'd otherwise never see—not to mention the knowledge of the back roads in some of the harder-to-find locales.

Through **Israel Wine Experience** (☎ 054/052–0604, www.israelwinexp.com), wine expert Oded Shoham and his staff offer customized half- and full-day tours and tastings. Fees vary, but a half-day tour of three wineries is about $400 for a group of up to 5 people.

PICK OF THE VINEYARDS

These wineries either have open tasting rooms, or visits can be arranged with an advance phone call. Note: most kosher wineries are open only a half-day on Friday, and are closed on Saturdays and Jewish holidays. Small tastes are usually free, but at most wineries a guided tasting costs between $10 and $18 per person for three to five wines.

Carmel Winery

GALILEE

❶ **Golan Heights Winery** Still the standard bearer for Israeli wines, this large producer has a welcoming visitor center and tours. Wines are made under the Yarden, Gamla, and Golan labels. Kosher. *Try: Single-vineyard Odem Organic Chardonnay; Yarden Syrah.* ✉ Rte. 87, Industrial Zone, Katzrin ☎ 04/696–8420 🌐 www.golanwines.com.

❷ **Chateau Golan** A French-style chateau houses an art-filled tasting room. It's open daily; call in advance. Not kosher. *Try: Plummy, balanced-tannin Eliad Cabernet blends.* ✉ Moshav Eliad, Ramat Hagolan ☎ 04/660–0026 🌐 www.chateaugolan.com.

❸ **Galil Mountain Winery** A sleek, modern low-lying stone-and-wood building offers views of the

WINES IN RESTAURANTS AND SHOPS

Even if you don't visit these wineries, look for vintages from these superior regional producers in restaurants or shops in Israel.

Clos de Gat

Galilee: Golan Heights and Chateau Golan in the Golan; Dalton and Galil Mountain in the Galilee

Shomron/Carmel: Recanati, Margalit, Amphorae

Samson/Central Coast: Carmel, Barkan, Soreq

Judean Hills: Sea Horse, Domaine du Castel, Clos de Gat

The Negev: Yatir, La Terra Promessa

Galil Mountain

vineyards and the winemaking facilities. These are great-value wines for the money. Kosher. *Try: Fruity, mineral-tinged Sauvignon Blanc.* ✉ Kibbutz Merom, Yiron ☎ 04/686–8740 🌐 www.galilmountain.co.il.

❹ **Tabor Winery** Set amid almond groves near Mt. Tabor in the Galilee, this intimate visitor center offers tastings and tours, plus a restaurant called Bordeaux. Kosher. *Try: Full-bodied, oaky Mas'ha 2003, a Cabernet-Shiraz-Merlot blend that is the winery's calling card.* ✉ Kfar Tavor, ☎ 04/676–0444 🌐 www.taborwinery.com.

SHOMRON/ CARMEL

❺ **Tishbi Winery** The vistor center at this fourth-generation winery offers harvest activities August–October. Kosher. *Try: Woodsy, berry-rich Pinot Noir.* ✉ 33 Hameyasdim St., Zichron Ya'akov ☎ 04/638–0435 🌐 www.tishbi.com.

❻ **Amphorae Winery** This boutique winery is set in a series of rustic, Tuscan-style stone buildings. Call in advance to arrange a visit. Not kosher. *Try: Balanced, full-bodied Cabernet Sauvignon.* ✉ Makura Farm, Kerem Maharal ☎ 04/984–0702 🌐 www.amphorae-v.com.

SAMSON/ CENTRAL COAST

❼ **Carmel Winery** One of two visitor centers for Carmel (the other is in Zichron Ya'akov near Haifa), this facility at the country's largest winery offers tours of the original underground cellars built by Baron Edmond de Rothschild, as well as the facility's original barrel room. Kosher. ✉ 25 Hacarmel St. Rishon LeZion ☎ 03/948–8851 🌐 www.carmelwines.com.

JUDEAN HILLS

❽ **Ella Valley** For about $16 groups of 10 or more can tour the winery and sample four vintages in a wood-bar tasting room. Kosher. *Try: Fruity Sauvignon Blanc.* ✉ Rte. 475, off Rte. 38, Netiv Halamed Heh ☎ 02/999–4885 🌐 www.ellavalley.com.

❾ **Flam Winery** Two dynamic brothers, the sons of a former chief winemaker for Carmel Mizrachi, run this well-regarded producer. Call to arrange a cheese and wine tasting. *Try: Woodsy, berry-rich Flam Reserve Merlot.* ✉ Eshtal Junction, Ya'ar Ha'kodshim ☎ 02/992–9923 🌐 www.flamwinery.com.

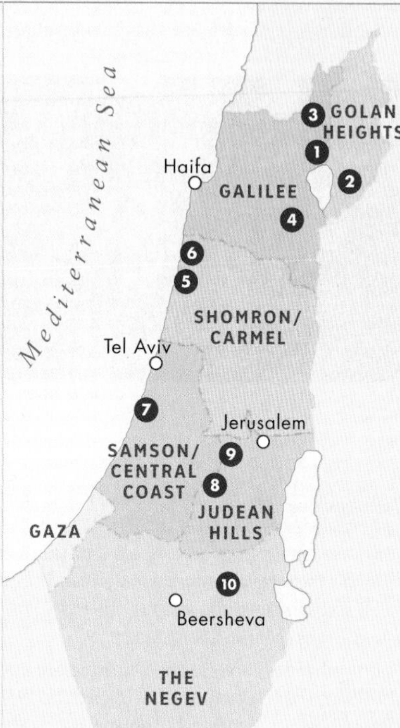

THE NEGEV

❿ **Yatir Winery** Generating great excitement, Yatir is a desert gem with promise. Call in advance. Kosher. *Try: Yatir Forest, whose grape blend varies from year to year; fruity, light Viognier.* ✉ Off Rte. 80, Tel Arad ☎ 08/995–9090 🌐 www.yatir.net.

Yatir Winery

MORE ISRAELI WINE RESOURCES

Pina BaRosh Wine Bar

WINE FESTIVALS

Annual wine festivals offer the opportunity to meet winemakers and taste their products, often in beautiful surroundings. Every July, Jerusalem's **Israel Museum** (☎ 02/670–8811 ✉ info@imj.org.il for dates) turns over its outdoor space at night for a weeklong wine festival featuring more than 150 wineries, food from local restaurants, and various other vendors. This Jerusalem tradition is highly recommended.

Up north, the **Golan Heights Winery** stages harvest festivals in September or October at their Katzrin headquarters (☎ 04/696–8420 ✉ ghwinery@golanwines.co.il).

The **Yoav Yehuda Wine Festival** (☎ 08/850–2240 🌐 www.yoav-exp.co.il) occurs every year during wine season (fall) and celebrates the more than two dozen wineries operating near Jerusalem in the Judean Hills and the surrounding area.

TASTING IN SHOPS AND BARS

Avi Ben, Jerusalem. This chain of retail wine shops offers free wine tastings every Friday from 11 to 2:30. On Thursday evenings look for winemaker-hosted tastings (NIS 20—NIS 50 per glass). ✉ 22 Rivlin St. ☎ 02/625–9703 ✉ 3 Harmonim St. ☎ 02/625–2339 🌐 www.avibenwine.com.

Methusaleh, Tel Aviv. Of the 160 selections at this new wine bar in the hipster Florentine neighborhood, nearly half are local, with many available by the glass. A custom-crafted flight of three Israeli wines ranges from NIS 28 to NIS 56. There's great food, too, from cheese and tapas to a full dinner menu. ✉ 16 Uriel Acosta St., ☎ 03/510–2923.

Pina BaRosh Wine Bar, Rosh Pina. A recent addition to the most famous B&B in funky Rosh Pina, near Tzfat, features more than 100 mostly northern Israeli wines. Wines by the glass are available every day from 8:30 AM to midnight, as are tastings, which range from NIS 74 to NIS 134. ✉ 8 Ha Chalutzim St. ☎ 04/693–7028 🌐 www.pinabarosh.com.

BRINGING IT HOME

Although you can ship wines home for personal enjoyment, the prices are prohibitively high, and your wines may get held up in U.S. Customs. A better bet is to save suitcase space for a few boutique bottles. Then, at the larger wineries, take notes on favorites and purchase them back home. **Skyview Wines & Spirits** in New York has the largest selection (🌐 www.skyviewwine.com ☎ 888/759–8466) from conventional wineries.

Wine clubs like **Israeli Wine Direct** (🌐 www.israeliwinedirect.com) are a source for smaller producers like Margalit, Pelter, Flam, and Clos de Gat. Wines are shipped to your home (not available in all states).

READING & PLANNING

An increasing number of resources are available for vino-tourists in Israel. The Web site **Wines Israel** (🌐 www.wines-israel.co.il), a great place to start, has an easy-to-read English-language section including information about the industry, winemaking history, wine routes, places to visit, and more.

Rogov's Guide to Israeli Wines (Toby Press, $19.95) is updated annually by Daniel Rogov, Israel's preeminent wine writer. It's a great resource for tasting wines.

local wine production. Included in the tour are a tasting of some four varieties and a seven-minute audiovisual presentation screened in the original wine cellar. Tours depart between 9 and 4 and must be reserved in advance. ✉ *2 Winery St.* ☎ *04/639–1788* 🌐 *www.carmelwines.co.il* 🎫 *NIS 22* 🕒 *Sun.–Thurs. 9–6, Fri. 9–1.*

Ramat Hanadiv. In the hills near Zichron Ya'akov, this sprawling garden is a fitting tribute to Baron Edmond de Rothschild. (*Hanadiv* means "the well-known benefactor.") At its center is the dignified tomb where Rothschild and his wife Ada lie buried. A 20-minute film in the welcoming visitor center tells of his legacy in Israel. Outside, curving paths are framed by rolling green lawns, abundant patches of flowers, and waving palms. Clearly marked trails lead to a 2,000-year old Roman farmhouse and a hidden spring. After all that legwork, the terraces of the on-site café beckon. A children's playground is set off to one side. ✉ *Southern end of Mt. Carmel, south of Zichron Ya'akov* ☎ *04/629–8111* 🌐 *www.ramat-hanadiv.org.il* 🎫 *Free* 🕒 *Sun.–Thurs. 8–4, Fri. 8–2, Sat. 8–4.*

5

WORTH NOTING

Bet Aaronson (Aaronson's House). About halfway down Hameyasdim Street is Bet Aaronson, whose late-19th-century architecture successfully combines art nouveau and Middle Eastern traditions. This museum was once the home of the agronomist Aaron Aaronson (1876–1919), who gained international fame for his discovery of an ancestor of modern wheat. The house remains as it looked after World War I, with family photographs and French and Turkish furniture, as well as Aaronson's library, diaries, and letters.

Aaronson and his two sisters became local heroes as leaders of a militant group dedicated to ousting the Turks from Palestine. Both sisters were in love with Aaron's assistant, Absalom Feinberg, who was killed in an ambush in the Gaza Strip. His remains were recovered some 50 years later from a grave marked simply by a date tree, the tree having sprouted from some dates in Feinberg's pockets. A tour in English is provided; the last one takes place at 1:30 pm. ✉ *40 Hameyasdim St.* ☎ *04/639–0120* 🎫 *NIS 15* 🕒 *Sun., Mon., Wed., and Thurs. 8:30–2:15, Tues. 8:30–3, Fri. 8:30–noon.*

Binyamin Pool. On Hameyasdim Street, near Bet Aaronson, is Binyamin Pool, a misnomer because it's actually the town's original water tower, built in 1891. Zichron Ya'akov was the first village in Israel to have water piped to its houses; Meir Dizengoff, the first mayor of Tel Aviv, came here to see how it was done. The facade resembles that of an ancient synagogue. ✉ *Hameyasdim St.*

First Aliya Museum. Commissioned by Baron de Rothschild, this building is a fine example of late-19th-century Ottoman-style architecture, built of white stone with a central pediment capped by a tile roof. The museum is dedicated to the lives of immigrants who came to Israel with the First Aliya (a period of settlement from 1882 until 1904). Life-size model displays of local immigrants (like Zachariya, the seed vendor, and Izer, the cobbler) illustrate how life was lived at that time. A film traces the struggles of a family who came from Europe in this difficult period of Israel's modern history. ✉ *2 Hanadiv St.* ☎ *04/629–4777* 🎫 *NIS 15* ⏲ *Mon. and Wed.–Fri., 9–2, Tues. 9–3.*

Ohel Ya'akov. On a prominent corner stands the old synagogue, Ohel Ya'akov, built by Baron de Rothschild in 1886 to satisfy the settlers' spiritual needs. It's only occasionally open to visitors. ✉ *Hameyasdim St. and Hanadiv St.*

WHERE TO EAT

$$$ MEDITERRANEAN ✕ **Haneshika.** The restaurant's huge courtyard with dark orange umbrellas is usually packed with diners. Inside, the place is small and cozy. For country-style eating, you might start with mozzarella gnocchi with sautéed mushrooms, or a zucchini and feta cheese terrine. Main courses include baked crabs in a sweet-and-hot chili sauce, lamb casserole with eggplant and pine nuts, and seafood and fennel salad. Apple crumble with a cinnamon-flavored sauce is a delightful dessert. ✉ *37 Hameyasdim St.* ☎ *04/639–0133* 🌐 *haneshika.co.il* ✍ *Reservations essential* ▭ *AE, DC, MC, V* ⏲ *No dinner Fri. Closed Sun.*

$ MIDDLE EASTERN ✕ **Hatemaniya shel Santo.** Grab a table in the courtyard if you want a tasty and authentic Yemenite meal. There's no menu—the waiter brings you soft pita bread, country black bread, a fresh vegetable salad, and a rugged hummus drizzled with olive oil. You can order stuffed vegetables or chicken, but make sure you also try the potato cakes and a plate of the small meat patties flavored with cilantro. It's all delicious and nicely washed down with Yemenite coffee or cold water with lemon and mint. ✉ *52 Hameyasdim St.* ☎ *04/639–8762* ▭ *AE, DC, MC, V* ⏲ *Closed Sat.*

$$ MEDITERRANEAN ✕ **Kashtunyo Wine Cellar.** An underground wine cellar is a happy place to hear about wines from owner Amos Meroz, whose hat is always rakishly tilted to one side. Eight tables covered with checkered cloths fill a small space defined by curving stone walls. Dishes of olives glisten on a tiny wooden bar in the dimly lighted room. Scores of wine bottles line the back wall, where you'll find vintages from Israel, Italy, Australia, California, France, and South Africa. You can enjoy cheese and stuffed grape leaves while learning from an expert. Or just sit quietly with your glass while French songs fill the air. ✉ *56 Hameyasdim St.* ☎ *04/629–1244* ✍ *Reservations essential* ▭ *AE, MC, V.*

$$$ ECLECTIC ✕ **Picciotto.** Pots of geraniums and rosemary and lavender bushes are at the entrance of this charming, eclectic eatery. The original settlers peer out sternly from photos on the vanilla-colored walls. A wood stove in the middle keeps everything cozy. The chef's lemon-cured salmon with cucumber dressing merits mention, as does the roasted eggplant with tomatoes and mint leaves. Each makes a fine introduction to main courses such as seafood pasta in white wine and wild herbs and lemony chicken breast with capers. For dessert, try the phyllo leaves filled with crème anglaise and seasonal fresh fruit. ✉ *41 Hameyasdim St.* ☎ *04/629–0646* ✍ *Reservations essential* ▭ *AE, DC, MC, V.*

WHERE TO STAY

¢ 🏨 **Bet Maimon.** On the western slopes of Zichron Ya'akov, this family-run hotel has a spectacular view of the coastal valley and the sea. The terrace restaurant serves both Middle Eastern and Eastern European lunches. The rooms are done up in blues and yellows. There's a pretty garden and a small aboveground pool. Guests who are less than fit will feel the climb to the sundeck on the roof; the three-story building has no elevator. **Pros:** city's best lodging; nice views. **Cons:** lots of steps to climb; old-fashioned feel. ✉ *4 Zahal St.* ☎ *04/639–0212* 🌐 *www.maimon.com* *25 rooms* *In-room: a/c, Wi-Fi. In-hotel: restaurant, pool, parking (free)* ▭ *AE, DC, MC, V.*

BENYAMINA

5 km (3 mi) south of Zichron Ya'akov, 55 km (34 mi) north of Tel Aviv.

Picturesque Benyamina, the youngest settlement in the area, was founded in 1922 and has several wineries. It was named after Baron Edmond de Rothschild, the head of the French branch of the famous family, who took a keen interest in the welfare of his fellow Jews in Palestine. (His Hebrew name was Benyamin.)

The advice of the viniculture experts Rothschild hired in the 1880s paid off handsomely, at least in this region—the fruit of the vines flourished in the 1890s. Rothschild's paternalistic system was not without its pitfalls, however; some of his administrators ruled his colonies like petty despots, trying, for instance, to impose use of the French language on the local settlers, who wished to speak Hebrew. Language notwithstanding, the Binyamina Winery was founded in 1952; you can find it at the end of the village by following the Hebrew signs that show a bunch of grapes.

5

GETTING HERE AND AROUND

You can easily reach Benyamina by train. If you're driving, take Route 4. Either option makes for a very pretty ride. Once you're here, you'll need a car to get around because public transport is uneven at best.

EXPLORING

Binyamina Winery. The large visitor center at the country's fourth-largest winery was once a perfume factory. It hasn't changed as much as you'd think, as cosmetics made from grape seeds are some of the products for sale here. You can also find olive oil, vinegar, and yes, even wine. The production facilities are next door in buildings surrounded by towering palm trees. Reservations are required for the 45-minute tour of the winery and barrel rooms, including a sampling of four or five wines. You can also do your tasting while having lunch or dinner in the restaurant that was once an orange packing facility. Or, you can simply drop in for coffee and cake. ✉ *17 Hanassi St.* ☎ *04/638–8643* 🌐 *www.binyaminawines.com* *Free* *Sun.–Thurs. 9–5; Fri. 9–noon.*

Tishbi Estate Winery. Among the hills and valleys of this pastoral area is one of the country's most esteemed wineries. The first vines were planted almost 120 years ago. Estate is the premier label (the Sauvignon Blanc and Chardonnay are among the best in Israel). At the country-style visitor center, it's a treat to eat breakfast, brunch or lunch under the grapevines in the courtyard. Apart from wine, you'll also find local cheeses, olive oil, honey, and wine jellies at the shop. A visit to the new chocolate tasting room is a treat. Call ahead to reserve the one-hour tour, which includes tastings and a visit to the old alembic distillery where their prized brandy is made. It's about 3 km (1½ mi) north of Benyamina. ✉ *Rte. 652* ☎ *04/628–8195* 🌐 *www.tishbi.com* 🎟 *Free* 🕑 *Sun.–Thurs. 8–5, Fri. 8–3.*

AKKO TO ROSH HANIKRA

One of the oldest port cities in the world, Akko has an Old City ringed by ancient ramparts. Inside are an 18th-century mosque, underground Crusader halls, and winding lanes leading past a marketplace and restaurants at the water's edge. North of Akko, wide beaches, two of them within nature reserves, follow one after the other up the coast. The *moshavim* and *kibbutzim* (rural agricultural settlements) in this area are often unusual settings for gourmet restaurants and upscale bed-and-breakfasts. Rosh Hanikra, at the top of the northern coast, has a cable car that carries you down to caves hollowed out by wildly crashing waves.

AKKO

Fodor's Choice ★

22 km (13½ mi) north of Haifa.

The Old City of Akko, a UNESCO World Heritage Site, is an enchanting mix of mosques, markets, and vaulted Crusader ruins (many of them underground). A walk through the cobbled alleys and outdoor market stalls brings you to a small port filled with fishing boats. When viewed from the surrounding ramparts, it's one of the country's prettiest views.

To reach the historic parts of Akko, you'll be driving through a modern city: a bustling, traffic-ridden metropolis of about 48,000 people. It's rather plain, so reserve judgment until you've seen the Old City.

GETTING HERE AND AROUND

From Haifa, you can get here via Route 4. A much slower but far prettier inland route takes you north on Route 70, passing through rolling hills and avoiding the drab satellite towns north of Haifa. There are direct buses from Haifa, and trains from Jerusalem and Tel Aviv (you may have to change trains). Once you are here, a car is the best way to get around.

From Akko's port, the *Queen of Akko* ferry makes a 40-minute jaunt around the bay. The cost is NIS 25. Two well-known companies, Egged Tours and United Tours, offer one-day trips to Akko from Haifa.

TIMING AND PRECAUTIONS

Plan on spending the better part of a day if you want to see everything, including the excellent presentation in the Turkish bathhouse. Women alone should exercise caution walking around at night.

ESSENTIALS

Vistor and Tour Information **Akko Visitor Center** (✉ *At the town entrance, just inside the stone arch* ☎ *04/995–6727* 🌐 *www.akko.org.il*). **Egged Tours** (☎ *03/920–3919* 🌐 *www.eggedtours.co.il*). **Queen of Akko** (☎ *050/555–1136*). **United Tours** (☎ *03/693–3412 or 03/522–2008* 🌐 *www.inisrael.com/united/index.html*).

CLOSE UP

Akko's History

History clings to the stones in the Old City of Akko, with each twist and turn along its streets telling another tale. The city's history begins 4,000 years ago, when Akko was first mentioned in Egyptian writings that refer to the mound northeast of its walls. The Old Testament describes in Judges 1 that after the death of Joshua the tribe of Asher was unable to drive the Canaanites from Akko, so they lived among them.

Akko has always been worth fighting for. It had a well-protected harbor, fertile hinterland, and a strategic position that linked Egypt and Phoenicia. Alexander the Great had such regard for Akko that he set up a mint here. Akko was Phoenician for long periods, but when the Hellenistic king Ptolemy II gained control in the 2nd century BC, he renamed it Ptolemais.

King Baldwin I led the Crusaders who conquered Akko in 1104, and the port city was the Crusaders' principal link to home. Commerce thrived, and the European maritime powers Genoa, Pisa, Venice, and Marseilles developed separate quarters here. After the disastrous defeat of the Crusader armies in 1187, Akko surrendered to Saladin, but Richard the Lionheart soon recaptured the European stronghold. In its Crusader heyday, Akko had about 40 churches and monasteries and a population of 50,000.

In the 13th century, after the conquest of Jerusalem by the Muslims, Akko became the effective capital of a shrunken Latin kingdom; it fell to the Mamluks in 1291 and lay in ruins for centuries. In 1749 Dahr el-Omar, the Bedouin sheikh, moved his capital from Tiberias to Akko and rebuilt the walls of the city.

Napoléon couldn't conquer the city in 1799, but the British captured it in 1918. With the founding of the State of Israel in 1948, many Arab inhabitants left Akko, though a good number remain. Akko's population now numbers about 46,000, with people living inside the Old City itself and in new developments pushing the city limits to the north.

EXPLORING AKKO

The walled city of Old Akko is relatively small and the well-signed sights are close to one another, making it easy to tour. You approach the Old City on Weizman Street (watch for signs that say Old Akko), proceeding through a breach in the surrounding walls. If you're driving, park in the large lot.

OLD CITY

Start your tour at the Akko Visitor Center, just inside the main entrance to the Old City. This is where you purchase tickets. A combination ticket that includes all sights in the Old City is NIS 27. A combination ticket that includes all the sights along with the Turkish bath is NIS 46.

Once you've bought your ticket, take the time to get a map of the area and see the seven-minute film on the history of the region. Before you enter the Old City, you might want to walk along the Ramparts and visit the Ethnography Center. To get there, ascend the steps at the opening in the city walls. The El-Jazaar Mosque, south of the main entrance, is

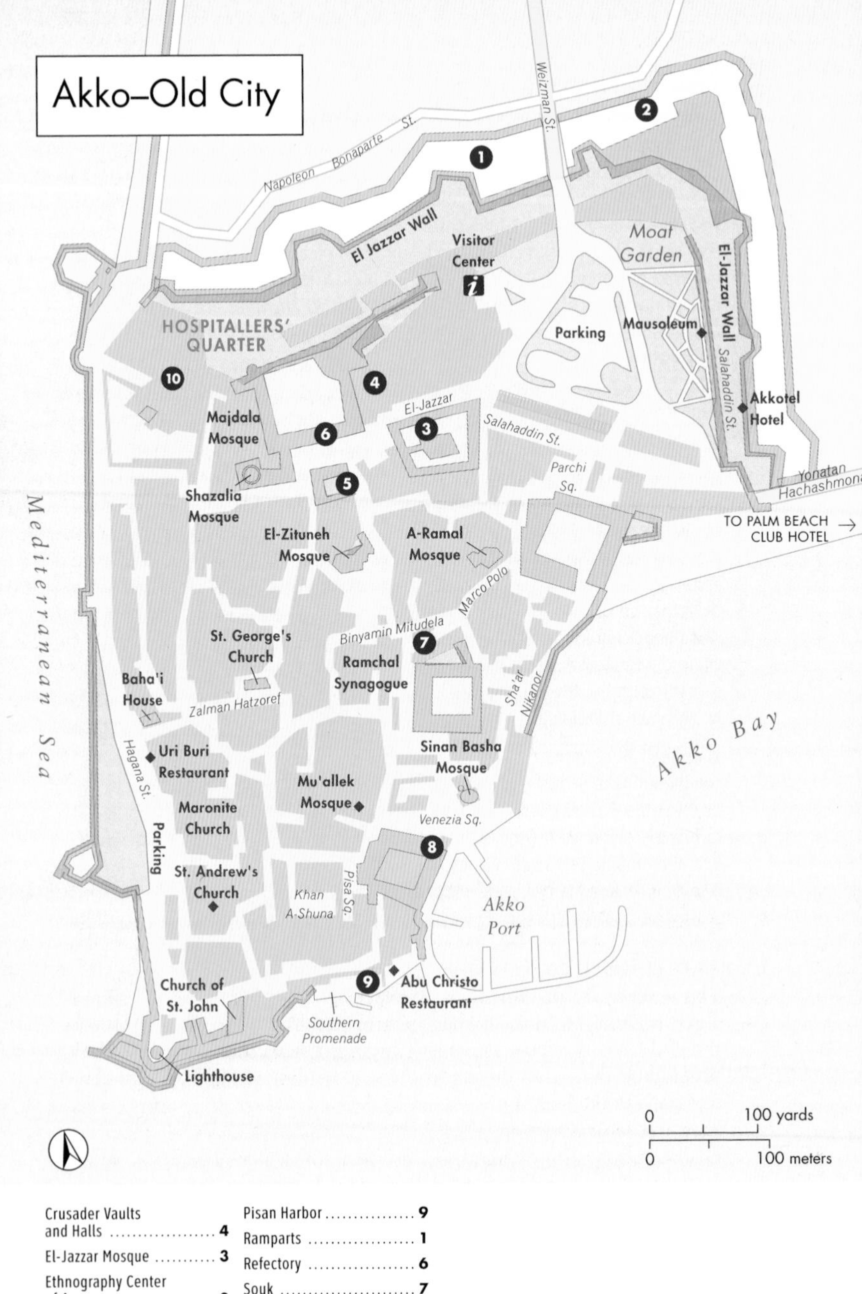

- Crusader Vaults and Halls **4**
- El-Jazzar Mosque **3**
- Ethnography Center of Acre **2**
- Khan el-Umdan **8**
- Museum of the Underground Prisoners .. **10**
- Pisan Harbor **9**
- Ramparts **1**
- Refectory **6**
- Souk **7**
- Turkish bathhouse **5**

also a good stop before entering the Old City. Deeper in the Old City are the fascinating Crusader Vaults and Halls, as well as many other sights. You will end up at the seaside walls of the Pisan Harbor.

WORD OF MOUTH

"For example, I spent an entire day in Akko. There were so many different sites that could fill up a day; then there was a lunch break, the market, and so on." –AlexA

TOP ATTRACTIONS

★ **Crusader Vaults and Halls.** Here you'll find a series of barrel-vaulted rooms known as the Crusader Vaults and Knights Halls. Six such halls have been discovered thus far. Arrows point the way through dimly lit vast rooms filled with ongoing reconstruction work, huge marble columns, and myriad archaeological pieces from the past. Archaeologists are always busy delving into the mysteries of Akko, but signs keep you on a safe path. Above this part of the Crusader city stands the Ottoman citadel, which you can glimpse from the courtyard. Built by Dahr el-Omar in the 18th century on the rubble-filled Crusader ruins, the citadel was the highest structure in Akko.

The different factions within Akko's walls probably sowed the seeds of the Crusaders' downfall here. By the mid-13th century, open fighting had broken out between the Venetians and Genoese. When the Mamluks attacked with a vengeance in 1291, the Crusaders' resistance quickly crumbled, and the city's devastation was complete. It remained a subdued place for centuries, and even today Akko retains a medieval cast. ✉ *1 Weizman St.* ☎ *04/991–1764* 🌐 *www.akko.org.il* 🎟 *Combination ticket NIS 27* ⏲ *Nov.–Mar., Sat.–Thurs. 9–4:15, Fri. 9–1:15; Apr.–Oct., Sat.–Thurs. 9–5, Fri. 9–2:15.*

★ **El-Jazzar Mosque.** This house of worship is considered one of the most beautiful in Israel. Ahmed el-Jazzar, who succeeded Dahr el-Omar after having him assassinated, ruled Akko from 1775 to 1804. During his reign he built this mosque along with other public structures. His cruelty was so legendary that he earned the epithet "the Butcher." (He is buried next to his adopted son in a small white building to the right of the mosque.)

Just beyond the entrance is a pedestal engraved with graceful calligraphy; it re-creates the seal of a 19th-century Ottoman sultan. Some of the marble and granite columns that adorn the mosque and courtyard were plundered from the ruins of Caesarea. In front of the mosque is an ornate fountain used by the faithful for ritual washings of hands and feet. Inside the mosque, enshrined in the gallery reserved for women, is a reliquary containing a hair believed to be from the beard of the prophet Muhammad; it is removed only once a year, on the 27th day of Ramadan.

The mosque closes five times a day for prayers, so you might have a short wait. Dress modestly. ✉ *Off El-Jazzar St.* 🎟 *NIS 6* ⏲ *Sat.–Thurs. 8–5, Fri. 8–11 and 1–5.*

5

NEED A BREAK?

In the plaza outside the El-Jazzar Mosque are outdoor restaurants where you can enjoy a falafel, fresh-squeezed orange or pomegranate juice, or coffee while watching the world go by.

Pisan Harbor. Climbing the stone steps at the water's edge, you can walk along the sea walls at the Pisan Harbor. Start at the café perched on high—a great lookout—and head west in the direction of the 18th-century Church of St. John. You'll end up at the southwestern extremity of Akko, next to the lighthouse. Head north along Haganah Street, which runs parallel to the crenellated western sea wall. After five minutes you'll reach the whitewashed, blue-trimmed Baha'i house (not open to the public), where the prophet of the Baha'i religion, Baha'u'llah, spent 12 years of his exile. His burial site is just north of Akko at the Baha'i Founder's Shrine and Gardens. ✉ *Southern tip of Akko.*

Refectory. The Refectory was once known as the Crypt of St. John—before excavation it was erroneously thought to have been an underground chamber. The dimensions of the colossal pillars that support the roof (they're girded with metal bands for extra support) make this one of Israel's most monumental examples of Crusader architecture. It's also one of the oldest Gothic structures in the world. In the right-hand corner opposite the entrance is a fleur-de-lis carved in stone, the crest of the French house of Bourbon, which has led some scholars to suggest that this was the chamber in which Louis VII convened the knights of the realm.

Just outside this room is an entrance to an extremely narrow subterranean passageway. Cut from stone, this was a secret tunnel that the Crusaders probably used to reach the harbor when besieged by Muslim forces. (Those who are claustrophobic can take an alternate route, which goes back to the entrance of the Turkish bathhouse and continues from there.) You'll emerge to find yourself in the cavernous vaulted halls of the fortress guard post, with a 13th-century marble Crusader tombstone at the exit. ✉ *Parking lot at 1 Weizman St.* ☎ *04/991–1764* 🌐 *www.akko.org.il* 🎫 *Combination ticket NIS 27* ⏲ *Nov.–Mar., Sat.–Thurs. 9–4:15, Fri. 9–1:15; Apr.–Oct., Sat.–Thurs. 9–5, Fri. 9–2:15.*

★ **Turkish Bathhouse.** Built for Pasha el-Jazzar in 1781, Akko's remarkable Turkish bathhouse was in use until 1947. Don't miss the sound-and-light show called "The Story of the Last Bath Attendant," set in the beautiful bathhouse itself. You follow the story, with visual and audio effects, from the dressing room decorated with Turkish tiles and topped with a cupola, through the rooms with colored-glass bubbles protruding from the roof domes, sending a filtered green light to the steam rooms below. ✉ *1 Weizman St.* ☎ *04/991–1764* 🌐 *www.akko.org.il* 🎫 *Combination ticket NIS 46* ⏲ *Nov.–Mar., Sat.–Thurs. 9–4:15, Fri. and Jewish holiday eves 9–1:15; Apr.–Oct., Sat.–Thurs. 9–5, Fri. and Jewish holiday eves 9–2:15.*

WORTH NOTING

Ethnography Center of Acre. There are two sections to this small but charming museum: one re-creates a 19th-century marketplace, including craftsmen's workshops such as a hatmaker and a blacksmith, filled

Now a museum, the 18th-century Turkish bathhouse in Akko receives light through a dome with glass bubbles.

with every last tool they'd need to make hats and horseshoes; the other room displays a traditional Damascene living room, complete with an astounding collection of furniture and accoutrements. To get here once you're up the steps to the Ramparts, keep an eye out for the short flight of stairs heading down to the left. ✉ *On the ramparts* ☎ *04/991–1004* 🎫 *NIS 15* ⏲ *Daily 10–4.*

Khan el-Umdan. In Venezia Square, in front of the port, is the Inn of the Pillars. Before you visit this Ottoman *khan*—the largest of the four in Akko—and the Pisan Quarter beyond, take a stroll around the port, with its small flotilla of fishing boats, yachts, and sailboats. Then walk through the khan's gate beneath a square clock tower, built at the turn of the 20th century. The khan served vast numbers of merchants and travelers during Akko's golden age of commerce, in the 18th century. The 32 pink-and-gray granite pillars that give it its name are compliments of Ahmed el-Jazzar's raids on Roman Caesarea. There was once a market at the center of the colonnaded courtyard. ✉ *Venezia Sq.*

Museum of the Underground Prisoners. Located at the sea's edge, this museum is in several wings of the citadel built by Dahr el-Omar and then modified by Ahmed el-Jazzar in 1785. It became a prison during the British Mandate. On the way in, you pass the citadel's outer wall; the difference between the large Crusader building stones and the smaller Turkish ones above is easy to spot. The original cells and their meager contents, supplemented by photographs and documents that reconstruct the history of the Jewish resistance to British rule in the '30s and '40s, illustrate prison life. During the Mandate, the citadel became a high-security prison whose inmates included top members of Jewish resistance organizations, among them Ze'ev Jabotinsky. In 1947 a dramatic prison breakout by leaders of the Irgun captured headlines around the world and provided Leon Uris's novel *Exodus* with one of its most dramatic moments. ✉ *Hahagana St.* ☎ *04/991–1375* 🎫 *NIS 10* ⏲ *Sun.–Thurs. 8:30–4:30, Fri. 8:30–1:30.*

WORD OF MOUTH

"We loved Akko: the market, the old town, the sea, the people. Fantastic place to spend the afternoon." –ljane

The Ramparts. As you enter the Old City, climb the blue-railing stairway on your right for a stroll along the city walls. Walking to the right, you can see the stunted remains of the 12th-century walls built by the Crusaders, under whose brief rule—just less than two centuries—Akko flourished as never before or since. The indelible signs of the Crusaders, who made Akko the main port of their Christian empire, are much more evident inside the Old City itself.

The wall girding the northern part of the town was built by Ahmed el-Jazzar, the Pasha of Akko, who added these fortifications following his victory over Napoléon's army in 1799. With the help of the British fleet, el-Jazzar turned Napoléon's attempted conquest into a humiliating rout. Napoléon had dreamed of founding a new Eastern empire, thrusting northward from Akko to Turkey and then seizing India from Great Britain. His defeat at Akko hastened his retreat to France, thus changing the course of history. Walk around to the guard towers and up an incline just opposite; there's a view of the moat below and Haifa across the bay. Turn around and let your gaze settle on the exotic skyline of Old Akko, the sea green dome of the great mosque its dominating feature. Walk down the ramp, crossing the rather messy Moat Garden at the base of the walls; straight ahead is the El-Jazzar Mosque.

Souk. At this outdoor market, stalls heaped with fresh produce alternate with specialty stores: a pastry shop with an astonishing variety of exotic Middle Eastern delicacies; a spice shop filled with the aromas of the East; a bakery with steaming fresh pita. You'll often see fishermen sitting on doorsteps, intently repairing their lines and nets to the sounds of Arabic music blaring from the open windows above. The loosely defined area twists and turns through the center of the Old City, but Marco Polo Street is a good place to begin your exploration.

NEED A BREAK?

In the souk, duck into the Oudah Brothers Cafe (✉ *Khan ha Frankim St.* ☎ *04/991–2013*) and enjoy a coffee, hummus, or kebab in the courtyard of the 16th-century Khan el-Faranj, or Franks' Inn. Note the 18th-century Franciscan monastery and tower to your left.

NEAR THE CITY

★ **Baha'i Founder's Shrine and Gardens.** For the Baha'is, this is the holiest place on earth, the site of the tomb of the faith's prophet and founder, Baha'u'llah. First you'll pass the gardens' west gate, open only to Baha'is. Take the first right (no sign) and continue to the unobtrusive turn, 500 yards up, to the north (main) gate. Baha'u'llah lived in the red-tile mansion here after he was released from jail in Akko, and was buried in the small building next door, now the Shrine of Baha'u'llah. Going through the black-iron gate, you follow a white gravel path in the exquisitely landscaped gardens, with a fern-covered fountain and an observation point along the way, until you reach the shrine. Visitors are asked to dress modestly. The shrine is on Route 4, about 1 km (½ mi) north of the gas station at Akko's northern edge. ✉ *Rte. 4* ☎ *04/835–8845* 🌐 *www.bahaigardens.org.il* 🎫 *Free* ⏲ *Gardens daily 9–4; Shrine Fri.–Mon. 9–noon.*

Lochamei Hageta'ot. Kibbutz Lochamei Hageta'ot was founded in 1949 by survivors of the German, Polish, and Lithuanian Jewish ghettos set up by the Nazis. To commemorate their compatriots who perished in the Holocaust, the kibbutz members set up the **Ghetto Fighters Museum,** which you enter to the right of the main gate. Exhibits include photographs documenting the Warsaw Ghetto and the famous uprising, and halls devoted to different themes, among them that of the Jewish communities before their destruction in the Holocaust; the death camps; and deportations at the hands of the Nazis. You can also see the booth in which Adolf Eichmann, architect of the "Final Solution," sat during his Jerusalem trial.

5

In a cone-shaped building, the adjacent **Yad Layeled** (Children's Memorial) is dedicated to the memory of the 1½ million children who perished in the Holocaust. It's designed for young visitors, who can begin to comprehend the events of the Holocaust through a series of tableaux and images accompanied by recorded voices, allowing them to identify with individual victims without seeing shocking details. There is a small cafeteria on the premises. The site is 2 km (1 mi) north of Akko on Route 4. ✉ *Kibbutz Lochamei Hageta'ot, Rte. 4* ☎ *04/995–8080* 🎫 *Free* ⏲ *Sun.–Thurs. 9–4.*

WHERE TO EAT

$$ SEAFOOD

✕ **Abu Christo.** In the Old City, this popular waterfront fish restaurant stands at one of the original 18th-century gates built by Pasha Ahmed el-Jazzar when he fortified the city after his victory over Napoléon. It's a family business that's been passed from father to son since 1948. The covered patio is an idyllic place to dig into earthy hummus with pine nuts, eggplant salad spiced with sumac, and other salads. Abu Christo serves the daily catch—often grouper, red snapper, or sea bass—prepared simply, either grilled or deep-fried. Shellfish such as jumbo shrimp and crabs, and grilled meats are also available. ✉ *Crusader Port* ☎ *04/991–0065* 🌐 *www.abu-christo.co.il* ✍ *Reservations essential* 💳 *AE, DC, MC, V.*

$$$ SEAFOOD Fodor's Choice ★

✕ **Uri Buri.** Known far and wide for its excellent fish and seafood, Uri Buri is housed in an old Turkish building. One room is furnished with sofas, copper dishes, and *nargillas* (water pipes). Everything on the menu is seasonal, and the fresh fish is steamed, baked, or grilled. Allow time to linger here—it's not your everyday fish fry. Two house specialties are gravlax and Thai-style fish; delicious seafood soup is another fixture. Or try the baby calamari with kumquats and pink grapefruit or Creole shrimp with five spices. Uri Buri is near the lighthouse, on one edge of the parking lot. ✉ *93 Haganah St.* ☎ *04/955–2212* ⚠ *Reservations essential* ▭ *AE, DC, MC, V* ⊗ *Closed Tues.*

WHERE TO STAY

$ **Akkotel.** This three-story hostelry, a former Turkish police station, is built into the city wall. Original wood doors lead into the small lobby where a painted plaster rosette decorates the gold ceiling. The lavish old-world decor has been updated: original bathrooms have been beautifully modernized and surprising touches of original stonework remain in the windows and walls. Double rooms are decorated in brown, caramel, and beige, and net curtains embroidered with flowers frame the windows. Each of the five family rooms has a loft with two beds so four people can settle in comfortably. The rooftop café showcases the lovely skyline of Old Akko. **Pros:** family run; unusual lodging; warm service. **Cons:** no pool; no parking. ✉ *Salahaddin St.* ☎ *04/987–7100* 🌐 *www.akkotel.com* *16 rooms, 2 suites* *In-room: safe, refrigerator. In-hotel: restaurant, Internet terminal, Wi-Fi hotspot* ▭ *AE, DC, MC, V.*

$ **Nes Ammim Guest House.** Founded in 1964, Nes Ammim is an ecumenical Christian settlement focusing on mutual respect and tolerance. Guests are invited to chat with members of the community, who are happy to take you around the beautifully landscaped grounds. Lodging options are either standard rooms or family apartments with kitchenettes. The setting, 10 km (6 mi) north of Akko, is picturesque and rural, once you get past the dismal approach road. To get here, drive north from Akko on Route 4. **Pros:** welcoming staff; good for families; modest price. **Cons:** basic rooms; few activities. ✉ *Off Rte. 4* ☎ *04/995–0000* *48 rooms, 13 apartments* *In-room: a/c, safe, refrigerator. In-hotel: restaurant, bar, pool, Internet terminal, Wi-Fi hotspot* ▭ *AE, DC, MC, V.*

$$ **Palm Beach Club.** A private beach with exceptional views and a country club with state-of-the-art facilities make this hotel a great deal, especially for families. There's a huge outdoor pool in a sprawling grassy area where wooden walkways lead down to the curving bay. The views are fantastic: on one side you can see Old Akko's blue domes, skinny minarets, and stone walls; on the other, the mountains behind Haifa. For youngsters there's a children's pool, and for adults a Turkish bath with wet and dry saunas. There's also a bar in the cheerful lobby. **Pros:** warm staff; great beach; lots of activities. **Cons:** small rooms. ✉ *Rte. 4* ☎ *04/987–7777* 🌐 *www.palmbeach.co.il* *97 rooms, 27 suites* *In-room: a/c, safe, refrigerator, Internet (some). In-hotel: 2 restaurants, room service, tennis courts, pools, gym, spa, Wi-Fi hotspot, parking (free)* ▭ *AE, DC, MC, V.*

SPORTS AND THE OUTDOORS

Just south of the Old City on the Haifa–Akko road is a sandy stretch of municipal beach in **Akko Bay,** with parking, showers, toilets, and chair rentals. Admission is NIS 10.

Despite modern boats, the old harbor in Akko retains echoes of past eras.

SHOPPING

David Miro (✉ *1 Weitzman St.* ☎ *04/955–3439*) sells a whole range of Israeli-made products. The jewelry that combines silver and gold is especially interesting; some incorporates Roman glass, some uses turquoise Eilat stone, and there's also hand-worked copperware and silver pieces.

EN ROUTE

To the west of Route 4, as you travel north from Akko, stands a segment of the multitiered **aqueduct** built by Ahmed el-Jazzar in the late 18th century to carry the sweet waters of the Kabri springs to Akko.

NAHARIYA

8 km (5 mi) north of Akko.

This crowded, vibrant seaside town was built along the banks of a river lined with eucalyptus trees. (The town's name comes from *nahar,* the Hebrew word for "river.") The town is popular with vacationing Israelis who throng the small shops along the main street. European visitors too appreciate the lively atmosphere and the white-sand beaches. One of the region's most beautiful stretches of sand is just at the end of the main street. Two others sit just north of town.

Although German was once the most common language here, you're now just as likely to hear Russian or Amharic (spoken by Ethiopians). In July and August, there's dancing in the amphitheater at the mouth of the river, and Israeli stars perform on the beach and in the town square.

GETTING HERE AND AROUND

There are direct buses from Haifa. Trains from Jerusalem and Tel Aviv travel at least twice a day to Nahariya. You might have to change trains along the way. By car, take Route 4 north of Akko. From a location 5 km (3 mi) north of Nahariya, Trek Yam takes you on an exciting 30-minute ride up the coast in a high-speed motorboat. The cost is NIS 70 per person.

ESSENTIALS

Tour Information **Trek Yam** (☎ *04/982–3671*).

EXPLORING

Byzantine Church. This church has an elaborate, 17-color mosaic floor, discovered in 1964, that depicts peacocks, other birds, hunting scenes, and plants. It was part of what experts consider one of the largest and most beautiful Byzantine churches in the Western Galilee, where Christianity rapidly spread from the 4th to the 7th century. To get here, head east on Haga'aton to Route 4, making a left at the stoplight and then the first right onto Yechi'am Street. From here take the third left and then an immediate right onto Bielefeld Street. ✉ *Bielefeld St.* *NIS 2.*

WHERE TO EAT

$$$$ MEDITERRANEAN Fodor'sChoice ★ ✕ **Adelina.** When dining at this stellar restaurant, you may wonder how you got so lucky. There's the knockout view of the Mediterranean from the stone terrace, the olive tree-shaded setting, and the wonderful Spanish-accented dishes prepared by Adelina. Cooking is done in the huge silver tabun oven as Spanish music drifts across the dark wooden tables. Try the paella marinara packed with shellfish, roast sirloin with bacon and tarragon, or broccoli cannelloni in a creamy pepper sauce. Move on to *knafe* (a local pastry) with pistachio ice cream. The eatery is about 8 km (5 mi) east of Nahariya. ✉ *Kibbutz Kabri, Rte. 89* ☎ *04/952–3707* *Reservations essential* *AE, DC, MC, V* *Closed Sun.*

$$ MEDITERRANEAN ✕ **BaNahala.** Be prepared for taste-bud overload at this lovely restaurant surrounded by pecan trees. Inside the old building, part of a family estate, wood tables are set with fresh flowers, chairs are made from woven rope, and one wall displays the charming faces of the owners as children. Outside, market umbrellas shade the tables on the huge wood-plank terrace. When the kids are finished choosing from their own menu, they can frolic on the lawn. For grown-ups there's everything from lamb kebabs with tahini to sweet red peppers stuffed with tangy cheese and risotto to tuna steak marinated in ginger. Top off the meal with baked cheesecake and berry sorbet. The comprehensive list of Israeli wines gives you a chance to sample local vintages. ✉ *17a Yitzhak Sadeh* ☎ *04/951–2074* *www.banahala.co.il* *Reservations essential* *AE, DC, MC, V* *Closed Sun.*

$$ MODERN ISRAELI ✕ **Ida.** On the main street, you'll recognize Ida by the white stucco building topped by a sign in big blue letters. Ida was the wife of the town's first mayor, and the couple lived here in the 1950s. The mood is friendly and relaxed. Gold roses are stenciled on several walls, and wood screens divide the interior into cozy areas. It's an impressive modern Israeli dining experience: start with duck confit with cranberry sauce, then move on to shellfish risotto with a creamy shrimp sauce or the panfried trout

with a coconut and carrot sauce. It'll be hard to say no to chocolate cheesecake as a finale. ✉ *48 Haga'aton Blvd.* ☎ *04/951–3444* ▭ *AE, DC, MC, V.*

> **WORD OF MOUTH**
>
> "I second the recommendation of Nahariya. Nahariya is right next to the fabulous Achziv beach, and it's a couple of miles from Rosh Hanikra. It's a much quieter experience than Haifa." –judyinjerusalem

$$ FRENCH ★ **La Crepe Jacob.** This popular place is in a small cottage with blue window frames and a flower-filled garden. A wood-burning stove keeps things cozy inside. Locally made goat cheeses cram the counter as you walk in. The hefty crepes, lovingly prepared by Betty and Jacob, come with fillings such as feta, ham, and mushrooms; smoked salmon and cheese; and tomato, onion, olives, cheese, and mushrooms. The banana and chocolate crepe is a delicious wrap-up. In addition, the menu includes heartier dishes like veal fillet with shrimp. It's about 3 km (2 mi) east of the city. ✉ *Moshav Ben Ami, Rte. 89* ☎ *04/952–0299* ▭ *AE, DC, MC, V* ⊗ *Closed Sun.*

$$ ECLECTIC **Penguin.** The doors to this casual institution opened in 1940—it's probably the oldest restaurant in the country. Three generations of the same family work here, and the walls carry enlarged photographs of how the place looked when it was just a hut. Stop off for coffee and cake, or make a meal of spinach blintzes with melted cheese, hamburger platters, or Chinese dishes. The management swears that the schnitzel gets accolades from Viennese visitors. Kids will enjoy the enclosed playground. ✉ *31 Haga'aton Blvd.* ☎ *04/992–8855* ▭ *AE, DC, MC, V.*

WHERE TO STAY

$$$$ ★ **Aromantica.** Varda, who makes every effort to provide a relaxing stay for guests, runs these comfortable country cottages in the rural farming settlement of Moshav Ben Ami. Her touches include chocolates left bedside, and complimentary wine, lemonade, and ice cream. A tiny rock fountain burbles outside the door of each tile-roofed cabin, and wind chimes provide soothing sounds. Inside, each room has clay-hued sofas, bright white pillows and coverlets, wood-burning stoves, and hot tubs. It's about 3 km (2 mi) east of the city. **Pros:** personal service; pretty location. **Cons:** not for families; a bit hard to find. ✉ *Rte. 89* ☎ *054/498–2302 or 04/982–0484* 🌐 *www.aromantica.co.il* *3 cabins* *In-room: a/c, kitchen* ▭ *AE, DC, MC, V* *BP.*

$$ **New Carlton.** A wood-paneled spa with eight treatment rooms, wet and dry saunas, a quiet lounge, and a fitness room make this a pleasant place to stay. These handsome facilities also include an outdoor pool surrounded by a grassy lawn. You can walk down the street to a wonderful beach, soaking up the flavor of a bustling town as you go. The guest rooms are tasteful, with taupe curtains, white duvets, and black-and-taupe carpets. Some rooms have balconies facing the pool. La Scala dance club attracts revelers with live music. **Pros:** helpful staff; amenities for business travelers. **Cons:** noisy lobby; crowded on weekends. ✉ *23 Haga'aton* ☎ *04/900–5555* *192 rooms, 4 suites* *In-room: a/c, safe, refrigerator. In-hotel: restaurant, room service, bar, pool, parking (free), Wi-Fi hotspot* ▭ *AE, DC, MC, V* *BP.*

5

At Rosh Hanikra, take a cable car down the cliffs for an up-close look at the sea grottoes.

$$$$ **Pinhas & Gaston.** Billed as a "holiday estate," this heavenly retreat offers four delightful guesthouses, each featuring carved-wood beds, down quilts, and well-equipped kitchens. Each has its own wooden deck, hot tub, and private pool; wicker lounge chairs under big market-style umbrellas face a tangerine orchard. If you can tear yourself away from all this luxury, bikes are available for a spin around the rural setting. Thoughtful touches, such as espresso machines in the kitchens, make the place feel like home. **Pros:** beautiful setting; romantic getaway. **Cons:** expensive rates; no Internet. ✉ *Moshav Liman, Rte. 4* ☎ *057/728–2828 or 04/952–6000* *4 houses* *In-room: a/c, kitchen, DVD. In-hotel: 4 pools, bicycles* *AE, DC, MC, V* *BP.*

$ ★ **Pivko Village.** Nestled among the trees on the grounds of a kibbutz, these roomy log cabins hold up to five people, making them a good bet for families. The amazing views from the wide windows and the hot tubs on the patios sweep from Haifa to the cliffs of Rosh Hanikra. The interiors are warm and comfortable, with separate living and sleeping areas. There are plenty of activities, such as horseback riding, hiking, swimming, and tennis. Breakfast is brought to your door. The excellent restaurant Adelina is right on the grounds. **Pros:** lots of activities; good restaurant. **Cons:** a bit hard to find. ✉ *Kibbutz Kabri, Rte. 89* ☎ *04/995–2711* *www.al-hagivah.co.il* *6 cabins* *In-room: a/c, kitchen, Internet. In-hotel: restaurant* *AE, DC, MC, V* *BP.*

$$$$ ★ **Villa Provence.** Hidden away in a rural settlement 10 km (6 mi) from the city, this out-of-the-ordinary lodging looks as though it was plucked from a French hillside. Inside the main building are six individually

decorated suites, each named for a French flower (the Lilac Suite is sweet as can be). Every piece of furniture and all the decorative accessories, from armoires to picture frames, have been hand-painted and decorated in Provençal style. Outside are a pool and a hot tub surrounded by chaise lounges. The breakfast, served in a dining room overlooking the pool or outside on the terrace, is organic. **Pros:** gorgeous setting; pretty pool. **Cons:** very expensive; no restaurants nearby. ✉ *Moshav Manot, Rte. 8911* ☎ *04/980–6246* 🌐 *www.villaprovence.co.il* *6 rooms* *In-room: a/c, refrigerator. In-hotel: Wi-Fi hotspot* *AE, MC, V* *BP.*

NIGHTLIFE AND THE ARTS

La Scala (✉ *23 Haga'aton St.* ☎ *04/900–5555*), Nahariya's flashiest disco, draws the over-30 crowd for standard dance tunes with a throbbing beat. It's in the passageway just west of the New Carlton. The cover charge on Friday is NIS 50; doors open at 10 pm.

5

SPORTS AND THE OUTDOORS

BEACHES

Nahariya's public bathing facilities at **Galei Galil Beach** (✉ *North of Haga'aton Blvd.*) are ideal for families. Apart from the lovely beach, facilities include an Olympic-size pool, a wading pool, a playground for children, changing rooms and showers, plus a snack bar. In peak season, the beach offers exercise classes early in the morning. The entrance fee is NIS 30.

★ Beautifully maintained because it's in the Achziv National Park, **Achziv Beach** (✉ *Rte. 2*) is great for kids. There are two huge lagoons along the sandy shore, one shallow, the other deep. There are also watchful lifeguards and playground facilities. In July and August, turtles lay their eggs on the beach. You can picnic on the grassy slopes or make use of the restaurant. Enter at the second sign for Achziv Beach, not the first. Admission, which is NIS 30, includes the use of showers and toilets.

Betzet Beach (✉ *Rte. 2*), a bit farther north of Achziv Beach, is part of a nature reserve and offers abundant vegetation, trees, and the ruins of an ancient olive press. There's a lifeguard on duty in season. Admission is free.

SCUBA DIVING

★ **Trek Yam** (☎ *04/982–3671*) takes scuba divers to explore the caves at Rosh Hanikra along the coast. The price of each trip is NIS 75. The company also offers Jeep trips and boating excursions. Reserve several days in advance.

ROSH HANIKRA

7 km (4½ mi) north of Nahariya and 38 km (24 mi) north of Haifa.

★

GETTING HERE AND AROUND

It's a short drive from Nahariya to Rosh Hanikra, the last destination on the country's northern coast. You'll need your own car, as there's no public transportation.

EXPLORING

> **WORD OF MOUTH**
>
> "If you are limiting yourself to coastal sites, then I would make sure to drive a bit farther north to Rosh Hanikra—there is a beautiful view and interesting caves; it's well worth the trip. Caesarea and Akko will occupy a full day." -Oreet

The dramatic white cliffs on the coast signal both Israel's border with Lebanon and the sea grottoes of **Rosh Hanikra.** Even before you get in line for the two-minute cable-car ride down to the grottoes, take a moment to absorb the stunning view back down the coast. Still clearly visible is the route of the railway line, now mostly a dirt road, built by the British through the hillside in 1943 to extend the Cairo–Tel Aviv–Haifa line to Beirut. After the descent, you can see the 12-minute audiovisual presentation called *The Sea and the Cliff.*

The incredible caves beneath the cliff have been carved out by relentless waves pounding away at the white chalky rock for countless years. Footpaths inside the cliff itself lead from one huge cave to another, while the sound of waves echoes off the water-sprayed rocky walls. Huge bursts of seawater plunge into pools at your feet (behind protective rails). It's slippery, so hang on to the children. ✉ *End of Rte. 4* ☎ *073/271–0100* 🌐 *www.rosh-hanikra.com* 🎫 *NIS 42* ⏲ *Nov.–Mar., Sat.–Thurs. 8:30–4, Fri. 9–4; Apr.–June, Sat.–Thurs. 9–6, Fri. 9–4; July and Aug., Sat.–Thurs. 8:30 am–11 pm, Fri. 8:30–4. Call to verify hrs.*

WHERE TO EAT

$$ ISRAELI ✕ **Diner ba Rosh.** This bright and breezy spot for Israeli fare has a fabulous view of the sea swirling and crashing below. The selection of beers on tap—all produced in the Golan Heights—range from pale ale to a tangy red lager. Starters include a bagel with corned beef and a baked potato with garlic sauce and fried onions. As a main course, the appealing casserole of beef and root vegetables simmered in beer is a sure hit, as are franks and sauerkraut, steaks, and burgers. ✉ *End of Rte. 4* ☎ *04/952–0159* 💳 *AE, DC, MC, V* ⏲ *Closed Sat.*

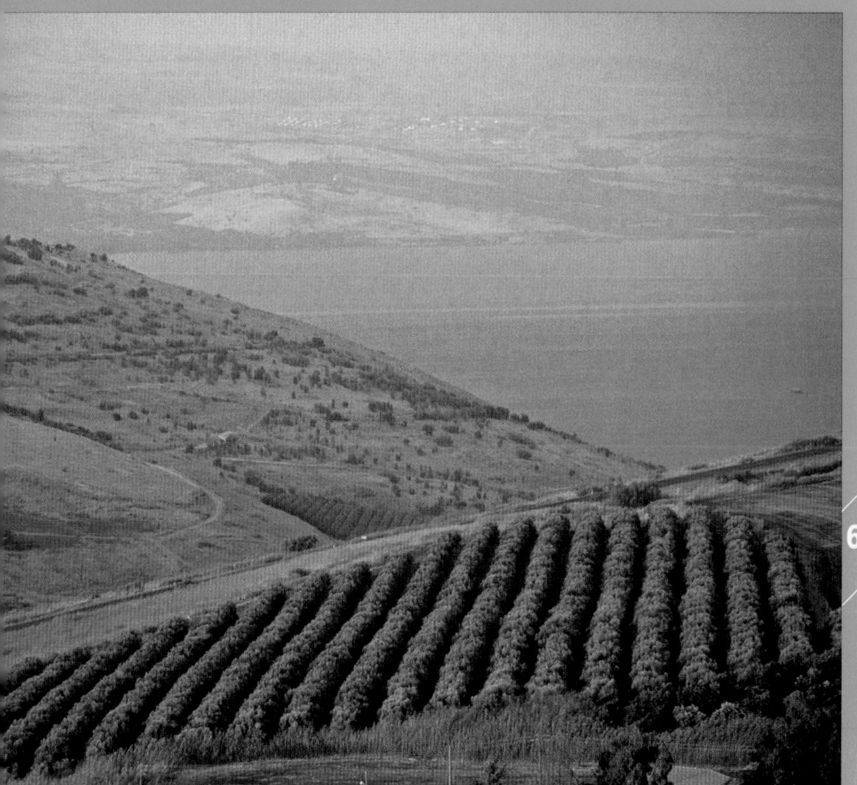

6

Lower Galilee

WITH NAZARETH, TIBERIAS, AND THE SEA OF GALILEE

WORD OF MOUTH

"We hit all holy sites in Galilee and made it to Beit Shean which is the coolest archaeology dig we've seen since Pompeii."

—semiretired

WELCOME TO LOWER GALILEE

National park at Beit She'an

TOP REASONS TO GO

★ **Sunset on the Sea of Galilee:** The lake at sundown is always evocative, often beautiful, and occasionally spectacular. Walk a beach, sip a drink, or take a sail as dusk slowly settles.

★ **Zippori:** The distant past is palpable at this archaeological site, once a worldly Jewish and Hellenistic city. Set amid woods, it has the loveliest ancient mosaics in the land.

★ **Nazareth:** Tradition and modernity collide in the town where Jesus grew up. Today it is a city of baklava and BMWs, new politics and ancient passions. Talk to a local as you sample Middle Eastern delicacies.

★ **Mt. Gilboa:** This little-visited region offers local beauty and grand views for the independent traveler who has a bit of time and no checklist of must-see famous sites.

★ **A spiritual source:** Tune your ear to the Galilee's spiritual reverberations. Listen as pilgrims chant a Mass at the Mount of Beatitudes or sit meditatively on Tabgha's shore.

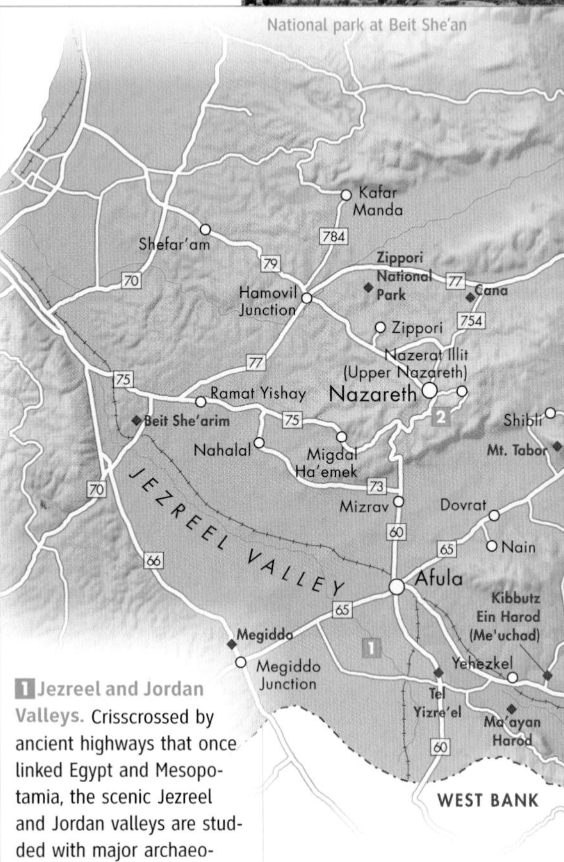

1 Jezreel and Jordan Valleys. Crisscrossed by ancient highways that once linked Egypt and Mesopotamia, the scenic Jezreel and Jordan valleys are studded with major archaeological and historical sites. Megiddo, corrupted in Greek as Armageddon, is known for a biblical battle and is prophesied to be the site of a future one. Zippori, also called Sepphoris, is a site with Jewish and Christian links. The Roman ruins at Beit She'an evoke the glory of one the richest cities in the eastern Mediterranean.

2 Nazareth and the Galilee Hills. The once-sleepy town of Nazareth, the site of Jesus' boyhood, has boomed in recent decades to become a regional center. The nearby hills, such as Mt. Tabor and Mt. Gilboa, are both biblical byways and part of the reforested landscape many find so entrancing.

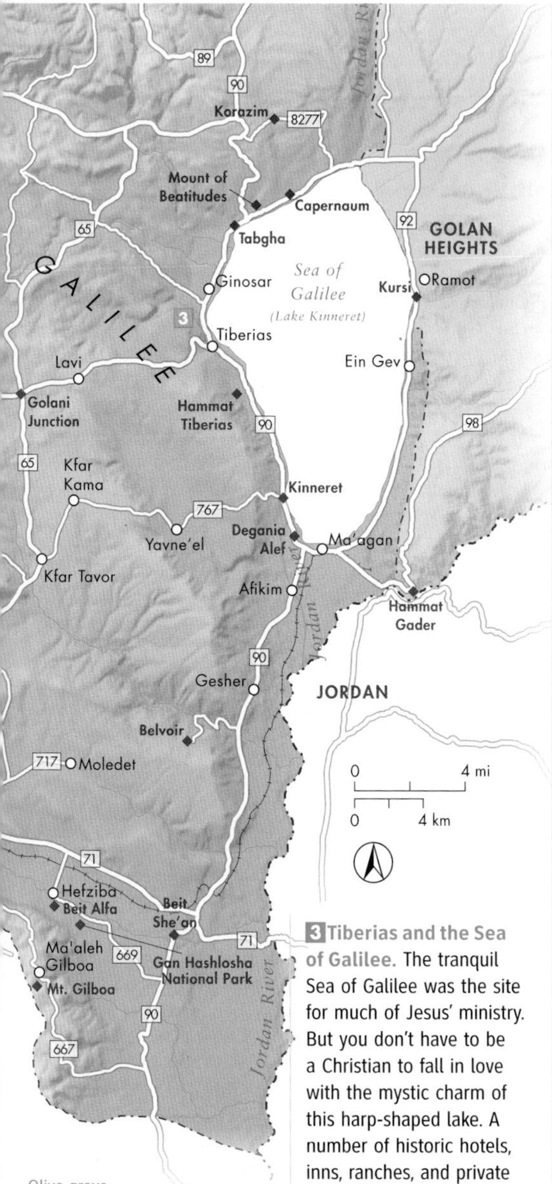

GETTING ORIENTED

The Hebrew word *gal* means "wave," and the Lower Galilee is indeed a hilly country, with deep valleys framed by mountain ridges. Not much more than a creek, the Jordan River cuts through the topography on the eastern border, first draining into the freshwater Sea of Galilee and then flowing south toward the Dead Sea. The Galilee is the storied land where King Saul lost his life fighting the Philistines; where the Romans built cities such as Beit She'an; where Jesus, who grew up in Nazareth, carried out much of his ministry; and where the Crusaders built and lost a kingdom. The lakeside resort city of Tiberias beckons with its hot springs and history.

Basilica of the Annunciation, Nazareth

3 Tiberias and the Sea of Galilee. The tranquil Sea of Galilee was the site for much of Jesus' ministry. But you don't have to be a Christian to fall in love with the mystic charm of this harp-shaped lake. A number of historic hotels, inns, ranches, and private villas ring the lake. The hot springs at Tiberias and Hammat Gader have been attracting guests since the time of Augustus Caesar.

Olive grove

6

LOWER GALILEE PLANNER

When to Go

The Galilee is prettiest in the spring months of March and April when it is covered with wildflowers, and its hills are draped in green. Summer can be torrid. Avoid the Sea of Galilee during Passover (March–April) and the High Holidays and Sukkot (September–October): although the weather is great at these times, half the country vacations here; rates soar.

Some hotels charge high-season rates during July and August; this is also true the week of Christmas. Weekends in general (Thursday night through Saturday night) are more crowded; some hotels hike rates substantially.

Special Walks

Two annual *Tza'adot* (Big Walks) take place in March or April: one along the shore of the Sea of Galilee (2½ km [1½ mi] and 9 km [5½ mi]), the other along the trails of Mt. Gilboa (routes range from 6 km [4 mi] to 40 km [25 mi] over two days). These mass rambles attract folks from all over the country and abroad. For details, contact **Israel Sport for All Association** (☎ *03/562–1441* ✉ *isfa@zahav.net.il*).

Getting Here and Around

Bus Travel: The Egged bus cooperative provides regular service from Jerusalem, Tel Aviv, and Haifa to Nazareth, Beit She'an, Afula, and Tiberias. There is no direct service from Ben Gurion International Airport; change in Tel Aviv or Haifa. There are several buses an hour from Tel Aviv to Afula (1½ hours). Bus 842 (*yashir*, or "direct") is quickest; Buses 829, 830, and 835 are express, stopping at major stations en route. Bus 823 from Afula to Nazareth (20 minutes) is infrequent. The 830 and 835 continue from Afula to Tiberias (about an hour). The 829 and 843 link Afula to Beit She'an (20 minutes) three times a day.

To get from Haifa to Tiberias, take the slow Bus 430 (about an hour), which leaves hourly from Merkazit Hamifratz. From the same Haifa station, the slow Bus 301 leaves two or three times an hour for Afula. Buses from Jerusalem to Beit She'an and Tiberias (Buses 961, 963, 966, and the slower 948) depart roughly hourly; change in Beit She'an for Afula, where you change again for Nazareth. Buses 961 and 963 continue to Tiberias. The ride to Beit She'an is about two hours, to Tiberias another 25 minutes. Bus 431 connects Nazareth and Tiberias once every two hours.

Car Travel: Driving is the best way to explore the Lower Galilee. Driving time from Tel Aviv or Jerusalem to Tiberias is two hours. Some newer four-lane highways are excellent, but some secondary roads may be in need of repair.

Signposting is clear (and usually in English), with route numbers clearly marked. Brown signs indicate most sights. The Lower Galilee is served by a number of highways. Route 90, going up the Jordan Valley to Tiberias and on to Metulla on the Lebanese border, is the most convenient road from Jerusalem. Routes 2 and 4, both multilane expressways, lead north from Tel Aviv. Turn east onto Route 65, then north onto Route 60 to get to Nazareth. Stay on Route 65 and turn east on Route 77 to reach Tiberias. While Route 6 is a modern superhighway, it is also an electronic toll road. If you're driving a rental car, you'll be charged for using it.

For more information about getting here and around, see the Travel Smart chapter.

Dining

Tiberias in particular and the Sea of Galilee in general have far livelier culinary options than other parts of Lower Galilee. Some places in the countryside are worth going out of your way for. Restaurant attire is casual.

The local specialty is the native St. Peter's fish (tilapia), though most restaurants serve the (still excellent) pond-bred variety. Meat dishes tend to be Middle Eastern: *shashlik* and kebabs (ground meat grilled on skewers) accompanied by hummus, pickles, and french fries. Most economical are *shawarma* (slices of spit-grilled turkey meat served in pita bread) and falafel. The cheapest eats are always at the stands at a town's central bus station.

Lodging

Tiberias, the region's tourist center, has hotels for budgets from deluxe to economy. Within a 20- to 30-minute drive are excellent guesthouses, some run by kibbutz residents and some on the Sea of Galilee. Nazareth has a couple of deluxe hotels and several older inexpensive ones that cater primarily to Christian pilgrim groups but also attract individual travelers and Israelis. Also in Nazareth, and to a lesser extent around Tiberias, are hospices run by Christian orders.

Bed-and-breakfasts have sprung up in profusion. Many are in or adjacent to private homes in rural farming communities; others are within kibbutzim. These are a good value, especially for families.

Many "guesthouses," as upgraded youth hostels are now called, are suitable for families; these are generally the cheapest deals.

WHAT IT COSTS

	¢	$	$$	$$$	$$$$
Restaurants	under NIS 32	NIS 32–NIS 49	NIS 50–NIS 75	NIS 76–NIS 100	over NIS 100
Hotels	under $120	$120–$200	$201–$300	$301–$400	over $400

Restaurant prices are per person for a main course at dinner in NIS (Israeli shekels). Hotel prices are in U.S. dollars, for two people in a standard double room in high season. Non-Israeli citizens paying in foreign currency are exempt from the 16% VAT tax on hotel rooms.

Top Festivals

Ein Gev, on the eastern shore of the Sea of Galilee, has an Israeli-music festival in the spring. Beit She'an revives its ancient Roman theater for a short series of events in October, and in May and December, Jacob's Ladder—the twice-annual folk festival—fills the air above Nof Ginosar, on the Sea of Galilee, with traditional folk and country music of the British Isles and North America.

Planning Your Time

It's possible to get a feeling for this region in a few days, but you can expand your trip to include some highlights of the Upper Galilee and the Golan including Tzfat (Safed). Tiberias, with its many accommodations, or the Sea of Galilee region is a good base for exploring archaeological sites—Beit She'an is impressive—as well as sites associated with the ministry of Jesus. Nazareth is worth a trip, either from Tiberias or en route to it from other areas. The Galilee is a low-key area with some lovely national parks and natural sites, including Mt. Tabor, if you choose to linger.

Tours

Both Egged Tours and United Tours have one-day tours around the region from Jerusalem and Tel Aviv that take in Nazareth, the Sea of Galilee, and other highlights.

Updated by Sarah Bronson

The Lower Galilee is a history-soaked region where scores of events in the Hebrew Bible and the New Testament took place. Blessed with forested hills, fertile valleys, gushing springs, and the Sea of Galilee, it has strong appeal. The graves of Jewish, Christian, Muslim, and Druze holy men attract those seeking spiritual solace, but the region is also the scene of earthly delights, including fine restaurants and spas.

To most Israelis, the Galilee is synonymous with "the North," a land of nature reserves and national parks. In short, they would claim, it's a great place to visit, but they wouldn't want to live there: it's provincial and remote. Still, the Lower Galilee has its own quiet beauty and varied landscape. Whatever your agenda is—spiritual, historical, recreational, or restful—savor your time here. Follow a hiking trail above the Sea of Galilee. Wade through fields of irises in the spring. Bathe in a warm mineral spa. Buy some good goat cheese.

Farming and tourism form the economic base. The region's kibbutzim and a smaller number of moshavim (Jewish family-farm villages) are concentrated in the Jezreel and Jordan valleys and around the Sea of Galilee. The rockier hill country is predominantly Arab (*Israeli* Arab; this is not disputed territory), and for the last half century the two communities—Jewish and Arab—have been attempting neighborly relations despite the ethnic tensions that swirl around them. By and large, they've succeeded.

Culture and entertainment are not this region's strong suits. A number of annual festivals and events are the highlights. Tiberias's pubs and restaurants probably come closest to providing lively nightlife, but there are worse ways to spend an evening than sitting by a moonlit lake washing down a good St. Peter's fish or a lamb shashlik with an excellent Israeli wine.

JEZREEL AND JORDAN VALLEYS

"Highways of the world cross Galilee in all directions," wrote the eminent Victorian scholar George Adam Smith in 1898. The great international highway of antiquity, the Via Maris (Way of the Sea), swept up the Mediterranean coast from Egypt and broke inland along three separate passes through the hills to emerge in the Jezreel Valley before continuing northeast to Damascus and Mesopotamia. It made the Jezreel Valley a convenient and frequent battleground. In fact, the Jezreel Valley heard the clash of arms so often that the very name of its most commanding tell—Har Megiddo (Mt. Megiddo), or Armageddon—became a New Testament synonym for the final apocalyptic battle of all time. Today, this and other ancient sites such as Beit She'an remain highlights here.

On a topographical map, the Jezreel Valley appears as an equilateral triangle with sides about 40 km (25 mi) long, edged by low mountains and with a narrow extension east to Beit She'an, in the Jordan Rift. From there, the Jordan Valley stretches like a ribbon north to the Sea of Galilee. Your first impression will be one of lush farmland as far as the eye can see. But as recently as 50 years ago, malarial swamps still blighted the area; some pioneering settlements had cemeteries before their first buildings were completed.

With a few exceptions, restaurants in this rustic area are confined to roadside cafeterias, lunchtime diners at or near parks, and small restaurants and snack bars in the towns of Afula and Beit She'an.

BEIT SHE'ARIM

20 km (12½ mi) southeast of Haifa, 25 km (15½ mi) west of Nazareth.

GETTING HERE AND AROUND

Driving from Tel Aviv, take Route 4 (the old Tel Aviv–Haifa Highway) to Furadis Junction, then turn east on Route 70. Continue to Yokneam Junction, then take Route 722 to Hashomrim Junction. Take the first left, and continue until you reach the national park.

EXPLORING

Chalk slopes are honeycombed with catacombs around the attractively landscaped site of ancient **Beit She'arim**—today Beit She'arim National Park. Orthodox Jews pilgrimage here to the Tomb of Judah ha-Nasi, chief editor and redactor of the Mishnah, the seminal text of rabbinic Judaism, but you don't need to be religious to appreciate the role this vast necropolis has played in the development of modern Judaism. The landscape is soothing, there are pleasant walking paths, and some of the caves have an Indiana Jones–intrigue. Equipped with a flashlight and free park brochure and map, you'll discover ornately carved sarcophagi that attest to the complex intercultural relations in the Roman world.

A Jewish town flourished here after the eclipse of Jerusalem brought about by Titus's legions in AD 70 and its reconstruction as a pagan town by Hadrian in AD 135. For generations Jews were denied access to their holy city and its venerated burial ground on the Mt. of Olives,

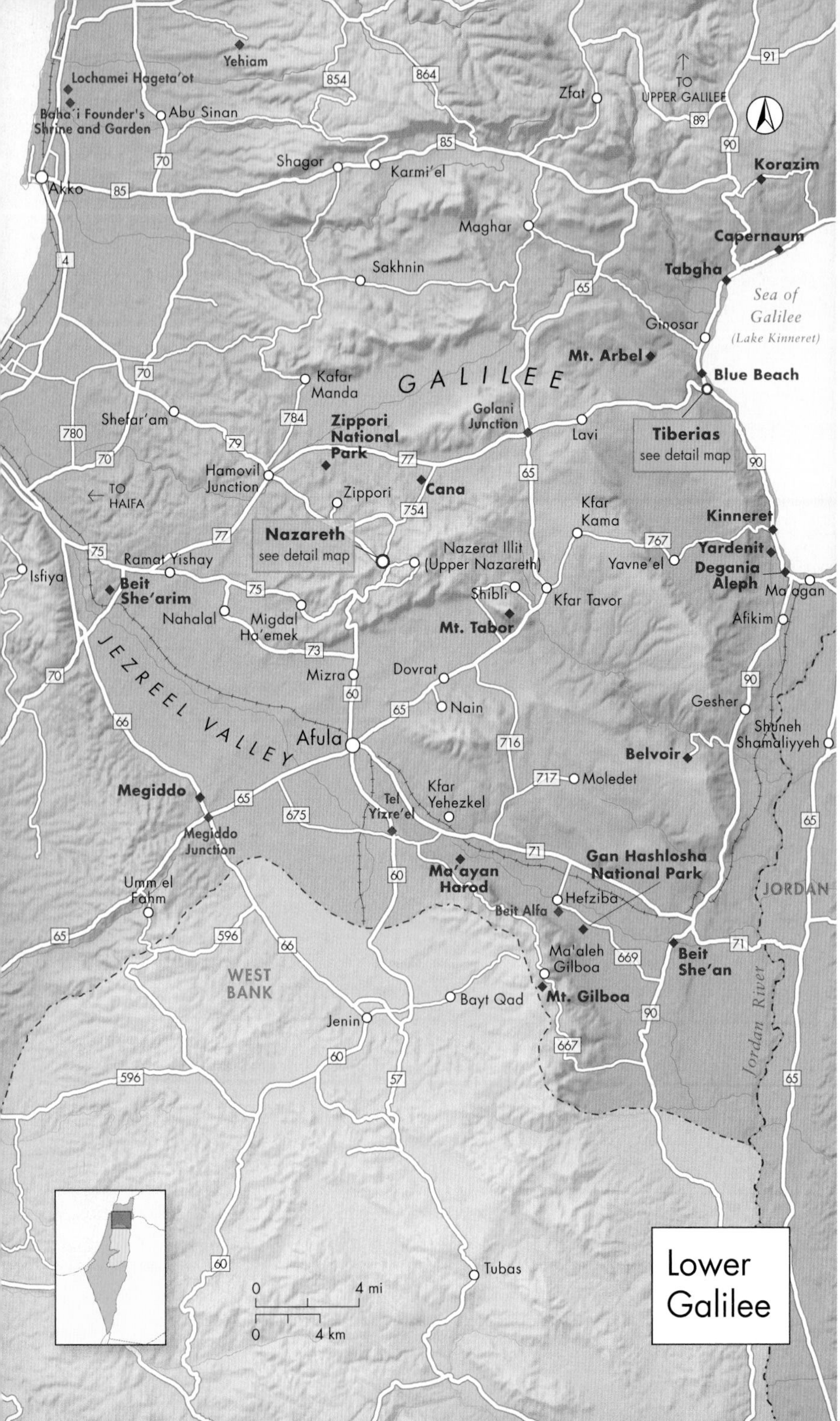
Lower Galilee
Yehiam
Lochamei Hageta'ot
Baha'i Founder's Shrine and Garden
Abu Sinan
Akko
Shagor
Karmi'el
Zfat
TO UPPER GALILEE
Korazim
Maghar
Capernaum
Tabgha
Sakhnin
Sea of Galilee
(Lake Kinneret)
Ginosar
Mt. Arbel
Blue Beach
GALILEE
Kafar Manda
Shefar'am
Zippori National Park
Golani Junction
Lavi
Tiberias
see detail map
Hamovil Junction
Cana
Zippori
TO HAIFA
Nazareth
see detail map
Kfar Kama
Kinneret
Yardenit
Nazerat Illit (Upper Nazareth)
Yavne'el
Degania Aleph
Ma'agan
Ramat Yishay
Isfiya
Beit She'arim
Shibli
Kfar Tavor
Nahalal
Migdal Ha'emek
Mt. Tabor
Afikim
JEZREEL VALLEY
Mizra
Dovrat
Nain
Gesher
Shuneh Shamaliyyeh
Afula
Belvoir
Megiddo
Moledet
Kfar Yehezkel
Tel Yizre'el
Megiddo Junction
Gan Hashlosha National Park
Ma'ayan Harod
JORDAN
Umm el Fahm
Hefziba
Beit Alfa
Ma'aleh Gilboa
Beit She'an
WEST BANK
Mt. Gilboa
Bayt Qad
Jenin
Jordan River
Tubas
0 4 mi
0 4 km
91
864
854
89
85
90
70
4
65
70
784
780
79
77
70
65
754
77
767
75
75
73
60
90
70
65
66
716
717
65
675
65
71
60
65
596
66
669
71
90
667
60
596
57
65
60

so the center of Jewish life and religious authority shifted first to Yavne, in the southern coastal plain, and then northward to the Lower Galilee.

By around AD 200 Beit She'arim had become the unofficial Jewish capital, owing its brief preeminence to the enormous stature of a native son. Rabbi Yehuda (or Judah) "ha-Nasi" (the Patriarch: a title conferred on the nominal leader of the Jewish community) was responsible for the city's inner workings and for its relations with its Roman masters. Alone among his contemporaries, Yehuda ha-Nasi combined worldly diplomatic skills with scholarly authority and spiritual leadership.

The rabbi eventually moved east to Zippori because of its more salubrious climate, and there gathered the great Jewish sages of his day and compiled the Mishnah, which remains the definitive interpretation of biblical precepts for religious Jews. Nonetheless, it was in his hometown of Beit She'arim that Yehuda ha-Nasi was finally laid to rest. If Beit She'arim was a magnet for scholars and petitioners in his lifetime, it became a virtual shrine after his death. With Jerusalem still off-limits, the town became the most prestigious burial site in the Jewish world for almost 150 years.

Two major expeditions in the 1930s and '50s uncovered a vast series of 20 **catacombs.** The largest of these is open to the public, with 24 chambers containing more than 200 sarcophagi. A wide range of carved Jewish and Roman symbols and more than 250 funerary inscriptions in Greek, Hebrew, Aramaic, and Palmyrene throughout the site testify to the great distances people traveled—from Yemen and Mesopotamia, for instance—to be buried here. Without exception, the sarcophagi were plundered over the centuries by grave robbers seeking the possessions with which the dead were often interred.

On Fridays and Saturdays, a newly excavated set of "lamp caves"—so named for the menorahs carved into the walls—are open and worth walking to the other side of the park to see. ✉ *Follow the signs in Kiryat Tivon, off Rte. 75 or 722* ☎ *04/983–1643* 🌐 *www.parks.org.il/ParksENG* 🎫 *NIS 20* ⏲ *Apr.–Sept. 8–5; Oct.–Mar. 8–4.*

MEGIDDO

★ *20 km (12½ mi) southeast of Beit She'arim, 2 km (1¼ mi) north of the Megiddo Junction, 12 km (7½ mi) west of Afula.*

GETTING HERE AND AROUND

A car is the best way to get here, as the site is poorly served by public transportation. You can reach the site by taxi from Afula.

ESSENTIALS

Taxi Contact **Yizre'el** (✉ *Afula* ☎ *04/652–3111*).

EXPLORING

Recognized by UNESCO as a World Heritage Site in 2005, Megiddo is an ancient city built on foundations even older: dating back to the biblical era. Today called **Tel Megiddo National Park,** it's one of the region's most impressive ruins. Allocate about 90 minutes to see the park.

Most people are fascinated by the ancient water system. In a masterful stroke, King Ahab's engineers dug a deep shaft and a horizontal tunnel through solid rock to reach the vital subterranean spring outside the city walls. With access secure, the spring's original opening was permanently blocked. There is nothing more than a trickle today, though, the flow perhaps choked by subsequent earthquakes. As you descend 180 steps through the shaft, traverse the 65-yard-long tunnel under the ancient city wall, and climb up 83 steps at the other end, look for the ancient chisel marks and hewn steps. A visit to the water system at noon offers a reprieve from the summer heat.

Apart from the ancient water system, don't miss the partially restored Late Bronze Age gate, perhaps the very one stormed by Egyptian troops circa 1468 BC, as described in the victory stela of Pharaoh Thutmose III. A larger gate farther up the mound was long identified with King Solomon (10th century BC)—Megiddo was one of his regional military centers—but has been redated by some scholars to the time of Ahab, a half century later. There is consensus, however, on the ruined stables at the summit of the tell: they were certainly built by Ahab, whose large chariot army is recorded in an Assyrian inscription.

Evidence indicates prehistoric habitation here as well, but among the earliest remains of the *city* of Megiddo are a round altar dating from the Early Bronze Age and the outlines of several Early Bronze Age temples, almost 5,000 years old, visible in the trench between the two fine lookout points.

A tiny museum at the site's entrance offers good visual aids, including maps, a video, and a model of the tell. A small gift shop alongside the museum sells handsome silver and gold jewelry, some incorporating pieces of ancient Roman glass. There is also a cafeteria. ✉ *National Park, Rte. 66* ☎ *04/659–0316* 🌐 *www.parks.org.il/ParksENG* 🎫 *NIS 25* ⏲ *Apr.–Sept. 8–5; Oct.–Mar. 8–4.*

MT. GILBOA AND ENVIRONS

Fodor's Choice ★ *24 km (15 mi) southeast of Megiddo via Rtes. 675 and 667, 10 km (7 mi) east of Afula.*

Visit Mt. Gilboa in February or March and you'll find yourself surrounded by people enraptured with the delicate purple iris native to these slopes. The views of the valley below and the hills of Galilee beyond are great year-round, but on a clear winter or spring day they're amazing, reaching as far as the snowcapped Mt. Hermon, far to the north. Afternoon is the best time to come.

Mt. Gilboa—actually a steep mountain range rather than a single peak—is geographically a spur of the far greater Samaria Range (the biblical Mt. Ephraim, today the West Bank) to the southwest. Half the mountain has been reforested with evergreens, while the other half has been left in pristine rockiness. Environmentalists prefer the latter, as it protects the wildflowers that splatter the slopes with color every spring. From the gravel parking area off Route 667, easy and well-marked trails

The archaeological layers at Megiddo include prehistoric remains and an ingenious biblical-era water system.

wind through the natural habitat of the rare black (actually deep purple) iris, which draws hordes of Israelis every spring.

Three thousand years ago, the Philistines rerouted the Israelites on Mt. Gilboa. Saul, the nation's first king, was wounded and took his own life on the battlefield. The next day, the Bible relates, when the Philistines came to plunder their fallen foes, they discovered the bodies of Saul and his sons. Seeking trophies, "they cut off his head, and stripped off his armor, and they fastened his body to the wall of [Beit She'an]" (I Samuel 31). In his eulogy for Saul and his son Jonathan, king-to-be David cursed the battlefield where "thy glory, O Israel" was slain: "Let there be no dew or rain upon you" (II Samuel 1).

GETTING HERE AND AROUND

Driving from Afula, follow Route 71 east, turn right on Route 675, then left on Route 667. There is no reliable public transportation.

EXPLORING

Ma'ayan Harod *(Spring of Harod)*, at the foot of Mt. Gilboa, is a small national park with huge eucalyptus trees and a big swimming pool fed by a spring. Today it's a bucolic picnic spot, but almost 3,200 years ago, Gideon, the reluctant hero of the biblical Book of Judges, organized his troops to fight a Midianite army that had invaded from the desert. At God's command—in order to emphasize the miraculous nature of the coming victory—Gideon dismissed more than two-thirds of the warriors and then, to reduce the force still more, selected only those who lapped water from the spring. Equipped with swords, ram's horns, and flaming torches concealed in clay jars, this tiny army of 300 divided into three companies and surrounded the Midianite camp across the

CLOSE UP

Kibbutz Life Then and Now

The founding fathers and mothers would probably be bewildered by life on a 21st-century kibbutz (a collective settlement, but literally translated as "a gathering"). Many of Israel's founders came from Russia in the early 20th century, inspired by Zionist ideals of returning to their ancestral homeland and a work ethic that regarded manual labor as an almost spiritual value. They were socialists who believed "from each according to his ability, to each according to his need."

EARLY DAYS

Degania, the first kibbutz, was founded in 1909 on the shores of the Sea of Galilee, where ten men and two women began to work the land. The utopian ideology, in which individual desires were subordinated to the needs of the community, was wedded to the need for a close-knit communal structure, in order to cope with forbidding terrain and a hostile neighborhood. Life was arduous, but their numbers grew.

Kibbutzim played a considerable role in molding the fledgling state, absorbing immigrants, and developing agriculture. By 1950, two years after Israel's independence, there were more than 200 kibbutzim. Their egalitarian ethos meant that all shared chores and responsibility—but also ownership of the means of production. The kibbutz movement became the world's largest communitarian movement.

GROWTH AND CHALLENGE

With time, many kibbutzim introduced light industry or tourism enterprises, and some became successful businesses. The standard of living improved, and kibbutzim took advantage of easy bank loans. When Israel's hyperinflation reached 454% during the mid-1980s, many communities found themselves bankrupt. Change became inevitable, and the movement peaked around 1990, when the almost 270 kibbutzim across the country reached 130,000 members. (An individual kibbutz can range from fewer than 100 to more than 1,000 members.)

THE KIBBUTZ TODAY

In today's Israel, many young "kibbutzniks," after compulsory military service or university studies, have found the kibbutz ethos stifling and have opted for the individualism and material attractions of city life. Despite the changes, city folk, volunteers, and tourists are still drawn to this rural environment, which offers a slower pace.

Only some 15% of kibbutz members now work in agriculture, though they account for a significant proportion of the national production. Industry, services, and tourism—including kibbutz guesthouses and hotels—are the real sources of income. Differential wage systems have been introduced, unemployment is growing, and foreign laborers often provide menial labor in fields and factories. All kibbutzim have abandoned children's dormitories, instead allowing parents to raise their children in a family home.

Many members of the older generation have become distressed by what they see as the contamination of pioneering principles. But reality bites hard, and ironically, only those kibbutzim that succeed economically can afford to remain socialist.

valley in the middle of the night. At a prearranged signal, the attackers shouted, blew their horns, and smashed the jars, revealing the flaming torches, whereupon the Midianites panicked and fled, securing an Israelite victory.

The spring has seen other armies in other ages. It was here in 1260 that the Egypt-based Mamluks stopped the invasion of the hitherto invincible Mongols. And in the 1930s, the woods above the spring hid Jewish self-defense squads training in defiance of British military law. ✉ *Off Rte. 71* ☎ *04/653–2211* 🌐 *www.parks.org.il/ParksENG* 🎫 *NIS 36* ⏲ *Apr.–June, Sept. 8–5; Oct.–Mar. 8–4; Jul. and Aug. 8–6.*

NEED A BREAK?

At Michal and Avi Barkin's goat farm (✉ *1 km [½ mi] east of Navot Junction [Rtes. 71 and 675], Kfar Yehezkel* ☎ *050/449–2799*), you can sample excellent cheeses over wine or coffee in the wooden reception room or enjoy a light meal of salads, toasted sandwiches, or hot stuffed pastries. The farm is open Friday, 2 to 10 pm, and Saturday, 4 to 10 pm.

Gan Hashlosha National Park, commonly known as Sahne, is considered one of the most beautiful places in the world, and not only by Israelis. The park was developed around a warm spring (28°C, or 82°F, most of the year) and a wide, still stream deep enough to dive into at spots, with artificial cascades in others. Lifeguards are on duty. Facilities include changing rooms for bathers, two snack bars, and a restaurant. Apart from swimming, this is also a very popular picnic spot. ✉ *Off Rte. 669* ☎ *04/658–6219* 🌐 *www.parks.org.il/ParksENG* 🎫 *NIS 36* ⏲ *Apr.–Sept. Sat.–Thurs. 8–5, Fri and holiday eves 8–4., Oct.–Mar. Sat.–Thurs. 8–4, Fri. and Jewish holiday eves 8–3. Last entrance one hour before closing.*

In 1928 members of Kibbutz Hefziba who were digging an irrigation trench discovered the ancient synagogue of **Beit Alfa,** now part of Beit Alfa Synagogue National Park. Their tools hit a hard surface, and excavation uncovered a multicolored mosaic floor, almost entirely preserved. The art is somewhat childlike, but that, too, is part of its charm. An Aramaic inscription dates the building to the reign of Byzantine emperor Justinian in the second quarter of the 6th century AD; a Greek inscription credits the workmanship to one Marianos and his son, Aninas. In keeping with Jewish tradition, the synagogue faces Jerusalem, with an apse at the far end to hold the ark. The building faithfully copies the architecture of the Byzantine basilicas of the day, with a nave and two side aisles, and the doors lead to a small narthex and a onetime outdoor atrium. Stairs indicate there was once an upper story.

Classic Jewish symbols in the top mosaic panel leave no doubt that the building was a synagogue: a holy ark flanked by lions, a menorah, and a shofar (ram's horn). The middle panel, however, is the most intriguing: it's filled with human figures depicting the seasons, the zodiac, and—even more incredible for a Jewish house of worship—the Greek sun god, Helios, driving his chariot across the sky. These images indicate more liberal times theologically, when the prohibition against making graven images was perhaps not applied to two-dimensional art. The last panel tells the story of Abraham's near-sacrifice of his son Isaac,

Panoramic views of the Galilee draw hikers to explore Mt. Gilboa.

captioned in Hebrew. Take time to watch the lighthearted but informative film. Allocate 45 minutes for a visit here. ✉ *Kibbutz Hefziba, Rte. 669* ☎ *04/653–2004* 🌐 *www.parks.org.il/ParksENG* 🎫 *NIS 20* ⏲ *Apr.–Sept. 8–5; Oct.–Mar. 8–4.*

WHERE TO EAT AND STAY

$$ MODERN ISRAELI Fodor's Choice ★ ✕ **Herb Farm on Mount Gilboa.** The sweeping panorama from the wooden deck and picture windows is attraction enough, but this family restaurant—operated by Yossi Mass, his wife Penina, and their son Oren—is also known for its fresh herbs. Homemade bread and a "salad basket" of antipasti are fine starters, but try one of the imaginative salads. Tempting entrées might include a tart of shallots, forest mushrooms, and goat cheese, or a colorful pie of beef, lamb, goose breast, tomatoes, pine nuts, and basil. Desserts make for an agonizing decision, so share. ✉ *Rte. 667, 3 km (2 mi) off Rte. 675* 📫 *Box 2402, Afula 18120* ☎ *04/653–1093* ✍ *Reservations essential* 💳 *AE, DC, MC, V* ⏲ *Closed Sun.*

$$ ISRAELI ✕ **Mizra Grill.** A short drive from the Gilboa region, Mizra is best known as a superior cafeteria with an excellent salad bar. In the late afternoon it becomes a good sit-down dinner restaurant, serving a variety of grilled meats. Kibbutz Mizra produces high-quality pork products, making its restaurant a magnet for those indifferent to kosher prohibitions. There is an adjacent high-end deli-supermarket. It's open from 8:30 am to 8:30 pm. ✉ *Rte. 60, entrance to Mizra* ☎ *04/642–9214* ✍ *Reservations essential* 💳 *AE, DC, MC, V.*

$ 🏨 **Kibbutz Ein Harod (Ichud) Guest Houses and Suites.** The 89-year-old Kibbutz has a strong business offering cabins and suites to meet every need, nestled in the kibbutz's lovely landscape. Choose from the simply appointed standard rooms (ask for a blue or green room, which are larger than the orange ones), family-friendly cabins with lofts and a shared yard, or ultraromantic luxury suites with private gardens and views of Mt. Gilboa. Children love the kibbutz playground, the swimming pool, and the chance to pet the cows and sheep in the dairy farm. Adults will appreciate the museum of art in the kibbutz next door, Ein Harod (Meuchad), with a permanent collection of Jewish art spanning cultures and genres. **Pros:** serene atmosphere; options for both families and couples. **Cons:** luxury suites are pricey on weekends. ✉ *Kibbutz Ein Harod (Ichud)* ☎ *052/830–9737* 🌐 *www.ein-harod.co.il/eng/164/Ein+Harod.html* *26 rooms, 10 cabins, 5 suites* *In-room: refrigerator, Wi-Fi. In-hotel: restaurant, pool* *AE, DC, MC, V.*

¢ **Ma'ayan Harod Guest House.** An example of how the facilities have been improved at many Israel Youth Hostel Association lodgings, rooms here are a cut above the usual hostel offerings, with TVs, refrigerators, and coffeemakers. The somewhat spartan bungalows have two single beds rather than doubles. **Pros:** convenient to national parks; air-conditioned rooms. **Cons:** rowdy teenage crowd; no evening activities. ✉ *Gidona* ☎ *04/653–1669* *mayanh@iyha.org.il* *28 rooms* *In-room: refrigerator* *AE, DC, MC, V* *BP.*

6

BEIT SHE'AN

23 km (14 mi) southeast of Afula, 39 km (24 mi) south of Tiberias.

The modern town of Beit She'an has little to offer visitors, but the past beckons. Unlike some archaeological sites that appear to be just piles of rocks, ancient Beit She'an is a gloriously rich ruin, complete with bathhouses, pagan temples, and public theaters. It's one of the country's most notable sites.

GETTING HERE AND AROUND

The national park is northeast of modern Beit She'an. From Route 90, turn west on Sha'ul Hamelech Street, and right after Bank Leumi.

EXPLORING

★ At the intersection of the Jordan and Jezreel valleys, this town has one spectacular site, **Beit She'an National Park.** A Roman theater was excavated in the 1960s, but the rest of Scythopolis, as this great Late Roman and Byzantine (2nd–6th centuries AD) city was known, came to light only in more recent excavations. The enormous haul of marble statuary and friezes says much about the opulence of Scythopolis in its heyday—especially when you remember that there are no marble quarries in Israel, and all that stone was imported from what is today Turkey, Greece, or even Italy.

A free site map available at the visitor center gives a good layout. In summer it's best to arrive early in the morning, as the heat quickly becomes insufferable. Better yet, consider returning in the evening for the engaging **sound-and-light spectacle,** inaugurated in 2008 and presented Monday, Wednesday, and Thursday from 7 pm to 9:30 pm and Saturday from 7:30 pm to 9:30 pm. Tickets cost NIS 40; reserve in advance and check times. Scythopolis's **downtown area,** now exposed, has masterfully engineered colonnaded main streets converging on a central plaza that once boasted a pagan temple, a decorative fountain, and a monument. An elaborate Byzantine bathhouse covered more than 1¼ acres. On the main thoroughfare are the remains of Scythopolis's amphitheater, where gladiatorial combats were once the order of the day.

The high tell dominating the site to the north was the location of Old Testament **Canaanite/Israelite Beit She'an** 2,500 to 3,500 years ago. Don't climb to the top for the meager archaeological remains, but rather for the fine panoramic view of the surrounding valleys and the superb bird's-eye view of the main excavations.

The semicircular **Roman theater** was built of contrasting black basalt and white limestone blocks around AD 200, when Scythopolis was at its height. Although the upper *cavea,* or tier, has not survived, the theater is the largest and best preserved in Israel, with an estimated original capacity of 7,000 to 10,000 people. The large stage and part of the *scaena frons* (backdrop) behind it have been restored, and Beit She'an hosts autumn performances as in days of yore.

✉ *Off Sha'ul Hamelech St.* ☎ *04/658–7189* 🌐 *www.parks.org.il/ParksENG* 🎫 *NIS 25* ⏲ *Apr.–Sept., Sat.–Thurs. 8–5; Oct.–Mar., Sun.–Fri. 8–4, Sat. 8–5.*

NEED A BREAK?

Bis Le'chol Kis (✉ *24 Merkaz Rasco* ☎ *04/658-7278*) translates loosely as "a bite for every budget." Falafel and shawarma are the bites, and they do them well. Instead of pita bread, you can opt to have your turkey-meat shawarma in a fresh, home-baked baguette. Air-conditioning in summer is a welcome relief. Look for this place in a small commercial center right next to the Egged Central Bus Station.

WHERE TO STAY

¢ **Beit She'an Guest House.** This modern limestone and basalt building is wrapped around a courtyard shaded by palm trees. Many rooms, including suites with private balconies, have great views east over the Jordan Valley. All are simply but agreeably furnished. The lobby café is a good spot to enjoy pizzas and sandwiches. Breakfast is included; other meals are available on request. Make sure to see the memorable mural humorously depicting life in ancient Beit She'an. **Pros:** convenient to the national park; pretty pool area. **Cons:** sometimes noisy with teenage groups; no evening entertainment. ✉ *126 Menachem Begin Blvd. [Rte. 90]* ☎ *04/606–0760* 🌐 *www.youth-hostels.org.il/english.html* *60 rooms, 2 suites* *In-room: no phone, refrigerator. In-hotel: pool, Internet terminal, parking (free)* 💳 *AE, DC, MC, V* *BP.*

NIGHTLIFE AND THE ARTS

The marvelous **Roman theater** (☎ *04/658–7189* ✉ *moked@npa.org.il*) hosts concerts, mostly by Israeli artists, every October.

The remains of the wealthy late Roman and Byzantine city of Beit She'an include a large public bathhouse.

BELVOIR

Rte. 717; turn off 12 km (7½ mi) north of Beit She'an; continue 5 km (3 mi) to site.

GETTING HERE AND AROUND

Driving north on Route 90 from Beit She'an, turn west on Route 717. While any bus traversing Route 90 will let off at the road, the fortress is high above the valley. It's a long hike, and don't count on getting a ride. The road from Ein Harod via Moledet is passable in dry weather but in very bad condition in places.

EXPLORING

The Crusaders chose their site well: they called it **Belvoir**—"beautiful view"—and it was the most invincible fortress in the land. The Hebrew name "Kochav Hayarden" (the Star of the Jordan) and the Arabic "Kaukab el Hauwa" (the Star of the Wind) underscore its splendid isolation. Today it's part of **Kochav Hayarden National Park.** The breathtaking view of the Jordan River valley and southern Sea of Galilee, some 1,800 feet below, is best in the afternoon. You don't need to be a military historian to marvel at the never-breached concentric walls.

The Hospitallers (the Knights of St. John) completed the mighty castle in 1173. In the summer of 1187, the Crusader armies were crushed by the Arabs under Saladin at the Horns of Hittin, west of Tiberias, bringing an end the Latin Kingdom of Jerusalem with one decisive battle. Their remnants struggled on to Tyre (in modern Lebanon), but Belvoir alone refused to yield; 18 months of siege got the Muslims no farther than undermining the outer eastern rampart. The Crusaders, for their part, sallied out from time to time to battle the enemy, but their lone resistance had become pointless. They struck a deal with Saladin and surrendered the stronghold in exchange for free passage, flags flying, to Tyre.

Don't follow the arrows from the parking lot; instead, take the wide gravel path to the right of the fortress. This brings you to the panoramic view and the best spot from which to appreciate the strength of the stronghold, with its deep, dry moat; massive rock and cut-stone ramparts; and gates. Once inside the main courtyard, you're unexpectedly faced with a fortress within a fortress, a scaled-down replica of the outer defenses. Not much remains of the upper stories; in 1220, the Muslims systematically dismantled Belvoir, fearing another Crusade. Once you've explored the modest buildings, exit over the western bridge (once a drawbridge) and spy on the postern gates, the protected and sometimes secret back doors of medieval castles. ✉ *National Park, Rte. 717, 5 km (3 mi) west of Rte. 90* ☎ *04/658–1766* 🌐 *www.parks.org.il/ParksENG* 🎫 *NIS 20* ⏲ *Apr.–Sept. 8–5; Oct.–Mar. 8–4.*

NAZARETH AND THE GALILEE HILLS

Remove the modern roads and power lines, and the landscape of this region becomes a biblical illustration. Villages are scattered haphazardly on the hillsides, and small farm-holdings crowd the valleys. Olive groves, the region's ancient resource, are everywhere. Hilltop views and modern pine forests, white-and-red houses, and decorative trees that dab the countryside provide visually arresting moments.

There are several New Testament settings here—Nazareth, where Jesus grew up; the Cana wedding feast; and Mt. Tabor, identified with the Transfiguration—but Jewish history resonates strongly, too. Tabor and Yodefat were fortifications in the Great Revolt against the Romans; Shefar'am, Beit She'arim (in a nearby valley), and Zippori were in turn the national centers of Jewish life (2nd–4th centuries AD); and latter-day Jewish pioneers, attracted to the region's untamed scenery, put down roots where their ancestors had farmed.

NAZARETH

Fodor's Choice ★ *25 km (15½ mi) east of Beit She'arim, 56 km (35 mi) east of Haifa, 15 km (9½ mi) north of Afula.*

The Nazareth, where Jesus grew up, was an insignificant village nestled in a hollow in the Galilean hills, but today's city of 65,000 pulses with energy. Apart from the occasional donkey plying traffic-clogged Paulus VI Street, there's little that evokes the Bible in contemporary Nazareth, unless you know where to look—and indeed, droves of Christian pilgrims come to pray at the awe-inspiring Basilica of the Annunciation or for quiet contemplation at one of Nazareth's many smaller churches.

For nonbelievers, Nazareth is a fascinating day or half-day stop; the Christian devout will want to spend a full day, if not two. If your goal is to experience Nazareth as Jesus did, plan a tour at Nazareth Village. The calmest days to visit are Wednesday, when many businesses close for a midweek sabbatical, and Sunday, the day of rest for the Christians who make up a third of the town. If you're looking for local color (and traffic jams), come on Saturday, when Arab villagers come to the big city to sell produce and buy goods.

GETTING HERE AND AROUND

If you're driving from Beit She'arim or Haifa on Route 75, Route 77 breaks off to the north—to Zippori, the Golani Junction, and Tiberias. Route 75 continues to skirt the north side of the picturesque Jezreel Valley as it climbs into the hills toward Nazareth; at the crest of the hill, Route 60 from Afula joins it. A turn to the left takes you down to Paulus VI, Nazareth's main drag. If you pick up Route 77 from the opposite side, from Tiberias and points north, a left turn onto Route 764 takes you into Nazareth's Paulus VI Street. Nazareth's Central Bus Station is downtown on Paulus VI Street, near the Basilica of the Annunciation.

Nazareth itself is mired in traffic but the historic and religious sites are all close together, so it's best to park and walk.

Both Egged Tours and United Tours run one-day tours three times a week that take in Nazareth, Capernaum, Tabgha, the Sea of Galilee, Tiberias, and the Jordan River. Current prices are US$79 from Tel Aviv, $82 from Jerusalem.

★ The Old City tour that begins daily at the Fauzi Azar Inn is unique in that it skips religious sites almost entirely (except on Sundays, when shops are closed), and focuses instead on the colorful sights, sounds, and smells of daily life in Nazareth. You'll be taken, for example, to shops in the souk where owners will let you taste their wares; to unique and charming gift shops far from city center; and to various coffee shops, whose managers will sit with you if they have time and answer your questions about Nazareth life and culture. The Fauzi Azar tour is also the only means of access for visitors to the St. George Greek Orthodox monastery, where you'll have the rare opportunity to see a priceless collection of icons and an underground cave where Christians hid from their enemies in the 5th century. Tours are daily at 9:30 am and costs NIS 20 plus NIS 15 to NIS 20 for tastings and site admissions.

Taxi Contacts **Abu el-Assal** (✉ *Nazareth* ☎ *04/655–4745*). **Diana** (✉ *Nazareth* ☎ *04/655–5554*).

Visitor and Tour Information **Egged Tours** (☎ *03/694–8888 or *2800* 🌐 *www.egged.co.il/Eng*). **Fauzi Azar Tour** (✉ *Old City* ☎ *04/602–0469* 🌐 *www.fauziazarinn.com*).

Tourist Information Office (✉ *Casa Nova St., Nazareth* ☎ *04/657–3003 or 04/657–0555*). **United Tours** (☎ *03/617-3315* 🌐 *www.unitedtours.co.il*).

EXPLORING

Baptist Church. Christianity speaks with many voices in Nazareth. The Baptist Church, a few hundred yards north of the Church of St. Gabriel, is affiliated with the Southern Baptist Convention of the United States. Sunday services (10:30 am) are conducted in Arabic with an English translation of the sermon; the Baptist school next door also offers services, with more English speakers, at the same time. Note that 2011 marks 100 years of Baptist presence in the Holy Land; call to find out

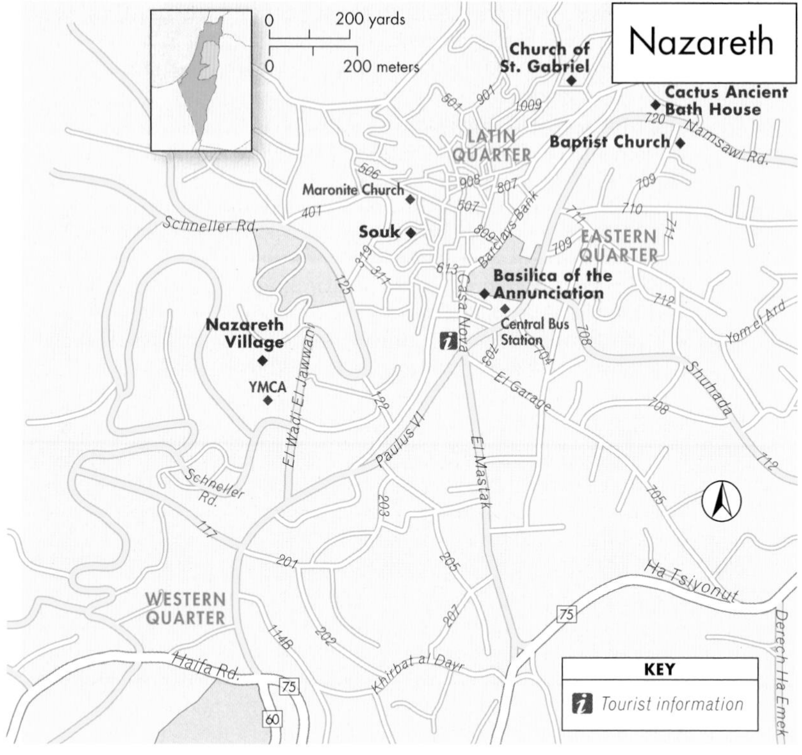

about celebrations. ✉ *Paulus VI St.* ☎ *04/657–6946 or 04/657–4370* 🌐 *www.lbc-nazareth.org.*

★ **Basilica of the Annunciation.** Casa Nova Street climbs steeply to the entrance of the Roman Catholic Basilica of the Annunciation, the largest church in the Middle East, consecrated in 1969. It enshrines a small ancient cave dwelling or grotto, identified by many Catholics as the home of Mary. Here, they believe, the angel Gabriel appeared to her and announced (hence, Annunciation) that she would conceive "and bear a son" and "call his name Jesus" (Luke 1). Pilgrim devotions suffuse the site throughout the day. Crusader-era walls and some restored Byzantine mosaics near the grotto bear witness to the antiquity of the tradition. The grotto is in the so-called lower church. Look up through the "well," or opening over the grotto, that connects with the upper church to the grand cupola, soaring 195 feet above you.

A spiral staircase leads to the vast upper church, the parish church of Nazareth's Roman Catholic community. Italian ceramic reliefs on the huge concrete pillars represent the Stations of the Cross, captioned in the Arabic vernacular. You now have a closer view of the cupola, its ribs representing the petals of an upside-down lily—a symbol of Mary's purity—rooted in heaven. It is repeatedly inscribed with the letter *M*. The huge mosaic behind the altar shows Jesus and Peter at the center and an enthroned Mary behind them, flanked by figures of the hierarchical church (to your right) and the charismatic church (to your left).

The artwork of the site, donated by Catholic communities around the world, is eclectic in the extreme but the more interesting for it. The portico around the courtyard just inside the main gate is decorated with striking contemporary mosaics, many depicting the Madonna and Child in styles and with facial features reflecting the donor nation. The massive main doors leading to the lower church relate, in bronze relief, the central events of Jesus' life; abstract stained-glass windows brilliantly counterpoint the dim lighting here. The large panels on the walls of the upper church, again on the theme of mother and child, include a vivid offering from the United States, a fine Canadian terra-cotta, and mosaics from England and Australia. Particularly interesting are the gifts from Japan (with gold leaf and pearls), Venezuela (a carved-wood statue), and Cameroon (a stylized painting in black, white, and red).

In the exit courtyard, a glass-enclosed baptistery is built over what is thought to have been an ancient mikvah, a Jewish ritual bath. The adjacent small Church of St. Joseph, just past Terra Sancta College, is built over a complex of rock-hewn chambers traditionally identified as the workshop of Joseph the Carpenter. Note that parking is hard to find; try Paulus VI Street or the side streets below it. ✉ *Casa Nova St.* ☎ *04/657–2501* 🎫 *Free* 🕓 *Hours vary by section. Grotto, 6 am–9 pm, Upper Basilica, 8–6, St. Joseph's Church, 7–6. Masses daily at 6:30 am (Italian) and 7:15 am (Arabic), and Sun. at 7, 8:30, 10, 5 pm, and 6 (all Arabic). Programs: Silent Prayer, daily 6–9 am, Nazareth's Rosary, Tues. 8:30 am, Eucharistic Adoration, Thurs. 8:30 am, Candlelight Procession, Sat. 8:30 am.*

6

NEED A BREAK?

Try the unbeatable Arab pastries at Mahroum Sweets (✉ *Casa Nova and Paulus VI Sts.* ☎ *04/656–0214*). It's clean, has bathrooms, and serves wonderful *bourma* (cylindrical pastry filled with whole pistachio nuts), cashew baklava, and great halvah. Don't confuse this place with Mahroum Bakery: look for the Arab pastries, not gooey Western cakes.

Church of St. Gabriel. The Greek Orthodox Church of St. Gabriel, about 1 km (¾ mi) north of the junction of Paulus VI and Casa Nova streets, is built over Nazareth's only natural water source, a spring dubbed Mary's Well. The Greek Orthodox, citing the noncanonical Gospel of St. James, believe it to be the place where the angel Gabriel appeared to Mary to announce the coming birth of Jesus. (On Paulus VI Street, at the bottom of the short approach to the church, is a round, white, stone structure marked "Mary's Well," but this is merely a modern outlet.)

The ornate church was built in 1750 and contains a stunning carved-wood pulpit and iconostasis (chancel screen), with painted New Testament scenes and silver-haloed saints. The walls are adorned with frescoes of figures from the Bible and the Greek Orthodox hagiography. A tiny "well" stands over the running water, and a modern aluminum cup gives a satisfying plop as it drops in. (The water is clean; the cup is more suspect.) ✉ *Off Paulus VI St.* ☎ *04/657–6437* 🎫 *Donation expected* 🕓 *Mon.–Sat. 8–5, Sun. after services–5.*

Nazareth Village. The shepherds, weavers, and other characters in this reconstructed Jesus-era community will delight children and adults alike. Using information gained from archaeological work done in the area, this attraction aims to reconstruct Jewish rural life as Jesus would have known it more than 2,000 years ago. Workshops, farms, and houses have been created with techniques that would have been used at the time. Interpreters in period costume cook and work at winepresses and looms, giving a sense of daily life. The village is geared toward Christian travelers but may also be of interest to others; there is a re-created synagogue and mikvah (ritual bath). Guided tours with different themes are offered; check in advance about these, as reservations are required. ✉ *5105 St., by the Nazareth YMCA downtown* ☎ *04/645–6042* 🌐 *www.nazarethvillage.com* 🎫 *NIS 50* ⏲ *Mon.–Sat. 9–5* (last tour at 3).

Souk. Full of the aroma of fresh spices, Nazareth's market, in the Old City, has something for everyone, from coffee sets to pastries to T-shirts and antiques. The old lanes are narrow and shops are tiny, with goods spilling into the street, but this souk is more orderly than those in many other Israeli cities. If it does get overwhelming, take a coffee break. ✉ *Casa Nova St. and vicinity.*

★ **Cactus Ancient Bath House.** In 1993, Elias and Martina Shama-Sostar were renovating their crafts shop when they discovered ancient steam pipes under the store. Further excavation revealed a huge, wonderfully preserved Roman-style bathhouse. Israel's Antiquities Authority has not made any official announcements about the site, but several historians who have visited speculate that the bathhouse may date from the 1st century AD. A one-hour tour takes you to the hot room, the heating tunnels, and the furnace. Coffee is served in the arched hall where wood and ashes were once kept. ✉ *Mary's Well Square* ☎ *04/657–8539* 🌐 *www.nazarethbathhouse.org* 🎫 *NIS 120 for up to 4 visitors* ⏲ *Mon.–Sat. 9–7 or by appointment* 💳 *AE, DC, MC, V.*

WHERE TO EAT

After a full day of visiting Nazareth's shrines, you can quench your thirst with the locals at one of the little Arab restaurants along Paulus VI Street. Dinner here usually means hummus, shish kebab, baklava, and the like. Decor is incidental, atmosphere a function of the clientele of the moment, and dinnertime early. Needless to say, reservations are not necessary, and dress is casual. If you're looking for more upscale dining, several high-end restaurants have opened in the past few years, serving both traditional Arab foods and fusion fare.

$$–$$$ MIDDLE EASTERN

✕ **Al-Reda.** In a magnificent 19th-century mansion with a *Thousand and One Nights* atmosphere, Al-Reda matches its magical setting with excellent Arab cuisine, from interesting salads (eggplant with cheese) and roasted lamb neck to kebabs and shashlik, as well as dishes with Indian or European influences. Pesto and grilled vegetables stuffed in a chicken breast is a good option, as are the variety of vegetarian choices. Don't pass up dessert. ✉ *23 Al Bishara St., next to the Basilica of the Annunciation* ☎ *04/608–4404* 💳 *AE, MC, V* ⏲ *No lunch Sun.*

$$–$$$ ECLECTIC Fodor's Choice ★

✕ **Annai.** In a 200-year-old mansion, Annai, which opened in 2009, is perhaps the most elegant restaurant in Nazareth—although there's not much competition. The eclectic menu includes a "New York" salad of

Shopping in Nazareth's popular market is a good introduction to this growing, largely Arab city.

baby shrimp and calamari in a chili-mayonnaise sauce, appetizers such as in-season vegetables with grilled goat cheese and date vinaigrette, and the house specialty, goose liver in cream sauce. There are three choices for seating: an outdoor terrace, an indoor area with traditional Middle Eastern accoutrements, and a second indoor area with more sleek, modern decor. ✉ *Bank Barclays St.* ☎ *077/789–0064* ▭ *AE, DC, MC, V.*

$$$ MIDDLE EASTERN ✕ **Diana.** Ranked among the region's best Arab restaurants, Diana doesn't fail to impress. Owner Duhul Safadi is most famous for his kebabs and lamb chops, but the fish and seafood dishes are all equally wonderful. There's a plant-filled terrace and a sophisticated dining room that would not be out of place in Tel Aviv. ✉ *Grand New Hotel, 51 Paulus VI St.* ☎ *04/657–2919* ▭ *AE, DC, MC, V* ⊙ *Closed Mon.*

$$ MIDDLE EASTERN ✕ **Tishreen.** The tile floors, stone walls, and dim lighting at this restaurant and bar named after a month on the Muslim calendar are the perfect setting for the Middle Eastern menu. Known for the wood-burning oven from which fresh breads emerge, try any of the inexpensive and popular kebabs, meat, and cheeses wrapped in bread, or the eggplant stuffed with pesto and cheese. Alcohol is served, too. ✉ *56 El-Bishara St., near Mary's Well St.* ☎ *04/608–4666* ▭ *AE, DC, MC, V.*

$$–$$$ MIDDLE EASTERN ✕ **Zan.** One of Nazareth's newest restaurants, Zan has a limited but interesting menu, and is known for its grilled lamb kebab covered with Arabic *shrak* bread. Also recommended is the shrimp in garlic and lemon sauce. The pleasant indoor seating area is adorned with a mural of Nazareth's Old City, but the walled garden, surrounded by pomegranate trees and grapevines, is the most atmospheric spot. ✉ *Haknissiya St.* ☎ *04/655–3388* ▭ *AE, DC, MC, V* ⊙ *Closed Sat.*

Nazareth's Basilica of the Annunciation has a venerable cave many Catholics believe was the home of Mary.

WHERE TO STAY

$ **Fauzi Azar Inn.** In a handsomely restored 200-year-old mansion in the heart of the Old City, Fauzi Azar offers dorm-style accommodations for backpackers, as well as private rooms with soaring ceilings for individuals and families. A traditional Arab breakfast is available in the communal dining hall, where you'll meet a variety of tourists, students, and long-term visitors. The inn is the starting point for the popular Jesus Trail hiking trip, which is organized by inn staff (*www.jesustrail.com*). The hotel is difficult to find, so call when you arrive in the city and the staff will pick you up. **Pros:** picturesque, historic building; reasonable rates; friendly staff; spotlessly clean. **Cons:** no elevator; little parking; hard to find the hotel; lack of amenities. *Old City* *04/602–0469* *www.fauziazarinn.com* *15 rooms* *In-hotel: Internet terminal, Wi-Fi hotspot* *MC, V* *BP.*

$ **Plaza.** The white–and–soft-pink stone of this building is the first hint that Nazareth has at last acquired an upscale hotel. Guest rooms have dark wood furnishings that lend a touch of class and since the hotel is on a hill, many rooms enjoy a view of Old Nazareth. A huge gym is another of the draws, as is the quality restaurant. The hotel offers guests a free tour of the Old City on Saturdays. **Pros:** pretty swimming pool; air-conditioning. **Cons:** no evening entertainment; far from Nazareth's shrines. *2 Hermon St., Upper Nazareth* *04/602–8200* *177 rooms, 7 suites* *In-room: safe, Internet. In-hotel: room service, bar, pool, gym, laundry service, Internet terminal, parking (free)* *AE, DC, MC, V* *BP.*

$ **Rimonim Nazareth.** As you walk through the doors, your first impression is likely to be that the place is rather staid. That's because the action is underground, where the adjoining bar, lounge, and dining room add a bit of buzz. Rooms are comfortable and well appointed; ask for one on the fourth floor so you'll have a balcony. The location—on Nazareth's main street, very close to Mary's Well—is a limited blessing; this is not a town that comes alive at night. **Pros:** convenient to the sights; air-conditioning. **Cons:** street noise; no evening entertainment. ✉ *1 Paulus VI St.* ☎ *04/650–0000* 🌐 *www.rimonim.com* *226 rooms* *In-room: safe, refrigerator. In-hotel: room service, bar, laundry service, Internet terminal, Wi-Fi, parking (free)* *AE, DC, MC, V* *BP.*

$ **St. Gabriel.** Sitting high on the ridge that overlooks Nazareth from the west, this hotel began life as a convent—hence the charming neo-Gothic church still in use today. Renovations extended the nuns' old cells, and half the rooms—which were renovated again in 2010—enjoy some of the city's greatest views. The reception area is furnished with inlaid tables, chairs, and mirrors in the old Damascene style, and the dining room prides itself on its local dishes. The garden and the view are perfect for unwinding at sundown. **Pros:** near the shrines; memorable views. **Cons:** no evening entertainment. ✉ *2 Salesian St., POB 2448, Nazareth* ☎ *04/657–2133 or 04/656–7349* 🌐 *www.stgabrielhotel.com* *60 rooms* *In-room: Wi-Fi. In-hotel: restaurant, laundry service, Internet terminal, parking (free)* *AE, DC, MC, V* *BP.*

6

SHOPPING

Shababik. If you're looking for handmade souvenirs, check out Shababik, which means "windows" in Arabic. The pottery, clothes, and home decor are all made by local women, and prices are reasonable. ✉ *Al-mutran St., Old City, Nazareth* ☎ *04/608–0747.*

ZIPPORI NATIONAL PARK

Village 5 km (3 mi) northwest of Nazareth off Rte. 79; site 3 km (2 mi) from village via bypass; 47 km (29 mi) east of Haifa.

GETTING HERE AND AROUND

Driving to this national park from Nazareth, follow Route 79 west and turn north at the signs. No buses service this route. If you don't have a car, take a taxi from Nazareth (agree on the price in advance, and consider asking the driver to wait).

EXPLORING

Fodor's Choice ★ The lush beauty and fantastic archaeological finds at Zippori make this well worth a visit, especially if you have an interest in Roman culture or the beginnings of Talmudic thought. Like many places during the Roman era, **Zippori**—known by Latin and Greek speakers in the classical world as Sepphoris—was a prosperous city where Jews and gentiles coexisted fairly peaceably. The extensive ruins at the much-visited Zippori National Park include Israel's finest Roman-era mosaics. The ancient city, situated on a high ridge with commanding views, can be visited in two hours. The key sites are relatively close together.

Zippori's multiple narratives begin with a Jewish town that stood here from at least the 1st century BC. Christian tradition reveres the town as the birthplace of the Virgin Mary. Zippori's refusal to join the Great Revolt of the Jews against the Romans (AD 66–73) left a serious gap in the rebel defenses in the Galilee, angering its compatriots but sparing the town the usual Roman vengeance when the uprising failed. The real significance of Zippori for Jewish tradition, however, is that in the late 2nd or early 3rd century AD, the legendary sage Rabbi Yehuda ha-Nasi, head of the country's Jewish community at the time, moved here from Beit She'arim, whereupon the Sanhedrin (the Jewish high court) soon followed. Rabbi Yehuda summoned the greatest rabbis in the land to pool their experience. The result was the encyclopedic work known as the Mishnah. Further commentary was added in later centuries to produce the Talmud, the primary guide to Orthodox Jewish practice to this day.

Zippori also had a cosmopolitan soul and by the 3rd century AD, it had acquired a mixed population of Jews, pagans, and Christians. The most celebrated find on the site is the mosaic floor of a Roman villa, perhaps the governor's residence, depicting a series of Dionysian drinking scenes. Its most stunning detail is the exquisite face of a woman, by far the finest mosaic ever discovered in Israel, which the media dubbed "the Mona Lisa of the Galilee." The restored mosaics are housed in an air-conditioned structure with helpful explanations. In other parts of the park, the so-called Nile Mosaic displays Egyptian motifs, and a mosaic synagogue floor (below the parking lot) is decorated with the signs of the zodiac, like those found in Beit Alfa and Hammat Tiberias.

If the mosaic floors bespeak the opulence of Roman Sepphoris, the relatively small Roman theater is mute evidence of the cultural life the wealth could support. Take a few minutes to climb the watchtower of Dahr al-Omar's 18th-century castle for the panoramic view and the museum of archaeological artifacts. About 1 km (½ mi) east of the main site—near the park entrance—is a huge section of ancient Zippori's water system, once fed by springs just north of Nazareth. The ancient aqueduct-reservoir is in fact a deep, man-made, plastered canyon, and the effect is extraordinary. ✉ *Off Rte. 79* ☎ *04/656–8272* 🌐 *www.parks.org.il/Eng* 🎫 *NIS 25* ⏲ *Apr.–Sept 8–5; Oct.–Mar. 8–4.*

CANA

8 km (5 mi) north of Nazareth on Rte. 754, 1 km (½ mi) south of junction of Rtes. 77 and 754; 50 km (31 mi) east of Haifa.

Near the large, modern Arab village of Kfar Kanna is the site of the ancient Jewish village of Cana, mentioned in the New Testament. Here Jesus performed his first miracle, turning water into wine at a wedding feast, thereby emerging from his "hidden years" to begin a three-year ministry in the Galilee.

GETTING HERE AND AROUND

Part of the sprawling suburbs of Nazareth, Kfar Kanna sits astride Route 754, linking Route 77 to the north and Route 79 to the south.

EXPLORING

Within the village, red signs lead to rival churches—one Roman Catholic, the other Greek Orthodox—that enshrine the scriptural tradition. (The alley to these churches is just wide enough for cars, and you can sometimes park in the courtyard of a souvenir store. If the street is blocked, park on the main road.)

The plaza of the Greek Orthodox St. George Convent is a peaceful spot. The First Miracle Church, on the grounds, is rarely open to visitors, but you can wander the landscape freely. On a lower plaza is a handsome statue of Jesus (surrounded, perhaps predictably, by souvenir shops).

The present Catholic **Cana Wedding Church** was built in 1881 on what the Franciscans believe to be the spot where the wedding at which Jesus performed this first miracle (John 2:1–11) took place. The quaint sanctuary is generally open to the public. Check out the basement, where stones and mosaics bear witness to the ancient building that was once on this site. ✉ *Churches St.* ☎ *04/651–7011* *Free* ⏲ *Apr.–Sept., Mon.–Sat. 8–noon and 2–6, Sun. 8–noon; Oct.–Mar., Mon.–Sat. 8–noon and 2–5, Sun. 8–noon.*

PLANT A TREE IN ISRAEL

Around the Golani Junction are groves of evergreens planted by visitors as part of the Plant a Tree with Your Own Hands project of the Jewish National Fund. Since the early 1900s more than 230 million trees have been restored to barren hillsides across Israel. At the **Planting Center**, a few hundred yards from the junction, you can choose a sapling, dedicate it to someone, and plant it yourself; the cost is $18 for adults. ✉ *Take Rte. 7707 off Rte. 77 east of Golani Junction at Lavi, then immediate left on secondary road* ☎ *050/546–9069* ⏲ *Sun.–Thurs. 8–3, Fri. 8–noon.*

6

EN ROUTE

One of the region's most strategic crossroads, **Golani Junction** is about 6 km (4 mi) east of Cana. It is named for the Israeli brigade that captured it in the War of Independence in 1948. A monument, a museum, and a McDonald's share the northeast corner of the intersection.

MT. TABOR

★ *16 km (10 mi) south of the Golani Junction off Rtes. 65 and 7266, 17 km (10½ mi) northeast of Afula.*

The domelike Mt. Tabor, the region's highest mountain, looms over one of the prettiest stretches of the Lower Galilee. Quilts of farmland kaleidoscope through the seasons as different crops grow, ripen, and are harvested. Modern woods of evergreens cover the hillsides.

Apart from the natural beauty, Mt. Tabor and its immediate surroundings have considerable biblical history. About 32 centuries ago, Israelite warriors of the prophetess-judge Deborah and her general, Barak, routed a Canaanite chariot army that had gotten bogged down in the mud. The modern kibbutz of Ein Dor, south of the mountain, is the site of ancient Endor, where King Saul unsuccessfully beseeched the spirit of the prophet Samuel for help before his fateful (and fatal) battle against the Philistines (I Samuel 28:3–25).

Continued on page 387

Jesus in the Galilee

Galilee beckons shyly. As in days of old, there is little of the frenetic pace and charged emotions of Jerusalem. For many Christians, the evocative, soft landscapes breathe new life into old familiar stories, and brush black-and-white scriptures with color. But curious visitors with less religious motivation will be drawn into Galilee's gentle charm. This tour of selected sights will speak to both.

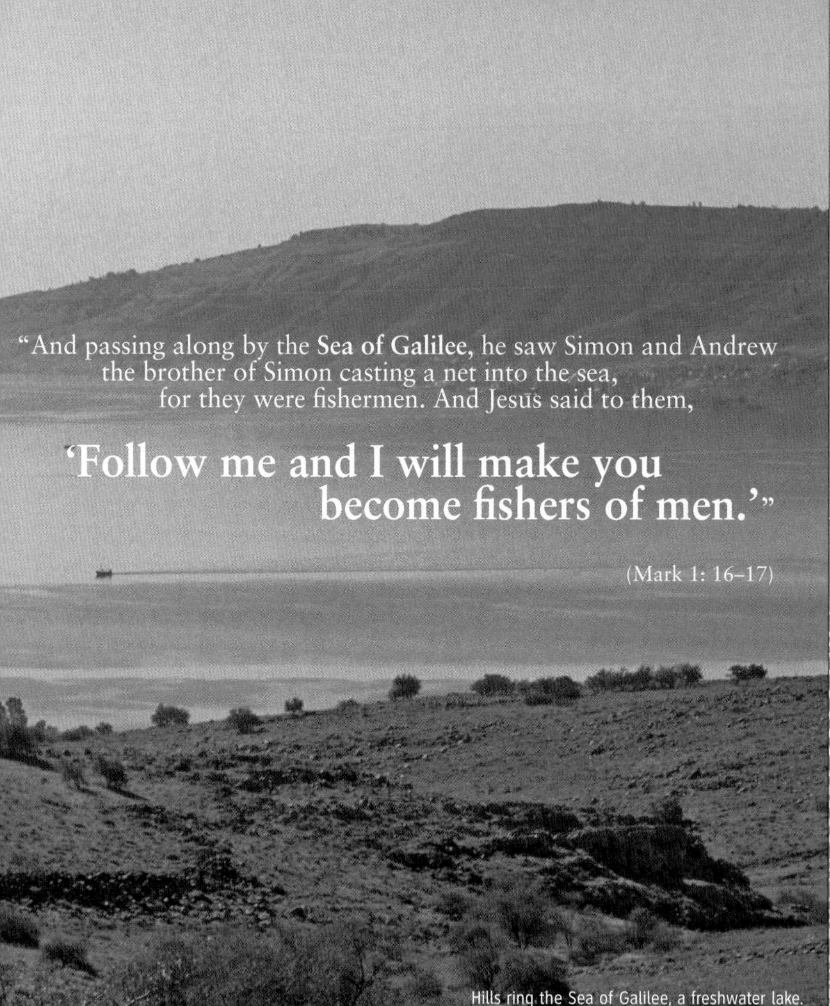

"And passing along by the **Sea of Galilee**, he saw Simon and Andrew
the brother of Simon casting a net into the sea,
for they were fishermen. And Jesus said to them,
'Follow me and I will make you
become fishers of men.'"
(Mark 1: 16–17)

Hills ring the Sea of Galilee, a freshwater lake.

Jesus was born in Bethlehem and died in Jerusalem, but it was in the Galilee that his ministry was forged. Over time, archaeologists and historians have unearthed many sites referred to in the New Testament. Today you can walk the hillsides, sail the Sea of Galilee, explore the ruins, and touch the churches of this beautiful region. Or you can sit under a tree and read scripture in the place where its narrative unfolded. If you have an eye for the contours of the land and an ear for echoes of the past, the experience can be unforgettable.

The activity and teachings of Jesus gain meaning and resonance from the landscape and social setting in which they emerged. Understand their context, and you will enhance your understanding of the events that have so shaped Western civilization.

By Mike Rogoff

RESTLESS SOCIETY, TURBULENT TIMES

Christ in the Storm on the Sea of Galilee by Jan Brueghel the Elder

The Romans came for the weekend in 63 BC and stayed for four centuries. Herod (later "the Great"), scion of a powerful political family, began his brutal reign as King of the Jews, courtesy of Rome, in 37 BC. He died in 4 BC, only a short time after the birth of Jesus (Matt. 2:1).

Herod's kingdom was divided among his three surviving sons: Archelaeus, Herod Antipas (who got Galilee, and Perea beyond the Jordan River), and Philip. It was Herod Antipas who executed John the Baptist (Matt. 14:10), and was in Jerusalem at the time of the crucifixion (Luke 23:7).

RIVAL THEOLOGIES

Jewish society in the land of Israel was anything but unified and placid 2,000 years ago. Two ideological streams dominated: the Sadducees were the establishment, many of them wealthy, led by the priestly class that controlled the Temple-based cult of Yahweh, the One God, in Jerusalem. They took religious texts literally, and rejected the idea of resurrection and an afterlife (Acts 23:6-9).

The Pharisees, on the other hand, drew their strength from the common people, offering a comforting belief in resurrection and an afterlife in a better world. Their rabbis, or teachers, would interpret biblical law, a practice that laid the groundwork for post-Temple Judaism as practiced until today.

Jesus himself came from the Pharisaic tradition, and "taught in their synagogues" (Luke 4:15). He was critical of the Pharisees' behavior, but not of their theology: They "sit on Moses' seat," he told his followers, "so practice and observe whatever they tell you" (Matt. 23:2).

SECTS AND CATACLYSM

Theological differences and domestic politics gave rise to numerous Jewish sects with strong religious agendas: the followers of Jesus, and of John the Baptist before him, were just two. One of the best known at the time were the Essenes, widely identified today as the monastic Jewish community that wrote the Dead Sea Scrolls.

There were other, less spiritual types like the Zealots—extreme nationalists who spearheaded the Great Revolt against Rome in AD 66. The cataclysm was not long in coming: Jerusalem and the Temple were razed in AD 70, four decades after Jesus' prediction that "there will not be left here one stone upon another" (Matt. 24:2).

Marriage Feast at Cana by Hieronymus Bosch

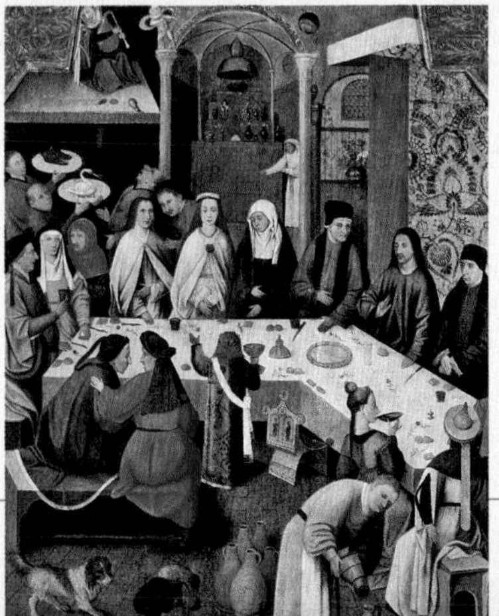

FACT, FAITH, AND TRADITION

The church on the Mount of Beatitudes has sweeping views of the Sea of Galilee.

Finding evidence of events or personalities in the distant past, the New Testament era included, is a kind of treasure hunt; and there is rarely an "X" to mark the spot. But when you do strike gold, through archaeological discoveries or ancient writings, for example, it thrills scholars and laypeople alike.

POPULATING ANCIENT MAPS

There are Galilean towns, like Nazareth and Tiberias, that have survived the centuries and are obviously genuine. Others, like Cana, are still debated. A lot of rocks have been turned over in the last three-quarters of a century, however, and archaeologists have exposed and identified Capernaum, Bethsaida, Chorazin (Korazim), Caesarea Philippi (Banias) in the Upper Galilee, and, to the satisfaction of many, Gennasaret (Ginosar) and Nain as well.

"TRADITIONAL" SITES: WHERE MEMORIES ENDURE

Other sites have been linked to events over time, though no evidence exists. Scriptural descriptions don't exactly offer geographical coordinates, and some locations that are still much visited by pilgrims are conjecture that has jelled into tradition. Visitors in the distant past often took local hearsay for hard fact when tour guides and other opportunists pointed out the very rock or glade or spring where this or that happened. It's not surprising that many traditional holy places are found so close to each other. Guides were often paid by the site—why should they journey unnecessary distances?

Events like the Sermon on the Mount, the Transfiguration, the feeding of the multitudes, the "feed my sheep" encounter of John 21, and the swine of the Gadarenes are all in this category. But for the faithful, the personal spiritual experience is more than a search for solid stones. It hardly depends on proof of where (or even whether) a particular event actually took place. Centuries of prayers and tears will sanctify a site, making it a remembrance place in the region where it all began.

TOURING THE CRADLE OF CHRISTIANITY

An astonishing three-quarters of the activity of Jesus recorded in the New Testament took place on, around, or within sight of the "Sea" of Galilee. The lake provided the largely Jewish towns and villages on its shores with a source of fresh water, a fishing industry, and a means of transportation.

Base yourself in Tiberias and head north, or clockwise, around the lake. The sights are close enough to see in a day. To visit Nazareth, Cana, and Mt. Tabor, 25 miles west of Tiberias, allot another day or be selective. Below are key places associated with Jesus, and scriptural references to them.

1 TIBERIAS *"... boats from Tiberias came near the place ..." (John 6:23).* Herod Antipas, son of Herod the Great, built the city as capital of the Galilee in AD 20. The town never lost its importance, and is today the region's urban center.

2 GINOSAR/GENNESARET Eight kms (5 mi) north of Tiberias, modern Ginosar is a kibbutz, with a museum that houses the extraordinary 1st-century-AD wooden boat found nearby. *"... they came to land at Gennesaret ... immediately the people recognized him ... and as many as touched [the fringe of his garment] were made well" (Mark 6:53–56).*

3 MT. OF BEATITUDES *"Seeing the crowds, he went up on the mountain, and when he sat down his disciples came to him ... 'Blessed are the poor in spirit ...'" (Matt. 5–7).* The traditional site of Jesus' Sermon on the Mount is set in hilltop gardens, with a church and a superb view of the lake.

4 TABGHA Two events in the life of Jesus are recalled in two churches here. The Multiplication was one: a famous 5th-century mosaic records the event. Crowds followed Jesus and evening came. What about food? *"'You give them something to eat' ... 'We have only five loaves here and two fish' ... 'Bring them ...' He looked up to heaven, and blessed ... And they all ate and were satisfied ... about 5,000 men, besides women and children" (Matt. 14: 15–21).*

The primacy of Peter is another. The beach and an attractively simple chapel recall the appearance of Jesus on the shore: *"'Have you any fish?' ... 'No' ... 'Cast the net' ... 'It is the Lord!' ... 'Simon [Peter] ... Do you love me? ... Feed my sheep'" (John 21:1–19).*

5 CAPERNAUM Jesus made this thriving Jewish town, now an archaeological site, the center of his ministry: *"He went and dwelt in Capernaum ..." (Matt. 4:13).* Here he preached— *"... and immediately on the sabbath he entered the synagogue and taught" (Mark 1:21).*

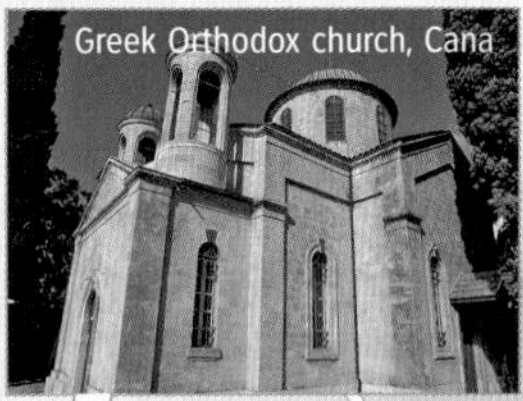

Greek Orthodox church, Cana

Basilica of the Annunciation, Nazareth

Mt. Tabor

Golani Junction
Lavi
9 Cana
65
Zippori
754
79
Kfar Kamma
Nazerat Illit (Upper Nazareth)
10 Nazareth
Kfar Tavor
Migdal Ha'emek
Shibli
Mt. Tabor
11
716

❻ BETHSAIDA This was the hometown of the disciples Philip, Andrew, and Peter (John 1:44), and the place where Jesus cured a blind man (Mark 8:22–25). The town was left stranded when its lagoon dried out, and eluded identification until recently.

Mosaic at Church of the Multiplication, Tabgha

❼ KURSI Jesus cured two madmen on the Golan Heights slopes, *"the country of the Gadarenes": ". . . a herd of swine was feeding . . . [the demons] came out [of the demoniacs] and went into the swine . . ." (Matt. 8:28–34).*

Synagogue at Capernaum

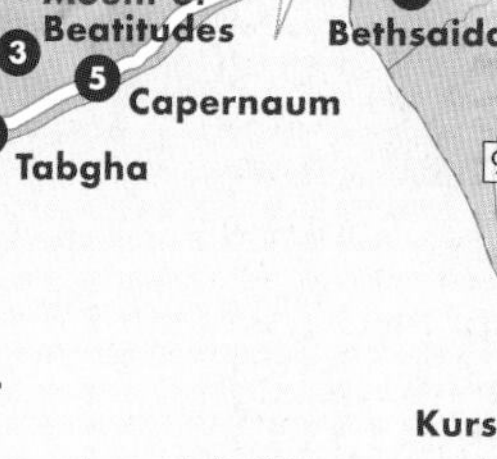

Ancient boat at Ginosar.

Baptism in the Jordan River

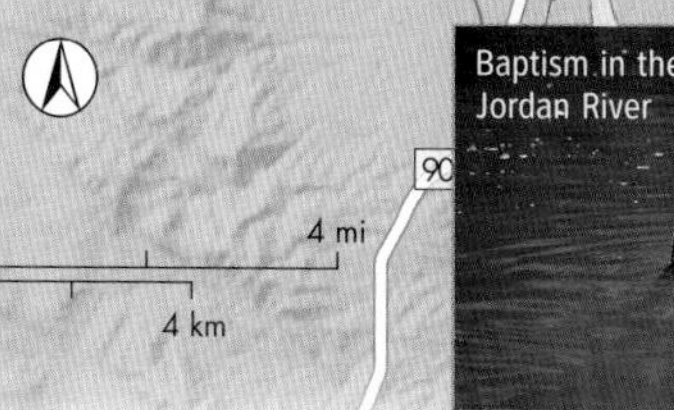

❽ JORDAN RIVER Today people come to be baptized in the Jordan in this northern region, but the New Testament story almost certainly refers to the river's southern reaches, near Jericho: *"Then Jesus came from the Galilee to the Jordan to John, to be baptized by him" (Matt. 3:13).*

❾ CANA When the wine ran out at a wedding feast, Jesus (after some persuasion) turned six stone jars-full of water into superior wine. *"This, the first of his signs, Jesus did in Cana of Galilee . . ." (John 2:1–11).*

Byzantine church at Kursi

❿ NAZARETH Here, the New Testament relates, an angel appeared to Mary to announce the coming birth of Jesus (Luke 1:26–38). It was here he grew up (his so-called "hidden years") and to Nazareth he returned as a teacher: *". . . he went to the synagogue . . . on the sabbath . . . he stood up to read . . . the prophet Isaiah . . ."(Luke 4:16–30).*

⓫ MT. TABOR In the event called "the Transfiguration," Jesus took three of his disciples *"up a high mountain apart,"* where they had a vision of him as a radiant white figure flanked by Moses and Elijah (Mark 9:2–8). Mt. Tabor has long been identified as the place, though some prefer Mt. Hermon in the far north.

TIPS FOR EXPLORING THE GALILEE

Greek Orthodox church at Capernaum

GETTING AROUND

Buses may be the cheapest way to see Israel, but they are not time-effective in the Galilee. Nazareth and Tiberias are easy to get to (and are 35 minutes apart), and a few less-frequent lines stop at Cana, Ginosar, and near Tabgha. Other Christian sites in the area are a fair hike from the highway or only doable by car.

HOLIDAYS, SERVICES, AND MORE

The Christmas and Easter celebrations that are so much part of the culture in many places are absent in Israel, where only 1.5% of its citizens are Christian. In the Galilee, the exception is Nazareth, with its lights and Christmas trees, and a traditional procession downtown at 3 PM on Christmas Eve. Many denominations are represented here, but Nazareth has no scheduled services in English.

In Tiberias, English-speakers can attend Catholic mass in St. Peter's Church (daily at 6:30 PM, Sundays at 8:30 AM) and occasional Protestant services at YMCA Penuel (just north of town) and St. Andrew's (opposite the Scots Hotel). A good source of information is the Web site of the Christian Information Center: www.cicts.org

■ **TIP→ For information about Nazareth Village, which re-creates the town as it was 2,000 years ago, and Yardenit, a group baptismal site, see the listings elsewhere in this chapter.**

VISITING SUGGESTIONS

Christian sites demand respectful behavior and conservative dress (no shorts, short skirts, or sleeveless tops). Photography is usually permitted, but professionals may require prior permission. Pay attention to advertised opening times and allow time for unexpected delays in getting there.

HIKING THE LANDSCAPE

Hikers can consider the Jesus Trail. Its primary route is 65 kms (40 mi) long, but you can select sections for a shorter hike. Organized tours are available. Visit www.jesustrail.com.

You can also walk or cycle along the footpaths of the new 60-km (37-mi) Gospel Trail, which traces the path that Jesus took along the Sea of Galilee. Visit www.goisrael.com.

CREATING SPECIAL MOMENTS IN THE GALILEE

- Carry a Bible and a good map.
- In fine weather, the Mount of Beatitudes is best in the afternoon, when the light is gentler on the lake and the hills.
- If you are unencumbered by luggage, and don't have a car to retrieve, stroll the easy trail from Mount of Beatitudes down to Tabgha (cross the highway with care), visit the two sites there, and then walk the 2-mi promenade that follows the highway east to Capernaum.
- The little beach of volcanic pebbles at Tabgha (the Primacy site) can be magical.
- Bethsaida is evocative—pure 1st century: no Byzantine, Crusader, or modern structures. It's never crowded, and offers a great place to sit with a view of the lake and read your favorite verses.

GETTING HERE AND AROUND

If you're driving, take Route 7266 through Shibli, a village of Bedouin who abandoned their nomadic life a few generations ago. A narrow switchback road starts in a clearing between Shibli and the next village, Dabouriya. Nazareth-based taxis often wait at the bottom of the mountain to provide shuttle service to the top. Watch out for them if you're driving your own car up; they come down in overdrive like the lords of the mountain they almost are.

EXPLORING

As far back as the Byzantine period, Christian tradition identified Mt. Tabor as the "high mountain apart" that Jesus ascended with his disciples Peter, James, and John. There, report the Gospels, "he was transfigured before them" (Matthew 17:2) as a radiant white figure, flanked by Moses and Elijah. The altar of the present imposing **Church of the Transfiguration,** which was consecrated in 1924, represents the tabernacle of Jesus that Peter suggested they build; those of Moses and Elijah appear as small chapels at the back of the church. Step up to the terrace to the right of the church doors for a great view of the Jezreel Valley to the west and south. From a platform on the Byzantine and Crusader ruins to the left of the modern church (watch your step), there is a panorama east and north over the Galilean hills. Fifty yards from the church, a Franciscan pilgrim rest stop has refreshments and bathrooms. ☎ *04/673–2283* 🎟 *Free* 🕒 *Daily 8–noon and 2–5.*

6

Jewish pioneers founded the veteran farming village of **Kfar Tavor** in 1901 in the shadow of the domed mountain from which it took its name. Not everyone farms today, and the village side streets, with single-family homes and well-tended gardens, feel like a nice piece of suburbia anywhere.

An excellent time-out from regular touring, the **Tabor Winery** was founded in 1997. The quality of its wines has risen steeply in the last decade. A 12-minute film and tasting are free. From late July through September, you can pay to stomp grapes the traditional way—a great family activity. ✉ *Visitors Center, POB 422, Kfar Tavor* ☎ *04/676–0444* 🌐 *www.taborwinery.com* 🎟 *Tours: NIS 19; family harvest by prior arrangement* 🕒 *Sun.–Thurs. 10–5, Fri. 10–3.*

In the same compound as the Tabor Winery, the charming **Marzipan Museum** contains explanations and delectable products made from locally grown almonds. If you have kids in tow, don't think twice about signing up for the fun marzipan-making workshop. (There's also a chocolate workshop.) Best of all, you get to take your creations home. ✉ *Kfar Tabor Visitor Center, Keren Kayemet L'Yisrael Avenue,* 📫 *POB 417, Kfar Tavor* ☎ *04/677–2111* 🌐 *www.shakedtavor.co.il* 🎟 *NIS 15* 🕒 *Sun.–Thurs. 9–6, Fri. 9–4, Sat. 10–6. Closes one hour earlier in winter.*

WHERE TO EAT

$$$ ISRAELI **Bordeaux.** The name hints at the restaurant's location, adjacent to the Tabor Winery. The style is "country," with warm wood decor inside and a great scenic deck for outside dining. With special effort made to use excellent local farm produce, the wide-ranging menu stretches from

modestly priced pastas, salads, and sandwiches to more sophisticated steaks, fish, and chicken dishes. A children's menu and good desserts contribute to the family-friendliness. ✉ *Kfar Tabor Visitors Center, Kfar Tavor* ☎ *057/944–3438* ⏲ *Closed Mon.* *Reservations essential* 💳 *AE, DC, MC, V.*

$$$ MIDDLE EASTERN

✕ **Sahara.** The menu at this Middle Eastern restaurant is a bit more sophisticated than that of its neighbors. Within the stone building with its landmark round tower is a spacious interior with stone floors and arches, wooden tables, and a centerpiece water cascade. Follow the excellent *mezze* (local salads) with traditional skewers of grilled meat, baked lamb, or one of the fish or chicken dishes. The Jordanian *mansaf* (a mix of rice, pine nuts, and pieces of lamb cooked with aromatic herbs) is an interesting discovery. ✉ *Rte. 65, next to gas station in Kfar Nin* ☎ *04/642–5959* *Reservations essential* 💳 *AE, DC, MC, V.*

EN ROUTE

If you're heading to the Sea of Galilee, take Route 767, which breaks off Route 65 at Kfar Tavor. It's a beautiful drive of about 25 minutes. The first village, **Kfar Kama,** is one of two in Israel of the Circassian (*Cherkessi*) community, Sunni Muslim non-Arabs from Russia's Caucasus Mountains who settled here in 1876. The unusually decorative minaret of the mosque is just one element of the tradition the community vigorously continues to preserve. On the descent to the lake, there is a **parking area** precisely at sea level. The Sea of Galilee is still more than 700 feet below, and the view is superb, especially in the afternoon. You meet Route 90 at the bottom of the road.

TIBERIAS AND THE SEA OF GALILEE

The Sea of Galilee is, in fact, a freshwater lake, measuring 21 km (13 mi) long from north to south and 11 km (7 mi) wide from east to west. Almost completely ringed by cliffs and steep hills, the lake lies in a hollow about 700 feet below sea level, which accounts for its warm climate and subtropical vegetation. This is Israel's Riviera-on-a-lake, replete with beaches and outdoor recreation facilities. Its shores are also dotted with sites hallowed by Christian tradition (note that several of these sites demand modest dress) as well as some important ancient synagogues. Tiberias itself is one of Judaism's four holy cities, along with Jerusalem, Hebron, and Tzfat.

The city of Tiberias is the logical starting base for exploration. One sightseeing strategy is to circle the Sea of Galilee clockwise from Tiberias (via Routes 90, 87, 92, and 98).

TIBERIAS

★ *38 km (23½ mi) north of Beit She'an, 36 km (23 mi) east of Nazareth, 70 km (43 mi) east of Haifa.*

As the only city on the Sea of Galilee, Tiberias, with a population of 40,000, has become the region's hub. The city spreads up a steep hillside, from 700 feet below sea level at the lake, to about 80 feet above sea level in its highest neighborhoods—a differential big enough to create significant variations in comfort levels during midsummer.

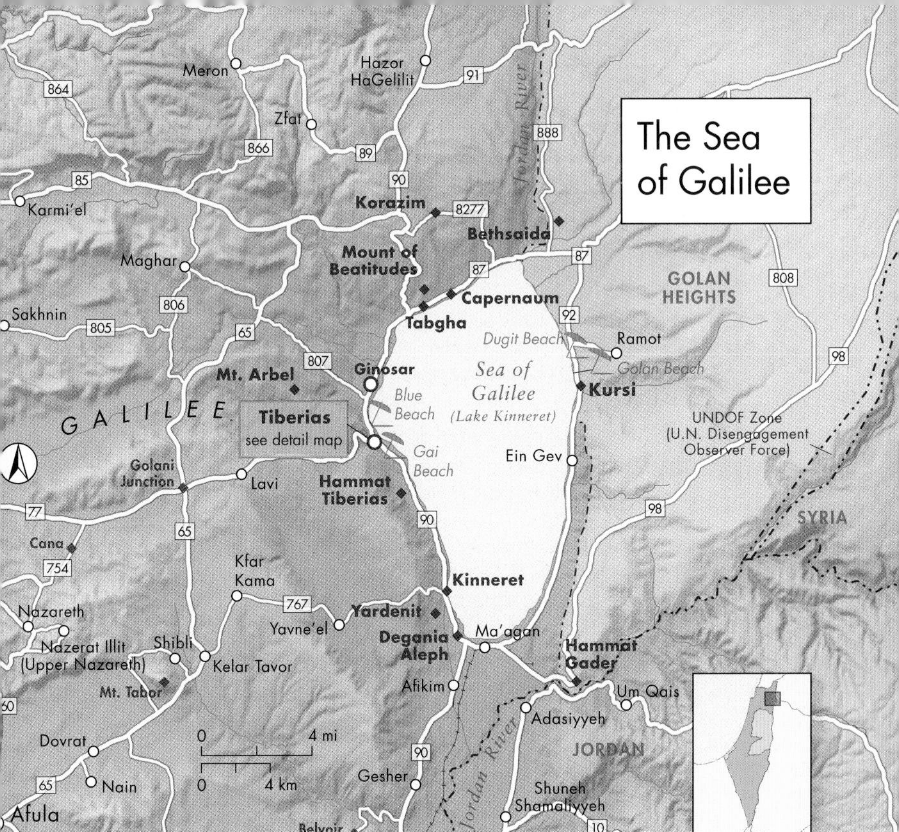

The splendid panoramic views of both the lake and the Golan Heights on the far shore deserved a better sort of development. Tiberias has little beauty and less charm, and although almost 2,000 years old, it still has the atmosphere of a place neglected for decades, if not centuries. It is at once brash and sleepy, with a reputation as a resort town based more on its location than its attractions. Travelers tend to see little of the town itself, sticking to the restaurants and hotels along the lake, and the boardwalk, which comes alive at night with vendors hawking clothes, jewelry, and knickknacks. Those traveling by car often skip the town altogether, opting for the numerous bed-and-breakfasts that dot the region.

GETTING HERE AND AROUND

The city sits astride the junction of Routes 90 and 77. Egged buses regularly serve Tiberias from Haifa, Nazareth, Tel Aviv, and Jerusalem. Haifa is one hour away, while Tel Aviv and Jerusalem are both two hours distant. Tiberias is small enough to walk to most locations, though given the punishing summer heat you may wish to have a taxi take you for even short jaunts.

Both Egged Tours and United Tours run one-day tours three times a week that take in Nazareth, Capernaum, Tabgha, the Sea of Galilee, Tiberias, and the Jordan River. Current prices are US$60 from Tel Aviv,

CLOSE UP

Tiberias Through Time

Tiberias was founded in AD 18 by Herod Antipas, son of Herod the Great, and dedicated to Tiberius, then emperor of Rome. The Tiberians had little stomach for the Jewish war against Rome that broke out in AD 66. They soon surrendered, preventing the vengeful destruction visited on other Galilean towns.

With Jerusalem laid waste in AD 70, the center of Jewish life gravitated to the Galilee. By the 4th century, the Sanhedrin had settled in Tiberias. Here Jewish oral law was compiled into what became known as the Jerusalem Talmud, and Tiberias's status as one of Judaism's holy cities was assured.

Tiberias knew hard times under the Byzantines, and further declined under the hostile Crusaders. Starting in the 1700s, newcomers from Turkey and Eastern Europe swelled the Jewish population, but an 1837 earthquake left Tiberias in ruins.

Relations between Jews and Arabs were generally cordial until the Arab riots of 1936, when some 30 Jews were massacred. During the 1948 War of Independence, an attack by local Arabs brought a counterattack from Jewish forces, and the Arabs abandoned the town. Today the citizenry is entirely Jewish, and abandoned mosques stand as silent monuments.

$64 from Jerusalem. Matan Tours, based in Tiberias, operates a guide-driven limo-van for a day tour of some Sea of Galilee sites and the Golan Heights. The cost is $45 per person.

ESSENTIALS

Bus Contact **Egged** (☎ *03/694–8888 or *2800* 🌐 *www.egged.co.il/Eng*).

Medical Contacts **Emergency Medical Service** (✉ *1 Kishon St., Tiberias* ☎ *04/671–7611*). **Superpharm** (✉ *1 Hayarden St., Tiberias* ☎ *04/671–6663*).

Taxi Contacts **Ha'emek** (✉ *Tiberias* ☎ *04/604–4888*). **Hagalil** (✉ *Tiberias* ☎ *04/980–8333*).

Visitor and Tour Information **Aviv Tours** (✉ *66 Hagalil St., Tiberias* ☎ *04/672–3510*). **Egged Tours** (☎ *03/694–8888 or *2800* 🌐 *www.egged.co.il/Eng*). **United Tours** (☎ *03/617–3315* 🌐 *www.unitedtours.co.il*).

EXPLORING

Foremost among Tiberias's many venerated resting places is the **tomb of Moses Maimonides** (1135–1204). Born in Córdoba, Spain, Maimonides—widely known by his Hebrew acronym, the "Rambam" (for Rabbi Moshe Ben Maimon)—won international renown as a philosopher, as physician to the royal court of Saladin in Egypt, and in the Jewish world, as the greatest religious scholar and spiritual authority of the Middle Ages. To his profound knowledge of the Talmud, Maimonides brought an incisive intellect honed by his study of Aristotelian philosophy and the physical sciences. The result was a rationalism unusual in Jewish scholarship and a lucidity of analysis and style admired by Jewish and non-Jewish scholars alike.

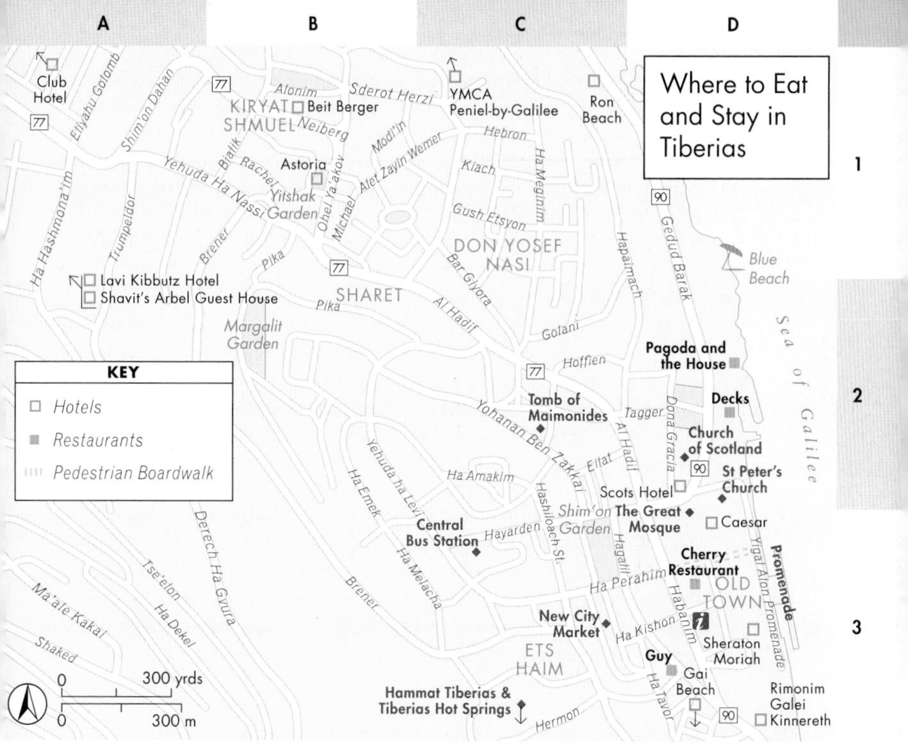

Where to Eat and Stay in Tiberias

KEY

□ *Hotels*

■ *Restaurants*

Pedestrian Boardwalk

Maimonides never lived in Tiberias, but after his death in Egypt, his remains were brought to this Jewish holy city for interment. His whitewashed tomb has become a shrine, dripping with candle wax and tears. To get here, walk two blocks up ha-Yarden Street, and turn right onto Ben Zakkai Street. The tomb is on your right, topped by a soaring spire of red steel girders. ✉ *Ben Zakkai St.* ☎ *No phone* 🎫 *Free* ⏲ *Sun.–Thurs. dawn–dusk, Fri. and Jewish holiday eves until 2 pm.*

★ Not to be confused with the nearby Tiberias Hot Springs (a modern spa where you can bathe), **Hammat Tiberias** is a national park that includes a notable mosaic floor, and the remains of an ornate 4th-century synagogue and ancient therapeutic baths. The Hammam Suleiman (Turkish bath), which was in use from 1780 until 1944, is now a museum. It's located just to the right of the park entrance. Hammat Tiberias is worth a half hour visit, though the experience parallels the more impressive ruins and hot springs in which you can soak at Hammat Gader.

The site has Israel's hottest spring, gushing out of the earth at 60°C (140°F) because of cracks in the earth's crust along the Syrian-African Rift. Alas, this is an archaeological site, so you don't get to try the waters here. The healing properties of its mineral-rich waters were already recognized in antiquity, as evidenced by the ruins of ancient towns—including an exquisite 4th-century AD mosaic floor of a synagogue.

Legend says that Solomon, the great king of Israel, wanted a hot bath and used his awesome authority to force some young devils below ground to heat the water. The fame of the salubrious springs spread far and wide, bringing the afflicted to seek relief. Seeing such gladness among his subjects, Solomon worried about what would happen when he died and the devils stopped their labors. In a flash of the wisdom for which he was renowned, Solomon made the hapless devils deaf. To this day, they have not heard of the king's demise and so continue to heat the water for fear of his wrath.

By the end of the Second Temple period (the 1st century AD), when settlement in the Sea of Galilee region was at its height, a Jewish town called Hammat (Hot Springs) stood here. With time, Hammat was overshadowed by its newer neighbor, Tiberias, and became known as Hammat Teverya (Tiberias Hot Springs). The benefits of the mineral hot springs were already legendary: a coin minted in Tiberias during the rule of Emperor Trajan, around AD 100, shows Hygeia, the goddess of health, sitting on a rock with a spring gushing out beneath it.

Parts of ancient Hammat have been uncovered near the road, bringing to light a number of ruined **synagogues.** The most dramatic dates from the 4th century AD, with an elaborate **mosaic floor** that uses motifs almost identical to those at Beit Alfa: classical Jewish symbols, human figures representing the four seasons and the signs of the zodiac, and the Greek god Helios at the center. The mosaics of Hammat Tiberias are among the finest ever found in Israel. Later cultures exploited the hot springs, too, as the small adjacent Turkish bath attests.

Behind Hammat Tiberias, a turquoise dome marks the **tomb of Rabbi Meir Ba'al Ha-Ness,** the "Miracle Worker," who supposedly took a vow that he would not lie down until the Messiah came—and was therefore buried in an upright position. His name has become an emblem for charitable organizations, and many a miracle has been attributed to the power of prayer at his tomb.

Hammat Tiberias is on the southern edge of Tiberias on Route 90. Although you can walk from the downtown hotels, the summer heat makes this unbearable. It's best to take a taxi. ✉ *Rte. 90, 2 km (1 mi) south of Tiberias, 7 km (4 mi) north of Kinneret.* ☎ *04/672–5287* 🌐 *www.parks.org.il/ParksENG* 🎫 *NIS 12* ⏲ *Apr.–Sept., Sat.–Thurs. 8–5, Fri. and Jewish holiday eves 8–4; Oct.–Mar., Sat.–Thurs. 8–4, Fri. and Jewish holiday eves 8–3.*

Tiberias Hot Springs, on the lake side of Route 90, is a modern spa fed by the mineral spring. In addition to sophisticated therapeutic services and facilities, it has a large, warm indoor mineral pool (35°C or 95°F) and a small outdoor one right near the lake's edge. A restaurant serves lunch. ✉ *Rte. 90* ☎ *04/672–8500* 🎫 *Pools: NIS 60, NIS 35, Sun.–Thurs. after 4 and Fri. after 2* ⏲ *Sun., Mon., and Wed. 8–8, Tues. and Thurs. 8 am–11 pm, Fri. 8–4, Sat. 8:30–6.*

WHERE TO EAT

At a right angle to the waterside promenade, the *midrachov* (pedestrian mall), between the Sheraton Moriah and Caesar hotels, has a wide range of affordable dining options. There are also a couple of budget places

The god Helios occupies the center of a spectacular 4th-century mosaic of the zodiac at Hammat Tiberias.

on Habanim Street. If you're into local color, look for the tiny, modest restaurants (where English really *is* a foreign language) on Hagalil Street and in the little streets that connect it to Habanim Street, like the pedestrian-only Kishon Street.

$$ ISRAELI **Cherry.** Centrally located on the Tiberias boardwalk, Cherry has become an institution for budget travelers. The menu, simple and familiar to Western visitors (bagel melts, pastas, omelets, and the like) offers satisfying and generous meals at reasonable prices. The St. Peter's Fillet, which is oven-baked in olive oil with herbs and garlic and served with antipasti. For a refreshing and healthy summer dessert, try the watermelon served with salty Bulgarian cheese, or treat yourself to a chocolate crepe. ✉ *4 Habanim Boardwalk* ☎ *04/679–0051* ⏲ *No dinner Fri.; open Sat. sundown to 1 am.* ✥ *3D*

$$$$ MODERN ISRAELI **Decks.** Built on a pier, this family-run restaurant is something of an institution, and the locals keep coming back for the great food. The kitchen specializes in delicious meats—steak, goose liver, or long skewers of veal and vegetables—grilled slowly over hickory wood. The bluefin tuna carpaccio, caught by the manager's brother, is a delicacy. An apple tart pan-baked at your table is the house dessert. ✉ *Lido complex, Rte. 90, at the exit from Tiberias north* ☎ *04/672–1538* ▭ *AE, DC, MC, V* ⏲ *Sun.–Thurs. noon–midnight; Fri. noon–6; Sat. half hour after sundown–midnight.* ✥ *2D.*

$ MIDDLE EASTERN **Guy.** Stuffed vegetables are the calling card at this kosher family-run restaurant (pronounced "guy"), whose name means "ravine" in Hebrew. The cook-matriarch Geula comes from a Tiberias family, but her Moroccan ancestry shines through in delicious dishes like eggplant stuffed with seasoned ground beef. There are good, if more conventional, Middle Eastern meat and salad options, but go for the excellent soups, and try some *kibbeh* (a Kurdish-Iraqi specialty of seasoned ground meat and bulgur). Although there is a menu, there are also daily specials so ask your waiter to recommend the tastiest treats, such as apricots or dates stuffed with rice. The restaurant faces the lake and is slightly set back from the sidewalk, opposite a small traffic circle; keep your eyes open or you'll miss it. It gets quite busy at lunchtime but is quieter at dinner. ✉ *63 Hagalil St.* ☎ *04/672–3036* ▭ *No credit cards* ⊙ *Closed Sat. and one hour before sundown on Fri.* ✥ *3D.*

$$$ ASIAN ✕ **Pagoda and the House.** This faux-Chinese temple (Pagoda) has an outdoor patio overlooking the lake and across the road (House, part of the same restaurant) is a maze of more intimate rooms entered through a garden. The menu is identical and kosher at both places, but Pagoda is closed on the Sabbath, while the House is open. Apart from the Chinese standards, try the Thai soups (such as the tasty hot-and-sour soup), the goose spareribs, or strips of beef with peanut sauce. There's a sushi bar, too. ✉ *Gedud Barak St. (Rte. 90)* ☎ *04/672–5513 or 04/672–5514* *Reservations essential* ▭ *AE, DC, MC, V* ⊙ *Pagoda: no dinner Fri. No lunch Sat. The House: no dinner Sat.–Thurs. No lunch Sun.–Fri.* ✥ *2D.*

WHERE TO STAY

$ **Astoria.** One of Tiberias's better moderately priced hotels, the Astoria is set away from the lake. Don't worry; there are still views from guest rooms. What it lacks in location, however, it makes up for in quality. It's comfortable, clean, and family run, with furnishings in attractive pastels. Large family rooms are available. **Pros:** good value; great views of the water. **Cons:** too far to walk downtown; basic decor. ✉ *13 Ohel Ya'akov St.* ☎ *04/672–2351* 🌐 *www.astoria.co.il* *88 rooms* *In room: refrigerator (some). In-hotel: bar, pool, spa, laundry service, Internet terminal, Wi-Fi, parking (free), no-smoking rooms* ▭ *AE, MC, V* *BP* ✥ *1B.*

¢ **Beit Berger.** This family-run hotel has spacious rooms, most with balconies. A car is an advantage here, but there is frequent public transportation downtown (except on the Sabbath). The hotel is self-catering, so the supermarket across the street is very convenient. Recent additions such as satellite TV have made this quite a bargain. **Pros:** reasonable rates; hillside views; kitchens. **Cons:** too far to walk downtown; no swimming pool. ✉ *27 Neiberg St.* ☎ *04/671–5151* *45 rooms, 2 apartments* *In-room: kitchen, refrigerator. In-hotel: bar, laundry service, Internet terminal, parking (free)* ▭ *AE, DC, MC, V* ✥ *1B.*

$$$ **Club Hotel.** Cascading down a hillside, this all-suites hotel offers an unimpeded view of the lake. Units sleep at least four, and the rate is the same up to that number. This classic vacation property has cheerful decor and an upbeat style, an all-season team to engage the kids, and a good health club to relax their parents. Downtown is less than 10 minutes away by car or cab. **Pros:** spectacular views; spacious rooms. **Cons:** crowded on weekends; away from downtown. ✉ *HaBanim St.* ☎ *04/671–4444* 🌐 *www.leonardo-hotels.com* *398 suites* *In-room:*

safe, refrigerator. In-hotel: restaurant, bar, tennis court, pool, gym, laundry service, parking (free) ▭ AE, DC, MC, V 🍴 BP ✣ 1A.

$$$$ **Gai Beach.** The rare lakeshore location is a big plus, and for some, so is the distance from the noisy downtown promenade. A marble lobby lounge is large and airy, though clusters of comfortable armchairs create intimacy. Guest rooms are tastefully furnished, if a bit small and slightly fraying; about two-thirds face the lake. Rooms on the two lower floors (there are three all together) have private balconies. The hotel gives you free access to the adjacent water park, with seven slides, a wave pool, and a children's pool, making it arguably the most family-friendly hotel in town. The guests-only spa has a very private feel. **Pros:** on the lake; gorgeous spa; far from the hubbub. **Cons:** a bit isolated; crowded on weekends. ✉ *Derech Hamerhatzaot, Rte. 90* ☎ *04/670–0700* 🌐 *www.gaibeachhotel.com* *198 rooms, 2 suites* *In-room: safe. In-hotel: restaurant, room service, bar, pools, gym, spa, beachfront, laundry service, parking (free), Wi-Fi* ▭ *AE, DC, MC, V* 🍴 *BP* ✣ *3D.*

$$ **Lavi Kibbutz Hotel.** With a new wing built in 2008, this guesthouse is keeping up with the times. Rooms are spacious, and many have good views. The kibbutz is religious and there is no checking in or out and use of cars between Friday and Saturday evening. That said, the atmosphere is welcoming for all, and waking up in peaceful rural surroundings has much to recommend it. The hospitality of kibbutz members offers visitors a look at life on one of Israel's 17 religious kibbutzim. Ask to see the synagogue furniture factory and the unique apparatus set up in the cowsheds to milk the cows on Saturday without violating the Sabbath. **Pros:** opportunity to experience kibbutz life; central location; good children's programs. **Cons:** no evening entertainment; Sabbath restrictions. ✉ *Rte. 77, Lavi, 11 km (7 mi) west of Tiberias* ☎ *04/679–9450* 🌐 *hotel.lavi.co.il* *188 rooms, 4 suites* *In-room: Wi-Fi (some). In-hotel: bar, tennis court, pool, gym, children's programs (ages 3–13), laundry service, Internet terminal, parking (free)* ▭ *AE, DC, MC, V* 🍴 *BP* ✣ *1A.*

$$$$ **Rimonim Galei Kinnereth.** It's easy to understand why this grand dame was a personal favorite of Israel's founding prime minister, David Ben-Gurion. Its location right on the lake is unbeatable, and the spa is a soothing complex suffused with incense and candles; a large whirlpool gurgles away in its own glassed-in gazebo. Guest rooms are nicely decorated and recently renovated, but they are neither extraordinary enough nor large enough to justify the rack rate. Breakfast and either lunch (on weekends) or dinner are included. **Pros:** convenient to Tiberias; lakeside swimming pool; quiet; sense of history. **Cons:** can be crowded on weekends and in July and August. ✉ *1 Eliezer Kaplan St.* ☎ *04/672–8888* 🌐 *www.rimonim.com* *120 rooms, 7 suites* *In-room: safe, refrigerator, Wi-Fi. In-hotel: bar, pool, gym, spa, beachfront, water sports, laundry service, Internet terminal, parking (free)* ▭ *AE, DC, MC, V* 🍴 *MAP* ✣ *3D.*

$ **Ron Beach.** The family-run Ron Beach is the northernmost hotel in Tiberias and has rare private lake frontage, though no beach. Most guest rooms are in a two-story building facing the water. The upper floor is made up of suites; the lower floor opens out to lawns and the pool area. There are also several large family rooms. All in all, it's a

6

To escape the heat or just have fun, take a ride on the Sea of Galilee.

great value. **Pros:** lakeside location; pretty pool. **Cons:** too far to walk to downtown; no beach. ✉ *Gedud Barak St.* ☎ *04/679–1350* 🌐 *www.ronbeachhotel.com* *122 rooms, 4 suites* *In-room: refrigerator. In-hotel: room service, bar, pool, laundry service, Internet terminal, parking (free)* ▭ *AE, DC, MC, V* 🍴 *BP* ✥ *1C.*

$$$ **Scots Hotel.** A former hospital, this hotel has been successfully reinvented as an upscale hotel. Two renovated older structures and one entirely new one produce a pleasingly asymmetrical complex filled with pleasant surprises, such as a roof terrace where you can have a drink or light meal, and an inviting courtyard with a waterfall. Everywhere are unexpected views of the lake. The aesthetics are wonderful, with nicely decorated rooms and well-appointed bathrooms. **Pros:** boutique-hotel feel; historic setting; central location. **Cons:** no nightly entertainment. ✉ *1 Gedud Barak St., at Hayarden St.* ☎ *04/671–0710* 🌐 *www.scotshotels.co.il* *50 rooms* *In-room: safe, refrigerator, Wi-Fi. In-hotel: room service, bar, pool, spa, laundry service, Internet terminal, parking (free)* ▭ *AE, DC, MC, V* 🍴 *BP* ✥ *2D.*

Fodor's Choice ★

$ **Shavit's Arbel Guest House.** Israel and Sarah Shavit make congenial hosts, with the bonus that he's a licensed tour guide and a chef. Their inn, which has whirlpools and wooden balconies, is surrounded by a riot of greenery, including an inviting *bustan* (a local-style garden redolent with fragrant herbs). Four apartments have a living room and a bedroom (one is wheelchair accessible); the fifth has two bedrooms. The rustic environment, 10 minutes from Tiberias and the Sea of Galilee, is pleasing, and the dining room transforms into a good-value à la carte restaurant in the evening. **Pros:** warm hospitality; delicious food. **Cons:** far from downtown Tiberias. ✉ *Rte. 7717, off Rte. 77, Arbel Village*

☎ 04/679–4919 🌐 www.4shavit.com 1 room, 5 apartments In-room: no phone, kitchen, refrigerator. In-hotel: restaurant, pool, laundry service ▭ AE, DC, MC, V 🍴 BP ✣ 2A.

WORD OF MOUTH

"Our hotel in Tiberias was right on the Sea of Galilee. I was surprised to learn it is actually a lake and the primary freshwater source for Israel. It was a beautiful lake and we were fortunate enough to see a rainbow over it. The next day we took a boat ride. Once again it was cold, with hard rain. But once we set sail, the sun came out and we had beautiful views." –P_M

$ **YMCA Peniel-by-Galilee.** Archibald Harte, founder of Jerusalem's landmark YMCA, built a lakeside retreat here in the 1930s and later bequeathed his property to the Jerusalem YMCA. You can still feel his presence walking on the pebbly beach, and relaxing in the common areas decorated with antique Damascene wood panels. Spacious guest rooms, most with lake views, are furnished simply but comfortably; two have kitchenettes. The pool is fed by a natural spring, with fish swimming in the clear water. A loyal clientele responds to the quiet charm of the place, making reservations essential. **Pros:** rustic appeal; reasonable rates. **Cons:** too far to walk to town; no evening entertainment. *✉ Off Rte. 90, 3 km (2 mi) north of central Tiberias ☎ 04/672–0685 🌐 www.ymca-galilee.co.il 12 rooms, 1 suite In-room: kitchen (some), refrigerator. In-hotel: 2 restaurants, pool, beachfront ▭ AE, DC, MC, V 🍴 BP ✣ 1C.*

NIGHTLIFE AND THE ARTS

Much of the entertainment, especially in the larger hotels in Tiberias, is of the live lounge-music variety: piano bars, one-man dance bands, and crooners. Thursday and Friday are "nightclub" nights at some hotels, with dance music for the weekend crowds. The clientele tends to be a bit older. Generally speaking, the younger set wouldn't be caught dead here, preferring to hang out at one of the few pubs, where the recorded rock music is good and loud and the beer is on tap.

The cultural center **Bet Gabriel** (*✉ 650 feet east of Tzemach Junction, west of Ma'agan ☎ 04/675–1175 🌐 www.betgabriel.co.il*) is located on the southern shores of the Sea of Galilee, only a 10-minute drive from Tiberias. Its fine architecture, beautiful garden setting, and concert facilities have established its popularity in the area. Tiberias's Tourist Information Office and major hotels carry information on the month's performances and art exhibits.

SPORTS AND THE OUTDOORS

BEACHES

The Sea of Galilee—a freshwater lake—is a refreshing but rocky place for a swim. You can recline on pleasant commercial beaches with amenities ranging from cafeterias to water parks, or on free beaches with minimal facilities. Note that the region has seen a drought over the past few years, so at this writing the water level is low. The numerous water parks with slides and pools remain popular.

September's **Kinneret Swim,** a tradition since 1953, has both amateur (3½ km [2 mi] and 1½ km [1 mi]) and competitive (1½ km [1 mi])

categories. At several locations around the Sea of Galilee you can hire pedal boats, rowboats, and motorboats and arrange to water-ski. Serious kayakers convene for an annual international competition in March.

Blue Beach (✉ *Rte. 90, at northern exit from Tiberias* ☎ *04/672–0105*) is one of the oldest establishments in the region. It's open May to October, and admission is NIS 40. Open May to October, **Gai Beach** (✉ *Rte. 90, at southern exit from Tiberias* ☎ *04/670–0713*) has a multislide water park in addition to swimming. Admission is NIS 70.

WALKING AND JOGGING

A **promenade** follows the lakeshore for about 5 km (3 mi) south of Tiberias, offering nice views of the lake and Golan Heights. As you leave the hotels behind, you appreciate the Sea of Galilee's mystic beauty. At this writing the promenade is being extended north of the city.

WATER SPORTS

Waterskiing and boat rentals are popular activities on the lake. You can ride in everything from large ferries to reproductions of the fishing boat St. Peter would have used. The recent drought has had an impact on ferries: ask your hotel or the tourist office about sailing opportunities.

Holyland Sailing (✉ *Tiberias Marina* ☎ *04/672–3006* 🌐 *www.jesusboats.com*) has five wooden boats that are replicas of those in use during the time of Jesus. The 45-minute cruises include historical commentary and concerts of traditional music. Sunset cruises are especially popular.

SHOPPING

Tiberias relies heavily on tourism yet has little in the way of shopping. The exception is jewelry. There are a few jewelry stores near the intersection of Habanim and Hayarden streets and in some of the better hotels. **Caprice** (✉ *Tabor St.* ☎ *04/670–0600*), a large diamond factory, introduces you to the industry with a video and a short tour of its workshops and small museum.

MT. ARBEL

★ *8 km (5 mi) northwest of Tiberias, off Route 7717.*

Magnificent views await at the top of the Arbel cliffs, and the relatively easy hiking trails take you into caves and to an ancient synagogue that once served a Jewish community in these spectacular heights. (You can drive up the mountain if you're not in the mood to hike).

The 2,600-acre Arbel National Park and Nature Reserve is on a plateau that slopes from the Arbel Valley to a cliff at the top of Mt. Arbel, above Lake Kinneret; the views are of the Sea of Galilee and the Golan Heights. The reserve has few trees but, depending on the season, there are a variety of flowers and small fauna. Jesus is said to have preached and performed miracles at the foot of the mountain.

Ancient texts indicate that the Seleucid Greeks conquered the Biblical-era Jews of Arbel as the Seleucids made their way to Jerusalem. Later, a few decades before the famous suicide of a group of Jewish zealots at Masada, a similar group from Israel's north barricaded themselves at Arbel. Roman historian Flavius Josephus describes a battle there in 37 BC between the Jews and Marc Antony, who had been sent by Herod the Great to suppress the Jewish rebellion. According to Josephus, the Jews were "lurking in caves . . . opening up onto mountain precipices that were inaccessible from any quarter except by torturous and narrow paths . . . the cliff in front of them dropped sheer down." Antony eventually crushed the rebels by lowering his soldiers into the caves from above, but the bravery and rashness of the rebels may be the source of the tradition saying that after the coming of the Messiah, the battle of the End of Days will take place at Arbel.

To get here from the Tiberias-Golani junction road (Route 77), turn at the Kfar Hittim junction to Route 7717. Turn right at the turnoff for Moshav Arbel, and before entering the moshav, turn left and drive 3.5 km to the site. ✉ *Rte. 7717* ☎ *04/673-2904* 🌐 *www.parks.org.il/ParksENG* 🎫 *NIS 20* 🕓 *Daily, summer 8–5, winter 8–4. Last entrance one hour before closing.*

GINOSAR

10 km (6 mi) north of Tiberias.

Many Israelis know Ginosar, a kibbutz founded in 1937, as the home of the late Yigal Allon (1918–80), commander of the crack Palmach battalions in the War of Independence and deputy prime minister of Israel in the 1970s under Golda Meir and Yitzhak Rabin. Travelers, however, come here to see the ancient fishing boat.

GETTING HERE AND AROUND

Egged buses frequently make the short trip here from the Tiberias Central Bus Station. Ask the driver to tell you where to get off.

EXPLORING

Kibbutz Ginosar's premier tourist attraction is a **wooden fishing boat** from the 1st century AD, found on the shore by two amateur archaeologists in 1986. Three years of drought had lowered the level of Lake Kinneret, and bits of the ancient wood were suddenly exposed in the mud. Excavated in a frenetic 11 days, the 28-foot-long boat became an instant media sensation. Given the frequency of New Testament references to Jesus and his disciples boating on the Sea of Galilee—including coming ashore at Gennesaret, perhaps today's Ginosar—the press immediately dubbed it the "Jesus Boat."

On the other hand, the startlingly vivid relic might have been a victim of the Roman naval victory over the rebellious Jewish townspeople of nearby Magdala in AD 67, as described by the historian Flavius Josephus. Whatever its unknown history, it is the most complete boat this old ever found in an inland waterway anywhere in the world. Today it is exhibited dry in all its modest but remarkably evocative glory in a specially built pavilion in the Yigal Allon Museum. A short video tells the story. ✉ *Nof Ginosar, Off Rte. 90* ☎ *04/672–7700* 🌐 *www.jesusboatmuseum.com* 🎫 *NIS 20* 🕓 *Sat.–Thurs. 8–5, Fri. 8–4; last entry 1 hr before closing.*

WHERE TO STAY

$ **Ginosar Village.** Its grand location—with a private beach right on the Sea of Galilee—makes this kibbutz guesthouse especially popular. Renovated in 2008, the inn is warm and inviting, with spacious balconies looking out over the Sea of Galilee. There is a morning tour of the lovely grounds, and the nearby museum is free to guests. The dinner buffet includes both meat and vegetarian choices, the latter offering outstanding blintzes with sweetened cheese. A more upscale property, the Nof Ginosar Hotel is also at the same location, with different facilities. **Pros:** convenient location; opportunity to experience kibbutz life; beautiful gardens. **Cons:** too far to walk to town; no evening entertainment. ✉ *Rte. 90* ☎ *04/670–0300* 🌐 *www.ginosar.co.il* *162 rooms* *In-room: refrigerator, Internet. In-hotel: bar, tennis court, pool, beachfront, laundry service, Internet terminal, parking (free)* ▭ *AE, DC, MC, V* *BP.*

KIBBUTZ MUSIC

Nof Ginosar hosts the twice-annual **Jacob's Ladder Festival** (🌐 *www.jlfestival.com*), a perennial favorite for folk-music fans. The music is eclectic, with international artists performing anything from Celtic to country classics. The crowd is equally diverse, coming from the United States, Canada, Britain, and around the world. The spring festival features several stages spread out on the kibbutz lawns, as well as impromptu jam sessions. The winter festival, in December, is held indoors. Book your room far ahead.

EN ROUTE

On Route 90, on your right a few miles north of Ginosar, is an electric substation that powers huge water pumps buried in the hill behind it. The Sea of Galilee is Israel's primary freshwater reservoir and the beginning of the **National Water Carrier,** a network of canals and pipelines that integrates the country's water sources and distribution lines. On the hill above is the small tell or mound of the Old Testament city of **Kinneret,** which dominated a branch of the Via Maris, the main highway of the ancient Near East. Scholars assume that the Hebrew name for the lake—Kinneret—comes from that of the most important city on its shores in antiquity. Romantics contend that the name derives from the lake's shape, which resembles the biblical *kinnor* (lyre).

TABGHA

★ *4 km (2 ½ mi) north of Ginosar, 14 km (8 mi) north of Tiberias, at Capernaum Junction (Rtes. 90 and 87).*

With a name that is an Arabic corruption of the Greek Heptaegon (Seven Springs), Tabgha is a cluster of serene holy places associated with Jesus' ministry in the Galilee. A promenade and hiking trails connect the shrines.

GETTING HERE AND AROUND

Tabgha is located off Route 87, a few hundred meters from the junction with Route 90. A promenade connects the Church of the Multiplication with the Church of the Primacy of St. Peter. A trail leads up to the Mount of Beatitudes, but the hike is best enjoyed going downhill, with the glorious views of the lake in front of you. Even without a car, Tabgha can be easily walked to from Route 90.

EXPLORING

The German Benedictines (Roman Catholic) dedicated the large, orange-roofed **Church of the Multiplication** in 1936 on the scanty remains of earlier shrines. The site has long been venerated as the "deserted place" (Mark 6:30–6:34) of the Gospels, where Jesus miraculously multiplied two fish and five loaves of bread to feed the crowds that followed him. The present airy limestone building with the wooden truss ceiling was built in the style of a Byzantine basilica to give a fitting context to the beautifully wrought 5th-century mosaic floor depicting the loaves and fishes in front of the altar. The nave is covered with geometric designs, but the front of the aisles is filled with flora and birds and, curiously, a Nilometer, a graded column once used to measure the flood level of the Nile for the purpose of assessing that year's collectible taxes. ✉ *Rte. 87* ☎ *04/670–0180* 🎫 *Free* ⏲ *Sun. 10–5, Mon.–Sat. 8:30–5.*

The austere, black basalt **Church of the Primacy of St. Peter,** 200 yards east of the Church of the Multiplication, is built on the water's edge, over a flat rock known as Mensa Christi (the Table of Christ). After his resurrection, the New Testament relates, Jesus appeared to his disciples by the Sea of Galilee and presented them a miraculous catch of fish. Three times Jesus asked the disciple Peter if he loved him, and after his reply of "You know that I love you," Jesus commanded him to "Feed my sheep." Some scholars see this affirmation as Peter's atonement for having thrice denied Jesus in Jerusalem after Jesus' arrest. The episode is seen as establishing Peter's "primacy" (Matthew 16:18) and, in the Roman Catholic tradition, that of the popes, his spiritual successors. The site was included in the itineraries of both Pope Paul VI in 1964 and Pope John Paul II in 2000. ✉ *Rte. 87* ☎ *04/672–4767* 🎫 *Free* ⏲ *Daily 8–noon and 2–5.*

6

MOUNT OF BEATITUDES

★ *8 km (5 mi) north of Ginosar, 3 km (2 mi) north of Capernaum Junction.*

Tradition identifies this tranquil hillside as the site of Jesus' most comprehensive teaching, recorded in the New Testament as the Sermon on the Mount: "And seeing the multitudes, he went up into a mountain; and when he was set, his disciples came unto him. And he opened his mouth, and taught them, saying: 'Blessed are the poor in spirit, for theirs is the kingdom of Heaven.'" (Matthew 5:3). In 2000, Pope John Paul II celebrated Mass with some 100,000 faithful a bit higher up the hill.

GETTING HERE AND AROUND

It's best to drive here. Lots of tourist buses make the journey, but there is no public transportation. It's on a spur road off of the main lake road, atop a hill.

EXPLORING

The domed **Roman Catholic church,** run by the Franciscan Sisters (Italian), was designed by the famous architect and monk Antonio Barluzzi (he was Mussolini's architect, and this church was commissioned by the

Churches are among the sights along the peaceful shores of the Sea of Galilee.

Fascist dictator of Italy) and completed in 1937. Windows are inscribed with the opening words (in Latin) of the Beatitudes, the initial "Blessed are" verses from the Sermon on the Mount. The terrace surrounding the church offers a superb view of the Sea of Galilee, best enjoyed in the afternoon, when the diffused western sun softens the light and heightens colors. Keep in mind this is a pilgrimage site, so dress modestly and respect the silence. Catholics and Protestants feel equally at home at this site, where the sisters also run a pilgrim hospice. ✉ *Rte. 8177, off Rte. 90* ☎ *04/679–0978* 🎫 *NIS 5 per vehicle* ⏲ *Apr.–Sept., daily 8–noon and 2:30–5; Oct.–Mar., daily 8–noon and 2:30–4.*

KORAZIM

Rte. 8277, at Rte. 90, 6 km (4 mi) north of Capernaum Junction.

GETTING HERE AND AROUND

Scenic Route 8277 offers some breathtaking views of the Sea of Galilee far below, but you'll need a car to enjoy them. There is no public transit to Korazim. Consider saddling up a horse from the stables at Vered Hagalil and riding here.

EXPLORING

The excavations at **Korazim** National Park are of interest to Jews, Christians, and Muslims. The extensive and often remarkable ruins, dating from the 4th or 5th century AD, are on the site of the ancient Jewish village that was condemned by Jesus for rejecting him (Matthew 11:21), and include a monumental basalt **synagogue** adorned with the stone carvings of plants and animals. One remarkable artifact, a decorated and inscribed stone "armchair" dubbed the Throne of Moses, is thought to have been used by the worthies of the community during the reading of the Torah. The park also includes the tomb of a Bedouin sheikh. The lake views from the site are also impressive.

Built on a basalt bluff a few miles north of the Sea of Galilee, the town of Korazim was renowned for its high-quality wheat. It also provided services and hospitality for travelers on the nearby high road to Damascus and the east.

✉ Rte. 8277 ☎ 04/693–4982 🌐 www.parks.org.il/ParksENG 🎫 NIS 20 ⏲ Apr.–Sept., Sat.–Thurs. 8–5, Fri. and Jewish holiday eves 8–3; Oct.–Mar., Sat.–Thurs. 8–4, Fri. and Jewish holiday eves 8–3.

WHERE TO STAY

$ **The Frenkels Bed and Breakfast.** Americans Etha and Irwin Frenkel retired to this rustic village on the border between the Lower and Upper Galilee and have made gracious hospitality a second career. Each spacious unit, set amid lovingly tended gardens and with tantalizing views of the Sea of Galilee, has its own distinct character, courtesy of combinations of wood and stone, cane furniture, tiles, and throw rugs. The atmosphere is one of warmth and intimacy. **Pros:** convenient to national parks; charming rooms. **Cons:** no evening entertainment; no telephones in room. *✉ Rte. 8277, Korazim ☎ 04/680–1686 🌐 www.thefrenkels.com 3 suites In-room: no phone, refrigerator, Wi-Fi. In-hotel: Internet terminal No credit cards BP.*

$$ ★ **Vered Hagalil Guest Farm.** When former Chicagoan Yehuda Avni and his Jerusalem-born wife Yonah came here in the 1960s, building this inn took a lot of imagination. While the stunning views of the Sea of Galilee were unbelievable, the site was barren hillside. The Avnis created something then unique in Israel: a ranch where guests can ride during the day and retire to luxurious rooms at night. The units, from cozy one-room cabins to larger, more luxurious cottages, combine wood and basalt rock. Some have wood-burning stoves and hot tubs overlooking the lake. The restaurant has a fine regional reputation for its hearty soups, salads, and steaks. **Pros:** best stable in the area; convenient to national parks; panoramic views. **Cons:** no evening entertainment. *✉ Rtes. 8277 and 90, Korazim ☎ 04/693–5785 🌐 www.veredhagalil.co.il 6 cabins, 25 cottages In-room: kitchen (some), refrigerator. In-hotel: restaurant, bar, pool, laundry service, Internet terminal AE, DC, MC, V.*

6

CAPERNAUM

3 km (2 mi) east of Tabgha and the Capernaum Junction, 17 km (10½ mi) northeast of Tiberias.

GETTING HERE AND AROUND

Capernaum is on Route 87, east of the intersection with Route 90. Since buses leave you a few miles from the site, it's best to drive.

EXPLORING

For Christians, Capernaum is among the most moving places in Israel, because it's where Jesus established his base for three years and recruited some of his disciples ("Follow me, and I will make you fishers of men"

[Matthew 4:19]). It is also the site of the **House of St. Peter,** the ruins of an actual home where Jesus is believed to have lodged.

Built astride the ruins of Peter's house is a modern Franciscan church, and many tourists are touched by the sight of this Christian house of worship and a beautifully manicured garden built next to the room where Jesus is believed to have slept. (There is also a red-domed Greek Orthodox monastery here, but it is seldom visited.)

Capernaum is also a site of interest to Jews, and the prosperity of the ancient Jewish community (it is Kfar Nahum in Hebrew) is immediately apparent from the remains of its **synagogue,** which dominates the complex. (It was excavated by the Franciscan friars in the early 20th century and partly restored.) The ancient Jewish community went to the expense of transporting white limestone blocks from afar to set the building off from the town's crudely built basalt houses. Stone benches line the inside walls, recalling the synagogue's original primary function as a place where the Torah was read. Once thought to date to the 2nd or 3rd century AD, the synagogue is now regarded by many scholars as belonging to the later Byzantine period (4th–5th centuries AD). It is certainly not the actual one in which Jesus taught, but since consecrated ground was often reused, the small earlier structure in the excavation pit in the present building's southeastern corner may have been.

Limestone reliefs that once graced the synagogue exterior represent a typical range of Jewish artistic motifs: the native fruits of the land, the biblical Ark of the Covenant, a seven-branched menorah, a shofar, and an incense shovel (to preserve the memory of the Temple in Jerusalem, where they were used prior to the city's destruction in AD 70). A small 1st-century mosaic from Magdala shows a contemporary boat, complete with oars and sails—a dramatic illustration of the many New Testament and Jewish references to fishing on the lake.

Jesus eventually cursed the people of Capernaum for failing to heed his message, saying "And you, Capernaum, will you be lifted up to the skies? No, you will go down to the depths. If the miracles that were performed in you had been performed in Sodom, it would have remained to this day. But I tell you that it will be more bearable for Sodom on the day of judgment than for you" (Matthew 11:23–24).

If you're visiting Capernaum, dress appropriately: you won't be allowed in if you're wearing shorts or a sleeveless shirt. ✉ *Rte. 87* ☎ *04/672–1059* 🎫 *NIS 3* ⏲ *Daily 8:30–11:30 and 3:30–4:45.*

SPORTS AND THE OUTDOORS

Northeast of Capernaum, the so-called kayaks of **Abukayak** (✉ *Jordan River Park, Rte. 888* ☎ *04/692–2245 or 04/692–1078* 🌐 *www.abukayak.co.il/*) are really inflated rubber canoes. Abukayak offers a serene one-hour paddle down the lower Jordan River, from March through November; a truck picks you up at the end. Life jackets are provided, and the trip is appropriate for young children.

EN ROUTE

Route 87 continues east past Capernaum and crosses the **Jordan River**—somewhat muddy at this point—at the Arik Bridge. Those raised on spirituals extolling the Jordan's width and depth are often surprised

Capernaum was the base of Jesus' Galilean ministry, but the synagogue remains date from a later era.

to find how small a stream it really is: seldom wider than 30 feet. The Jordan enters the Sea of Galilee just a few hundred yards downstream.

BETHSAIDA

6 km (4 mi) north of Capernaum.

GETTING HERE AND AROUND

Route 87 provides an easy drive around the Sea of Galilee for Christian pilgrims visiting the major Galilean sites related to the life of Jesus. At the north side of the lake, where Route 87 ends, turn at Bet Tzida junction onto Route 888; Jordan River Park and Bethsaida will be on your left. There is a parking fee of NIS 50 per vehicle.

EXPLORING

Not to be confused with the Bet Tzida Nature Reserve farther south, Jordan River Park at Bethsaida is said to have been the home of apostles Philip, Andrew, and Peter (according to John 1:44 and 12:21), as well as one of the wives of King David. Here archaeologists have partially excavated an ancient fishing village, including the remains of several homes that, while now only rubble, provide an idea of how communal life was once lived here. Now, as then, the village affords a view of the Sea of Galilee (though the shore moved drastically, relative to the town, in an earthquake in 363 AD). A shaded and serene sitting area includes arrows pointing to other Christian sites around the lake. Other than the sitting area, shade is limited here, so bring a hat and plenty of water. ✉ *Rte. 888* ☎ *04/692–3422.*

KURSI AND THE EASTERN SHORE

Kursi is 17 km (10½ mi) southeast of Capernaum on Rte. 92, 5 km (3 mi) north of Ein Gev.

Kursi, where Jesus healed two men possessed by demons (Matthew 8:28–32), is today a park incorporating the ruins of a Byzantine monastery. The eastern shore of the Sea of Galilee is far less developed than the western and northern sides, and the relatively rural character remains today, even as negotiations sputter along between Israel and Syria about returning this area to the control of Damascus.

GETTING HERE AND AROUND

Route 92 follows the eastern shore of the Sea of Galilee while Route 87 circles to the north of the lake. You can reach Kursi either by driving north or south from Tiberias. Whether you circle the lake clockwise or counterclockwise, the views are often breathtaking.

EXPLORING

Huddling under the imposing cliffs of the Golan Heights, where Route 789 climbs away from 92, **Kursi**'s national park is linked with the New Testament story of a man from Gadara (other gospels mention Gerasa) who was possessed by demons. Jesus exorcised the spirits, causing them to enter a herd of swine grazing nearby, which then "rushed down the steep bank into the lake, and perished in the waters" (Matthew 8:32). Fifth-century Byzantine Christians identified the event with this spot and built a monastery. It was an era in which earnest pilgrims inundated the holy places, true and new, and the monastery prospered from their gifts. The partly restored ruins of a fine Byzantine church are a classic example of the basilica style common at the time; the ruined monastery is higher up the hillside. ✉ *Rte. 92* ☎ *04/673–1983* 🌐 *www.parks.org.il/ParksENG* 🎫 *NIS 13* ⏲ *Apr.–Sept., Sat.–Thurs. 8–5, Fri. and Jewish holiday eves 8–4; Oct.–Mar. daily 8–4.*

WHERE TO EAT AND STAY

$$ SEAFOOD ✕ **Ein Gev Fish Restaurant.** At lunchtime this popular establishment on the eastern shore bustles with tour groups, but it's a fine dinner option, too. Famous for St. Peter's fish, it has added sea bream, trout, and gray mullet to the menu, as well as entrées such as quiche, pizza, pasta, salads, and omelets. In fine weather, sit on the large outdoor terrace, and take in the view across the lake to Tiberias. Watch for the signs for Kibbutz Inn Ein Gev. ✉ *Kibbutz Ein Gev* ☎ *04/665–8136* ⏲ *No dinner Fri., closed Sat.* 💳 *AE, DC, MC, V.*

$$$–$$$$ ISRAELI ✕ **Habikta.** The wood cabin in which Habikta (literally "the cabin") is housed, and its heavy antique furniture, evoke the smoked meats for which it's best known. The chicken and steaks, smoked over cherrywood and grape vines, come with access to the generous salad buffet. Try the whole chickpeas coated in cumin and green onions, or the coriander tossed with slivered almonds and lentils. ✉ *Moshav Ramot, Golan Heights* ☎ *04/679–4016* 🌐 *www.67356183.com* ⏲ *Closed Fri. and Sat.* 💳 *AE, DC, MC, V.*

$$ 🏨 **Beit Ram Sheraf.** The four suites owned by Judit Sheraf and Avi Ram are the perfect place for a family weekend: each cottage has a double bedroom, a living room that sleeps three, a kitchenette, a Jacuzzi, and a

private yard with a barbecue grill and a hammock or swing set. A generous Israeli breakfast can be brought to your cabin for an extra fee. The large private pool is open from April to October; the grounds also have an outdoor Jacuzzi, massage room, and a DVD library. **Pros:** heated pool; child-friendly atmosphere. **Cons:** relatively expensive. ✉ *Ramot, Golan Heights* ☎ *052/284–4013* 🌐 *www.beit-ram.co.il* *4 cottages* *In-hotel: pool, Internet terminal, Wi-Fi* ▭ *AE, MC, V.*

$ **Ein Gev Holiday Village.** Located on the palm-shaded eastern shore, this complex offers several options: spacious motel-style rooms, some with a view; waterfront units with sunset-watching patios; apartments designed for families; and older family cottages (called *kafriot*), some close to the water, others not. All have fully equipped kitchenettes, and an on-site market means you can cook your own meals. About a mile north, Kibbutz Ein Gev, which runs the village, has a famous fish restaurant, a small harbor, and a wagon-train ride. **Pros:** convenient to national parks; beachfront setting. **Cons:** no evening entertainment. ✉ *Rte. 92, 12 km (7½ mi) north of Tzemach Junction, Ein Gev* ☎ *04/665–9800* 🌐 *www.eingev.com* *184 rooms* *In-room: kitchen. In-hotel: restaurant* ▭ *AE, DC, MC, V* *BP.*

¢ **Ma'agan.** At the southern tip of the Sea of Galilee, this kibbutz has arguably the most enchanting view of all the properties around the lake. Furnishings are comfortable but not luxurious. Choose between regular guest rooms or spacious suites with living rooms (and a fold-out sofa), a small bedroom, a kitchenette, and a patio. The food is unmemorable, but the facilities—sandy beach, swimming pool near the shore, extensive lawns—make it the best deal around. There is a smaller pool and a play area for kids. **Pros:** pretty beach; convenient location. **Cons:** no evening entertainment. ✉ *Rte. 92, 1 km (½ mi) east of Tzemach Junction* ☎ *04/665–4411* 🌐 *www.maagan.com* *36 rooms, 112 suites* *In-room: kitchen (some). In-hotel: bar, pool, beachfront, water sports, laundry facilities, Internet terminal, parking (free)* ▭ *AE, DC, MC, V* *BP.*

$$ **Ramot Resort Hotel.** High in the foothills of the Golan Heights, this hotel is only a few minutes from good beaches and a water park. Its main building has comfortable guest rooms with private balconies and fabulous lake views. The deluxe wood chalets have whirlpool tubs, saunas, entertainment systems, and other perks. There are also cabins for families on more limited budgets. Free guided tours of the area are available in summer. As of this printing, all rooms, plus the lobby and dining room, were set for upgrading in 2011. **Pros:** convenient to national parks; cooler temperatures than at the lake; beautiful vistas. **Cons:** no evening entertainment. ✉ *East of Rte. 92* ☎ *04/673–2636* 🌐 *www.ramot-nofesh.co.il* *80 rooms, 25 chalets, 18 cabins* *In-room: Wi-Fi. In-hotel: bar, pool, laundry service, parking (free)* ▭ *AE, DC, MC, V* *BP.*

NIGHTLIFE AND THE ARTS

The **Ein Gev Spring Festival** (☎ 04/675–1175 ✉ *bg@betgabriel.co.il*) once hosted the likes of Bernstein and Rampal, Dietrich and Sinatra, but the focus today is Israeli vocal music, from traditional to contemporary. It is held on Kibbutz Ein Gev during Passover (in April) but is organized by Bet Gabriel. E-mail for details; put the festival in the subject line.

SPORTS AND THE OUTDOORS

The shoreline of the Sea of Galilee has receded somewhat with the low level of the water, and the bottom now drops precipitously. Keep a close eye on children.

BEACHES

Dugit Beach (✉ *Rte. 92, 8 km [5 mi] north of Ein Gev* ☎ *04/673–1750* 🎫 *NIS 50 per car*) is a stone's throw north of Golan Beach. The two are now under one management and provide similar recreational facilities, but Dugit has lifeguards.

Golan Beach (✉ *Rte. 92, 7 km [4½ mi] north of Ein Gev* ☎ *04/673–1750*) is the best-known beach on the northeastern shore of the lake. There are powerboat, rowboat, kayak, and pedal-boat rentals; waterskiing; and inflatable, boat-towed "bananas." There is no lifeguard, though.

WATER PARK

Lunagal, a popular water park within Golan Beach, has pools, waterslides, and other diversions for kids. ✉ *Rte. 92, 7 km (4½ mi) north of Ein Gev* ☎ *04/667–8000* 🎫 *NIS 60 Apr.–June, Sept., and Oct.; NIS 80 July and Aug.* ⏲ *Call for hrs.*

HAMMAT GADER

10 km (6 mi) east of Tzemach Junction on Rte. 98, 22 km (14 mi) southeast of Tiberias, 36 km (22½ mi) northeast of Beit She'an.

GETTING HERE AND AROUND

Whether you're driving via Tiberias (Route 90) or the Golan Heights (Route 98), this highway is one of the most captivating in Israel with expansive views across the Yarmuk River into Jordan. Don't leave the roadway. The minefield signs mean exactly what they say.

EXPLORING

Hammat Gader is popular with Israelis, who come for the freshwater and mineral pools, giant waterslide, alligator farm, performing parrots, petting zoo, and restaurants. It has history, too: in its heyday, this was the second-largest spa in the Roman Empire (after Baiae, near Naples). Built around three hot springs, Hammat Gader's impressive complex of baths and pools attests to the opulence that once attracted voluptuaries and invalids alike. The large number of ancient clay oil lamps found in one small pool is proof of nighttime bathing and a hint that this area might have been set aside for lepers, to keep them out of sight of the regular patrons. ✉ *Rte. 98* ☎ *04/665–9964 or 04/665-9966* 🌐 *www.hamat-gader.com* 🎫 *NIS 77–87* ⏲ *Jun.–Sept. 7 am–5 pm daily; Oct.–May Mon.–Fri. 7 am–11 pm, Sat. 7–9, Sun. 7–5.*

WHERE TO STAY

$$$ **Spa Village.** Though only a few yards from the recreation park at Hammat Gader, this quiet Thai-style complex is a world apart. The superbly outfitted wooden cabin-suites have hot tubs that use thermal mineral water from the nearby springs; a few have their own saunas.

Treatment rooms and exercise equipment are for hotel guests only. The warm mineral-pool area, a serene oasis by day, is almost mystical when you take the torch-lighted waters at night. The rest of the park is free for hotel guests. On weekends (Thursday and Friday nights), there is a minimum two-night stay. **Pros:** sybaritic experience; tropical gardens; pampering staff. **Cons:** no evening entertainment. ✉ *Rte. 98, Hammat Gader* ☎ *04/665–5555* 🌐 *www.spavillage.co.il* *29 suites* *In-room: safe, refrigerator, Wi-Fi. In-hotel: restaurant, pool, spa, laundry service, Internet terminal, parking (free)* 💳 *AE, DC, MC, V* 🍽 *BP.*

DEGANIA, KINNERET, AND YARDENIT

Degania Aleph: 10 km (6 mi) south of Tiberias; Kinneret: 2 km (1 mi) northwest of Degania Aleph.

Degania and Kinneret, two historic kibbutzim founded in the early 20th century, contain museums and historic graveyards worth a visit. Also nearby is Yardenit, a baptism site for Christians.

GETTING HERE AND AROUND

Both Degania Aleph and Kinneret are south of Tiberias along Route 90. If you take a bus, ask the driver in advance about stopping.

6

EXPLORING

The first kibbutz, the collective village of **Degania Aleph** was founded in 1909 by Jewish pioneers from Eastern Europe and established here at its permanent site on the banks of the Jordan River the following year. (Aleph is the *A* of the Hebrew alphabet; don't confuse the kibbutz with its younger neighbor, Degania Bet.) Near the entrance is a small Syrian tank of World War II vintage. On May 15, 1948, the day after Israel declared its independence, Arab armies invaded it from all sides. Syrian forces came down the Yarmuk Valley from the east, overran two other kibbutzim en route, and were only stopped here, at the gates of Degania. A teenager with a Molotov cocktail set alight the lead tank.

Within restored stone buildings of the early kibbutz is the museum of **Beit Gordon** *(A. D. Gordon House)*, named for the spiritual mentor of the early pioneers. It houses two collections: one devoted to the region's natural history, the other examining the history and archaeology of human settlement in the surrounding valleys. Among the prehistoric sites represented is Ubeidiya, just south of the kibbutz and Israel's oldest human settlement, which scholars now date back to 1¼ million years ago. ✉ *Near Rte. 90* ☎ *04/675–0040* *Museum: NIS 13* ⏲ *Sun.–Thurs. 10–2, Fri. 10–1, Sat. with advance registration only.*

A short drive from Degania Aleph is Degania Bet, where you can smell the **Galita Chocolate Farm** long before you get to it. In addition to the "bar" serving hot and cold chocolate drinks, and a tempting gift shop, Galita has eight different chocolate-making workshops for adults, children, or both. Reservations aren't required but advance notice will ensure you can enjoy the activities in English. ✉ *Kibbutz Degania Bet, off Route 90* ☎ *04/675–5608* 🌐 *www.galita.co.il* *Entrance and film free. Workshops: NIS 40–180.* ⏲ *Sun.–Thurs. 10–6, Fri. 10–5, Sat and holidays 10–6.*

Across the Jordan from Degania, **Kinneret** was founded in 1911 as the country's second kibbutz, taking its name from the Hebrew word for the Sea of Galilee. The serene **Kibbutz Kinneret Cemetery** includes the grave of Rachel *Hameshoreret* (Rachel the Poetess), a secular shrine for many Israelis. The cemetery offers a superb view of the lake, the Golan Heights, and majestic Mt. Hermon. Among the other distinguished denizens of this ground are pioneer leaders of the early Zionist movement. A few steps down from the clearing is Rachel's grave, identified by the low stone seat attached to it. The pebbles left on her grave by visitors (a token of respect in the Jewish tradition) are a tribute to Rachel's renown and to the romantic hold she has on the national imagination. Born in Russia in 1890, she became a poet of national stature in Hebrew; she died in 1931. Rachel wrote with great sensitivity of the beauty of this region and with passion—knowing that her end was near—of her frustrated dream of raising a family. Her tombstone is eloquently devoid of biographical information; it carries only her name and four lines from one of her poems: "Spread out your hands, look yonder: / nothing comes. / Each man has his Nebo / in the great expanse." (✉ *Off Rte. 90, 600 yd south of junction with Rte. 767* ☏ *04/675–9500 kibbutz office*)

On a picturesque bend of the Jordan River where huge eucalyptus trees droop into the quiet water is **Yardenit,** developed as a baptism site for Christian pilgrims. The baptism of Jesus by John the Baptist (John 1:28) is traditionally identified with the southern reaches of the Jordan River, near Jericho. However, that area was controlled by Jordan from 1949 to 1967 and then became a hostile frontier between Israel and Jordan following the Six Days' War. Pilgrims began to seek out accessible spots beyond the conflict zone. You'll often see groups of pilgrims being immersed in the river amid prayers and hymns and expressions of joy but despite the crowds, the atmosphere is orderly and spiritual. Snacks and souvenirs are available. The white robes required to enter the water become transparent when wet, so bring a bathing suit or large towel. ✉ *Off Rte. 90* ☏ *04/675–9111* 🌐 *www.yardenit.com* 🎫 *Free entrance to site, robe rental $10.* 🕒 *Sun.–Thurs. 8–5, Fri. 8–4. Last baptism one hour before closing.*

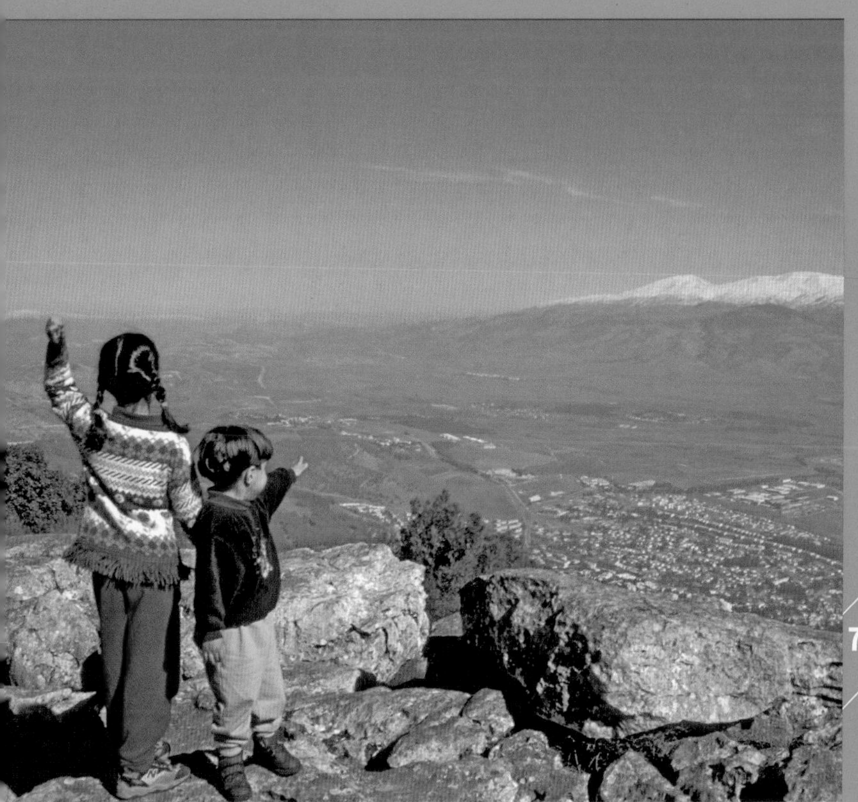

7

Upper Galilee and the Golan

WITH TZFAT (SAFED)

WORD OF MOUTH

"Tour some of the areas in the Golan—so many archeological sites, Tzfat . . . Banias, lots to see and it is gorgeous . . . great wines to drink . . ."

—risab

WELCOME TO UPPER GALILEE AND THE GOLAN

TOP REASONS TO GO

★ **The Old City of Tzfat:** While the tiny historic synagogues offer a rare taste of Jewish houses of worship from bygone days, the galleries are saturated with contemporary colors and shapes.

★ **Kayaking on the Jordan River:** A cool ride downriver can be a strenuous adventure or a tame family float; either way, it adds an interesting accent to a trip to the northern Galilee.

★ **The Hula Nature Reserve:** The Hula Reserve provides shelter for hundreds of species of birds, some 500 million of which fly over the Hula Valley twice a year on their migrations between Europe and Africa.

★ **Hermon River Nature Reserve:** Hike to the Banias waterfall and the Crusader ruins, and pick up a freshly baked pita from the Druze mill along the way.

★ **Gamla:** This is the site of the Jews' heroic last stand following a siege by the Romans in AD 67. Aside from its history, it offers a challenging hike or an easy amble, all with glimpses of wildlife.

1 Tzfat (Safed) and Environs. At 3,000 feet above sea level, Tzfat is Israel's highest city, known for being the center of Kabbalah, or Jewish mysticism. Although it's one of several holy sites in Israel, this city north of the Sea of Galilee has a spiritual dimension found nowhere else. Its twisting passageways, vestiges of the Ottomans and the Crusaders, caught the attention of artists, who make this one of the country's most enchanting destinations every spring and summer.

2 Upper Hula Valley. Situated between the Golan Heights, Naftali Ridge, and the Beqaa Valley, the Upper Hula Valley is best known for the Tel Dan Nature Preserve. Spread out over 800 acres, it's a prime spot for hiking, cycling, or picnicking. Bustling Kiryat Shmona and sleepy Metulla are the region's largest communities.

3 Golan Heights. This region's main geographic feature is the Sea of Galilee, the country's main water reservoir. This is the northernmost part of the country, and from Mt. Hermon you can gaze out over Lebanon and Syria. The Golan Heights draws visitors throughout the year to its relaxing countryside, inventive restaurants, and leading wineries.

Nimrod's Fortress

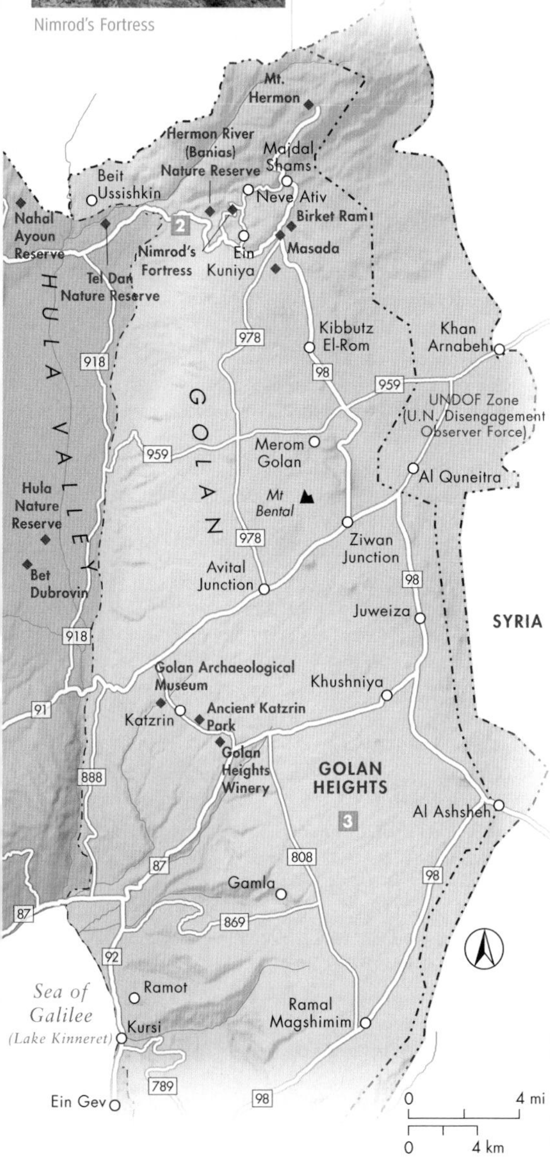

Mt. Hermon
Hermon River (Banias) Nature Reserve
Majdal Shams
Beit Ussishkin
Neve Ativ
Nahal Ayoun Reserve
2
Birket Ram
Nimrod's Fortress
Ein Kuniya
Masada
Tel Dan Nature Reserve
HULA VALLEY
978
Kibbutz El-Rom
Khan Arnabeh
918
98
959
GOLAN
UNDOF Zone (U.N. Disengagement Observer Force)
959
Merom Golan
Hula Nature Reserve
Al Quneitra
Mt Bental
978
Ziwan Junction
Bet Dubrovin
Avital Junction
98
Juweiza
SYRIA
918
Golan Archaeological Museum
Khushniya
91
Katzrin
Ancient Katzrin Park
Golan Heights Winery
888
GOLAN HEIGHTS
Al Ashsheh
3
87
808
98
Gamla
87
869
92
Sea of Galilee (Lake Kinneret)
Ramot
Ramal Magshimim
Kursi
789
Ein Gev
98
0 4 mi
0 4 km

GETTING ORIENTED

The undulating hills of Western Galilee push upward into sharp limestone and basalt formations, bordered on the north by Lebanon and on the east by the volcanic, mountainous Golan Heights, beyond which lies Syria. The major cities—Tzfat in the rugged Galilee mountains and Katzrin in the Golan Heights—are a study in contrasts. The former is immersed in Jewish mysticism, and the latter is the result of a hardheaded determination to secure Israel's border with Syria by establishing a modern town in what was once a battlefield.

Ancient oil press at Gamla

UPPER GALILEE AND THE GOLAN PLANNER

Getting Here

Only one airline flies from Tel Aviv to the small airport of Mahanayim, near Rosh Pina: Ayit operates a few 35-minute flights each day.

There is no transportation at the airport except for taxis. However, you can arrange for a rental car to be waiting at the airport. From the airport it's 10 km (6 mi) to Tzfat and 30 km (19 mi) to Kiryat Shmona.

When to Go

Unlike other parts of the country, there is no best time of the year to tour the Upper Galilee and the Golan. The range of colors is wonderful in spring, when hillsides are covered with wildflowers. Summer brings families traveling with children, as well as music and culinary festivals; days can be hot, but the low humidity makes it manageable. Wine fans appreciate the area in autumn during harvest time at the vineyards. Nights can be cold year-round. In winter, more precipitation means gushing streams and gray skies.

Getting Around

Bus Travel: Local Egged buses stop at all major sights in this region (there is always a kibbutz, a town, or some other small residential settlement nearby). Avoid buses if you're on a tight schedule, as they tend to be infrequent.

Car Travel: The Upper Galilee and the Golan are a three-hour, 180-km (112-mi) drive from Tel Aviv; a 1½-hour, 60-km (37-mi) drive from both Akko and Nahariya; and four hours from Jerusalem, which is 200 km (124 mi) to the south.

There are a few different ways to get here. From Tiberias and the Sea of Galilee, Route 90 runs north between the Hula Valley, on the east, and the hills of Naftali, on the west.

The more rugged Route 98 runs from the eastern side of the Sea of Galilee up through the Golan Heights to Mt. Hermon. Near the top of Route 98 you can pick up Route 91, which heads west into the Upper Galilee.

From the Mediterranean coast there are several options, but the main one is Route 85 from Akko. Route 89 runs parallel to Route 85 a little farther north, from Nahariya, and has some gorgeous scenery.

From Haifa take Route 75 to Route 77, turning onto Route 90 at Tiberias, or Route 70 north onto Route 85 east. If you're starting from Tel Aviv, drive north on Route 4 or 2 to Hadera; from there you'll head northwest on Route 65, exiting onto Route 85 east.

The state of Israel's roads is generally fair to good, but in the Upper Galilee in particular, some roads are still two-lane. Drive cautiously. Try to avoid driving during peak hours (usually late Thursday and Saturday afternoons), when city folk crowd the roads back to Jerusalem and Tel Aviv after a day out in the country.

There are plenty of gas stations along Route 90 and in the towns, such as Katzrin (Route 87) and Tzfat (Route 89). Most are open daily but close by 9 pm, so it's best to fill up during the day.

For more information on getting here and around, turn to Travel Smart Israel.

Planning Your Time

A day trip to the Golan Heights from Tiberias is doable, but there's something about the lush foliage of the forests and the mountain air of the Golan that makes you want to linger. Three or four days is ideal to explore the region, including wine tasting, hiking a piece of wilderness, country meals, kayaking, or just kicking back in a room with a stunning view. The ideal way to see this area is by car, though local buses will get you almost anywhere you want to go if you have time. Note that touring the Upper Galilee and Golan is usually very safe but if security demands unusual caution, certain areas may be temporarily inaccessible.

Dining and Lodging

The Upper Galilee and the Golan's crisp, appetite-whetting air is an exquisite backdrop for some excellent restaurants. Fresh grilled Dan River trout, Middle Eastern fare prepared by Druze villagers, or home-style Jewish cooking in Tzfat are all regional fare. Excellent local wines enhance any meal: try the Mt. Hermon red, Gamla Cabernet Sauvignon, and Yarden Cabernet Blanc and Merlot. In a few places (such as Tzfat), it can be hard to find a restaurant open on Shabbat (sundown Friday until sundown Saturday).

There are few grand hotels here, but the ample selection of guesthouses and inns ranges from ranch-style to home-style. As the tourist industry has developed, many kibbutzim and moshavim have added hotels (or guest wings attached to homes); some also arrange tours, from rafting to Jeep excursions. Rooms in kibbutz guesthouses can be reserved directly or through the Kibbutz Hotels chain, a central reservation service based in Tel Aviv, although not all the kibbutzim are represented. **Israel Kibbutz Hotels** (☎ *03/560–8118* 🌐 *www.kibbutz.co.il*).

WHAT IT COSTS

	¢	$	$$	$$$	$$$$
Restaurants	under NIS 32	NIS 32–NIS 49	NIS 50–NIS 75	NIS 76–NIS 100	over NIS 100
Hotels	under $120	$120–$200	$201–$300	$301–$400	over $400

Restaurant prices are per person for a main course at dinner in NIS (Israeli shekels). Hotel prices are in U.S. dollars, for two people in a standard double room in high season. Non-Israeli citizens paying in foreign currency are exempt from the 16% VAT on hotel rooms.

Visitor Information

Beit Ussishkin Nature Museum has information about area nature reserves, natural history, and bird-watching. The Israel Nature and Parks Authority staff are good resources for planning itineraries that include their sites in other parts of the region and the country. The visitor information service at Moshav Beit Hillel is especially helpful, with a wide selection of bed-and-breakfast accommodations in the moshav, which is in the heart of the Hula Valley tourist region. The Tiberias Tourist Information Office can furnish information on the entire region. The Tourist Information Center–Upper Galilee can also provide information; it's open weekends and holidays only.

Contacts **Beit Ussishkin Nature Museum** (✉ *Kibbutz Dan, Rte. 99, Upper Galilee* ☎ *04/694–1704*). **Israel Nature and Parks Authority Northern District** (✉ *Megiddo National Park, Rt. 66* ☎ *04/659–0316* 🌐 *www.parks.org.il*). **Tourist Information Center–Upper Galilee** (✉ *Mahanayim Junction, intersection of Rtes 90 and 91, just west of Mahanayim, about 5 km northeast of Tzfat* ☎ *04/693–6945*).

7

Updated by Sarah Bronson

"Israel's Little Tuscany" has long been a nickname for the Upper Galilee. The green countryside, the growing numbers of both large-scale and boutique wineries, and the laid-back atmosphere have attracted urbanites for weekend jaunts (and sometimes for good).

The mountain air is redolent with the fragrance of spice plants; visitors can hike, cycle, or ride horses along trails that range from easy to challenging; and opportunities for kayaking, bird-watching, and other outdoor pursuits abound. These are the best vacation treats, all in a fascinating historical setting.

The main geographical feature of this region is towering Mt. Hermon, known as Israel's "sponge." Huge volumes of water from winter snow and rainfall soak into its limestone, emerging at the base of the mountain in an abundance of springs that feed the Jordan River and its tributaries and provide half of Israel's water supply. The water also sustains lush vegetation that thrives year-round and is home to wildcats, hyraxes, gazelles, and hundreds of species of birds.

This water and the strategic vantage points of the Galilee mountaintops and the Golan Heights have made the region a source of political contention since time immemorial. Over the centuries, Egyptians, Canaanites, Israelites, Romans, Byzantines, Muslims, Crusaders, and Ottomans locked horns here; in the 20th century alone, the borders have been changed by Russia, Britain, France, and of course, Israel and Syria.

Borders are not the only things that have shifted here. A geological fault line, the Syrian-African Rift, cuts straight through the 30-km (19-mi) Hula Valley; in 1837 an earthquake razed Tzfat and Tiberias, though no significant rumbles have been heard since. Extinct volcanic cones give the Golan its unusual topographic profile.

With all this water and fertile soil, the region has long been an agricultural center and is today studded with apple and cherry orchards, fishponds, sunflowers, and vineyards. The pastoral beauty and variety of outdoor activities attract visitors from elsewhere in Israel and the world, supplying the region's other main industry: tourism.

Proximity to Lebanon and Syria does not ordinarily deter people from visiting the Upper Galilee and the Golan. On the contrary, the combination of an exciting past with a gorgeous natural setting is precisely the draw here.

Over the last century, both Jews and non-Jews have faced hardships and hurdles in this region. Yet the tenacious Galileans will say there's no better place to live. Only four hours' drive from hectic Tel Aviv and visceral Jerusalem, visitors find this is truly another world.

TZFAT (SAFED) AND ENVIRONS

In the southern part of the Upper Galilee, attractions range from the narrow streets and historic synagogues of Tzfat to the wilderness of the Hula Nature Reserve. Other sites, like Mt. Meron, pair scenic appeal with spiritual importance. At Rosh Pina you can shop and dine where the Galilee's first Zionist pioneers labored. Or you can just relax at an inn or a kibbutz guesthouse and enjoy the wooded scenery.

TZFAT

33 km (20 mi) north of Tiberias, 72 km (45 mi) northeast of Haifa.

Tzfat attracts artists who look for inspiration, travelers charmed by its cobbled alleys, and religious people in search of meaning—a rare example of harmony between the secular and the spiritual. The city is known for its spiritual, even sacred, vibe and its breathtaking views.

It doesn't take long to walk all of Tzfat's Old City, but allow plenty of time to poke around the little cobbled passages that seem to lead nowhere, to linger over some minute architectural detail on a building from another time, or to browse through shops filled to overflowing with locally made art. And it's almost impossible to get lost; Yerushalayim (Jerusalem) Street is a good orientation point—it runs through the heart of the Old City, encircles the Citadel, and from there, steps lead down to the two main areas of interest, the Old Jewish Quarter and the adjacent Artists' Colony. There is no way to avoid the hilly topography, so remember to wear comfortable walking shoes. As the town is largely Orthodox, modest dress is recommended when visiting synagogues. For women, this means a longish skirt or long pants and at least a short-sleeve top; for men, long pants are appropriate.

Tzfat hibernates from October through June, when the city's artists move to their galleries in warmer parts of the country. This does not mean you should leave Tzfat out of your itinerary during those months; there is enough to occupy the curious wanderer for at least a few hours, and much of it is free. In the summer, especially during July and August, Tzfat is abuzz with activity: galleries and shops stay open late, klezmer music (Eastern European Jewish "soul music") dances around corners, and the city extends a warm welcome to everyone.

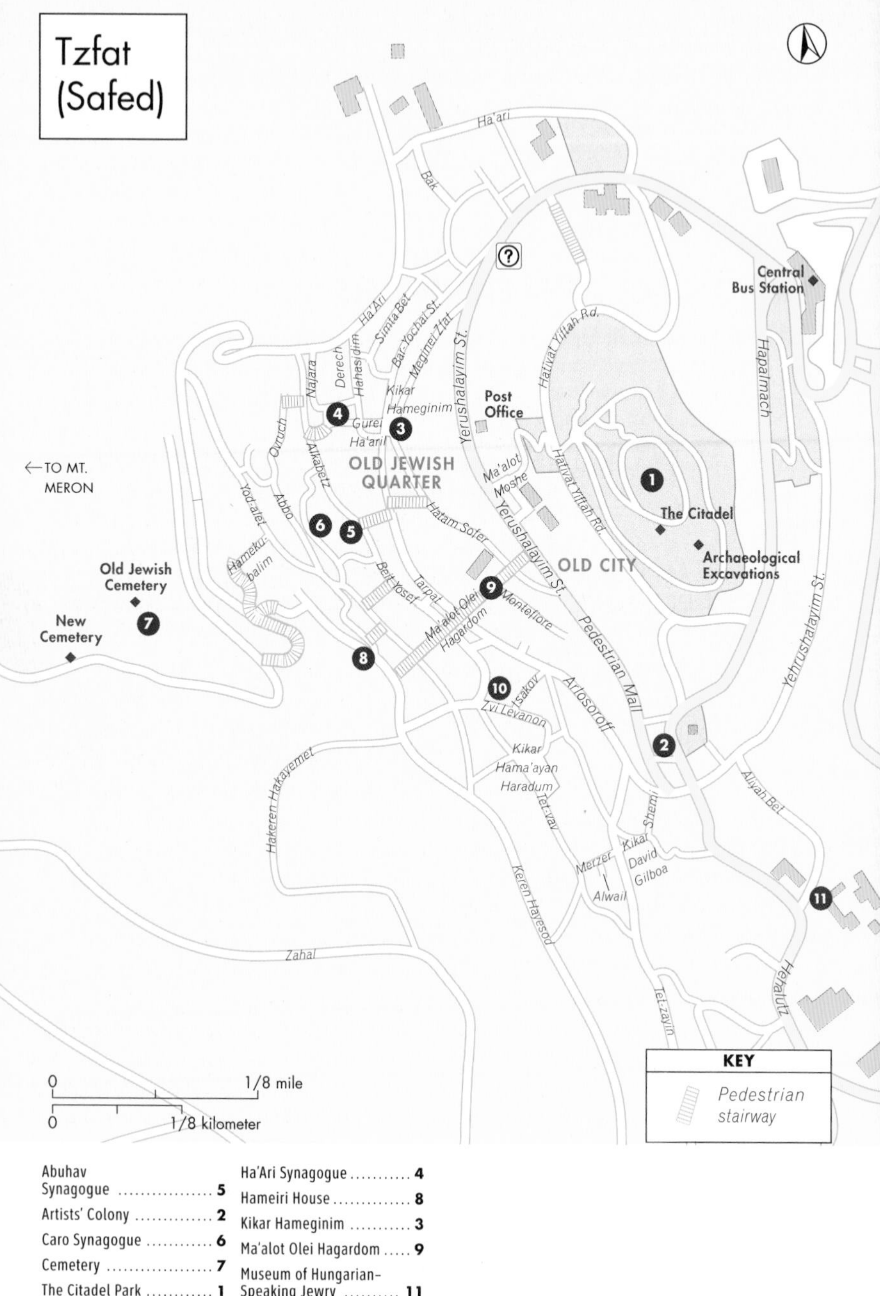

- Abuhav Synagogue 5
- Artists' Colony 2
- Caro Synagogue 6
- Cemetery 7
- The Citadel Park 1
- General Exhibition 10
- Ha'Ari Synagogue 4
- Hameiri House 8
- Kikar Hameginim 3
- Ma'alot Olei Hagardom 9
- Museum of Hungarian-Speaking Jewry 11

CLOSE UP

What Is Kabbalah?

Kabbalah, which means "receiving," is an ancient study of Jewish mysticism that gained popularity in the 13th century. Tzfat has been the main center for Kabbalah scholarship since the 16th century, making it one of Judaism's four holiest cities (along with Jerusalem, Tiberias, and Hebron).

Kabbalah, as opposed to formal rabbinical Judaism, is about reading between, behind, and all around the lines. Each letter and accent of every word in the holy books has a numerical value with particular significance, offering added meaning to the literal word. One of the most popular Kabbalistic concepts is that of *tikkun olam*, or "fixing the world." According to Jewish mystics, the universe was "broken" by God in order to make room for the physical realm. Thus the quest of humankind is to repair the universe through good works and service of God.

Although classical Kabbalah studies are intertwined with those of the Bible and the Talmud, not all religious Jews study Kabbalah. In fact, tradition holds that a person studying Kabbalah must be at least 40 years old and have a thorough knowledge of other Jewish texts. Outside of Hasidic Judaism, which has incorporated some Kabbalah into its worldview, many mainstream Orthodox Jews do not study Kabbalah at all, preferring to focus on matters of the perceivable world.

7

GETTING HERE AND AROUND

If you're driving to Tzfat from Jerusalem, take Route 6 north. If you're starting in Tel Aviv, head north on Route 2. Either way, you'll want to turn east on Route 65, then north on Route 90, then west on Route 89 to Tzfat. If your journey starts in Haifa, head north on Route 4, then east on Route 89 to Tzfat. Egged runs at least one bus daily to Tzfat from Tel Aviv, at least seven from Jerusalem, and at least 35 from Haifa.

In Tzfat the private company Nativ Express runs eight local bus lines. The Hamavreek taxi company in Tzfat will pick up incoming travelers at the Mahanayim Airport and take them to various destinations in the region. Buses from Tzfat central bus station, at the entrance to the city, head to most towns in the region.

Both of Israel's major bus companies, Egged Tours and United Tours, offer one- and two-day guided tours of the region, departing from Tel Aviv and Jerusalem.

Within the Old City, the many streets closed to traffic make it difficult to drive from one place to another. You may have to drive around the perimeter of the city rather than through it. The best way to get around is on foot.

ESSENTIALS

Bus Contacts **Egged** (☎ **2800* 🌐 *www.egged.co.il*). **Nativ Express** (☎ *1/599–559–5599* 🌐 *www.nateevexpress.com*).

EXPLORING

TOP ATTRACTIONS

Abuhav Synagogue. This large Sephardic synagogue is named for a 14th-century Spanish scribe, one of whose Torah scrolls found its way here with the Spanish Jewish exiles 200 years later. A look around reveals several differences between this synagogue and its Ashkenazi counterparts, such as the Ha'Ari; for example, the walls are painted the lively blue typical of Sephardic tradition, and the benches run along the walls instead of in rows (so that no man turns his back on his neighbor).

Every detail is loaded with significance: there are three arks—for the three forefathers, Abraham, Isaac, and Jacob (the one on the right is said to be the Abuhav original)—and 10 windows in the dome, referring to the Commandments. The charmingly naive illustrations on the squinches include a depiction of the Dome of the Rock (referring to the destruction of the Second Temple) and pomegranate trees, whose 613 seeds are equal in number to the Torah's commandments. The original building was destroyed in the 1837 earthquake, but locals swear that the southern wall—in which the Abuhav Torah scroll is set—was spared. ✉ *Abuhav St.* ☎ *04/692–3885* ⏲ *Open Sun.–Thurs. 9–5, Fri. 9–1.*

Artists' Colony. The colony, set in Tzfat's old Arab Quarter, was established in 1951 by six Israeli artists who saw the promise hidden in Tzfat's war-torn condition; for them, the old buildings, the fertile landscape, and the cool mountain air fused into the magic ingredients of creativity. Others soon followed until, at its peak, the colony was home to more than 50 artists, some of whom exhibit internationally. Most galleries are open only in the spring and summer, from about 10 am to 6 pm. ✉ *Old City of Tzfat.*

Caro Synagogue. Tucked among art galleries, the Caro appears quite run-down, but it is considered one of the Old City's most interesting and even charming synagogues by those who feel a deep spiritual connection to the great scholar after whom it was named. Rabbi Yosef Caro arrived in Tzfat in 1535 and led its Jewish community for many years. He is the author of the Shulchan Aruch, the code of law that remains a foundation of Jewish religious interpretation to the present day, and this synagogue is said to have been Caro's study hall. It was destroyed in the great earthquake of 1837 and rebuilt in the mid-19th century. If you ask, the attendant might open the ark containing the Torah scrolls, one of which is at least 400 years old. A glass-faced cabinet at the back of the synagogue is the *geniza*, where damaged scrolls or prayer books are stored (because they carry the name of God, they cannot be destroyed). The turquoise paint here—considered the "color of heaven"—is believed to help keep away the evil eye. ✉ *Alkabetz St.* ☎ *04/692–3284.*

General Exhibition. An important stop in a tour of the Artists' Colony, the works inside this large space are a representative sample of the work of Tzfat's artists, ranging from oils and watercolors to silk screens and sculptures, in traditional and avant-garde styles. The permission of the Muslim authorities was required to organize the exhibition, as it is housed in the old mosque, easily identified from afar by its minaret. The Artists' Colony has recognized the growing presence of artists from the former Soviet Union, and the adjacent building holds the **Immigrant Artists' Exhibition.** In either facility, if any works catch your fancy, just ask directions to the artist's gallery for a more in-depth look at his or her work. ✉ *Isakov and Zvi Levanon Sts.* ☎ *04/692–0087* 🌐 *www.artistcolony.co.il* 🎟 *Free* ⏲ *Sun.–Thurs. 10–5; Fri., Sat., and Jewish holidays 10–2.*

Ha'Ari Synagogue. This Ashkenazi synagogue has associations going back to the 16th century. It is named for a rabbi who left an indelible mark on Tzfat and on Judaism: Isaac Luria, known to all as the Ari, Hebrew for "lion" and an acronym for Adoneinu Rabbeinu Itzhak ("our master and teacher Isaac"). In his mere three years in Tzfat, he evolved his own system of the Kabbalah, which drew a huge following that would influence Jewish teaching the world over. Even more astounding is that he died in his midthirties; it is generally said that one should not even consider study of the Kabbalah before the age of 40, when one reaches the requisite level of intellectual and emotional maturity.

The pale colors of this tiny Ashkenazi synagogue contrast sharply with its olive-wood Holy Ark, a dazzlingly carved tour de force with two tiers of spiral columns and vibrant plant reliefs. (The Sephardic Ari Synagogue, where the rabbi prayed, is farther down the quarter, by the cemetery. The oldest of Tzfat's synagogues, this 16th-century structure has especially fine carved wooden doors.) ✉ *Ha'Ari St.* 🎟 *free* ⏲ *Sun.–Thurs. 9:30 until afternoon prayer service (about 20 min. before sunset), Fri. 9:30–1.*

7

Hameiri House. Difficult to find, this centuries-old stone building houses a museum documenting the life of the Jewish community of Tzfat over the past 200 years, with notations in both Hebrew and English. ✉ *Keren Hayesod St.* ☎ *04/697–1307* 🎟 *NIS 14* ⏲ *Sun.–Thurs. 8:30–2:30, Fri. and holidays 8:30–1:30.*

WORTH NOTING

Cemetery. Old and new cemeteries are set into the hillside below the Old Jewish Quarter. The old plots resonate with the names and fame of the Kabbalists of yore, as their graves are identifiable by sky-blue markers. It is said that if the legs of the devout suddenly get tired here, it is because they are walking over hidden graves. The new cemetery holds the graves of members of the pre-State underground Stern Gang and Irgun forces, who were executed by the British in Akko's prison (⇨ *Chapter 5*). In a separate plot, bordered by cypresses, lie the 21 Tzfat teenagers killed by terrorists in 1974—they were taken hostage while on a field trip in the northern Galilee town of Ma'alot. ✉ *Below Keren Hayesod St.* 🎟 *Free.*

Citadel Park. In Talmudic times, 1,600 years ago, hilltop bonfires here served as a beacon to surrounding communities heralding the beginning of the lunar month, the basis for the Jewish calendar. In the 12th century, the Crusaders grasped the strategic value of this setting and built

Tzfat is an artsy village in the northern Galilee known for being the birthplace of Kabbalah (Jewish mysticism).

the Citadel. The Muslim sultan Baybars conquered it in 1266, leaving only the scattered pieces you see today.

The Jewish settlement outside the Citadel's walls grew and prospered during and after the Crusader era, becoming a center of Kabbalah studies. When the departing British Mandate forces left the town's strategic positions to the Arab forces, the remains of the Citadel again became a battleground between Jews and Arabs. ✉ *Old City.*

Kikar Hameginim. "Defenders' Square," in the Old Jewish Quarter, was once its social and economic heart. A sign points to a two-story house that served as the command post of the neighborhood's defense in 1948—hence the plaza's name. ✉ *Bar Yochai St.*

Ma'alot Olei Hagardom. Part of Tzfat's charm is its setting, on the slope of a hill. This *ma'alot,* or stairway, which extends from Yerushalayim Street to Keren HaYesod Street, forms the boundary between the Old Jewish Quarter and the Artists' Colony. It is named for Tzfat freedom fighters executed by the British during the mandate. ✉ *Off Yerushalayim St.*

Memorial Museum of Hungarian-Speaking Jewry. The founders of this museum are Tzfat residents and Holocaust survivors Hava and Yosef Lustig. The exhibits in the museum's three small rooms, including letters, children's books, drawings, items of clothing, and more, tell of the everyday life of communities and individuals in the Hungarian-speaking Jewish pre-Holocaust world. The computer database has information about 1,700 Jewish communities in Hungary, Transylvania, Slovakia, and other countries. ✉ *Old Ottoman government center, Independence Sq.* ☎ *04/692–5881* 🌐 *www.hjm.org.il* 🎫 *NIS 15* 🕙 *Sun.–Fri. 9–1.*

WHERE TO EAT

> **WORD OF MOUTH**
>
> ". . . spent an entire day exploring Tzfat. Tzfat is seen on foot but is a small village and definitely worth a visit." —hat

¢ MIDDLE EASTERN **Azamra.** This popular local eatery's upstairs dining room has benches and tables inlaid with Middle-Eastern designs, walls painted the soft shade of blue found inside local synagogues, and colorful carpets from all over the region. The strikingly dressed owner and chef, Ronen Jarufi, makes each meal to order. Choose from a variety of Yemenite breads—*lachuch*, *malawa*, or *jachnun* are all good picks—and he'll top it with homemade cheese and his own hot sauce. The place also stocks books about Kabbalah and CDs of evocative Jewish music. *18 Elkabetz St. 50/225–4148 No credit cards Closed Sat.*

$$$ ISRAELI **Bat Ya'ar.** Its wooded mountaintop setting enhances this timbered restaurant's delicious food. A meaty bowl of bean stew, eaten by the fireplace, is a pleasure any time of year. Outside is a playground for children. Hour-long family nature activity packages are offered, as well as horseback-riding excursions. Bat Ya'ar is 5 km (3 mi) north of Tzfat. It's best to call for directions. *Birya Forest 04/692–1788 www.batyaar.co.il Reservations essential AE, DC, MC, V.*

$$$ VEGETARIAN Fodor's Choice ★ **Ein Camonim.** The Galilee Hills make perfect pastureland for livestock—in this case, goats—and here you can taste the fresh output of Ein Camonim's dairy. The all-you-can-eat menu includes a platter of goat cheeses, a selection of home-baked breads, and a variety of fresh salads. There's a half-price menu for children 12 and under. The specialty shop next door sells the dairy's cheeses, olives, and other homemade products. The eatery is 20 km (12½ mi) southwest of Tzfat, 5 km (3 mi) west of Kadarim Junction. *Rte. 85, Doar Karmiel 04/698–9894 AE, DC, MC, V.*

$$ ECLECTIC **Gan Eden.** The setting, a charming stone house with both indoor and outdoor seating, lends great atmosphere to this family-run kosher eatery. Taking in the view of Mt. Meron (the restaurant's name means "paradise"), the place is best known for its fish, especially its fillets of sea bass and sea bream. What they call calzones are actually dumplings stuffed with salty Tzfat cheese and served with a delicious salad of lettuce, cranberries, and walnuts. Gan Eden serves no meat or chicken. *Mt. Canaan Promenade, Gedud Hashlishi St. 33 04/697–2434 AE, MC, V Closed Sat.*

WHERE TO STAY

$$$ **Canaan Spa.** This elegant hotel on the outskirts of Tzfat knows how to pamper its guests. In addition to conventional Swedish massage, you can enjoy reflexology or aromatic massages or hot-stone treatments. Paintings and sculptures adorn public areas that are coordinated in tranquil colors for an effect of refined luxury. Facilities include tennis and basketball courts and a 1½-acre private forest. The price includes brunch and dinner. **Pros:** truly relaxing atmosphere; great pool; fabulous brunch. **Cons:** remote location; not for families. *Mt. Canaan Promenade, Gdud Hashlishi Street 04/699–3000 www.canaanspa.com 116 rooms, 8 suites In-room: a/c, safe, refrigerator. In-hotel: restaurant, tennis court, pools, spa, no kids under 14 AE, DC, MC, V MAP.*

7

$ **Joseph's Well.** At Kibbutz Amiad, 10 km (6 mi) south of Tzfat, this lodging has clusters of rooms sharing private patios. Each room is like a cozy studio apartment, with pine furnishings and chintz curtains. They all have a coffee corner with an electric kettle, and tea and coffee. Breakfast is served in the kibbutz dining room. Joseph's Well offers few activities but is a good base for exploring the Upper Galilee. **Pros:** informal; terrific for children; a peek into kibbutz life. **Cons:** plain decor; don't expect sophisticated breakfast. *Kibbutz Amiad, off Route 90, M.P. Upper Galilee, 12335 04/690–9829 www.amiad-inn.com 27 rooms In-room: a/c, no phone. In-hotel: pool AE, DC, MC, V.*

$$ **Ruth Rimonim.** Built 200 years ago for a Turkish sultan, this spectacular castle was transformed into a hotel in 1961. Since then it has enjoyed a reputation for charm and excellence. The stone-walled rooms, many of which have vaulted ceilings, are both comfortable and rustic; the former stables serve as a dining room. Half the rooms have mountain views. **Pros:** romantic; nice pool; central location. **Cons:** pool is open only in summer; some older rooms are small. *Artists' Quarter, Off Tel Zayin St., Tzfat 04/699–4666 www.rimonim.com 77 rooms In-room: a/c, refrigerator. In-hotel: 2 restaurants, bar, pool, gym, Wi-Fi hotspot AE, DC, MC, V.*

¢ **Safed Inn.** On the outskirts of Tzfat, the Safed Inn caters especially well to families and budget travelers. There's a courtyard for barbecuing, pretty garden where the kids can play, a fully stocked kitchen, and homey dining room where breakfast is served. Standard rooms are simple but clean. For a bit more, the deluxe rooms have featherbeds, whirlpool tubs, and parquet floors. **Pros:** Very good value. **Cons:** Owner can be a bit brusque; no kids in deluxe rooms. *Mount Canann Promenade, off Gdud Hashlishi St. 04/697-1007 www.safedinn.com 20 rooms In-room: a/c. In-hotel: laundry service AE, DC, MC, V BP.*

NIGHTLIFE AND THE ARTS

Every July or August, Tzfat hosts the **Klezmer Festival** (*04/692–7484 www.safed.co.il/klezmer-festival-safed.html*), and there could be no better setting for three days of "Jewish soul music" than this mystical, cobbled-lane city. Many events are street performances and therefore free. Keep in mind that Tzfat practically bursts at the seams at this time, with revelers both religious and secular.

SPORTS AND THE OUTDOORS

★ In the Birya Forest 5 km (3 mi) from Tzfat, the **Bat Ya'ar Ranch** (*04/692–1788 www.batyaar.co.il*) offers outdoor fun for the whole family including pony rides, rope bridges between trees, and outdoor bowling with wooden lanes and balls. Horseback riding is NIS 130 per person.

SHOPPING

Safed Candles (*Najara St., near Ha'Ari Synagogue 04/692–1093*) has grown from a one-room workshop to a huge space filled with the pleasant aroma of beeswax and the bright colors of hand-decorated Sabbath, Havdalah, and Hanukkah candles.

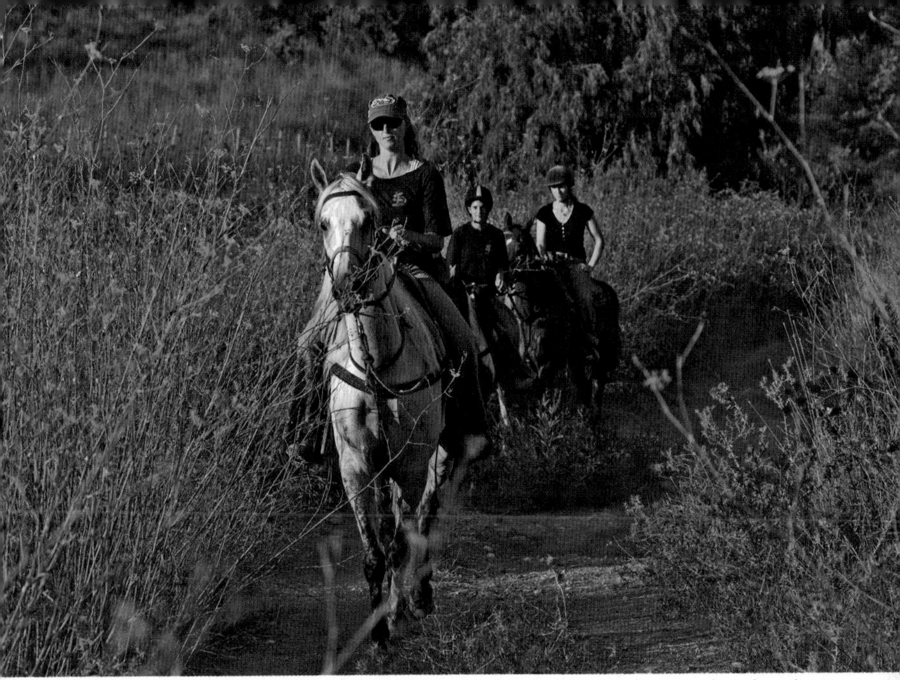

Getting on horseback is a popular activity in the Galilee, with its verdant hills, quiet forests, and gentle paths.

MT. MERON

21 km (13 mi) west of Tzfat on Route 89.

GETTING HERE AND AROUND

From Tzfat take Route 89 west, following signs to "Tomb of Rashbi." A security guard will check the trunk of your car before you ascend to the parking lot.

EXPLORING

Mt. Meron. The spiritual importance of Tzfat extends beyond the city limits to Mt. Meron, a pilgrimage site both for ultra-Orthodox Jews and nature lovers.

Meron has for centuries drawn thousands upon thousands of Orthodox Jews to pay homage to the great rabbis of the Roman era who are buried at the eastern foot of the mount. The most important site on Mt. Meron—and one of the holiest places in Israel—is the **Tomb of Rabbi Shimon Bar Yochai,** survivor of the Bar Kochba Revolt of almost 2,000 years ago. The simple building that houses the tomb is a place for quiet reflection and prayer, though you may encounter a bar mitzvah or other festive event in the courtyard outside.

Bar Yochai is said to have fled from the Romans with his son Elazar after the fall of Jerusalem to a cave at Peki'in, not far from here, where he remained for 13 years. The faithful, beginning with the 16th-century mystics who settled in Tzfat, believe that from his cave-hideout Bar Yochai penned the *Zohar* (the Book of Splendor), his commentary on the first five books of the Hebrew Bible. Others claim that the Zohar

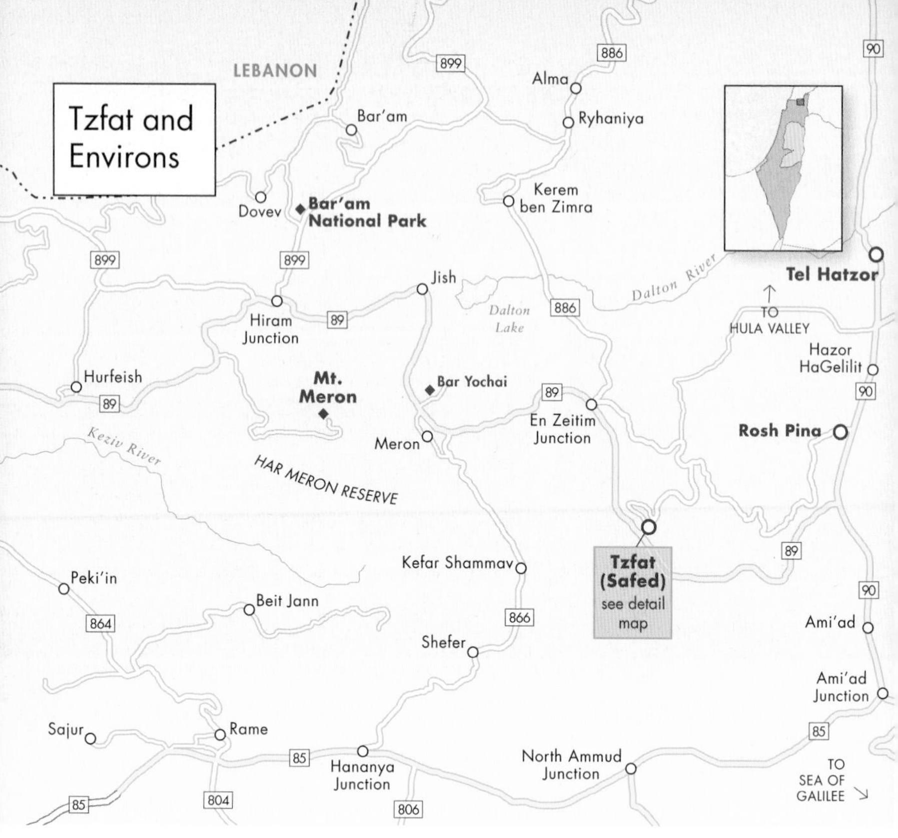

dates from 13th-century Spain. Nevertheless, the constant flow of visitors is evidence of the pilgrims' devotion to the great rabbi and rebel.

The pilgrimage is still celebrated en masse on Lag Ba'Omer, the festive 33rd day of the seven solemn weeks that begin with Passover and end with *Shavuot* (Pentecost). At this time Mt. Meron comes alive as a grand procession arrives on foot from Tzfat, carrying Torah scrolls and singing fervently. Bonfires are lighted, with celebrations lasting days. Many ultra-Orthodox Jews still uphold the tradition of bringing their three-year-old sons here on Lag Ba'Omer for their first haircuts.

WHERE TO EAT AND STAY

So many families in Moshav Amirim operate bed-and-breakfasts and small restaurants (all vegetarian) that the village has become a popular weekend destination. The community, about 4 km (2½ mi) north of the junction of Route 89 and Route 866, has everything from single rooms to suites. The lodgings and eateries operate under the collective name of **Amirim Holiday Village** (✉ *Moshav Amirim* ☎ *04/698–9571* ✉ *alitamirim@hotmail.com*)

$$$ VEGETARIAN ✕ **Dalia's.** The cheerful chef at this restaurant, the oldest dining establishment in Moshav Amirim, is a former nutritionist, so you know everything on the menu is wholesome as well as toothsome. The set menu includes, among other items, almond and peanut patties in onion sauce and tomatoes stuffed with wheat and barley, as well as a beautiful array of salads and soups. Dessert, consisting of yogurt with fresh fruit, is served with a big helping of fresh air and scenery. It's a bit hard to find, so call for directions. ✉ *Moshav Amirim, on the entrance road into the village* ☎ *04/698–9349* ✍ *Reservations essential* ▭ *AE, DC, MC, V.*

$ VEGETARIAN ✕ **Stupp's.** A local institution, Stupp's is managed by psychologist-turned-foodie Eiries Stupp, whose parents founded this kosher dairy eatery. The atmosphere is mildly Italian, with a Galilean twist. The menu has something for everyone: pastas, salads, and burgers with soy cheese. The house specialties include phyllo dough filled with mushrooms and walnuts, and corn bread creamed with cheddar. Reservations are required on summer evenings. ✉ *Moshav Amirim, on the entrance road into the village* ☎ *04/698–0946* ▭ *AE, DC, MC, V* ⏲ *Closed Sat.*

$$–$$$ **Hase'uda Ha'aharona.** This lodging's peculiar choice of name (it means "The Last Supper") shouldn't stop you from enjoying its magnificent views of the Golan Heights, the Sea of Galilee, and the Galilee mountains. The owners, Bella and Laurence, have outfitted each of the suites in classic style with furnishings they collected while traveling through Europe. They are happy to prepare gourmet breakfasts, lunches, and dinners, but many guests skip breakfast because each room has a kitchen stocked with a selection of cereal, yogurt, fruit, and other delicacies. **Pros:** pretty pool; cozy; tasty food. **Cons:** not much for nonvegetarians; need a car to get around. ✉ *Moshav Amirim, on the entrance road into the village* ☎ *04/698–9788* 🌐 *www.haseudah-haacharonah.com* *7 rooms* *In-room: a/c, kitchen, Wi-Fi. In-hotel: pool, spa* ▭ *AE, DC, MC, V.*

SPORTS AND THE OUTDOORS

At **Eretz Hagalil Jeeps** (✉ *Moshav Amirim* ☎ *04/698–0434 or 050/531–6140* 🌐 *www.eretz-hagalil.co.il*), Yoram Zarchi takes off-road aficionados on two-hour excursions through the Galilee and the Golan, taking in sites of natural beauty and historical significance along the way. Trips cost NIS 590 to NIS 650 per person.

Malkiya Stables (✉ *Kibbutz Malkiya, Rte. 899* ☎ *052/281–6293*) offers spectacular mountain views on its rides. Ask about trail rides of one to four hours for ages seven and up. The stables are about 29 km (18 mi) north of Khiram Junction.

BAR'AM NATIONAL PARK

15 km (9 mi) northwest of Meron, 40 km (25 mi) northwest of Tzfat.

GETTING HERE AND AROUND

From Tzfat, head west on Route 89, then north on Route 899. After 3 km (1½ mi), turn right onto a dirt road. There's no bus service to Bar'am.

EXPLORING

In an otherwise deserted spot lie the ruins of **Bar'am**, one of the best-preserved ancient synagogues anywhere. Like most other synagogues uncovered in this area, this structure dating from the 3rd century faces south, toward Jerusalem; unlike any other, however, this one has lavish architectural elements, such as an entrance with a segmental pediment, and freestanding giant columns in front. The interior, which resembles that of other Galilean synagogues of the Talmudic period (3rd to 8th centuries AD), is less well preserved. Rows of pillars in the prayer hall apparently served as supports for the ceiling, and the building may have had a second story. A section of the facade's lintel, now in the Louvre in Paris, contains the Hebrew inscription "May there be peace in this place, and in all the places of Israel. This lintel was made by Jose the Levite. Blessings upon his works. Shalom." Allow at least an hour to wander around. ⊠ *Rte. 899* ☎ *04/698–9301* *NIS 12* ⊙ *Apr.–Sept. Mon.–Thurs. 8–5, Fri. 8–3; Oct.–Mar. Mon.–Thurs. 8–4, Fri. 8–3.*

ROSH PINA

Fodor's Choice ★

10 km (6 mi) east of Tzfat, 25 km (15½ mi) north of Tiberias.

The restored village of Rosh Pina is a gift-shop and gallery-browser's delight, and the dilapidated wooden doors and stonework of some still-abandoned premises are part of the charm.

Rosh Pina—literally "cornerstone"—gets its name from Psalm 118:22: "The stone that the builders rejected has become the chief cornerstone." This verse inspired the Galilee's first Zionist pioneers, who came from Romania in 1882, determined to build a village. They bought this land, at the foot of the mountain ridge east of Tzfat, and arrived with all they needed, right down to the timber for construction.

The Romanians derived their main livelihood at Rosh Pina from the production of silk by silkworms; the philanthropist Baron Edmond de Rothschild donated the necessary mulberry trees. However, the rewards of their efforts were elusive: residents walked around in silk scarves but had nothing to eat. Eventually, the immigrants moved away, and for decades the village was inhabited only by squatters. Today it's a vacation destination and a year-round residence for 2,500 people.

GETTING HERE AND AROUND

From Tel Aviv, you can fly into the small airport of Mahanayim, near Rosh Pina, or there are daily buses from Tzfat, Tiberias, and Haifa. If you're driving from Tzfat, head east on Route 89, then north on Route 90.

ESSENTIALS

Taxi Contacts **Meir Taxi** (☎ *04/693–5735*).

EXPLORING

The two-story **Schwartz Hotel**, on Ha'elyon Street, built in 1890, was the first rest house in the Galilee. Today it is a mere skeleton of the original, but try to imagine what it was like to check in here after a long, tiring journey on foot and enjoy the tranquil view of the Sea of Galilee below and white-capped Mt. Hermon to the north. ⊠ *Ha'elyon St.* ☎ *No phone.*

The **synagogue** is usually locked, but ask around and you might find someone to open it for you. The interior remains as it was when it was built in the mid-1880s; the dark pews made of the timber brought from Romania have aged gracefully. The ceiling has painted depictions of palm trees and biblical motifs. ✉ *Ha'elyon St.* ☎ *No phone.*

The **Old Rosh Pina Office** occupies the house that belonged to Professor Gideon Mer, a leading expert on malaria in the 1930s. Legend has it that Mer used to inject his wife and children with experimental remedies in his efforts to combat malaria in this region. (All survived.) The British were so impressed with Mer's work that they sent him to Burma to fight malaria epidemics there. Implements and household items from the early days of Rosh Pina are on display. Next door, a colorful audiovisual presentation showcases the founding of this pioneering community. ✉ *Hachalutzim St.* ☎ *04/693–6603* *NIS 15* ⏲ *Sun.–Thurs. 8:30–5, Fri. and Sat. 8:30–1.*

WORD OF MOUTH

"Rosh Pina is a fabulous small 'boutique' town with marvelous (and expensive!!) boutique hotels, restaurants, Old City, etc." —Flame123

WHERE TO EAT

$$$ CONTEMPORARY Fodor's Choice ★ **Auberge Shulamit.** This charming inn takes its name from the original Hotel Shulamit, where the 1948 Armistice Treaty was signed. Among the menu's delectables—along with the home-smoked meats—are chestnut soup in season, shrimp with wild rice, and an elegant array of desserts. If you can't bear to leave, the inn has three French country–style guest rooms. ✉ *1 David Shub St.* ☎ *04/693–1485* 🌐 *www.shulamit.co.il* *Reservations essential* 💳 *AE, DC, MC, V.*

$$$$ ARGENTINEAN **Babayit Shel Rafa.** The sizzling steaks of his native Argentina figure prominently on Rafa's menu. The best starters are the pickled tongue and the meat or corn empanadas. Entrées include roast beef and a sausage and lamb casserole with rice and green beans. Vegetarians shouldn't despair, as the rich vegetable, mozzarella, prune, and almond stew is delicious. Business lunches, served daily from noon to 5 pm, are tasty and economical. ✉ *Hachalutzim St., Old Rosh Pina restoration site, next to the Old Rosh Pina Office* ☎ *04/693–6192* *Reservations essential* 💳 *AE, DC, MC, V.*

$ ISRAELI **Chocolata.** The original arched stone basement of the old synagogue is the setting of this romantic restaurant. In addition to the usual fresh salads, pastas, and sandwiches, there are unusual dishes like artichokes filled with cheese. True to its name, the kitchen serves a host of chocolate delights, including 37 different kinds of pralines made by the house chocolatier. ✉ *Old Rosh Pina, east lower entrance to the synagogue* ☎ *04/686–0219* *Reservations essential* 💳 *AE, DC, MC, V.*

$$ ECLECTIC **Ja'uni.** The century-old structure that houses Ja'uni once served as a post office, then as an armory. The menu is seasonal and eclectic. The Spanish-style tapas menu changes daily, and may include roasted peppers, zucchini or fried cabbage in tahini, or eggplant in ginger, honey, and soy sauce. The outdoor seating is pleasant and there is live music on summer evenings. ✉ *30 David Shub St.* ☎ *04/693–1881* 💳 *AE, DC, MC, V.*

$$$$ STEAK Fodor's Choice ★ **Meat-balim.** Go easy on the appetizers here, as you'll want to save room for this sleek, modern kosher eatery's savory meat dishes. Those in the know recommend the generous veal entrecôte and the lamb chops in a flavorful sauce of caramel, oranges, mint, and ginger. Avoid the

7

Visit Rosh Pina for its charming streets, shops, and galleries.

creamy desserts, which don't contain real dairy. The extensive wine list is a pleasure, however. ✉ *Hagalil St.* ☎ *04/686–0107* ⏲ *Sun.–Thurs. 11 am–1:30 am, Fri. 11–4 summers; closed winters, Sat. closed winters; summers open 30 minutes after sundown—1:30 am* ▭ *AE, DC, MC, V.*

WHERE TO STAY

Rosh Pina is a budding center of tourism for this region, and many residents are now opening their homes as bed-and-breakfasts.

$$ Fodor's Choice ★ **Ahuzat Hameiri.** This stunning mansion has been in the Hameiri family since it was built in the late 1880s. The current generation has renovated the rooms and landscaped the grounds with an elegant touch. Most rooms have stained-glass doors and vaulted ceilings; it's worth asking for one of the pair that has private terraces. A full Israeli breakfast is delivered to your door. **Pros:** breathtaking views. **Cons:** no pool; many steps to rooms. ✉ *1 Hachalutzim St.* ☎ *050/653–2530* 🌐 *www.hrp.co.il* *9 rooms* *In-room: a/c. In-hotel: laundry service* ▭ *MC, V.*

$ **Kfar Hanassi Tourism.** These accommodations at Kfar Hanassi give you a real taste of communal life. The one- and two-room units overlook a garden, and each has a barbecue and full kitchenette. Boldly colored sheets and dhurrie rugs add a country touch. Meals are in the kibbutz's communal dining room. Several artists live and work at Kfar Hanassi, and you're welcome to visit their studios. Guided hikes to the mountainous Jordan River area northeast of the kibbutz are available, and there are plenty of other activities to keep kids occupied, too. **Pros:** great for families; friendly. **Cons:** basic rooms; no restaurant. ✉ *Kibbutz Kfar Hanassi, 5 km from Rt. 90, next to Mahanayim airport* ☎ *04/691–4870* *www.k-hanassi.co.il* *20 units* *In-room: a/c, no phone, kitchen, Wi-Fi. In-hotel: tennis court, pool* *AE, DC, MC, V.*

$$$$ **Mizpe Hayamim.** With a splendid view of the Sea of Galilee, this hotel specializes in pampering its clients. Its spa features such treatment as the olive-branch massage and other rubdowns with oils distilled from wildflowers. About half the rooms are suites with their own whirlpool tubs. The organic restaurant is known throughout the region, and the lobby has an herbal-tea corner open around the clock. A gallery sells local artwork, and a gift shop offers homemade breads, cheese, and other products. **Pros:** great food; enchanting walking paths; pretty pool. **Cons:** need a car to get around; not a place for families. *Tzfat Rd. 89* *04/699–4555* *www.mizpe-hayamim.com* *100 rooms* *In-room: a/c. In-hotel: restaurant, room service, gym, spa, no kids under 10* *AE, DC, MC, V* *MAP.*

$$ **Villa Tehila.** Amichai and Tehila Yisraeli bought what was a run-down 19th-century farm in Rosh Pina and started converting the stables, storehouse, and dairy into a charming guesthouse. Thirty years later, Villa Tehila retains its old-world character: the simply appointed rooms, which overlook a central courtyard, have the original stone walls and are decorated with antiques. Children will enjoy feeding the ponies, turtles, parrots, chinchillas, and llama. There's a pub on the premises, open only on weekends. **Pros:** child-friendly; pool open year-round. **Cons:** some rooms very small; courtyard dimly lit at night. *7 Hachalutzim St.* *04/693–7788* *www.villa-tehila.co.il* *11 rooms* *In-room: a/c, refrigerator. In-hotel: pool, laundry service, Internet terminal* *AE, DC, MC, V.*

SHOPPING

The Well. Sigal Eshet-Shafat and her husband Inbar used to sell typical handicrafts, but it turned out that their jams, dressings, and liqueurs were what attracted the clientele. The on-site coffee shop lets you sample the store's delights and sign up for the occasional cooking class. The onion jam is a favorite for both dairy and meat dishes. *Beit Wilkomitz, end of Hachalamoniot Way, Old Rosh Pina* *04/693–0340* *Sun.–Thurs. 10:30–1, Fri. 10:30–3.*

NIGHTLIFE AND THE ARTS

Blues Brothers Pub. The atmosphere in this small stone basement may best be described as "happy Gothic." Inexpensive meals are served to the mainly youthful clientele. *Villa Tehila, 7 Hachalutzim St.* *04/693–7788.*

Julian. Although it's also a restaurant, this is probably the closest thing in the area to a trendy bar. It's in what used to be the region's customhouse: over a century ago it marked the boundary between British and French jurisdictions. Options include wines, draft beer, whiskeys, and cocktails. *46 Derech HaGalilee* *04/693–0207.*

7

TEL HATZOR

8 km (5 mi) north of Rosh Pina, 14 km (9 mi) east of Tzfat.

GETTING HERE AND AROUND

From Tzfat, head east on Route 89, then north on Route 90.

EXPLORING

Tel Hatzor is a good stop for archaeology buffs—its massive mound is made up of the remnants of 21 cities. The excavation and restoration of some of these antiquities have produced fascinating results.

On the Via Maris—the major trade route linking Egypt and Mesopotamia—Hatzor is referred to several times in documents from ancient archives in both lands, and scholars believe a huge archive may someday be found here.

The Book of Joshua (11:13) notes that Joshua destroyed Canaanite Hatzor in the 13th century BC, and Israelites resettled it. Its next heyday came three centuries later, when King Solomon decided it would serve him well as a regional military and administrative center, like Megiddo and Gezer. In 732 BC, Hatzor met its end when invading Assyrian king Tiglath Pileser III conquered the Galilee and forced its Israelite inhabitants off the land in chains and into exile.

The huge site is divided into two areas: the **Upper City,** which comprised the most ancient settlements, and the **Lower City,** first settled in the 18th century BC. Only the Upper City, covering less than a fifth of the total excavation site, is open to the public. The **Hatzor Museum** (on the grounds of Kibbutz Ayelet Hashachar, across the highway) houses figurines, weapons, stone pots, and other artifacts unearthed in the two areas; others are at the Israel Museum in Jerusalem. It's open by appointment. ✉ *Tel Hatzor National Park, Rte. 90* ☎ *04/693–7290* 🎫 *NIS 18* ⏲ *Park and museum Apr.–Sept., Sat.–Thurs. 8–5, Fri. 8–4; Oct.–Mar., Sat.–Thurs. 8–4, Fri. 8–3.*

HULA NATURE RESERVE

8 km (5 mi) north of Tel Hatzor, 24 km (15 mi) northeast of Tzfat.

GETTING HERE AND AROUND

From Tzfat, head east on Route 89, north on Route 90.

EXPLORING

★ The **Hula Nature Reserve** contains the last vestige of wetlands preserved after the rest were drained in the 1950s to create arable land. Over the years it became apparent that in addition to affecting water quality in the Sea of Galilee, draining the wetlands had destroyed the habitat of millions of birds that came to the Hula Valley on their migrations between Europe and Africa.

Pelicans, wild geese, storks, cranes, plovers, and raptors once again have a sanctuary here, and the swampy waters abound with carp, catfish, and perch. There are rare thickets of papyrus, and you might see a water buffalo or two. A 1-km hiking trail offers great views of the entire reserve. The visitor center has informative displays of the history of the valley and the 800-acre reserve. There's an observation tower, snack bar, and pleasant picnic area. Parts of the public areas are wheelchair accessible. ✉ *East of Rte. 90* ☎ *04/693–7069* 🎫 *Park NIS 18; visitor center NIS 15* ⏲ *Park Sun–Thurs. 8–4, Fri. 8–2; visitor center Sun–Thurs. 10–4, Fri. 10–2.*

NEED A BREAK?

For a rest stop with a bit of history, try Ahuzat Dubrovin (✉ *East of Rte. 90, Yesod Hama'ala* ☎ *04/693–7371* 🎫 *NIS 10* ⏲ *Mon.–Thurs. 10:30–4, Fri. 10:30–2*), near the entrance to the Hula Nature Reserve. The Dubrovins, a family of Russian immigrants who converted to Judaism and moved here in 1909, once owned this reconstructed farmhouse. The property was eventually donated to the Jewish National Fund and opened to the public in 1986. An exhibit in the former family home highlights the old days of the Hula Valley. A kosher restaurant specializes in smoked meat dishes.

UPPER HULA VALLEY

The sights that hug the border with Lebanon show contrasting sides of Israel. The bustling town of Kiryat Shmona and sleepy Metulla bear eloquent witness to the varying fortunes of Israel's relationships with its Arab neighbors. Tel Dan Nature Reserve, on the other hand, draws visitors with its antiquities, surging river, and lush, wild beauty.

7

KIRYAT SHMONA

45 km (28 mi) north of Tiberias, 39 km (24 mi) north of Tzfat.

The major urban center in the Upper Hula Valley, Kiryat Shmona is known for the cable car up Manara Cliff. For years, the instability in neighboring Lebanon profoundly affected life in the town, and by 1982 the spate of terrorist attacks had reached such proportions that Israel responded by invading Lebanon, the first stage of what would become the First Lebanon War. Kiryat Shmona was again in the news in 1996 when Hezbollah terrorists launched a focused and continued attack on the town and its environs using Katyusha rockets. The Israel Defense Forces responded by targeting Hezbollah's bases in southern Lebanon in a campaign that became known as the Grapes of Wrath. In 2006, Hezbollah again lobbed rockets into northern Israel, sparking the Second Lebanon War.

GETTING HERE AND AROUND

From Tzfat, head east on Route 89, then north on Route 90. There are at least 16 buses daily from Tel Aviv, at least 19 from Haifa, and 4 from Jerusalem.

ESSENTIALS

Taxi Contacts **Hatzafon Taxi** (☎ *04/694–2333*).

EXPLORING

The Kiryat Shmona–Kibbutz Manara cable car at **Manara Cliff** (✉ *Kibbutz Manara, Rte. 90* ☎ *04/690–5830* 🎫 *NIS 49 weekdays, NIS 59 weekends* ⏲ *Open daily Mar.–Jul. and Sept.–Oct. 9:30–5; Aug. 9:30–7; Nov.–Feb. 11–4. Last cable car leaves 30 min. before closing*) gives you a bird's-eye view of the Hula Valley. It has one station midway on the 1,890-yard trip, where the adventurous can step out and do some rappelling and dry sliding (a roller-coaster-like activity), or try the climbing wall. One option is to take the cable car up and mountain bike down. There's also the thrill of a 600-foot zip line. If you opt to remain in the cable car, the trip takes eight minutes each way, overlooking cliffs and green hills from a height of some 850 yards. At the bottom are a trampoline and other attractions for kids. There is wheelchair access to the cable car and upper station.

Perched on the northern edge of Kiryat Shmona is **Tel Hai,** meaning "hill of life," which played an important role in Israel's history. In the aftermath of World War I, while Britain and France bickered over control of the upper Hula Valley, bands of Arabs often harassed the Jewish farms, and finally overran Tel Hai in 1920. Only Kibbutz Kfar Giladi was successful in defending itself.

Following this incident, Tel Hai resident Josef Trumpeldor and seven comrades were called on to protect the place. Trumpeldor already had a reputation as a leader in the czar's army in his native Russia, where he lost an arm fighting. Fired by Zionist ideals, he had moved to Palestine in 1912 at the age of 32. During the final battle in 1920, Trumpeldor and his comrades were killed and it is for them that Kiryat Shmona—City of the Eight—is named. It is said that Trumpeldor's last words were: "It is good to die for our country." He is buried up the road from the museum, beneath the statue of a lion.

The heroic last stand at Tel Hai was important not only because it was the first modern instance of Jewish armed self-defense, but also because the survival of at least two of the Jewish settlements meant that when the final borders were drawn by the League of Nations in 1922, these settlements were included in the British-mandated territory of Palestine and thus, after 1948, in the State of Israel. ✉ *Off Rte. 90.*

The **Tel Hai Courtyard Museum** displays agricultural tools used in Trumpeldor's time. A moving audiovisual show highlights the history of the place. ✉ *Off Rte. 886* ☎ *04/695–1333* 🎫 *NIS 22* ⏲ *Sun.–Thurs. 9–4, Fri. and Sat. 10–3.*

WHERE TO EAT

$$$ SEAFOOD ✕ **Dag al Hadan.** Fresh trout and a glass of wine, in a shady copse by the gurgling Dan River—it's as good as it sounds, which is why Dag al Hadan draws crowds on weekends. This was the first restaurant in the region to specialize in the fish the Dan yields in abundance; you can see the trout ponds in a small installation on the grounds. The same management also runs a café next door where light vegetarian meals are served. The restaurant, opposite Kibbutz Hagoshrim, is tucked away behind the main road, but it's large and well signposted. ✉ *Beit Hillel, off Rte. 99, near Kiryat Shmona* ☎ *04/695–0225* ✍ *Reservations essential* 💳 *AE, DC, MC, V.*

$$ ECLECTIC ✕ **Focaccia Bar.** This family restaurant in the Alonim Mall serves a good selection of pastas and pizzas, as well as meat dishes with a Middle Eastern touch. It sits opposite Kibbutz Ma'ayan Baruch. ✉ *Off Rte. 9, near Kiryat Shmona* ☎ *04/690–04474* 💳 *AE, DC, MC, V.*

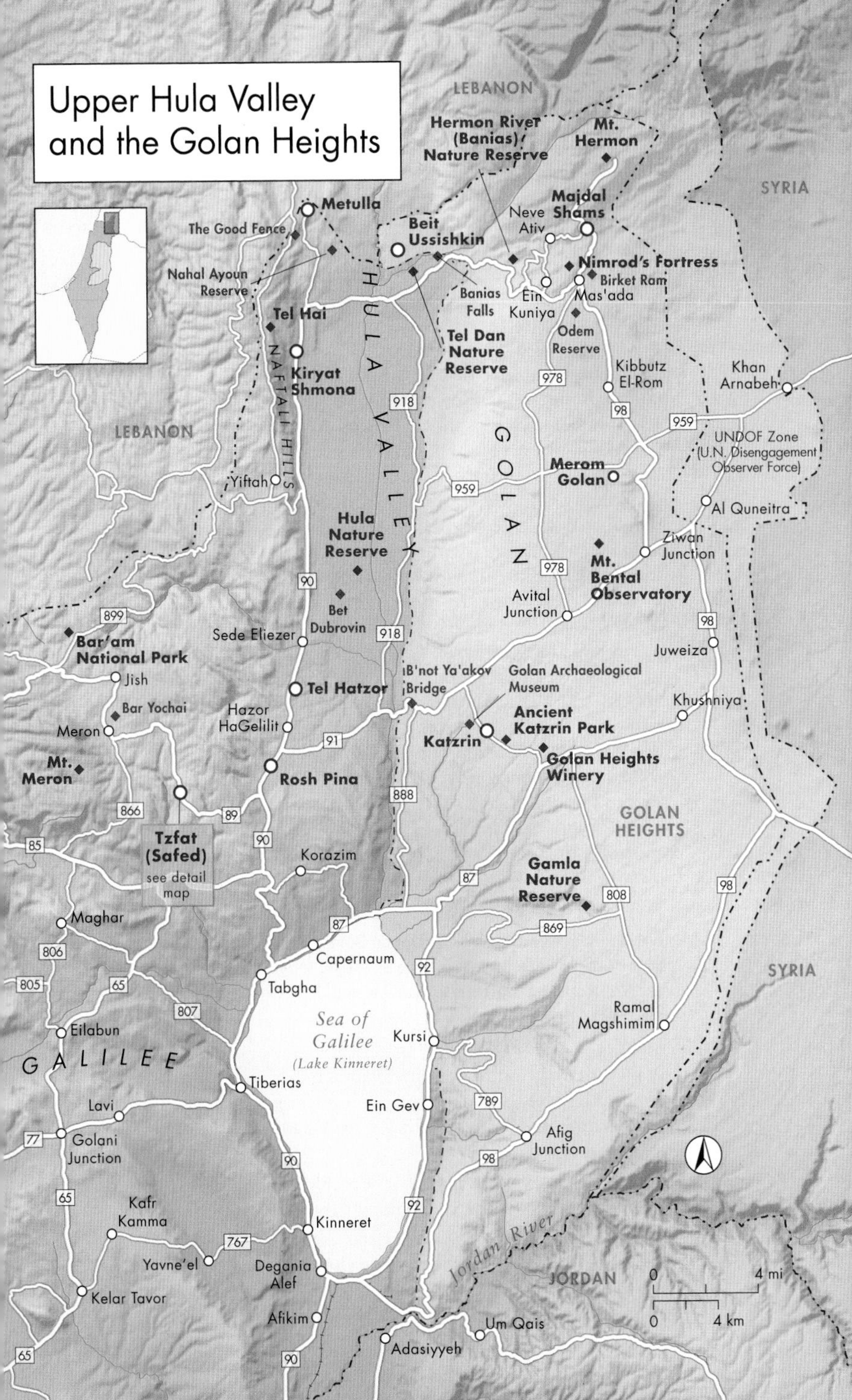
Upper Hula Valley and the Golan Heights
LEBANON
Hermon River (Banias) Nature Reserve
Mt. Hermon
SYRIA
Metulla
The Good Fence
Nahal Ayoun Reserve
Beit Ussishkin
Majdal Shams
Neve Ativ
Nimrod's Fortress
Birket Ram
Mas'ada
Ein Kuniya
Banias Falls
Tel Hai
HULA VALLEY
Tel Dan Nature Reserve
Odem Reserve
Kiryat Shmona
NAFTALI HILLS
Kibbutz El-Rom
Khan Arnabeh
LEBANON
GOLAN
UNDOF Zone (U.N. Disengagement Observer Force)
Merom Golan
Yiftah
Al Quneitra
Hula Nature Reserve
Ziwan Junction
Mt. Bental Observatory
Avital Junction
Bet Dubrovin
Sede Eliezer
Bar'am National Park
Jish
Juweiza
B'not Ya'akov Bridge
Golan Archaeological Museum
Tel Hatzor
Bar Yochai
Hazor HaGelilit
Meron
Ancient Katzrin Park
Khushniya
Katzrin
Golan Heights Winery
Mt. Meron
Rosh Pina
GOLAN HEIGHTS
Tzfat (Safed) see detail map
Korazim
Gamla Nature Reserve
Maghar
Capernaum
Tabgha
SYRIA
Sea of Galilee (Lake Kinneret)
Kursi
Ramal Magshimim
Eilabun
GALILEE
Tiberias
Ein Gev
Lavi
Golani Junction
Afig Junction
Kafr Kamma
Kinneret
Jordan River
Yavne'el
Degania Alef
JORDAN
Kelar Tavor
Afikim
Um Qais
Adasiyyeh
0 4 mi
0 4 km
918 959 978 98 90 899 91 888 866 89 85 87 808 869 806 805 65 807 92 789 77 767

WHERE TO STAY

$$ **Hagoshrim Kibbutz Hotel.** The waters of the Hermon River flow right through Hagoshrim—under a glass-topped channel set in the ceramic tile of the lobby and then through the property. While the rooms are simply decorated, the lobby is especially pleasant, with blond-wood furniture and colorful cushions and throw rugs. Gosh, the kosher restaurant, specializes in meat dishes. Kayaking and guided walking tours are available. **Pros:** wide selection of activities; nice common areas. **Cons:** basic decor; can get loud in summer. ✉ *Rte. 99, east of Kiryat Shmona, Upper Galilee* ☎ *04/681–6000* 🌐 *www.hagoshrim-hotel.co.il* *164 rooms* *In-room: a/c, refrigerator. In-hotel: restaurant, bar, pool, gym, Wi-Fi hotspot* *AE, DC, MC, V.*

$ **Kibbutz Hotel Kfar Giladi.** Atop a hill behind Tel Hai is one of the country's oldest and largest kibbutz hotels. It is run very efficiently but retains a homey atmosphere. The rooms are on the plain side, but some have lovely views of the Hula Valley and Mt. Hermon. The gift shop has some unusual handcrafted items, many made by members of the community. The Beit Hashomer Museum, which explores the history of the kibbutz and the vicinity, is on the grounds. **Pros:** good value; lovely indoor and outdoor swimming pools. **Cons:** basic decor; uninspired food. ✉ *Rte. 886, Upper Galilee* ☎ *04/690–0000* 🌐 *www.kfar-giladi.co.il* *170 rooms* *In-room: a/c, refrigerator. In-hotel: pools, gym, Wi-Fi hotspot* *AE, DC, MC, V.*

$$ **Pastoral Kfar Blum Hotel.** Kibbutz Kfar Blum owns this deluxe hotel in the northern Hula Valley. The rooms are spacious and elegantly appointed. The spa offers unusual experiences such as a Turkish hammam and a rain cave. The kibbutz offers kayaking on the Jordan River and a chamber-music festival every summer. **Pros:** excellent room appointments; lovely spa; variety of programs for children. **Cons:** room rates are pricey; some construction noise. ✉ *Off Route 90, near Kiryat Shmona, Kfar Blum* ☎ *04/683–6611* 🌐 *www.kfarblum-hotel.co.il* *120 rooms* *In-room: a/c, refrigerator, Wi-Fi, safe. In-hotel: restaurant, bar, tennis courts, pool, spa* *AE, DC, MC, V.*

THE ARTS

For the classically minded, **Upper Galilee Local Council** (✉ *Upper Galilee* ☎ *04/681–6640*) hosts **Chamber Music Days** each year in late July and early August, a nationally renowned festival of chamber music in a pastoral setting.

SPORTS AND THE OUTDOORS

A plethora of outfits organize water-sports trips in this region, and almost all hotels can make reservations for you. The minimum age for kayaks and other water "vehicles" is usually six.

BOATING

Sde Nechemia (✉ *Kibbutz Huliot, Rte. 99* ☎ *04/694–6010*), near Kiryat Shmona, offers boating and tubing trips for NIS 70 per person.

KAYAKING

Hagoshrim Kayaks (✉ *Kibbutz Hagoshrim, off Rte. 99 near Kiryat Shemona* 🌐 *www.kayak.co.il* ☎ *04/681–6034*) has a 5-km (3-mi) "family" course that lasts 1½ hours and a 6-km (4-mi) "stormy" course that expands on the family course and lasts almost two hours. The family course costs NIS 75 per person, the stormy course NIS 95 per person.

Kibbutz Kfar Blum (✉ *Beit Hillel, off Rte. 9778* ☎ *04/690–2616*) rents two-person rubber kayaks for 1½-hour or two-hour runs. The cost is NIS 75 per person for the short course and NIS 109 per person for the long course. Kayaks are available from March through October; call ahead to inquire at other times of the year. The same site has a climbing wall, a rope park, a zip line across the water, and archery, at NIS 100 to NIS 159 per person for the full package.

Jordan Source (✉ *Kibbutz Sde Nechemia, off Route 9779* ☎ *04/694–6010 Ext. 3*) runs a 3½-hour kayaking trip (this one can be rough) costing NIS 75 per person and a 1½-hour trip for NIS 50 per person.

OFF-ROAD VEHICLES

Easy Track (✉ *Moshav She'ar Yashuv, near Rte. 99* ☎ *04/690–4440* 🌐 *www.mbez.co.il*), a company based in the northern Hula Valley, offers wind-in-your-hair ways to explore the countryside, in self-drive dune buggies (driver's license required) or on 1½-hour guided Jeep trips.

METULLA

7 km (4 mi) north of Kiryat Shmona, 46 km (28 mi) north of Tzfat.

Israel's northernmost town, Metulla, is so picturesque that it's hard to believe this tranquil spot is just a stone's throw from a contentious border.

The tensions of the Middle East dissipate here in the charm of the European-style limestone buildings that line Metulla's quaint main street, and the city itself seems to have changed little since its founding as a farming settlement in 1896. The numerous signs offering *zimmer* (German for "room") for rent enhance the Continental atmosphere. Even the weather is decidedly un-Mediterranean, with refreshingly cool mountain breezes carrying whiffs of cypress and spice plants in summer, and snow in winter.

GETTING HERE AND AROUND

From Tzfat, head east on Route 89, then north on Route 90.

EXPLORING

Nahal Ayoun Nature Reserve. In summer, the stream that gives this nature reserve its name slows to a trickle because the water is channeled away to irrigate agricultural fields. In winter, however, the water gushes, becoming a beautiful backdrop for hiking and picnicking. The towering Oven Fall is the most famous of the reserve's four waterfalls. Two trails meander through the reserve; the shorter one, taking about half an hour, begins and ends in the lower parking lot and goes to Oven Fall. The longer one, taking 1½ hours, begins in the upper parking lot and leads downstream. ✉ *East of Rte. 90* ☎ *04/695–1519* 🎫 *NIS 23* ⏲ *Apr.–Sept., Sat.–Thurs. 8–5, Fri. 8–3; Oct.–Mar., Sat.–Thurs 8–4, Fri. 8–3.*

7

In the Upper Hula Valley, you'll find the Tel Dan Nature Reserve and the Hermon River (Banais) Nature Reserve.

WHERE TO EAT

$$$$ STEAK ✕ **Hatachana.** This ranch-style steakhouse, whose name means "The Mill," raises its own cattle, so you're assured of the finest T-bones, as well as tasty sausages, lamb chops, and hamburgers. Each entrée comes with grilled vegetables and either fries or a baked potato, so it's certain that you won't go away hungry. It gets crowded, so reservations are a good idea. ✉ *1 Harishonim St.* ☎ *04/694–4810* 🌐 *www.tachana.co.il* 💳 *AE, D, MC, V.*

SPORTS AND THE OUTDOORS

The multistory **Canada Centre** (✉ *1 Harishonim St., POB 281* ☎ *04/695–0370* 🌐 *www.canada-centre.co.il*) has just about everything a sports complex can offer. You can spend the whole day here, playing basketball, ice-skating, working out, bowling, swimming, zooming down the waterslide, or taking aim on the shooting range.

TEL DAN NATURE RESERVE

25 km (15½ mi) southeast of Metulla, 15 km (9 mi) northeast of Kiryat Shmona, 50 km (31 mi) northeast of Tzfat.

GETTING HERE AND AROUND

From Tzfat, head east on Route 89, then turn north on Route 90. Once you pass Kiryat Shmona, turn right (east) on Route 99. The reserve is near Kibbutz Dan.

EXPLORING

★ The **Tel Dan Nature Reserve** is hard to beat for sheer natural beauty. A river surges through it, and luxuriant trees provide shade. A host of small mammals lives here—many partial to water, such as the otter and the mongoose—as well as the biblical coney, also known as the hyrax. This is also the home of Israel's largest rodent, the nocturnal Indian crested porcupine, and its smallest predator, the marbled polecat. The reserve has several hiking trails; a short segment, on a raised wooden walkway, is wheelchair accessible.

Dan was a majestic city in biblical times. According to Genesis, Abraham came here to rescue his nephew Lot and, five centuries later, Joshua led the Israelites through the area to victory. Fine ruins from several epochs lie here. Among them are the 9th-century BC city gate and the cultic site where King Jeroboam set up a golden calf to rival the Jerusalem Temple. Just inside the city gate is the platform for a throne, where the city's king pronounced judgment. One of the site's most extraordinary finds is an arched gateway dating from the 18th-century BC Canaanite period, more than a millennium earlier than scholars had previously thought. ✉ *North of Rte. 99* ☎ *04/695–1579* 🎫 *NIS 23* ⏲ *Apr.–Sept., Sat.–Thurs. 8–5, Fri. 8–3; Oct.–Mar., Sat.–Thurs. 8–4, Fri. 8–3; last entrance 1 hr before closing.*

Adjacent to the Tel Dan Nature Reserve, the **Beit Ussishkin Museum** has interesting exhibits about the flora, fauna, and geology of the Hula Valley, the Golan Heights, and the Jordan River. The audiovisual presentations are concise and informative. ✉ *Kibbutz Dan, off Rte. 99* ☎ *04/694–1704* 🎫 *NIS 18* ⏲ *Sun.–Thurs. 8–4, Fri. and Jewish holiday eves 8–2, Sat. 10–3.*

WHERE TO STAY

$$ **Pausa-Gourmet Galilee Inn.** Leaders in Israel's Slow Food movement own this beautiful boutique hotel, and their minimalist taste is reflected in the lovely and warm setting. The carefully landscaped and tranquil grounds include a boccie court, herb and vegetable gardens, and orchards that produce the ingredients used in the inn's kitchen. Meals are served family style; the Spanish, Japanese, and Israeli food is served at a massive wooden table. **Pros:** unforgettable meals; lovely decor; outdoor hot tub. **Cons:** remote location; small rooms; no pool. ✉ *Moshav She'ar Yashuv, Rte. 99* ☎ *054/690–4434* 🌐 *www.pausa-inn.co.il* *8 rooms* *In-room: a/c, no phone. In-hotel: restaurant, no kids under 14* 💳 *AE, D, DC, MC, V.*

THE GOLAN HEIGHTS

Considered the most fertile land in Israel, the Golan Heights is known for its many fine wineries. As you drive through these verdant hills, covered with wildflowers in the spring, you'll also see abundant olive groves and apple and cherry orchards; fruit picking is a popular tourist activity: cherries from mid-May through June and figs in August and September.

The region was once volcanic, and many symmetrical volcanic cones and pronounced reliefs dominate the landscape, particularly in the

CLOSE UP

The City of Pan

The name *Banias* is an Arabic corruption of the Greek *Panias* (Arabic has no *p*), the original name given to the area that, in the early 4th century BC, was dedicated to the colorful Greek god Pan, the half-goat, half-human deity of herdsmen, music, and wild nature—and of homosexuals and nymphs. The Banias Reserve encompasses the ruins of this ancient city.

Herod the Great ruled the city in the 1st century AD; his son Philip inherited it and changed the city's name to Caesarea Philippi, to distinguish it from the Caesarea his father had founded on the Mediterranean coast. The city continued to flourish until after the Muslim conquest in the 7th century AD, when it declined into little more than a village. In the 10th century AD, Muslim immigration brought renewed settlement and Jews also came to Banias (as it became known sometime during the 7th century).

In the early 12th century, Crusaders held Banias, who saw it as a natural border between their kingdom and the neighboring Muslim realm, whose center was Damascus. The Muslims recaptured Banias in 1132, but the city declined in importance and was taken over by Bedouin chieftains. It became a small village, which it remained until the Israel Defense Forces (IDF) conquered the area in the 1967 Six Days' War and its inhabitants abandoned it.

Upper Golan. The gentle terrain and climate of the rest of the region have historically attracted far more settlement than the less hospitable northern Upper Galilee. Today it's home to Jewish, Druze, and Alawite communities.

You can explore the area by joining a guided tour, perhaps galloping away on a horse or zipping by in a four-wheel-drive vehicle.

HERMON RIVER (BANIAS) NATURE RESERVE

20 km (12½ mi) east of Kiryat Shmona, 50 km (31 mi) northeast of Tzfat.

GETTING HERE AND AROUND

From Tzfat, head east on Route 89, then turn north on Route 90. Once you pass Kiryat Shmona, go east on Route 99.

EXPLORING

★ **Hermon River (Banias) Nature Reserve.** One of the most stunning parts of Israel, this reserve contains gushing waterfalls, dense foliage along riverbanks, and the remains of a temple dedicated to the god Pan. There are two entrances, each with a parking lot: the sign for the first reads Banias Waterfall; the other is 1 km (½ mi) farther along the same road and is marked Banias.

The **Banias Spring** emerges at the foot of mostly limestone Mt. Hermon, just where it meets the basalt layers of the Golan Heights. The most popular short route in the reserve is up to the **Banias Cave,** via the path that crosses the spring. Excavations have revealed the five niches hewed out of the rock to the right of the cave; these are what remain of Hellenistic and Roman temples, depicted in interesting artist's renderings. Three of the niches bear inscriptions in Greek, mentioning Pan, the lover of tunes, Echo, the mountain nymph, and Galerius, one of Pan's priests. All early references to the cave identify it as the source of the spring, but earthquakes over the years have changed the landscape, and the water now emerges at the foot of the cave rather than from within it.

The Banias Reserve offers three interconnected hiking trails—ask for the English-language trail map and advice at the cashier's booth. One, which passes a Crusader gate, walls, and moat, takes about 45 minutes. The second, also about 45 minutes, explores the magnificent 1,613-square-foot palace complex dating to the reign of Herod's grandson, Agrippa II, on top of which are the ruins of what is thought to have been the marketplace of the day: a string of single chambers along a well-preserved section of wall might well have been shops. The third is a 90-minute trail leading past the **Officers' Pool,** built by the Syrians, and a water-operated flour mill, to the thundering 33-meter-high **Banias Waterfall.** The trails are spiced with the pungent aroma of mint and figs, and studded with blackberry bushes. If time is short, you may prefer to take a brief walk to the falls, return to your car, then drive on to the second entrance to see the caves and the spring where the Hermon River originates. The cost of admission covers entry to both sites.

If you're ready for a real hiking challenge and can have a car waiting at the other end, a long, very steep trail leads from the parking lot at the Banias Nature Reserve through the oak and thorny broom forest up to Nimrod's Fortress, a 40- to 60-minute climb. ✉ *Off Rte. 99* ☎ *04/695–0272* 🎫 *NIS 23* ⏲ *Apr.–Sept., Sat.–Thurs. 8–5, Fri. 8–4; Oct.–Mar., Sat.–Thurs. 8–4, Fri. 8–3; last entrance 1 hr before closing.*

NEED A BREAK?

A few minutes' walk along the trail leading to the waterfall is the ancient flour mill and a stall where Druze villagers make their traditional pita (bigger and flatter than the commercial version), which is not only baked on the premises but also milled here. Pull up a rock, and for a few shekels you'll be served a large rolled-up pita with *labane* (white goat's cheese) and Turkish coffee.

NIMROD'S FORTRESS

5 km (3 mi) east of Hermon River (Banias) Nature Reserve, 58 km (36 mi) northeast Tzfat.

GETTING HERE AND AROUND

From Tzfat, head east on Route 89, then turn north on Route 90. Once you pass Kiryat Shmona, go east on Route 99. Once you pass the Hermon River Nature Reserve, turn north on Route 989. The fortress is on the left.

EXPLORING

★  **Nimrod's Fortress.** The dramatic views of this towering, burly fortress perched above Banias, appearing and disappearing behind each curve of the narrow road that leads to it, are part of the treat of a visit to Nimrod's Fortress (Kal'at Namrud). And once you're there, the fortress commands superb vistas, especially through the frames of its arched windows and the narrow archers' slits in its walls.

In 1218 the Mameluke warlord al-Malik al-Aziz Othman built this fortress to guard the vital route from Damascus via the Golan and Banias, to Lebanon and to the Mediterranean coast, against a Crusader *reconquista* after their 1187 defeat. It changed hands between Muslims and Christians in the succeeding centuries, as both vied for control of the region. During one of its more interesting periods, from 1126 to 1129, a fanatic sect of Muslims infamous for their murderous violence occupied Nimrod's Fortress. Before heading out to track down their enemies, the cutthroats are said to have indulged in hashish, thus earning the nickname *hashashin* (hashish users), from which the word *assassin* is derived.

Nimrod's Fortress is a highlight for kids, with a ladder down to a vaulted cistern, a shadowy spiral staircase, and unexpected nooks and crannies. A path leads up to the fortress's central tower, or keep, where the feudal lord would have lived. ✉ *Nimrod's Fortress National Park, Rte. 989* ☎ *04/694–9277* 💰 *NIS 20* ⏲ *Apr.–Sept., daily 8–5; Oct.–Mar. 8–4; last entrance 1 hr before closing.*

MT. HERMON

12 km (7½ mi) northeast of Nimrod's Fortress, 25 km (15½ mi) northeast of Kiryat Shmona, 66 km (41 mi) northeast of Tzfat.

GETTING HERE AND AROUND

From Tzfat, head east on Route 89, then turn north on Route 90. Once you pass Kiryat Shmona, go east on Route 99. At Mahanayim Junction turn east on Route 91, then north on Route 98.

EXPLORING

The summit of **Mt. Hermon**—famous as Israel's highest mountain, at 9,230 feet above sea level—is actually in Syrian territory. Its lower slopes attract Israelis to the country's only ski resort. Summer is arguably the most interesting time on the Hermon, though: after the winter snows melt, hikers can discover chasms and hidden valleys here, the long-term result of extremes in temperature. A powerful array of colors and scents emerges from the earth as the summer sun draws out cockscomb, chamomile, and scores of other flowers and wild herbs. Approaching from Nimrod's Fortress, you'll pass **Moshav Neve Ativ,** designed to look like a little piece of the Alps in the Middle East, complete with A-frame chalet-style houses, a handful of which have guest rooms. A detour through the old Druze village of **Majdal Shams** offers a number of good eateries.

SKIING

The slopes of **Mt. Hermon** (☎ *04/698–1337* 🌐 *www.skihermon.co.il*) have little to offer the serious, or even the novice, skier. There is a chairlift to the top, year-round—NIS 38 for entrance and the lift—the better to enjoy the place in summer, when it's bursting with wildflowers. A track sled that spirals down a 950-yard course is another attraction. To get to Mt. Hermon, take Route 99 east to Route 989 north to Neve Ativ.

WORD OF MOUTH

"The road to Nimrod's Fortress was steep and winding. Surprises were everywhere—an underground cistern, a spiral stairway that descended into darkness, and underground passages. The ancient fortress gave spectacular views of the valleys below." —photo by Keith_Marks, a Fodors.com member

Israel's highest mountain—Mt. Hermon, at 9,230 feet—gets plenty of snow in winter and spring.

Ein Kiniya, which appears across a valley on your left as you head east into the Golan on Route 99, is the most picturesque of the several Druze villages around here. The houses are built of the black basalt typical of the Golan.

MAJDAL SHAMS

Majdal Shams may not look like much, but the Druze town is a hub for skiers in the winter and berry pickers in the fall. It's also a year-round destination for wine lovers because of the local vineyards, and foodies, as Druze cuisine is renowned in the region.

Unlike their counterparts in the Galilee, the Druze of the Golan Heights are not, for the most part, Israeli citizens. They do, however, consider themselves an important part of the country's cultural landscape.

GETTING HERE AND AROUND

From Kiryat Shmona, head east on Route 99, then turn north at Masadeh onto Route 98, which will take you directly into Majdal Shams. The streets aren't signed, so it's a good idea to call ahead for directions to your hotel.

EXPLORING

Odem Mountain Winery (✉ *Moshav Odem* ☎ *04/687–1122* 🌐 *www.harodem.co.il*), a family-owned boutique winery located between Majdal Shams and Merom Golan, produced its first harvest in 2003. In 2010 it produced 70,000 bottles, mostly dry reds but also a crisp Chardonnay. The 30-minute tours of the vineyards are available by appointment throughout the year.

A nice complement to the Odem Winery, **De Karina Artisan Gourmet Chocolates** (✉ *Kibbutz Ein Zivan, Golan Heights,* ☎ *04/699–3622* 🌐 *www.de-karina.co.il* 🎫 *22 NIS, workshops 45-59 NIS* ⏲ *Open, Sun.–Thurs. 9–5, Fri. 9–3*) was founded by a third-generation chocolatier from Argentina. In addition to a heavenly chocolate shop, there are factory tours and chocolate-making workshops. Try the "Mt. Hermon Chocolates"—milk chocolate cones topped by white chocolate "snow." All tours and workshops are by advance arrangement only.

WHERE TO EAT AND STAY

$$$ ECLECTIC ✕ **The Milkman and the Witch.** Located in Nimrod, a short drive from Majdal Shams, this whimsical restaurant is decorated with smiling witch dolls and boasts a magnificent view of volcanic lakes and cherry fields. The staff is attentive and friendly, and the food is hearty. The chef specializes in casseroles, such as salmon cooked with coconut milk, ginger, and oranges. Another tasty dish is the lamb simmered in white wine and served with root vegetables. ✉ *Nimrod Tzafon* ☎ *04/687–0049* 🌐 *www.witch.co.il* ⏲ *AE, MC, V.*

$ ECLECTIC ✕ **Undefined.** Named for the nationality most local Druze have listed on their documents, this eatery adds a touch of sophistication to this small town. It serves a mix of Asian and Italian dishes; try the tasty whole eggplant stuffed with tahini, or one of the succulent steaks. ✉ *Main road* ☎ *050/764–1699* ✍ *Reservations required* ⏲ *AE, MC, V.*

$ 🏨 **Toskana in the Hermon.** Owner Shoky Ayob has channeled the spirit of Italy in his beautiful bed-and-breakfast. The castlelike exterior is faced with golden-hued Jerusalem stone, while the interior is bathed in soothing browns, tans, and maroons. Since the same rate applies to all rooms, ask for one with a balcony view of either Majdal Shams or Mt. Hermon and Syria. During the summer, your room includes free admission for fruit picking at a nearby cherry farm. **Pros:** lovely accommodations; bargain price. **Cons:** no elevator; no pool. ✉ *Masadeh* ☎ *050/752–8623* 🌐 *www.toskana.co.il* 🛏 *9 rooms* 👍 *In-room: a/c, kitchen. In-hotel: laundry service* 💳 *AE, DC, MC, V.*

SPORTS AND THE OUTDOORS

At **Buggy B'Hermon** (☎ *050/520–0222* 🌐 *www.buggyhermon.co.il*), Saleh Nakleh and his staff offer rides around the Golan in all-terrain vehicles. There's also guided hiking, berry picking, and (for groups of eight or more) sumptuous traditional Druze meals cooked by his wife and served on the deck of the cabin high in their cherry fields.

MEROM GOLAN

20 km (12½ mi) south of Mt. Hermon, 46 km (28 mi) northeast of Tzfat.

Kibbutz Merom Golan was the first settlement built in the Golan after the Six Days' War. Its fields and orchards are typical of local kibbutzim. Apples and cherries are especially good in these parts. Another popular attraction is the nearby Mt. Bental Observatory.

7

GETTING HERE AND AROUND

From Tzfat, head east on Route 89, then north on Route 90. At Mahanayim Junction turn east on Route 91, then north on Route 98. Merom Golan is on the left.

Mt. Bental Observatory. From the top of this volcanic cone, once a military outpost, Mt. Hermon rises majestically to the north and the Syrian side of the Golan stretches eastward as if it's on the palm of your hand. Opposite is the ruined town of Kuneitra, captured by Israel in 1967, lost and regained in the 1973 Yom Kippur War, and returned to Syria in the subsequent disengagement agreement—it is now a demilitarized zone. Modern Kuneitra is in the distance. The cluster of white buildings south of old Kuneitra houses the United Nations Disengagement Observer Force. A pine-cabin shop serving delicious herb teas and snacks is the perfect place to get out of the wind that often sweeps this peak. The observatory is near Kibbutz Merom Golan; from Rte. 98 or Rte. 959, follow the signs along the rural roads to the observatory—it's between the geological park and the airstrip. ✉ *Off Rte. 98 and the "Fruit Path".*

WHERE TO EAT

$$ STEAK ✕ **Cowboys' Restaurant.** This is the best corral this side of the Israel-Syria disengagement zone. Saddle-shape stools at the bar and cattle hides on the walls contribute to the frontier atmosphere. But it's the grub—specifically the hearty steaks and the house specialty, chicken breast stuffed with smoked meat—that packs 'em in. ✉ *Kibbutz Merom Golan, off Rte. 959* ☎ *04/696–0206* ▭ *AE, DC, MC, V.*

KATZRIN

20 km (12½ mi) south of Merom Golan, 38 km (23½ mi) northeast of Tiberias, 35 km (22 mi) northeast of Tzfat.

Katzrin, founded in 1977 near the site of a 3rd-century town of the same name, has a suburban feel, despite its strategic location and attendant sensitivity. The water here, which comes straight from the basalt bedrock, is delicious and makes your skin feel like silk.

GETTING HERE AND AROUND

From Tzfat, head east on Route 89, then north on Route 90. At Mahanayim Junction turn east on Route 91, then south on Route 9088.

ESSENTIALS

Visitor Information **Kessem HaGolan Visitor Center** (✉ *Rte. 9088* ☎ *04/696–3625*).

EXPLORING

The **Golan Archaeological Museum** has a fascinating collection of animal bones, stones, and artifacts that put the region into historical and geographical perspective. Among the exhibits is a Bronze Age dwelling reconstructed from materials excavated nearby. Don't miss the moving film on the history and last stand of Gamla, the "Masada of the North," during the Great Revolt against the Romans (AD 66) and its rediscovery by archaeologists 1,900 years later. The museum is run in conjunction with the Ancient Katzrin Park. ✉ *Katzrin commercial center, near the corner of Shayon and Daliyot streets* ☎ *04/696–1350* 🌐 *www.museum.*

The ancient ruins of the synagogue at Gamla are surrounded by rolling green hills and rocky terrain.

golan.org.il *NIS 24, includes Ancient Katzrin Park* *Sept.–May, Sun.–Thurs. 9–4, Fri. 9–2; June–Aug., Sun.–Thurs. 9–6, Fri. 9–4.*

Ancient Katzrin Park, 2 km (1 mi) east of downtown Katzrin, is a partially restored 3rd-century Jewish village. The Katzrin synagogue has decorative architectural details, such as a wreath of pomegranates and amphorae in relief on the lintel above the entrance. The complexity of its ornamentation reflects the importance of the city. Built of basalt, the synagogue was used for 400 years until it was partly destroyed, possibly by an earthquake, in AD 749. Two reconstructed buildings, the so-called House of Uzi and House of Rabbi Abun, are attractively decorated with rope baskets, weavings, baking vessels, and pottery (based on remnants of the originals), and lighted with little clay oil lamps. *Rte. 87* *04/696–2412* *www.museum.golan.org.il* *NIS 24, includes Golan Archaeological Museum* *Sept.–May, Sun.–Thurs. 9–4, Fri. 9–2; June–Aug., Sun.–Thurs. 9–6, Fri. 9–4, Sat. 10–4.*

The **Golan Heights Winery** caught the world's attention with its award-winning Yarden, Gamla, and Golan labels. The area's volcanic soil, cold winters, and cool summers, together with state-of-the-art winemaking, have proven a recipe for success. The shop sells the full line of wines, including the Katzrin Chardonnay, the Yarden Gewürtztraminer, and the Yarden Cabernet Sauvignon, as well as sophisticated accessories for the oenophile. Call ahead for tour information. *Rte. 87, 2km south of Katrin* *04/696–8435* *www.golanwines.co.il* *NIS 20* *Sun.–Thurs. 8–6:30, Fri. 8–2.*

WHERE TO EAT

The commercial center of Katzrin, the "capital" of the Golan Heights, has a number of falafel stands, a couple of restaurants, and a pizzeria, making it a perfect midday stop for travelers.

$ ISRAELI **Ochel Beiti.** This tiny and unassuming kosher eatery in the old commercial center may not look impressive, but the Yemenite flavors and aromas certainly are. The restaurant's name means "home cooking." Shalom, the owner, chief cook, and bottle washer, makes a hearty meat soup, served alongside fluffy pitas and tangy salsa. Middle Eastern salads, kebabs, and other local favorites are on offer. ✉ *Katzrin old commercial center, off Derech Hahermon and Daliyot streets* ☎ *04/696–2120* ▭ *No credit cards* ⊙ *Closed Sat.*

NIGHTLIFE

Within Katzrin Park, there's a **pub** (✉ *Off Derech Hahermon* ☎ *04/685–0449*) in a century-old Syrian dwelling, with a selection of 10 different beers on tap and a dairy menu. Having a drink among the ancient ruins is reason enough to make a detour if you're staying in the area.

GAMLA NATURE RESERVE

20 km (12 mi) southeast of Katzrin.

GETTING HERE AND AROUND

From Tzfat, head east on Route 89, then south on Route 90. Turn east on Route 87, then south on Route 808. Watch for Gamla signpost.

EXPLORING

Gamla Nature Reserve. Aside from the inspiring history of "the Masada of the North," the beauty of Gamla's rugged terrain, softened in spring by greenery and wildflowers, is truly breathtaking. Griffon vultures soar above and gazelles can often be seen bounding through the grasses. The main story of the camel-shaped Gamla (the name *Gamla* comes from *gamal,* the Hebrew word for "camel") goes back to the year AD 67, when at the beginning of the Great Revolt, Vespasian launched a bloody attack here that ended seven months later, when the 9,000 surviving Jews flung themselves to their deaths in the abyss below the town. The vivid descriptions of the battle, as written by Flavius Josephus in *The Jewish War,* are engraved in stones along the trail site: "Built against the almost vertical flank, the town seemed to be hung in the air"—exactly the impression visitors still have as they approach the site.

Because Gamla was never rebuilt, the relics of the battlefield still eerily match the ancient sources, among them the fortifications, 2,000 "missile stones," and a large number of arrowheads. From a much earlier period (probably the 2nd millennium BC), there are about 200 **dolmens** scattered in the area—strange basalt structures shaped like the Greek letter "pi," probably used for burial. There is an excellent film on the story of Gamla at the Golan Archaeological Museum in Katzrin. ✉ *Off Rte. 808* ☎ *04/682–2282* 🎫 *NIS 25* ⊙ *Apr.–Sept. daily 8–5, Oct.–Mar. 8–4. Last entry one hour before closing.*

8

Eilat and the Negev

WITH A SIDE TRIP TO PETRA

WORD OF MOUTH

"Sde Boker is a kibbutz in the Negev Desert. Most famously known for being the final resting place of David Ben-Gurion, Israel's first prime minister. Hiking trails leading into the desert begin here, and, sometimes, nature blesses you with a chance encounter."

—photo by Keith_Marks, a Fodors.com member

WELCOME TO EILAT AND THE NEGEV

TOP REASONS TO GO

★ **Coral Reserve, Eilat:** Put on a snorkel, and marvel at the brilliant-colored fish and entrancing corals at one of the world's finest protected coral reefs.

★ **Hiking the desert:** Explore the splendid scenery, deep wadis, rugged heights, and steep cliff faces of the Negev. The mountains of Eilat and the desert craters offer spectacular hikes.

★ **Makhtesh Ramon:** This giant crater is an utterly unique geological phenomenon, with hundreds of rock formations and multihued cliffs.

★ **Side trip to Petra:** Just over the border in Jordan, Petra's awe-inspiring Treasury (the Khazneh), carved into a rose-red cliff, is one of many archeological treats at this UNESCO World Heritage site.

★ **Timna Park:** Trek across the lunarlike landscape, making sure to see this desert park's famous red-hued Solomon's Pillars and its 20-foot mushroom-shaped rock formation.

Solomon's Pillars, Timna Park

1 Eilat and Environs. Sun-drenched Eilat, a resort town on the shores of the Red Sea, brims with luxury hotels, restaurants, duty-free shopping, and the Negev's only nightlife. It's just south of Timna Park, which is not to be missed.

2 The Heart of the Negev. In the very center of the upside-down triangle that makes up the Negev, you'll find several of the region's top sites, including Ben-Gurion's desert home and grave, as well as the ancient Nabatean city of Avdat.

3 Beersheva. The biblical city of Beersheva, a World Heritage Site, is Israel's fourth-largest city and makes a great jumping-off point for trips around the Negev.

Bedouin men in the Negev

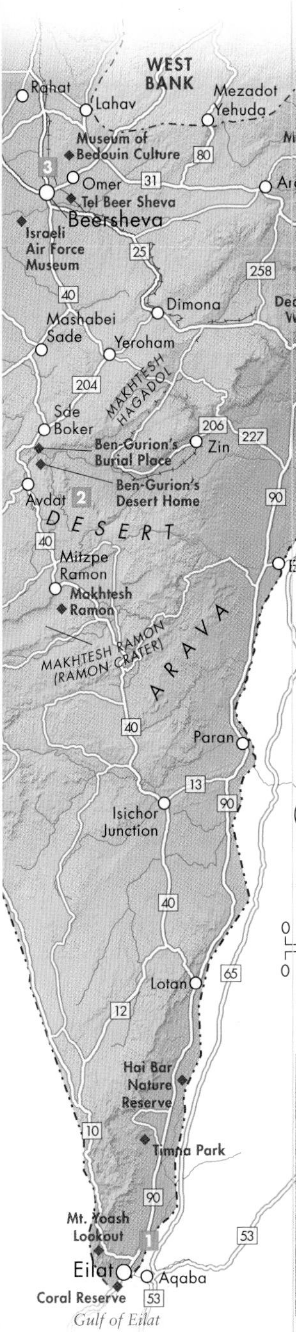

GETTING ORIENTED

There are three basic areas in the inverted triangle of the Negev, Israel's southern desert that make up the southern part of the country. The first, and farthest south, is carefree Eilat, with the Underwater Observatory at Coral Beach, and Timna Park. Eilat is also a convenient jumping-off point for a trip to Jordan and the splendid ruins of the ancient city of Petra. Next is the Negev's heart, with sites such as Ben-Gurion's desert home and grave, the ancient Nabatean-Roman-Byzantine ruins at Tel Avdat, and the amazing Makhtesh Ramon (Ramon Crater). The third, in the north, includes the capital city of Beersheva.

Bird—watching in the Sde Boker desert

Petra

EILAT AND THE NEGEV PLANNER

When to Go

October through May is the best time to explore the Negev. In early March, scarlet, bright yellow, white, and hot pink desert flowers burst out against the brown desert earth; March is also when Eilat's International Bird-watchers' Festival takes place. In January and February it's dry and cold, especially at night. Scorching-hot conditions prevail in the summer, from June through September (though it's very dry).

Desert Precautions

To remain comfortable and safe, respect certain rules of the desert. Drink two quarts of water a day in winter, and one quart per hour in summer. Keep a jerrican (which holds five gallons) of water in your car, plus extra bottles. Water fountains found along the way don't always work. Flash floods pose an occasional danger from September through March, especially after rainfall farther north. If even a small amount of water is flowing across the road, wait for it to stop (it can take a while); it can be a sign of imminent flooding. Driving at night is not recommended; plan to reach your destination by 5 pm in winter and by 8 pm in summer.

Getting Here and Around

Air Travel: Flights to Eilat take off from Ben Gurion Airport (about halfway between Jerusalem and Tel Aviv), Sde Dov Airport in north Tel Aviv, and Haifa Airport. Two domestic airlines serve Eilat: Arkia (☎ *09/8644444* 🌐 *www.arkia.com)* and Israir (☎ *03/7954038* 🌐 *www.israirairlines.com)*. In Eilat, the airport is actually in the middle of the city. From there, it's about a five-minute cab ride to hotels and a ten-minute walk to the center of town.

Bus Travel: The national bus company, Egged (☎ *03/694-8888 or *2800* 🌐 *www.egged.co.il*) provides frequent bus service to Beersheva from Tel Aviv and Jerusalem; each takes about 1½ hours. Buses run from Tel Aviv to Eilat at least four times a day and twice at night and take 4½ to 5 hours. Service from Jerusalem to Eilat takes about 4½ hours. You can reserve Eilat bus tickets up to two weeks in advance, recommended for weekend travel. Within Eilat, Bus 15 starts at the Central Bus Station (entrance to town) and runs through the hotel area to pick up passengers and take them to points south.

Car Travel: The only way to see the Negev Desert comfortably and efficiently is to drive (air-conditioning in summer is a must). Beersheva is 113 km (70 mi) southeast of Tel Aviv and 83 km (52 mi) south of Jerusalem. To get to Eilat from Tel Aviv, the most direct way is Route 40 south to Beersheva, which takes about five hours.

Taxi Travel: In Eilat, the preferred way of hopping from one place to another is by taxi. Rides don't usually cost much more than NIS 35, and you can hail a cab on the street.

Train Travel: Israel Railways provides service only between Tel Aviv and Beersheva. There's frequent service (except on Saturday, when just two trains run, and both late in the evening) from the north to Beersheva all day; the trip takes 1½ hours.

For more information on getting here and around, see Travel Smart Israel.

Visitor Information

Hours vary at the region's tourist information offices and visitor centers—so phone ahead. In Eilat, pick up the useful "Events in Eilat" brochure from the tourist information office.

Tours

Eilat Friendly Tours books excursions and offers guide service in and around Eilat. *For tour operators for outdoor activities in Eilat, check the listings in the Sports and the Outdoors section of Eilat.*

Eilat Friendly Tours (🌐 *friendlytours-online.com*).

Dining and Lodging

Although Eilat is nestled at the southern tip of a desert, there are all sorts of cuisines to choose from when you're dining out: Italian, Indian, French, Argentinean, Yemenite, and Thai among them. There's excellent sea fish here, including delicacies such as *denise* (sea bream). In the rest of the Negev, with the notable exception of the Mitzpe Ramon Inn, plan to dine in humble surroundings—typically a roadside diner—on meals that are apt to reflect the cook's ethnic background.

Visitors who keep kosher should note that while most hotels serve kosher meals, few of the restaurants in Eilat are kosher, including chains with kosher branches elsewhere.

Hotels in sunny Eilat run from family-style to huge, lush, and luxurious. Pleasure comes first: business facilities on a modest scale are available in larger hotels, whereas a beautiful and luxurious spa with a wide range of facilities is an important feature of each large hotel. Even many of the smaller hotels have installed spas. In Eilat, a few hotels operate on an all-inclusive basis. High season is Hanukkah/Christmas, Passover/Easter, and July and August.

WHAT IT COSTS

	¢	$	$$	$$$	$$$$
Restaurants	under NIS 32	NIS 32–NIS 49	NIS 50–NIS 75	NIS 76–NIS 100	over NIS 100
Hotels	under $120	$120–$200	$201–$300	$301–$400	over $400

Restaurant prices are per person for a main course at dinner in NIS (Israeli shekels). Hotel prices are in U.S. dollars, for two people in a standard double room in high season. Non-Israeli citizens paying in foreign currency are exempt from the 16% VAT on hotel rooms.

Planning Your Time

As you drive along the Negev's scenic roads, you'll pass stretches of flat, uninhabited countryside under hot, blue skies, punctuated by the odd acacia tree, twisting wadi, or craggy mountain. In winter delicate desert flowers decorate the landscape. If you want to skip the desert-driving experience, you might limit your trip to Eilat. In Eilat you can stay at a luxurious hotel, relax on the sunny shore, take a cruise on the bay, visit the underwater observatory, and dive or snorkel amid the coral reefs.

Most Negev sites open at 8:30 am and close by 4 pm in winter and 5 pm in summer. Keep in mind that outside Eilat, restaurants close early on Friday for the Jewish Sabbath, and since the main meal of the day is served at noon in the desert, lunch may be history if you arrive after 1:30; roadside diners close at around 1:30 pm.

Updated by Benjamin Balint

With its stark mountains, dramatic wadis, the Nabatean city of Avdat, colorful Bedouin encampments, and the spectacular Ramon Crater, the Negev—a word meaning "dry" in Hebrew—is much more than simply "a desert." The Negev contains Israel's most dramatic natural scenery, with its rugged highlands, as well as Eilat, a resort town set on the Red Sea, with luxury hotels, hot restaurants and bars, and duty-free shopping.

The region also has an abundance of historical sites and ruins. You can visit the kibbutz home and grave of Israel's founding father and first prime minister—David Ben-Gurion, the man who first dreamed of settling the desert—and on the same day, you can tour the millennia-old ruins at Tel Beersheva, visited by the biblical patriarch Abraham. For those seeking adventure, the Negev is the place to take camel treks and Jeep tours, spend the afternoon hiking, or scuba dive in the Red Sea.

If all this isn't enough, the Negev offers the ideal base for a day trip or overnight visit to Petra in Jordan. The rose-red remains of this ancient city of the wealthy Nabateans, who controlled a spice route that stretched from Arabia to the Mediterranean, are carved into towering sandstone cliffs. Petra's gigantic monuments and royal tombs, 2,000 years old, are exceptional treasures, even in a region filled with antiquities.

The Negev makes up about half the country's land area, yet is home to only 8% of its population. The ancient Israelites had fortifications here, as did the Nabateans and the Romans after them. The region's first kibbutzim were established in the early 1940s, with new immigrants sent south after the War of Independence, in 1948. Two years later, people started trickling into Eilat, which was nothing but a few rickety huts. The desert itself was made to bloom, and the semiarid areas between Tel Aviv and Beersheva became fertile farmland. Today, agricultural settlements throughout the Negev make use of advanced irrigation to raise tomatoes, melons, olives, and dates that are exported to winter markets in Europe.

EILAT AND ENVIRONS

The Arava Plain comes to an abrupt end where it meets the Bay of Eilat, home to Israel's southernmost town: the sun-drenched resort of Eilat. The Gulf of Eilat gives way to the Red Sea, which lies between the Sinai Mountains to the west and Jordan's Edom Mountains to the east. The Jordanian port of Aqaba is directly across the bay—Eilat residents will eagerly point out the Jordanian royals' yacht and vacation villa—and to the southeast is Saudi Arabia. The Sinai Desert is just over the Egyptian border.

Most travelers fly into or whiz down to Eilat to flop down on its beaches and snorkel or scuba dive among its tropical reefs. But if you have time, explore the vast desert landscape to the north of Eilat. You'll find cliffs, canyons, and unique geological formations at Timna Park, and indigenous animals at Hai Bar Nature Reserve. Both make good side trips from Eilat; just leave time for a sunset stop at Mt. Yoash. Another option is to explore ancient Petra, over the border in Jordan.

EILAT

307 km (190 mi) south of Jerusalem, 356 km (221 mi) south of Tel Aviv.

A legend says that after the Creation, the angels painted the earth. When they got tired, they spilled their paints: the blue became the waters of Eilat, and the other colors became its fish and coral. Whether or not this is true, add to this rainbow of colors Eilat's year-round warm weather, its superb natural surroundings of sculptural red-orange mountains, and its prime location on the sparkling Red Sea—whose coral reefs attract divers from all over the world—and you've got a first-rate resort.

Eilat, a city of about 50,000, is now Israel's prototypical "sun-and-fun" destination, with some 12,000 hotel rooms, and its relaxed cadences depart from the usual Israeli bustle. But its strategic location as a crossroads between Asia and Africa has given it a long place in history. According to the Bible, the Children of Israel stopped here as they fled from Egypt into the Promised Land, and King Solomon kept his fleet in the area. Later, because of its position on a main trade and travel route, Eilat was conquered by every major power: the Romans, Byzantines, Arabs, Crusaders, Mamluks, Ottoman Turks, and, most recently, the British, whose isolated police station, called Umm Rash Rash (headquarters of their camel corps), was the first building in modern-day Eilat. When David Ben-Gurion visited in 1935, he envisioned an international port here, and in 1945 Shimon Peres, today president of Israel, led a camel trek to the area. "Shards of coral and beautiful large seashells are scattered on the shore," he reported. "A lone boat, its sail bent to the wind, delivers foodstuff from Aqaba to Umm Rash Rash. White-winged kingfishers pounce on their prey. A gulf with a natural port pleads for life."

The Israelis took the area in March 1949, the last action of the War of Independence. The modern town was founded in 1951 and developed as a port in 1956 after the Egyptian blockade of the Tiran Straits was lifted.

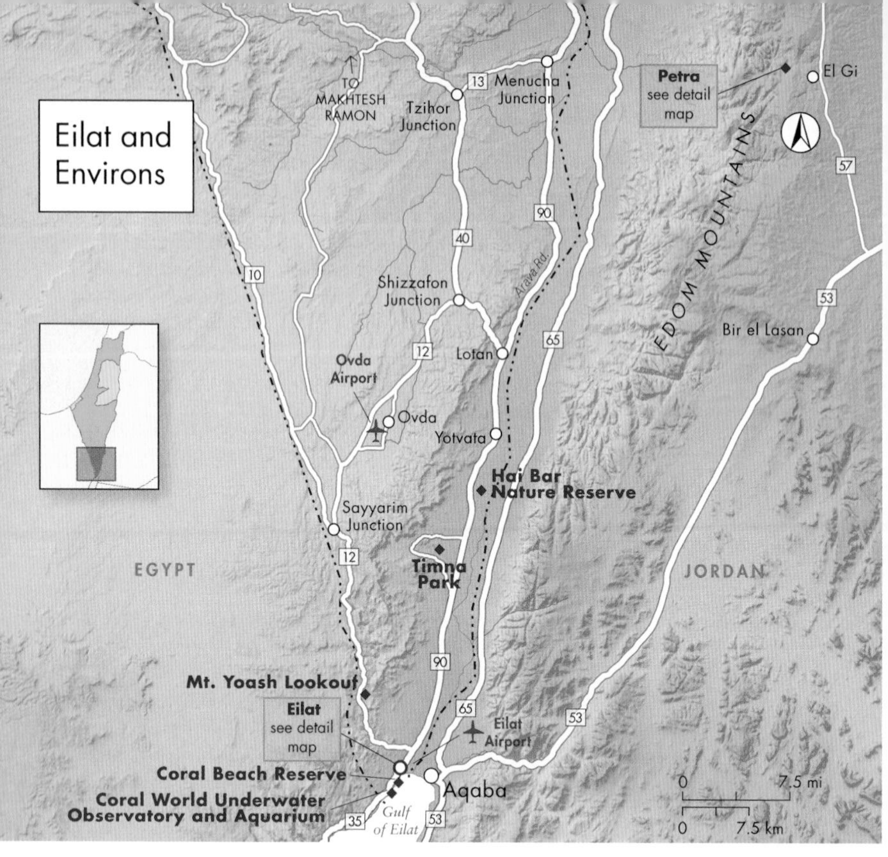

Most travelers are persuaded that Eilat's natural assets more than make up for its undistinguished architecture and overdevelopment. For wherever you are in Eilat, a glance eastward presents you with the dramatic sight of the granite mountain range of Edom, whose shades of red intensify toward evening, culminating in a crimson sunset blaze over the Red Sea. This incongruous name for a body of water that's brilliantly turquoise along the shore is the result of a 17th-century typographical error by an English printer: in setting the type for an English translation of a Latin version of the Bible, the printer left out an "e" and thus "Reed Sea" became "Red Sea." The name was easily accepted because of the sea's red appearance at sunset.

GETTING HERE AND AROUND

The most direct way to Eilat from both Tel Aviv and Jerusalem is via Beersheva. From Tel Aviv, Route 40 south runs directly to Beersheva. To reach Beersheva from Jerusalem, take Route 1 west to the Route 6 turnoff. Follow Route 6 southbound; after Kiryat Gat it turns into Route 40 south, which leads into Beersheva. Leave Beersheva via Route 25 (marked "Dimona—Eilat"), driving 69 km (43 mi) to the Arava Junction. Turn right (south) onto Route 90 (Arava Road), and travel straight to Eilat. The trip takes about five hours. For bus travel between Eilat,

Tel Aviv, Jerusalem, and points in between, the national bus company, Egged, provides widespread service.

VISITOR INFORMATION

Eilat Tourist Information Office (✉ *Arava Road, corner of Yotam Blvd., across from Mull Yam shopping center* ☎ *08/637–2111* ⏲ *Sun.–Thurs. 8–6, Fri. and Jewish holiday eves 8–2*).

Eilat Central Bus Station (✉ *Ha-Tmarim Blvd. 12, next to Shalom Mall*).

EXPLORING

Start exploring Eilat with a walk along the seaside **promenade,** beginning at Herod's Hotel, near the Jordanian border. The 3-km (2-mi) promenade is also known as the Peace Walk, since it is hoped that one day it will continue to Aqaba, Jordan. Purple and pink bougainvillea pour down from the Royal Beach Hotel's terrace above; add to your enjoyment by stopping for an ice cream from one of the stands. If you're here at sunset, sit and savor the show-stopping view of the Red Sea turning red, with the dark, reddish-gray shapes of the Edom Mountains to the east and the rugged Eilat Mountains to the west. On a clear day, you can see as far as Saudi Arabia and Egypt.

A stroll past swanky hotels and loads of shops, coffee bars, and restaurants, with palm-lined beaches on the other side, brings you to the Dutch Bridge, which opens for tall-masted vessels. On one side is the lagoon, or inner marina, where yachts are anchored and various small craft are for hire; on the other is the marina, where cruise boats of all types wait to sally forth. The promenade winds along beside more beaches, covered with sunbathers. The scene includes sophisticated strollers, the backpack crowd, artists doing quick portraits, vendors selling earrings, and tattoo artists, all accompanied by strolling street performers. At the intersection of Durban and Arava streets (at the roundabout), you can continue along the waterfront, with the Mul Yam shopping mall all on your right, until you reach a small palm-filled plaza with a tiny, cement block–shaped building with a statue of four fighters raising a comrade aloft while a flag "flies" above. This is Umm Rash Rash, where the Israelis first took control of the Gulf of Eilat in March 1949, as determined by the United Nation's partition plan. The small building—the only one that existed then—is a far cry from today's luxury resorts.

NEED A BREAK?

At the western end of the promenade, at the Mul Yam shopping mall (identified by the seahorse over its entrance), is an outdoor café that feeds the crowd with ice cream, sweet drinks, and good coffee. Locals turn out in force here to sip, chat, and watch the tourists go by.

★ **Coral World Underwater Observatory and Aquarium.** One of Eilat's star attractions can be recognized by its tall space-needle structure punctuating the waves just offshore. Located 8 km (5 mi) south of the city center, this is the largest aquarium complex in the Middle East. Plan to spend several hours here (there's a cafeteria for lunch on the premises). The **Aquarium's** 12 windows provide views of rare fish so magnificent and so Day-Glo colorful that it's hard to believe they're real; there's an unlighted room where phosphorescent fish and other sea creatures glow in the dark. And there are turtle and stingray pools, too. Don't miss feeding time (11 am daily) in the 650,000-liter **Shark Pool.** The anaconda snakes, poisonous frogs, and piranha are fed in the **Amazonas** exhibit at 3 pm. Captain Jaws takes you on a sea journey during an audiovisual show presented in a simulated-motion theater with moving seats at the **Oceanarium.**

WORD OF MOUTH

"Eilat is really nice in the winter when it's very cold elsewhere. I would not miss Eilat, and you could visit the coral beach . . . and Kings City—a new biblical theme park."—danharris76

A 300-foot wooden bridge leads to the **Underwater Observatory.** Head down the spiral staircase and into the sea—you are now 15 feet underwater, where two round, glass-windowed halls, connected by a tunnel, offer stunning views of the surrounding coral reef, home to exotic tropical fish. The **Observatory Tower**—reached by stairs—gives coastal views of Israel's neighboring countries. There's a café up here. You can also take a ride on a glass-bottom boat, or on a 100-ton yellow submarine that dives to 60 meters. Bus 15 runs to and from downtown Eilat every half hour. ✉ *Rte. 90 (Eilat–Taba Rd.)* ☎ *08/636–4200* 🌐 *www.coralworld.com/eilat* 🎫 *NIS 79, NIS 89 including Oceanarium* ⏲ *Sat.–Thurs. 8:30–5, Fri. and Jewish holiday eves 8:30–4.*

Kings City. This gigantic fairy-tale castle looms behind the hotels on the northern beach. Kings City, a biblical theme park on three levels, offers three distinct sections of sophisticated entertainment, and there's a high-flying water ride to boot. The **Cave of Illusions** has, among other interactive diversions, hands-on games that test your mental acuity, a jail to test your ability to escape, a huge maze, and a large, endless kaleidoscope. Next, you reach the **Bible Cave** in an elevator that descends almost 200 feet underground to an immense cavern where humanlike robots reenact Bible stories about King Solomon and other tales. In the **Journey to the Past** you see 3-D films of pharaohs in ancient Egypt, and then there's the thrilling 10-minute waterfall ride that ends in a huge splash (you're in a boat). **David's Spiral** includes two slides, one of them 150 feet long. There's a kid-friendly restaurant, a café, a bar, and a gift shop, too. You'll need three to four hours to do this park justice. It's located at the end of the promenade, next to the eastern lagoon. Note that children less than 1 meter tall (about 3 feet) are not admitted, and the park is handicapped accessible. ✉ *East Lagoon, next to Herod's Hotel* ☎ *08/630–4444* 🌐 *www.kingscity.co.il* 🎫 *NIS 118* ⏲ *Sun.–Thurs. 9–10, Fri. 9–three hours before Shabbat.*

★ **Coral Beach Reserve.** Less than 1 km (½ mi) south of Eilat, this is one of the finest and most densely populated coral reefs in the world. Close to the shoreline, the reef is 1¼ km (¾ mi) long and is zealously guarded by the Israel Nature and Parks Authority. The most northern reef in the world, it contains over 100 types of coral and 650 species of fish. In the lagoon, divers and snorkelers take two bridges, or a trail marked by buoys, to get to the reef wall. Stunning multicolored fish and soft and hard corals are your rich reward. There are hot showers, snorkel rental, and a snack bar on the premises. Kids should be over five to

The Red Sea, just off the coast of Eilat, offers spectacular snorkeling and scuba diving.

snorkel—younger ones can fool around on the beach. ✉ *Rte. 90 (Eilat–Taba Rd.) opposite the Eilat Field School* ☎ *08/637–6829* 🌐 *www.parks.org.il* 🎫 *NIS 30* ⏲ *April–September 9–6; October–March 9– 5.* 8

WHERE TO EAT

Eilat has so many restaurants that you can easily dine on a different cuisine each night over a long holiday. Savor the finest local seafood and fresh fish; charcoal-grilled meats of every kind; or Chinese, Indian, Thai, and Italian cuisine and other ethnic meals, reflecting Israel's many waves of immigration. Many restaurants offer outdoor seating, often near the water or amid pots of pink bougainvillea. Outdoor cafés serve café *hafuch* (strong coffee with a frothy, hot-milk topping) and light food, such as cheese toast (grilled-cheese sandwiches) and salads, as well as rich cakes, ice cream, iced drinks, and various other coffee concoctions.

$$$ ECLECTIC ✕ **Eddie's Hideaway.** As the name suggests, Eddie's is slightly hard to find and not within walking distance of the hotel strip. The affable Eddie ("I consider each guest a visitor in my own home—a friend," he says) prepares straightforward but delicious food, which makes it easy to understand why his restaurant—one of the oldest in Eilat—is worth seeking out and earns such stellar reviews, especially for its delicious steaks. Devotees also appreciate the shrimp and fish dishes. Savor the filet Dijon (filet mignon graced with mustard and brown sugar), the schnitzel cordon bleu, or Shanghai fish with hot soybean paste. Inquire if Eddie has prepared a "daily"—a dish he particularly likes to cook. Note that on Saturday only lunch is served. ✉ *68 Almogim St. (enter from Elot St.)* ☎ *08/637–1137* ✍ *Reservations essential* 💳 *AE, DC, MC, V* ⏲ *Closed Sun. No lunch* ✥ *2A.*

$$ ASIAN ✕ **Ginger Asian Kitchen and Bar.** A duo of Thai chefs presents an Asian fusion and sushi cuisine of delicate spiciness at this spiffy New York look-alike. It's small, but the menu's huge. Recessed lighting contributes to the chic vibe, as do the off-white walls and black leather chairs. Start with plump *kioza* dumplings stuffed with chicken, goose, and vegetables or shrimp tempura on avocado with miso sauce, then try the Jakarta (chicken or beef with eggplant and zucchini with an Indonesian sweet sauce) or exotica (chicken or seafood dressed with coconut milk and chili paste and scattered with basil leaves). Finish off with an almond and butter pastry, topped with caramelized bananas and ginger parfait. A lighter bar menu is served from midnight until 3 am Thursday to Sunday night. ✉ *Yotam St. across from the Imax* ☎ *08/637–2517* 🌐 *www.gingereilat.com* ✍ *Reservations recommended* ▭ *AE, DC, MC, V* ✣ *3A.*

$$$$ ITALIAN ✕ **La Cucina.** Right here on the North Beach Promenade, you'll find a little slice of Tuscany at this restaurant with arched wooden windows, paintings of Italian cities, a fireplace, and bougainvillea spilling over the outdoor terrace. If you love thin-crust pizza, try Cucina's, which is crunchy as a cracker and especially delicious when topped with seafood. Other good bets are fried spinach ravioli with ricotta cheese, and peppered fillet of beef medallions in a cream and Gorgonzola sauce. Passion-fruit and forest-berry sherbet flavored with lemongrass makes a cool ending. ✉ *North Beach Promenade beneath the Royal Beach* ☎ *08/636–8932* ✍ *Reservations essential* ▭ *AE, DC, MC, V* ✣ *4D.*

$$ MOROCCAN ✕ **Lalo.** This lunch restaurant, one of the most established in Eilat, is a top-drawer example of Moroccan-Israeli ethnic cooking, by a mother-and-son team. Upon your arrival, five different salads (including cauliflower, tahini, eggplant, and hot peppers) are set quickly upon the table. The menu may confront you with foods you've never eaten before, but it rewards any adventuresome choices you make. Consider such delicacies as beef cooked with hummus (a house specialty); tongue; calves' brains served straight up with Moroccan spices; succulent couscous with vegetables, chickpeas, and tender chicken; and spicy-hot fish. No fancy pitas are served here—just plain bread. Dessert is specially prepared fruit, such as oranges cooked until thick and soft, accompanied by tea with mint. You might also try the homemade jams. ✉ *259 Horev St., Shkunat Alef* ☎ *08/633–0578* ▭ *AE, DC, MC, V* ⏲ *Sun.–Thurs. 2–5, closed Fri. and Sat. No dinner* ✣ *4B.*

$$$ SEAFOOD Fodor's Choice ★ ✕ **Last Refuge.** Locals hold this fish and seafood restaurant (known in Hebrew as Hamiflat Ha'acharon) in high regard and take their guests from "up north" here as a real treat. The dining room, with dark wood paneling and nautical motifs, spills onto a spacious balcony, where diners eat beside the water, looking at Jordan across the way. Presented with a flourish are fish or crab soups, freshly caught charcoal-grilled Red Sea fish, lobster (order in advance), jumbo shrimp, and creamed seafood served in a seashell. A Refuge specialty is stir-fried, small, spicy sea crabs, prepared in olive oil and garlic. Start with the *coquille* (shell) of seafood. Weekends tend to be extra busy, so it's smart to reserve several days ahead (and to ask for balcony seating). ✉ *Rte. 90, across from*

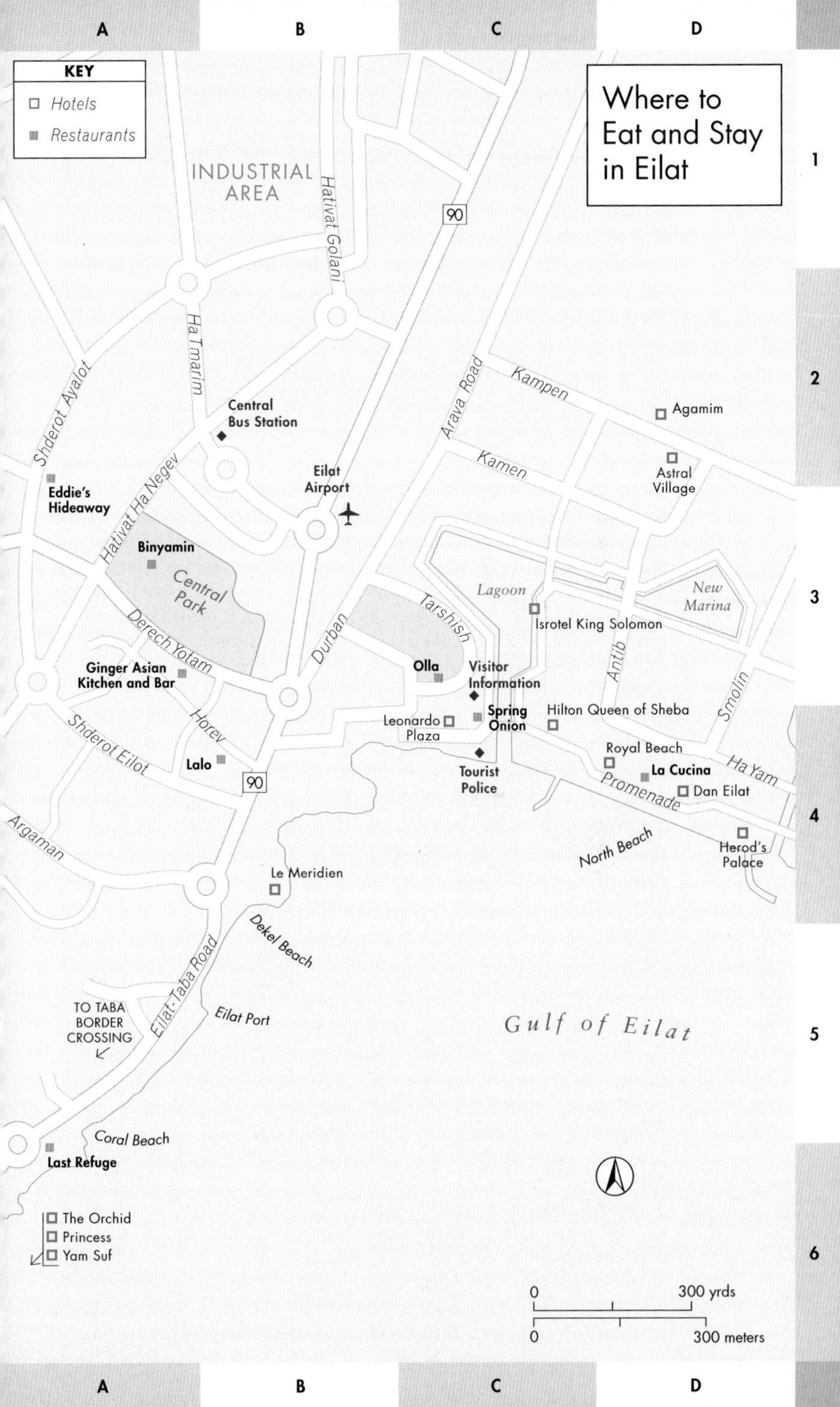

A
B
C
D
KEY
Hotels
Restaurants
Where to Eat and Stay in Eilat
1
2
3
4
5
6
INDUSTRIAL AREA
Hativat Golani
90
Ha Tmarim
Shderot Ayalot
Central Bus Station
Hativat Ha Negev
Eilat Airport
Eddie's Hideaway
Binyamin
Central Park
Arava Road
Kampen
Agamim
Kamen
Astral Village
Lagoon
New Marina
Isrotel King Solomon
Tarshish
Durban
Derech Yotam
Ginger Asian Kitchen and Bar
Olla
Visitor Information
Antib
Smolin
Leonardo Plaza
Spring Onion
Hilton Queen of Sheba
Horev
Shderot Eilot
Lalo
Tourist Police
Royal Beach
La Cucina
Ha Yam
Promenade
Dan Eilat
Argaman
North Beach
Herod's Palace
Le Meridien
Dekel Beach
Eilat-Taba Road
TO TABA BORDER CROSSING
Eilat Port
Gulf of Eilat
Coral Beach
Last Refuge
The Orchid
Princess
Yam Suf
0
300 yrds
0
300 meters
A
B
C
D

the Isrotel Yam Suf hotel, Coral Beach ☎ *08/637–3627* ♤ *Reservations essential* ▭ *AE, DC, MC, V* ✣ *5A.*

$$$ TAPAS ✕ **Olla.** Far and away the best tapas bar in Eilat, this restaurant has leather-backed booths and tastefully subdued lighting. The bar level, extraordinarily lively on weekends, offers some of the best bartending in the city. As for the tapas, try the goose-liver slices on caramelized apple with figs, the shrimp coated in *kadaif* (a honey-drizzled shredded phyllo pastry), and the mussels in cream with Roquefort cheese. Ask manager Dror Harush for special recommendations. Downstairs, and under the same management, is a new and enticing meat restaurant called Rak Bsarim where you can choose your cut of meat, butcher-style, or try the 300 gram (two-thirds of a pound) lamb ribs from the Golan or the foie gras marinated in red wine sauce with chili pepper confiture. ✉ *Tarshish 17, Bell Hotel* ☎ *08/632–5566* ⊕ *www.olla-tapas.co.il* ♤ *Reservations essential* ▭ *AE, DC, MC, V* ✣ *3C.*

$$ VEGETARIAN ✕ **Spring Onion.** Vegetarians, front and center! Diners come to this two-story restaurant (called Batzal Yarok in Hebrew) for the city's largest selection of garden-fresh salads with interesting toppings, as well as delicately cooked vegetable quiches, fresh fish, sushi, blintzes, and wonderfully authentic pizzas. Noodles tossed with vegetables in ginger and soy sauce make an appetizing dish. They also serve cheese toast—try the one with Bulgarian cheese, olive oil, and black olives. Portions are large (it's acceptable to split a dish); if you have room, opt for a wedge of cream cake. Beer and wine are available. Both floors are crowded and sometimes claustrophobic, but there's plenty of outdoor seating. ✉ *Bridge House, near the bridge on the promenade* ☎ *08/637–7434* ▭ *MC, V* ✣ *3C.*

WHERE TO STAY

$$ ★ **Agamim.** With a name that means "lakes," this water-garden hotel, also part of the Isrotel chain, was designed with pure relaxation in mind. Built in 2002, the compound of four-floor buildings is set amid palm trees, emerald grass, and tropical plants, around a lagoon-shaped pool with hammocks and swing chairs. Pale green wicker chairs invite leisure time on the nearby terrace. Many rooms (all the same size) sit right over the curving waterways that flow from the pool, and all have balconies. Recessed lighting in the rooms casts a soft light on striped sofas, bedspreads, and curtains of tobacco, blue, dark green, and dark rose, along with dark turquoise rugs. **Pros:** one of Eilat's more laid-back hotels; great pool area. **Cons:** it's a 10- to 15-minute walk to the beach; not convenient for strollers or wheelchairs. ✉ *Kampan St., North Beach* ☎ *08/630–0300* ⊕ *www.isrotel.co.il* ♁ *In-room: a/c, safe, refrigerator. In-hotel: 2 restaurants, bar, pools, gym, spa, children's programs (ages 3–12), laundry service, Internet terminal* ▭ *AE, DC, MC, V* 🍽 *CP* ✣ *2D.*

$$ **Astral Village.** Not exactly otherworldly, but certainly fun for a family, this affordable compound that opened in 2005 consists of small, trim cottages in beige stucco, with wooden shutters and red-tile roofs. White-frame windows with red-and-white flowers planted out front look out onto the huge pool, where holiday activity is centered. Music plays, palm trees sway. The cheerful turquoise-trimmed dining room is

off the lobby. **Pros:** near the marina; good value; staff is eager to please. **Cons:** a 10-minute walk to the beach. ✉ *Kempen St. near King Solomon's Palace hotel* ☎ *08/636–6888* 🌐 *www.astralhotels.co.il* *170 rooms, 12 suites* *In-room: a/c, TV, safe, refrigerator. In-hotel: restaurant, bar, pool, gym, spa, children's programs (ages 3–10)* *AE, DC, MC, V* *CP* ✥ *2D.*

$$$$ Fodor's Choice ★ **Dan Eilat.** The glitzy 14-floor, U-shape Dan is on the North Beach Promenade near the Jordanian border. Its design, by internationally acclaimed Israeli architect Adam Tihani, effectively combines snazzy high style with comfort. The two connecting two-story lobbies feature a winding glass stairway (as scary as it sounds), craggy rock walls with a water cascade, floating ceiling sculptures, a huge aviary, and a rock pool with iguanas. The spacious blue–and–terra-cotta rooms have blond-wood furnishings, and the dresser mirror can be adjusted to reflect the sea. If you can, reserve one of the terrace suites, which feature a large balcony and indoor Jacuzzi. Two pools—a 20-meter pool for serious swimmers and an active pool with waterslide—anchor the large, lush outdoor area, which includes the Grotto, a casual poolside restaurant specializing in juicy hamburgers and hot dogs. Children can play in the supervised "Danyland" playroom or in the toddler's pool. The 13th and 14th floors have been recently renovated. **Pros:** great location on the beach; excellent breakfasts (marked with nutritional symbols to mark low sodium and no added sugars offerings) and superb dinners prepared by chef Ofir Kedem. **Cons:** sometimes noisy; crowded dining room. ✉ *North Beach Promenade* ☎ *08/636–2222* 🌐 *www.danhotels.co.il* *374 rooms, 48 suites* *In-room: a/c, safe. In-hotel: 2 restaurants, bar, pools, gym, squash courts, spa, children's programs (ages 3–10), laundry service, Internet terminal* *AE, DC, MC, V* *CP* ✥ *4D.*

8

$$$$ ★ **Herod's Palace.** Herod's—designed with the legendary king in mind—is all about over-the-top opulence and palatial pizzazz. Until late 2007 part of the Sheraton chain and now part of the Fattal Hotels Group, it's really three hotels in one. The dramatic 12-story lobby, decorated with Italian wrought-iron chandeliers, carved marble planters, and mosaics graces the Palace, the main building. The Vitalis is a spa hotel with large public areas (no children allowed). The Forum is designed to host conventions, and includes the largest ballroom in Eilat, with a seating capacity of 1,200. Touches of luxury are apparent everywhere, from the minaret towers that greet you outside to Romanesque domes, arches, bridges, and niches inside, all designed by well-known architect Yoav Igra (also one of the hotel's investors) to convey Israel's archaeological flavor. Rooms are spacious, with warm, dark-wood furniture and lush curtains. Unlike the Dan, where you can't see the sea from the pool, the Herod's pool sits at the end of an avenue of palm trees—it looks as though it flows straight into the sea. **Pros:** widest, quietest beach in Eilat; no cell phones in public areas; the largest hotel in Eilat. **Cons:** furniture is worn in some rooms. ✉ *North Beach, Box 4201* ☎ *08/638–0000* 🌐 *www.herodshotels.com* *Palace: 296 rooms, 33 suites. Vitalis: 52 rooms, 4 suites. Forum: 104 rooms, 20 suites* *In-room: a/c, safe, DVD (some), Wi-Fi (some). In-hotel: 4 restaurants, room service, bar, pools,*

CLOSE UP

Kids in the Negev

Think of the Negev as a huge sandbox for kids. There's lots to do and enjoy: alpaca rides, camel trips, Jeep excursions, snorkeling, floating in the Dead Sea, boat rides on the Red Sea, smearing on mud. And children like the kind of food prevalent in the Negev, such as french fries and schnitzel (fried breaded chicken cutlets). Even fancy restaurants have these on their menus, to please the young ones. The hotels in Eilat go out of their way to cater to kids, trying to outdo one another with their children's sections, often called Kiddyland. These are separate facilities on the hotel grounds, filled with every imaginable distraction, from toys and crafts to PlayStations, and there are qualified supervisors on hand. Many hotels employ staff trained to keep kids entertained. And even in upscale restaurants at night, it's not unusual to see baby strollers parked beside the candlelit tables.

spa, beachfront, bicycles, children's programs (ages 2–12), laundry service, Internet terminal ▭ *AE, DC, MC, V* 🍽 *CP* ⊕ *4D.*

$$$$ **Hilton Queen of Sheba.** The imaginary palace King Solomon built for the queen is what Hilton International set out to construct with this imposing example of grandeur: a palatial entrance capped with a pillared dome rises between two turrets, with a wing of more than 200 rooms on either side. Khaki-colored curtains cover the windows of the 40-foot-high lobby, and Italian mosaics of biblical animals cover the floor. The queen must have loved cats—images of them are everywhere. The bedrooms have gold-framed mirrors, taupe-and-orange carpeting, Egyptian-motif black-and-taupe bedspreads and curtains, and marble bathrooms with hand-painted murals. Rooms on even-numbered floors have balconies (some with Jacuzzis) facing the sea or the marina. Opened in late 1999, the 14-floor hotel was developed by Itzhak Tshuva (who recently snapped up Manhattan's Plaza Hotel) and designed by the Romanian-born architect Shlomo Gertner. Transparent gold-cage elevators offer views of the atrium as they rise. **Pros:** prime location, close to both seafront and shops; stunning views of the Eilat Bay and mountains. **Cons:** late-night music from the boardwalk can be disturbing to rooms on lower floors; lines for the dining room at dinner are sometimes annoyingly long. ✉ *8 Antib Rd., North Beach* ☎ *08/630–6666* 🌐 *www.hilton.com* *479 rooms, 20 suites* *In-room: a/c, safe, kitchenette (some). In-hotel: 4 restaurants, bar, pools, gym, spa, children's programs (ages 3–10)* ▭ *AE, DC, MC, V* 🍽 *CP* ⊕ *4C.*

$$$ ★ **Isrotel King Solomon.** Solomon's entire court could easily have been accommodated at the oldest member of Isrotel's chain. It's a huge and comfortably utilitarian family hotel with an expansive lobby furnished in beige wicker with gray upholstery. The staff attends to guests' every need, and everything runs like clockwork. The commodious dining room is open market–style and serves Chinese and other foods. Breakfast selections are vast, and eating on the leafy, shaded terrace is a pleasure. Palm-fringed pools (one with a 50-meter waterslide) overlook the lagoon, and the children's "house" offers all-day entertainment.

Garden-terrace suites have their own hot tubs. **Pros:** perhaps Eilat's most child-friendly hotel, with a jamboree, arts-and-crafts workshops, computer rooms, games, and supervised activities; rooftop lounge with free Internet access. **Cons:** not on the beachfront; noisy; food is uninspired. ✉ *Lagoon Promenade, North Beach* ☎ *08/636–3444* 🌐 *www.isrotel.co.il* *398 rooms, 22 suites* *In-room: a/c, safe, refrigerator. In-hotel: restaurant, room service, bar, pools, tennis courts, gym, spa, children's programs (ages 2–10), laundry service* 💳 *AE, DC, MC, V* *CP* ✣ *3C.*

$$ ★ **Le Meridien.** Enter this dandy hotel, and the first thing you'll see through its glass walls is a breathtaking view of the shimmering sea and Jordanian mountains beyond. This all-suite lodging (rooms house four to six guests) maintains a refined air. Each suite in the hotel's two seven-story towers has its own balcony. The spacious lobby lounge has a bar and a dance floor (there's a quiet lobby as well), and waiters sing in the pub at night. Parents can keep an eye on their children in the Kids' Club via a closed-circuit system transmitted to their in-room TV. The spa offers the last word in beauty and health treatments, and there's a beach exclusively for hotel guests. **Pros:** lovely views; a short walk from the Mul Hayam shopping area. **Cons:** late-night music from the hotel's club may disturb some guests; not much of a beachfront; pool closes early. ✉ *Arava Rd., Box 2120* ☎ *08/638–3333* 🌐 *www.fattal.co.il* *246 suites* *In-room: a/c, cable TV, safe, refrigerator. In-hotel: 2 restaurants, room service, bar, pool, gym, spa, beachfront, children's programs (ages 3–10), laundry service* 💳 *AE, DC, MC, V* *CP* ✣ *4B.*

$$$ **Leonardo Plaza.** The hotel formerly known as the Sheraton faces the beach from the promenade near the marina, and everything is within walking distance. A decorator's touch is needed in the lobby and reception area. That being said, the pleasant dining room was renovated in 2004, and the western wing got a makeover a year later. The rooms, along outside corridors, have carpets in shades of blue and white, dark blue bedspreads, and gold-and-blue curtains. Most rooms face the sea or pool, and 14 have in-room hot tubs. American tour groups and French visitors are partial to this place. The fourth-floor business lounge has fax and Internet facilities. **Pros:** well-situated beachfront location, in the middle of the promenade; extensive kids' activities. **Cons:** within earshot of the beachfront discos; Internet is expensive. ✉ *North Beach Promenade, Box 135* ☎ *08/636–1111* 🌐 *www.leonardo-hotels.com* *301 rooms, 7 suites* *In-room: a/c, safe, refrigerator, Wi-Fi. In-hotel: 2 restaurants, room service, bar, pools, spa, beachfront, children's programs (ages 4–10), laundry service, Internet terminal* 💳 *AE, DC, MC, V* *CP* ✣ *4C.*

$$ **The Orchid.** Teak furnishings from the Far East, and high wood beams characterize this Asian-themed hotel on the quiet South Beach. Also here are opulent luxury villas with extraordinary views of Eilat Bay, many of them with private Jacuzzis. The pool offers views of the mountains and a small waterfall. **Pros:** just across from the aquarium; free shuttle to downtown Eilat every hour; free bike rental for guests; good kosher Thai restaurant. **Cons:** you have to wait for a cart to take you up the steep hill to the rooms; if you visit during the winter, bear in mind

8

that the rooms are unheated. ✉ *South Beach, Box 994* ☎ *08/636–0360* 🌐 *www.orchidhotel.co.il* *168 rooms, 16 villas* *In-room: a/c, safe, refrigerator. In-hotel: 2 restaurants, room service, bar, pools, spa, laundry service, Internet terminal* ▭ *AE, DC, MC, V* ✣ *6A.*

$$$$ Fodor's Choice ★ **Princess.** The southernmost hotel in Israel (it's five minutes from the Egyptian border), the Princess, which has recently completed a two-year renovation, is one of Eilat's most luxurious hotels. Owned by Frankfurt businessman Alexander Tessler, it has a light-filled reception area facing a two-story sheer rock cliff through a soaring glass wall; the public spaces are dazzlingly white with gold trim. The pool area—the largest in the city—is a country club in itself, where squiggle-shape pools connected by bridges afford views of charcoal gray mountains across the bay. Down at the serene snorkeling beach, reached by a short tunnel under the road, two jetties lead to the water, and suntanning beds beckon. The spa in this self-contained resort is ultramodern, and the two restaurants, under the direction of well-known Israeli chef Peter Hummel, offer superb fare. **Pros:** elegant business lounge on the 15th floor; chic Moscow–New York nightclub downstairs; free shuttles every hour into town for sightseeing. **Cons:** far from the action in Eilat; mobbed with kids during summer vacation. ✉ *Rte. 90 (Eilat–Taba Rd.), Box 2323* ☎ *08/636–5555* 🌐 *www.eilatprincess.com* *338 rooms, 64 suites (including 7 "theme suites" and 8 "club suites," each with an outdoor Jacuzzi)* *In-room: a/c, TV, safe. In-hotel: 2 restaurants, room service, bar, tennis courts, pools, gym, spa, beachfront, children's programs (ages 2–10), laundry service, Internet terminal, parking (free)* ▭ *AE, DC, MC, V* *CP* ✣ *6A.*

$$$$ **Royal Beach.** At the jewel in the Isrotel chain's crown, guests discover a magical blend of comfort, glamour, and sophistication. Opened in 1994, across the promenade from the beach, the colossal Royal Beach is Eilat's answer to Miami's South Beach. It has a serene atrium with cushy, smoky green leather couches. Three-story glass windows bring graceful bamboo and palm trees inside. A large terrace—crammed with multicolored flowers, overhead fans, and kilim rugs—faces the Bay of Eilat, providing especially stunning views at sundown. Rooms are decorated in warm blue; all have comfortable sofas and chairs, and a balcony. Suites come with whirlpool tubs. For the best views, ask for a higher floor. **Pros:** pleasant pool area graced by palm trees and waterfalls; excellent seaside location. **Cons:** laissez-faire staff; apart from the suites, the rooms are small. ✉ *North Beach* ☎ *08/636–8888* 🌐 *www.isrotel.co.il* *363 rooms, 19 suites* *In-room: a/c, safe, Wi-Fi. In-hotel: 4 restaurants, room service, bar, 3 pools, spa, beachfront, children's programs (ages 3–10), laundry service* ▭ *AE, DC, MC, V* *CP* ✣ *4D.*

$$ **Yam Suf.** Just across from the Coral Beach, this swank Isrotel hotel, formerly known as the Ambassador, is made up of three wings: an L-shape, three-floor wing still called the Ambassador, where all rooms have balconies and face the sea; the Garden Wing, comprising two three-floor buildings with rooms and suites that have private gardens; and the Diver's Wing, which faces the Manta Dive Center (offering five- and two-day certification courses) and has nine rooms that can each accommodate four guests. The hotel's entrance, facing the Eilat

Mountains, is up a palm-lined drive; inside, the decor is modern and lively. The color scheme of the guest rooms is particularly attractive, with marine blue, khaki, and sunny yellow tones. Just across the road are the beach and a seafood restaurant. **Pros:** great beach for snorkeling; very close to the aquarium and the Last Refuge fish restaurant. **Cons:** bland food; not within walking distance to central Eilat. ✉ *Rte. 90 (Eilat–Taba Rd.)* ☎ *08/638–2222* 🌐 *www.isrotel.co.il* *237 rooms, 14 suites* *In-room: a/c, safe, refrigerator. In-hotel: restaurant, bar, 3 pools, gym, spa, diving, children's programs (ages 3–10), laundry service, Internet terminal* *AE, DC, MC, V* *CP* ✥ *6A.*

NIGHTLIFE AND THE ARTS

For an overview of local events, pick up a copy of the detailed leaflet "Events and Places of Interest," available at the tourist information office. For the coming week's arts and entertainment information, check out Friday's *Jerusalem Post* magazine, or the *Herald Tribune*'s *Haaretz Guide,* both of which carry listings for Eilat.

BARS AND CLUBS

Most hotels in Eilat have a piano bar (some with space for cutting loose), and many have dance clubs; all are open to the public. Pubs abound; top bands perform at several, and at many you can even get a decent meal. Other dancing options are beach parties, where bronzed bodies groove to recorded music all night; keep an eye out in town for English-language posters listing times and places. Admission is free. On Friday night, join Eilatis who gather at the Aqua Sport beach at sunset.

At the Princess Hotel, **Moscow-New York** (✉ *Eilat–Taba Rd.* ☎ *054/770-0286*) tops the disco bill, with mirrored walls, fluted columns, and a checkered dance floor. **Platinum** (✉ *North Beach Promenade* ☎ *08/636–3444*), at the Isrotel King Solomon hotel, has well-known DJs and trendy twentysomethings. Good bands are the claim to fame at the very popular **Three Monkeys Pub,** where live music begins most nights at 11 pm (✉ *Royal Beach Promenade* ☎ *08/636–8888*).

8

ISRAELI FOLK DANCING

★ At the **Etzion Gaver School** (✉ *Sheshet Hayimim St., entrance on Argaman St.* ☎ *057/810-4273* *NIS 25*) you can learn how to folk dance on weeknights starting at 9 (call ahead to verify times).

MUSIC FESTIVALS

★ Two of the country's most important music events have long taken place in Eilat. Both festivals feature internationally acclaimed musicians. Check with the tourist office for details. **The Red Sea International Music Festival** (🌐 *redseaclassicalfestival.com*), a series of classical concerts under the direction of Valery Gergiev, takes place in late December or January. The world-class **Red Sea Jazz Festival** (🌐 *redseajazzeilat.com*) is held in Eilat's cargo port in the last week of August.

THEATER

★ **WOW** (✉ *Isrotel Royal Garden, North Beach* ☎ *08/638–6701* 🌐 *www.isrotel.co.il* *NIS 105*) is a 1½-hour show (performances are daily 11 am to 9 pm with vaudeville sketches, magicians, jugglers, and gravity-defying circus acrobatics—all in a 3-D video-art setting. The best of its kind in Israel.

After a day at the beach, secure a seat with a waterside view at one of Eilat's many restaurants.

SPORTS AND THE OUTDOORS

Many of the activities outlined below can be arranged through your hotel or a travel agency. Several tour operators maintain desks in hotel lobbies and will take reservations there.

BEACHES

★ Beach managers, who ensure the cleanliness of their sections and provide open-air showers and (for a fee) deck chairs, operate Eilat's beautiful beachfront—the **North Beach** and the **South Beach.** Look for beaches with the large white sign that says public authorized swimming zone, along with the wooden lifeguard huts on stilts; lifeguards are usually on duty until 4 or 5 in the afternoon. The beaches are free, and many turn into clubs after nightfall, with thatched-roof restaurants and pubs, contemporary music, and dancing. Beach No. 2, at the Leonardo Plaza, and Beach No. 3, on the northern promenade near the Dan Hotel, are particularly pleasant.

Families favor North Beach, which runs northeast from the intersection of Durban and Arava streets up to the marina and the bridge. Here you can go paragliding or rent a paddleboat or a "banana" (a plastic boat towed by a motorboat). Farther along, after the bridge and opposite the Queen of Sheba, Royal Beach, Dan, and Herod's hotels, lies a beautifully landscaped series of beaches. Young people tend to hang out at the southernmost beaches, near the dive centers (south of the port, along the Eilat–Taba Road). The southern beaches share the coast with the Underwater Observatory and the Coral Reserve.

The Eilat municipality has in recent years made a number of beaches wheelchair accessible. The best is opposite the Neptune Hotel, where a wheelchair path leads from the promenade to the water's edge.

BIRD-WATCHING

★ **International Birding and Research Center**. More than a billion birds migrate annually through these skies to and from Africa along the Rift Valley, and bird-watching enthusiasts come for the spectacle, at its height in late March. The nonprofit birding center offers Jeep bird-watching tours (NIS 220 for four hours) to see Eastern Imperial Eagles, Lanner Falcons, Western Reef Herons, Oriental Skylarks, and many other species, as well as night tours to experience the nocturnal life of the Arava Desert. (✉ *Entrance to Eilat, turn off Route 90 at the sign to the Rabin Border Crossing (the Eilot interchange) and follow the signs* ☎ *057/776–9103 or 050/767–1290* 🌐 *www.birdsofeilat.com*)

BOATING AND WATER SPORTS

You've got to get out on the water if you're in Eilat; choose from an array of water-ski, Jet-ski, banana-ride, or parasailing adventures. There are boat-rental and water-sports facilities at both Eilat's marina (near the bridge) and Coral Beach, south of the port on the Eilat–Taba Road (Route 90).

The **Red Sea Sports Club** (✉ *Bridge House* ☎ *08/638–2240* ✉ *Manta Diving Center, Coral Beach* ☎ *08/637–0688* 🌐 *www.redseasports.co.il*) rents paddleboats, canoes, and mini speedboats. It also offers waterskiing lessons, parasailing, and cruises to Taba on a Spanish schooner (four hours, NIS 155). You can also charter a 150-horsepower speedboat piloted by a water-ski instructor for about NIS 300 per half hour.

8

DESERT TOURS

How better to experience the rugged beauty of the desert than on a sure-footed animal perfectly adapted to the terrain? At Eilat's **Camel Ranch** (☎ *08/637–0022* 🌐 *www.camel-ranch.co.il*) off the Eilat–Taba road, you can take a half-day excursion (four hours), or sunset tour (two hours). The ranch is closed on Sunday.

RAPPELLING

Jeep Sea (✉ *Bridge House, near the marina* ☎ *08/633–0133* 🌐 *www.weekend.co.il/eilat/jeepsi*), which specializes in desert tourism, runs customized Jeep tours and rappelling (known in Israel as snappelling) trips for both novices and experienced rappellers. Call ahead to reserve.

SCUBA DIVING AND SNORKELING

★ In Eilat you'll find everything from beginner's courses to expert PADI (Professional Association of Diving Instructors) five-star dive centers; snorkeling and scuba diving are extremely popular activities here. Eilat Bay is located at the northern tip of a coral reef that extends from the equator.

Aqua Sport International Red Sea Diving Center (✉ *Coral Beach* ☎ *08/633–4404* 🌐 *www.aqua-sport.com*) is a British-owned company that for over 45 years has been operating PADI-certified diving courses in both Eilat and Taba, as well as snorkeling cruises to the most magnificent sections of the reef.

Families (ages eight and older) have fun "snuba" diving at **Caves Reef** (☎ *08/637–2722* 🌐 *www.snuba.co.il*), south of the Underwater Observatory on the South Beach. In this snorkeling-diving hybrid, you breathe through tubes connected to tanks carried in an inflatable raft on the surface. The price, NIS 200 per person, includes instruction, a practice session, and a guided underwater tour that goes no deeper than 20 feet. Reserve in advance.

Coral Beach Nature Reserve (✉ *Eilat–Taba Rd., Coral Beach* ☎ *08/637–6829* 🎫 *NIS 30* ⏲ *Daily 9–5*) is a veritable utopia for qualified divers who want to get close to the region's fabulous fish and corals. Facilities include hot showers, lockers, and a small restaurant.

Lucky Divers (✉ *5 Simtat Zukim, near the Mul Yam Shopping Center* ☎ *08/632–3466* 🌐 *www.luckydivers.com*) is Eilat's only PADI Gold Palm five-star diving center, which for 30 years has been offering all manner of dive courses from two-hour introductory dives (NIS 220) to a five-day open water certification course (NIS 1,100).

At the Isrotel Yam Suf hotel, **Manta Diving Club** (✉ *Eilat–Taba Rd., Coral Beach* ☎ *08/637–6569* 🌐 *www.redseasports.co.il*) is an excellent diving center.

TENNIS AND SQUASH

The two squash courts at the **Dan Hotel** (☎ *08/636–2222*) are available to guests and nonguests for NIS 45 for 40 minutes.

Courts at the **Isrotel Sport Club Hotel** (✉ *North Beach* ☎ *08/630–3333*) are open to guests of the several Isrotel properties at the hourly rate of NIS 40; you can rent rackets and balls.

SHOPPING

Eilat is a duty-free zone; all items are exempt from VAT (value-added tax) and/or purchase tax. Articles such as bathing suits and jewelry sold in chain stores are less expensive in Eilat branches, as are items that are price-controlled, like gas, cigarettes, and alcohol.

SHOPPING CENTERS AND MALLS

One of Eilat's two shopping malls, **Mul Yam** (✉ *Arava Rd. and Yotam St.*) is at the entrance to town and is noted for made-in-Israel products. Here you can stroll along with the chattering crowd, stop for a drink of freshly squeezed orange or carrot juice, and perhaps pick up a lottery ticket at the stand outside the Israel Jewelry Exchange shop. Then check out such stores as **Intima** for women's soft and sexy lingerie; **Gottex** for famous swimwear; **Honigman** for women's sweaters, shirts, and skirts; and **Fox** for cheeky casual clothing for adults and children. There's also a bookstore, drugstore, and several coffee shops. Outside the mall, on the promenade going west, are one-after-the-other tacky but fun stalls selling hats, T-shirts, and earrings. Also, a branch of **Rockport** sells Teva sandals and other shoes.

The two sections of **Kanion Adom and Shalom Plaza** (✉ *HaTmarim Blvd., across from the entrance to the airport*) are connected by a café-filled passage. You'll find a variety of shops, but this is on a smaller scale than Mul Yam. There is a notable absence of tacky souvenir and gift shops.

HOTEL BOUTIQUES

Along the beachside promenade, on the ground level of each hotel, you'll pass one boutique shop after another. You'll find at least 40 stores and lots of restaurants, pubs, and coffeehouses—Cafe Aroma, which is open 24/7, is a good bet for a chocolate croissant, Greek salad, or orange cake. If you'd rather sun and play during the day, you'll still have plenty of time to shop at night—these places are open until 9 pm or later (except Friday night). Here's a sampling of some of the best.

At Herod's Palace hotel, **Cardo** (☒ *North Beach* ☎ *08/638–0000*) is an intriguing marketplace carrying unusual paintings, sculptures, Judaica, old-style objets d'art, Moroccan furnishings such as painted and inlaid mirrors, boxes and frames, gifts, and wall hangings. Stop at **Emporium** (☎ *08/633–9495*) on the promenade near Herod's Palace to browse familiar designer names, such as DKNY, Polo, and Calvin Klein. **H. Stern** (☒ *Hilton Queen of Sheba hotel* ☎ *08/633–1525*) has an excellent reputation for high-quality gold and diamond pieces, pearls, and also a small selection of silver sculptures by the well-known artist Frank Meisler. **Laline** (☒ *Promenade near Queen of Sheba hotel* ☎ *08/633–5713*) carries Israeli-made soap, body-care products, and candles. Look for Breitling and Cartier timepieces at **Padani** (☒ *Royal Beach hotel* ☎ *08/633–6627*). You'll find everything from resort wear and cosmetics to T-shirts, jewelry, and toys at **Royal Beach Rotunda** (☒ *Royal Beach Hotel* ☎ *08/636–8811*).

WINE TASTING

For an early evening sampling of "Private Collection" Carmel wines produced in the Shomron region, drop by Eilat's oldest wine shop, **Ha-Martef** (☒ *Sheba shopping center [Canion Shva]* ☎ *08/637–2787*). Owner Itzik Ben Adiva will happily bring you up to date on Israel's burgeoning viniculture scene in his modest, jam-packed shop. It's in the industrial area close to Eddie's Hideaway and next to Lisa Fish—look for wall-size murals of women treading grapes. Ha-Martef ("the cellar" in Hebrew) is open Sunday through Thursday, 8 to 2 and 5 to 8.

HAI BAR NATURE RESERVE

35 km (21½ mi) north of Eilat on Route 90, between Kibbutz Yotvata and Kibbutz Samar.

GETTING HERE AND AROUND

The reserve is located on the Dead Sea–Eilat (Route 90) road, between kibbutzim Yotvata and Samar. Look for the sign for Hai Bar and Predator Center, opposite entrance to Kibbutz Samar. Drive 1½ km (1 mi) to entrance. The reserve is also accessible via Egged Bus 390 from Tel Aviv, Bus 397 from Beersheva, or Bus 444 from Jerusalem.

EXPLORING

The Hai Bar Nature Reserve makes a good day trip from Eilat and can be combined with a visit to the Timna Park. The reserve consists of a 12-square-km (4½-square-mi) natural habitat for biblical-era animals and birds and the Predator Center. The reserve was created not only as a refuge for animals that were almost extinct in the region but also as a breeding ground for animals set free in the Negev. Opened to the public in 1977, the area re-creates the ancient savanna landscape of acacia groves and includes a salt marsh. Roaming around are stripe-legged wild asses, addaxes, gazelles and ibex, the Arabian oryx (antelope), and other desert herbivores. Ostriches come prancing over, ready to stick their heads into your car windows. Try to be here in the morning, when the animals are most active. You need a car and a CD player if you want a "guided tour"; you rent the CD for a few shekels and off you go. It takes about 45 minutes.

The 20-square-km (7¾-square-mi) **Predators Center** houses local birds and beasts of prey: foxes, wolves, spotted leopards, and striped hyenas. As you watch the hyena, notice that its front legs are stronger than its rear legs, enabling it to carry heavy prey a long distance. The birds of prey hang out in gigantic cages, where you'll see, among other species, the only lappet-face vultures left in Israel, with average wingspans of about 10 feet. In the pitch-black **Nightlife Room,** watch nocturnal animals that are active when we sleep: owls, desert hedgehogs, scorpions, and Egyptian fruit bats. ✉ *Rte. 90, 35 km (21 mi) north of Eilat* ☎ *08/637–6018* 🌐 *www.parks.org.il* 🎫 *NIS 39 (Predator Center only, NIS 25)* ⏲ *Sun.–Thurs. 8:30–5, Fri. and Sat. 8:30–4.*

NEED A BREAK?

If you're looking for fantastic kibbutz-made ice cream, stop by Yotvata Rest Inn (☎ *08/635–7229*), next to a gas station on Route 90 between the Hai Bar Reserve and Timna Park, 40 km (25 mi) north of Eilat. The kibbutz of the same name is across the way, and their dairy products are much loved by Israelis: cheeses, chocolate milk, yogurt, puddings, and ice cream (try the *pitaya*, or dragonfruit, flavor). Hot dishes (chicken or beef) and sandwiches are available as well. There's also a tourist information center at the entrance. Open 24 hours.

TIMNA PARK

Fodor's Choice ★ *25 km (15 mi) north of Eilat; 15 km (9 mi) south of Hai Bar Nature Reserve.*

GETTING HERE AND AROUND

From Hai Bar Nature Reserve, return to Route 90 south toward Eilat. Turn right after 15 km (9 mi) at sign for Timna Park and Timna Lake. A 3-km (2-mi) access road (which passes Kibbutz Elifaz) leads to the entrance booth. The reserve is also accessible via Egged Bus 390 from Tel Aviv, Bus 397 from Beersheva, or Bus 444 from Jerusalem.

EXPLORING

Timna Park is a lunarlike desert landscape interspersed with amazing geological shapes and ancient archaeological sites, surrounded by beautifully colored cliffs in a range of shades from sandy beige to rich red and dusky black. The granite Timna Mountains (whose highest peak is 2,550 feet) encompass the park's spectacular collection of rock formations and canyons. Millions of years of erosion have sculpted shapes of amazing beauty, such as the red-hued **Solomon's Pillars** (sandstone columns created by rare patterns of erosion, not by the biblical king) and the 20-foot-high freestanding **Mushroom**. The late-afternoon hours provide unusual light for spectators and photographers alike.

WORD OF MOUTH

"There are some great places around and close to Eilat. Just to mention one—Timna Park is not to be missed." —eri

People have also left their mark here. South of the pillars are the remains of a small **temple** built in white sandstone by Egyptians who worked the mines 3,400 years ago, during the Egyptian New Kingdom (the time of Moses); the temple was dedicated to the cow-eared goddess Hathor. This Lady of the Rock was the patroness of miners, as you can discover at the multimedia presentation, "Mines of Time." In the temple, archaeologists have discovered a snake made of copper (*nehushtan* in Hebrew)—according to Numbers 21:4–9, Moses made a serpent in the wilderness to heal people suffering from snake bites, and the snake remains a symbol of healing to this day. Near the temple, a path and stairway lead up to the observation platform overlooking the valley. Above the platform is a rock-cut inscription whose hieroglyph you can see clearly with the aid of a sighting telescope. It shows Ramses III offering a sacrifice to Hathor. You can also explore a life-size replica of the biblical tabernacle.

When you arrive, ask for the explanatory pamphlet, which shows the driving route in red. Because of the park's size (60 square km [23 square mi]), we suggest driving from sight to sight and exploring each on foot; some of the sights are several kilometers apart. A small building just inside the entrance screens a multimedia video (with a revolving stage and 360-degree screen) detailing humanity's 6,000-year-old relationship with the Timna area, starting with the ancient Egyptians who established the world's oldest known copper mines here. Take note of the 8,000 stone circles discovered in the park: they once led to mine shafts, one of which you can explore. The bright teal rock known as Eilat stone, a byproduct of copper mining, is today a trademark of Israeli jewelry. Wall panels explain the valley's fascinating geological makeup.

Experienced hikers can pick up a map detailing various serious hikes that take from 7 to 10 hours to complete. They're best done in winter (summer daytime heat exceeds 100 degrees). Watch out for old mine shafts, take adequate water, and *be sure* to let the staff at the gate know you are going, and when you plan to return. You can also rent bikes and paddleboats near the small lake. Multimedia sunset stargazing tours, accompanied by actors and darbooka-playing musicians, run through July and August. ✉ *Rte. 90* ☎ *08/631–6756* 🌐 *www.timna-park.co.il* 🎟 *NIS 44* ⏲ *Sat.–Thurs. 8–4, Fri. 8–3.*

8

NEED A BREAK?

Here's a surprise in the desert landscape, right in Timna Park: a lake (man-made), where you can take out a paddleboat. Nearby is Solomon's Khan, a rest house with goodies and refreshing drinks for the worn-out traveler. ✉ ***Timna Park*** ☎ ***08/631–7850.***

OFF THE BEATEN PATH

Mt. Yoash. This lookout along the border road with Egypt is an easy trip from Eilat. Notice the huge storage tanks as you drive along Route 12; they belong to the Eilat–Ashkelon oil pipeline. After you pass the tanks, you enter the Eilat Mountains Nature Reserve, with Nahal Shlomo, a dry riverbed, on your left. Drive 12 km (7½ mi) into the reserve and turn left at the orange sign for Mt. Yoash; then drive another 1 km (½ mi), bearing right up a rough, steep, and winding stone road. Park and take in knockout views of the alternating light and dark ridges of the Eilat Mountains; the cities of Eilat and Aqaba; the mountains of Edom, behind Aqaba; the start of the Saudi Arabian coastline and the Nahal Geshron gorge, emptying into the Red Sea at Taba; and the plain of Moon Valley and the mountains of Sinai, in Egypt. A beautiful two-hour hiking trail begins in the parking lot. The Jordanian army operated a strategic post here at the summit until March 1949, when Israeli forces took it during the last campaign of the War of Independence. The raising of a makeshift Israeli flag here (an event commemorated by a sculpture next to the Mul Yam shopping mall in Eilat) marked the end of the war. To get to Mt. Yoash, leave Eilat from the junction of Route 90 (Arava Road) and Yotam Boulevard, traveling west on Yotam (which becomes Route 12), with a tourist center on the left.

THE HEART OF THE NEGEV

The area extending from the Negev Highlands to Eilat offers a wide range of sights: Mitzpe Revivim, a reconstructed desert outpost; David Ben-Gurion's kibbutz home and grave site; an icy desert pool at Ein Avdat; the 2,000-year-old Nabatean hilltop stronghold of Avdat; and the immense Makhtesh Ramon (Ramon Crater). You'll also have the opportunity to meet the Negev's indigenous people, the Bedouin.

MITZPE RAMON AND MAKHTESH RAMON

Fodor's Choice ★ *On Route 40, between Beersheva and Eilat, 21 km (13 mi) south of Avdat, 80 km (50 mi) south of Beersheva.*

The raison d'être of **Mitzpe Ramon,** a town of 5,500 people on the northern edge of the crater, founded in 1951 by workers building the road to Eilat, is to serve as an access point to the magnificent giant crater, and as a center of ecotourism and hiking. Visitors love the area because of its pure air and natural beauty. The local main road runs through the crater on its way to Eilat, a promenade winds along its edge, and a huge sculpture park sits on its rim. Outdoor enthusiasts will enjoy exploring the geology, nature (note the metal fences around the trees to keep the ibex from eating the leaves), and stunning scenery by foot, mountain bike, or Jeep. The winter weather here is cool and pleasant.

Israel's most spectacular natural sight, and one of the largest craters in the world, the **Makhtesh Ramon (Ramon Crater)** in the heart of the Negev is a place of unparalleled serenity and breathtaking views. The crater's walls are made from layers of different-color rock beds containing fossils of shells, plants, and trees. At one time under the sea, the makhtesh floor is today covered with heaps of black basalt, the peaks of ancient volcanoes, jagged chunks of quartzite, natural prism rock, and beds of multicolor clays.

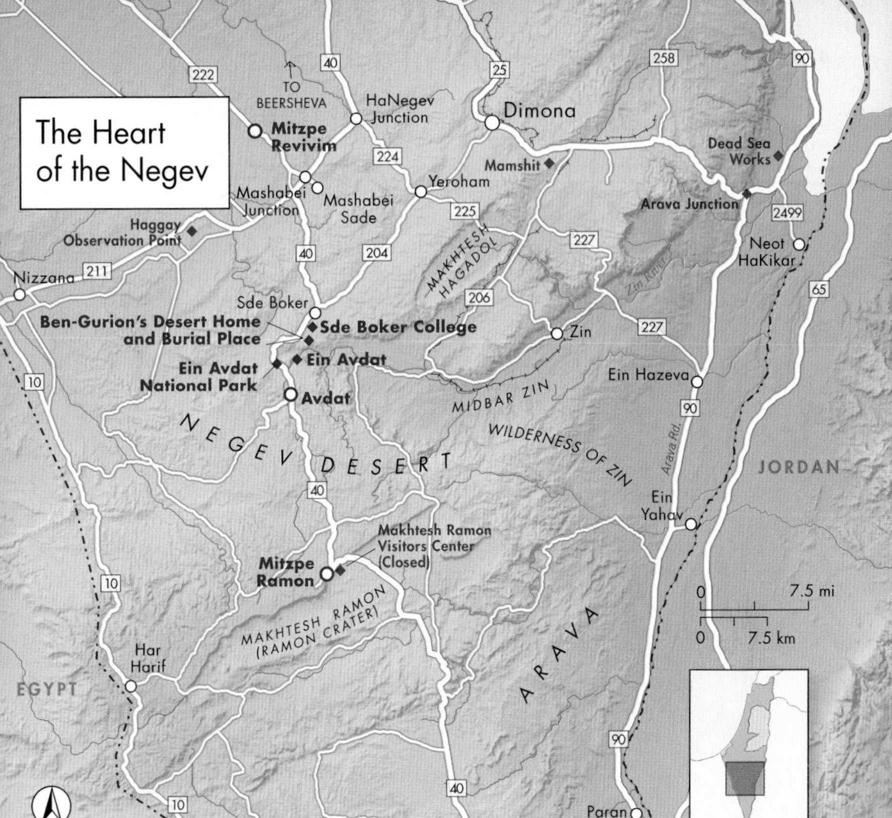

GETTING HERE AND AROUND

On Route 40, between Beersheva and Eilat, 21 km (13 mi) south of Avdat, 80 km (50 mi) south of Beersheva. Egged Bus 392 runs four times a day from Beer Sheva to Mitzpe Ramon (an hour and three-quarters drive); there are no direct buses from Jerusalem.

If you're continuing south to Eilat, you can still see the crater, as Route 40 goes right through it; just try to plan your day so that you won't be driving to Eilat after dark. There are no gas stations between Mitzpe Ramon and Yotvata, a distance of more than 100 km (62 mi).

VISITOR INFORMATION

Mitzpe Ramon Visitor Center (✉ *Top of the main street, Box 340, Mitzpe Ramon* ☎ *08/658–8691 or 08/658–8620*). The visitor center, at the very edge of the *makhtesh*, will be closed for two years, starting in August 2011. It remains a distinctive structure, however, to be used as a landmark and point of reference. More specific information can be found at 🌐 *www.parks.org.il*.

EXPLORING

Makhtesh Ramon (Ramon Crater). This immense depression is 40 km (25 mi) long, 10 km (6 mi) wide, and at its deepest, measuring 2,400 feet. Because it's a phenomenon known only in this country (there are two others in the Negev), the Hebrew term *makhtesh* is now accepted usage.

By definition, a makhtesh is an erosion valley walled with steep cliffs on all sides and drained by a single watercourse.

You can take a walk (about 1 km, or ½ mi) along the **Albert Promenade,** which winds east to west along the edge of the crater from the visitor center to the cantilevered observation platform hanging over the rim. This is not the time to forget a camera—the view is overwhelming. The promenade is fashioned from local stone, as is the huge sculpture by Israel Hadani, the back of which faces town and represents the crater's geological layers.

With the crater as a magnificent backdrop, the **Desert Sculpture Park** exhibits a far-flung collection of 19 huge contemporary stone sculptures. The park took shape in 1962 with the work of a group of prominent Israeli and foreign sculptors under the direction of Negev artist Ezra Orion. Their idea was to add to the natural stone "sculptures" with geometrical rock formations of similar design. The sculptors brought their chosen rocks and formed their desert works of art with minimal hand shaping. Ibex often wander through. ✉ *Turn off the main road near gas station at sign marked "Ma'ale Noah."*

For a look at one of the crater's geological subphenomena, drive into the makhtesh to see the **Carpentry,** a hill of black prismatic rock that appears to be neatly sawed. A path goes up to a wooden walkway, built to protect nature's artwork from travelers' feet. Long ago, the sandstone was probably hardened and slightly warmed by volcanic steam, and the rocks split into prisms. ✉ *Rte. 40, going south.*

One of nature's works is the **Ammonite Wall,** which is on the right just as you finish the descent on route 40 from Mitzpe Ramon into the crater itself (on its northeastern edge). A sign indicates a distance of 5 km (3 mi), which applies to the marked hike in the crater (for fit walkers only—take water). The rock face, which is actually part of the crater wall, contains hundreds of ammonite fossils, which look like spiraled rams' horns and are indeed named for the Egyptian god Ammon, who had the head of a ram.

Alpaca Farm. Just to the West of Mitzpe Ramon near the rim of the Ramon Crater is this farm, with its herd of 600 sweet-faced alpacas and llamas. Young and old get a kick out of feeding the animals, even if they receive the occasional spit in the face from these long-lashed creatures. Children weighing less than about 50 pounds can take a llama ride; horseback rides (some at night) and tours are available to all. You can also weave wool on a loom, and everyone loves to watch the shearing at Passover. ✉ *Turn off main road onto Ben Gurion Boulevard opposite gas station at the town's main roundabout* ☎ *08/658–8047* 🌐 *www.alpaca.co.il* *NIS 25; NIS 150 for 1.5-hour horse ride along the crater rim* ⏲ *Daily 8:30–6:30 (8:30–4:30 in winter).*

EN ROUTE

It's a **scenic drive** through the Ramon Crater on Route 40. The Negev wadis increase in size from their source in the Sinai, and cut through the Negev on their way to the Arava Valley, to the east. The sight of the Edom Mountains on the eastern horizon is beautiful, especially in the light of late afternoon.

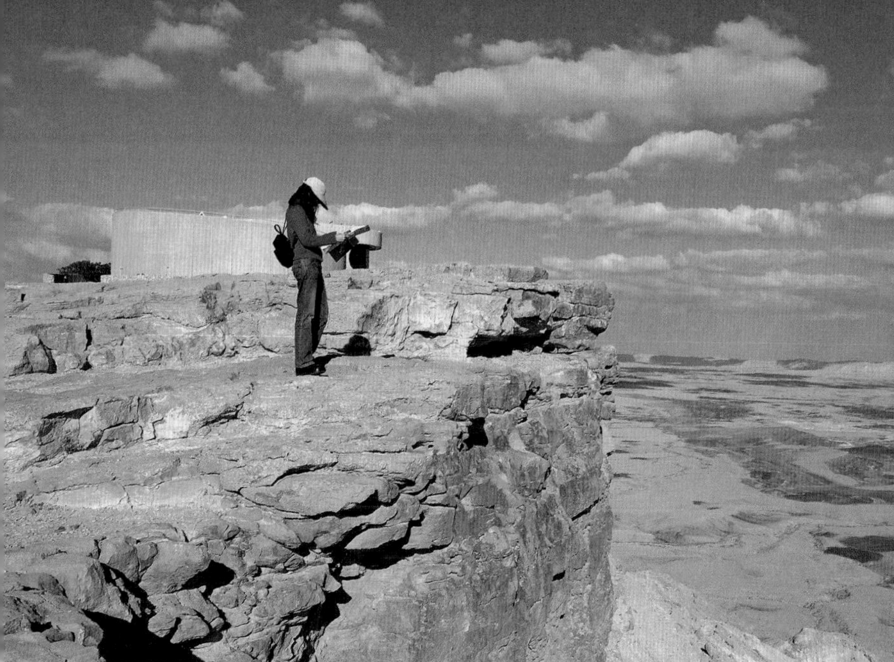

Makhtesh Ramon (Ramon Crater), shown in the valley below, is one of the Negev's top sites.

South of the crater on Route 40, near the Shizafon Junction, stop at Kibbutz Neot Smadar, home both to an arts center with stained glass, ceramics, and textile workshops, and to a farm shop that sells dates, cheeses, almonds, olive oil, and herbal creams.

After the Tzichor Junction with Route 13 (which connects Route 40 with the parallel north–south highway Route 90), you'll see limestone strata that have "folded" over the millennia. After the Ketura Junction (where Route 40 ends), there are breathtaking views of the Arava Valley (on your left), which marks the Israel–Jordan border and is part of the Great Syrian-African Rift, a fault line formed millions of years ago. From here, Route 90 leads straight to Eilat (52 km [33 mi]). It's not advisable to take Route 12 to Eilat if you're finishing this tour after a long day's drive or toward dark; Route 90 is the more direct and safer road.

WHERE TO EAT AND STAY

¢ CAFÉ ★ **Cafeneto.** Ah, the taste of a flaky croissant and the enticing scent of cappuccino—in the desert! You can get a full Israeli breakfast here (including local cheese, omelets, and vegetables) as well as sandwiches such as the "Baghdadi" (hard-boiled egg, roasted eggplant, tomato, cucumbers, scallions, parsley, and tahini). Or you might try a salad of finely chopped vegetables with mint, coriander, lemon, and olive oil. Sip an iced chai, fresh juice, espresso, or a latte with shredded chocolate on the terrace. Open until 10 pm. ✉ *Nahal Tsiah 5, near the camel observatory, Mitzpe Ramon* ☎ *08/658–7777* ✍ *Reservations not accepted* 💳 *AE, DC, MC, V.*

$ ISRAELI **Ha-Havit.** If you're lucky enough to get a window table at Ha-Havit ("the beer barrel"), you'll be sitting right on the edge of the crater, and the scenery may just overshadow whatever's on your plate. At this pub-restaurant, you can choose from fairly predictable fare including onion soup, pasta, meatballs, chicken, schnitzel, hummus, and stuffed mushrooms. You can raise a toast to the spectacular view with beer or wine. On Tuesday night, Ha-Havit morphs into a disco, and soldiers come to dance the night away. ✉ *Beside Mitzpe Ramon visitor center at the end of Maale Ben Tor St.* ☎ *08/658–8226* *Reservations not accepted* *DC, MC, V.*

$$$ ★ **Chez Eugene.** This expensive but unpretentious new boutique "restaurant-hotel" is pure elegance. Six suites feature a wine bar and fireplace and contemporary art books, and a minimalist high-ceilinged decor designed to capture the pure desert light. Enjoy pampering massages, yoga, and romantic walks—but most of all enjoy the culinary delights prepared by chef Yair Feinberg, like leek and thyme puff pastry with a touch of foie gras, or pasta with braised eggplants, feta from the desert, and pine nuts. The frequently changing menu also includes goat cheese from the Naot Farm, herbs from the Negev, meat from Beersheva and seafood from the fishponds of Kibbutz Mashabei Sadeh and Kibbutz Revivim. **Pros:** ideal for couples looking for a haven of serenity. **Cons:** no views; situated in the old industrial area. ✉ *Har Hardon 8/1, Spice Quarter, Mitzpe Ramon* ☎ *08/653–9595* *6 suites, some with private patio and Jacuzzi* *AE, DC, MC, V* *CP.*

$ ★ **Desert Home.** Here's a little piece of heaven on the outskirts of Mitzpe Ramon: a building with five lovely guest rooms designed for couples, each with a covered terrace facing the surrounding desert hills. In this two-story, sand-colored, adult-oriented inn that's fenced with tree branches, each room has a bleached-wood floor, handmade wood furniture, and pale lime, mauve, or blue walls, a double bed with bright-white pillows and taupe spread, a white fan overhead (in addition to individual air-conditioning), and a blue sofa with Moroccan cushions. The wood kitchenette sparkles with shiny utensils, and there's a microwave. **Pros:** lots of privacy; breakfast of local delicacies delivered to your room each morning. **Cons:** remote location; not geared for children. ✉ *70 En Shaviv* ☎ *052/322–9496* *5 rooms* *In-room: a/c, refrigerator, no phone. In-hotel: Jacuzzi, no kids under 16* *No credit cards* *BP.*

$ ★ **Ramon Inn.** There's nothing rugged about a stay at this charming desert hotel. The four-story building has no elevator, but the accommodations are entirely comfortable. Stay in a pastel-and-white studio apartment (for one or two) or a two- or three-room suite (for four to six guests); suites have well-equipped kitchenettes. The lobby has an open fireplace for chilly winter nights. The 20-yard-long heated indoor swimming pool would not be out of place at any luxury hotel. Helpful staff are happy to arrange for Jeep tours, horseback tours with instructors from the nearby Alpaca Farm, or moonlit tours when there is a full moon. Even if you're not staying here, the restaurant ($$) is worth a visit; hearty buffet meals are enlivened by condiments made by local cooks. **Pros:** ideal for mountain bikers looking to take advantage of the craters many trails; ask staff about "cyclists' packages." **Cons:** no views to speak of; other than the crater, which is a daytime activity, not much to do nearby at night. ✉ *1 Ein Akev St., Mitzpe Ramon* ☎ *08/658–8822* 🌐 *www.isrotel.co.il* *96 rooms* *In-room: a/c, safe, kitchen, refrigerator. In-hotel: restaurant, room service, bar, pool, gym, bicycles, laundry facilities* *AE, DC, MC, V* *CP.*

$ ★ **Succah in the Desert.** In the middle of nowhere (but accessible by unpaved road) is this out-of-the-ordinary encampment of huts (like the portable dwellings used by the Children of Israel when they wandered in this desert). On a rocky hillside are eight isolated dwellings, 150 meters apart, each made of stone and wood, with a palm-frond roof. For the rugged traveler seeking the starkness and purity of the desert, it's an appealing example of ecotourism. Each succah has a carpet on its earthen floor and a mattress with cozy blankets; household essentials include a tea corner, a clay water jar, and copper bowls for ablutions. The units are solar-powered, and there's an ecological-toilet cabin. Guests eat in the communal succah. You can ask a staff member to pick you up from outside the Ramon Inn. Plan to arrive before dark. **Pros:** homemade vegetarian breakfasts and dinners included in the price; great for stargazing. **Cons:** can be cold during the desert nights; difficult to reach without a car. ✉ *On road to Alpaca Farm, 7 km (4½ mi) west of Mitzpe Ramon, Box 272* ☎ *08/658–6280* 🌐 *www.succah.co.il* *8 units that sleep 2, 1 unit that sleeps 10, all with shared bath* *AE, DC, MC, V* *MAP.*

SPORTS AND THE OUTDOORS

ARCHERY

Desert Archery (☎ *050/534–4598* 🌐 *www.desertarchery.co.il*) offers trips where you hike through a desert course while shooting arrows at targets—a kind of cross between archery and golf. Suitable and safe for children.

JEEP AND HIKING TOURS

A hike, or a ride in a Jeep, is an unforgettable way to immerse yourself in the landscape.

Camel-supported hikes, rappelling excursions, and Jeep and mountain-bike trips are run by **Adam Sela Tours** (☎ *050/530–8272* 🌐 *www.adamsela.com*), which offers ecological tours and Bedouin visits as well. **Society for the Protection of Nature in Israel** (*SPNI* ☎ *03/638–8666*) often includes the Negev heartland in its guided trips.

MOUNTAIN BIKING AND RAPPELLING

★ Treat yourself to a thrilling bike ride: **Negev Land (Tiyulei Eretz Negev)** (☎ *050/998–8144* 🌐 *www.negevland.co.il*) rents mountain bikes for the day. It also offers Jeep tours, rappelling with instructors, and rents climbing equipment. Closed on Saturdays.

SWIMMING

You'll find a large indoor pool at **Ramon Inn** (✉ *1 Ein Akev St., Mitzpe Ramon* ☎ *08/658–8151*).

SHOPPING

Next to the visitor center, the **Amonit Gallery** (☎ *08/658–6166*) has a rather unusual selection: jewelry and batiks made by the owner, Bedouin drums, Armenian pottery, T-shirts with pictures of local animals, and desert stones and fossils.

Alpaca Farm (☎ *08/658–8047*) sells skeins of alpaca wool—light as a feather, soft as down, and warm as toast. There are cozy hats, too.

★ For all-natural, environmentally friendly, handmade, deliciously scented cosmetics, soaps, and body-care products that make ideal gifts, visit **Naturescent** (✉ *Har Ardon 22 in the industrial area.* ☎ *08/653–9333* 🌐 *www.naturescent.co.il*)

AVDAT

Fodor's Choice ★ *On Route 40, 21 km (13 mi) north of Mitzpe Ramon, 101 km (63 mi) south of Beersheva.*

GETTING HERE AND AROUND

On the Beersheva-Mitzpe Ramon road (Rte. 40), a 15-minute drive south of Sde Boker.

EXPLORING

The remains of the Nabatean city of **Avdat,** a 12-acre acropolis, looms on a hilltop over the spice route between Petra and Gaza. The Nabateans were seminomadic pagans who came here from northern Arabia in the 3rd century BC. With their prosperous caravan routes connecting the desert hinterland to the port city of Gaza, on the Mediterranean coast, they soon rose to glory with a vast kingdom whose capital was Petra (in present-day Jordan). Strongholds to protect the caravans were established along these routes, usually a day's journey apart.

The name "Avdat" is the Hebrew version of Oboda (30 BC–9 BC), a deified Nabatean king who may have been buried here. Another king of Avdat, Aretes, is mentioned in the New Testament. The prominent local dynasty intermarried with the family of Herod the Great, and in AD 106 the Romans finally abolished the Nabatean kingdom. The Nabatean temple on Avdat's "acropolis" left almost no remains, but its magnificence can be imagined from its restored gateway. Most of the remains on the acropolis date from the 3rd, 4th, and 5th centuries—the Christian Byzantine period. The city continued to flourish until it was sacked by the Persians in AD 620 and was rediscovered only in the 20th century.

Start at the **visitor center,** where you can learn about the Nabateans in a 10-minute video, see examples of what these ancient traders actually transported across the desert, and examine archaeological artifacts found in the excavations. Be sure to pick up the Israel Nature and Parks Authority's excellent explanatory brochure and map of the site. Drive up the road (save your energy for walking around the site itself), stopping first at the sign for the **Roman burial cave.** Park, and walk the 300 feet for a quick peek. The 21 double catacombs cut into the rock date from the 3rd century BC.

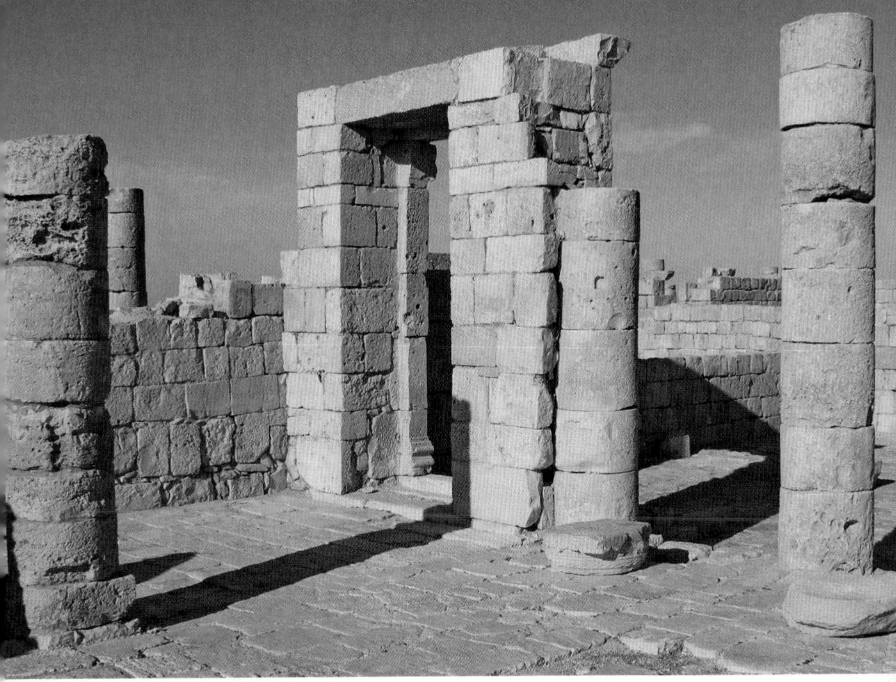

These ruins in the ancient Nabatean city of Avdat are perched more than 2,000 feet above sea level.

Back in your car, drive up to the lookout point at the restored Roman building (note the watchtower with an inscription dating to the late third century). The cultivated fields below were re-created in 1959 in order to see if the ancient Nabatean and Byzantine methods of conserving the meager rainfall (measured in millimeters) for desert farming would still work. The proof is in the cultivated crops and orchards before you.

Using the Israel Nature and Parks Authority's map, you can trace the lifestyle of these former locals at sites that include a reconstructed three-story Roman tower; a rare Nabatean pottery workshop; a Byzantine winepress; cisterns; two Byzantine churches; and a large baptismal font (to accommodate the converted). Near the baptismal font you can walk down the steps to see 6th-century AD Byzantine dwellings, each consisting of a cave (possibly used as a wine cellar) with a stone house in front of it. At the bottom of the hill, north of the gas station, is a Byzantine bathhouse. There is an eatery that serves light meals at the visitor center. ✉ *Rte. 40* ☎ *08/655–1511* 🌐 *www.parks.org.il* 🎫 *NIS 25* ⏲ *Apr.–Sept., Sat.–Thurs. 8–5, Fri. and Jewish holiday eves 8–4; Oct.–Mar., Sat.–Thurs. 8–4, Fri. and Jewish holiday eves 8–3.*

EIN AVDAT AND SDE BOKER

14 km (9 mi) north of Avdat on Route 40.

Ein Avdat (Avdat Spring) lies at the foot of the narrow canyon dividing the plateau between the ancient Nabatean city of Avdat and Kibbutz Sde Boker, in Ein Avdat National Park. The park encompasses the remains of one of the famed ancient Nabatean cities along the Incense Route, the road over which precious incense, perfumes, and spices were brought from Arabia across the Negev and to the Mediterranean ports. Ask for the explanatory leaflet when you pay. Lock your car, taking valuables with you. On the way, it's worth taking a reflective pause in Sde Boker, where Israel's first prime minister, dedicated to the dream of making the Negev flourish, lived and is now buried.

Ein Avdat National Park is located off the Beersheva–Mitzpe Ramon road (Route 40). To get to the lower entrance, head down the curving road from Ben-Gurion's grave. The upper entrance is about 5 km to the south.

Ben-Gurion's home and grave is also along Route 40; driving north, you'll see the sign for Ben-Gurion's Home directing you to turn right immediately after Kibbutz Sde Boker. Egged Bus 392 runs to Sde Boker from Beersheva four times a day (45-minute ride).

The college is just next door to Ben-Gurion's home and grave. Enter through the gate with the traffic arm, next to the "Ben-Gurion's memorial" sign.

EXPLORING

Ben-Gurion's Desert Home and Burial Place. Thousands of people make their way to this pilgrimage site every year. David Ben-Gurion (1886–1973), Israel's first prime minister, was one of the 20th century's great statesmen. He regarded the Negev as Israel's frontier, and hoped that tens of thousands would settle there. When Ben-Gurion resigned from government in 1953 (later to return), he and his wife Paula moved to the isolated, brand-new **Kibbutz Sde Boker** to provide an example for others. "Neither money nor propaganda builds a country," he announced. "Only the man who lives and creates in the country can build it." And so, the George Washington of Israel took up his new role in the kibbutz sheepfold. In February 1955 he became prime minister once more, but he returned here to live when he retired in 1963. (He moved back to his Tel Aviv residence some months before his death, at the age of 87, in 1973.)

Set amid the waving eucalyptus trees is Paula and David Ben-Gurion's simple dwelling, a testament to their typically Israeli brand of modesty and frugality. Ben-Gurion's small Negev home is commonly known as "the hut," owing to its humble appearance. It's a one-story wooden home with a small kitchen, an eating corner with a table and two chairs, and simple furniture throughout. Visitors such as United Nations Secretary-General Dag Hammarskjöld drank tea with Ben-Gurion in the modest living room. Ben-Gurion's library shelves contain 5,000 books (there are 20,000 more in his Tel Aviv home, on Ben-Gurion Boulevard). His bedroom, with its single picture of Mahatma Gandhi, holds the iron cot on which he slept (often only three hours a night) and his slippers on the floor beside it. The house is exactly as he left it.

Next door, in another painted-wood building, is an exhibition whose themes are the story of Ben-Gurion's extraordinary life, original documents that show the leader's strong ties to the Negev, and the Negev today in light of Ben-Gurion's dream. A film showing the footage of kibbutz members actually voting on his acceptance into their community is shown in the **visitor center**; the shop here sells gifts, jewelry, and books about the "Old Man," as he was known locally.

Fodor's Choice ★ **Ben-Gurion's Grave** (☎ *08/655-5684* 🎫 *free* ⏲ *open all day, daily*) just 2 mi south of the Desert Home is often visited at the same time. Walk through the beautiful garden until you reach the quiet, windswept plaza; in the center are the simple raised stone slabs marking the graves of David and Paula Ben-Gurion (she died five years before her husband). The couple's final resting place—selected by Ben-Gurion himself—commands a view of Zin Valley's geological finery: a vast, undulating drape of stone that changes hue as the daylight shifts. The cluster of greenery and palm trees to the right on the valley floor marks Ein Avdat (Avdat Spring). ☎ *08/656–0469* 🌐 *www.bgh.org.il* 🎫 *NIS* 12 ⏲ *Sun.–Thurs. 8:30–4, Fri. and Jewish holiday eves 8:30–2, Sat. and Jewish holidays 10–4; last admission ½ hr before closing.*

WORD OF MOUTH

"You have two weeks which is enough time to drive to Eilat. I would plan on driving one day and stopping on the interesting sights. You could go one way through Mitzpe Ramon, see the Ramon Crater, Avdat, Sde Boker and visit Ben-Gurion's home (very interesting how the first prime minister of Israel lived). Visit his grave—one of the most beautiful sights in the desert." —eri

NEED A BREAK?

By the gas station just to the south of the entrance to Ben-Gurion's Desert Home on Route 40 at Sde Boker is a small café called Menta (☎ *08/657–9938*), which is open 24 hours, and offers tasty cappuccino, espresso, muffins, and sandwiches.

Sde Boker College. Ben-Gurion envisioned a place of learning in the desert. Sde Boker College, which specializes in environmental studies, became part of Ben-Gurion University of the Negev, whose main campus is in Beersheva. Although there isn't a great deal to see, the **National Solar Energy Center** (☎ *08/659–6934*), where a research program investigates new ideas for harnessing solar energy and alternative energy technologies, offers one-hour guided tours. For the traveler, the college, just 2 miles south of Sde Boker proper, is primarily a place to eat and possibly spend the night. The commercial center in the middle of the campus has a restaurant, a supermarket open until 8 pm, a post office, and the field school (among the largest in Israel) of the **Society for the Protection of Nature in Israel.** ✉ *Sde Boker College, Sde Boker* ☎ *08/653–2016* 🌐 *www.boker.org.il.*

NEED A BREAK?

In the mood for a zinfandel (or a cabernet sauvignon or merlot) in the desert? Call San Francisco–born kibbutznik Zvi Remak (☎ *050/757–9212*), and he'll lead you on his bicycle to his garage winery behind Ben-Gurion's home. Tasting is done on a barrel by the front door of what was once a kibbutz shower room.

★ **Ein Avdat National Park.** Water flowing from Ein Avdat has cut a beautiful, narrow canyon through the area's soft white chalk forming a

Continued on page 492

ADVENTURES

The Negev—a word that means "dry" in Hebrew—is a desert that covers more than half of Israel's land area, yet remains a wilderness waiting to be explored.

At first glance, the Negev appears to be a monolithically desolate landscape. But take a closer look and you'll find an impressive variety of sights: stark ridges, enormous erosion craters, serpentine wadis (dry riverbeds) and gorges, sun-scorched mesas, burnt cliffs, sculptured sandstone, treeless plains and sand dunes.

The Negev Desert

N THE NEGEV

Since the days of the biblical patriarchs, the Negev has played host to ancient Egyptian miners, Bedouin herders, and Nabatean spice merchants who made the Negev the trade crossroads of Asia, Africa, and Europe.

With its sense of remoteness, the Negev

base that invites fast-paced adventures. Whether you choose to explore it by jeep or camel, or experience its Bedouin culture, or take a stargazing or bird-watching trip, time spent in this giant desert wonderland won't disappoint.

ACTIVE ADVENTURES

There are several ways to explore the Negev. Popular choices include hiking in craters and near the Dead Sea, perching yourself atop a camel, or taking a Jeep excursion across the desert.

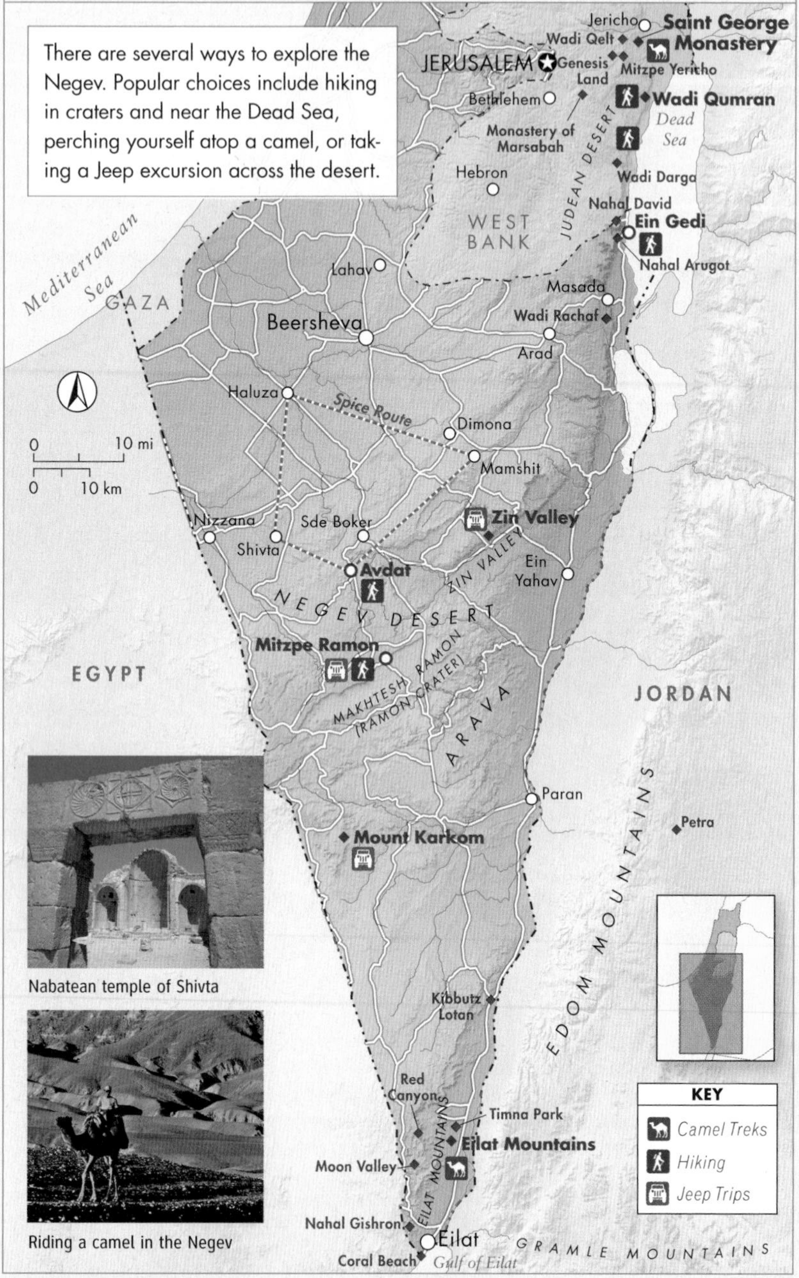

Nabatean temple of Shivta

Riding a camel in the Negev

KEY

- *Camel Treks*
- *Hiking*
- *Jeep Trips*

HIKING TRIPS

Hiking in the Negev

Israel's trails are excellently marked, and well signposted in both English and Hebrew. Although some guided one-day hikes are in English, don't dismiss hikes in Hebrew; English-speakers in the group are often glad to translate.

THE DEAD SEA

The labyrinth of rocky, brush-covered canyons and wadis found here are eminently hikable. Spend the day exploring one of several in the region, such as **Wadi Qumran,** where the Dead Sea Scrolls were discovered. The most accessible hikes are in **Ein Gedi**, a lush oasis with waterfalls, springs, and shade. The **Ein Gedi National Park** encompasses two wadis, Nahal David and Nahal Arugot, and has the area's best maintained trails.

THE SPICE ROUTE

Many of the ancient towns found in the heart of the Negev were once part of the Spice Route, which stretched from south Arabia to the Mediterranean, and flourished from the 3rd century " # to the 2nd century AD. One of the most spectacular of these towns, all of which are in complete ruin, is **Avdat**.

These cities, now in ruins, reflect the rich trade in frankincense and myrrh from south Arabia to the Mediterranean, which flourished from the 3rd century BC until the 2nd century AD. You'll see remains of the fortresses, irrigation systems, and caravanserai.

THE CRATERS

The Negev has three stunning craters: the Large Crater, the Small Crater, and Makhtesh Ramon (Ramon Crater), said to be the largest erosion crater on earth, at about 24 miles (40km) long, 5 miles (8 km) wide, and 1,600 feet (500 m) deep. Each has well-marked trails that lead past dizzying cliffs of multi-hued stratified rock.

HOW TO GO **A visitors' center** on the edge of Makhtesh has maps and helpful rangers. A safe, interesting, alternative is a guided, off-the-beaten-track hike. If you are planning a multi-day hike and prefer having gear and food provided, you can easily arrange a private tour. ■ TIP→ **Summer temperatures can easily reach 100 degrees, so drink a liter of water every hour.**

CAMEL TREKS

(left) A camel trip through the Negev. (right) Greek Orthodox Saint George Monastery

If you'd like to give your feet a rest, but still experience the desert up close, a camel ride is just the thing.

The local Bedouin name for camels is Ata Allah, or God's gift. The animal has traditionally provided both transport—a camel can go 5–7 days with little or no food and water—and milk. And meat from young male camels is a delicacy of the Arabian diet.

After you mount, the camel lurches forward rump first, which means you should lean back to avoid getting "camelpulted." Once you get going, however, riding is surprisingly comfortable. A walking camel moves both feet on one side of its body, then both feet on the other. This long-strided gait suggests the rolling motion of a boat, which explains the camel's other nickname in this part of the world: "ship of the desert." The reins used to steer a camel, unlike a horse's reins, are attached to a bit inserted in the nose, so be gentle. Since camels travel in single-file, however, you won't have to worry too much about steering your beast.

Common routes, which can run up to half-day, take you through the **Eilat Mountains**, or to the lip of **Wadi Qelt** (known in Hebrew as Nahal Prat), home to the beautiful **Greek Orthodox Saint George Monastery**, often stopping at a shady oasis along the way.

HOW TO GO **Eilat's Camel Ranch** (enter just after the Texas Ranch opposite Coral Beach) is one place that offers tours for every taste: a daily tour at 4:30 ventures into the desert mountains and canyons (affording fabulous sunset views). Or try the two-hour tour on which you ride for an hour, then savor a desert meal including vegetables and goat cheese. Finally, you might try the family ride, which lasts 1½ hours. The ranch is closed Sunday.

A Nubian ibex, often seen in the Ramon Crater.

JEEP TRIPS

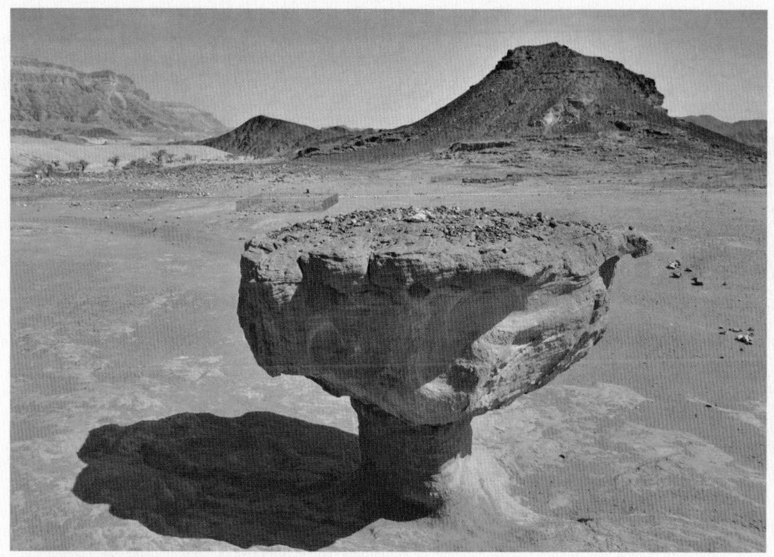

"Mushroom Rock," one of the many sandstone formations found in Timna Park.

After visiting the Negev, Mark Twain described it as "a desolation that not even imagination can grace with the pomp of life and action." Had he roared through the desert on the back of a 4x4, the American writer might have taken a different view.

Many jeep tours whisk you through the **Ramon Crater**, the **Zin Valley** (a desert moonscape punctuated by natural springs), or **Mount Karkom** (an ancient sacred mountain where you can see rock art, stone circles, geoglyphs, and cultic altars).

Other than the lurching off-road excitement, one of the advantages of jeep tours is the high standard of guiding. Licensed Israeli guides undergo rigorous training, and most have developed an amazing feel for the contours of the landscape. Guides will introduce you to the desert's geologic past and present habitat, and describe Israel's sophisticated water and soil conservation programs.

HOW TO GO From Eilat, the well-established **Red Sea Sports Club** leads jeep safaris through the **Granite Mountains** around Eilat to lookout points above **Moon Valley**, with a descent into the **Red Canyon** where you walk for an hour and take in the natural beauty. The cost is NIS 140 per person. Another experienced company, **Jeep Sea**, offers a 1½-hour "Desert Glimpse" tour, with a view of the hot-pink flamingos near Eilat; the cost is NIS 65. Jeep Sea also provides a four-hour trip to the Red Canyon (including hiking) for NIS 140 per person.

SPECIAL-INTEREST ACTIVITIES

Hiking, trekking, and zooming across the desert in a jeep aren't the only ways to experience the Negev. Try spending an overnight in a Bedouin tent, joining an archaeological dig, or bird-watching.

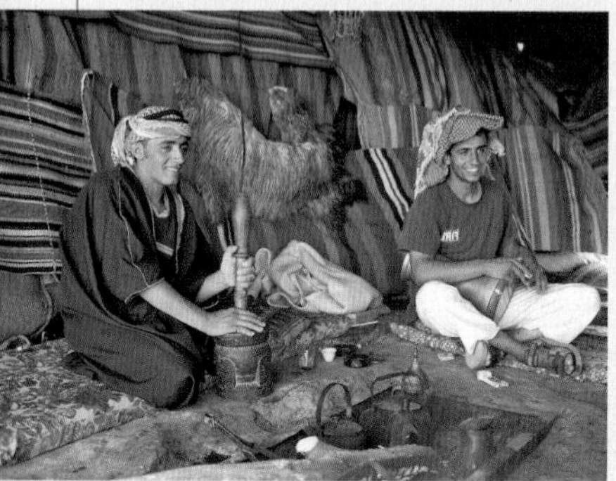

A Bedouin hospitality tent

THE BEDOUIN EXPERIENCE

Spending a day with Bedouins usually involves making a meal. You'll sit on beautiful woven mats and dine on *labane* (thick, tangy yogurt), *taboun* (Bedouin bread) with hummus, fresh-baked pita with zatar, goat cheese, and skewered meat. The feast is then washed down with sweet mint tea or black cardamom-spiced coffee. Sometimes there's belly dancing and music played on traditional instruments like the shabbaba, a kind of flute, and the rababa, a one-string violin. As you're soaking it in, smoke a *nargilla* (water pipe) with your host, and ask him about the herbal expertise and plant lore that are so intrinsic to Bedouin culture.

STAYING OVERNIGHT Staying overnight in a Bedouin tent is a worthwhile experience as part of your time in the Negev. The two best Bedouin outfitters are **Khan Shayarot** (☎ 08/653–5777), on route 40, about 20 minutes north of Mitzpe Ramon, and **Kashkhar** (☎ 050/668–9743), which is a family-run and organizes night-tracking tours, located a little more than a mile north of Avdat, also on route 40.

THE BIBLICAL EXPERIENCE

Visit **Genesis Land**, (Eretz Breishit) (☎ 02-9974477), where Israeli actors bring Biblical stories to life in the landscape in which they took place. You might be greeted by Eliezer, who'll lead you to Abraham's tent to enjoy meats, shepherd casseroles, and pita with zatar. Activities can include letter-writing with a quill on parchment, baking bread, or making pottery. Or, you can take a camel ride to the Monastery of Marsabah or the nearby Ein Mabua oasis.

STAYING OVERNIGHT Stay the night (Genesis Land offers accommodation either in Abraham's tent or a cabin), allows you to watch the sun set and the moon rise over the stark Judean hills, and put yourself into the rhythms of an ancient and simpler way of life.

ASTRONOMY

If stargazing is your thing, the Negev offers an awesome nightly spectacle, completely free of light pollution.

HOW TO DO IT To peer at some constellations and nebulae, visit Tel Aviv University's world-class **Wise Observatory** (☎ 08/6588133), located on a high plateau in the central Negev, 5 km west of the town of Mitzpe Ramon. Astronomers here recently discovered a planetary system–a star and two giant planets. The best—most cloudless—season to visit is June through August.

ECOTOURISM

Over the past decade, the Negev has incubated the development of ecotourism for the naturalistically minded. For this experience, you can visit one of several kibbutzim, which have traditionally engaged in environmentally friendly practices. Visitors can learn how the kibbutz deals ecologically with waste disposal, grows organic agriculture, reuses solid waste for alternative building, composts, and recycles.

Working on a kibbutz

HOW TO DO IT A good place to start is **Kibbutz Lotan**, 55 km (33 mi) north of Eilat. The kibbutz, which was awarded a prize for ecological villages, also conducts tours to familiarize visitors with mud huts that do not use electricity. (Tours leave daily at 9 AM from the parking lot in front of the holiday village.) The kibbutz also offers tours that introduce visitors to birds' migratory paths and local agriculture like date harvesting. (These tours depart at 10 AM from the parking lot.)

Another recommended Negev company with expert guides is the ten-year-old **Beerotayim Ecotourism Center**, which offers everything from 3-hour donkey rides to 8-day combined camel and 4 x 4 excursions (bring your own sleeping bag). Wadi Beerotayim itself lies in the western Negev Highland, near the Sinai–Negev border, and offers an excellent base for exploring the Ramon Crater.

Sifting for artifacts on an archaeological dig

DESERT DIGS

In late 2008, a British tourist visiting Israel discovered almost 300 24-carat gold coins dating from the 7th century at a dig where she had been volunteering. If you fancy working in the dust under a blazing sun in the hopes of finding treasure, take part in one of several ongoing archaeological digs.

HOW TO DO IT The best resource to volunteer for digs that appeal to you is the **Israel Ministry of Foreign Affairs** Web site (🌐 www.israel-mfa.gov.il).

BIRD-WATCHING

Millions of birds fly over Eilat and the Negev on their journey between winter grounds in Africa and summer breeding grounds in Eurasia. Migration takes place between mid-February and the end of May, and between early September to late November (spring is the larger of the two migrations). Lanner falcons, imperial eagles, long-legged buzzards, oriental skylarks, white storks, Egyptian vultures, and desert eagle owls—all these and many more come to visit.

HOW TO DO IT The **International Birding and Research Center**, just north of Eilat, is aflutter year-round (except August, when it closes); it's open Sunday–Thursday 8:30–5. The center conducts half- and full-day trips with names like "Morning Birder," "Desert Birding Trip," and "The Grouser." Binoculars are provided. Prices range from NIS 15 to NIS 230 per person per trip.

Blackstart

marvelous oasis that offers the ideal respite from your arduous Negev travels. Walk toward the thickets of rushes, and look for ibex tracks, made with pointed hoofs that enable these agile creatures to climb sheer rock faces. It's not easy to spot an ibex—their coats have striped markings that resemble the rock's strata. Rock pigeons, Egyptian vultures (black-and-white feathers, bright yellow beak, and long, pinkish legs), and sooty falcons nest in the natural holes in the soft rock and in cliff ledges.

The big surprise at Ein Avdat is the Ein Marif pools of ice-cold, spring-fed water, complete with splashing waterfall. To reach this cool oasis, shaded by the surrounding cliffs, walk carefully along the spring and across the dam toward the waterfall. Swimming and drinking the water are not allowed (you'll not be *sorely* tempted, though—the water is swarming with tadpoles), but enjoying the sight and sound of water in the arid Negev certainly is. The trail leads through stands of Euphrates poplars, and by caves inhabited by monks during Byzantine days, and then continues up the cliff side (using ladders and stone steps), but you can't follow it unless your party has two cars and leaves one at the destination. The easier and more common option is to walk along the streambed from the lower entrance to the Ein Marif pools at the foot of the waterfall, return along the same path. ✉ *Ein Avdat National Park, Advat, Route 40* ☎ *08/655–5684* 🌐 *www.parks.org.il* 🎫 *NIS 25* ⏲ *Apr.–Sept., Sun.–Thurs. 8–5, Fri. and Jewish holiday eves 8–4; Oct.–Mar., Sun.–Thurs. 8–4, Fri. and Jewish holiday eves 8–3; last admission 1 hr before closing.*

EN ROUTE

For an eagle's-eye view of the waterfall and spring below, turn off Route 40 at the orange sign for Ein Avdat to get to the **Ein Avdat Observation Point.** Below you is the white canyon carved out by the Zin River, with its waterfall (most of the year) tumbling into a pool surrounded by greenery. From the lookout, a path leads around the top of the cliff (be very careful), enabling you to see the rope marks in the rock; these have been created over the years by Bedouin pulling up water buckets. For information on the hike from here to ancient Avdat, consult the Field School at Sde Boker College.

MITZPE REVIVIM

36 km (22 mi) southeast of Beersheva.

On Route 40, the Beersheva-Mitzpe Ramon road, turn onto Route 222 at Mashabim Junction after Kibbutz Mashabei Sade, then drive 9 km (6 mi) to turnoff to Retamim on your left, following signs to the Mitzpe.

Mitzpe Revivim, the southernmost Jewish outpost during the early settlement of the country, played a strategic role in the defense of the Negev. It's now essentially a museum on a tiny kibbutz. In 1943, in a desolate and empty Negev, three such outposts were set up to gauge the feasibility of Jewish settlement in the southernmost part of the country; one of these was Mitzpe Revivim (*mitzpe* means "lookout," and *revivim* means "rain showers"). Revivim's very presence, along with a handful of other Negev settlements, influenced the United Nation's decision to include the Negev as part of the State of Israel in the 1947 partition plan. During the War of Independence, Egyptian soldiers besieged isolated Mitzpe Revivim, and a hard battle was won by a small band of pioneers and Palmach soldiers. You can enter its Byzantine caves, which once served as command bunker (the radio crackles original messages) and field hospital; climb the lookout tower; and see WWII-era Dakota C-47 and Piper Cub planes used to bring supplies and evacuate the wounded. A one-page "self guide" brings the rooms to life. Snacks, drinks, and Revivim's fine Halutza olive oil are available at the visitor center. ✉ *Kibbutz Revivim, Rte. 222* ☎ *08/656–2570* 🎫 *NIS 14* ⏲ *Sun.–Thurs. 8–4, Fri. and Jewish holiday eves 8–noon.*

EN ROUTE

Driving north along Route 40, you'll see a sign on the left for the **Haggay Observation Point,** which offers a glorious first glimpse of the **Wilderness of Zin**—stark, flat, beige terrain—and **Kibbutz Sde Boker.** Except for the greenery of the kibbutz, the area looks just as it did to the wandering Children of Israel making their way from Egypt to the Land of Canaan more than 3,000 years ago, no doubt complaining all the while about the lack of figs, vines, and water. (Along this stretch of Route 40, you'll pass through areas where signs announce "firing zone." The signs indicate closed military areas, which you may not enter without proper authorization. It's perfectly safe to travel on the main roads; just don't wander off them.)

Continue north along Route 40 and just before passing the turnoff to Golda Park (featuring a lake filled by the floodwaters of the Revivim River), you'll come to the gas station at **Mashabim Junction,** which also serves as a roadside café (good for stocking up on bottled water).

BEERSHEVA

Beersheva's emblem depicts a tamarisk tree, representing the biblical past, and a pipe through which water flows, symbolizing the city's modern revival. Four thousand years ago, the patriarch Abraham dug wells (*be'er* in Hebrew) here and swore an oath (*shevua*) over seven (*sheva*) ewes with the king of Gerar, who vowed to prevent his men from seizing the well. And it was here that Abraham planted a grove of tamarisk trees. Isaac built an altar here, the prophet Elijah found refuge here from Jezebel, and King Saul constructed a fort here. It's easy to envision these scenes today thanks to the cloaked figures of Bedouin shepherds with their sheep and goats on the hillsides surrounding the city.

Beersheva is now the fourth-largest city in Israel, with a population of some 200,000. It houses a major university, named after David Ben-Gurion, an Israel Aircrafts Industries complex, a high-tech center, and a regional hospital serving Bedouin shepherds, kibbutzniks, and other desert dwellers. Largely blue-collar, the city is struggling to accomodate thousands of recent immigrants, many from Ethiopia and the former Soviet Union.

The famed Bedouin market, once a source of some of Israel's best ethnic handicrafts, has been hit hard by modern times (especially the competition of cheap imports from the Far East) and isn't what it used to be. But it now has a permanent location, and you might still find something authentic. Most intriguing are the Bedouin themselves, sitting cross-legged with their goods spread out on the ground.

Tel Beersheva, just outside the city, is the site of biblical Beersheva and could easily be the site of Abraham's well. An expression from the Book of Judges, "from Dan to Beersheva," once indicated the northern and southern boundaries of the Land of Israel. UNESCO declared it a World Heritage site in July 2005.

Romans and Byzantines built garrisons in Beersheva, but in subsequent centuries the city was abandoned. In 1900 the Ottoman Turks, who had ruled Palestine since 1517, rebuilt Beersheva as their Negev district center (the present Old City). They set aside an area for a Bedouin market, which still takes place every Thursday. During World War I, when the British took Beersheva from the Turks, the city rapidly expanded; in October 1948 it was conquered by Israel.

From time immemorial, Beersheva has acted as a crossroads. In antiquity, the city straddled the intersection of two ancient important international road junctions: The "Way of the Sea" (Via Maris) which extended along the shoreline in the west, and the King's Highway (the Valley Route) in the east. Today, because it's quite close to Tel Aviv and Jerusalem, this unpretentious city serves as a jumping-off point for Negev travel—main roads branch out from here; buses serving the Negev depart from here; and trains from the north end up in Beersheva. If your schedule permits, stay overnight in Beersheva for a glimpse of a growing desert city with an interesting citizenry.

GETTING HERE AND AROUND

Beersheva is 113 km (70 mi) southeast of Tel Aviv and 120 km (75 mi) southwest of Jerusalem. The drive from either Tel Aviv or Jerusalem takes about 1½ hours. To Beersheva from Tel Aviv, take Route 2 (the Ayalon Highway) south until the turnoff marked "Beersheva—Ashdod." After this you'll be on Route 41, which runs into Route 40 after 6 km (4 mi). Continue on Route 40 to Beersheva; there are clear signs all the way.

To reach Beersheva from Jerusalem, take Route 1 west to the Route 6 turnoff. Follow Route 6 southbound; after Kiryat Gat it turns into Route 40 south, which leads into Beersheva.

The Israel Air Force Museum is 7 km (4½ mi) west of Beersheva on a narrow desert road that pushes past the city's drab outskirts.

For the Museum of Bedouin Culture, at the Lehavim Junction on Route 40, turn east onto Route 31, and turn in at the brown sign for the Joe Alon Center. It's 95 km (57 mi) south of Tel Aviv, 24 km (14 mi) north of Beersheva.

Tel Beersheva is 2 km (1¼ mi) east of Beersheva, on the road between Beersheva and Shoket Junction (route 60), near the Bedouin town of Tel Sheva.

VISITOR INFORMATION

Beersheva Tourist Information Office (✉ *1 Derech Hebron, corner of Kakal St., on the southern edge of the old city* ☎ *08/623–4613*).

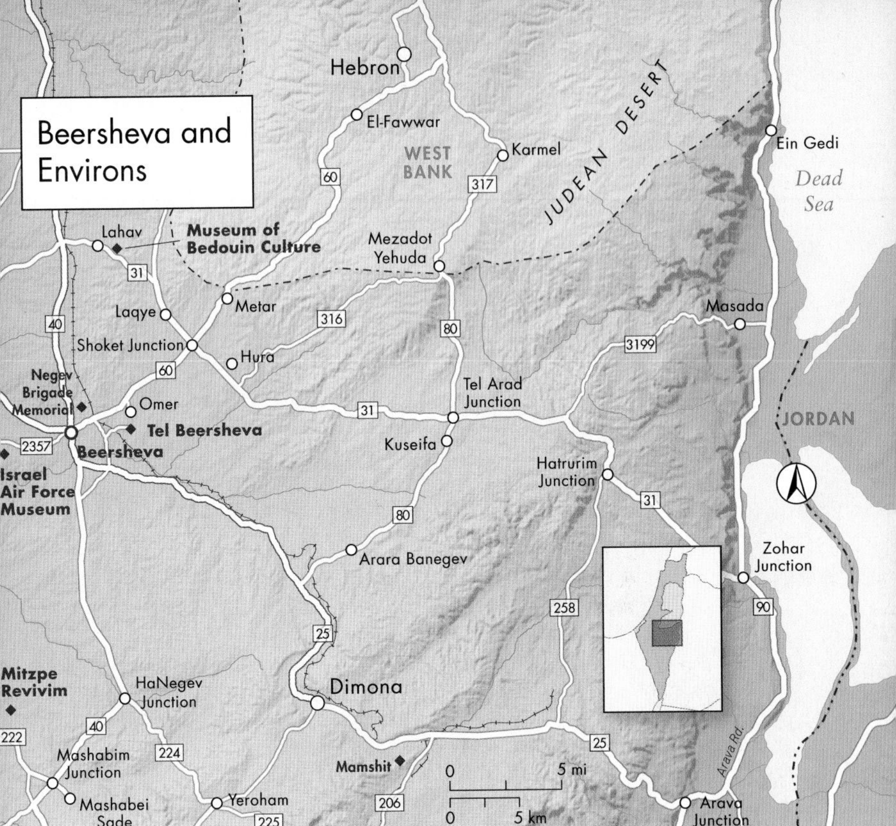

EXPLORING

★ **Israel Air Force Museum.** For plane lovers, this is a field of dreams. The open-air Israel Air Force Museum (housed on the active Hatzerim Air Force Base) is a gigantic concrete field with more than a hundred airplanes and helicopters parked in rows. The fighter, transport, and training (plus a few enemy) aircraft tell the story of Israel's aeronautic history, from the Messerschmitt—obtained in 1948 from Czechoslovakia, and one of four such planes to help halt the Egyptian advance in the War of Independence—to the Kfir, the first fighter plane built in Israel. The young air force personnel who staff the museum lead tours that take about 1½ hours and include a movie shown in an air-conditioned Boeing 707 used in the 1977 rescue of Israeli passengers held hostage in a hijacked Air France plane in Entebbe, Uganda. Another attention-getting display is a shiny, black Supermarine Spitfire with a red lightning bolt on its side, flown by Ezer Weizmann, the IAF's first pilot, and later President of Israel. The museum also houses an antiaircraft exhibit and a rare collection of historical and instructive films. Tours are available in English and French. ✉ *Rte. 2357; follow Joe Alon Rd. due west out of Beersheva* ☎ *08/990–6855* 🎫 *NIS 30* ⏲ *Sun.–Thurs. 8–5, Fri. 8–1 pm.*

★ **Museum of Bedouin Culture.** Once off the main road, you'll drive through the Lahav pine forest adjacent to Kibbutz Lahav to reach the Joe Alon

DID YOU KNOW?

Dromedary camels, such as this one, have been used in the Negev for thousands of years, and are particularly well suited for transporting heavy loads through the desert.

Center, whose centerpiece is this one-of-a-kind museum focusing on the Bedouin people, who have long populated the Negev. The study center (marked with an orange sign) is named for the late Colonel Joe Alon, a pilot who took a great interest in this area and its people. Housed in a circular, tentlike building designed by Israeli architect Tzvi Lissar, the museum tells the story of the Bedouin's rapid change from a nomadic to a modern lifestyle through tableaux of life-size mannequins. The tableaux are grouped by subject: wool spinning and carpet weaving, bread baking, the Bedouin coffee ceremony, wedding finery (including a camel elaborately decorated for the event), donkeys and camels at work, and toys made from found objects such as pieces of wire and wood. The tools and artifacts—most handmade, and many already out of use in modern Bedouin life—form an outstanding collection. Admission includes a cup of thick coffee in a real Bedouin tent, where the sheikh performs the coffee ceremony over an open fire. ✉ *Rte. 325 off Rte. 31* ☎ *08/991–3322* 🌐 *www.joealon.org.il* 🎫 *NIS 20* 🕑 *Sun.–Thurs. 9–4.*

★ **Tel Beersheva.** Tel Beersheva, biblical Beersheva—traditionally associated with the patriarch Abraham—is a mound of ruins created by nine successive settlements. Archaeologists have uncovered two-thirds of a city dating from the early Israelite period (10th century BC). Because of the site's significance for the study of biblical-period urban planning, UNESCO has recognized Tel Beersheva as a World Heritage Site. At the top of the tell is the only planned Israelite city uncovered in its entirety, which includes sophisticated waterworks and a fascinating reconstructed horned altar. A fine example of a circular layout typical of the Iron Age, the city is believed to have been destroyed around 706 BC by Sennacherib of Assyria. At the northeastern end, outside the 3,000-year-old city gate, is a huge well (the deepest in Israel, and more than 6 feet in diameter) which apparently once reached groundwater 90 feet below. This ancient well served the city from its earliest times, and scholars speculate that it could be the well that is documented in the Bible as Abraham's Well (Genesis 21:22–32). The observation tower is rather ugly, but it does afford beautiful views. ✉ *Rte. 60* ☎ *08/646–7286* 🌐 *www.parks.org.il* 🎫 *NIS 13* 🕑 *Apr.–Sept., Sun.–Thurs. 8–5, Fri. and Jewish holiday eves 8–3; Oct.–Mar., Sun.–Thurs. 8–4, Fri. and Jewish holiday eves 8–2.*

8

OFF THE BEATEN PATH

Neve Midbar. This spacious health spa (for daytime visits) centers on a pool of natural thermo-mineral waters pumped up from deep underground, at a temperature of 39°C (around 102 °F). The spa also has two freshwater pools and a shallow pool for babies. A hot tub, sauna, various massages, and aromatherapy treatments make for an unusual desert experience. A gift shop, kosher restaurant, and coffee shop share the premises. ✉ *Rte. 222, 20 minutes' drive south from Beersheva* ☎ *08/657–9666* 🕑 *Sun., Mon., Wed., and Sat. 9–6, Tues. and Thurs. 9 am–10 pm; Fri. 9–4.*

WHERE TO EAT AND STAY

$$$$ CONTINENTAL

✕ **Ahuzat Smilansky.** On a tree-lined street with old-fashioned streetlights, you'll find this perfect venue for a rarified dining experience. Located in a renovated Ottoman-era building in Beersheva's Old City, the rustic restaurant and tapas bar has an outdoor balcony, high ceilings, floors enhanced with arabesque tiles, and an inner courtyard. Candle boxes hang from the walls, and dark-wood padded chairs and beautifully set tables give serene elegance to the lovely setting. The chef and owner, Yariv Eitani, apprenticed in Provence before returning to his hometown. The creatively prepared dishes don't disappoint: start with furnace-baked Camembert or smoked duck in aspic and move on to such main courses as saffron salmon, roasted eggplant ravioli, lamb osso buco, and beef skewers with date and onion chutney. ✉ *23 Smilansky, Old City* ☎ *08/665–4854* *Reservations essential* ▭ *AE, DC, MC, V* ⊗ *No lunch Fri.–Sat.*

$$ CONTEMPORARY **Pitput.** The name of this grilled-meat restaurant means "chatter" in Hebrew, and the young crowd definitely lives up to this moniker. The washed beige walls are hung with shadow boxes filled with wine corks and coins. The staff here is congenial and the food attractively presented. Sitting outside on the busy sidewalk or inside listening to recorded jazz or blues, diners have a range of selections besides the meat specialties like entrecôte hamburgers: salads, omelets, blintzes from cheese to salmon, pasta, grilled fish with grilled vegetables, and pizza. Cheese sandwiches are made on sesame-seed rolls called *begeles*. Half bottles of Yarden wine are available. You can't go wrong by finishing with hot homemade pecan pie or cheesecake with fresh fruit. There's live music some evenings and the restaurant is wheelchair accessible. ✉ *122 Herzl St., in the "Big" shopping center* ☎ *08/628–9888* ▭ *AE, DC, MC, V.*

$ **Leonardo Negev.** Formerly the Golden Tulip, this is the only large hotel in town, and it provides up-to-date lodgings, especially for business travelers, who make use of three floors and a business lounge. The twelve-floor building's beige-and-brown stone reflects its desert surroundings, and arched windows soften the city's square look. Guest rooms are comfortably outfitted with wicker chairs, and the curtains and bedspreads form a snappy color scheme of red, green, and butterscotch. Good reading lights are a welcome touch. Rooms on the business floor are equipped with safes and minibars. The breezy outdoor patio, with bubbling fountains, is a cool place to relax in the hot desert climate. The hotel's outdoor pool is open from April to October. **Pros:** good rates for what you get; for those using Beersheva as a base for a Negev road trip, easy location at the entrance to the city. **Cons:** dull, nondescript setting; Internet costs extra. ✉ *4 Henrietta Szold St., near City Hall* ☎ *08/640–5444* 🌐 *www.fattal.co.il* *210 rooms, 48 suites* *In-room: a/c, TV, kitchen (some), Wi-Fi. In-hotel: restaurant, room service, bar, pool, gym, spa, laundry service* ▭ *AE, DC, MC, V* *BP.*

NIGHTLIFE AND THE ARTS

BARS

Join Ben-Gurion University students for a beer and delicious pub food at **Coca Bar** (☎ *08/623–3303*), behind the "Gimmel" student dorms on Arlozorov Street.

MUSIC

The Israel Sinfonietta Beer Sheva (☎ *08/626–6422* 🌐 *http://english.isb7.co.il*) is a well-regarded symphonic group founded in 1973 under the conduction of Doron Salomon. Its concert hall seats more than 700.

CLOSE UP

Bedouin Culture

Bedu, the Arabic word from which the name Bedouin derives, simply means "inhabitant of the desert." Some 160,000 Bedouin, seminomadic Arab tribesmen and full citizens of Israel, live in the Negev. The present-day Bedouin of the Negev (and the Sinai) trace their origins to nomads of the Arabian Peninsula who wandered west 400 to 600 years ago. The exceptions are members of the Jebeliya tribe, descendants of East European slaves sent by Emperor Justinian to serve Greek monks at St. Catherine's Monastery at Mt. Sinai. The slaves slowly adopted the Bedouin way of life, and they still serve the monks from their desert nearby.

Since Israel gained independence in 1948, the Bedouin's urbanization and integration into Israeli society has been difficult. The Negev's Bedouin men have loyally served in the Israeli army, and some have lost their lives doing so. Starting in the late 1960s, however, the Israeli government built seven Bedouin towns, the largest of which is Rahat (a settlement of over 40,000 residents ten minutes north of Beersheva), and encouraged resettlement. Their simple, nomadic way of life becomes more difficult to maintain each year as they resist these policies.

Earning a living. The Bedouin's main livelihood is the raising of livestock, camels and black goats in particular. The animals supply milk, meat, hair for weaving, and dung for burning as fuel. The wanderings of the Bedouin are driven by the unending search for grazing land and water for their flocks. Marriages are arranged, taking family interests into account. It is not uncommon today for a man to have two wives, the first wife and a younger one to help her. The Bedouin boast one of the highest birth rates in the world.

The family is structured as a business. Men, who work as herders, make decisions about buying and selling livestock as well as finding new pastures. Women and children do the cooking, weaving, searching for firewood, and often caring for the flocks.

Hospitality and heritage. A Bedouin proverb says, "He who shares my bread and salt is not my enemy." Bedouin are known for their warm hospitality. It is not only a pleasure to extend hospitality but the Bedouin see it as a duty. A Bedouin host would never fail to invite a stranger into his tent. And refusing a Bedouin's invitation would be unthinkable because it would deny the host an opportunity to display his kindness. Having the honor of being invited by a Bedouin host to drink sweet tea or coffee, made over an open fire in his tent, is an unforgettable experience. A Bedouin tent is customarily divided into two sections by a woven curtain known as a *ma'nad*. Having been welcomed into a tent, guests are honored, respected, and nourished, frequently with cardamom-spiced coffee, and music played on a traditional instrument called the *rababa*, a one-string violin.

A rich heritage of poetry has been passed down through the generations by word of mouth. Only in the past few years have these words been recorded, written in their original Arabic, and preserved by scholars who recognize that the Bedouin way of life is rapidly slipping away.

THEATER

Once a year, in March or April, the **Light Opera Group of the Negev** (☎ *08/641–4081*), a nonprofit group of amateur singers, presents performances of Gilbert and Sullivan and other light operas and musicals in English like *My Fair Lady* and *South Pacific*.

SHOPPING

Although the Negev is still home to the Bedouin, many of today's Bedouin women are less inclined than yesterday's to stay home weaving. An eagle's eye and a saint's patience will guide your search through the bundles and stacks of rather ordinary stuff at the **Bedouin market,** where you can find goods made by elder generations. The market starts at daybreak each Thursday and lasts until early afternoon; south of the Old City, it's on the eastern side of the huge outdoor market site near the bridge, at Derech Eilat and Derech Hebron streets. (A goat and sheep sale takes place once in a while.) The best time to visit is 6 am, an hour or so later in winter. Walk to the back, passing coffee and tea sellers. For sale, if you can find them, are embroidered dresses, yokes, and side panels from dresses; woven camel bags; bales of wool; rugs; earrings, bracelets, amulets, and nose rings; coin headbands (used as dowry gifts); tassels; copperware; and *finjans* (Bedouin coffee pots).

An elegant desert wine shop? You may be surprised by the state-of-the-art design, stock of imported and local wines, and well-informed staff (including owner Oded Arnat) at **Wine Aficionado (Aninei Ha-Yayin)** (✉ *117 Trumpeldor St., across the street from the Muslim cemetery* ☎ *08/628–9444*).

EN ROUTE

On Route 40 northeast from Beersheva to Arad is the large and impressive **Monument to the Negev Brigade,** designed by Israeli artist Danny Karavan and built during the 1960s. The monument's 18 symbolic parts and Hebrew text tell the story of the Palmach's Negev Brigade, which halted the Egyptian attack during the War of Independence after the birth of the State of Israel in 1948. Framed by two acacia trees, the tower offers a great view of Beersheva and the surrounding desert.

SIDE TRIP TO PETRA

Poet Dean Burgon called Petra, the ancient city of dazzling facades tucked into the mountains of southern Jordan, the "rose-red city, half as old as time." Situated between the Red Sea and the Dead Sea, Petra is about two hours north of Eilat, and four hours south of the Jordanian capital Amman. Its boulevards, temples, and splendid tombs (800 in all) secreted among the high cliffs, evoke incomparable mystery and grandeur. Once inaccessible to all but an intrepid few, it is now easier to reach and has become an increasingly popular destination since the Israel-Jordan border was opened in 1994.

Petra (called Rekem in the Dead Sea Scrolls) lies in the biblical region of Edom. According to Genesis, the Edomites were descendants of Esau, Jacob's brother and rival. Edom's fertile land was a magnet that desert dwellers couldn't ignore, but the Edomites were careful to keep it exclusive. When Moses led the Israelites to the Promised Land and asked to pass through Edom, he was denied.

By the 7th century BC, a new group had swept in from Arabia: the Nabateans. It is their spectacular tombs and carved monuments that draw travelers to Petra today. With a wealthy empire that at its height reached from Damascus to the Sinai, the Nabateans controlled the region's trade routes, their caravans bearing frankincense and myrrh, Indian silks, and African ivory.

WORD OF MOUTH

"I had expected Petra to be the high point of my trip to Jordan, and it was. I can't stress too strongly that this is a must-see site. I also can't stress too strongly that you need . . . plenty of time, and you need to climb some steps. . . . The colors of the veined rocks were breathtaking (and hopelessly photogenic)—beautiful multicolored swirls that seemed almost too regular to be natural." —thursdaysd

Most of Petra's famous tombs—which fuse Graeco-Roman, Egyptian, and Mesopotamian styles—were carved during the 1st century AD, before the Nabatean kingdom was subsumed into the Roman Empire. Although the combination of a necropolis and a capital city may seem strange today, this custom was common among ancient peoples, who established cemeteries at the entrances to many of their capitals. The presence of tombs of the rich and powerful near the city's major monuments was perhaps part of a cult of the dead. When travelers came to the city, they would leave offerings at the tombs to ensure the success of their journeys.

Gradually, Christianity replaced the old religion, and churches were built in Petra. Around the same time, the rise of sea trade began to precipitate Petra's decline, as ancient traders learned that they could use prevailing winds to hasten ships across the sea. Some Arabian goods began to come to Egypt and its Mediterranean ports via the Red Sea. It didn't help that a series of earthquakes left a ruinous mark on the city.

After Petra's takeover by the Muslims in 633, alliances and crossroads changed and the rest of the world lost interest in the area. The Crusaders built fortifications among the ruins in the 11th century, but after their 1189 surrender to the Muslim warrior Saladin, the city sank into oblivion. Only the local Bedouin knew its treasures. It was not until 1812 that Swiss explorer Johann Ludwig Burckhardt rediscovered Petra, providing the Western world with its first contemporary description of the marvels of this Nabataean caravan-city. It is now justly recognized as a United Nations World Heritage Site.

TOP ATTRACTIONS

Colonnaded Street. The Romans built the main street of Petra in the early 1st century BC. In typical Roman style, it became the city's major thoroughfare, suitable for both commerce and grand ceremonial processions. After the Roman annexation of the Nabatean kingdom, the street was restored, as noted in an inscription dated AD 114 and dedicated to Emperor Trajan. The original marble paving stones as well as remains of statues of deities still stand, including those depicting Hermes (messenger of the gods) and Tyche (goddess of fortune). In

8

PETRA PLANNER

When to Go

Summer temperatures hit 100 degrees, but it can get chilly and rainy in January and February. In all seasons, sturdy shoes are essential for negotiating the rocky, uneven terrain. If traveling during the Muslim holy month of Ramadan, some services may not be available. Check with your hotel or the tourist office ahead of time.

Touring Petra

A number of operators run tours to Petra that you can reserve in advance from Eilat. They're a good option if you want to see the highlights without worrying about logistics. (*www.petraisrael.com* offers tips on arranging tours to Petra from Israel.)

Visitor Information

Petra's visitor center (*03/215–6029* *www.petrapark.com* *1-day pass JD 50; 2-day pass JD 55* *Summer 6–6; winter 6–4*), next to the site entrance, has brochures and you can arrange local guides for a basic two-hour Petra tour for a flat fee of JD 15. A modern, new visitor center is planned and construction is underway. It's expected to be finished in early 2012.

Getting Here and Around

Air Travel: El Al and Royal Jordanian Airlines both fly to Amman, Jordan's capital, from Tel Aviv's Ben Gurion Airport. This option has limited appeal, as you must be at the airport two hours before flight time for the 15-minute flight, then drive three hours from Amman to Petra.

Twice a week, Arkia airlines offers one-day guided tours in which you fly from Tel Aviv to Eilat at 6:30 am, drive to Petra in an air-conditioned bus, spend three hours walking through Petra, and take a return flight arriving in Tel Aviv at 9 pm. The rate per person is $312 (*www.arkia.com*).

Bus Travel: To get to Petra from Aqaba—the Jordanian town just across the border that shares the Red Sea shore with Eilat—two buses a day run at a cost of JD 5, but there is no specific timetable.

To get to Petra from Amman, public buses run from Amman's Mujema Al Janoub, or the South Bus Station. They depart when full. Three private bus companies offer air-conditioned service between Petra and Amman: **Alpha** (*06/582–7623*); **Jett** (*06/569–6151*); and **Trust** (*06/581–3449*).

Car Travel: A parking area on the Israeli side of the border makes it possible to drive a rental car here, but only cars registered to their drivers can be taken into Jordan. For those taking longer trips, rental cars are available in Aqaba and Petra. Hidab Hotel can book rental cars from local agencies. There is an Avis agency in the Moevenpick Hotel in Petra and in Aqaba. The Hertz office in Petra is located next to the Palace Hotel on the main street of Wadi Musa.

Taxi Travel: Once you cross into Jordan from Eilat, shared taxis are available on the Jordanian side of the border to take you into Aqaba, where you can rent a car or take the bus to Petra if the scheduling is right. A shared taxi to Aqaba costs about JD 10, which is divided among the passengers. If your time in Petra is limited, consider taking the faster but costlier private taxi, which will run you JD 45 to JD 50; be prepared to negotiate.

Crossing the Border

The closest border crossing to Petra is just north of Eilat at what is called the Arava crossing. Cross the border early in the morning to avoid waiting in line behind large tour groups and aim to be in Petra before noon. When crossing back from Jordan to Israel, bring JD 6 for the Jordanian exit tax.

Americans need a visa to enter Jordan. It can be bought on the spot for about NIS 88.

Most visitors take a taxi to the Jordan border from Eilat (10 minutes, NIS 35), walk across, and catch a taxi to Petra on the other side (about JD 45). The Arava border crossing, just north of Eilat, is open Sunday to Thursday 6:30 am to 10 pm, Friday and Saturday 8 to 8. The crossing is closed on the religious holidays Yom Kippur and Id el Fitr. Two other border crossings might be convenient under certain circumstances. The Allenby Bridge crossing (known in Jordan as the King Hussein crossing, four hours' drive from Petra) is about 45 minutes from Jerusalem. If you plan to enter Jordan at the Allenby Bridge, the most direct route from Jerusalem to Amman, you'll need to obtain your visa ahead of time at the Jordanian Embassy in Tel Aviv or in your country of origin. Remember to bring a passport photo. The northern Beit She'an border crossing (five hours' drive from Petra) is approximately 40 minutes from Tiberias.

Before traveling to Jordan, make sure to check your government's travel advisory and always exercise caution.

Money Matters

The Jordanian unit of currency is the dinar, abbreviated JD. The exchange rate at press time was approximately JD 0.7 to the U.S. dollar. You can change money at the Moevenpick, next to the entrance to Petra.

WHAT IT COSTS

	¢	$	$$	$$$	$$$$
Restaurants	under JD 3	JD 3–JD 4	JD 4–JD 5	JD 5–JD 7	over JD 7
Hotels	under $35	$35–$50	$50–$65	$65–$110	over $110

Restaurant prices are in Jordanian dinar, for one main course at dinner. Hotel prices are in U.S. dollars, for two people in a standard double room in high season.

Planning Your Time

An overnight (two-day) trip to Petra is optimal. Be prepared for a lot of walking: it's about 2 miles from the entry to the Basin restaurant.

Begin at the Horse Square and walk through the narrow, mysterious Siq to the Treasury, Petra's most magnificent facade. From there, continue along what was once the city's main street, lined with monuments from Petra's glory days. Walk along the Colonnaded Street to the Basin for lunch. The route back is the same but the sun striking the rocks at different angles reveals new dimensions of the site's beauty; note that the way back is uphill. The horse-drawn carriages you'll see are meant only for the infirm, but they can be hired, gypsy-cab style, by tired pedestrians. Expect to pay about JD 40 from the entry to the Treasury or JD 40 from the Basin to the entry. In the evening, enjoy the sunset from a hotel balcony or rooftop terrace. Check at the visitor center to see if the Petra by Night tour is on.

On the second day, you can return to the Treasury and explore other sites, perhaps making the climb up to the Monastery. There are lots of well-stocked souvenir shops by the visitor center if you want some souvenirs or gifts.

AD 363 an earthquake devastated Petra and the surrounding region, and the street never returned to its former glory.

> **WORD OF MOUTH**
>
> "You can definitely do Petra in a day [from Israel], but it is a really long day. It takes a while to get through the border, then get on a bus or van for the two-to-three hour drive to Wadi Musa before you even actually walk around Petra. If you like walking, you could spend a long time wandering around and exploring—more time than you might be allowed for a day trip. We did the day trip, and wished that we had taken a more relaxing two-day tour." —ALF

Great Temple. No one can say for sure who was worshipped at this temple, or if it was the seat of the city's government. But the dozens of columns that adorn its courtyards, beautifully restored in recent years by archaeologists from Brown University, attest to its ancient grandeur; it even boasted its own theater, which some scholars believe may have been a meeting hall for Petra's rulers.

Qasr al-Bint. This structure's full name, which translates as the "Palace of the Daughter of Pharaoh," derives from a legend that the pharaoh's daughter promised she would marry the man who could channel water to the city where she lived. When she had to choose between two winners, she asked each how he had managed his appointed task. The one whose answer she preferred won her hand. In fact, the structure was the most important temple in Petra, built in the early 1st century AD. As in the Temple of the Winged Lions, the identity of the deity worshipped here isn't known, but a statue depicting him or her—perhaps Dushara, the greatest deity of the Nabatean pantheon—certainly stood in the temple's inner sanctum. A giant marble hand, part of a colossal statue, was discovered here in 1959.

Siq. The main entrance to Petra, in ancient times as in ours, is through the Siq (meaning "cleft"), a narrow, 1200-meter long canyon between towering walls of astonishing red and purple-hued stone. Bands of Nabatean paving stones are still visible along the way. Votive niches, some of which contain inscriptions dating from the 2nd and 3rd centuries AD, show that this road served as much as a ceremonial path as a passageway. Your first glimpse of the magnificent Treasury, after you've walked a hundred meters or so through the narrow Siq, will take your breath away. Film buffs may recall Harrison Ford galloping through this area in *Indiana Jones and the Last Crusade.*

Theater. This semicircular amphitheater is a clear sign of the extent to which the Nabateans, like most other peoples of this region, had adopted Roman culture. The Nabateans apparently had no qualms about building a theater in a cemetery; their stonemasons even cut into some of the existing tombs (the remains of which you can see at the back of the rock-cut theater) to do so. The capacity of the theater has been estimated at 7,000.

★ **Treasury.** The Siq opens suddenly onto Petra's most famous monument, known locally as the Khazneh. This 130-foot-high structure displays a splendid frontage graced by a number of mythological figures adopted

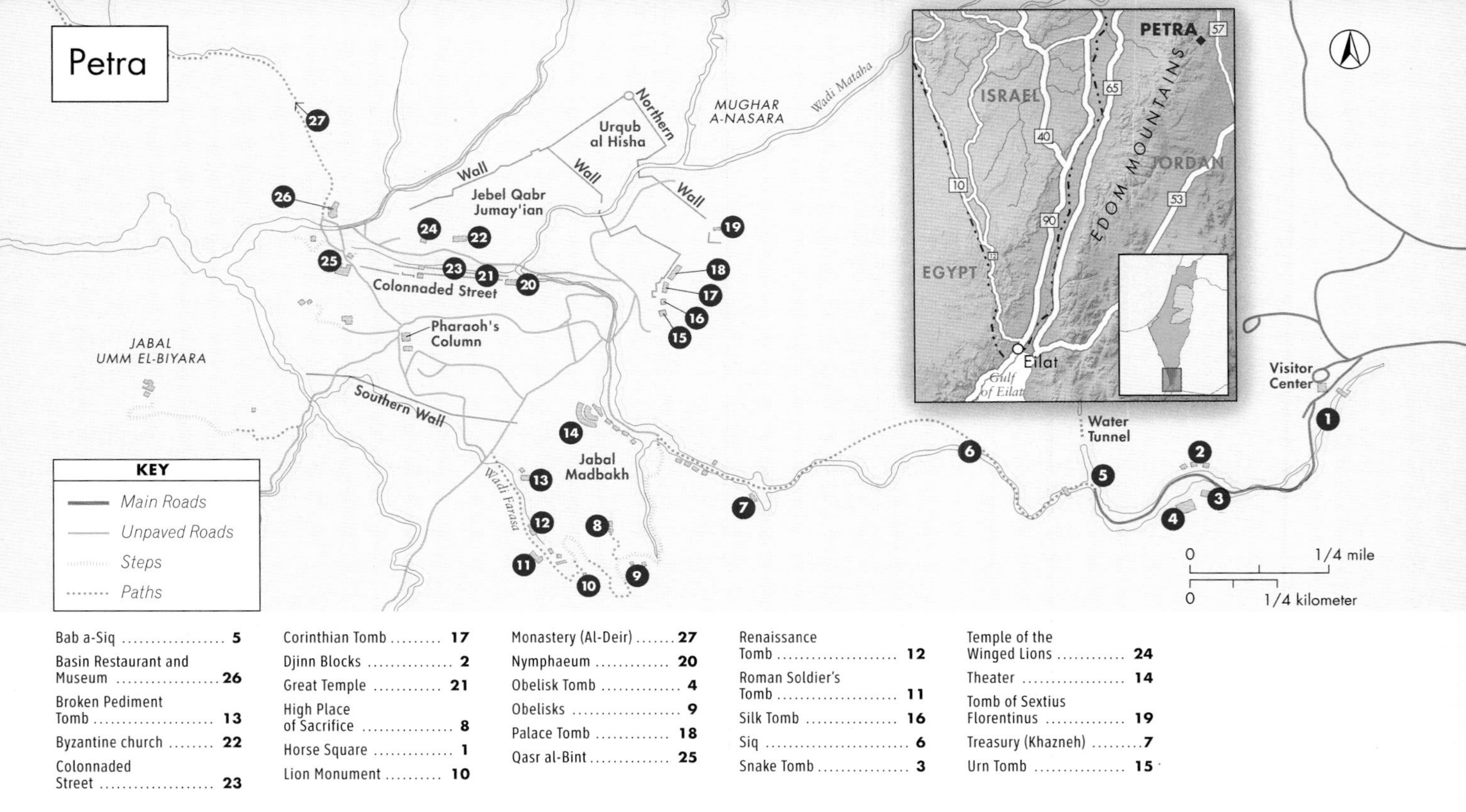
Petra
KEY
Main Roads
Unpaved Roads
Steps
Paths
PETRA
EDOM MOUNTAINS
ISRAEL
JORDAN
EGYPT
Eilat
Gulf of Eilat
57
65
40
10
53
90
12
Visitor Center
Water Tunnel
0
1/4 mile
0
1/4 kilometer
MUGHAR A-NASARA
Wadi Mataha
Northern
Urqub al Hisha
Wall
Wall
Wall
Jebel Qabr Jumay'ian
Colonnaded Street
Pharaoh's Column
JABAL UMM EL-BIYARA
Southern Wall
Jabal Madbakh
Wadi Farasa
Bab a-Siq 5
Basin Restaurant and Museum 26
Broken Pediment Tomb 13
Byzantine church 22
Colonnaded Street 23
Corinthian Tomb 17
Djinn Blocks 2
Great Temple 21
High Place of Sacrifice 8
Horse Square 1
Lion Monument 10
Monastery (Al-Deir) 27
Nymphaeum 20
Obelisk Tomb 4
Obelisks 9
Palace Tomb 18
Qasr al-Bint 25
Renaissance Tomb 12
Roman Soldier's Tomb 11
Silk Tomb 16
Siq 6
Snake Tomb 3
Temple of the Winged Lions 24
Theater 14
Tomb of Sextius Florentinus 19
Treasury (Khazneh) 7
Urn Tomb 15
8

by the Nabateans from Greek and Roman worship. Castor and Pollux (who after their deaths became the two brightest stars in the constellation Gemini), Amazons, Gorgons, eagles, and other creatures march across the Khazneh's rosy facade. Between the columns of the *tholos* (the rounded section above the tympanum) are the remains of a female deity holding a cornucopia; she is believed to be al-Uzza, the patroness of Petra and the Nabatean version of Aphrodite, goddess of love.

The full Arabic name for this monument is Khazneh Fara'un, or Pharaoh's Treasury. It was assumed by archaeologists to be a royal tomb, and legends of treasures allegedly secreted within have drawn grave robbers to this place for centuries. The urn carved at the top of the tholos was thought to be the hiding place for the hoard. The Bedouin have been taking potshots at it for generations in the hopes of dislodging its contents, a practice whose results are still visible.

WORTH NOTING

Bab a-Siq. The Gate of the Cleft opens onto the Siq, the canyon-lined passageway leading to the main sights. From here you can spot the remains of a Nabatean water tunnel, built to divert flood waters from coursing through the narrow cleft and flooding the necropolis. A dam, constructed for the same purpose in the second half of the 1st century AD, was restored by the Jordanians after particularly serious flooding some years ago.

Broken Pediment Tomb. One of a series of facades carved into the western face of Jabal Madhbah, or the Mount of the Altar, this tomb is characterized by the broken-off gable of its roof, supported by four pilasters topped with Nabatean capitals.

Byzantine Church. Richly decorated with mosaics in the characteristic style of the period, this church (discovered by the American archaeologist Kenneth Russell, and excavated in the 1990s) appears to have been destroyed by fire soon after its construction, perhaps in a severe earthquake that took place in AD 551. The remains, including a spectacular mosaic floor, have undergone only partial conservation. One hundred and forty papyrus scrolls were found here.

Corinthian Tomb. Set among some of Petra's finest tombs is one named for the large number of Corinthian capitals, now badly deteriorated, that once decorated its facade.

Djinn Blocks. The function of these three large structures is unclear; they may have been connected to Nabatean worship, perhaps symbolizing one of their deities. In Arabic, *djinn* refers to malevolent spirits, a common theme in Arab folklore.

★ **High Place of Sacrifice.** An ancient flight of stairs cut into the rock—and restored by the Jordanian Department of Antiquities—leads to the summit of Jabal Madhbah, or the Mount of the Altar. Its peak, besides offering spectacular views of Petra below, contains a rectangular court surrounded on three sides by benches in the triclinium style of the Roman dining room; in the center of the court is a raised block of stone, on which the priest may have stood. To the west are two altars accessed by steps, in front of which is a channel into which the blood of the sacrificial animal drained.

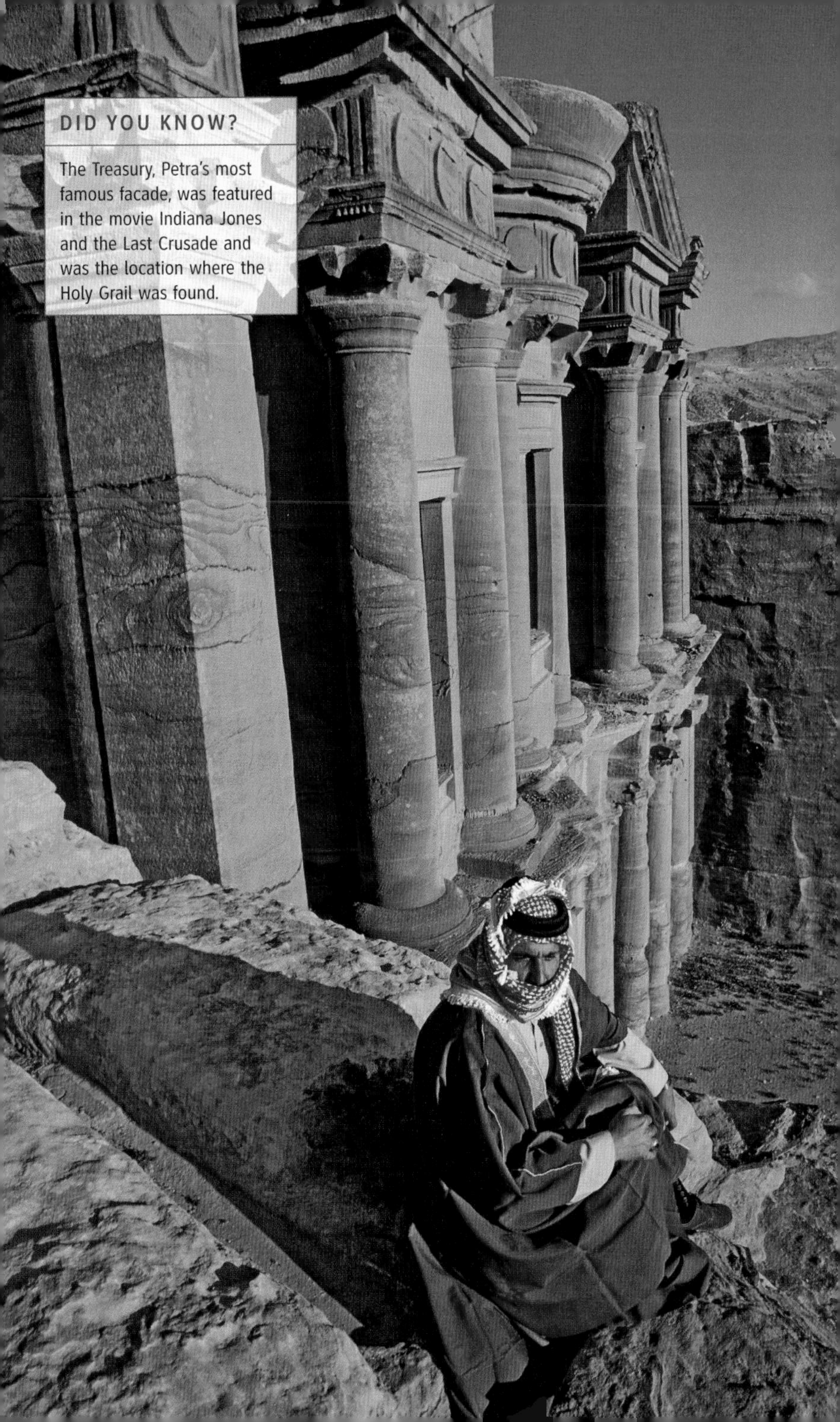

DID YOU KNOW?

The Treasury, Petra's most famous facade, was featured in the movie Indiana Jones and the Last Crusade and was the location where the Holy Grail was found.

Horse Square. Horses used to be the conveyance of choice for the approximately 1-km (½-mi) trip to Petra's main antiquities. Your entry ticket currently entitles you to a horseback ride (no carriage) along the first 800 yards of the path before it narrows to become the Siq; you'll still be expected to tip though (about 5JD), and many people skip this.

Lion Monument. Surface runoff fed this fountain on the path to the High Place via a channel leading to the lion's mouth, from which water once streamed.

★ **Monastery (Al-Deir).** Second only to the Treasury in its magnificence, the Monastery is reached at the end of a winding uphill 4-km (2½-mi) trail. It's larger than the Treasury (it stands 170 feet wide), but less impressively ornate. An inscription was discovered nearby referring to "the symposium of Obodas the God." From this inscription, archeologists deduced that the Monastery was built 2,000 years ago as a meeting place for members of the cult of Obodas. Either tomb or temple, it holds a spacious chamber cut deep into the mountainside, and offers sweeping views of the adjacent gorges.

Museum. Petra's museum, which has restrooms, is in the same building as The Basin restaurant. Displays include a small number of Nabatean artifacts, such as jewelry and pottery.

Nymphaeum. Dedicated to the water nymphs, this fountain was used for both refreshment and worship. The fountains of the two-story structure were fed by a water channel that continued along Petra's main street.

Obelisk Tomb. This upper story of a two-story tomb is named for the four freestanding obelisks that decorate its facade. The lower story, the Triclinium Tomb, was so named because three walls of the empty room are lined with *triclinia*, a Latin word for this kind of bench. Sacred memorial feasts to honor the dead were held here.

Obelisks. On the terrace below the High Place stand two obelisks hewed from the bedrock, examples of a common method of representing deities in the ancient Near East. Some scholars believe them to be representations of Dushara and al-Uzza; others believe they are simply the remains of quarries.

Palace Tomb. This unfinished tomb is one of the few in Petra not carved entirely out of the rock. Many of the tomb's constructed segments have fallen away, so it's hard to ascertain its original dimensions. At the base of the Palace Tomb are the remains of the northern city wall, built after the 1st century BC.

Renaissance Tomb. This tomb, bearing a pediment with three urns, bears a close resemblance to the Tomb of Sextius Florentinus, in the main part of the city. It may have been created around the same time, the first third of the 1st century AD.

Roman Soldier's Tomb. The headless figure in the niche of this unusual tomb's facade is dressed in typical Roman military garb, while the friezes and floral capitals appear more typical of Nabatean architecture before the Roman annexation. Directly opposite the Roman Soldier's Tomb is a triclinium; the rubble in between was probably once a colonnaded courtyard connecting the two edifices.

WORD OF MOUTH

"Once you're in Petra, you start descending the valley (meaning you'll be going uphill on the way back). Make sure you have comfortable shoes." —W9London

Silk Tomb. The striations of natural color in the Silk Tomb's rock make it one of Petra's finest and certainly the easiest to spot. The ribbons of rock flow across the facade like a multicolored silk scarf blowing in the wind.

Snake Tomb. No outward decoration marks this tomb, but 12 burial niches are carved into the floor inside. The name comes from a rough wall relief that shows two snakes attacking what may be a dog. Notice also the horse-and-rider relief above it.

Temple of the Winged Lions. This impressive building overlooking the Colonnaded Street takes its name from the sculptures that serve as capitals for its columns. The identity of the deity worshipped within is unknown, but votive figurines suggest that it may have been Isis, Egyptian goddess of the heavens and patroness of fertility. An inscription dates the construction of the temple to around AD 27, during the reign of Aretas IV.

Tomb of Sextius Florentinus. This is one of the few Petra monuments that can be dated with certainty: the name of this Roman governor of Arabia who died in office in AD 128 appears in the Latin inscription over the tomb's doorway.

Urn Tomb. Named for the vaselike decoration at the top of its pediment, this is the largest of Petra's royal tombs. It is supported by a series of vaults at its lower level, dubbed *al makhamah* (the law court) by the locals for some long-lost reason; the upper level was called *a-sijn* (the prison). Although originally carved around AD 70, according to an inscription within, Petra's Byzantine Christians turned the Urn Tomb into a church in AD 446.

8

WHERE TO EAT AND STAY

Dining in the town closest to the antiquities site of Petra—Wadi Musa—ranges from simple, inexpensive fare to the elegant and pricey, with little in between. Both dining experiences, however, have one thing in common: courteous service and a welcoming spirit. Don't be put off by the plainness of the center-village eateries mentioned here. The locals enjoying their meal at the next table will remind you that the best fare is often to be had at such unostentatious restaurants.

Petra has many lodging options. You can choose from luxurious to money-saving accommodations; both can be found adjacent to or near the site. The hotels closest to the site obviously provide the most convenient access to Petra and save you taxi money. A short car drive away in Wadi Musa are several good hotels, with some on the ridge above Wadi Musa. Taybet Zeman, in the village of Taybeh 9 km (5½ mi) from Petra, is the farthest from the site, but its uniquely authentic flavor is well worth the ride. All rooms have a private bath unless otherwise indicated.

$$–$$$ MIDDLE EASTERN ✕ **Al-Arabi.** This is a reliable place for a quick, inexpensive lunch, where diners can get a substantial meal, including mixed grill (their specialty), shawarma, barbecued meats, and hummus. The interior is very simple but bright. Look for the red sign on the left as you walk uphill. ✉ *Main St., Wadi Musa* ☎ *03/215–7681* ▭ *AE, MC, V.*

> **WORD OF MOUTH**
>
> "Hint: if you have any Israeli shekels left over, spend them in Petra on food, souvenirs, etc. In the hotel they only wanted dinars or dollars, but in historic Petra, EVERY vendor was happy to take shekels—just make sure you know the exchange rate before you leave Israel!" —Pitzikat

$$$$ MIDDLE EASTERN ✕ **The Basin.** This buffet restaurant owned by the Crowne Plaza Hotel is in the antiquities site of Petra at the end of the Colonnaded Street. The only one inside the site itself, it serves hummus, baba ghanoush, and a variety of salads. It may not be the most imaginative meal you'll ever have, but the shaded patio offers a pleasant midday break. ✉ *Petra* ☎ *03/215–6266* ▭ *AE, MC, V.*

$$$ MIDDLE EASTERN ✕ **Petra Zeman.** The specialty here is *maklouba,* a chicken-and-rice dish that the locals call "upside down" because servers seem to enjoy the diners' reaction as they turn the pot upside down with a flourish on the serving tray at the table. This is also a great place to try the Jordanian national dish, *mansaf*—lamb in a tangy yogurt sauce served over rice. Dessert, here and everywhere in town, means a tiny cup of strong coffee spiced with *hel* (cardamom) and a dish of baklava, or one of the many kindred versions of this Middle Eastern honey-and-pistachio sweet. ✉ *Main St., Wadi Musa* ☎ *79/553–6391* ▭ *AE, MC, V.*

$$$$ **Crowne Plaza Petra.** The three-story Crowne Plaza is conveniently adjacent to Petra's entrance. Next door is the Petra Cave, the hotel's bar-discothèque, with nightly live Arabic and Western music, and "hubbly-bubblies"—water-pipes—for those who want to try smoking tobacco the traditional Middle Eastern way. Rooms are clean and serviceable, and although none has a balcony, many offer stunning views. **Pros:** excellent location; refreshing pool. **Cons:** outdated furnishings; small rooms. ✉ *Tourism St., Wadi Musa* ☎ *03/215–6266* 📠 *03/215–6977* 🌐 *www.petra.crowneplaza.com* *147 rooms, 3 suites, 31 hillside chalets* *In-room: a/c, safe, Internet. In-hotel: 3 restaurants, bar, tennis court, pool, gym, Internet terminal* ▭ *MC, V.*

$$$$ **Marriott Petra.** This excellent three-floor hotel is located on the ridge above Petra, somewhat farther away than the other hotels, though free shuttle service to the Petra entrance is available. Most rooms offer spectacular views of the Petra Valley below. A marble-floor lobby and high atrium of white stone arches greet you. Guests can take advantage of the spa with Turkish bath and sauna, and visit the Bedouin tent behind the hotel. **Pros:** stunning sunset views; Petra's best Italian restaurant, L'Affresco. **Cons:** 15-minute drive to Petra entrance; does not change Israeli currency. ✉ *Queen Rania Al Abdallah St., Wadi Musa* ☎ *03/215–6407* 🌐 *www.marriott.com/hotels* *99 rooms, 1 suite* *In-hotel: 2 restaurants, bar, pool, spa, Wi-Fi hotspot* ▭ *MC, V.*

$$$$ **Moevenpick.** One good reason to stay here is the unmatched location. Located just steps from the entrance to Petra, this five-floor, Swiss-run hotel has comfortable rooms with blond-wood furnishings and gold-framed mirrors, some with balconies. A beautiful Oriental

interior courtyard with arabesques, a fountain, and palm trees is the ideal place for an afternoon coffee, after which you can enjoy the sunset from the roof garden, or take a refreshing dip in the outdoor pool. **Pros:** the hotel's sumptuous Al Iwan restaurant is the best in Wadi Musa; the breakfast buffet is excellent; quiet. **Cons:** no views to speak of; slow Internet. *Box 214, Wadi Musa 03/215–7111 www.moevenpick-petra.com 183 rooms In-hotel: 2 restaurants, bar, pool, gym AE, DC, MC, V.*

$$$$ **Taybet Zeman.** Nine kilometers (5½ mi) from Petra, on the outskirts of the town of Taybeh, this charming lodging was once a Bedouin village. Abandoned for years, it was eventually revamped into a serene hotel that has every modern amenity but has been designed to steep guests in aspects of Bedouin culture that have all but disappeared. Rooms are spacious and decorated in authentic Bedouin style with throw rugs and wall hangings—a colorful counterpoint to the natural stone walls. They open onto alleys and small courtyards. At the hotel's souk (market) you can watch handcrafted items being made. The central courtyard has a spice garden, and its yields are served in the hotel's excellent restaurant, where the menu mixes Eastern and Western favorites. The buffet is worth a trip in itself. The hotel has one wheelchair-accessible room. **Pros:** on a ridge high above Petra, the hotel offers views of the mountains of Edom, especially from the Diwan, its garden terrace; excellent service. **Cons:** not within walking distance to the entrance to Petra; no air-conditioning in many rooms, and some rooms, while quaint, are rather dark. *Queen Ranya St., Wadi Musa 03/215–0111 105 rooms In-hotel: restaurant, pools, laundry facilities AE, MC, V.*

NIGHTLIFE AND THE ARTS

The **Petra by Night** candlelit walk of Petra is atmospheric. Strolling through the Siq as shadows play on the canyon walls allows you to appreciate another side of the magnificent carved city. Music is played on traditional instruments such as the rababa. The two-hour event occurs Monday, Wednesday, and Thursday at 8:30 pm (JD 12). Check for availability at the Petra visitor center. It's recommended to do this first, if you arrive in the evening, and then go back and do a thorough visit the next day; it can seem anticlimactic if you already know what to expect. Keep in mind that the walk through the Siq to the treasury is about a kilometer, downhill on the way in, and back up the same route out; there are no carriage rides at night. (*03/215–6029*).

SHOPPING

Petra's handicraft specialty is the work of its "sand artists"—artisans who fill bottles with sand in a variety of hues and complex designs. They can customize the purchase by writing a name or other text in the sand. The artists work and sell their unique wares in shops in Wadi Musa, as well as in the Siq.

HEBREW VOCABULARY

Many people in Israel speak at least one other language, in addition to Hebrew, and most can get by in English. So the chances of getting too lost for words are slim. At the same time, your traveling experience can be enriched by having at least a few words to share in conversation or to use while touring and shopping, even at the local grocery store. Here are some basic words and expressions that may be of use during your stay. Please note that the letters "kh" in this glossary are pronounced like the "ch" in chanuka or the Scottish loch.

GREETINGS AND BASICS

ENGLISH	HEBREW TRANSLITERATION	PRONUNCIATION
Hello/good-bye/peace	Shalom	shah-**lohm**
Nice to meet you	Na'im me'od	nah-**eem** meh-**ohd**
Good morning	Boker tov	boh-ker **tohv**
Good evening	Erev tov	eh-rev **tohv**
Good night	Layla tov	lahy-lah tohv
How are you?	Ma shlomekh?	mah shloh-**maykh**
How are you? (to a man)	Ma shlomkha?	mah shlohm-**khah**
How are you?	Ma nishma?	mah-nee-**shmah**
Fine	Beseder	beh-**say-dehr**
Everything is fine	Hakol beseder	hah-kohl beh-**say-dehr**
Is everything okay?	Hakol beseder?	hah-kohl beh-**say-dehr**
Very well	Tov me'od	tohv-meh-**ohd**
Excellent/terrific	Metzuyan	meh-tzoo-**yahn**
Send regards!	Timsor dash!	teem-sohr **dahsh**
Thank you	Toda	toh-**dah**
Thank you very much	Toda raba	toh-dah rah-**bah**
See you again	Lehitra'ot	leh-heet-rah-**oht**
Yes	Ken	kehn
No	Lo	lo
Maybe	Oolai	**oo**-ligh
Excuse me/Sorry	Slicha	slee-**khah**
Again/Could you repeat that?	Od pa'am	ohd pah-**ahm**

	ENGLISH	HEBREW TRANSLITERATION	PRONUNCIATION
DAYS			
	Today	Hayom	hah-**yohm**
	Tomorrow	Machar	mah-**khahr**
	Yesterday	Etmol	eht-**mohl**
	Sunday	Yom Rishon	yohm ree-**shohn**
	Monday	Yom Sheni	yohm sheh-**nee**
	Tuesday	Yom Shlishi	yohm sh-**leeshee**
	Wednesday	Yom Revi'i	yohm reh-**vee**
	Thursday	Yom Chamishi	yohm kha-mee-**shee**
	Friday	Yom Shishi	yohm shee-**shee**
	Saturday, Sabbath	Shabbat	yohm shah-**bat**
NUMBERS			
	1	Echad	eh-**khad**
	2	Shtayim	shtah-**yeem**
	3	Shalosh	shah-**lohsh**
	4	Arba	ah-**rbah**
	5	Chamesh	chah-**maysh**
	6	Shesh	shehsh
	7	Sheva	**sheh**-vah
	8	Shmoneh	**shmoh**-neh
	9	Teisha	**tay**-shah
	10	Esser	**eh**-sehr
	11	Achad esreh	ah-**chahd** eh-**sreh**
	12	Shteim esreh	sh**taym** eh-**sreh**
	20	Esrim	eh-**sreem**
	50	Chamishim	khah-mee-**sheem**
	100	Me'a	may-**ah**
	200	Ma'tayim	mah-**tah-yeem**

ENGLISH	HEBREW TRANSLITERATION	PRONUNCIATION
USEFUL PHRASES		
Do you speak English?	Ata medaber anglit?	ah-ta meh-dah-ber ahng-**leet**
I don't understand (man)	Ani lo mevin	a-**nee** loh meh-**veen**
I don't understand (woman)	Ani lo m'vina	a-**nee** m'veena
I don't know (man)	Ani lo yodea	a-nee loh yoh-**day**-ah
I don't know (woman)	Ani lo yodaat	a-nee loh yoh-**dah**-aht
I am lost (man)	Ani avud	a-nee ah-**vood**
I am lost (woman)	Ani avuda	a-nee ahvoo-**dah**
I am American	Ani Amerika'i	ah-nee ah-mer-ee-**kah**-ee
I am British	Ani Briti	ah-**nee bree**-tee
I am Canadian	Ani Canadi	ah-**nee** kah-**nah**-dee
What is the time?	Ma hasha'a?	mah hah-shah-**ah**
Just a minute	Rak rega	rahk **reh**-gah
Minute, moment	Rega	**reh**-gah
Now	Achshav	ahkh-**shahv**
Not yet	Od lo	ohd loh
Later	Achar kach	ah-**khahr** kahkh
I would like	Hayiti mevakesh	hah-**yee**-tee m-vah-**kehsh**
Where is..?	Eifo..?	**ay**foh
The central bus station	Hatachana hamerkazit	hah-tah-khah-**nah** hah-mehr-kah-**zeet**
The bus stop	Tachanat ha'autobus	tah-khah-**naht** hah-oh-toh-**boos**
The train station	Tachanat harakevet	tah-khah-**naht** hah-rah-**keh-veht**
The city center	Merkaz ha'ir	mehr kahz hah-**eer**
The post office	Hado'ar	hah-**doh**-ahr

ENGLISH	HEBREW TRANSLITERATION	PRONUNCIATION
A pharmacy	Beit mirkachat	bayt meer-**kah**-khaht
A public telephone	Telefon tziburi	teh-leh-**fohn** tzee-boo-**ree**
A good restaurant	Mis'ada tova	mee-sah-**dah toh-vah**
The rest rooms	Hasherutim	hah-shay-roo-**teem**
Right	Yemina	yeh-**mee**-nah
Left	Smola	s-**moh**-lah
Straight ahead	Yashar	yah-**shar**
Here	Kan	kahn
There	Sham	shahm
Do you have a (vacant) room?	Yesh lachem cheder (panui)?	yehsh lah-**chehm khed**-ehr (pah-**nooy**)
Is it possible to order a taxi?	Efshar lehazmin monit?	ehf-**shahr** leh-hahz-**meen** moh-**neet**
Taxi	Monit	moh-**neet**
A little	k'tzat	keh-**tzaht**
A lot	harbe	hahr-**beh**
Enough	maspik	Mah-**speek**
I have a problem	Yesh li ba'aya	yehsh lee bah-**yah**
I don't feel well (man)	Ani lo margish tov	ah-**nee** loh mahr-**geesh** tohv
I don't feel well (woman)	Ani lo margisha tov	ah-**nee** loh mahr-**gee-shah** tohv
I need a doctor (man)	Ani tzarich rofe	ah-**nee** tzah-**reech** roh-**feh**
I need a doctor (woman)	Ani tzricha rofe	ah-**nee** tzree-**khah** roh-**feh**
Help	Ezra	Eh-**zrah**
Fire	Dleika	duh-leh-**kah**

DINING

ENGLISH	HEBREW TRANSLITERATION	PRONUNCIATION
I would like	Hayiti mevakesh	hah-**yee**-tee m-vah-**kehsh**
Some water, please	Mayim, bevakasha	mah-**yeem** beh-vah-kah-**shah**

ENGLISH	HEBREW TRANSLITERATION	PRONUNCIATION
Bread	Lechem	**leh**-khehm
Soup	Marak	mah-**rahk**
Meat	Bassar	bah-**ssahr**
Chicken	Off	ohf
Vegetables	Yerakot	yeh-rah-**koht**
Dessert	Kinuach	kee-**noo**-ahkh
Cake	Ooga	**oo**-gah
Fruit	Perot	peh-**roht**
Coffee	Cafe	kah-**feh**
Tea	Te	teh
fork	Mazleg	mahz-**lehg**
spoon	Kapit	kah-**peet**
knife	Sakin	sah-**keen**
plate	Tzalachat	tzah-**lah**-chaht
Napkin	Mapit	mah-**peet**
Food	Ochel	**oh**-khehl
Meal	Arucha	ah-roo-**khah**
Breakfast	Aruchat boker	ah-roo-**khaht boh**-ker
Lunch	Aruchat tzaharayim	ah-roo-khaht tzah-hah-**rah**-yeem
Dinner	Aruchat erev	Ahroo-**khaht eh**-rehv
Do you have a menu in English?	Yesh tafrit be'anglit?	yehsh tahf-**reet** beh- ahng-**leet**
A pita filled with falafel	Manat felafel	mah-naht feh-**lah**-fehl
Without hot sauce	Bli charif	blee khah-**reef**
It's tasty, delicious	Zeh ta'im	zeh tah-**eem**
I don't like the taste	Zeh lo ta'im li	zeh loh tah-**eem** lee
The check, please	Cheshbon, bevakasha	Khehsh-bohn beh-vah-kah-**shah**

ENGLISH	HEBREW TRANSLITERATION	PRONUNCIATION

SHOPPING

ENGLISH	HEBREW TRANSLITERATION	PRONUNCIATION
Do you have..?	Yesh lecha..?	yesh leh-khah
Milk	Chalav	khah-**lahv**
(Orange) Juice	Mitz (tapuzim)	meetz (tah-poo-**zeem**)
Butter	Chem'a	khem-**ah**
Cream cheese	Gevina levana	geh-vee-**nah** leh-vah-**nah**
Hard cheese	Gevina tzehuba	gevee-**nah** tzeh-**hoo**-bah
Sausage	Naknik	Nahk-**neek**
Jelly	Riba	**ree**-bah
Sugar	Sukar	**soo**-kahr
Ice cream	Glida	**glee**-da
Map	Mapa	**mah**-pa
Cigarettes	Sigariyot	see-gahr-ee-**yoht**
Telephone card (for public phones)	Telecart	teh-leh-**kahrt**
That one, please	Et zeh, bevakasha	eht zeh, beh-vah-kah-**shah**
May I see it?	Efshar lir'ot?	ehf-**shahr** leer-**oht**
How much does it cost?	Kama zeh oleh?	**kah**-ma zeh **ohleh**
That's expensive!	Yakar!	yah-**kahr**
No, it's too expensive	Lo, zeh yakar midai	loh, zeh yah-**kahr** meed-**igh**
Too big	Gadol midai	gah-dohl meed-**igh**
Too small	Katan midai	kah-tan meed-**igh**
Perhaps there is a discount ?	Yesh hanacha oolai	Yehsh hah-na-**khah** oo-ligh oo-**ligh**
I'll take it	Ani ekach et zeh	ah-nee eh-**kakh** eht zeh

PALESTINIAN ARABIC VOCABULARY

Arabic is spoken by all Arab citizens of Israel (about 20% of the Israeli population) and in the West Bank and Gaza. The areas where you're most likely to hear Arabic are East Jerusalem, Jaffa, and Nazareth, and in the popular sites of the West Bank, Bethlehem and Jericho (when these are open to travelers). Many people in these areas speak some English, but a little Arabic will come in handy with some vendors and taxi drivers or when you are in more rural areas and villages. It helps to have a written address for a taxi ride as well. You may run into small differences in dialect and accent between villages and cities, but for the most part Palestinians dialects are similar.

Some letters in Arabic do not have English equivalents. This glossary tries to approximate Arabic sounds. The letter 'r' is always rolled. When you see 'gh' at the start of a word, pronounce it like a French 'r', lightly gargled at the back of the throat. Any double letters should be extended: 'aa' is pronounced as an extended 'ah'; 'hh' is an extended 'h' sound; 'ss' is an extended hiss.

GREETINGS AND BASICS

ENGLISH	ARABIC TRANSLITERATION	PRONUNCIATION
Hello/ peace be upon you	salamou alaikom	sah-**lah**-moo aah-**lay**-kom
(reply) Hello/ and peace be upon you	wa aalaikom essalaam	wah aah-**lay**-kom **ehss**-sah-**ahm**
Good-bye	maa issalameh	**maah** is-**ah-lah**-meh
Mr./ Sir	sayyed	**sigh**-yed
Mrs./ Madam	sayyida	**sigh**-yee-dah
Miss	anisseh	**ah**-niss-say
How are you? (man speaking)	keif hhalak	kayf **hah**-luck
How are you? (woman speaking)	keif hhalik	kayf **hah**-lik
Fine, thank you	bi kheir elhhamdilla	bee **khayr** el-**ham**-dihl-lah
Pleased to meet you	tsharrafna	tshahr-**ruhf**-nah
Please (man)	min fadlak	min **fahd**-lahk
Please (woman)	min fadlik	min **fahd**-lik
Thank you	shokran	shohk-rahn
God willing	Inshallah	ihn-**shahl-lah**
Yes	aah or naam	aah or naahm
No	la	lah

ENGLISH	ARABIC TRANSLITERATION	PRONUNCIATION
I'm Sorry (man)	mit assif	miht **ass**-sef
I'm Sorry (woman)	mit assfeh	miht **ass**-feh

DAYS

Today	eliom	el-**yohm**
Tomorrow	bokra	bok-rah
Yesterday	embarehh	ehm-**bah**-rehh
Sunday	il ahhad	**il ah**-had
Monday	Ittinein	it-tee-**nayn**
Tuesday	ittalata	it-tah-**lah**-tah
Wednesday	il 'arbaa	il **ahr**-bah-**aah**
Thursday	il khamees	il khah-**mees**
Friday	iljumaa	il zhum-**aah**
Saturday	issabet	**iss-sah**-bet

NUMBERS

1	wahed	**wah**-hed
2	tinein	tee-**nayn**
3	talati	tah-**lah**-tee
4	arbaa	**ahr**-bah-aah
5	khamseh	**khahm**-seh
6	sitteh	**sit**-teh
7	sabaa	sub-**aah**
8	tamanyeh	tah-**mah**-nee-**yeh**
9	tisaa	**tiss**-aah
10	aashara	**aah**-shah-rah
11	ihhdaaesh	ihh-**dah**-ehsh
12	itnaaesh	it-**nah**-ehsh
20	ishreen	iish-**reen**
50	khamseen	khahm-**seen**
100	meyyeh	**may**-yeh
200	mitein	**mee**-tain

ENGLISH	ARABIC TRANSLITERATION	PRONUNCIATION
USEFUL PHRASES		
Do you speak English?	btihki inglizi?	btih-**kee** in-**glee**-zee?
I don't understand (man)	mish fahem	mish **fah**-him
I don't understand (woman)	mish fahmi	mish **fah**-meh
I don't know (man)	mish aarif	mish **aah**-ref
I don't know (woman)	mish aarfi	mish **aahr**-fee
I'm lost (man)	ana dayih	ah-nah **dah-yeh**
I'm lost (woman)	ana dayaa	ah-nah **dah**-ye-aah
I am American (man)	ana amriki	ah-nah ahm-**ree-kee**
I am American (woman)	ana amrikiyya	ah-nah ahm-**ree-key**-yah
I am British (man)	ana baritani	ah-nah bah-**ree-tah-nee**
I am British (woman)	ana baritaniya	ah-nah bah-**ree-tah-nay**-yah
What is this?	eish hada?	aysh **hah**-dah?
What time is it?	Addeish el wa'ed?	Ahd-**daysh**-el **wah**-ed
Where is?	wein?	wayn?
The train station	mahattit iltrain	mah-huht-**tit il-train**
The bus station	mahattit el buss	mah-**huht**-tit el **buhss**
The intracity bus station	mahattit el bus eddakheli	mah-huht-**tit el** buhss **ed**-dah-**khe-lee**
The taxi station	mujammaa el takasi	moo-**jam**-maah el tah-**kah**-see
The airport	el matar	el mah-**tahr**
The hotel	el oteil	el **ooh**-tayl
The cafe	el ahwi	el ah-**weh**
The restaurant	el mataam	el **matt-aahm**
The telephone	el tiliphon	el tih-lih-**fohn**

ENGLISH	ARABIC TRANSLITERATION	PRONUNCIATION
The hospital	el mostashfa	el moos-**tash**-fah
The post office	el bareed	el bah-**reed**
The rest room	el hammam	el huhm-**mahm**
The pharmacy	el saydaleyyeh	el sigh-dah-**lay-yeh**
The bank	el bank	el bahnk
The embassy	el safara	el sah-fah-**rah**
Right	yameen	yah-meen
Left	shmal	shmahl
Straight ahead	doughri	doo-ghree
I would like a room	beddi ghorfi	bed-dee **ghor-fih**
A little	shway or aleel	shway or ah-leel
A lot	kteer	kteer
Enough	bikaffi	bee-kaf-fee
I have a problem	aandi moshkili	aahn-dee **moosh**-keh-lee
I am ill	ana mareed	ah-nah mah-reed
I need a doctor	beddi daktor	bed-**dee** dac-**tor**
Help	saadoonee	**saah-doo**-nee
Fire	naar or harika	naahr or hah-**ree**-kah
Caution/ look out	entebeh or owaa	in-teh-beh or ohw-**aah**

DINING

I would like	beddi	behd-dee
Water	mayy	muhyy
Bread	khobez	kho-bihz
Vegetables	khodra	khod-rah
Meat	lahhmi	**lahh**-meh
Fruits	fawakeh	fah-**wah**-keh
Cakes/ Sweets	helou/ halaweyyat	**heh**-loo/ hah-lah-**way-yaht**
Tea	shay	shahy
Coffee	ahwi	ah-weh

ENGLISH	ARABIC TRANSLITERATION	PRONUNCIATION
A fork	shokeh	show-keh
A spoon	maala a	**maah**-lah ah
A knife	sikkeen	sick-**keen**
A plate	sahin	sah-hin

SHOPPING

I would like to buy	beddi ashtri	bed-**dee** ahsh-tree
cigarettes	sagayer or dokhkhan	sah-**gah**-yer or dokh-**khahn**
a city map	khareeta lal madeeni	khah-**ree**-tah lahl mah-**dee**-nee
a road map	khareeta lal tareek	khah-**ree**-tah lahl tah-**reek**
How much is it?	addaish ha o	**ad**-daysh **ha** oh
It's expensive	ghali	**ghah**-lee

Travel Smart Israel

WORD OF MOUTH

"Renting a car is one way to see Israel—but in Tel Aviv parking is horrid (and the traffic can be too). There is a train system in Israel, and it is good for going from city to city. Within cities, there are great bus systems. There are also, of course, taxis."
–Elkaz

"A car can be expensive—depending on type of car (size, and manual versus automatic). For one person it won't be worth it. Don't consider a car for major cities (Tel Aviv, Jerusalem, Haifa). Even for a trip 'out of town' a tour is probably more worthwhile for a single person. Add in admission prices to some sights, and a tour may be cheaper."
–AlexA

www.fodors.com/community

GETTING HERE AND AROUND

AIR TRAVEL

The least expensive airfares to Israel are often priced for round-trip travel and must be purchased well in advance. Airlines generally allow you to change your return date for a fee; most low-fare tickets, however, are nonrefundable.

Flights to Israel tend to be least expensive from November through March, except for the holiday season at the end of December. Prices are higher during the Jewish New Year's holidays (usually in September) and during Passover (usually in April).

Flying time from New York to Israel is approximately 11 hours; from Los Angeles, it's about 18 hours (including the usual stopover in Europe or New York). International passengers are asked to arrive at the airport three hours prior to their flight time in order to allow for security checks.

From North America, the New York City area's international airports offer the highest number of nonstop flights, with El Al Airlines, Continental, United, and Delta providing service. Direct flights are also available on El Al from Los Angeles and Toronto and on US Airways from Philadelphia. Major European carriers—including Air France, Alitalia, British Airways, Brussels Airlines, Czech Airways, Iberia, KLM, Lot, Lufthansa, Malev, Swissair, Turkish Airways, and Virgin Atlantic—have daily flights from the United States and on to Israel with stopovers in their domestic hub airports.

Because Israel is slightly smaller than New Jersey, it's often more efficient to drive within the country than fly. The exception is the resort city of Eilat, which is 360 km (224 mi) south of Tel Aviv on the Gulf of Eilat. There are flights several times a day from Tel Aviv and daily from Haifa.

Reconfirmation obligations differ from airline to airline (and change from time to time); be certain to check with your carrier for all legs of your journey.

Airline Security Issues **Transportation Security Administration** (*www.tsa.gov*).

AIRPORTS

Israel's main airport, Ben Gurion International Airport (TLV) is a few miles southeast of Tel Aviv. The airport has towering interior walls of Jerusalem stone adorned with sixth-century Byzantine mosaics that were discovered during construction. A soothing fountain lies in the center of the departure hall, ringed by leather and chrome armchairs. The spacious food court serves Middle Eastern cuisine and fast-food favorites. From Sde Dov Airport (SDV), about 4 km (2½ mi) north of the city center, domestic airlines fly to Eilat in the south and to Haifa or Rosh Pina in the north.

Charter flights between Europe or Russia and the southern resort town of Eilat land either at Ovda Airport (VDA) or Eilat Airport (ETH).

Airport Information **Ben Gurion International Airport** (*03/975–5555* *www.iaa.gov.il*). **Eilat Airport** (*08/636–3838* *www.iaa.gov.il*). **Ovda Airport** (*08/637–5880* *www.iaa.gov.il*). **Sde Dov Airport** (*03/698–4500* *www.iaa.gov.il*).

GROUND TRANSPORTATION

The quickest and most convenient way to get to and from the airport is by taxi. Taxis are always available outside the arrivals hall. Fares are approximately NIS 185 to Tel Aviv and NIS 280 to Jerusalem.

From the airport, trains depart for Tel Aviv every 25 minutes. They will take you to the city in 25 minutes for NIS 14. Trains continue on to Herzliya, Netanya, Haifa, Akko, and Nahariya. Direct train service to Jerusalem won't commence until 2016.

The Nesher shuttle service takes you to Jerusalem for NIS 50. The 10-passenger *sherut* taxis (limo-vans) depart whenever they fill up. The main disadvantage is that if you're the last passenger to be dropped off, you may tour the city for an hour while the driver discharges the other passengers. To get to Ben Gurion Airport from Jerusalem the same way, call Nesher to book a place, preferably a day in advance. A "special" taxi (as opposed to a shared sherut) costs about NIS 280, with a 25% surcharge after 9 pm and on Saturday and holidays.

If you depart for the airport from central Tel Aviv by car or taxi at rush hour (7 to 9 am, 5 to 7 pm), note that the roads can get clogged. Allow 45 minutes for a trip that would otherwise take only about 20 minutes.

Taking the bus from Ben Gurion Airport to Jerusalem is tedious. You need to board the Egged local shuttle (line 5, fare NIS 5.30) for a 10-minute ride to the Airport City commercial complex, and wait there for the Jerusalem-bound Egged bus (line 947, fare NIS 23). It runs to Jerusalem's Central Bus Station approximately every 30 minutes during the day, less frequently in the evening.

Contacts **Egged** (☎ *03/694–8888 or* 🌐 *www.egged.co.il/eng*). **Nesher** (☎ *599/500–205; 02/625–3233 or 02/623–1231 in Jerusalem* 🌐 *www.neshertours.co.il/english.asp*).

FLIGHTS

The national carrier, El Al Israel Airlines, is known for maintaining some of the world's strictest security standards. It is not necessarily the cheapest carrier, especially from the United States. Continental, Delta, and US Airways often have cheaper nonstop fares, and some European airlines have better prices if you don't mind a stopover in their hub cities. Within Israel, Arkia Israeli Airlines and Israir Airlines have flights from Tel Aviv to Eilat and Haifa. Royal Jordanian Airlines flies the 45-minute route between Tel Aviv and Amman.

To Israel **Continental Airlines** (☎ *800/523–3273 for U.S. reservations, 800/231–0856 for international reservations* 🌐 *www.continental.com*). **Delta Airlines** (☎ *800/221–1212 for U.S. reservations, 800/241–4141 for international reservations* 🌐 *www.delta.com*). **El Al Israel Airlines** (☎ *212/768–9200 or 800/223–6700 in the U.S.; 03/977–1111 in Israel* 🌐 *www.elal.co.il*). **Royal Jordanian Airlines** (☎ *03/516–5566* 🌐 *www.rja.com.jo*). **US Airways** (☎ *800/428–4322 for international reservations* 🌐 *www.usairways.com*.

Within Israel **Arkia Israeli Airlines** (☎ *03/690–3712* 🌐 *www.arkia.com*). **Israir Airlines** (☎ *03/795–4038* 🌐 *www.israirairlines.com*).

BIKE TRAVEL

Biking has really taken off in Israel, and tens of thousands of people hit the trails every year. With mountains, deserts, and wooded hills, this small country is ideal for bicycling. Off-road adventure tours take you to remote archeological sites and other places not reachable by car. Although keep in mind, the going can get rough due to the extreme heat much of the year, the winding and hilly roads, and aggressive drivers. Biking is best enjoyed from September to June. Trains don't accept bikes, but buses do.

Israel Bike Trails has a Web site with comprehensive bike trail information listing elevations and level of difficulty. Several companies offer organized guided bike tours throughout the country, including Israel Cycling. Biking maps in English are hard to find. Serious bikers use the Israel Hiking and Touring Maps published by the Society for the Protection of Nature. At this writing, only one in this series (#20, Eilat Mountains) has been published in English.

Bike Contacts **Israel Bike Trails** (🌐 *www.israelbiketrails.com*). Israel Cycling (☎ *050/460–6550* 🌐 *www.israelcycling.com*). **Society for the Protection of Nature** (☎ *03/638–8688* 🌐 *www.teva.org.il/english/ecotourism*).

BOAT TRAVEL

Several large cruise companies, including Celebrity, Holland America, Oceania, Regent Seven Seas, and Royal Caribbean, have Mediterranean itineraries that include stops at the Israeli ports of Ashdod and Haifa. In addition, the Israeli company Mano sails from Haifa to many points in the Mediterranean between April and November.

At the time of this writing, Varianos Travel announced that limited ferry service between Israel and Greece and Cyprus will resume in summer 2011.

FERRY CONTACTS

Cruise Lines **Celebrity Cruise** (☎ *800/760–0654* 🌐 *www.celebritycruise.com)* **Holland America** (☎ *877/932–4259* 🌐 *www.hollandamerica.com*). **Oceania Cruises** (☎ *800/531–5619* 🌐 *www.oceaniancruises.com*). **Regent Seven Seas** (☎ *877/505–5370* 🌐 *www.rssc.com*). **Royal Caribbean** (☎ *866/562–7625* 🌐 *www.royalcaribbean.com*).

Cruises from Haifa **Mano Maritime** (☎ *972–4–860–6666* 🌐 *www.man.co.il*). **Varianos Travel** (☎ *357/2268–0500* 🌐 *www.varianostravel.com*).

BUS TRAVEL

Buses can take you almost anywhere in Israel. City bus routes are run exclusively by Egged, except in metropolitan Tel Aviv, where Dan provides some competition. Buses in Israel are clean, comfortable, and air-conditioned. Intercity bus fares vary according to the distance traveled. During weekday rush hours allow time for long lines at the obligatory security checks to enter the bus station. Buses are often overcrowded on Saturday nights after Shabbat and always on Sunday mornings when it looks like the entire Israeli army is returning to base after a weekend at home.

The Central Bus Station in Tel Aviv resembles the work of a mad scientist. The stark concrete building has multiple entrances on several levels, endless corridors, and a confusing array of platforms. It's all topped off by dozens of kiosks selling fast food and cheap merchandise. By contrast, Jerusalem's Central Bus Station is clean, well organized, and easy to navigate. There's a pleasant food court, an ATM, an efficient information desk, and branches of some of the country's best-known stores.

Although the buses resemble those in most other countries, there are a few quirks. When you're in Jerusalem, remember that the ultra-Orthodox population primarily uses Buses 1 and 2, which service the Western Wall area. It's generally accepted that women sit separately in the rear of the bus. Women should never sit in an empty seat next to an ultra-Orthodox man and shouldn't be offended if a man would rather stand than sit beside them in an empty seat. (And in case you're wondering, ultra-Orthodox women generally accept this arrangement.)

Frequent bus service is available between Jerusalem and Tel Aviv. Egged Bus 405 runs from the Tel Aviv Central Bus Station, and Bus 480 from the Arlozorov Street terminal, each with two to five departures per hour, depending on the time of day (NIS 19.70). There is a similar service to Jerusalem from most major cities, terminating at the Central Bus Station. The two small bus stations in East Jerusalem are for private, Palestinian-operated bus lines, with daily service to West Bank towns such as Bethlehem and Jericho.

FARES

For both local and long-distance travel, drivers accept payment in shekels. Drivers on the long-distance buses will grumble when they have to make change for a bill over NIS 100, so make sure to have smaller denominations. Unless you're running to catch a bus, it's almost always faster to buy your ticket at the station. On city buses you don't need exact change.

For travel between major cities and within each city, Egged offers good rates on packs of 10 or more tickets and monthly passes that give you an unlimited number of rides. These may be purchased at any city bus station or on the bus. These are particularly good for children and senior citizens, who get large discounts. Children under age five ride free whether or not they occupy their own seat.

The fare on all city routes is NIS 6.20. If you'll be taking another bus within 75 minutes, ask for a free *ma'avar*, or transfer ticket. Intercity fares are based on distance traveled. The one-hour trip between Tel Aviv and Jerusalem will cost you about NIS 20, while the three-hour journey between Tel Aviv and Tiberias runs about NIS 47. There are no advance reservations except to Eilat.

SCHEDULES

All bus service is available Sunday to Thursday from 5:30 am to 12:30 am. Keep in mind that public transportation in all cities except Haifa ceases to run on Jewish holidays and on Shabbat, which lasts from sundown Friday afternoon to an hour after sundown Saturday evening. Be sure to give yourself extra time if traveling just before Shabbat.

Every large bus station has an information booth where you'll generally be able to find schedule and platform information in English. Bus maps in English are virtually nonexistent—just tell the clerk where you want to go and you'll probably get a handwritten map.

TOURS

Egged operates Route 99, a two-hour circle tour of Jerusalem for visitors. Its distinctive red double-decker buses are equipped with audio explanations in eight languages (via individual headphones). The route begins at the Central Bus Station at the city's western entrance, and its 24 stops include the Machaneh Yehuda market, the edge of the downtown, Mt. Scopus, City of David, Dung Gate, Mt. Zion, Jaffa Gate, City Hall (Safra Square), King David Hotel (and other hotels en route), Haas Promenade, Jerusalem (Malcha) Mall, the railway station at the Biblical Zoo, Mt. Herzl, Yad Vashem, Israel Museum, the Knesset, and the Supreme Court. Departures are Sunday to Thursday at 9 am, 11 am, 1:30 pm, 3:45 pm, and 6 pm (the last tour does not operate from November to February). On Friday and the eves of Jewish holidays, the last bus leaves at 1:30 pm. The cost is NIS 60 for one full trip, NIS 80 for a one-day ticket (unlimited transfers), and NIS 130 for an unlimited two-day ticket; children's discounts are available.

In Tel Aviv, Dan operates the hop-on, hop-off Route 100. The two-hour circuit, which begins at the Reading Terminal in north Tel Aviv, departs Sunday to Thursday at 9 am, 11 am, noon, 1 pm, 2 pm, 3 pm, and 4 pm. On Friday, buses leave until 2 pm. The fare is NIS 45. There are 28 stops along the way, including Tel Aviv University, Dizengoff Center, and Carmel Market.

Bus Information Dan (☎ *03/639–4444* 🌐 *www.dan.co.il/english/default.asp*). **East Jerusalem Bus Station** (✉ *Sultan Suleiman St., opposite Damascus Gate, East Jerusalem* ☎ *054/449–3088*). **Egged** (☎ *03/694–8888* 🌐 *www.egged.co.il/eng*). **Jerusalem Central Bus Station** (✉ *224 Jaffa Rd., Romema* ☎ *03/694–8888*).

CAR TRAVEL

The Hebrew word for a native-born Israeli is *sabra,* which literally refers to a prickly cactus with sweet fruit inside. You'll meet the sweet Israeli if you get lost or have automotive difficulties—helping hands are quick to arrive—but behind the wheel, Israelis are prickly, aggressive, and honk their horns far more than their Western counterparts. Try not to take it personally.

Some travelers will feel more comfortable hiring a driver, and there are plenty of ways to find someone reliable. Ask for recommendations at your hotel. Every hotel has taxi drivers that serve their guests and most are familiar with all parts of the country and will be happy to quote you a daily rate. For one day, the rate should be around NIS 800.

Israel's highways are numbered, but most people still know them simply by the towns they connect: the Tiberias–Nazareth Road, for example. Intersections and turnoffs are similarly indicated, as in "the Eilat Junction." Orange signs indicate tourist sites; national parks signs are on brown wood.

ADDRESSES

In Israel, streets are generally named after famous people or events, meaning that almost every community has a Herzl Street and a Six-Day War Street. Don't worry about the "boulevard" or "alley" attached to many street names—Israelis just use the proper name. You won't find a Jabotinsky Street and a Jabotinsky Alley in the same city. What you might encounter is a street that will change names after a couple of blocks. Street numbers follow the standard format, with odd numbers on one side and even numbers on the other. Larger apartment buildings often have several entrances marked by the first three or four letters of the Hebrew alphabet.

If you know history, you'll have an easier time finding your way around Jerusalem's neighborhoods. In Baka the streets are named after the biblical tribes, in Rehavia they're medieval Jewish scholars, and in Old Katamon the brigades who fought in Israel's War of Independence are honored with street names.

There are four towns in Israel that have functioning Old Cities dating from either biblical times (Jerusalem), the Crusader period (Akko and Jaffa), or the Middle Ages (Tzfat). Streets and alleys in these areas have names, but often not numbers.

GASOLINE

Gas stations are to be found at regular intervals along the country's major highways, except in the Negev. On highways they're generally always open, while those in the city tend to close at midnight. Prices are standardized, so it doesn't matter which station you choose. Most offer both full- and self-service pumps. If you go the full-service route, ask for a *kabbalah* (receipt). Attendants do not expect to be tipped. Most rental cars take unleaded gas, which at the time of this writing costs NIS 6.40 per liter. Most stations accept international credit cards.

PARKING

In Tel Aviv, Jerusalem, and Haifa, parking laws are stringently enforced. Expect a ticket of NIS 150 on your windshield if you've overstayed your welcome at a paid parking spot. Cars will be towed if parked in a no-parking zone. Pay attention to the curb, as parking is forbidden where it is painted red. In downtown areas, parking is permitted only where there are blue and white stripes on the curb or where there are meters. Meters cost NIS 4.60 per hour and accept 5, 2, and 1 shekel coins. Pay-and-display cards may also be used and are for sale at post offices, kiosks, and lottery booths.

Sound complicated? Stick to parking lots. Covered and open parking lots are plentiful in the major cities, and cost around NIS 15 per hour or NIS 70 per day.

RENTAL CARS

In Jerusalem, a combination of walking and taking cabs or a guide-driven tourist limo-van is often more time effective—and, in the case of the former, more cost effective—than a rental car. This has become especially true of late with the increase in traffic and the confusion caused by road construction. Exceptions are the more distant West Jerusalem sights and panoramic overlooks, which have plenty of free parking. On the east side, a rental car is often more of a bother than a boon, and cabs are the way to go. If you plan on heading north to the Golan or Upper Galilee, a rental car will be a significant time-saver over bus travel.

Rental rates in Israel start at around $50 per day and $200 per week for an economy car with unlimited mileage. The cars here are generally smaller than similar

American models. Minivans and four-wheel-drive vehicles are very popular and should be reserved well in advance, especially during high season. Allow plenty of time to pick up and drop off your vehicle if you're renting from a city office.

Drivers must be at least 24 years old. Your own driver's license is acceptable in Israel, but an International Driver's Permit is still a good idea. This international permit is universally recognized, so having one in your wallet is extra insurance against problems with the local authorities.

RENTAL CARS IN THE WEST BANK

There are no restrictions on driving Israeli rental cars into West Bank areas under Israeli control (known as Area B). However, your rental car insurance coverage does not extend to West Bank areas under Palestinian control (known as Area A). If you rent from companies at the airport, in Tel Aviv, or in West Jerusalem, you won't be able to drive the car to Bethlehem, Jericho and other towns under the Palestinian Authority. If you plan on visiting these areas by car, use Green Peace or one of the other Palestinian-operated companies in East Jerusalem. Passing through the checkpoints within Israel is usually stress free, as tourist vans and rental cars are routinely waved through with no need to show identification.

If your rental car comes with a GPS system, check to see if it includes or excludes West Bank routes. If the West Bank is excluded, the GPS will route your journey from Jerusalem to the Dead Sea along a circuitous three-hour route instead of a more direct one that takes less than an hour. Even if you're using GPS, it's always a good idea to discuss possible routes with your rental car company if you plan on passing through the West Bank.

Rental Agencies **Avis** (☎ *800/638–4016*). **Best** (☎ *800/220–015* 🌐 *www.best-car.co.il*). **Budget** (☎ **2200* 🌐 *www.budget.co.il*). **Eldan** (☎ *800/938–5000* 🌐 *www.eldan.co.il*). **Green Peace Car Rental** (☎ *02/585–9756* 🌐 *www.greenpeace.co.il*). **Sixt** (☎ *70/050–1502* 🌐 *www.sixt.co.il*).

ROAD CONDITIONS

Israel's highway system is very modern and has signs in English as well as Hebrew and Arabic. Route 6, the main north–south toll road, can save significant time on longer journeys. The highway starts at the Maahaz Junction south of Kiryat Gat and ends about 87 km (54 mi) north at the Ein Tut Junction near Yokneam. Electronic sensors read your license plate number and transmit the bill according to the distance you travel, to your rental-car company. Expect to pay around NIS 60 to drive the length of the highway.

Route 1 is the chief route to Jerusalem from both the west (Tel Aviv, Ben Gurion Airport, Mediterranean coast) and the east (Galilee via Jordan Valley, Dead Sea area, Eilat). The road from Tel Aviv is a divided highway that presents no problems except at morning rush hour (7:30 to 9), when traffic backs up at the entrance to the city. For this reason, some drivers prefer Route 443—via Modi'in—which leaves Route 1 just east of the Ben Gurion Airport, and enters Jerusalem from the north (most convenient for East Jerusalem locations). Route 1, which enters Jerusalem under the Bridge of Strings, is more convenient for Givat Ram, West Jerusalem, downtown, and Talbieh.

Jerusalem, Haifa, and Tel Aviv are all clogged with traffic during the workday. Central Jerusalem is now almost completely closed to private vehicles, with traffic routed around the periphery. Don't consider driving in Jerusalem if you're not comfortable negotiating narrow spaces or parking in tight spots.

If you're driving through the Negev, watch out for camels that can come loping out of the desert and onto the road. In the winter rainy season, sudden flash floods sometimes cascade through the *wadis* (streambeds that are usually dry) with little warning, washing out roads. It's best to postpone your desert trip if there's heavy rain in the forecast.

The desert can be unbelievably hot, even in the winter. It's a good idea to carry extra water—both for yourself and for your car—while driving at any time of year.

ROADSIDE EMERGENCIES

In case of an accident or roadside emergency, call either the police or Shagrir, the national breakdown service. English-speaking assistance is generally available.

The local representative of AAA is Memsi. Should anything happen to your rental car, call your rental company for roadside repair or replacement of the vehicle.

Automobile Associations Memsi (*03/564–1111 in Tel Aviv, 02/625–0661 in Jerusalem www.memsi.co.il*).

Emergency Services Police (*100*). **Shagrir** (*03/557–8888*).

RULES OF THE ROAD

More Israelis have been killed by car accidents than in all of the nation's wars combined. Use extra caution when driving a car here. By law, drivers and all passengers must wear seat belts at all times. Police crack down on drunk driving; the legal blood-alcohol limit is .05%. It's against the law to use a cell phone while driving.

Speed limits vary little across Israel: motorways (represented with blue signs) have speed limits of either 90 or 100 kph (56 or 62 mph). The exception is Route 6, where the limit is 110 kph (68 mph). Highways with green signs have speed limits of 80 or 90 kph (50 or 56 mph). Urban roads are 50 or 60 kph (31 or 37 mph).

Headlights must be turned on in daylight when driving on intercity roads from November through April 1. A flashing green traffic light indicates that the red stoplight is about three seconds away and you should come to a halt.

Children, ages nine and under, must be seated in age-appropriate car seats, and children under 14 are not allowed in the front seat.

LIGHT RAIL TRAVEL

At the time of this writing, Jerusalem's long-delayed light rail service was scheduled to go into operation in summer 2011. Once on track, the rail system will ease travel through the Old City and other downtown areas of interest to travelers. Check for updates on the site operated by the company building the line, CityPass.

Information CityPass (*www.citypass.co.il*).

TAXI TRAVEL

Taxis are an affordable way to get around. If you need to get somewhere fast or are unfamiliar with the area, a taxi is your best bet, and you can hail one on the street or request one by phone. On the whole, drivers are knowledgeable, cheerful, and like to practice their English with tourists.

Taxis are white sedans with a yellow sign on the roof. The sign lights up to indicate availability. According to law, taxi drivers must use the meter (be firm when you request this) unless you hire them for the day or for a trip out of town, for which there are set rates. If you're pressed to take the cab at a set price, you can ask your hotel staff for an estimate of the cost of your journey. In such a case, agree on the price before you begin the journey and assume that the driver has built in a tip. In the event of a serious problem with the driver, report his cab number (on the illuminated plastic sign on the roof) or license-plate number to the Ministry of Tourism or the Ministry of Transport.

Certain shared taxis or minivans have fixed rates and run fixed routes, such as from Tel Aviv to Haifa or from the airport to Jerusalem; such a taxi is called a *sherut* (as opposed to a "special," the term used for a private cab). Some sheruts can be booked in advance.

Eight- or ten-seat sheruts are an option if you're traveling between Jerusalem and Tel Aviv. They operate from outside Tel Aviv's Central Bus Station seven days a week, departing when they fill up (fare NIS 20). They end their journey with stops opposite the Jerusalem Central Bus Station and near Zion Square in the downtown area. A "special" cab costs about NIS 270, with a 25% surcharge after 9 pm and on Saturday and holidays.

Taxi Contact **Nesher** (☎ *599/500-205 or 02/625-3233*).

Jerusalem Taxi Contacts **Hapalmach** (☎ *02/679-2333 or 02/679-3333*). **Hapisgah** (☎ *02/642-1111 or 02/642-3333*). **Ha'ooma/ Habira** (✉ *1 Harav Kook St., near Zion Sq., Downtown* ✉ *Central Bus Station, Romema* ☎ *02/538-9999*). **Rehavia** (☎ *02/625-4444 or 02/622-2444*). **Smadar** (☎ *02/566-4444*).

Eilat Taxi Contacts **Taba** (☎ *08/633-3339*). **London** (☎ *08/996-3789*). **Massada Taxis** (☎ *08/642-2222*). **Netz Taxis** (☎ *08/627-0808*).

TRAIN TRAVEL

Until new tracks are completed in 2016, train travel between Jerusalem and Tel Aviv is more a pleasant and scenic excursion than an efficient way to travel between the two cities. The journey currently takes 1 hour and 45 minutes, compared to 45 minutes by bus. It's a comfortable ride, and many just do it for the attractive scenery. The train, which departs every two hours, runs between Jerusalem's Malcha Station and Tel Aviv's Savidor Station (popularly known as Arlozorov Street terminal). There are connections to Haifa and other destinations to the north. Service ends midafternoon on Friday and resumes about two hours after dark on Saturday. (A similar schedule applies to Jewish religious holidays.) The adult fare to or from Tel Aviv is NIS 21.50 one-way, NIS 39 round-trip.

Other cities—including Ashkelon, Beersheva, Beit Shemesh, Haifa, Herzliya, Akko, and Nahariya—are easily reachable by train from Tel Aviv. There are no different classes of service. All carriages are clean, spacious, and comfortable with well-upholstered seats. They are often crowded, however.

All train stations post up-to-date schedules in English. Complete schedules are also available on the Web site of the Israel Railway Authority. Tickets may be purchased at the ticket office in the station. There's no train service on Saturdays or Jewish holidays.

Purchase your train tickets with cash or credit card at the station ticket booth before you board. Reservations are not accepted for train travel.

Information **Israel Railways** (☎ *03/577-4000 or *5770* 🌐 *www.rail.co.il*).

ESSENTIALS

ACCOMMODATIONS

Israel once had a reputation for having mostly utilitarian lodgings, but today you can check into luxury resorts, chic boutique hotels, and rural bed-and-breakfasts. There are also some more unusual offerings, including Christian hospices (meaning hostelries, not facilities for the ill) and kibbutz hotels (purpose-built lodgings on the grounds of collective communities). *For more information, see the Israel Lodging Primer in Chapter 1.*

Apartment and House Rental Contacts **Good Morning Jerusalem** (☎ *02/623–3459* 🌐 *www.accommodation.co.il*). **Israel Holiday Apartments** (☎ *09/772–7163* 🌐 *www.holidayapartments.co.il*). **Kleiman Real Estate** (☎ *052/238–0638* 🌐 *www.kleimanrealestate.com*). **Vacation Rental By Owner** (🌐 www.vrbo.com/vacation-rentals/asia/israel).

Bed-and-Breakfast Contacts **Bed and Breakfast in Israel** (🌐 *www.b-and-b.co.il*). **Good Morning Jerusalem** (☎ *02/623–3459* 🌐 *www.accommodation.co.il*). **Home Accommodation Association of Jerusalem** (☎ *02/645–2198* 🌐 *www.bnb.co.il*). **Weekend** (🌐 *www.weekend.co.il*). **Rural Tourism in Israel** (🌐 www.zimmeril.com).

Christian Hospice Contacts **GoIsrael** (☎ *888/77–ISRAEL* 🌐 *www.goisrael.com*). **Guided Tours Israel** (☎ *315/876–9917* 🌐 *www.guidedtoursisrael.com/christian-accommodation-israel.html*).

Home Exchange and Vacation Rental Contacts **Flathunting** (🌐 *www.flathuntingisrael.com*). **Sabbatical Homes** (🌐 *www.sabbaticalhomes.com*). **Vacation Rental By Owner** (🌐 www.vrbo.com/vacation-rentals/asia/israel).

Hostel Contacts **Hostelling International—USA** (☎ *301/495–1240* 🌐 *www.hiusa.org*). **Israel Hostels** (☎ *No phone* 🌐 *www.hostels-israel.com*). **Israel Youth Hostel Association** (☎ *02/655–8406* 🌐 *www.iyha.org.il*).

WORD OF MOUTH

Did the resort look as good in real life as it did in the photos? Did you sleep like a baby, or were the walls paper thin? Did you get your money's worth? Rate hotels and write your own reviews in Travel Ratings or start a discussion about your favorite places in Travel Talk on www.fodors.com. Your comments might even appear in our books. Yes, you, too, can be a correspondent!

Kibbutz Hotel Contact **Kibbutz Hotels Chain** (☎ *03/527–8085* 🌐 *www.kibbutz.co.il*).

COMMUNICATIONS

INTERNET

Most hotels in Israel have connections for laptops, and larger hotels typically offer wireless access. Ask about the price, as some charge as much as $20 per day for the privilege. You can also find Internet access at the Tel Aviv and Jerusalem central bus stations and in many cafés. Jerusalem has free Wi-Fi Internet access in the downtown area, on Emek Refaim Street, and at Safra Square. Ben Gurion Aiport and the Eilat Airport also offer free Wi-Fi.

Contacts **Cybercafes** (🌐 *www.cybercafes.com*) lists over 4,000 Internet cafés worldwide.

PHONES

Israel's phone numbers have seven digits, except for certain special numbers that have four to six digits. Toll-free numbers in Israel begin with 177, 1800, 1700, or 1888. When calling an out-of-town number within Israel, be sure to dial the zero that begins every area code.

The country code for Israel is 972. When dialing an Israeli number from abroad, drop the initial 0 from the local area code. The country code for Jordan is 962. When dialing from Israel, dial 00962 and the area code 3 before land-line numbers in

Petra; for Amman, use 00962 and the area code 6. When dialing within Jordan, add a 0 before the area code.

CALLING WITHIN ISRAEL

Making a local call in Israel is quite simple. All public telephones use phone cards that may be purchased at newspaper kiosks and post offices. Pick up the receiver, insert the card in the slot, dial the number when you hear the tone, and the number of units remaining on the card will appear on the screen. One unit equals two minutes.

The area codes for dialing between cities within Israel are Jerusalem (02); Tel Aviv (03); Netanya and Herzliya (09); Haifa, Galilee, Tiberias, Tzfat, and Nazareth (04); Eilat and the Negev (08).

Pay phones are found in shopping malls, bus stations, gas stations, and at booths on main streets. On public phones, the number you're dialing appears on a digital readout; to its right is the number of units remaining on your card.

Dial 144 for directory or operator assistance. Operators all speak English. Dial 188 for an international operator.

CALLING OUTSIDE ISRAEL

When calling internationally direct from Israel, first dial the international access code and then the country code. The international access code for the United States and Canada is 001, and the country code for each is 1.

You can make international calls using a telecard from a public phone. A call from Israel to most countries costs about 25¢ per minute.

By dialing Israel's toll-free numbers (1800 or 177) and the number of your long-distance service, you can link up directly to an operator in your home country. This service works from all public phones and most hotel rooms.

Access Codes **AT&T Direct** (☎ *180/949–4949*). **MCI WorldPhone** (☎ *180/940–2727*). **Sprint International Access** (☎ *180/938–7000*).

MOBILE PHONES

If you have a multiband phone and your service provider uses the world-standard GSM network (as do T-Mobile, Cingular, and Verizon), you can probably use your phone abroad. Roaming fees can be steep, however: 99¢ a minute is considered reasonable. And overseas you normally pay the toll charges for incoming calls. It's almost always cheaper to send a text message than to make a call, since text messages have a very low set fee (often less than 5¢).

If you just want to make local calls, consider buying a new SIM card (note that your provider may have to unlock your phone for you to use a different SIM card) and a prepaid service plan in the destination. You'll then have a local number and can make local calls at local rates.

■ TIP→ If you travel internationally frequently, save one of your old mobile phones or buy a cheap one on the Internet; ask your cell-phone company to unlock it for you, and take it with you as a travel phone, buying a new SIM card with pay-as-you-go service in each destination.

It is significantly cheaper to rent a cell phone at Ben Gurion Airport than to use your cell phone from abroad. Rental booths are in the arrivals hall.

Several Israeli cell-phone rental companies offer tourists a phone for 65¢ per day. ATS offers free incoming calls, local calls inside Israel at 24¢ per minute, and 33¢ per minute to the United States. If you order the phone in advance, it will be waiting for you on the day of your arrival.

Contacts **ATS** (☎ *50/571–3972* 🌐 *www.atsisrael.com*). **Cellular Abroad** (☎ *800/287–5072* 🌐 *www.cellularabroad.com*). **Mobal** (☎ *888/888–9162* 🌐 *www.mobalrental.com*). **Planet Fone** (☎ *888/988–4777* 🌐 *www.planetfone.com*).

CUSTOMS AND DUTIES

For visitors with nothing to declare, clearing customs at Ben Gurion Airport requires simply following the clearly marked green line in the baggage claims hall. Lines are generally short, with very little wait. Customs inspectors rarely examine luggage. The red line for those with items to declare is next to the green line. Those over 17 may import into Israel duty-free: 250 cigarettes or 250 grams of tobacco products; 2 liters of wine and 1 liter of spirits; ¼ liter of eau de cologne or perfume; and gifts totaling no more than $200 in value. You may also import up to 15 kg of food products, but no fresh meat.

Pets are not quarantined if you bring a certificate issued by a government veterinary officer in your country of origin issued within seven days prior to travel. The certificate must state that the animal has been vaccinated against rabies not more than a year and not less than one month prior to travel. Dogs and cats less than three months old will not be admitted. At least 48 hours prior to arrival, pet owners must send a fax to the Ramla Quarantine Section stating the name of the owner, animal species, age, flight number, and approximate arrival time.

Information in Israel Israel Customs Authority (☎ *02/666–3784* 🌐 *www.mof.gov.il/customs/eng*). **Ramla Quarantine Station** (☎ *03/968–8963* 📠 *03/960–5194*).

U.S. Information U.S. Customs and Border Protection (🌐 *www.cbp.gov*).

EATING OUT

Israeli restaurants are sophisticated and varied, as one would expect from a country with immigrants from dozens of countries. Be sure to sample the culinary traditions of the Middle East at neighborhood restaurants known as *steakiya*. Here you'll fill up on dishes such as hummus and warmed pita bread accompanied by a variety of skewered grilled meats, mounds of french fries, and an astonishing array of fresh salads. Restaurants in Eilat, Haifa, and Tel Aviv take advantage of their seaside location to serve the best in seafood dishes, and in any major city it's not difficult to find authentic Thai, Italian, Indian, Latin American, Chinese, French, Indonesian, Japanese, even American food.

While "kosher" once meant "boring," the number of inventive kosher restaurants is growing. Restaurants certified as kosher by the local rabbinate in every city are required to display a dated and signed Hebrew certificate. All the major hotels throughout the country are kosher and their restaurants and cafés welcome nonguests. The Friday editions of the *Jerusalem Post* and *Haaretz* newspapers both carry extensive restaurant listings and note kosher restaurants. The Web site eLuna is a good source for listings, reviews, and discount coupons for kosher eateries. *For more information on Israeli cuisine, see Flavors of Israel in Chapter 1.*

Kosher restaurant resource eLuna (🌐 *www.eluna.com*).

MEALS AND MEALTIMES

Hotels serve a huge, buffet-style breakfast called *arukhat boker*, comprising a variety of breads and rolls, eggs, oatmeal, excellent yogurt, cheeses, olives, vegetable and fish salads, and such American-style breakfast foods as pancakes and granola. You can find the same spread at many cafés. Outdoor coffee shops serving salads, sandwiches, cakes, and delicious coffee abound. Every city and small town has modestly priced restaurants that open in midmorning and serve soup, salad, and grilled meats.

Many restaurants offer business lunch specials or fixed-price menus, but à la carte menus are most common. A service charge (*sherut*) of 10% to 15% is sometimes levied and should be noted separately on your bill.

Because Friday is not a workday for most Israelis, Thursday night is the big night out at the start of the weekend, when cafés and restaurants fill up quickly.

PAYING

Credit cards are widely accepted in restaurants, but always check first. Tips of between 12% and 15% can be paid in cash only. If you are dining in a smaller town or village, make sure you have sufficient cash with you, as credit cards are sometimes not accepted.

RESERVATIONS AND DRESS

Dress in all but the most expensive Israeli restaurants is generally casual. Apart from the restaurants in five-star hotels, men won't need a jacket and tie, and anything goes for women. Israeli restaurants in the larger cities fill up in the evening. Unless you're dining early—before 7 pm—reservations are advised for all except the smallest neighborhood restaurants.

WINES, BEER, AND SPIRITS

Wine has deep roots in Israeli culture. Israel is one of the earliest wine-producing areas in the world, and the symbol of Israel's Ministry of Tourism is a cluster of grapes borne on a pole by two men. Wineries built during the 19th century are still producing wine today, and a plethora of boutique wineries have sprung up in the past decade. Dalton, Castel, Ben Ami, Golan, and Carmel's Rothschild Series are good bets and are found on many Israeli wine lists. *(For more information see "The Wines of Israel" in Chapter 5.)* As for spirits, those with a taste for Greek *ouzo* may enjoy the comparable, local *arak*. Sabra is a locally produced chocolate- and orange-flavored liqueur.

The local brews in Israel are Maccabi (lager) and Goldstar (bitter), while Carlsberg, Heineken, and Tuborg are popular imports. Beer is most commonly available by the bottle, but some bars serve it on draught.

ELECTRICITY

The electrical current in Israel is 220 volts, 50 cycles alternating current (AC); wall outlets take Continental-type plugs, with two round prongs.

WORD OF MOUTH

Was the service stellar or not up to snuff? Did the food give you shivers of delight or leave you cold? Did the prices and portions make you happy or sad? Rate restaurants and write your own reviews in Travel Ratings or start a discussion about your favorite places in Travel Talk on www.fodors.com. Your comments might even appear in our books. Yes, you, too, can be a correspondent!

If your appliances are dual-voltage, you'll need only an adapter. Don't use 110-volt outlets marked for shavers only for high-wattage appliances such as blow-dryers. Most laptops operate equally well on 110 and 220 volts and so require only an adapter.

EMERGENCIES

Israel has an extremely sophisticated emergency response system and a high percentage of citizens who are trained medics. If you find yourself in any kind of medical or security emergency in a public place, the professional and citizen response will be instantaneous.

To obtain police assistance at any time, dial 100. For emergency ambulance service, run by Magen David Adom, dial 101. To report a fire, dial 102. Emergency calls are free at public phones.

MEDICAL CENTERS

Emergency rooms in major hospitals are on duty 24 hours a day in rotation; the schedule is published in the daily press. In an emergency, call Magen David Adom to find out which hospital is on duty that day for your specific need (orthopedic or gastric, for example). Be sure to take your passport with you. There will be a fee.

EILAT AND THE NEGEV

Two hospitals serve the Negev: Soroka in Beersheva, and Yoseftal in Eilat. Both have English-speakers on staff and 24-hour emergency rooms (bring your insurance documents). Both may be approached for emergency dental problems.

JERUSALEM

The privately run Terem Emergency Care Center in Jerusalem offers first aid and full medical attention, 24 hours a day, at its Romema clinic, and more limited hours at its other two Jerusalem locations.

A private dental clinic offers emergency service Sunday and Monday 8 to 6, Tuesday to Thursday 8 to 8, and Friday 8 to 1. Call first: when the office is closed, the call is automatically transferred to an on-call dentist.

The major hospitals in Jerusalem are Hadassah Ein Kerem, Sha'arei Zedek near Mt. Herzl, Bikur Holim downtown, and Hadassah Mt. Scopus.

TEL AVIV

Ichilov Hospital, which is in north Tel Aviv, is about a 10-minute drive (depending on traffic) from the heart of downtown. There's a 24-hour emergency room. Be sure to bring your passport with you. You will be provided with all records in English for your insurance providers at home. If you need an ambulance, you can call 101 to reach Magen David Adom.

Foreign Embassies **U.S. Embassy** (✉ *71 Hayarkon St., Tel Aviv* ☎ *03/519–7575*).

General Emergency Contacts **Magen David Adom** (✉ *2 Alkalai St., Tel Aviv* ☎ *101 for emergencies; 02/652–3133 in Jerusalem; 03/546–0111 in Tel Aviv*).

Eilat and the Negev Hospital Contacts **Soroka Hospital** (✉ *Hanessi'im St., Beersheva* ☎ *08/640–0111*). **Yoseftal Hospital** (✉ *Yotam St., Eilat* ☎ *08/635–8011*).

Jerusalem Hospital Contacts **Bikur Holim** (✉ *Strauss St., Downtown* ☎ *02/646–4111, 02/646–4113 emergency room*). **Hadassah Ein Kerem Hospital** (✉ *Ein Kerem* ☎ *02/677–7111 (including emergency room), 02/677–9444 children's emergency room*). **Hadassah Mt. Scopus** (☎ *02/584–4111 or 02/584–4333*). **Sha'arei Zedek** (✉ *Mt. Herzl* ☎ *02/655–5111, 02/655–5509 emergency room*). **Terem Emergency Care Center** (✉ *Bet Yahav, 80 Yirmiyahu St., Romema* ☎ *1–599–520–520 general line, 02/509–3333 Romema main branch*).

Tel Aviv Hospital Contact **Ichilov Hospital** (✉ *6 Weizmann St., Center City* ☎ *03/697–4444*).

HEALTH

No vaccinations are required to visit Israel. The country has one of the world's most advanced health care systems. Most doctors at emergency clinics and hospitals in Israel speak English. Emergency and trauma care is among the best in the world.

It is safe to drink tap water and eat fresh produce after it's been washed, but take care when buying food from outdoor stands; make sure the food is hot and cooked in front of you. Imodium and Pepto-Bismol are available over the counter at every pharmacy.

Heat stroke and dehydration are real dangers if you're going to be outdoors for any length of time: a sun hat and sunblock are musts, as is plenty of bottled water (available even in the most remote places) to guard against dehydration. Take at least 1 liter per person for every hour you plan to be outside. Use sunscreen with SPF 30 or higher. Most supermarkets and pharmacies carry sunscreen in a wide range of SPFs, but it is much more expensive than in the United States.

U.S. brands of mosquito repellent with DEET are available in pharmacies and supermarkets. Wear light, long-sleeved clothing and long pants particularly at dusk when mosquitoes like to attack.

Yad Sarah is a nationwide voluntary organization that lends medical equipment and accessories such as wheelchairs, crutches, and canes. There is no charge, but a contribution is expected. It's open Sunday to Thursday 8 to 7 and Friday 8 to noon. Equipment can be returned elsewhere in the country.

OVER-THE-COUNTER REMEDIES

At the pharmacy (*beit mirkachat*) it is easy to find many of the same over-the-counter remedies as you would at home. Everyday pain relievers such as Tylenol and Advil are widely available. Medication can be obtained from pharmacies, which are plentiful. English is spoken in the majority of pharmacies. Locally produced medication is fairly inexpensive, but expect to pay more for drugs that are imported.

The daily press publishes the addresses of pharmacies on duty at night, on Saturday, and on holidays. This information is also available from Magen David Adom. In Jerusalem, Super-Pharm Nayot is open Sunday to Thursday 8:30 am to midnight, Friday 8:30 am to 3 pm, and Saturday one hour after the Sabbath ends until midnight. Its downtown location has slightly shorter hours.

In Eilat, the Michlin Pharmacy will deliver to your hotel and is open Sunday to Thursday 8 to 2 and 4 to 8:30, Friday 8 to 3. Super-Pharm is open daily 9:30 am to 1 am. There are also pharmacies in Arad, Beersheva, and Mitzpe Ramon.

Health Contacts Michlin Pharmacy (✉ *Opposite Central Bus Station, Eilat* ☎ *08/637–2434*). **Super-Pharm** (✉ *5 Burla St., Nayot, Jerusalem* ☎ *02/649–7555* ✉ *3 Hahistadrut St., Downtown, Jerusalem* ☎ *02/624–6244* ✉ *Kanion Mul Yam, Eilat* ☎ *08/634–0880*). **Yad Sarah** (✉ *124 Herzl Blvd., Bet Hakerem* ☎ *02/644–4444*).

HOURS OF OPERATION

Sunday is a regular workday in Israel. All government offices and most private offices and travel agencies are closed on Friday and Saturday as well as for all Jewish religious holidays. Businesses are generally open by 8:30 am in Israel.

Although hours can differ among banks, almost all open by 8:30 Sunday to Thursday. Most close at 12:30 and then reopen on Monday and Thursday from 4 to 7 pm. Banks are closed on Jewish religious holidays and on Friday and Saturday except in Muslim areas, where they're closed Friday only. In Christian areas they're open Saturday morning and closed Sunday.

Museums don't have a fixed closing day, so although they're usually open 10 to 6, and often on Saturday mornings, confirm the schedule before you go.

Most local pharmacies close at 7 pm. Large chain stores, such as Super-Pharm and NewPharm, are usually open until 10 pm. In most cities a few drugstores are open all night, on a rotating basis. Daily listings can be found in English-language newspapers.

Shops generally open at 9 or 9:30; neighborhood grocery stores usually open around 7. A few shops still close for a two- or three-hour siesta between 1 and 4. Most stores do not close before 7 pm; supermarkets are often open later, and in large cities, there are all-night supermarkets. Arab-owned stores usually open at 8 and close in late afternoon. Mall hours are 9:30 to 9:30 Sunday to Thursday. Friday, the malls that close for Shabbat shut down about two hours before sundown and reopen two hours after sunset on Saturday evening. Outside Jerusalem, some malls keep regular hours on Saturday, while others stay closed.

MAIL

The post office does it all: handles regular and express letters, sends and receives faxes, accepts bill payments, sells phone cards and parking cards, handles money transfers, and offers quick-delivery service. Nearly every neighborhood has a post office, identified by a white racing deer on a red background. English is almost always spoken. The main branches are usually open from 8 until 6 or 7, and small offices are usually open Sunday to Tuesday and Thursday 8 to 12:30 and 3:30 to 6, Wednesday 8 to 1:30, and Friday 8 to noon. In Muslim cities the post office is closed Friday, in Christian towns it's closed Sunday, and in Jericho it's closed Saturday.

It takes about 7 to 12 days for mail to reach the United States from Israel.

In mailing addresses, the abbreviation M.P. stands for Mobile Post (M.P. Gilboa, for example). You'll see this as part of the address in more rural areas.

Tourists who want to receive mail at a local post office should have it addressed to "Poste Restante" along with the name of the town. Such mail will be held for pickup free of charge for up to three months. Mail delivery from Israel is reliable.

SHIPPING PACKAGES

Most stores offer shipping to international destinations. If you choose to send your purchases home yourself, you'll find all the supplies you need at any local post office, but be prepared to wait in a long line for service. Be sure to bring picture ID with you. Boxes and labels are available in various sizes, and you may insure your package. Parcels are generally secure when mailed from Israel. To Canada and the United States, it takes approximately two weeks by air and up to three months by surface mail. Quicker, more expensive alternatives are FedEx and UPS.

Express Services **EMS Service** (☎ *03/538–5909* 🌐 *www.israelpost.co.il*). **FedEx** (☎ *1700/700–339* 🌐 *www.fedex.com/il*). **UPS** (☎ *1800/834–834* 🌐 *www.ups.com/content/il/en/contact/index.html*).

MONEY

Israel is a moderately priced country compared to Western Europe, but it's more expensive than many of its Mediterranean neighbors. Prices are much the same throughout the country. To save money, try the excellent prepared food from supermarkets (buy local brands), take public transportation, eat your main meal at lunch, eat inexpensive local foods such as falafel, and stay at hotels with kitchen facilities and guest houses. Airfares are lowest from late October to early December and from late January to early March.

Sample prices: cup of coffee, NIS 12; falafel, NIS 10; beer at a bar, NIS 20; canned soft drink, NIS 10; hamburger at a fast-food restaurant, NIS 20; short taxi ride, about NIS 30 to NIS 35; museum admission NIS 32; movie, NIS 35.

Prices throughout this guide are given for adults. Substantially reduced fees are almost always available for children, students, and senior citizens.

TIP→ Banks never have every foreign currency on hand, and it may take as long as a week to order. If you're planning to exchange funds before leaving home, don't wait till the last minute.

Currency Conversion **Google** (🌐 *www.google.com*). **Oanda.com** (🌐 *www.oanda.com*). **XE.com** (🌐 *www.xe.com*).

ATMS AND BANKS

Your own bank will probably charge a fee for using ATMs abroad; the foreign bank you use may also charge a fee. Nevertheless, you'll usually get a better rate of exchange at an ATM than you will at a currency-exchange office or even when changing money in a bank. And extracting funds as you need them is a safer option than carrying around a large amount of cash.

TIP→ PIN codes with more than four digits are not recognized at ATMs in Israel. If yours has five or more, remember to change it before you leave.

The main branches of all the banks—Hapoalim, Leumi, Discount, First International—are in Jerusalem's downtown area, but they are arguably the last resort for changing money. Several times a week they have morning hours only (different banks, different days), they give relatively low rates of exchange, and it usually involves waiting in line and having the clerk fill out paperwork.

Banks in the Negev towns and Eilat have their own hours and closing days, which vary. ATMs (called *kaspomats* in Israel) are generally not enclosed but rather installed in a wall, usually next to a bank.

ATMs are ubiquitous all over Israel. Look for machines that have stickers stating that they accept foreign credit cards or that have a PLUS, NYCE, or CIRRUS sign. All have instructions in English. Almost all ATMs now have protective shields around the keypad to prevent anyone seeing your PIN.

With a debit card, the ATM will give you the desired amount of shekels and your home account will be debited at the current exchange rate. Note that there may be a limit on how much money you are allowed to withdraw each day and that service charges are usually applied. Make sure you have enough cash in rural areas, villages, and small towns where ATMs may be harder to find.

The banks and the exchange bureaus in the downtown Jerusalem and Jewish neighborhoods close early on Friday and reopen on Sunday morning.

CREDIT CARDS

Throughout this guide, the following abbreviations are used: **AE,** American Express; **DC,** Diners Club; **MC,** MasterCard; and **V,** Visa.

It's a good idea to inform your credit-card company before you travel, especially if you're going abroad and don't travel internationally very often. Otherwise, the credit-card company might put a hold on your card owing to unusual activity. Record all your credit-card numbers—as well as the phone numbers to call if your cards are lost or stolen—in a safe place. Both MasterCard and Visa have general numbers you can call (collect if you're abroad) if your card is lost, but you're better off calling the number of your issuing bank, since MasterCard and Visa usually just transfer you to your bank; your bank's number is usually printed on your card.

All hotels, restaurants, and shops accept major credit cards. Israelis use credit cards even for $5 purchases. Plastic is also accepted at banks for cash advances, although some banks will accept one card but none of the others. For cash advances using a Visa card, go to the Israel Discount Bank or Bank Leumi; with a MasterCard go to Bank Hapoalim or the United Mizrahi Branch.

Most credit cards offer additional services, such as emergency assistance and insurance. Call and find out what additional coverage you have.

Reporting Lost Cards **American Express** (☎ *800/528–4800 in the U.S. or 336/393–1111 collect from abroad* 🌐 *www.americanexpress.com*). **Diners Club** (☎ *800/234–6377 in the U.S. or 303/799–1504 collect from abroad* 🌐 *www.dinersclub.com*). **MasterCard** (☎ *800/627–8372 in the U.S. or 636/722–7111 collect from abroad* 🌐 *www.mastercard.com*). **Visa** (☎ *800/847–2911 in the U.S. or 410/581–9994 collect from abroad* 🌐 *www.visa.com*).

CURRENCY AND EXCHANGE

Israel's monetary unit is the new Israeli shekel, abbreviated NIS. There are 100 agorot to the shekel. The silver one-shekel coin is the size and shape of an American dime, but thicker. Smaller-value bronze coins are the half-shekel and the 10-agorot coin (both of which are larger than the shekel). There is also a 2-shekel round coin (silver), a 5-shekel hexagonal coin (silver), and a similar-size 10-shekel coin (bronze center, silver rim). Paper bills come in 20-, 50-, 100-, and 200-shekel denominations.

Dollars are widely accepted at hotels and shops, less so at restaurants. As of this writing, the exchange rate was about 3.45 shekels to the U.S. dollar.

In Israel, the best rates are at ATMs or at the myriad of currency-exchange shops (typically marked Change) in and around the central areas of the large cities. In Jerusalem you'll find these around Zion Square and the Ben Yehuda Street pedestrian mall, and at a few strategic locations elsewhere in the city (Jerusalem Mall, German Colony neighborhood, Jewish Quarter).

PACKING

Israel is a very casual country, and comfort comes first. For touring in the hot summer months, wear cool, easy-care clothing. If you're coming between May and September, you won't need a coat, but you should bring a sun hat that completely shades your face and neck. Take one sweater for cool nights, particularly in the hilly areas (including in and around Jerusalem) and the desert. Also take long pants to protect your legs and a spare pair of walking shoes for adventure travel. A raincoat with a zip-out lining is ideal for October to April, when the weather can get cold enough for snow (and is as likely to be warm enough in the south for outdoor swimming). Rain boots may also be a useful accessory in winter. Pack a bathing suit for all seasons.

Note that many religious sites forbid shorts and sleeveless shirts for both sexes—a light scarf comes in handy to throw over the shoulders. Women should bring modest dress for general touring in religious neighborhoods.

Along with the sun hat, take plenty of sunscreen, insect repellent, and sunglasses in summer. Essentials such as contact-lens solution and feminine hygiene supplies are available everywhere, but are more costly than in North America.

PASSPORTS AND VISAS

U.S. citizens, even infants, need only a valid passport to enter Israel for stays of up to 90 days. Make sure your passport is valid for at least six months after your travel date or you won't be permitted entry. No health certificate or inoculations are required.

Israel issues three-month tourist visas free of charge at the point of entry when a valid passport is presented. Some countries, particularly those in the Middle East, refuse to admit travelers whose passports carry an Israeli visa entry stamp. If you're concerned about regional mobility, you can ask the customs officer at your point of entry to issue a tourist visa on a separate piece of paper; you can also apply for a second passport and include a letter with the application explaining that you need the passport for travel to Israel. Be advised that it is not unheard of for Israeli customs officers to stamp passports despite requests not to do so; if you plan to travel repeatedly between Israel and those Arab states still hostile to Israel, a second passport is advisable.

Notarized consent from parents is required for children under 18 traveling alone, with one parent, or in someone else's custody.

RESTROOMS

Public restrooms are plentiful in Israel and similar in facilities and cleanliness to those in the United States. At gas stations and some parks, toilet paper is sometimes in short supply, so you might want to carry some with you. Few public sinks, except those at hotels, have hot water, but most dispense liquid soap. Occasionally you may be asked to pay one shekel at some facilities.

SAFETY

For the latest governmental travel advisories regarding travel to and within Israel, check with the U.S. State Department. The Israel Ministry of Tourism includes a section on its Web site with a nonalarmist perspective on visiting Israel during periods of unrest. For the latest local news, check the English-language papers *Haaretz* or the *Jerusalem Post*, available online.

General Information and Warnings **Israel Ministry of Tourism** (*www.goisrael.com*). **U.S. Department of State** (*www.travel.state.gov*).

Online News ***Haaretz*** (*www.haaretzdaily.com*). ***Jerusalem Post*** (*www.jpost.com*).

TAXES

A value-added tax (VAT) of 16% is charged on all purchases and transactions except tourists' hotel bills and car rentals paid in foreign currency (cash, traveler's checks, or foreign credit cards). Upon departure, you are entitled to a refund of this tax on purchases made in foreign currency of more than $100 on one invoice; but the refund is not mandatory, and not all stores provide VAT return forms. Stores so organized display "tax-vat" signs and give 5% discounts, or you can inquire.

Keep your receipts and ask for a cash refund at Ben Gurion Airport. Change Place Ltd. has a special desk for this purpose in the duty-free area. If you leave from another departure point, the VAT refund will be sent to your home address.

As of this writing, Israel has no departure tax.

TIME

Israel is two hours ahead of Greenwich Mean Time. Normally, New York and Montréal are seven hours behind; California is 10 behind. From late March until early September, Israel operates on Daylight Saving Time. When the Daylight Saving Times do not match, the time difference is reduced by one hour.

Time Zones **Timeanddate.com** (*www.timeanddate.com/worldclock*).

TIPPING

There are no hard-and-fast rules for tipping in Israel. Taxi drivers do not expect tips, but a gratuity for good service is in order. If you have negotiated a price, assume the tip has been built in. If a restaurant bill does not include service, 15% is expected—round up if the service was particularly good, down if it was dismal. Hotel bellboys should be tipped a lump sum of NIS 10 to NIS 20, not per bag. Tipping is customary for tour guides, tour-bus drivers, and chauffeurs. Bus groups normally tip their guide NIS 20 to NIS 25 per person per day, and half that for the driver. Private guides normally get tipped NIS 80 to NIS 100 a day from the whole party. Both the person who washes your hair and the stylist expect a small tip—except if one of them owns the salon. Leave NIS 10 per day for your hotel's housekeeping staff, and the same for spa personnel.

TOURS

Although Israel is a very small country, its wealth of different terrains, climate zones, and historical periods can make it overwhelming to tackle on your own. But should you join an organized tour? That depends on whether this is your first visit to Israel, if you have friends or family in the country, and how much local color you want to take in.

If it's your first time in the Middle East and you're looking for a general overview of the main historic, religious, and natural sites, an escorted tour can be both efficient and cost effective.

All package tours are led by licensed tour guides and include visits to Jerusalem, Tel Aviv, Masada, and the Dead Sea. It's not difficult to find itineraries tailored to your religious affiliation or areas of interest. If an organized trip is not for you, a private tour with a licensed guide is another option.

Dozens of companies offer guided tours at a variety of price levels. Package deals include hotels, meals, transportation, guides, and admission fees. But all tours are not equal—be sure to check out the itinerary to make sure it matches your pace, and whether the accommodations and restaurants are up to snuff.

SIGHTSEEING GUIDES

Licensed tour guides must undergo a rigorous two-year training program with annual continuing education required to maintain their credentials. Licensed guides can put together a complete customized itinerary for your group or take you for a couple of days on a private guided tour. Many are native English speakers and have fascinating backgrounds they are happy to share with you.

Freelance guides may approach unaccompanied travelers near the Jaffa Gate in the Old City of Jerusalem and other places on the beaten path. These guides are not licensed, so it's impossible to know whether the tour they're offering is worthwhile or if they're planning on taking you to their best friend's souvenir stall. It's best to ignore them and walk on.

Contacts **Israel Tour Guides** (*www.tour-guides.co.il*).

GUIDE-DRIVEN VEHICLES

Modern, air-conditioned limousines and minibuses driven by expert, licensed guides are a great way to see the country for anyone whose budget can bear it. At this writing, the cost was $450 to $550 per day; add another $100 for bigger vans. An additional $150 to $200 per night is charged for the driver's expenses if he or she sleeps away from home. Half-day tours are also available, and you may hire a guide without a car.

Guided Limousine Tours and Superb Limousine Services offer good vehicles and knowledgeable guides. Haifa-based Abboud Tours, run by Israeli Christian Abboud Maroun, specializes in private minibus tours of Jerusalem and the Dead Sea, Nazareth and the Galilee, and the fascinating walled city of Akko.

Contacts **Abboud Tours** (*04/852–5077* *www.abboudtours.com*). **Guided Limousine Tours** (*03/642–1649* *www.glt.co.il*). **Superb Limousine Services** (*03/973–1780* *www.superb.co.il*).

GENERAL-INTEREST TOURS

Several major international tour companies offer all-inclusive trips geared to the general traveler. These generally cover all the major sights and include midlevel accommodations. D.D. Travel, Escorted Globus Tours, Isramworld, and Trafalgar Tours all have one- to two-week trips that are perfect for first-time visitors to Israel. British-based Longwood Holidays is another well-established company offering weeklong tours, with optional extensions in Eilat or Tel Aviv, at very competitive prices.

On a smaller scale, two Israeli-based companies—Egged Tours and United Tours—offer one- or two-day bus tours to many parts of Israel and the Palestinian Authority, including Bethlehem and Jericho. Prices start at $100 per person for one-day tours and $240 per person for two-day tours. These tours are good options for solo travelers or for people who don't want to be part of a tour for their entire trip.

Contacts **D. D. Travel** (866/403–8457 www.ddtravel-acc.com/tours.htm). **Egged Tours** (700/707–577 *www.eggedtours.com*). **Escorted Globus Tours** (*800/942–3301* *www.escortedglobustours.com*). **Isram** (800/223–7460 *www.isram.com*). **Longwood Holidays** (*20/8418–2516* *www.longwoodholidays.co.uk*). **Trafalgar Tours** (*866/544–4434* *www.trafalgartours.com*). **United Tours** (*03/617–3315* *www.unitedtours.co.il*).

SPECIAL-INTEREST TOURS

ART

Haifa-based Israel My Way offers exciting five-day "Art Lover" tours that include the latest exhibits at the country's top museums, studio visits with local artists, and a chance to take in the best of Israeli music, opera, and dance.

Contacts **Israel My Way** (77/300–5717 www.israelmyway.co.il).

BIKING

Israel's EcoBike Cycling Vacations offers an eight-day countrywide bike tour as well as one-day Tel Aviv and Jerusalem trips. The Jerusalem Cyclists Club can give you advice about local conditions and recommend routes. They organize one-day tours from Jerusalem on occasional Saturdays. For Saturday tours in Tel Aviv and Jaffa, try the Tel Aviv Bicycle Club. Walkways runs countrywide one- to two-week trips with professional guides. These tours combine cycling and hiking along biblical paths around the Carmel area, the coastal plain, the Galilee, the Red Sea, the Sinai Desert, as well as Petra in Jordan.

TIP→ Most airlines accommodate bikes as luggage, provided they're dismantled and boxed.

Contacts EcoBike (☎ *077/450–1650* ⊕ www.ecobike.co.il). **Jerusalem Cyclists Club** (☎ *02/643–8386*). **Tel Aviv Biker's Association** (☎ *03/566–9667* ⊕ www.bike.org.il/taba/index_e.html). **Walkways** (☎ *02/534–4452* ⊕ *wwwwalk-ways.com*).

BIRD-WATCHING

Spring is the best time for bird-watching in Israel. Eilat, in southern Israel, hosts an annual Spring Migration Festival every March. The Kibbutz Lotan Center for Birdwatching offers bird-watching tours for small groups during the winter and spring around Eilat and Lotan. Many people report spotting more than 100 species.

Contacts **Kibbutz Lotan Center for Birdwatching** (☎ *800/200–075* ⊕ www.*birdingisrael.com*).

HIKING

Israel is a hiker's paradise, with terrains ranging from desert to forest to mountains. Try a segment or two of the 580-mi Israel National Trail if you want to experience the diversity of the landscape. For hiking the Galilee, the 36-mi Jesus Trail combines rugged scenery with historic and religious sites. Israel Extreme can create an itinerary for you, while Women Walkers arranges hiking tours of Israel exclusively for women.

The Society for the Protection of Nature in Israel, or SPNI, runs a "field schools" across the country, and conducts city walks and nature hikes. SPNI no longer offers English-speaking tours, but for nature hikes, where the experience matters more than the explanations, you might want to consider it. Most guides speak English. Many tours are family-oriented, but require you to have your own vehicle.

Contacts **Israel Extreme** (☎ *052/647–8474* ⊕ *www.israelextreme.com*). **Israel National Trail** (☎ *03/638–8719* ⊕ *www.israelnationaltrail.com*). **Jesus Trail** (⊕ *www.jesustrail.com*). **Society for the Protection of Nature in Israel** (☎ 03/638–8688 ⊕ *www.*teva.org.il/english). **Women Walkers** (⊕ *www.womenwalkers.com*).

JEWISH EDUCATIONAL TOURS

Keshet runs customized guided tours from one to ten days, focusing on Judaism and Jewish history. An experienced team of Jewish educators and guides staff Keshet.

Contact **Keshet** (☎ *646/358–4058* ⊕ *www.keshetisrael.co.il*).

WINE

See the Wines of Israel feature in Chapter 5.

Contact **Amiel Tours** (☎ *03/538–8444* ⊕ *www.amiel.com*).

TRIP INSURANCE

Comprehensive trip insurance is valuable if you're booking a very expensive or complicated trip (particularly to an isolated region) or if you're booking far in advance. Comprehensive policies typically cover trip cancellation and interruption, letting you cancel or cut your trip short because of illness, or, in some cases, acts of terrorism in your destination. Such policies might also cover evacuation and medical care. Some also cover you for trip delays because of bad weather or mechanical problems as well as for lost or delayed luggage.

Another type of coverage to consider is financial default—that is, when your trip is disrupted because a tour operator, airline, or cruise line goes out of business. Generally you must buy this when you book your trip or shortly thereafter, and it's available to you only if your operator isn't on a list of excluded companies.

Always read the fine print of your policy to make sure that you're covered for the risks that most concern you. Compare several policies to be sure you're getting the best price and range of coverage available.

Insurance Comparison Info **Insure My Trip** (☎ *800/487–4722* 🌐 *www.insuremytrip.com*). **Square Mouth** (☎ *800/240–0369* 🌐 *www.squaremouth.com*).

Comprehensive Insurers **Access America** (☎ *800/284–8300* 🌐 *www.accessamerica.com*). **AIG Travel Guard** (☎ *800/826–4919* 🌐 *www.travelguard.com*). **CSA Travel Protection** (☎ *800/873–9855* 🌐 *www.csatravelprotection.com*). **Travelex Insurance** (☎ *888/228–9792* 🌐 *www.travelex-insurance.com*). **Travel Insured International** (☎ *800/243–3174* 🌐 *www.travelinsured.com*).

VISITOR INFORMATION

The Israel Ministry of Tourism has a toll-free information line and information-packed Web site. They also have a free iSrael iPhone and iPad app, available on iTunes.

Contacts **Israel Government Tourism Office** (🌐 *www.goisrael.com*).

WORD OF MOUTH

Before your trip, be sure to check out what other travelers are saying in Talk on www.fodors.com.

ONLINE TRAVEL TOOLS

Drive Israel provides comprehensive coverage if you're going to rent a car and seek out your own accommodations. The Israel Nature and Parks Authority has info about the country's outdoor attractions, including where to buy discounted admission cards. The Index Tourism site has a good roundup of useful tips about Israel.

Contacts

Drive Israel (🌐 *www.drive-israel.com*). **Focus Multimedia Online Magazine** (🌐 *www.focusmm.com/israel/is_anamn.htm*). **Israel Nature and Parks Authority** (🌐 *www.parks.org.il*). **Index Tourism Israel Tourism Guide** (🌐 *www.index.co.il/tourism*).

INDEX

A

B

N

O

P

Q

R

PHOTO CREDITS

1, Mikhail Levit/Shutterstock. 2 (top left), erela, Fodors.com member. 2 (top right), RJun, Fodors.com member. 2 (center left), GeneZ, Fodors.com member. 2 (center right), rooneyroo, Fodors.com member. 2 (bottom left), Keith_Marks, Fodors.com member. 2 (bottom center), leahzzzz85, Fodors.com member. 2 (bottom right), GeneZ, Fodors.com member. 5, Israel images/Alamy. Chapter 1: Experience Israel: 8–9, John Norman/Alamy. 10, David Shankbone/wikipedia. 11 (left), Israel Ministry of Tourism. 11 (right), Odelia Cohen/Shutterstock. 12 (top right), Israel Ministry of Tourism. 12 (top left), PhotoStock-Israel/Alamy. 12 (bottom left), Israel Ministry of Tourism. 12 (bottom right), kavram/Shutterstock. 16 and 17 (left), Israel Ministry of Tourism. 17 (right), Israel Ministry of Tourism. 18 (left), Bomshtein/Shutterstock. 18 (top center), David Shankbone/wikipedia. 18 (bottom center), Israel Ministry of Tourism. 18 (top right), Amit Erez/iStockphoto. 18 (bottom right), Israel Ministry of Tourism. 19 (top left), Arkady Mazor/Shutterstock. 19 (bottom left), Mikhail Levit/Shutterstock. 19 (top center), Judy Balint. 19 (bottom center), wikipedia.org. 19 (right), Judy Balint. 20 and 21, Elan Fleisher/age fotostock. 22 and 23 (left), Israel Ministry of Tourism. 23 (right), Mordechai Meiri/Shutterstock. 24, Gisella Caroti. 25 (left), phogel/Flickr. 25 (right), Mikhail Levit/Shutterstock. 26, Bantosh/wikipedia. 27 (left), David Masters/Flickr. 27 (right), Benjamin Balint. 28, Ariy/Shutterstock. 29, InterContinental Hotels and Resorts. 30, Pina BaRosh Wine Bar. 31 (left and right), Avi Ganor. 32, Noam Armonn/iStockphoto. 33 (left), hoyasmeg/Flickr. 33 (right), Elisei Shafer/Shutterstock. 34, Israel Ministry of Tourism. 35, Jonathan Nackstrand/Shutterstock. 37 (left), Gadi Dagon. 37 (right), ogimogi/Flickr. 38, Noam Armonn/Shutterstock. 39 (left), Vitaliy Berkovych/Shutterstock. 39 (right), Howard Sandler/Shutterstock. 40, Ella/Shutterstock. 47, Kord.com/age fotostock. 48 (top left), Lebrecht Music and Arts Photo Library/Alamy. 48 (bottom left and right), wikipedia.org. 49 (top left), The London Art Archive/Alamy. 49 (top center), wikipedia.org. 49 (bottom left), Mikhail Levit/Shutterstock. 49 (right), Israel Ministry of Tourism. 50 (left), North Wind Picture Archives/Alamy. 50 (top right), The Print Collector/Alamy. 50 (bottom right) and 51 (top left and bottom left), wikipedia.org. 51 (right), Israel images/Alamy. 52 (left), wikipedia.org. 52 (top right), INTERFOTO Pressebildagentur/Alamy. 52 (bottom right), Robert Judges/Alamy. Chapter 2: Jerusalem: 53, Nicole_pappas, Fodors.com member. 58, Eyal Nahmias/Alamy. 66, Israel Ministry of Tourism. 67 (left), Elan Fleisher/age fotostock. 67 (right), Israel Ministry of Tourism. 68 (left), Israel images/Alamy. 68 (top right), Mikhail Levit/Shutterstock. 68 (bottom right), Jason Moore/Alamy. 69, North Wind Picture Archives/Alamy. 70, Mikhail Levit/Shutterstock. 71 (top), Israel Ministry of Tourism. 71 (bottom), Mikhail Levit/Shutterstock. 72, Israel images/Alamy. 73 (top left), Mikhail Levit/Shutterstock. 73 (top right), wikipedia.org. 73 (bottom), TNT Magazine/Alamy. 74, Joel Carillet/iStockphoto. 75 (top), David Sanger Photography/Alamy. 75 (bottom), Alvaro Leiva/age fotostock. 77 (top), Mikhail Levit/Shutterstock. 77 (bottom), Israel Ministry of Tourism. 78, ARCO/J Erichsen/age fotostock. 79 (top), Corbis. 79 (bottom), Joshua Haviv/iStockphoto. 80, Terry J Alcorn/iStockphoto. 81, Robin Laurance/age fotostock. 83, moris kushelevitch/Alamy. 89, Alvaro Leiva/age fotostock. 98, ARCO/J Erichsen/age fotostock. 101, Kord.com/SuperStock. 107, Israel Ministry of Tourism. 111, Eitan Simanor/Alamy. 124, Howard Sandler/Shutterstock. 125 (top), 8828810875/Shutterstock. 125 (bottom), Adem Demir/Shutterstock. 141, Hemis.fr/SuperStock. 146 (top), The Inbal Jerusalem Hotel. 146 (left bottom), Amit Geron .146(Right bottom), The David Citadel Hotel, Jerusalem. 155, Israel Ministry of Tourism. 162, Chadica/Flickr. 165, Dallas & John Heaton/age fotostock. Chapter 3: Around Jerusalem and the Dead Sea: 169, markdewd, Fodors.com member. 170 and 171 (left), Paul Prescott/Shutterstock. 171 (right), phardt, Fodors.com member. 174, Joseph Calev/Shutterstock. 180, R. Matina/age fotostock. 183, ARCO/J Erichsen/age fotostock. 186, Israel images/Alamy. 187, Gisella Caroti. 188 (top), Israel images/Alamy. 188 (bottom), Roger Cracknell 18/Israel/Alamy. 189 (top left), Hanan Isachar/Alamy. 189 (bottom left), Israel images/Alamy. 189 (top right), Ppja/wikipedia.org. 189 (center right), PhotoStock-Israel/Alamy. 189 (bottom right), Israel images/Alamy. 190, Terence Mendoza/Shutterstock. 191 (top), David Shankbone/wikipedia.org. 191 (bottom), Israel images/Alamy. 198, Steve Vidler/SuperStock. 199, Hemis.fr/SuperStock. 201 (top), Images&Stories/Alamy. 201 (bottom), Yvette Cardozo/age fotostock. 202 (left), Bruno Morandi/SuperStock. 202 (right), Eitan Simanor/Alamy. 209 and 213, Israel images/Alamy. 216, Jon Arnold Images Ltd/Alamy. Chapter 4: Tel Aviv: 219 and 220, Israel Ministry of Tourism. 221 (top), Dmitry Pistrov/iStockphoto. 221 (bottom), Israel Ministry of Tourism. 224, Elan Fleisher / age footstock. 225, Israel Ministry of Tourism. 226, Gadi Dagon. 233, LOOK Die Bildagentur der Fotografen GmbH/Alamy. 234, Israel Ministry of Tourism. 235 LOOK Die Bildagentur der Fotografen GmbH/Alamy. 238, Dave Houser/ImageState/photolibrary.com. 242, Yael Pincus. 246, Arkadiy Yarmolenko/Shutterstock. 247 (top), Paul Cowan/Shutterstock. 247 (bottom), Andrea Skjold/Shutterstock. 249, rooneyroo, Fodors.com member. 255, LOOK Die Bildagentur der Fotografen GmbH/Alamy. 256, Israel Ministry of Tourism. 265 (top left), Hotel Montefiore . 265 (top right), Sheraton Tel Aviv Hotels & Towers. 265 (bottom left), InterContinental Hotels and Resorts. Tel Aviv. 265 (bottom left), Assaf Pinchuk. 266, Eddie Gerald/Alamy. 269, Gadi Dagon. 270 (top left), Israel images/Alamy. 270 (top right), Israel Ministry of Tourism. 270 (bottom right), Benjamin Balint. 271 (top left), Israel Ministry of Tourism. 271 (top right and bottom right), Avi Ganor. 272 (top left), PhotoStock-Israel/Alamy. 272 (top right and bottom right), 275, and 279, Eddie Gerald/Alamy. 280, Kevin Galvin/Alamy. Chapter 5: Haifa and the Northern Coast: 283, Russell Kord/Alamy. 284, erela, Fodors.com member. 285 (top), Nathan Chor/Shutterstock. 285 (bottom), Paul Prescott/Shutterstock. 288, Arkady Mazor/Shutterstock. 293, GeneZ, Fodors.com member. 297, Eitan Simanor/Alamy. 298, Rafael Ben-Ari/Alamy. 304, Israel images/Alamy. 314, mgplessner, Fodors.com member. 319, Vitaliy Berkovych/Shutterstock. 328 (left), Eddie Gerald/Alamy. 328-29, Rina Nagila. 330 (top left), Bernard Edelstein. 330 (bottom left), Golan Heights Winery. 330 (right), Eddie Gerald/Alamy. 331 (top), Sea Horse Winery. 331 (bottom), Clos de Gat. 332 (top left), Daniel P. Acevedo/age fotostock. 332 (bottom left), Clos de Gat. 332 (right), Carmel Winery. 333 (top), Galil Mountain Winery. 333 (bottom), Carmel Winery. 334, Pina BaRosh Wine Bar. 343, Israel Ministry of Tourism. 347, R. Matina/age fotostock. 350, Eddie Gerald/Alamy. Chapter 6: Lower Galilee: 353, Jon Arnold Images Ltd/Alamy. 354, erela, Fodors.com member. 355 (left), Noam Armonn/iStockphoto. 355(right), Israel Ministry of Tourism. 358, Mary Lane/iStockphoto. 363, Jon Arnold Images Ltd/Alamy. 366, Israel images/Alamy. 369 and 375, Israel Ministry of Tourism. 376, Alexandre Grigoriev/Shutterstock. 380-81 (top), Jon Arnold/age fotostock. 380 (bottom), Israel Ministry of Tourism. 382 (top and bottom), www.wga.hu. 383 and 384 (top left), Israel Ministry of Tourism. 384 (bottom left and right) and 385 (top left), Israel images/Alamy. 385 (top center), Tomasz Parys/Shutterstock. 385 (top right and bottom right), Israel images/Alamy. 385 (bottom left), Israel Ministry of Tourism. 386, Paul Prescott/Shutterstock. 393 and 396, Israel images/Alamy. 402, Johnny Stockshooter/age fotostock. 405, Tomasz Parys/Shutterstock. Chapter 7: Upper Galilee: 411, Israel images/Alamy. 412, wikipedia.org. 413 (top), Yory Frenklakh/Shutterstock. 413 (bottom), Israel Ministry of Tourism. 416, PhotoStock-Israel/Alamy. 422, Helio San Miguel. 425, Eddie Gerald/Alamy. 430, PhotoStock-Israel/Alamy. 438, Niall Benvie/Alamy. 443, Keith_Marks, Fodors.com member. 444, Israel images/Alamy. 447, Israel Ministry of Tourism. Chapter 8: Eilat and Negev: 449, Keith_Marks, Fodors.com member. 450 (top), Yory Frenklakh/Shutterstock. 450 (bottom), zepperwing, Fodors.com member. 451 (left), Paul Prescott/Shutterstock. 451 (right), urosr/Shutterstock. 454, Paul Prescott/Shutterstock. 459, Elisei Shafer/Shutterstock. 468, Benjamin Balint. 477, Eddie Gerald/Alamy. 481, Israel Ministry of Tourism. 484-485, Josef F. Stuefer/Shutterstock. 486 (top), Israel images/Alamy. 486 (bottom), Alan Keohane/age fotostock. 487, Israel images/Alamy. 488 (top left), James Margolis/iStockphoto. 488 (top right), Bomshtein/Shutterstock. 488 (bottom), Ester Inbar/wikipedia.org. 489 (top), kavram/Shutterstock. 489 (bottom), blickwinkel/Alamy. 490 (left), Israel Ministry of Tourism. 490 (right), Eddie Gerald/Alamy. 491 (top), Yvette Cardozo/Index Stock Imagery/photolibrary.com. 491 (center), Kibbutz Lotan. 491 (bottom), ARCO/D. Usher/age fotostock. 496, RIEGER Bertrand/Hemis photolibrary.com. 507, RIEGER Bertrand/age fotostock.

ABOUT OUR WRITERS

Benjamin Balint, a writer based in Jerusalem, has written about Israeli culture for the *Wall Street Journal, Haaretz, the Jerusalem Post,* and the *Los Angeles Review of Books.* His book *Running Commentary* came out last year. Benjamin updated the "Eilat and the Negev" and "Around Jerusalem and the Dead Sea" chapters. Contact him at benjamin.balint@gmail.com.

Judy Lash Balint fell in love with Jerusalem on her first trip as a teenager and has made the holy city her home since 1998. Judy updated Travel Smart Israel and several sections of Experience Israel. An award-winning writer, blogger, and Jerusalem correspondent for several U.S.-based news outlets and Web sites, Judy shares her passion for Jerusalem through her writing as well as by leading private briefing seminars for visitors. Contact her at judy.balint@gmail.com

Sarah Bronson, a native of Boston, is a Jerusalem-based freelance writer, reporter, editor, and teacher. Her work has appeared in the *New York Times, Glamour,* and *Executive Traveler.*

Born in Montréal, **Judy Stacey Goldman** has lived in Israel for many years, where she works as a professional tour guide. She has also co-authored three books about off-the-beaten-track tourism and cuisine in Jerusalem and Tel Aviv. Judy writes the "Haifa and the Northern Coast" chapter, and also updates her features on "Street Food in Israel" and "Holiday Foods in Israel." Contact Judy at judebob@netvision.net.il.

Dina Kraft is a Tel Aviv–based journalist who writes for the Jewish Telegraphic Agency, the *New York Times,* and the *Financial Times,* among others. Dina updated the "Tel Aviv" chapter, adding many new places, and wrote the "Bauhaus Style in Tel Aviv" feature. Contact her at dinakraft@gmail.com.

Mike Rogoff, a professional tour guide and writer, has been exploring the byways of Israel with visitors of all persuasions since the early 1970s. South African-born and Jerusalem-based, Mike is a recipient of the Israel government's Guide of the Year award, and has contributed to Fodor's Israel since 1985. He updated most of "Experience Israel" as well as "Jerusalem Exploring" and the "Jesus in the Galilee" and "Jerusalem: Keeping the Faith" features. Contact Mike at rogoff@netvision.net.il.

Jessica Steinberg is a writer based in Jerusalem who has covered Israeli business, travel, life, culture, and fashion for the *New York Times,* the *International Herald Tribune, Women's Wear Daily, Hadassah,* and *Tablet.* She blogs regularly about Israeli life for Israelity and produces Expeditions, an online Israel travel magazine. Jessica updated sections of the "Jerusalem" chapter and the "Experience" chapter. She can be reached at jessica@netvision.net.il.

Adeena Sussman is a food writer, recipe developer, and cooking instructor who has written about Israeli food and wine and created Israeli-inspired recipes for publications including *Food and Wine, Sunset,* and *Hadassah.* Based in New York, she updated her feature on "The Wines of Israel" and "Flavors of Israel." Adeena's Web site is adeenasussman.com.